Hitler's Rival

HITLER'S RIVAL

Ernst Thälmann
in
Myth and Memory

RUSSEL LEMMONS

UNIVERSITY PRESS OF KENTUCKY

Scholarly publisher for the Commonwealth,
serving Bellarmine University, Berea College, Centre College of Kentucky,
Eastern Kentucky University, The Filson Historical Society, Georgetown
College, Kentucky Historical Society, Kentucky State University, Morehead
State University, Murray State University, Northern Kentucky University,
Transylvania University, University of Kentucky, University of Louisville,
and Western Kentucky University.
All rights reserved.

Editorial and Sales Offices: The University Press of Kentucky
663 South Limestone Street, Lexington, Kentucky 40508-4008
www.kentuckypress.com

17 16 15 14 13   5 4 3 2 1

Library of Congress Cataloging-in-Publication Data

Lemmons, Russel, 1962-
  Hitler's rival : Ernst Thälmann in myth and memory / Russel Lemmons.
     pages cm.
  Includes bibliographical references and index.
  ISBN 978-0-8131-4090-2 (hardcover : alk. paper) —
  ISBN 978-0-8131-4091-9 (epub) — ISBN 978-0-8131-4092-6 (pdf)
  1. Thälmann, Ernst, 1886-1944. 2. Communists—Germany—Biography.
3. Communism—Germany—History—20th century. 4. Germany—Politics
and government—1918-1933. 5. Socialism—Germany—History—20th
century. 6. National socialism. 7. Propaganda, Communist—Germany
(East) I. Title.
  HX274.7.T47L46 2013
  335.43092—dc23
  [B]   2012043894

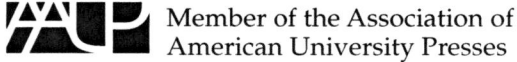

For "Sunshine"

Contents

Abbreviations

AIZ	*Arbeiter Illustrierte Zeitung*
CDU	Christian Democratic Union
Comintern	Communist International
CPSU	Communist Party of the Soviet Union
CPUSA	Communist Party in the United States of America
DEFA	Deutsche Film Aktiengesellschaft
DKP	West German Communist Party
DVP	German People's Party
ECCI	Executive Committee of the Communist International
FDJ	Free German Youth
FRG	Federal Republic of Germany
FSJ	Free Socialist Youth
GDR	German Democratic Republic
IML	Institute for Marxism–Leninism
KAPD	Communist Workers' League of Germany
KJVD	Communist Youth League of Germany
KPD	German Communist Party
NATO	North Atlantic Treaty Organization
NSDAP	National Socialist German Workers' Party
PDS	Party for Democratic Socialism
POW	prisoner of war
RFB	Red Front Fighters' League
SBZ	Soviet Zone of Occupation
SED	Socialist Unity Party
SPD	German Social Democratic Party
Ufa	Universium-Film Aktiengesellschaft
USPD	Independent Social Democratic Party
VVN	Association for the Victims of Nazi Persecution

Introduction

Myths have always played in important role in legitimizing politics, and among these myths is that of the fallen hero. Homer's *Iliad* and *Odyssey* promote cults of romanticized heroes—such as Achilles and Hector—who died so that others might live. Plato in his *Republic* calls for the building of altars to commemorate those who perished in order to preserve Greek culture. Jesus of Nazareth's sacrificial death plays a central role in Christian theology.[1] The Christian cult of the saints—with the emphasis it placed on the humble origins of Christian martyrs—had the effect of democratizing heroism. In the eyes of early Christians, ordinary people could accomplish extraordinary things by freely giving their lives for their savior.[2] This understanding of heroic death—emphasizing the modest origins of the fallen—took deep root in the United States, where an elaborate mythology surrounds those who died for the republic. The Lincoln Memorial, the Tomb of the Unknown Soldier, and the Vietnam Veterans' Memorial are among the most obvious examples of this phenomenon. The implication in each of these examples is clear: a cause worth dying for is one worth fighting for.[3]

Even in recent—supposedly more sophisticated—times, the cult of the fallen hero who dies in order to further a political cause has continued to play a vital role, especially in legitimizing "totalitarian" governments on both the right and the left. As Nina Tumarkin has pointed out in her two very successful books, *Lenin Lives!* and *The Living and the Dead,* the Soviet Union based its legitimacy on the cult of the fallen hero, first of Vladimir Ilich Lenin, then of those who perished during the Great Patriotic War against fascism. Although Lenin might not literally have died in battle against the class enemy, his unceasing effort to promote the benefit of the toiling masses undoubtedly contributed to his demise at a relatively young age—at least in the eyes of Soviet propagandists.[4] As the Russian cult of the Second World War's dead shows, these heroic martyrs need not be identifiable as individuals and can be an entire category of people, sometimes incorporating millions. Indeed, one of the characteristics of twentieth-century political culture was that many of these martyrs were nameless heroes who died not for fame and glory, as Achilles did, but rather for the common good. As built on traditions going back to early Christianity, martyrs became, in the context of the modern mass state, ordinary people rather than exceptional individuals exhibiting uncommon bravery. In short, everyone could be a champion of virtue and truth and give his or her life for the benefit of future generations. The people of modern Israel, for example, have legitimized their state—at least in part—based on the sacrifices of the Jews of Masada and the victims of the Holocaust.[5] In the contemporary United States, the site of the World Trade Center, where more than 3,000 Americans perished on 11 September 2001, has become "sacred ground." These victims have become, in the eyes of many of their fellow citizens, martyrs who died in order to preserve the American way of life.

Political movements in twentieth-century Germany have also made extensive use of hero cults in their quest for legitimacy. The National Socialist German Workers' Party (NSDAP) constructed an elaborate pantheon of heroes, including figures such as Horst Wessel and Herbert Norkus. Party propaganda chief Joseph Goebbels incorporated their deaths into important propaganda motifs long before the National Socialist (Nazi) Party "seizure of power" (Machtergreifung). The cult of the fallen, drawing upon the massive wellspring of grief following the Great War—compellingly analyzed by historians George L. Mosse, Jay W. Baird, and Allen J. Frantzen, among others—continued to play a vital role throughout the Third Reich, reaching its peak in the war for Lebensraum against the Soviet Union.[6] The heroism of previous generations helped to justify the sacrifices endured by Germans living in the Third Reich, playing a vital role in the leadership's effort to inspire and mobilize the masses in the war against Jewish Bolshevism. In the case of Germany, however, the effort to appeal to average people through the invocation of cults of heroic death was not limited to the far right of the political spectrum.[7]

The German Left, building upon centuries of tradition deeply rooted in the Christian west, also made use of elaborate hero myths. Karl Liebknecht and Rosa Luxemburg, murdered by right-wing thugs in January 1919, became the first prominent martyrs of German communism.[8] Members of the German Communist Party's (KPD) paramilitary organization, the Red Front Fighters' League (RFB), who were killed in street brawls with Nazis, also became heroes in the Communist pantheon. The most important hero for the German Left, however, was

Ernst Thälmann. Scholars have only begun to analyze the Thälmann cult, which spanned from 1925, when he became leader of the KPD, to the early 1990s, after the German Democratic Republic (GDR) had collapsed and its former citizens began the search for the meaning of their four-decade experiment with socialism.[9]

Ernst Thälmann was born in Hamburg in 1886. Although his parents could best be characterized as petit bourgeois, Thälmann went to work in Hamburg's dockyards, where he became an ardent supporter of the German Social Democratic Party (SPD). Following the Great War, in which he fought on the front lines, Thälmann came to sympathize with Karl Liebknecht and Rosa Luxemburg's Spartakusbund (Spartacus Union), becoming an ardent supporter of the Bolshevik experiment in Russia. During the 1920s, he not only joined the nascent KPD but also participated in a series of labor actions in the city of his birth, most famous among them the Hamburg Uprising of October 1923. As a result of the notoriety he garnered during the German October, Thälmann emerged as an increasingly prominent figure in the German Communist movement, becoming party chairman in 1925 and running for president of the republic that same year. As KPD chief, he led the party along a path that saw it become an instrument of Soviet foreign policy and carried out the Stalinization of the KPD. He also led the KPD during the fateful years preceding the Nazi "seizure of power."

It was during this period, the final years of the Weimar Republic, that the "Thälmann myth" took root. Although party leaders assured that no German figure would come to eclipse either Lenin or Joseph Stalin in importance among the KPD's rank and file, party propagandists touted Thälmann and his movement as the only alternative to a Nazi dictatorship and years of oppression and warfare. The dock worker from Hamburg became the archetypal antifascist, placing the welfare of the proletariat above all else. He was, in the eyes of KPD propagandists, a true *Arbeiterführer*, "leader of workers," a toiler among toilers. In 1932, Thälmann again ran for president, in this instance against both the incumbent, Paul von Hindenburg, and the Nazi leader, Adolf Hitler. His party's campaign literature depicted Thälmann as the only sensible alternative to the other candidates, each of whom was supposedly the willing tool of German capitalism and imperialism. The party line held that only the KPD chief understood how to deal with the hardship brought about by the economic depression; he alone recognized the overwhelming need to rescue the nation through the introduction of the Soviet model. Although Thälmann lost the election, the campaign played an important role in making him Germany's most visible leftist politician.

A few weeks after Hindenburg had named Hitler chancellor, Thälmann was arrested. Although—or, perhaps, *because*—he spent the next eleven and a half years in prison and was murdered under the führer's direct order in August 1944, the Thälmann myth survived. Opponents of the Third Reich—and not only those on the extreme left—consistently invoked his name, making the worker from Hamburg a symbol for all those who languished in Germany's prisons and concentration camps because of their opposition to Hitler fascism. The Soviet Communist International (Comintern) organized a massive campaign ostensibly to secure Thälmann's release. Prominent cultural and political figures, German and non-German alike, both Communists and non-Communists, demanded his release. A Thälmann Battalion—composed largely of leftist German exiles—fought on the republican side in the Spanish Civil War. Writers as politically diverse as Thomas Mann and Johannes Becher eulogized him following his death. German communism had generated its most prominent martyr.

Thälmann's death at the hands of his fascist enemies only served to give the myth more resonance, and in the postwar years the Thälmann legend became one of German communism's most important propaganda themes. Cries of "Ernst Thälmann ist unter uns!" ("Ernst Thälmann is among us!") could be heard in the speeches of every prominent German Communist. His legacy became especially important to the leaders of the KPD's successor party, the Socialist Unity Party (SED), which came to dominate the Soviet Zone of Occupation (SBZ) and later the GDR. Seeking to legitimize a separate, socialist German state in the face of the growing economic success of the Federal Republic of Germany (FRG), East Germany's leaders insisted that their country's existence rested upon German socialism's heritage of antifascism, and the Thälmann myth came to play a pivotal role in this narrative. Thälmann became "Deutschlands unsterblicher Sohn," Germany's eternal son, the cornerstone of the SED's antifascism myth and the mythological founder of the East German state.

GDR leaders incorporated the Thälmann legend into their political propaganda. Willi Bredel, a leading figure in Communist cultural circles, published a highly hagiographic biography, *Ernst Thälmann: Ein Beitrag zu einem politischen Lebenbild* (Ernst Thälmann: A Contribution to a Political View of His Life) in 1948. East Germany's filmmaking concern, Deutsche Film Aktiengesellschaft, made several movies regarding the legacy of this worker from Hamburg. Two of these films, *Ernst Thälmann—Sohn seiner Klasse* (Ernst Thälmann—Son of His Class, 1954) and *Ernst Thälmann—Führer seiner Klasse* (Ernst Thälmann—Leader of His Class, 1955), were major productions, costing millions of marks and directed by the GDR's most prominent filmmaker, Kurt Maetzig. These epics were arguably the most important East German propaganda films ever made. As part of the celebrations surrounding the one hundredth anniversary of Thälmann's birth in 1986, a two-part biopic premiered on East German television. Indeed, the anniversaries of Thälmann's birth and death had become important "holy days" in the GDR's civic religion, complete with mass demonstrations, quasi-religious rituals, and special editions of the SED's official organ, *Neues Deutschland.*

Thälmann's image also became prominent in East German art, and he was the subject of numerous socialist-realist paintings and sculptures. Posters urging the people of the GDR to "fight like Thälmann" made their appearance, and innumerable parks, town squares, factories, memorials, and buildings bore his name. His visage adorned placards carried alongside those of Karl Marx, Friedrich Engels, Lenin, and Stalin. The most prominent German among the SED's pantheon of immortals, a division of the Communist youth organization, the Thälmann Pioneers, bore his name. The governing party's massive propaganda machine adapted the Thälmann legend to appeal to youth in other ways. Irma, the slain Communist's daughter, wrote a children's book about her father, in which she emphasized his love for Germany's young people. Max Zimmering penned *Buttje Pieter und sein Held* (Buttje Pieter and His Hero, 1951), the first of several East German children's novels to lionize the fallen KPD chief. Teachers and youth leaders taught their charges songs about the martyred Communist leader, and students studied his life as part of the GDR's school curriculum.

Academic historians also incorporated Thälmann's image into their *Geschichtspropaganda* (historical propaganda). The "official" East German biography, written by an author collective from the Institute for Marxism–Leninism built upon the longstanding tradition of incorporating religious motifs into the Thälmann myth. This eight-hundred-page tome concludes with a quotation from Georgi Dimitrov that Thälmann was "blood of blood, flesh of flesh of the German working class and the entire international proletariat,"[10] a clear invocation of Christian images of the Eucharistic sacrifice embodied in the Roman Catholic and Eastern Orthodox liturgies. Other biographies appeared, as well as scores of articles in scholarly journals in which a heavily idealized Thälmann was the subject. Marking the Hamburg native's one hundredth birthday, scholars from throughout the Soviet bloc held a special conference in March 1986. The proceedings were published under the title *Ernst Thälmann—unsere Partei erfüllt sein Vermächtnis* (Ernst Thälmann—Our Party Fulfills His Legacy).[11]

Much can be learned from a detailed study of the Thälmann cult. For example: What does the myth tell scholars about the self-understanding of German Communists and the ways that party leaders viewed the legitimacy of their movement? What were the origins of the myth? In what ways—if any—did the ideology of German communism evolve between 1925, when Thälmann became chairman of the KPD, and the collapse of the GDR more than six decades later? How accurate was the image of Thälmann that the KPD and SED sought to propagate? What do the inaccuracies incorporated into the legend tell us? How were various media used to propagate the legend? How were traditional—especially Christian—themes incorporated? How was the Thälmann myth refashioned to coincide with the SED's agenda? In what ways did it remain consistent? How much influence did Soviet propaganda techniques have on the GDR's techniques? What role did intellectuals—especially academic historians—play in the propagation of the myth? What role did East German political propaganda, with its emphasis on the antifascism myth, play in the cold war? How successful was German Communist propaganda in the short and long terms? Why did antifascism, a theme that apparently once had so much resonance, ultimately fail?

Hitler's Rival: Ernst Thälmann in Myth and Memory seeks not only to address these questions but also to analyze closely a major theme in German Communist propaganda over the course of more than sixty years. Other scholars have dealt with this subject, a handful of them in some detail. Alan Nothnagle dedicates an entire chapter of his *Building the East German Myth: Historical Mythology and Youth Propaganda in the German Democratic Republic, 1945–1989* to the Thälmann legend. René Börrnert has also done valuable work concerning the SED's use of the Thälmann myth to appeal to East German youth. Indeed, his *Wie Ernst Thälmann treu und kühn! Das Thälmann-Bild der SED im Erziehungsalltag der DDR* is an encyclopedic account of every important manifestation of the Thälmann legend from 1946 to 1989—although it concentrates its efforts on the period since the 1960s. Because Börrnert deals with so much during the course of a relatively brief narrative, no single manifestation of the myth is the subject of a more than cursory analysis. In contrast, the collection of essays *Ernst Thälmann: Mensch und Mythos*, edited by Peter Monteath, delves into only a handful of the manifestations of the legend, limiting the examples upon which the authors of the work can draw. In short, although these fine books have much to tell scholars regarding the Thälmann myth, much work remains to be done.

These are not the only historiographical lacunae that this book seeks to fill, however. Hitherto, scholars who have written about the Thälmann legend have dealt exclusively with the years after the Second World War, ignoring the genesis of the legend in the final decade of the Weimar Republic. Previous historians have also ignored the developments in the myth during the years between Adolf Hitler's "seizure of power" and the signing of the German–Soviet Nonaggression Pact, during which the Comintern launched a major propaganda campaign ostensibly to secure Ernst Thälmann's release from a German prison cell. In other words, the first two chapters of this book are concerned with subject matter that no other historian has covered. Further, the book's greater scope permits an investigation into the evolution of the Thälmann legend over the course of more than six decades, a longer period of time than previous works. In short, the contribution of *Hitler's Rival* lies both in its approach to the subject matter and the scope of events to be considered.

Whenever scholars deal with the GDR's political culture, they find themselves confronting the totalitarian model, a contentious paradigm that has been the subject of far too much scholarly interest to be addressed definitively here. Although the account that follows demonstrates that there is much to be said for the argument that the SED sought ultimately to control every politically significant aspect of the lives of East Germany's citizens, the strengths and weaknesses of the totalitarian model are not this book's primary concern. Rather, *Hitler's Rival* approaches its subject in a novel way—using the "political religions" model. Although other scholars have investigated East German political propaganda as a manifestation of totalitarianism, only Randall L. Bytwerk has categorized the SED's ideology as a "political religion."[12] Bytwerk's valuable work, however, is a general overview of Nazi and SED propaganda, concentrating its efforts on comparing and contrasting the propaganda of the two German dictatorships. As a result, Bytwerk's book is relatively short on concrete examples, and it deals with the East German antifascism myth, including the Thälmann legend, only in passing. *Hitler's Rival* seeks to analyze the East German antifascism myth—as manifested in the Ernst Thälmann legend—through the prism of political religions. This approach is the product of more than a decade of research on East German political propaganda, during which I repeatedly noticed the striking religious motifs—originating for the most part in Roman Catholic Christianity—found in almost every aspect of the Thälmann myth. Indeed, the parallels between the Thälmann legend propagated by German communism and Christian stories and ritual are so striking that there is little doubt but that Communist propagandists quite consciously looked to Christianity—ironically a religious view that they aggressively rejected—for their models concerning the best ways to appeal to the masses. Whenever possible, the GDR leadership sought to reserve Sundays for the celebrations of the most important events in the country's political religion. Antifascist Martyr's Day, for example, was on the second Sunday in September, not only linking the celebrations to the traditional Christian Sabbath but supplanting them.

The contention that the mass political movements of the twentieth century—fascism and communism—can be viewed as political religions originated with Eric Voegelin (1901–1985). Born in Cologne, Voegelin grew up in Vienna and as a young man earned his doctorate in political science. Typically for a German-trained academic of his generation, Voegelin possessed a broad but deep knowledge of the humanities and social sciences. A staunch opponent of National Socialism, in 1933 he published two books highly critical of the racist turn he saw in central European politics, *Race and State* and *The History of the Race Idea,* both appearing in 1933. These books were banned in the Third Reich. Then Voegelin began work on *Political Religions,* in which he analyzed the striking similarities between the political movements of his time and the world's great religions, especially Christianity. The *Anschluss* in 1938 preempted its publication in Austria, but the book eventually appeared in Stockholm the following year. The Nazi annexation of Austria also convinced Voegelin that it was advisable to leave Europe, and he immigrated to the United States, where he took a position at Louisiana State University and later the Hoover Institution. Voegelin continued to publish extensively for the remainder of his life, and in works such as *Science, Politics, and Gnosticism* and "Ersatz Religion," he further developed his ideas concerning "political religions."[13]

Voegelin carefully analyzed the highly ritualized nature of the twentieth century's mass political movements. Both fascism and Bolshevism constructed an elaborate political mythology, he maintained, around practices usually associated with the world's great religions. Fascists and Communists incorporated quasi-religious rites, public oath taking, elaborate commemorative ceremonies, and highly stylized rituals into the public manifestation of their political movements, hoping thereby both more completely to socialize adherents to the party's teachings and to win new converts to its cause. Further, political leaders at both extremes invoked heroes from the past—Marx, Engels, Lenin, great kings and military leaders, not to mention martyrs to the cause—as examples to be followed by all true believers. These figures served as the political equivalent of Moses, Muhammad, Paul, or Jesus—prophets, saints, and saviors who had struggled on behalf of the movement, thereby granting it a legitimacy it might not otherwise have had. Further, political religions developed their own versions of Satan and his minions, enemies of morality and truth. On the left, the enemy was the expropriating classes, who, like the devil, must be defeated in order for good to triumph. On the right, those outside the nation—the Jews in the case of National Socialism—played a similar role. Even more elaborate mythologies developed, seeking to explain the course of history and the reasons why the party's ultimate triumph was assured. Revolutionary Marxism, for example, developed its own Eden myth, harkening back to the days of "primitive communism"—a veritable heaven on earth—supplanted by class exploitation, which was the Communists' version of original sin. Indeed, as Michael Burleigh has pointed out, Marxism inherited its lineal view of history—with a narrative beginning and ending at fixed points in time—from Christianity. These political mass movements even developed their own concepts of transcendence, which could be achieved only through the complete, uncritical embracing of the cause. Fascism and communism also created their own standards of orthodoxy, which resulted in the development of sectarianism and eventually a concept parallel to the religious notion of heresy. The political deities of fascism and communism were jealous gods who would brook no rivals. Indeed, the similarities between political and theistic religions were so extensive, Voegelin maintained, that totalitarian ideologies can best be understood as a species of the immanence heresy, under which heaven could be achieved on earth and one need not wait for the next life to experience perfection. Also like Christianity, these ideologies were chiliastic, the ultimate victory of the movement being inevitable if only its adherents would remain true to the cause. Finally, the leaders of these political movements, Voegelin concluded, were "Gnostics"—those with special knowledge and pow-ers who could lay the foundations of this earthly paradise. The party elite's monopolistic control over the propagation of a political religion is one of the characteristics that distinguish it from the more run-of-the-mill phenomenon of civic religion. Another important—if more difficult to pin down—distinction between political religions and civic religions is the former's omnipresence. In political religions, there is no sphere into which a citizen can escape in order to avoid exposure to the governing party's official ideology.[14]

Since the 1930s, Voegelin's model has gone in and out of fashion among scholars. One important reason for this shift is that, although the Austrian philosopher's paradigm can be useful to our understand-ing of twentieth-century mass politics, there is the distinct danger of committing the fallacy of the perfect analogy, and at least some authors have given in to this temptation.[15] In order to avoid this possibility, a scholar must remember that although the similarities between politi-cal and theistic religions are profound, the differences must be kept in mind as well. Recent scholarship has shown that Voegelin's model can be a useful analytical tool. Michael Burleigh—himself an advocate of the political religions paradigm—phrases the distinction eloquently: "A puddle contains water, but it is not an ocean." Although political mass movements might assume the outward, more public qualities of theistic religions, the former are concerned completely with transient matters. Only theistic religions can deal with eternal concerns and exis-tential questions that require adherents to address matters of ultimate importance. In short, as Burleigh explains, political religions "cari-catured fundamental patterns of religious belief, in modern societies where sacralized collectives, such as class, nation, or race, had already partly supplanted God as objects of mass enthusiasm or veneration."[16] This is why political religions were impossible prior to the French Revolution; they have succeeded, albeit temporarily, only under con-ditions where traditional theistic religions have been in decline. With the triumph of positivism and the widespread acceptance of Friedrich Nietzsche's insistence that "God is dead," large numbers of people liv-ing in the modern West launched a quest for another deity, one more in keeping with the times, a political religion, such as Marxism–Leninism or National Socialism, that could claim "scientific" roots. Adherents of political religions ultimately discovered that their new belief systems failed to satisfy them in long run because these movements were quite obviously unable to achieve their goals. Fascism was defeated as the result of a cataclysmic war; Marxism–Leninism never delivered on its promises of eternal peace and material abundance for all; and "real, existing socialism" proved to be a sham. The earthly paradise promised by party leaders, rather than approaching ever more quickly, seemed to become an ever more distant dream. As a result, the people of Eastern Europe—when given the opportunity—rejected the utopian vision of Marxism–Leninism, choosing instead the much more concrete accomplishments of representative government and the European-style social market economy. Whether these new, "post-totalitarian" gods will deliver or disappoint remains to be seen.

An effective way of understanding the history of German communism is to view it in the broader context of the twentieth century's failed political religions. Like the Soviet model upon which it drew, German communism adopted the outward trappings of religion in order to win adherents and ultimately triumph—at least temporarily—in a significant portion of Germany. The antifascism myth, with the fallen KPD chief Ernst Thälmann at its center, was a vital component of German Communists' quasi-religious worldview. A careful analysis of the Thälmann myth will provide valuable insight into the development of the political religion of German communism. For almost seventy years, from his rise to prominence as a result of the failed Hamburg Uprising in 1923 to the GDR's final days, Thälmann was a central figure in German Communist propaganda. The nine chapters that follow seek to trace the history of the mythology surrounding Ernst Thälmann from its origins in the late Weimar Republic to its swan song in the period immediately following German unification.

Chapter 1, "'Heil Moskau!'" begins with a brief overview of Ernst Thälmann's life prior to his becoming KPD chief in 1925. This chapter not only seeks to provide valuable background concerning the martyr at the center of German communism's most important legend but also supplies data against which later Communist accounts of the proletarian leader's life can be checked for accuracy. "'Heil Moskau!'" then turns to Thälmann's role in the Stalinization of the KPD and the implications that this development had for German Communist propaganda, especially that surrounding the dock worker from Hamburg. From 1925, when Thälmann launched the first of his two bids for the presidency of the Weimar Republic, the Soviet model heavily influenced the message of the party's political campaigns. Indeed, when opponents accused the KPD of being nothing more than a tool of the Soviet Union and its leader a mere lackey of Stalin, they were not far off the mark.

The KPD's ideology originated in Moscow, and under Thälmann's leadership the party was little more than the Comintern's instrument. The first chapter concludes with an analysis of the KPD's propaganda during the Weimar Republic's final years, during which Thälmann and his comrades sought to depict the SPD as a greater danger to the proletariat than the Nazis. In the months preceding Hitler's "seizure of power," the KPD's attempt to appeal to Social Democratic workers was deeply flawed and half-hearted at best, bringing into question Communists' later claim to have been Germany's most determined opponents of "Hitler fascism."

Chapter 2—"'Ernst Thälmann Must Be Won Like a Battle!'"—examines the development of the Thälmann legend during the years 1933 to 1944, when the Nazi leadership imprisoned the KPD chief. Following his arrest a few weeks after Hitler became chancellor, Thälmann became in many quarters representative of all the political prisoners held in the Third Reich. He emerged as a symbol for all of those who had opposed National Socialism and paid a heavy price for their antifascist convictions. Indeed, the Comintern launched a Free Thälmann campaign, designed ostensibly to secure the KPD chief's release. The chapter goes into some detail concerning the propaganda that this campaign generated, paying special attention to the religiously inspired symbolism of so much of the imagery created about the party leader from Hamburg. As the evidence makes clear, however, the Comintern actually had little interest in securing the harbor worker's release, and the campaign was much more about increasing Soviet influence among European leftists. In other words, in the eyes of the Soviets and German Communists, the leader from Hamburg was more valuable as a propaganda weapon languishing in a Nazi jail cell than he would have been if released and sent to Moscow. Indeed, when in August 1939 the Soviet Union signed the Nonaggression Pact with Nazi Germany—the time at which the KPD chief's release was most likely to be secured—the Free Thälmann campaign was abandoned.

Chapter 3, "'We Are Building upon the Foundations Created by Ernst Thälmann,'" opens with official reaction to the news that the KPD chief had been murdered and concentrates on the early postwar years, a period in which the Thälmann legend became a central component of KPD and SED propaganda, first in the SBZ and then in the GDR's early years. During the 1940s and 1950s, the image of Ernst Thälmann—"Germany's eternal son"—played an important role in almost every major propaganda campaign that the KPD and SED launched. Postwar

German Communists used every medium at their disposal to link the policies of their party with the Ernst Thälmann "legacy." The modest worker from Hamburg became in many ways the symbolic founder of the GDR, the giant upon whose shoulders postwar German socialism would be constructed.

Chapter 4, "'A Great National Deed,'" witnesses an evolution in the organization of this book's narrative. It marks the first of several chapters dealing with a central motif of the Thälmann legend, largely abandoning the chronological organization of the first three chapters. This chapter deals with what was arguably the most important manifestation of the Thälmann legend in the entire history of the GDR: Kurt Maetzig's two epic films, *Ernst Thälmann—Sohn seiner Klasse* (Ernst Thälmann—Son of His Class, 1954) and *Ernst Thälmann—Führer seiner Klasse* (Ernst Thälmann—Leader of His Class, 1955). "'A Great National Deed'" seeks, first of all, to investigate the politics of film biography in the GDR during the 1950s, examining the influence that Stalinist cultural policies had on East Germany. Here one witnesses the party leadership's heavy-handed intervention into the filmmaking process. Also, the narrative turns once again to the theme of political religions, interpreting Maetzig's films through the image of Thälmann as a secular saint in the GDR's official state religion. Finally, chapter 4 investigates instances in which filmmakers and party officials falsified the historical record in order to create an image of the fallen party leader more amenable to the themes of East German propaganda.

The fifth chapter, "'Out of Your Sacrificial Death Grows Our Socialist Deed,'" is concerned with the most important location for commemoration of Ernst Thälmann—Buchenwald Concentration Camp. The martyred Communist leader was murdered in the camp, so it should come as no surprise that he would become the most important single figure in commemoration rituals held at the site. Among the tens of thousands who had died in Buchenwald were many Communists, Social Democrats, and others on the political left. Thälmann became, in East German propaganda, representative of all of those who had died in the camp, an integral component of the SED's effort to create a mythology under which all those who had died at the hands of the Nazis contributed to the effort to build socialism in Germany. In the case of Buchenwald, there was also an ongoing effort to link the Thälmann myth with the East–West ideological struggle, the cold war.

The sixth chapter, "'We Can Look Forward to a Happy Future,'" analyzes the ways that SED propagandists sought to adapt the Thälmann legend in order to appeal to East German youth—a group vital to the ultimate success of German socialism. Because other scholars—Nothnagle and Börrnert—have written about the role of the Thälmann legend in the propaganda of the Free German Youth (Freie Deutsche Jugend), chapter 6 concentrates instead on close readings of books and stories published for the GDR's youth in which the martyred party chief makes an appearance. It makes clear that there was a quasi-religious tone to appeals made to East German youth.

The next chapter, "'Ernst Thälmann Is Still among Us,'" continues to develop this theme. In this case, however, it approaches the subject through an analysis of the role of the Thälmann myth in the writing of East German historians, concentrating on two biographies, one published in 1948—just before the founding of the GDR—by Willi Bredel and the other produced by an author collective at the Institute for Marxism–Leninism and appearing in 1980. At first glance, the two works are markedly different. Bredel's biography is striking because of its many inaccuracies, perpetuated in order to make the narrative of Thälmann's life more useful to the propagation of the antifascism myth. Bredel, like Maetzig, seeks to portray the fallen KPD chief as a secular saint, a quasi-religious figure whose death legitimized German socialism. The institute's biography, however, is—at least superficially—more scholarly, complete with footnotes, which are absent from Bredel's work. The 1980 book also abandons many of the outright fabrications found in the earlier publication, although it commits some striking sins of omission. Indeed, upon closer examination, the institute's biography stands in the same tradition as the earlier book. Both are heavily steeped in the religious imagery of sacrificial death.

The penultimate chapter of the book, "'Not All Who Have Died Are Dead,'" returns to a more chronological organization. Chapter 8 analyzes the Thälmann myth during the last decade of the GDR's existence. Although it deals with subject matter from throughout the 1980s—such as the trials of Wolfgang Otto, one of the men accused of murdering Ernst Thälmann—it concentrates on the events surrounding the commemoration of the fallen KPD chief's one hundredth birthday. By the mid-1980s, the SED leadership faced another crisis of legitimacy as the Soviet leadership launched its policies of perestroika (restructuring) and glasnost (openness), trends with which the GDR leadership had little sympathy. As a result, the Thälmann centenary celebrations became a repudiation of the calls for reform emanating from Moscow and a celebration of the supposed material accomplishments of "real, existing socialism." In this context, SED propaganda elevated the fallen KPD chief from the position of the prophet of a future Germany to the savior of German socialism. The cryptoreligious motifs found in the Thälmann legend are once again striking.

The final chapter, "Imprisoned, Murdered, Besmirched," analyzes the controversy surrounding the fate of the Ernst Thälmann National Monument on Berlin's Greifwalderstraße during the months following unification. Whereas many Germans, especially from the "old states," sought to raze the massive fifty-ton bronze Thälmann Monument and hundreds like it across the former East Germany, many "children of the GDR" sought to preserve them. An investigation of this dispute provides an opportunity to reach some tentative conclusions concerning the effectiveness of the Thälmann legend and the antifascism myth. This final chapter also provides a useful coda to the book, an analysis of the more than six decades during which the leaders of German communism sought to propagate the Thälmann legend.

Although it is important in the context of an introduction to describe what a book is, it is equally vital to explain what it is not. First and most important, *Hitler's Rival* is *not* a biography of Ernst Thälmann—although biographical elements play a role in the narrative. The book is also *not* a history of the KPD and SED and even less so of the GDR. It is, rather, an analysis of the Thälmann *legend* from its origins in the mid-1920s through the unification of Germany and just a bit beyond. Further, it is *not* a book primarily concerned with the effectiveness of the antifascism myth or East German political propaganda—although it does touch on these subjects provisionally. Nor is the book a comparative study—although in order to understand the Thälmann legend better I do on occasion compare it to other political myths, such as the Lenin and Stalin cults in the Soviet Union. I do this, however, primarily for the purposes of tracing the origins of motifs to be found in the Thälmann legend. In other words, *Hitler's Rival* is ultimately an analysis of a major theme in the propaganda of German communism, traced over the course of more than sixty years.

It might also be helpful to mention something concerning the way that certain terms are used in the text. When the words *myth* and *legend* appear, they say nothing—as they might in a more colloquial context—about the veracity of the ideas being analyzed. In short, what is meant by these terms is simply stories that explain and seek to provide some type of meaning. As the reader will discover, some of the myths and legends propagated by German Communists were true; others were not. Much the same applies to the use of the word *cult*. A "cult" is simply an activity in which one engages in response to a myth or legend. In other words, although the reader will discover many instances in which I make judgments concerning the activities of KPD and SED leaders—many of them harsh—my use of the terms *myth, legend,* and *cult* does not reflect any moral stance or judgment concerning the subject under consideration. Indeed, all societies have myths, legends, and cults. Rather, the use of these terms is the natural result of the contention that the antifascism myth and the Thälmann legend were manifestations of the political religion of German communism.

1

"Heil Moskau!"

Whenever biographers wanted to depict Ernst Thälmann as having had an exemplary proletarian upbringing, they had to invent one.[1] Neither of his parents came from a working-class background. His father, Jan, was born in the town of Weddern in Holstein on 11 April 1857. After military service in Potsdam, he moved to Hamburg, where in 1884 he married Maria Kopheisz, who was younger than her husband by around seven months. Like Jan, she had been born in a small town, Kirschwerder in Vierlanden, not far from Hamburg. The couple had two children: Ernst, born on 16 April 1886, and a daughter, Frieda, born about a year later. Neither parent exhibited any interest in working-class politics, and Jan, under his son's influence, would join the KPD only in 1923.[2]

Among the most important—and clearly the most interesting—sources regarding Ernst's childhood is a brief autobiography ("Mein Lebenslauf") penned by the Communist leader, probably in 1935, for his Nazi captors. Written in preparation for his trial for treason—although Thälmann never did see his day in court—the "Lebenslauf" provides not only important information regarding Ernst prior to his joining the KPD, but also valuable insight concerning the way that Thälmann saw himself as well as how he wanted his captors, not to mention posterity, to view him. In short, the "Lebenslauf" affords one of the few instances in which Thälmann had the opportunity to contribute to the creation of the mythology that would emerge about him following his death.[3] Hence, a close analysis of this document can provide an illuminating point of departure for an examination of the Thälmann myth.

Thälmann began his statement with a brief chronicle of his family's origins, the place of birth of his parents, and so forth. But he very quickly moved on to accounts of what he experienced as a child growing up in Hamburg. The city was dominated by arguably Germany's most important harbor, which employed around 30,000 people at the turn of the twentieth century. Hamburg's working class was among the most radicalized and organized in the country, and the city was known as one of Germany's "fortresses of socialism." Although an electoral system that favored the bourgeoisie assured that the mercantile classes dominated local politics, after 1890 the city consistently elected SPD deputies to all three of its Reichstag seats.[4] Hence, although Ernst contended that his "education at home and at school was in no way socialist, rather one could almost rightly contend that it was the opposite," and that his parents were an "antisocialist" influence, he did see working-class life firsthand, claiming to be more influenced by "the experiences, events and reality of everyday life [*Volksleben*]."[5]

Ernst claimed to have witnessed many of the inequities of the capitalist system simply by walking the streets of Hamburg. But much of the young boy's introduction to "everyday life" came through his father's business. Maria Thälmann's family was apparently reasonably well off, and she had brought some money to her marriage with Jan.[6] This enabled Jan, shortly after his son's birth, to purchase a tavern in Hamburg's harbor district, which helped to introduce young Ernst to the city's proletarian culture. The Thälmanns, in contrast to their customers, had petit bourgeois aspirations. Jan, Ernst recalled, "belonged to every possible bourgeois and military association," and Maria was devoutly religious—although Jan was not. Maria was apparently disturbed by her son's lack of religiosity—Ernst claims always to have seen the deceit inherent in religion—and it was a bone of contention between them. Ernst claimed to have asked Maria repeatedly why her God did not do more for the poor, hungry people whom he saw every day. Even as a child, the future Communist leader asserts, he saw through his mother's unsatisfying replies.[7]

In spite of his parents' outlook, Ernst's childhood was anything but the bourgeois ideal, and his experiences of "everyday life" went well beyond the confines of his father's public house. He learned a great deal in what he calls "the hard school of childhood [*Kinderlebens*]."[8] In 1892, for example, both of Ernst's parents were convicted of receiving stolen property and sentenced to two years in prison. Not much is known about this incident, but in the early 1950s Frieda recalled that "when our parents were convicted and sent to jail, we children were placed in foster care. I [went] to a Frau Fischer, Ernst was taken in by a family on Koppelstraße."[9] After his release from prison, Jan was forbidden to return to his previous occupation and went to work at the post office. This position did not work out either, and he eventually established a delivery business, transporting goods—mostly coal, fruit, and potatoes—throughout the city. Young Ernst often accompanied his father on his trips, many of which took him deep into Hamburg's proletarian districts as well as down to the docks, the coal yard, and the train station. Looking back on these experiences with the hindsight of some thirty-five years, Ernst maintained that he was struck by the injustice, the disparity between rich and poor, that he witnessed while accompanying his father. But when he asked his parents about these discrepancies, they were unable to provide him with a credible response.[10]

Nor did he find answers to his questions in school, where he received a petit bourgeois education. He was a solid but not excellent student who enjoyed "history, biology, folklore [*Volkskunde*], arithmetic, gymnastics and sports the most." He "had the least, or hardly any, enthusiasm for the study of religion." He wanted to continue beyond a rudimentary education and learn a trade or become a teacher. Although his parents could afford to provide their son with further training, Jan balked at the idea. Ernst would be more useful in the family business, and so he went to work for his father after graduation (*Schulentlassung*).[11]

Other things contributed to Ernst's education much more than school—and not just what he saw while wandering the streets of Hamburg. Beginning when he was around ten years old, an impressionable age, a series of events occurred that he later claimed had a profound influence on his development: the 1896 Hamburg dock strike, the Dreyfus Affair, and the Boer War. These incidents showed him that the injustices he witnessed daily were repeated on a much larger scale. The problems with which he was personally familiar were simply manifestations of worldwide, systematic inequities. Extensive reading in the works of such writers as "Schiller, Kleist, Herder, Goethe, and especially the history of the Germans and their struggles" also contributed to his emerging "self-consciousness."[12]

Shortly after leaving school, the sixteen-year-old experienced something that had a "tremendous influence upon my way of thinking and my imagination [*geistige Vorstellung*]." One day he saw a red poster that called the entire adolescent population of Hamburg to a "graduation celebration in the great hall of the Union Headquarters": "I went there alone. It was two o'clock in the afternoon. The great hall was full to the breaking point. I was astonished, and I was excited. Only youths of my age. What a mass of people, what fire, what vivacity, what enthusiasm in this group of youths. The hymn of thousands, what an effect, what joy, what an effect it worked upon me! My confirmation in [Pastor] Ruckteschell['s] Church in Eilbeck was but a small experience in comparison. Then came what was for me the great[est] experience. The day's speaker made his appearance." The speaker began with an attack on capitalism, the system responsible for the conditions in which working-class youths, such as those present, had to live. "Young comrades," he shouted, "you were born in what is becoming an historical time . . . ," a time when the workers were "ever willing and proud to raise the red banner of socialism again and again." It was a time for action, a time in which they must "seize the future of working humanity in their young hands." It was a time when socialism's inevitable victory was within their grasp. When the speaker was finished, young Ernst "stood alone among the thousands" as they sang several proletarian songs before "all of them stormed to the exit," overpowered by revolutionary fervor.[13]

As Ernst left the hall, he noticed that a table selling proletarian literature had been set up and saw a brochure entitled *How Do I Become a Co-struggler for Socialism?* As he purchased it for twenty pfennigs, he remembered the speaker's words: "The future of humanity lies on your shoulders!" He walked "alone into the street. Fantasies developed in my spirit: [W]hat are the [proper] paths? How can I help? What must I do? What steps should be followed?" The perplexed but excited young man wandered down to the harbor and sat on a bench. He thought about his life up until that time: "[S]hould he never get to know the human experience from another side, view the depths of the human soul only from a single perspective?" He thought long and hard, coming to the conclusion that his "parents' home was too narrow and passive [*kampflos*], but what should I do to change this, where is the way out of this situation?" He read the brochure all the way through, and "his thoughts concentrated upon the idea of socialism," but he could not discover a concrete solution to his problems. After sitting pensively for hours upon the bench, with no "plan for a way out of this problem," he went home and continued to work in his father's business.[14]

His experience on that Sunday afternoon continued to haunt him. Over the following months, the teenager became "more mature and self-conscious." Ernst worked hard in Jan's business, putting in more hours than his father's other employees but getting paid less. Jan justified this lower pay by pointing out that Ernst, as his son, would one day inherit the business. But the young man felt exploited and, insisting that he would move out of his parents' home if Jan refused to meet his demands, managed to secure an increase in pay; but it was not enough, and Ernst became increasingly determined to leave home. Events only reinforced his decision. One day he left the family's horse and wagon in the street, and "through no fault of my own" it was "stolen and damaged." As a result, he received a "sound thrashing" from his father. The next day, while Jan was making a delivery, Ernst quit his job and left home. He departed with all of his belongings in his suitcase and the three marks his mother had given him in his pocket, but "without any kind of destination."[15]

The sixteen-year-old was now unemployed and homeless. At first, he stayed in the Concordiahaus, a flophouse in St. Pauli for Hamburg's dispossessed. He then began to look for a job, without much success. Thälmann recalled, "Now I got to know the bitter necessity of earning my own daily bread, without having my parents or others to fall back upon." He found himself "in a struggle with that bitter power, hunger." In spite of his desperate straits, Ernst was ultimately not alone. Among those whom he met while searching for a job was a young man who worked for a local theater. His new friend, who lived in virtual penury with his seventy-eight-year-old mother, offered to take him on as a tenant for a couple of marks per week. The homeless youth eagerly agreed. The accommodations were modest, to say the least. "It was a basement apartment on Kleinen Wasserstraße in Altona, with only two rooms and a kitchen." His landlady proved to be remarkably compassionate. "She was as poor as a mouse herself, yet she let me live with her and fixed me coffee and breakfast in the morning" in spite of his inability to pay the modest rent. Ernst was learning that the poor, unlike their wealthy exploiters, could exhibit human kindness, which "made a deep impression" on him.[16]

The young man's search for employment proved fruitless, and so he began to do volunteer work at the Ernst-Drucker Theater, where his roommate worked. It was, Thälmann recalled, a working-class theater, so he learned a great deal. The actors were poorly paid and often deeply in debt. Yet they sometimes managed to give him "a little pocket money" to make sure that he did not starve. Once again, he experienced the generosity of the downtrodden firsthand. Of course, these circumstances could not continue indefinitely, and when he heard about the possibility of work in the harbor, he jumped at the opportunity.[17]

Although Ernst found a job, he remained perpetually underemployed. His first employer was a "Jewish-capitalist harbor operation," the "granary and warehouse firm Nathan, Philipp & Co, Grasbrook, an exploitation firm of the first rank, known as one of the worst-paying firms in Hamburg's harbor [district]." He continued to work down at the docks, moving between temporary positions, including jobs in warehouses, a "guano mill," and a "fish mill," all in the harbor district. "Here [he] . . . received [his] initial fundamental first-hand experiences of the capitalist system of exploitation and its methods, without having yet read Marx and Engels." Thälmann and other young workers were paid by the day and moved from job to job, and he "slowly became acquainted with the general conditions of workers in Hamburg's harbor." Because he and his peers were temporary and unorganized—nonunion labor was known as "wild" or "blue"—their prospects remained limited. Unionized workers held them in contempt, and no one seemed interested in these young laborers' plight. Thälmann, at last finding the purpose he had been searching for, set about to change these circumstances.[18]

The future Communist leader joined the SPD on 15 May 1903 at the youthful age of seventeen. Eight months later he joined a trade union, the Central Association of Transportation Workers of Germany, which later became simply the German Transport Workers' Union. "From a material perspective," the latter was clearly more important to him, so it might be surprising that Thälmann joined the party before the union. But looking back upon these developments over three decades later, he interpreted this sequence of choices as evidence that the "ideal side" was more important to him at the time. Thälmann also saw these events as another important turning point in his life. "Now begins my truly political life in the arena of the life struggle," he recalled. Shortly thereafter, he participated in his first strike, a work stoppage carried out by Hamburg's brewery workers—he had a job delivering bottles of beer at the time.[19]

From the outset, Thälmann was an active organizer, concentrating his efforts on Hamburg's young workers. "The working youth was only very weakly organized, especially weakly in Hamburg's harbor district." Neither the older workers nor union officials seemed very concerned about this situation. "The [union] bigshots [*Bonzen*] sat there like grandmothers, one hiding himself behind the other in order to avoid doing anything." Thälmann, with the help of "two other hard-working and willing young comrades," decided to take matters into his own hands. Receiving no help from the union hierarchy, they had to act on their own, devising a plan designed to appeal to their peers. "All paths and methods were pondered in our three heads, in order to show the bigshots that, even if they didn't want it, something good could also happen without them."[20]

Perhaps drawing upon personal experience, the three young men decided to arrange a mass assembly, for which they raised the princely sum of two hundred marks. They distributed flyers and hung posters throughout the harbor district. The posters read:

Extrablatt!!

Working youth of the entire Hamburg harbor district!

You have asked twelve questions—answers will be given to you. 500 working-class youths, your working brothers from the harbor district will give you the answers themselves! Make sure you make time—you have to hear the solemn oath of the 500!

Between 650 and 700 young workers attended the mass rally, making it a "surprisingly huge success." Their "efforts had born fruit," and some 200 young workers joined the labor movement that day. But Thälmann's and his comrades' work was just beginning. Over the next several weeks, they visited each of the new members at home, urging him to engage in "active struggle" for the labor movement. These 200 new adherents as well as the 300 or so young people already organized aggressively recruited more members. "In six months the number of organized youths in the union rose from 300 to around 1,600 to 1,800." More mass rallies were called, and yet more young people joined the union. "The older members were surprised and partly pleased about this surprise. The bigshots smelled danger." But there was nothing they could do to hinder the success of Thälmann and his comrades, and, facing up to reality, the union established a new youth organization.[21]

After performing his obligatory military service at the age of twenty, Thälmann took a job as a trimmer on the ship *America*. Although he gave up on the life of a sailor—he found it "too crude and wild"—after only three trips, the job did give him an opportunity to visit the United States. "The days in America were a surprise for me, a new world with advanced technology. A different communal life than in Germany." The "privileges of [American] women" particularly struck him, and although he approved, he found them, somewhat paradoxically, "almost unnatural." Overall, Thälmann developed a largely positive view of the United States, where he found "social relations [*Lebensverhältnisse*] far better than in Germany."[22]

Rejecting a vocation as a sailor, Thälmann, now a young man in his twenties, held a number of jobs—as a granary worker, in a coal bunker, and with a moving company. In 1910, he secured a permanent post as a driver for a laundry service, one of the largest in the city, owned by Gustav Welscher. Although he rose to the position of foreman, he diligently sought to organize his fellow workers. "Through . . . [his] untiring efforts," the company became 100 percent unionized. He also met his future wife, Rosa Koch, "a new storm, a new happiness," whom he married in 1915. When asked to sever his ties with the crew of workers as one of his obligations as foreman, he quit. Rather than abandon his principles, according to his "Lebenslauf," he turned down the opportunity to earn significantly more money. Instead, Thälmann went to work as a driver for another laundry service, Frauenlob. He later moved to the Trump laundry, where, by this time, Rosa also worked. But Trump closed at the start of the Great War.[23]

The years between the time Thälmann was sixteen and the outbreak of war had been important ones for him. As he put it, "I was very active in union and political matters and gradually became a well-known personality."[24] By the age of twenty-two, he had held numerous important positions in the trade union movement, including local leader of the drivers' union, representative to Hamburg's Union Cartel, youth delegate and delegate to the German Transport Workers' Union assembly. He had also held numerous positions in the local SPD, including district party leader and district secretary, eventually acquiring a position with the Adviser's Commission of Hamburg-Altona and Wandsbeck. These and several other posts employed "almost all of . . . [his] free time."[25]

Like millions of other Europeans of his generation, Thälmann was drafted to fight in the Great War. Unlike the fascist movements of the interwar years, the "front experience" was not central to Marxism–Leninism. In general, the extreme Left viewed the war not from the perspective of the trenches but instead emphasized its socioeconomic dimension; it was an imperialist war. Although combat was undoubtedly among the most memorable experiences of Thälmann's life—it was for practically everyone who endured it—he apparently did not consider it important to his political development.[26] In a "Lebenslauf" that consists of thirteen published pages of closely printed text, only a single paragraph is concerned with Thälmann's experiences in the

First World War, and that paragraph is mostly a simple list of his post-ings, what battles he fought in, and a single sentence regarding the four times he was wounded on the Western Front. He also earned several decorations, including an Iron Cross, although he did not record why he received these awards. The young man from Hamburg participat-ed in several major engagements, including the Battle of the Somme, where he was wounded in an artillery barrage. He summed up his ex-periences on the Western Front quite succinctly: "Entered [the army] as a simple cannoneer and also left as a simple cannoneer."[27] Unlike the National Socialists, Communists typically downplayed their war experience.

Upon demobilization, Thälmann returned to his native Hamburg, where he shared a modest two-room apartment with his spouse. Once again he had to settle for a series of temporary jobs, which had the advantage of providing him with the free time necessary to wander the working-class districts of Hamburg and continue to learn about proletarian life in the city. He did not participate in the soldiers' coun-cil movement, which he "judged from the beginning as a movement sentenced to death, because it was not socialist." The political situation in the early years of the Weimar Republic was in a constant state of flux, and, like so many radicals, Thälmann left the SPD for the Inde-pendent Social Democratic Party (USPD), serving as a delegate to the first party conference, held in Berlin in March 1919. At the October 1920 party conference in Halle, he "decided for the program of the left and for association with the Communist International. . . . Ninety-eight per cent of the Hamburg Organization of the USPD supported" him in this decision. Whereas at the end of 1920 the vast majority of the Hamburg USPD joined the People's Communist Party of Germany, he joined the KPD and participated in every party congress. Thälmann became chief of the organization in his native city, a position he held until he became national party chairman in 1925.[28] The autobiographical document con-cludes at this point.

Thälmann's 1935 "Lebenslauf" is of interest for a variety of reasons. First and most obviously, it provides a firsthand account of his life up to the point when he joined the KPD. It covers the part of Thälmann's life about which the least is known, and it is an important primary source. It provides the background, from the subject's own pen, needed to ex-amine later Thälmann biographies, especially those written during the late 1940s and early 1950s, which often relate largely fictional, albeit very detailed, accounts of these years.[29] The "Lebenslauf" provides a text against which these later accounts can be read for factual inaccuracies. An examination of these falsifications can prove to be a valuable asset to any effort to understand the Thälmann myth. After all, later biographers were extremely unlikely to manufacture events from whole cloth unless they wanted to support a particular point of view. This topic, however, is taken up later, in chapter 7.

What is of more interest at this point is what Thälmann was trying to accomplish when writing this "Lebenslauf." One clearly must take into account the audience for whom the imprisoned Communist leader was writing: his Nazi captors. He made no effort to defend himself. Indeed, from the Nazis' point of view, the 1935 "Lebenslauf" was a highly incriminating document. Thälmann readily admitted to having been a member of the KPD—there was no point in denying that. He also made it obvious that his sympathies continued to lie with the outlawed movement. Yet the "Lebenslauf" was clearly written with a political purpose in mind, one that went beyond simply recording the events of its subject's early life. In the end, Thälmann wrote for more than his fascist jailers because he obviously had little hope of winning them over. He was also writing for posterity. After all, although he might have expected never to leave a Nazi prison, he firmly believed that the defeat of the fascists was inevitable and that one day he might be thought of for his efforts against the Hitler regime, and he was trying to manipulate the way he would be remembered. In other words, he was making his own contribution to the future Thälmann myth.

An excellent paradigm for dissecting Thälmann's 1935 "Lebenslauf" is provided by socialist realism, a cultural—in this case, literary—model that was just coming into its own at the time the account was written. If viewed through this prism, it becomes abundantly clear what Thälmann was trying to accomplish. As Katarina Clark argues in her classic work on the subject, *The Soviet Novel*, a socialist-realist text is a ritualized "sort of parable for the working-out of Marxism–Leninism in history."[30] Although it is unclear how much the KPD chief knew about this literary movement emerging on Europe's far left, as an avid Stalinist he would have been aware of the general direction of the Comintern's cultural politics. If the "Lebenslauf" is viewed from the perspective of socialist realism, it becomes much easier to detect the motifs Thälmann used and understand the points he was trying to make. The fact that the "Lebenslauf" is not a novel, but a highly stylized autobiography, does not undermine this interpretation because socialist realism came to permeate all aspects of Stalinist culture.

Clark points out that at the center of any socialist-realist text is the "positive hero," "a relatively modest figure, usually a . . . worker, administrator, or soldier." He or she is the Soviet "Everyman," whose experiences represent the Marxist–Leninist view of history, culminating in the victory of communism. His or her experiences are to be based in a very concrete recreation of reality, of the life of the average worker. The "positive hero's" experiences represent one of the central themes of Leninism, the transition from "spontaneity" to "consciousness." This transition is, as Clark puts it, "*the* subtext of socialist-realism." "Spontaneity" is the "positive hero's" condition at the beginning of the narrative. He or she confronts conditions in an unorganized or naive manner. The hero knows that something is wrong but is not quite sure why or what do to about it. He or she seeks understanding but cannot obtain it because of a lack of ideological sophistication. As Lenin pointed out himself, this lack is not necessarily a "negative category" because it is a fundamental step to attaining "consciousness." By the end of the narrative, however, the "positive hero" has achieved consciousness, and he or she understands what is wrong and knows how to go about fixing it because the hero is no longer ideologically unsophisticated but has embraced the teachings of Marx, Lenin, and Stalin. A new world is opened for the protagonist, and for the first time things make sense.[31]

Thälmann's 1935 narrative is similar to this pattern. His parents were an "anti-socialist" influence, and growing up in an apolitical family, he was naive; he had no proletarian "consciousness." Yet "the experiences, events and reality of everyday life" began to change him. He knew that something was wrong; he could see it as he wandered the streets of Hamburg. The events he described—the poverty, the unemployment, the exploitation—were unaffected, tangible, gritty. He saw firsthand that a few were rich, whereas the many starved. But he did not know why. His parents would not tell him; he got no satisfying responses at school, nor did he find the answers he sought in the German classics. Thälmann was an archetypal example of a "spontaneous" average person seeking "consciousness," although unaware of it.

Then one day, as the result of a single event, his ideological transition began. He went to a socialist rally, where the experience moved him. The young people, the speaker, the singing—all had a "tremendous influence upon . . . [his] way of thinking and . . . [his] imagination." He read a pamphlet, which also made a dramatic impression upon him. Thus began his ideological transformation; he was "more mature and self-conscious," but his journey was not complete. More firsthand experience was needed, in this case his personally being exploited by the capitalist system, first of all by his own father. After he moved out of his parents' house, he was homeless and unemployed. But this situation permitted him to experience the generosity and compassion of the working classes, first with his landlady, who refused to put him in the street even when he could not pay his modest rent, then among the actors at the proletarian theater, who gave him a little money so that he would not go hungry. Thälmann's efforts to find a job contributed to his growing consciousness, and his problems did not go away even after he found a post. He observed the tension between the young temporary workers and the mature permanent workers, and that such disunity only worked to the capitalist exploiters' benefit. All this led Thälmann to join a trade union, for which he became an intensely active recruiter, as well as the SPD.

In his "Lebenslauf," Thälmann emphasized that all these things had happened to him even before he read the writings of Karl Marx and Friedrich Engels.[32] His experiences, not the writings of socialism's greatest thinkers, had led him to socialism. This sequence is important to the "spontaneity–consciousness" paradigm because it emphasizes the inevitability of Thälmann's metamorphosis, which mirrors the historical evolution of the German working classes and the ineluctable victory of communism. Thälmann's conversion was typical; he was an average German worker, and his experiences were repeated untold millions of times. His development personified the progress of the entire German proletariat and the approaching victory of communism. Neither the Nazis nor anyone else could stand in the way of this historical inevitability.

Thälmann's "Lebenslauf" mirrors socialist realism in a variety of other ways. For example, there is an emphasis on what Clark calls an "is/ought-to-be dichotomy."[33] For example, the older unionized workers held the younger unorganized workers in contempt. But all of the workers were in the same boat—they all were exploited by the capitalist classes, and their disunity only helped their enemies. They ought to be working together to build a socialist future for all of the dock workers. Also, on several occasions in his narrative, Thälmann describes the party "bigshots" who were content with the way things were and sat around "like grandmothers." They contrasted unfavorably with the experiences of his first trip to the Soviet Union in 1921, where he came to the "compelling conclusion that there are leaders in the workers' movement . . . who are ready to fight for socialism."[34]

As Clark points out, the socialist-realist hero also exhibits numerous distinct personality traits. For example, he or she rejects traditional religion.[35] Thälmann spurned both his mother's Christianity and the religion taught him in school; yet the hero, like the medieval saint, leads an ascetic life.[36] Thälmann underscores in several instances in his 1935 account that he always lived in extremely modest circumstances and that he had no interest in accumulating material goods. Also, like the classic socialist-realist hero, he was a man of action, who saw injustice and was determined to put things right. He was bound to take what "is" and create what "ought to be."[37] This ability to take action is evidence of another characteristic of the "positive hero": devotion, a cryptoreligious zeal that makes him or her determined never to surrender. Indeed, it can be argued that for the socialist-realist hero, the workers' movement *is* his or her religion.[38] Whether seeking to unionize the young workers in Hamburg's harbor district or carrying out his activities as an SPD representative, Thälmann continuously exhibited this level of dedication, according to his narrative. Even his marriage to Rosa fits the socialist-realist paradigm. Their relationship is mentioned only briefly and even then in sterile, unemotional terms. Thälmann simply describes the working conditions they shared and how circumstances affected his political development. His marriage is of interest only insofar as it helped him to attain consciousness; even love is subject to the dialectic—it is politicized. Nothing is beyond the purview of Marxist–Leninist ideology.[39]

Although Thälmann's narrative exhibits many, indeed most, of the characteristics of a classic socialist-realist text, it does not exhibit all of them. For example, there is no "mentor/disciple" relationship in the text. Further and most obvious, there is no martyrdom, although it can be argued that the situation that Thälmann faced when writing the text anticipated one.[40] But it is an extremely rare socialist-realist text that incorporates *all* of the quintessential characteristics of the genre.

This reading of Thälmann's 1935 "Lebenslauf" raises some interesting issues. We will never know whether he sought purposefully to write this brief autobiography within the socialist-realist paradigm, and it does not matter. As the leader of the KPD from 1925 until his imprisonment, he clearly would have been familiar with Stalinist culture, which by 1933 had completely come to dominate discourse within the Comintern and all of its satellite parties. Indeed, Thälmann has become infamous for the role he played in Stalinizing the KPD. How closely the "Lebenslauf" follows the motifs of socialist realism is evidence of how completely its author had absorbed the elements of Stalinist culture, even if he might have been completely unaware that he was following a particular Soviet model. As Clark and others have argued, socialist realism grew organically out of Soviet culture. It was not a paradigm created by the Stalinist state, but rather by the authors themselves. It evolved as the result of the classic Leninist dialectic of "spontaneity/consciousness," a concept with which Thälmann, for all of his lack of intellectual sophistication, was undoubtedly familiar, and it is not surprising that he incorporated this motif into this brief autobiography.[41] Given how central this dichotomy was to Leninist–Stalinist ideology, it would be surprising if Thälmann had not incorporated many of the elements of socialist realism into his "Lebenslauf" because the theory behind it was a vital component of his worldview.

In this instance, the socialist-realist paradigm served Thälmann well. It enabled him to communicate effectively with both his short- and long-term audiences, his Nazi captors and posterity. The way he constructed his narrative makes it clear that a Leninist worldview was not the product of having read Marx or of some alleged "Jewish influence"—as his captors claimed. It was the outgrowth of everyday experience, shared by millions of people all over the world, which was what made the victory of socialism inevitable. The fascists might be able to hold him in prison, but they could not ultimately win. His "Lebenslauf" made it clear that the victory of Marxism–Leninism–Stalinism was inescapable, as was the ultimate destruction of Hitler fascism. History was on Thälmann's side.

The "Lebenslauf" relates the way that Thälmann hoped to be viewed not only by his Nazi captors, but also by future generations. He wanted to be remembered as an average man who, because he had adopted the teachings of Marx, Lenin, and Stalin, had accomplished a great deal. A modestly educated, often unemployed harbor worker had risen to become the leader of the KPD, the most vibrant force opposing the fascist menace. If this Communist "everyman" could accomplish so much on behalf of socialism, so could others. Thälmann sought to present himself as a model for a future Bolshevik Germany, and all of these motifs would one day become important themes in the Thälmann legend.

Although Thälmann's pre-KPD years became a vital component of the myth, clearly other events came to eclipse them. Among the milestones in the Communist leader's life were the events of October 1923, the famous Hamburger Aufstand (Hamburg Uprising). This aborted revolution, which convulsed the streets of Hamburg for several days, would one day be lionized in poetry, prose, and film. Thälmann was central to these events, which would be interpreted as his first serious attempt to undermine the fascist "system" that was coming increasingly to dominate Germany. The Hamburger Aufstand would play a critical role in catapulting Thälmann to prominence in the KPD and help to secure him a position first on the Central Committee, then as party chairman. Hence, a brief recounting of the aborted 1923 revolution in Hamburg is important to understanding later and largely mythologized renditions of Thälmann's political and ideological maturation.

By 1921, Thälmann had been elected to the Reichstag and was one of Hamburg's two most important Communist politicians, the other being Hugo Urbahns. In many ways, the two men complemented each other well. Whereas Thälmann was an astute organizer and a spirited man of action who represented the concrete interests of the party rank and file, Urbahns, who sought to imbue the workers' movement with Marxist–Leninist ideals, represented the party's intellectual faction. Their different approaches and temperaments also led to a certain amount of animosity between them. Urbahns, who was willing to cooperate with the Social Democrats and underscored the importance of electoral victories, tended to sympathize with the party's right wing. He was a firm advocate of a "united front" strategy, which emphasized the importance of cooperation within the entire proletarian movement, Communist and non-Communist alike.[42]

Thälmann, in contrast, was a staunch leftist, emphasizing the importance of revolutionary action, including political violence. He sought to organize the workers under the banner of the KPD and led them in a series of general strikes designed to destroy the fledgling Weimar Republic and create a Bolshevik Germany. He was among the most prominent representatives of this position at the Third Comintern Congress, held in June and July 1921. This gathering, which spent a great deal of time discussing the situation in Germany, provided Thälmann with his first opportunity to visit the Soviet Union. He was among the delegates who most staunchly opposed the rightist course, arguing that Germany was ripe for revolution.[43] He, like other KPD leftists, had no interest in compromise, and any united front was a temporary tactic to be pursued only as long as it benefitted his own faction. Electoral victories mattered only as far as they provided the opportunity to undermine the republic's bourgeois institutions, and any notion of cooperating with the SPD, the party that most ardently supported the Weimar Constitu-

Ernst Thälmann in January 1932. Courtesy of the German Federal Archive.

tion, would be abandoned when the time was ripe for revolution. In the meantime, ostensible cooperation with the Social Democrats and the free trade unions provided the opportunity to convert as many of their members to the Communist cause as possible. Indeed, the SPD and free trade union leadership was not to be taken seriously. Events on 27 June 1922, when the police, under orders from Weimar authorities, fired upon striking workers only bolstered the leftists' case, and the idea of a united front was abandoned for the time being.[44]

Thälmann's positions on these matters, which were also widespread among the party's rank and file, helped to increase his influence within the movement. He was particularly popular with the party's large contingent of unskilled laborers. The dock worker from Hamburg spoke their language. He was one of their own. Thälmann also exhibited a certain amount of awkward charisma that, as Ruth Fischer—who would later become his political opponent—pointed out, added to his appeal.

> Thälmann was a big man and rather stout. As a youth he had gone to sea in the merchant marine, and he still retained the rolling gait of a sailor. He had a poor education, and Marxist terminology and foreign expressions were always a struggle for him; but his wide experience and excellent political instinct helped him from the beginning of his career. He was a very emotional orator, shouting, sometimes almost incoherently, and tearing off his white collar—a gesture that was invariably greeted with cheers. He won his audiences, however, by the seriousness of his convictions and the passion of his arguments. His hatred of the "generals"—of Hindenburg and Ludendorff—and his irreconcilable opposition to the regrouping of German imperialist forces were beyond question.[45]

Of course, the dock worker's hat and the leather jacket, which he wore almost constantly, added to this image as an average worker, one of the rank and file himself. His nickname, "Teddy," served to contribute to his "common man" image. Even what Werner Angress calls his "notorious predilection for mixed metaphors" proved to be to his advantage. His use of such phrases as "the hour of the moment" and "like a stillborn child which has lost its way in the sand" apparently served to set him apart from the more intellectual leaders of the movement.[46] Workers who did not comprehend the subtleties of dialectical materialism could comprehend what Thälmann had to say, and this anti-intellectual charm would serve him well over the subsequent years.

His increasing popularity assured the Hamburg native an ever more important place in the movement. In April and May 1923, for example, Thälmann was among a number of prominent Communists summoned to Moscow for a secret meeting of the Executive Committee of the Communist International (ECCI). The Moscow leadership sought to heal the ever-widening rift between the party's two main factions. Although the leftists were taken to task for their obstructionism—that is, their unwillingness to take the now defunct "united front" seriously—the Comintern came to the conclusion that more of them needed to be added to the KPD Central Committee. Perhaps their addition would quell the disputes within the party. In any case, it appeared that, for the time being at least, the Left was ascendant. Hence, on 16 May 1923, Thälmann was among four prominent leftists elected to the KPD's governing body.[47]

His new position as one of the party's national leaders assured that Thälmann would play a prominent role in the approaching German October. A successful dock strike in Hamburg, in which the city's harbor was completely shut down for three days and several workers were killed in clashes with the police, led some KPD leaders, including Thälmann, to conclude that the prospects of a revolution had reached an apogee. In late August 1923, KPD Central Committee chairman Karl Brandler was summoned to Moscow to discuss the situation in Germany and assess the plausibility of creating a Bolshevik republic in the near future. At first, Brandler opposed the idea as premature, and, as a result, other KPD leaders more amenable to the proposal—including Thälmann—were summoned to Moscow. The KPD's left wing, allied with the Soviet leadership, won the day, and by the time the conclave ended in early October, the determination was reached to launch an insurrection later in the month. Thälmann would play an instrumental role in subsequent developments.[48]

The sequence of the events surrounding the German October remains a subject of controversy, but the basics of what happened can be related here briefly. In January 1923, in response to Berlin's defaulting on its reparations payments for the war, French and Belgian troops occupied the Ruhr River Valley, Germany's industrial hub, hoping to force compliance. In response, the Germans pursued a policy of passive resistance, which in turn led to the collapse of the German economy and an inflationary spiral without precedent in European history.[49] The parliamentary system created at Weimar was on the verge of collapse, and extremists on both the right and left considered the economic crisis to be the death knell of the republic and sought to take advantage of the situation.

These were the conditions under which the Moscow meetings in August 1923 took place. The KPD and the Comintern held that, given the widespread discontent throughout Germany, the country was ripe for a revolution similar to the one that occurred in Russia just six years earlier. The German revolution was to begin on 23 October. But the party leadership, meeting in Chemnitz, called off the rebellion at the last minute. Most of the potential participants received word of this decision, but the German October proceeded in Hamburg. Thälmann was ringleader of events in his home city, a circumstance that would have a dramatic effect on his subsequent political career.

Exactly why the revolution transpired in Hamburg even though the Central Committee had successfully called off the uprising in the remainder of the country remains uncertain. There are at least three potential explanations. First of all, it is possible that Thälmann never received notification from the Central Committee, but this means that Hamburg was the only major city in the entire country not to receive news of the cancellation, which seems unlikely. Another alternative is that Thälmann received notification too late and that events were already under way in Hamburg when the courier arrived from Chemnitz. If this was the case, Thälmann continued the action even after he received word that the plan had been abandoned elsewhere. Finally, it is also possible that he was notified in time but decided to proceed anyway. If either of these last two explanations reflects actual events, then apparently Thälmann hoped that circumstances in Hamburg would serve as a catalyst for the spread of the revolution throughout Germany. In any event, he most likely disobeyed the dictates of his fellow Central Committee members, hardly the actions of a leader imbued with strict party discipline.[50] Nonetheless, the events of October 1923 would become a vital component of the Thälmann myth.

The Hamburg party leader, who had visited Chemnitz before the Central Committee reached the decision to abort the uprising, returned to Hamburg on 22 October. All buildings owned by the KPD were closed to non-Communists. On the early morning of 23 October, Communist revolutionaries erected barricades throughout Hamburg. Around 4:15 AM, about 1,300 Communist insurgents stormed twenty-six police stations throughout the city, hoping to acquire weapons and lead the entire proletariat against its bourgeois oppressors. But in the end only about 5,000 workers participated in the rebellion. As Ruth Fischer points out, "The Hamburg workers fought under the illusion that all Germany was fighting, that Russia would soon intervene," although the Hamburg leadership eventually came to know otherwise. When the expected expansion of the revolution evaporated, and it became clear to the insurgents in Hamburg that they fought alone, the uprising disintegrated. It was over by the end of 24 October.[51]

That is, it was over everywhere except in the proletarian district of Barmbeck, where Thälmann and his cohort continued to fight, hoping against hope that conditions would escalate and that the Soviets would intervene. By the end of 25 October, Thälmann and his exhausted men surrendered their weapons. The German October had failed miserably. Twenty-one of the insurgents were dead, and another 175 were wounded. Seventeen policemen lost their lives, and sixty-nine of them were injured during the course of the fighting.[52] The national government established a special court to deal with the insurgents. It met until January 1924, trying 443 accused revolutionaries, about one-quarter of whom were convicted of various crimes and received sentences ranging from a few months in prison to the death penalty. Among those convicted, the average sentence was incarceration for around fifteen months. Thälmann was charged with "high treason," but he had immunity from prosecution as a member of the Reichstag. The Hamburg court sought to have his immunity lifted, which led Thälmann to flee to the Soviet Union. The Reichstag, however, refused to sanction the court's actions, and he was able to return to Germany in July 1924.[53]

The entire event should have been an embarrassment to the party, but this was anything but the case. As Werner T. Angress explains, "German Communists . . . endowed the [Hamburg] uprising with a symbolic significance it never warranted. The Hamburg barricades became the party's Thermopylae, and Thälmann its Leonidas."[54] A mythology quickly developed surrounding Thälmann's role in the events of October 1923. The KPD propaganda machine insisted that he had not been defeated and that the revolution had failed because of the timidity of others, both on the KPD's right wing and in the Comintern. If all of the insurgency's leaders were as steadfast as Thälmann, the party line maintained, it could not have possibly failed. In short, Thälmann became the ultimate symbol of the self-sacrificing, determined revolutionary who could serve as a model for every good Communist.[55] In a speech given on the third anniversary of the uprising, Thälmann himself likened the Hamburger Aufstand to Russia's 1905 revolution: "There like here, a few hundred workers struggled to the death for the entire working class. . . . There like here, the fighters on the barricades left the battle undefeated." The party had learned valuable lessons from the events of 23–25 October: the danger of "opportunism" and the necessity of winning over the masses to the revolutionary course. But, like the 1905 revolutionaries, the KPD was assured ultimate victory, and the days of the bourgeois order were numbered. Thälmann and his comrades had not fought in vain; rather, they helped to pave the way for the inevitable victory of socialism.[56]

Thälmann's position as the KPD's Leonidas was solidified at the Comintern's Fifth World Conference in January 1924, where he publically castigated Grigori Zinoviev for abandoning the German proletariat in its hour of need. Zinoviev's position, as we now know, was in eclipse, and Thälmann's star was ascending. To a large extent because of his actions in the German October, the Hamburg native was elected to the Comintern's Presidium.[57]

Thälmann's elevation to the Comintern's ruling body was indicative of the Left's success at the Fifth World Conference. The Moscow leadership favored Thälmann's faction because of its willingness to participate actively in the Bolshevization of the KPD. The KPD lost any semblance of independence from the Third International, and it was coming increasingly under Soviet domination. The party's left wing eagerly acceded to these developments. Thälmann, for one, benefitted dramatically from this turn of events, and he would remain loyal to the line coming out of Moscow for the rest of his political career, even when it contradicted his own predilections. He proved to be extremely adept at taking Moscow's orders. After all, these changes assured that significant numbers of his political opponents were purged from the party. The KPD leadership, especially Thälmann and his closest political allies, was becoming the instrument of Moscow, and developments within the German party came increasingly to mirror the power struggle within the Soviet Union, assuring the Stalinization of the KPD. The fact that the Comintern abandoned the "united front" strategy in January 1924 undoubtedly served to make these circumstances easier for the Left to swallow. Indeed, undoubtedly to the Left's delight, the Fifth World Congress adopted the "social fascist" line, which maintained that the SPD was a bourgeois organization with much more in common with Germany's right-wing parties than with the KPD. The Comintern determined that "[a]s bourgeois society decays, all bourgeois parties, particularly social democracy, take on a more or less Fascist character. . . . Fascism and social democracy are two sides of the same instrument of big capitalist dictatorship." Zinoviev was even blunter when he stated that "international social democracy has now become a wing of fascism." The KPD quickly adopted this position, which would have dramatic consequences during the final years of the Weimar Republic.[58]

Although the KPD's stance concerning "social fascism" proved to be damaging to the republic in the long run, it proved advantageous to the party's left wing, especially to Thälmann, who was rapidly emerging as his faction's most prominent leader, as can be seen in the events following Reichspräsident Friedrich Ebert's sudden death at the end of February 1925. Because Ebert, as Weimar's first chief executive, had been appointed to his post by the Reichstag, the republic faced its first presidential election. At a 3 March meeting of the KPD's Central Committee, Wilhelm Pieck, who was sympathetic to the party's right wing, maintained that a candidate from his faction had the best chance of winning or at least garnering a significant number of votes. Weimar had stabilized following currency reform, and so Pieck and many other German Communists believed that the time was not ripe for a fanatically revolutionary candidate. He therefore tried to convince the Central Committee to nominate the right-wing Communist Clara Zetkin. But the party was firmly in the hands of the Left, and Thälmann was the clear choice. As Ruth Fischer explains, "The German Politburo selected him because of his status within the party as the personification of the revolutionary German worker."[59] Thälmann was, however, unelectable—but it would turn out that the same could be said regarding the other parties' candidates.

The 1925 presidential election indicates how deeply divided Germany remained in spite of the economic stabilization. Because of the KPD's leftward course and the subsequent abandonment of the "united front," the working-class parties remained divided, each nominating its own candidate. The Social Democrats named Otto Braun, and he and Thälmann would be targeting many of the same voters. The Catholic Center Party (Zentrum) designated Wilhelm Marx as its candidate, and the German People's Party (DVP) and a conglomeration of other right-wing groups nominated Karl Jarres, the mayor of Duisburg. There were also three minor candidates, including the NSDAP's nominee, Erich Ludendorff. Even more damaging than the division between the proletarian parties was the split between the two largest pro-Weimar parties, the SPD and the Zentrum. Clearly no one, certainly not Thälmann,

Campaigning for Ernst Thälmann, March 1925. Courtesy of the German Federal Archive.

would secure the majority necessary under the Weimar Constitution to get elected on the first ballot, which would be held on 29 March 1925.[60]

The fact that Thälmann had no chance of getting elected did not stop him from conducting a vigorous campaign. On 13 March, the Communist candidate began his effort in earnest, making numerous speeches to mass assemblies all over Germany. His message was simple and would remain consistent throughout the remainder of his political career: the "exploitative system" of Weimar Germany had to go. It would be replaced by a "Workers' Republic" modeled on the Soviet Union. Thälmann's position on German foreign policy was in harmony with his domestic program—he demanded a rejection of close cooperation with the Western powers in favor of an alliance with the Soviet Union, the only country that truly cared about the fate of the German proletariat. The KPD's positions on these issues were consistent with what was coming out of the Comintern in Moscow. Joseph Stalin, who dominated Soviet politics, viewed close cooperation between Germany and the Western powers—namely, Great Britain and France—as contrary to Russian interests. Hence, the KPD was to do all that it could to undermine cordial relations with the West. Thälmann, who supported this stance, had no difficulty maintaining the party line.[61]

Although Thälmann's 1925 bid for Germany's presidency would not play nearly as important a role in the development of the legend as his 1932 campaign against Paul von Hindenburg and Adolf Hitler, it is worth analyzing briefly. One can see the genesis of many of the most important components of the Thälmann myth in the KPD propaganda of 1925. For example, after he gave a campaign speech in Munich, some of the workers in attendance presented the Communist candidate with a red banner, the words "To the fighters on Hamburg's barricades" emblazoned on it.[62] The Hamburg Uprising was already becoming an important component of Thälmann's persona.

This was not the only prominent motif of later years that can be seen in the 1925 campaign, however. The Communist daily *Rote Fahne* (Red Flag) characterized Thälmann as the "Red Candidate," the "Candidate of the Workers," the "Candidate of the Revolution." The Communist leader was "the only Workers' Candidate," the solitary presidential hopeful who sought the benefit of the average working man and the only laborer among the competitors. He alone would "complete the work of November 1918" and eradicate the "bourgeois republic."[63] Appealing to German nationalism, he opposed the Treaty of Versailles, insisting it subverted the interests of the German proletariat and benefited only the imperialists in London and Paris. As the Communists consistently pointed out, the only European power that opposed Versailles was the Soviet Union, which was willing to cooperate with the German people to the advantage of the working class everywhere. Only Leninist Russia, seeking the advantage of the toiling masses, rejected the imperialists' policies.[64] A common man himself, Thälmann would govern on behalf of Germany's working people. Hand in hand with the Soviet people, only he could assure Germans a peaceful, prosperous future.[65]

Another theme that ran throughout the campaign concerned the crowds that came to hear Thälmann speak. Communist campaign literature constantly stressed their size and composition. Headlines in *Rote Fahne*, for example, bellowed that "20,000 Proletarians Demonstrate in the Sportpalast—Tens of Thousands on the Streets" and "30,000 Hamburg Workers Demonstrate for Thälmann." The accompanying articles likewise emphasized the magnitude and determination of his support.[66] By implication, workers who did not support the KPD's nominee could not be considered true proletarians. The message was clear: the overwhelming support that Thälmann received from average German voters assured his victory and the ultimate triumph of Marxism–Leninism.

The newspaper sought to create the illusion of an instinctual mass support. The workers allegedly stood behind him simply because they knew what was in their own interests. This approach was fairly typical of Communist and later National Socialist political propaganda in the Weimar Republic. In fact, it has long been integral to mass politics, and *Rote Fahne* was simply incorporating a motif that preceded the rise of twentieth-century political movements by centuries.[67]

Rote Fahne also lauded its candidate in poetry incorporating these themes:

> And yet there stands a "red boulder"
> A man like you in a worker's coat
> What you experience, he also experiences
> Proletarian, is your decision still difficult?
>
> All of you who suffer in drudgery
> And are tormented by hunger,
> Away with the lies and treason!
> Thälmann is your candidate![68]

This dreadful verse, which at least has the virtue of rhyming in the original German, also attacked Thälmann's opponents. Braun, the candidate of the hated Social Democrats, or "social fascists"—traitors to the toiling classes—naturally came in for the most malicious attacks. In a poem entitled "For Whom Will We Vote," *Rote Fahne* referred to Braun as a "Rat Catcher" who is just keeping "the position warm" for the right-wing candidate, Jarres. Wilhelm Marx was, of course, merely the tool of the Vatican, one of the bourgeoisie's candidates, who would do nothing for the working man.[69]

These attacks on the two status quo candidates mirrored the KPD's position concerning the Weimar Republic, which, as the party saw it, was a regime dominated by the bourgeoisie, interested only in the profits accrued by the capitalist exploiting classes. The exploiting class would stop at nothing to defeat a Thälmann candidacy, *Rote Fahne* insisted. The paper claimed, for example, that an attempt on the Communist candidate's life was narrowly averted. Someone, a tool of the business moguls who dominated the system, apparently planned to throw a hand grenade at Thälmann as he traveled to give a speech in Berlin's Sportpalast. Only the diligent work of the KPD's paramilitary wing, the RFB, averted disaster. The capitalist exploiters were clearly willing to go to any lengths to assure their continued domination of Germany.[70] The proletariat could expect only exploitation, denigration, and hunger from such a system. This government must be destroyed and replaced with a revolutionary, socialist, Bolshevik, pro-Soviet "workers' republic" if the German people really wanted progress. There was no other choice.

In the end, the vast majority of German voters cast their ballots for non-Communist candidates, but a majority could not agree on any of the presidential aspirants. Thälmann received around 1.9 million votes, or only 7 percent of the total, which was more than 800,000 fewer votes than his party had gotten in the most recent Reichstag election. This number placed him a very distant fourth in the contest. Jarres, the rightist candidate, came in first with almost 10.5 million votes, or almost 39 percent. Braun placed second with 7.8 million votes, and Marx third with almost 4 million votes. No one was close to receiving the majority needed to secure victory on the first ballot. A second election was scheduled for four weeks later, when only a plurality of votes would be needed to secure victory.[71]

In light of the 29 March election fiasco, questions arose regarding whether Thälmann should run in the second election or not, which was scheduled for 26 April. These concerns became even more acute when Field Marshal Paul von Hindenburg, the hero of the battle of Tannenberg, announced on 7 April that he would seek the presidency in order to secure national stability. Hindenburg was a staunch monarchist, but very popular, so in response to his announcement the pro-Weimar parties decided to unite behind Wilhelm Marx, who would run again as the pro-republic candidate.[72] Hindenburg's candidacy only increased the pressure on Thälmann to sit out the second election. The contest between Hindenburg and Marx would be a close one, and Thälmann's candidacy might take enough votes from Marx to assure a Hindenburg victory. Comintern chief Zinoviev, fearing just such a scenario, suggested that the KPD stay out of the second election, but the KPD Central Committee decided on 11 April to place its candidate on the second ballot.[73] Rote Fahne, explaining this controversial decision, insisted that there was no significant difference between the "civilian dictator Marx and the military dictator Hindenburg." Both represented the bourgeoisie, and the Communists had no interest in the politics of exploitation. From the KPD's perspective, it did not matter who won, and "every class-conscious worker stands against Hindenburg and Marx and for Thälmann!"[74]

The KPD propaganda machine did not put nearly as much effort into the April election as it had into the previous month's contest. *Rote Fahne*, for example, allocated much more space to an ongoing railroad strike and the approaching Reichstag elections. The Communists read the writing on the wall, and although their candidate campaigned, the party's efforts were halfhearted at best. Meanwhile, the KPD's positions on the major issues facing Germany remained unchanged. Although Thälmann garnered around 60,000 more votes on 26 April than in the previous month's election, his share of the total fell to 6.4 percent. Hindenburg won with slightly more than 14.5 million votes, or 48 percent. Marx, the republican candidate, received a little more than 13.75 million votes. Given the fact that the vast majority of the Communist votes probably would have gone to Marx, it can be argued that Thälmann's effort cost the center candidate the election. An avowed monarchist became president of the Weimar Republic, which did not bode well for the supporters of the centrist or left-wing parties, especially the workers who voted for the Communist Party. Overall the election not only was a washout for the republic but also—in the long run—proved catastrophic for the KPD.[75]

In spite of his abysmal showing in the 1925 campaigns, Thälmann continued to accrue influence within the KPD. The reasons behind this outcome had more to do with events in the Soviet Union—especially the power struggle following Lenin's death—than with what was going on in Germany. The Soviet government and its international surrogate, the Comintern, sought to bring the KPD and other parties in the Third International under increased Soviet influence. These developments reflected considerations of Soviet domestic politics rather than the international situation. As Stalin tightened his hold over Russia and the Comintern, he sought to assure that the international Communist parties within the Soviet orbit were Bolshevized, which in this context meant Stalinized. Indeed, the theme of the Fifth Comintern Congress, which met from 21 March to 6 April 1925, was the "Bolshevization of the parties of the Communist International."[76] Although Thälmann could not attend the meeting because of the presidential campaign, he was in sympathy with its goals. One of the attributes of Stalinization was the purging of the Comintern's intellectuals, beginning with Stalin's attacks upon Zinoviev and Leon Trotsky in the 1920s, culminating with the removal of Nikolai Bukharin and his supporters. The Hamburg Communist leader firmly supported these moves. Thälmann was eager to drive the intellectuals out of the KPD as well and hoped to Stalinize the party under his own leadership. Perhaps, as was the case with his Soviet mentor, Thälmann's actions were the product of more than just political expediency. Like Stalin, he had a deep-seated distrust of the intelligentsia. This attitude was probably a product of envy as well as of the fact that he was simply incapable of understanding the subtleties of intellectual debate. He was a man of action, not a party theorist, and Lenin and Stalin told him all that he needed to know concerning Marxism. In any case, Thälmann was the eager tool of his Soviet master.[77]

Stalin and the Comintern helped to prepare the way for Thälmann's purge of his party's intellectuals. Two of the figures who had dominated the KPD in the first half of the 1920s, Ruth Fischer and Arkadi Maslow, had, from the Comintern's point of view, shown too much independence in the past. Fischer, who had become the party's chairman about a year earlier, publicly challenged the Bolshevization of the KPD at the party's Tenth Congress in July 1925. To make matters worse, Maslow held that the Comintern had repeatedly failed to take the Social Democratic traditions of German Marxism into account, as it should. The German working class was simply not as radical as the Comintern would have liked, Maslow insisted, and any notions regarding a Communist revolution in Germany had to be abandoned for at least ten years. Fischer agreed with this position, making it clear that she was willing to work with the bourgeois parties to preserve the republic—at least for the time being. In this position, she was also in agreement with views expressed by Zinoviev earlier in the month. But Zinoviev's authority was in decline, and appeals to his opinion would hardly win Fischer support from the increasingly Stalinist Comintern. The KPD's far Left turned on Fischer and Maslow, mouthpieces of the moderate Left, the result of which was that three more ultraleftists— Hans Weber, Arthur Rosenberg, and Werner Scholem—were elected to the Central Committee in July. In August 1925, Fischer, Maslow, and Thälmann were summoned to Moscow, where the Fischer–Maslow faction was chastised for its excessive intellectualism, which caused it to be out of touch with the party membership. Further, Fischer and Maslow were called on the carpet for their indifference to the trade union movement, which was near and dear to Thälmann's heart. In the eyes of the Comintern, they needed to do more to organize workers under Communist auspices. Thälmann accused his comrades of disobeying direct orders from the Comintern, and on 11 August the KPD's Presidium voted that all members of the party's Central Committee had to agree with the "new course" taken by the Communist Party of the Soviet Union (CPSU), a move that undermined Trotsky, Zinoviev, and Lev Kamenev—all intellectuals. In the end, Moscow forced Fischer to resign her position as head of the party, and in November she and Maslow were driven from the KPD Central Committee.[78] A more submissive leadership had to be found, and on 1 September 1925, at the age of thirty-nine, Ernst Thälmann was elected chairman of the KPD.[79] He eagerly performed the tasks assigned him. An "Open Letter" explaining the recent changes appeared in *Rote Fahne*, accusing the former leadership of placing too much faith in the bourgeois parliamentary system, an example of "right deviation." To make matters worse, the Communist trade union movement had languished under Fischer's leadership. Finally, the old leadership, *Rote Fahne* reported, was never willing to enforce party discipline, and the KPD had become too ideologically diverse, little more than a debating society, rendering it politically impotent. Especially dangerous to party stability was the ultra-Left, which allied itself with Trotsky and Zinoviev. Mirroring events in Moscow, the KPD would abandon the course championed by Fischer and other party intellectuals. The Comintern, shifting rightward, decided that international capitalism had entered a temporary period of stabilization and that revolution was unlikely in the immediate future.[80] Ironically, the new KPD leadership would pursue much the same line as that proposed by the recently ousted party intellectuals. Thälmann's party would seek a "united front from below," although it would steadfastly refuse to cooperate with the SPD leadership. The new party chief never abandoned his goal of destroying the SPD. The Social Democratic leadership remained the "social fascists" and traitors to the proletariat's cause. Cooperation was to occur only with the SPD rank and file. Thälmann had won the day, but he had to put on hold any aspirations he had with an eye to revolution in the near future. The same conviction—which witnessed the temporary abandonment of global revolution—had become dominant in Moscow, where Stalin used it to emasculate his rivals politically.[81]

Thälmann proved remarkably adept at anticipating and following the often convoluted line coming out of Moscow. Although hardly an intellectual, he was an astute politician—otherwise he could not have survived the twisted course of Communist politics during the late 1920s. He adapted quickly to the course of events in the Soviet Union and foresaw the effects that they would have upon the KPD. For example, Thälmann conformed quickly to Stalin's program of "Socialism in One Country," introduced in 1928, which justified Stalin's assault upon his former ally Bukharin. Like its Soviet counterpart, the KPD experienced yet another purge of those unsympathetic with the new line coming out of Moscow. Once again, the Soviet Union's interests came first; the "Socialist Fatherland" must be protected. The Comintern's Sixth World Conference introduced another change in course in July and August 1928. Stalin feared that Germany's Great Coalition government under Hermann Müller was too pro-Western and was preparing, alongside Great Britain and France, for war against the Soviet Union. In response, the Comintern declared that the years of stabilization beginning in 1923 were at an end and that Europe was entering a period of "capitalist reconstruction" in which the contradictions in capitalism would become more acute. Although this change made an "imperialist" assault upon the Soviet Union more likely, a consequence that must be resisted at any cost, it also made the situation in Germany and the rest of Europe more ripe for revolution. Stalin was moving against his erstwhile allies on the right and ordered the KPD to resist the policies of the Great Coalition with all of the forces at its disposal. In other words, it must move back to the left. Thälmann, a determined revolutionary never enamored with the idea of a stabilization period, adapted quite quickly to the new circumstances. He was an ardent admirer of the Soviet Union, considered its preservation the most important objective of any good Communist, and eagerly lauded Stalin's policies. In addition, this latest purge of the KPD further solidified his position within both Germany and the Comintern.[82]

But just as Thälmann's influence was at its apex, a scandal erupted that almost led to his expulsion from both the Politburo and the Central Committee. In 1927, Thälmann had appointed a close personal friend and drinking companion, John Wittorf, to lead the party in Hamburg. Wittorf was apparently a compulsive gambler who ended up embezzling 1,850 marks to pay off some of his debts. When Thälmann discovered what Wittorf had done, he attempted to conceal his old friend's indiscretion. But word leaked out, and the Communist newspaper *Volkswille* (Will of the People), operated by some of Thälmann's political enemies, published the story. His opponents now had the ammunition to oust their party chief in spite of the support he had among the rank and file, not to mention Moscow. On 23 September 1928, the Politburo sacked Wittorf and his Hamburg cronies. On 25 September, after Thälmann announced that he would abide by whatever decision the party leadership reached, it recommended that he be removed temporarily from the Politburo and the Central Committee until the Comintern could decide his fate. Only three members of the Central Committee, which confirmed the Politburo's decision, stood by him. But the pliable Thälmann was too important to Stalin and his allies. In response, Moscow sent its representative, David Petrovsky-Bennett, to Berlin to smooth things over. In addition, Stalin called the entire KPD Politburo to a meeting in Moscow, where he made it clear that he backed his beleaguered German ally. In the end, at a 2 October meeting the KPD Politburo voted ten to nothing—with three abstentions—in support of a resolution that the German Communist leader "should remain in the party leadership despite his grave political errors."[83] Stalin saved Thälmann in his hour of need, evincing the German Communist's value to his Soviet master. Needless to say, this support only encouraged the restored KPD leader to become even more subordinate to Moscow's wishes, a situation that worked out well for Stalin. Further evidence that Thälmann's value to the new Moscow leadership was more important than success in Germany can be seen in the fact that in the year or so preceding the scandal KPD membership dropped by around 15,000, from 145,000 to 130,000, and even the former number was down by half from 294,000 on the eve of the German October in 1923. The German party leader's kowtowing to Moscow clearly had little appeal to the German proletariat, although it should be pointed out that the party's paramilitary wing, the RFB, had a membership of 127,000 in August 1927. But most of the RFB members were non-Communists, although the organization was under complete party control. The KPD's shrinking membership was apparently not very dedicated, and there was a great deal of turnover. Whereas younger people, those between twenty-five and forty, were overrepresented—undoubtedly a good thing for the party—women were underrepresented, composing only 16.5 percent of the membership, as opposed, for example, to the SPD's 21 percent female membership.[84] Although his party was in disarray, Thälmann maintained his position because of his eager adherence to the Stalinist line, a circumstance that would have dramatic consequences in the years to come.[85]

Evidence of Thälmann's servility to Moscow can be seen in his continued efforts to Stalinize the KPD, which was evident in the evolution of its agitation and propaganda (agit-prop) apparatus. Willi Münzenberg—a staunch Communist who rose to prominence at about the same time as Thälmann—oversaw the metamorphosis of KPD propaganda. Born in Erfurt in August 1889, he created a massive media empire, incorporating press, film, radio, and publishing. While he put the resources of his International Workers Aid at the KPD's disposal, he worked his way up the party hierarchy, becoming an important figure in its youth organization. This Communist media tsar, among Thälmann's closest political allies, became a member of the Central Committee in 1927. Münzenberg's newspapers, publications, and films continuously and vociferously lauded the USSR's accomplishments, while seeking to undermine the institutions of the Weimar Republic. Münzenberg and his media empire would play an important role in KPD propaganda until his death in 1940.[86] Another important component of this transformation was the RFB, founded in 1924, with Thälmann becoming its largely symbolic chief a year later and Willy Leow running its daily affairs. This paramilitary wing of the party, established primarily as a propaganda troop, became involved in what amounted to a civil war with the Nazi paramilitary organization the Sturmabteilungen (SA, Storm Sections), during the republic's final years. At the RFB's foundation, its primary goal was to create an image of the KPD as a well-organized political machine, certain one day to bring revolution to Germany. As Ruth Fischer recalls, under Thälmann

> [u]niformed Communists, young men with a good bearing, marching in military formation under disciplined command, became a frequent and popular sight in Germany; and when their bands played workers' songs and military marches in the market squares, they attracted big crowds. League members marched in formation to all Communist meetings and, standing at attention at the side of the platform, greeted each speaker with a raised fist salute and *"Rot Front! Heil Moskau!"* They guarded the entrance to the hall and protected party members distributing literature; at street meetings they surrounded the speakers' platform. When Clara Zetkin or Ernst Thälmann spoke, they formed an honor guard, standing at attention while the Communist dignitary made a ceremonious inspection.[87]

The RFB's participation altered the character of KPD rallies, which, as Fischer put it, "changed from the rather dull Social Democratic pattern to a cross between new-style Russian propaganda and American advertising. Party affairs were enlivened by organized mass choruses, and figures of the party's enemies were burned in effigy. The rifle clubs of this period used the faces of [Austen] Chamberlain [British foreign secretary] and other enemies of Soviet Russia as targets."[88] Every Communist Party event, however minor, became an opportunity to spew forth pro-Soviet, anti-Weimar propaganda. Much as in the Soviet Union, spectacle became more important than substance, and the magnitude of the demonstration took precedence over the message presented.[89]

This message was simple. The Weimar Constitution assured the continued domination of the bourgeoisie and the exploitation of the masses. The only hope for the German people, indeed for all of humanity, lay with the Soviet Union, the brainchild of the glorious Lenin, who became the most important figure in KPD propaganda. A Lenin cult, similar to that developing in Stalinist Russia, pervaded the pages of the German Communist press.[90] Lenin's visage—often alongside those of Marx, Engels, and occasionally Stalin—adorned rostrums where KPD leaders spoke. Lenin's birthday and the anniversary of his death became solemn celebrations on the calendar of the KPD's secular religion. Efforts to link Lenin with the German revolutionary movement manifested themselves in the "LLL" commemorations that marked important anniversaries in the lives of Lenin, Karl Liebknecht, and Rosa Luxemburg.[91]

Liebknecht and Luxemburg, murdered by right-wing thugs in January 1919, had been important symbols for the German Left since the early years of the Weimar Republic. Only a few days following their deaths, Paul Levi, speaking at a memorial in their honor, touted them as representative of all of those revolutionaries throughout the world who in recent years had given their lives in service to the proletariat. They became shining examples of all that was progressive in the human spirit. They had established the German Communist Party, the speaker pointed out, as well as its official newspaper, *Rote Fahne*. The pair had fought diligently, over a period of decades, for the benefit of the toiling masses. It was right, Levi insisted, that they always be remembered.[92]

Since his rise to prominence in the KPD, Thälmann had been an outspoken advocate of the Liebknecht–Luxemburg myth, seeking to link their sacrifice with the accomplishments of Lenin and the Soviet Union, not to mention the KPD's future achievements. As early as June 1926, at a ceremony commemorating the seventh anniversary of Luxemburg's funeral, Thälmann, anticipating the ways that future East German leaders would manipulate his memory, sought to link himself with the sacrifice made by the two fallen founders of the KPD (see chapter 3). While Wilhelm Pieck gave the keynote speech, Thälmann stood alone before the party's Liebknecht–Luxemburg memorial, dressed in his RFB uniform, his right fist raised in defiance of the capitalist exploiters. By implication, the new Communist leader was receiving the party founders' blessing. To elevate them and invoke their legacy was to exalt himself and his party.[93]

Liebknecht and Luxemburg, however, were problematic symbols for the Stalinized KPD. Both had shown a great deal of independence from Moscow, and Luxemburg had had the audacity to disagree publicly with Lenin, the infallible founder of the Soviet Union.[94] But Thälmann, recognizing the importance of these two figures to German communism, refused to abandon remembrance of them and their legacy to the "social fascists." As he put it in the final days of the Weimar Republic, "We have no intention of diminishing the importance of Rosa Luxemburg, Karl Liebknecht, Franz Mehring, and other comrades who formed the left radical wing of pre-war social democracy. We have no intention of denying their solid revolutionary traditions. And we certainly do not want to leave them to the social fascists . . . , who defame the dead. Rosa Luxemburg and others belong to us, belong to the Communist International and the KPD, to whose founding they contributed."[95] However, Thälmann made it abundantly clear that his party would tolerate no ideological deviation based on Luxemburg's anti-Leninist views. He made this point quite clearly on more than one occasion, and he usually made an effort to criticize the Communist martyr for her disagreements with Lenin even when he gave a speech praising her. On 19 February 1932, for example, he was quite blunt: "We must also clearly point out: on every question upon which Rosa Luxemburg had an opinion different from Lenin's, her position was wrong."[96] Thälmann could have his cake and eat it, too. A woman whose most famous statement was "Freedom is always the freedom to think differently" would ironically become a Stalinist icon.[97]

The Liebknecht–Luxemburg cult is of interest because of the many ways that it anticipated the Thälmann myth of the post–Second World War years. The pair had given their lives in the struggle against bourgeois exploitation and fascist militarism, making the ultimate sacrifice for the benefit of international socialism. Somewhat artificially, they were linked with the accomplishments of Lenin and the Soviet Union, providing legitimacy for their ideological heirs in the KPD of the 1920s and 1930s. Decades later East Germany's governing Socialist Unity Party would use Thälmann's legacy (*Vermächtnis*) to legitimize its rule, and many of the same motifs would be incorporated. But linking Thälmann to Lenin and the socialist experiment in Russia, concerning which Luxemburg was quite critical, was much more legitimate. Hence, although the Liebknecht and Luxemburg myths would be incorporated into the GDR's secular religion, the Thälmann legend would eclipse them both, but no one would ever overshadow Lenin in the SED pantheon.

Liebknecht and Luxemburg were not the only Communists to sacrifice their lives for the German proletariat during the Weimar years. Hundreds of lesser-known Communists, members of the rank and file, were killed in street fights with members of other political parties, especially the NSDAP. These men, most of whom were members of the party's paramilitary wing, the RFB, also became martyrs in the Communist pantheon. They were sacrifices presented on the altar of world revolution, men who had willingly given their lives to make Germany a better place for all working people. They were also to serve as examples to others, including proletarian adherents of the SPD. As Thälmann put it himself in September 1930, "In reality, the fight against the fascist forces of the bourgeoisie, which shows our party to the Social-Democratic workers as the only anticapitalist and antifascist force, is the strongest support of their disengagement from the social fascist leaders."[98] This is an interesting statement on Thälmann's part. Although he was perfectly willing to engage in what amounted to a small-scale civil war against the "Hitler fascists," crushing the "social fascists" by winning over their working-class supporters remained his primary goal. Even after the Nazi electoral breakthrough in September 1930, Hitler and his minions were of secondary importance to Thälmann. The primary enemy remained, ultimately, the German Social Democratic Party. In spite of this fact, it is for his fight against Hitler and National Socialism during the final two and a half years of the Weimar Republic that Thälmann would be most widely remembered. His struggle against "Hitler fascism" would also go on to become the central component of the postwar Thälmann myth.

The NSDAP won 18.3 percent of the vote in the 14 September 1930 Reichstag elections. This shocking development made the viciously antidemocratic party the second largest in the German Parliament, trailing only the SPD, which garnered 24.5 percent of the vote. The KPD's portion of the vote rose by 2.5 percent, when compared to the previous election held in May 1928, to 13.1 percent. When the KPD and NSDAP totals were combined with those achieved by other groups on the extreme left and right, the antirepublican parties garnered nearly 60 percent of the votes cast. The Weimar Republic faced its most serious crisis.[99]

But Thälmann and the KPD refused to panic. *Rote Fahne*, downplaying the Nazis' success, insisted that the "most important thing about the results of the Reichstag election of 14 September" was "the electoral victory of the Communist Party." Meanwhile, also attempting to explain how the results amounted to a KPD victory, the party chairman insisted that "one Communist vote has more weight than ten to twenty National Socialist votes combined" because the KPD voters were such ardent revolutionaries.[100] Further, Thälmann insisted, because of the crisis faced by the bourgeoisie, the republic's days were numbered, and the Nazis were not a threat in the long run. Hitler's ultimate failure would only increase KPD support among disaffected NSDAP voters. In short, the Nazi success was a good thing because it would speed up the timetable of revolution. The success of National Socialism represented the last gasp of monopoly capital in Germany. Thälmann continued to underestimate the long-term danger that Hitler's party posed even as late as February 1932, when he said in a speech delivered in his home town of Hamburg that "Hitler must come to power first, then the requirements for a revolutionary crisis [will] arrive more quickly." In the eyes of the KPD, the fascist dictatorship had begun with the rise of Heinrich Brüning to Germany's chancellorship, and the SPD, which promoted a false consciousness among its working-class members, remained the foremost threat to the proletariat.[101]

This is not to suggest that Thälmann did not respond at all to the success of Hitler fascism. In keeping with a Comintern order issued at the end of February 1930, the KPD began somewhat halfheartedly to pursue, once again, a "united front from below." Although the Communists would continue to castigate the Social Democratic leadership as "social fascists," the Communists attempted to appeal to the SPD rank and file. Social Democratic workers were not to be treated as enemies, but as potential comrades to be won over to the Communist cause. Thälmann also hoped to attract workers who supported the NSDAP.[102] Most famously, in July 1932, at a meeting held in the KPD headquarters, the Karl Liebknecht House, Thälmann established Antifascist Action, an organization created to fight against the "Brown Pest" that was killing the KPD's youngest, most determined members in the political street battles that plagued the republic's final years. In keeping with the "united front" tactic, one did not have to be a member of the Communist Party to join Antifascist Action, and Social Democratic workers would be actively recruited. But Thälmann continued to insist that cooperation with the SPD rank and file was a temporary development and that this "moderate wing of fascism" had to be vanquished. His unwillingness to change his attitude toward the SPD doomed Antifascist Action to failure from its conception.[103] Yet the creation of this organization would become an important component of the Thälmann myth.

The most intriguing illustration of Thälmann's fight with Hitler fascism, however, was the 1932 presidential campaign, which saw him run against the leader of German fascism, Adolf Hitler. A thorough analysis of this campaign provides an opportunity to understand the Thälmann myth at its genesis, to comprehend the "raw material" with which later myth builders would work. In addition, such an investigation provides the opportunity to compare the actual events of the 1930s with the myth that emerged in the postwar years, this book's central purpose.

Like its predecessor seven years earlier, Thälmann's second presidential bid took place under unusual circumstances. The aging Paul von Hindenburg's term was supposed to end, under the terms of the Weimar Constitution, in the spring of 1932, but the country, because of the Depression and the consequent rule by presidential decree, was on the verge of collapse. Both Chancellor Brüning and the pro-Weimar parties agreed that, for the good of Germany, the current president should remain in office. But Hindenburg was eighty-four years old, and, in spite of the fact that everyone agreed that he would easily win reelection, he had no interest in undergoing the rigors of another campaign. Brüning, therefore, attempted to get the incumbent's term extended extraconstitutionally, but that would take a two-thirds vote in the Reichstag. He failed to secure this supermajority because the Nazis and Communists—not for the first or last time—cooperated to defeat Brüning's measure. Each of these parties, staunch opponents of Weimar democracy, sought to accelerate the collapse of the republic for its own ends.[104]

Under these conditions, Hindenburg considered not running for reelection. First of all, he and many of his advisers were afraid that he could not endure the rigors of a campaign. Brüning got around this problem by promising Hindenburg two things. First, the elderly president would not have to campaign; Brüning would do that for him. Hindenburg would make only one speech during the course of the contest. Second, the chancellor promised the president that he would secure a majority for him on the first ballot, thereby making a run-off unnecessary. Another reason for Hindenburg's hesitancy was that in 1932, in

contrast to 1925, he would have the support of the SPD, an organization he despised, and he considered not running in order to avoid this
distasteful prospect. To his chagrin, many of those who had supported
him in the previous election would vote for another candidate. But,
as Brüning pointed out, the only realistic alternative to Hindenburg's
reelection was a Hitler presidency, and the elderly field marshal hated
the Austrian corporal even more than he disliked the Social Democrats.
Finally, Brüning convinced Hindenburg that his reelection might serve
as an initial step toward reestablishing the monarchy, an eventuality
that the conservative incumbent found attractive. Hindenburg agreed
to run, announcing his candidacy on 16 February 1932.[105]

Hitler, fearing that a defeat in the election would break the Nazis'
momentum, also hesitated before announcing his candidacy on 22 February. Theodor Duesterberg would represent the Harzburg Front, a conglomeration of several right-wing political organizations.[106] There was
never any doubt regarding who the KPD candidate would be, and in
mid-January Ernst Thälmann announced that he would seek the presidency once again.[107] He would run as the only alternative to fascism
and war, and antifascism would be a central theme of his campaign.

Brüning failed to deliver on his promise to secure a majority for
Hindenburg on the first ballot, and two elections were held. The Nazi
leader, putting up a determined fight in both campaigns, came in second in each. Thälmann came in a distant third in both contests, securing around 14 percent of the vote in the first on 13 March and only
about 10 percent on 10 April.[108]

Thälmann's propaganda line was consistent throughout both campaigns. In keeping with the Communist Party's ideology, its candidate's
personality was not an important issue—in sharp contrast to the Hitler
and Hindenburg camps. The KPD, as always, emphasized the condition of the downtrodden working class, which was suffering because of
the ongoing economic depression. The proletariat recognized that only
the Communist candidate could address its problems, and—so the
Communists would have it—millions of Germany's most productive
citizens stood behind Thälmann's candidacy. Articles and photographs
in Münzenberg's *Arbeiter Illustrierte Zeitung* (*AIZ*, Workers' Illustrated
Newspaper), for example, emphasized the KPD candidate's links with
the masses. Images of Thälmann in this and other publications almost
invariably showed him speaking before a huge crowd, dwarfed by the
historical forces that stood behind him.[109]

An article in the *AIZ* gave examples of the widespread support that Thälmann had among the toiling masses. Entitled "Wen will das Volk?" (Whom Do the People Want?), the author of the piece, which comprised two full pages of the magazine, asked around twenty Thälmann voters—from a cross-section of the German proletariat—their reasons for supporting the Communist. Excerpts from their answers were given, complete with photographs of all those quoted. A war invalid, for example, shown sitting in his wheelchair, explained that he supported the Communist candidate because only Thälmann would keep Germany out of war. Four unemployed workers gave the following response: "That isn't even a question for us anymore. As class-conscious workers we can never vote for the honorary president of the Stahlhelm [a right-wing paramilitary organization] and the signer of the emergency decrees [granting the chancellor special powers] that surrendered our honor—rather only for the class-conscious leader of workers Thälmann!" A coal salesman insisted that the German people knew what to expect from Hindenburg—more of the same failed policies that had led to the current economic catastrophe. "We are going to vote for Thälmann because, if we want to make things different, we must fight side by side with the working classes," he concluded.[110] Many of Thälmann's campaign posters emphasized this theme as well. One red placard, for example, dominated by the Communist leader's visage, promised "Work, Bread, Freedom, [and] Socialism" to those who supported his candidacy. Another placard promised that Thälmann would pursue the policies that had proven so successful in the Soviet Union, "the land of socialist construction, the land without capitalists—without unemployed—without fascism and militarism."[111] The Communists promised the German people change and an end to the failed policies of the past. As always, Lenin and Stalin's Soviet Union showed the way to permanent peace and prosperity. Only Marxism–Leninism could rescue the German people from eternal deprivation. Russia, the KPD insisted, should be Germany's model, a sentiment making Thälmann susceptible to propaganda depicting him as the agent of a foreign power. *Der Angriff* (The Attack), the daily paper of Berlin's NSDAP gauleiter, Joseph Goebbels, reported that the Communist candidate was "not the leader of the German proletariat. . . . He is the caretaker of the Russian leadership and can do anything only on its orders. . . . Thälmann can never be a leader because he is not allowed to have his own opinions."[112] One did not have to be a Nazi to have sympathy with this sentiment, but Thälmann stuck to his guns, promising the German people peace and prosperity under a Soviet-style system.

Not only did Communist propaganda in the 1932 presidential campaign paint a rosy picture of life following the creation of a Bolshevik Germany, it also portrayed, in the most graphic ways possible, the results of a Hindenburg or Hitler victory. Thälmann, as usual painting his political enemies with an extremely broad brush, put it this way in one of his campaign speeches: "Lay the decisive questions before the three bourgeois candidates [Hitler, Hindenburg, and Duesterberg] and consider their answer[s], which they gave long ago by the way they have behaved: [H]ow do the three candidates of the bourgeoisie stand on the capitalist system? How do they stand on the problem of fascism? How do all three of them stand together on imperialist war?" The Communist candidate then went on—correctly, as it turned out—to insist that "Herr Hitler pursues war against the Soviet Union."[113] In this case, Thälmann's ideology served him well. All German Communists believed that a Nazi takeover would lead to a German–Soviet war—that is, after all, what fascists did, make war. The fact that Thälmann warned the German public numerous times about this danger would become another important component of the postwar myth. Yet, as always, Thälmann's KPD had an extremely broad definition of "fascist." A fascist was anyone, including Social Democrats, who was not a Communist, so both Hitler and Hindenburg fell within this very broad category. The Communist leader would go to his grave believing that the SPD represented the forces of "social fascism" and was no better than Hitler's party. This example establishes not only how dogmatic Thälmann was, but also how seriously he and his party underestimated the NSDAP.

The danger of a Russo–German war if either the Nazi leader or the incumbent were elected became a dominant theme in the KPD campaign. One Communist flyer put it quite succinctly when it stated that "[w]hoever votes for Hindenburg votes for Hitler; whoever votes for Hitler votes for war!"[114] Both candidates were a danger to Europe's peace because only war could assure the continued domination of the exploiting classes they represented—if only temporarily. *AIZ* insisted that the bourgeoisie wanted conflict because it believed that "war brings work and colonies!" War was the only solution that the capitalists could offer to the economic crisis, more hardship for the workers on top of the troubles that they already had to endure. As long as the forces of exploitation and militarism remained at the political helm, international conflict was inevitable, and things would only get worse for the vast majority of the German people.[115]

KPD propaganda maintained that a Thälmann victory could bring an end to capitalist domination and the catastrophe it engendered. Only the victory of a man who would embrace the Soviet Union could stop an otherwise inevitable imperialistic war. Of all the presidential candidates, only Thälmann understood the nature of the real enemy—fascism, whether it was the extreme version of the NSDAP or the apparently more "moderate" type represented by the Social Democrats. He had dedicated his life to the cause of peace, socialism, and antifascism, all of which were inextricably linked. Thälmann, who had witnessed the horrors of war firsthand, would defeat capitalism and end the fascist threat not only to Germany, but also to the Soviet Union, the only place on earth where the proletariat had been freed from the chains of capitalist exploitation. The voters, the Communist campaign machine insisted, should follow Thälmann and the party into a glorious socialist future.[116]

Thälmann had by 1932 become a vital component of the KPD's emerging antifascism myth. According to this narrative, only the Communists stood against the forces of German fascism. The Social Democrats, who had supported the right-wing Hindenburg in the 1932 election, remained the "social fascists" no better than the Nazis. Only the KPD and its leader were willing to take a stand against National Socialism by attacking its roots in the capitalist system. The Communists represented the interests of the workers as well as of all other progressive elements—members of the KPD and "fellow travelers"—in German society. Communism and antifascism were identical; there was no separating them. This myth, all the more powerful because of the element of truth it contained, would become the cornerstone of German Communist propaganda for the next fifty-seven years, from Hitler's seizure of power and the proletarian resistance against Nazi rule to the collapse of the GDR in 1989–1990. The memory of Ernst Thälmann and his valiant fight against Hitler fascism would become an important component of this myth.

Another event that came to play an important role in the myth commenced on 31 October 1932, when Thälmann traveled secretly (and illegally) to Paris, where he addressed the French Communist Party. Here he gave one of his most famous speeches, in which he denounced before an almost entirely French audience the terms of the largely French-imposed "Diktat of Versailles" and its sequel, the "thieving Young Plan," under which Germany had agreed to pay France a staggering amount of reparations. He insisted that, following the approaching

revolution, proletarian governments would "never recognize the imperialist treaty." It was a tool of the capitalists and must be abrogated in the
name of socialist justice and international proletarian solidarity. Those
present, at least according to KPD accounts, greeted the speech with
thunderous applause. *Rote Fahne* called Thälmann's trip and subsequent
address an "historic hour," "a call for the proletariat to take the offensive" against the international bourgeoisie and the forces of fascism.[117]

Yet it is clear, his rhetoric notwithstanding, that Thälmann and the
KPD seriously underestimated the dangers Nazism presented. The
position of the German Communist Party coincided with that of Stalin, who refused to permit his German comrades to make more than
the most half-hearted of overtures to the Social Democrats. The Soviet
leader, who still considered the SPD's westward orientation a more immediate danger to the USSR than the Nazi menace, branded any serious attempt at cooperation with the Social Democrats as "anti-party
heresy" or "provocation by agents of international capitalism." Robert C. Tucker maintains that Stalin approached the German situation
purely from the point of view of realpolitik, always doing what he
thought was best for the Soviet Union, and he thus may very well have
consciously aided the Nazi seizure of power. The Soviet leader maintained that the Social Democrats were a more immediate threat than the
Nazis. He apparently believed that should Hitler become chancellor,
Germany would be involved in diplomatic maneuvering against the
Western powers rather than against the Soviet Union. Such a scenario would neutralize Germany, Britain, and France for the foreseeable
future. According to Heinz Neumann, Stalin said at the end of 1931,
regarding the possibility of a Nazi takeover in Germany, "Don't you believe, Neumann, that if the Nationalists seize power in Germany they
will be so completely occupied with the West that we'll be able to build
up socialism in peace?" In short, the contention that a Nazi takeover
was the precursor to a Communist revolution was an excuse for Stalin
to pursue policies he believed favorable to the Soviet Union. Further,
the Russian leader undoubtedly knew that a Nazi government would
persecute German Communists viciously.[118] Stalin sold out the KPD,
and Ernst Thälmann, who still believed that revolution was imminent,
was his unwitting accomplice.

Events in November 1932 might very well have reinforced the KPD
chief's belief that a revolution in Germany was imminent. This month
witnessed the Berlin Transport Workers strike, perhaps the most significant labor action in the history of the Weimar Republic. The strike was

also the most noteworthy example of cooperation between the Communists and the Nazis in their efforts to undermine the hated "system." Thälmann apparently interpreted the fact that many members of the Nazi and independent trade unions continued to strike even after their leaders had called for an end to the work stoppage as an indication that non-Communist workers were becoming radicalized. As a result, the party chief might have hoped that these groups would support the KPD in its revolutionary effort after the Hitler fascists came to power. Thälmann would be sorely disappointed in this expectation, not only by the non-Communist workers, but also by his Soviet masters, who had abandoned the idea of another German October following a Nazi seizure of power. After Hitler came to power, orders from Moscow insisted that the KPD not act too hastily. The German revolution was once again to be postponed.[119] Although Thälmann's reaction to this development is not known, it is easy to imagine that the "Leonidas of German communism" was disappointed by his Soviet masters' hesitancy to approve dramatic action on the part of the KPD.

As always, Thälmann and his cronies ultimately pursued the line out of Moscow, and there would be no Communist revolution launched in January 1933. Initially, even as the new regime began to persecute its political opponents, some KPD leaders' response was remarkably subdued. Central Committee member Wilhelm Pieck, for example, insisted in a speech delivered shortly after Hitler's appointment that from the Communist perspective not much had changed: "As gravely as we regard the situation, we are by no means pessimistic. Instead of bread, potatoes, coal, the government offers only promises and terror, and this must have a demoralizing effect on the labouring people in the NSDAP. . . . *For the present* our task is limited to making the workers capable of action for the struggle for their existence."[120] The German Communist Party made no serious effort to organize an armed resistance against the new government. Just a week after Hindenburg had named Hitler chancellor, however, the party leadership's tune would change dramatically.

On 7 February, a secret meeting of around forty of the KPD's most prominent leaders was held in Berlin's Sporthaus Ziegenhals to discuss the situation. During the course of the assembly, Thälmann made what became his most famous speech, in which he outlined his interpretation of the situation. The whole world was watching the German workers, he began, who faced "the most difficult struggle" in the party's history. At last, following a week of violence against all of Hitler's opponents, Thälmann recognized the gravity of the situation. He went on to explain how "the current situation" had come about. In January, the combined forces of the bourgeoisie, the Nazis and Social Democrats, had "taken over the offensive from us." In the previous months, the workers' movement had experienced a series of dramatic victories, and there had been—as could be seen, for example, in the Berlin Transport Workers strike—a "sharpening" of class conflict. In response, the forces of capitalism had created the "Hitler–Hugenberg–Papen cabinet" to crush the workers' revolutionary impulse. In short, the success of the Communist movement had led to the current situation, and Germany remained on the brink of revolution.[121]

Under the circumstances, the *"greatest danger* [was] the *underestimation of the Hitler regime."* But the workers likewise had to avoid an "overestimation" of the new government because that might undermine the party's determination to remain *"ready to resist"* Hitler and his minions. In preparation for the armed struggle, Thälmann proposed a united front with the SPD, the free trade unions, and even the Christian trade unions, who would organize a general strike aimed at toppling the regime, the result of which would be civil war. The time was right for action, not the spouting of slogans. Rather, circumstances warranted "undivided mass actions" carried out by "the proletariat in all its forms." After a long quotation from Lenin, Thälmann went on to explain that if the Nazis experienced the success he expected in the upcoming Reichstag elections, "the Hitler Party would use such a vote" to justify "further fascist assaults on behalf of the state for the securing and expansion of its power." Everything necessary must be done to prevent this eventuality. Even the party youth organization must be militarized in defense of the workers. It must be clear to everyone in Germany, not just Communists, that this course of action was the only legitimate one. "That means the realization of all of the following: the fascist dictatorship struck and smashed to pieces! Forward in this struggle! Forward in your revolutionary duty for the victory of the German working class!"[122] Thälmann apparently did not get to finish his speech. Walter Ulbricht, Berlin's party chief, received word that the assembly's security had been breached, and the meeting—and the party leader's speech—ended abruptly.[123]

Thälmann no longer underestimated the dangers that Hitler and his party posed. The new regime would not collapse under its own weight or disintegrate because it could not deal effectively with the economic crisis. It must be defeated violently by the German people.

At last, Thälmann recognized the severity of the crisis and was willing to cooperate with anyone, even the "social fascists," to destroy the nascent regime. On 27 February, the KPD chief published an "open letter" to this effect. Insisting that the "fascist assassins who rage against the workers with daggers, revolvers, and bombs [make] no distinction whether they carry the membership card of the KPD, the SPD, or the Christian trade unions in their pocket," he stated that the Nazis must be smashed by any means necessary.[124] The new regime presented such a danger to the workers' movement that he and the Communist Party would cooperate with all antifascists, no matter what their political allegiance. But his potential allies refused to heed his call. Cooperation with the KPD had long meant accepting Communist domination, and many antifascists anticipated—probably correctly—that even the dire circumstances created by Hitler's assuming the chancellorship had not eliminated this precondition for partnership with Thälmann's party. Although Thälmann finally recognized the threat that the Third Reich posed for the KPD, it did not do him much good. His party had burned its bridges to other anti-Nazi political movements long ago.

As a result of Thälmann's incompetence—not to mention his incessant kowtowing to a Soviet leadership interested only in the survival of the Bolshevik experiment in Russia—he had failed his people in its greatest hour of need. Insisting, as his Soviet masters contended, that there was no significant difference between social democracy and National Socialism, Thälmann and his party had done nothing to stop the Nazi seizure of power—indeed, they had welcomed it as what they considered to be the dying breath of German imperialism. The KPD chief's incompetence, coupled with the ideological solipsism emanating from Moscow, caused him to make a series of enormous blunders, not the least being his refusal to cooperate with the SPD leadership in any significant way. The KPD and its Soviet masters had changed their ideological position so many times that when it became necessary for Thälmann and his Russian superiors to make a principled stand against National Socialism, they were simply incapable of doing so. By the time that the proletarian leader from Hamburg recognized the enormity of the crisis that his movement faced, it was simply too late for the German Communist Party to alter the course of events. Years of living up to the motto "Heil Moskau!" had rendered Thälmann and his associates unable to appreciate the severity of the crisis facing them until it was too late.

Following the 28 February 1933 fire in the German Reichstag building and President Hindenburg's emergency decrees restricting civil liberties, around 4,000 Communist Party officials were arrested under orders from the Prussian minister of the interior Hermann Goering. The KPD chairman went into hiding, taking sanctuary in a secret apartment located in the area surrounding Berlin's Kaiserallee. But one of his comrades, Alfred Kattner—in all likelihood the victim of torture at the hands of the SA—gave information to the Gestapo concerning the party chief's whereabouts, and Thälmann went into custody on 3 March. The Hamburg Communist may have led his party's Thermopylae, but he would never get the opportunity to command its Plataea.[125]

By the time Ernst Thälmann entered Berlin's Moabit prison in March 1933, he had accomplished a great deal. Rising from obscurity in Hamburg, he had become one of the most important figures in the Communist Party, playing a vital role in the party's Stalinization. The modest dock worker from Hamburg was a central figure in the failed 1923 uprising, earning a reputation as a man of action and staunch advocate of the proletarian cause. In spite of his limited education, Thälmann was twice the presidential candidate of a major political party, survived a serious political scandal, and became Joseph Stalin's most loyal political ally in Germany. An important component of the Stalinization process was the creation of a massive media empire under the direction of Willi Münzenberg, a propaganda apparatus that helped to make Thälmann a significant figure in the politics of the late Weimar Republic. As a result of his prominence within the KPD, however, Thälmann was imprisoned by the Nazis. The same media machine that had presented him as the only viable option to a Hitler dictatorship, assuring him the German führer's undiluted hatred, would now mount a massive campaign ostensibly crafted to secure Thälmann's release from prison.

2

"Ernst Thälmann Must Be Won Like a Battle!"

Ernst Thälmann spent the remainder of his life, more than eleven years, in prison, much of his time consumed in preparation for a trial that would never occur. Although he was accused of the most serious political crimes—namely, planning to overthrow the German government through violent revolution and participating in the conspiracy that led to the 28 February Reichstag fire—his high profile assured that he would not be simply interned in a concentration camp and forgotten, like so many other opponents of National Socialism. Further, his prominence led the Nazi leadership to hope that he might become useful to the Third Reich—as a weapon in the ongoing propaganda battle with the Communists or even as a prominent convert to the Nazi cause. In order to facilitate the latter possibility, however unlikely, Nazi propaganda chief Joseph Goebbels made sure that Thälmann received information—newspapers and other periodicals—about events in the outside world, especially materials depicting conditions in the Soviet Union, particularly during the purges and, from 1941, the Russo–German War.[1]

At first, his Nazi jailers did not make a serious attempt to cut Thälmann off completely from the outside world. This was possibly the result of incompetence on their part, but it is more likely that the regime hoped to use the Communist leader as a kind of "back channel" to the German Left in exile and, perhaps more important, the Comintern. As a result, neither Thälmann's wife, Rosa, nor his daughter, Irma, were searched before their visits to his cell—at least prior to 1937—thus permitting them to smuggle letters into and out of the jail at Moabit, where he was held, which allowed Thälmann to carry out an extensive correspondence with his comrades outside of Germany. On one occasion, Irma was even able to smuggle a small camera into the visitation room, allowing her to take one of the most famous photographs of her father, sitting across the table from her. Thälmann's lawyers, Erich Wandschneider and Fritz Ludwig, also served as conduits through whom information could pass. The prisoner was also allowed to receive at least some of his mail.[2]

The most interesting but probably the least reliable channel through which intelligence could be passed was a series of couriers, assigned by the exiled KPD leaders to facilitate contact with the Communist leader. Hans Kippenberger, chief of the KPD's secret Military Apparatus in Berlin, was in charge of these operatives. He was also a close friend of Thälmann's, having played an important role in the 1923 Hamburg Uprising.[3] Kippenberger's three agents, code-named "Adam," "Humboldt," and "Auge," were probably Kippenberger himself, a Communist named Wilhelm Thebert, and the Military Apparatus chief's secretary Änne Kerff. They picked up whatever information they could concerning their imprisoned leader, often by simply hanging out around the jail and listening to whatever rumors circulated. In addition, the couriers managed to make contact with some prison employees. The regime apparently got wind of the Communist contacts in Moabit and, in 1937, moved Thälmann to Hannover and later Bautzen, hoping to decrease the possibility of a jail break. The prison workers served not only as sources of information, but also as avenues through whom written materials could be passed.[4]

In 1936, Kippenberger was called to Moscow, where he became a victim of Stalin's purges, which had such a dramatic effect on the KPD. His replacement was Hermann Nuding, who was himself purged in 1938 or 1939. Nuding's successor was Paul Bertz, who survived the war. The couriers fell victim to the purges as well, making their replacement necessary. Each courier periodically produced reports, often written in a muddled prose indicative of the ad hoc manner in which they accumulated information. One courier's messages, for example, usually began with the words "Comrade Thälmann unchanged in prison." Walter Trautzsch (code-named "Edwin") regularly met with Rosa in order to get information that could be passed on to his superiors. The written reports were in turn smuggled across the German–Czechoslovakian border, eventually working their way to Moscow. The 1939 German annexation of the remainder of Czechoslovakia blocked this route, and subsequent reports passed through Switzerland before proceeding on to the Soviet Union. The couriers' observations, coupled with the materials smuggled in and out of prison by Rosa, Irma, and Thälmann's lawyers, assured that the Communist leader had a surprising amount of contact with his comrades and that they were remarkably well aware of his circumstances.[5]

Moabit had been designed during the nineteenth century in the midst of a reform of Germany's penal institutions, and each inmate had his own cell.[6] As a result, although Thälmann had almost no contact with his fellow prisoners, the conditions of his incarceration were relatively benign, especially when compared to the suffering endured by thousands of his comrades confined to concentration camps. He initially had special privileges not afforded other prisoners. He was permitted much more reading material than other inmates, and Rosa was allowed to bring him special packages containing food, including "sardines, asparagus salad, grapes, figs, dates, ham, and different sorts of sausage," not to mention butter—all luxuries unavailable to other inmates.[7] The prisoner also, with at least his captors' tacit approval, received hundreds, if not thousands, of letters and post cards, in addition to flowers on his birthday.[8] Further, delegations, such as one from the 1935 International Penal Congress, were permitted to view Thälmann and the conditions of his incarceration, assuring that he was being treated well, although they were not always allowed to speak with him. When, for example, the Penal Congress delegation visited the imprisoned Communist leader, they were shown his cell, which contained a stack of newspapers and a "half-smoked pipe" that the jailers presented "as evidence of good treatment." Although the callers were allowed to see him from a distance, which permitted them to conclude that he was in good health, when they asked to speak with him, prison officials responded that "[h]e wants to be let alone."[9] Perhaps most important of all, the Nazis made no serious effort to restrict Thälmann's correspondence with comrades in the Soviet Union. Engaged in a propaganda war with international communism and its "fellow travelers," the Nazi regime sought to undermine Comintern claims that it was mistreating Germany's most famous political prisoner.

In 1936, under orders issued by the Ministry of Justice, many of Thälmann's privileges were rescinded. Although the reasons behind the regime's actions remain obscure, they were probably a response to the ongoing effort to secure the Communist leader's freedom, an effort that became especially intense around the time of his fiftieth birthday. For whatever reason, however, guards began to watch Rosa and Irma more carefully, and the two women could no longer bring the captive special packages. To make matters worse, officials more carefully censored Thälmann's mail, all of it passing through the local Gestapo office. Finally, in 1937, authorities moved him to a prison in Bautzen, holding him under semi-isolated conditions, permitting no visitors except his wife and daughter. As a result, during the years 1940 and 1941, Rosa smuggled letters that her spouse had written to Stalin out of Germany, which she accomplished by simply showing up at the gates of the Soviet embassy and asking to speak with Russian officials. Over the next year or so, she visited the embassy at least eleven times.[10] To make matters worse, guards kept a closer eye on Thälmann and his visitors, trying harder to overhear his conversations with his wife. Irma found it ever more difficult to secure a place in one of the local schools. The changes occurred around the same time that the regime moved him to Bautzen, preempting any escape attempts. These altered circumstances also made it more difficult for Comintern agents to recruit prison personnel for their mission.[11]

Whenever Thälmann met with Rosa—Irma did not always accompany her mother—a guard was in the room, assuring that they could not discuss anything of consequence, such as plans to break him out of jail. In October 1937, Rosa wrote a letter to the Prussian minister of the interior, Hermann Goering, complaining about her husband's deteriorating situation. She attempted to deliver the message personally to Goering's suite in the Hotel Atlantic, only to be forcibly removed from the hotel lobby by three men—but she accomplished her mission, and Goering received the letter. He replied the next month, granting at least some of Rosa's requests. Irma received a place at a local high school, for example, and Goering permitted Rosa two hours alone with her husband for Christmas in 1937. As a result, the fifty-one-year-old Rosa Thälmann became pregnant in spite of her relatively advanced age. Through one of the KPD couriers, she requested money from the party to travel to another country to terminate her pregnancy and received the funds. But this was not the only money Rosa received from the Comintern. She had no means of support because of her husband's imprisonment, and it was highly unlikely that she could find a job to support herself. Yet Rosa and Irma could not go into exile—they were much too important as agents of the Comintern. Hence, Rosa received intermittent payments from the Comintern—2,000 marks, for example, in November 1939. It was unthinkable that the spouse of Germany's most famous antifascist should go hungry, and the KPD continued to support Irma and her mother.[12]

In spite of the hardships Rosa faced, it seems that she had no wish to leave Germany—at least not without her husband. German authorities made it increasingly clear that Thälmann would never receive his day in court; they did not even indict him until December 1934. Although the indictment was supposed to be kept secret, Thälmann's lawyer, Ludwig, smuggled at least one copy of it out of Germany. Ludwig's client had been charged with attempting to overthrow the government violently and, in an example of hypocrisy extreme even by Nazi standards, with undermining the German Constitution.[13] The secrecy of the charges indicated how much the regime feared the prospect of another public trial of a major Communist figure. Hitler and his henchmen did not want to endure a setback in their propaganda battle with the Comintern comparable to the one involving Georgi Dimitrov, whom they had arrested on 9 March 1933, not quite a week after they took the KPD leader. As one of the Third International's representatives in Berlin, Dimitrov was accused of having conspired to set the 28 February Reichstag fire and to establish a Bolshevik Germany. Manacled for five months, until an international uproar led to the removal of his chains, Dimitrov was held in Moabit, the same prison as his comrade Thälmann.[14] The court refused to accept any of the eight defense attorneys he chose, and Dimitrov decided to defend himself. His trial began in September, the Bulgarian Communist putting up a brilliant defense, maintaining that the fire was not the product of a Communist conspiracy. Rather, from an objective Marxist point of view, setting the fire would have been counterproductive because it would have undermined the party's effectiveness among the German proletariat. The Comintern and the KPD were interested in proletarian revolution, not vandalism. Dimitrov even tried—although the court refused permission—to call Thälmann to testify about the anti-Communist character of the Reichstag fire. Indeed, he strongly implied that the Nazis had started the conflagration themselves in order to justify their efforts to crush the international workers' movement. The highlight of the trial took place on 4 November 1933, when Dimitrov questioned the Prussian prime minister, Hermann Goering, making the Nazi leader look like a buffoon and establishing that some prosecution witnesses had perjured themselves.[15] The embarrassment experienced by the regime only escalated when on 23 December the court acquitted Dimitrov as well as several of his supposed co-conspirators. Yet the accused were not released from custody until 27 February 1934, after an eight-week-long intensification of the international campaign to secure their liberation.[16] The Nazi regime had suffered a serious propaganda defeat—international opinion accepted Dimitrov's contention that the German regime had started the Reichstag fire for political reasons.

The German Communist leader initially hoped that he, too, might receive a trial and be acquitted. Some time in 1933, Thälmann wrote to the prosecutor's office, addressing the charges against him. Contending that the KPD never had a plan to overthrow the government violently, he wrote that "[t]he politics of the party are a mass politics and have nothing to do with a political putsch." Pursuing much the same line as Dimitrov, Thälmann contended that when the time was ripe, the KPD would come to power through the natural dialectical order of things. Setting fires to public buildings and other forms of vandalism were never a component of the party's platform.[17] A similar approach had worked for Dimitrov, and the German government, determined not to suffer another propaganda debacle, repeatedly postponed Thälmann's trial. In November 1935, Hitler, according to Goebbels, made the decision to delay judicial proceedings in order to "put an end to the publicity as soon as possible."[18] The international crusade ostensibly designed to secure Thälmann's release was evidently having some effect on the German government, which became more determined to dampen the publicity surrounding the case. The Free Thälmann campaign was ironically making it less likely that he would be liberated by the German court system, which could happen only if there were a trial. It became clear to both Thälmann and his spouse that they could never hope for a legal avenue to liberty. Nazi officials, maintaining that "the death penalty or lifetime imprisonment" were "not legally possible" for him and that the Communist prisoner represented a real threat to the regime, ultimately decided in the fall of 1935 that Thälmann would be held in long-term "protective custody."[19]

As a result, the couple began to pursue other options, one of which was to break him out of prison. According to the standard East German biography, an elaborate plan was devised in late 1934. One of Thälmann's guards, Emil Moritz, was a Communist agent who had access to the keys to the KPD chief's cell. Under cover of darkness, the prisoner would be smuggled through the employees' exit and escorted by an armed guard to an apartment on Stresemannstraße, around twenty minutes away. Disguised as an "old woman," he would be spirited across the border into Czechoslovakia. According to this account, the Nazis got suspicious because Moritz oiled the hinges on Thälmann's cell door, evidently to aid an escape. As a result, Moritz was transferred to another wing of Moabit prison and later arrested. At this point, the plot was abandoned because Stalin considered it too dangerous.[20] The reasons for abandoning the scheme remain unclear but add credence to later claims that neither Stalin nor the KPD leadership really wanted Thälmann out of prison. Thälmann himself raised the possibility that he could be swapped for a German prisoner held in the Soviet Union—he even proffered a suggestion regarding the person for whom he would be exchanged. Similar arrangements had been worked out previously, and this option was especially viable during the years of the German–Soviet rapprochement, 1939–1941. During this period, Stalin negotiated with other fascist governments to secure the release of some of his comrades, the ECCI functionary Mátyás Rákosi and the Romanian Communist Anna Pauker, for example.[21] Although Rosa passed this suggestion on to Moscow, the KPD chief's pleas fell on deaf ears. One of the couriers, Walter Trautzsch, remembered that, upon relaying the suggestion that a prisoner exchange be pursued, his bosses in Moscow rejected the idea outright.[22]

Both the Communist leader and his spouse eventually came to the conclusion that for a variety of reasons the Comintern would make no serious effort to secure his freedom. In October 1936, recognizing that her husband's release would undermine the newfound influence of many in the KPD and the Comintern, Rosa told one of her contacts, "I believe that many comrades are afraid that Thälmann will one day get out of prison. Yes, it is better for the party if he is in prison; otherwise you won't have as many propaganda possibilities."[23] The prisoner, who was less interested in the propaganda opportunities presented by his captivity than were his comrades in Moscow and Paris, was even more explicit in his criticism: "Why are you being such shitheads [Scheißkerle] and letting me sit here?" he wrote to them.[24]

There were a variety of answers to this question. First, as Rosa pointed out, her spouse was a valuable tool in the ongoing propaganda war between Hitler's Germany and Stalin's Soviet Union (discussed later in this chapter). There was more to the situation than that, however. If it were the only reason that Thälmann's comrades allowed him to languish in a Nazi prison, they would have made a serious effort to secure his release during the two years following the German–Soviet Nonaggression Pact, when there was effectively no antifascist propaganda coming out of Moscow. By this time, of course, the German Communists in Moscow were preoccupied with Stalin's purges and had other concerns, and freeing their ostensible leader was not foremost in their minds. There clearly was more behind their inaction, however. His comrades ultimately viewed their incarcerated leader as a political threat. Immediately after Thälmann's imprisonment, John Schehr became the new, temporary leader of the KPD, but he soon fell victim to the Gestapo.[25] At this point, Walter Ulbricht assumed the post—although Thälmann continued to be reelected, for propaganda purposes, to the Central Committee and the Politburo and remained officially the party's chairman.[26] Ulbricht insisted that his predecessor stand trial in Berlin for the good of the party, and Wilhelm Pieck—Ulbricht's closest ally on the Central Committee and future president of the GDR—wrote Thälmann a letter in which he made suggestions concerning trial strategy. The real reasons why they would thwart efforts to secure Thälmann's release, however, are obvious. If the imprisoned KPD leader were liberated and came to Moscow, Ulbricht and Pieck would lose much of their influence.[27] Thälmann had become the most important symbol of the Comintern's antifascist campaign, and under the circumstances it would have been almost impossible to deny him the leadership of the party.

Ulbricht and his allies on the KPD's Politburo were not the only prominent figures to consider Thälmann a political danger. Even more important, so did Stalin, who hastened to abandon his erstwhile protégée when it became politically expedient to do so. After all, Dimitrov's international popularity rivaled the Soviet leader's own, undoubtedly to Stalin's chagrin. He did not want another possible rival who was famous throughout Europe for giving the fascists a black eye. Thälmann had become the most celebrated figure in the antifascist movement, a fact that the paranoid Stalin presumably found threatening. As early as 2 May 1934, just two months after Dimitrov's release, the Soviet leader openly criticized Thälmann. "*Thälm[ann]* did not understand the national question. I spoke with him once in 1930. He did not understand . . . [p]rolet[arian] internationalism and nationalism."[28] Stalin's vague condemnation did not relate the real reason he disliked the KPD leader, which was simple jealousy, but it indicated that Thälmann's standing was deteriorating only a year into his imprisonment. To add insult to injury, the German Communist had seen fit to criticize the Soviet leader. The subject of Stalin's purges came up in a July 1937 conversation with Rosa and a prison guard, and one of the couriers' reports recorded Thälmann's response: "The whole thing [the purges] made a great impression upon him, and he was very disturbed. He said that one should not do such things. There are other ways and methods to render people harmless. But simply to shoot them—that he did not like." Thälmann changed his mind by September, however, finding things "totally in order." After all, he conceded, the Soviet Union had accomplished a great deal, as could be seen in the recent successful polar expeditions.[29] Like so many, the imprisoned KPD leader came to the conclusion that the progress made by the Russian people more than compensated for the regime's "excesses." Stalin, of course, did not overlook even a temporary straying from the party line. Anyone who criticized him was a danger, and Thälmann's statements concerning the purges likely helped convince the Russian leader that it was better to leave the German in prison. Without the Soviet leader's approval, any plan to secure Thälmann's release was doomed from the outset. In short, from a political point of view, no one of importance in the Russian capital, German exile or Russian, had any interest in procuring the KPD leader's release.

Thälmann had become the most prominent symbol of the antifascist movement—undoubtedly to the consternation of the Soviet leader, infamous for his dislike of anyone whose star might eclipse his own. After several years in fascist prisons, Thälmann had become internationally famous and, like Dimitrov, would have been all but untouchable if freed from Bautzen. Whereas Thälmann was valuable to the workers' movement while he was in a Nazi prison, he could quickly become a liability for the Soviet dictator as a free man. Whether Thälmann would have been Stalin's rival remains unknown—what is important is that Stalin quite probably suspected that he would be.[30]

The letters that the German Communist wrote in prison contributed to Stalin's concern. Most of what Thälmann wrote in his cell was, from the Comintern's perspective, harmless, such as the letters written to his daughter and notes to his comrades in Moscow, urging them to carry on the struggle against fascism and war. Much of this correspondence would be published by East German authorities in the years after the Second World War.[31] Yet the couriers' reports, including Thälmann's criticism of the purges, and a considerable portion of what Thälmann himself wrote while in prison—most notably his twenty-four letters to Stalin—would only see the light of day following the GDR's collapse.

Little is known concerning Stalin's personal response to Thälmann's letters, although there are a couple of interesting clues in Dimitrov's diary. On 21 December 1940, for example, the then Comintern chief received a phone call from the Soviet foreign minister Viacheslav Molotov. Moscow had recently received a letter from Thälmann, and, asking Dimitrov to examine the document, Molotov wanted "to make certain if it is really Thälmann's handwriting." There evidently was some concern regarding the content of the letter, although exactly what that concern was remains uncertain. In his 15 October 1941 diary entry, a few months after the German invasion of the Soviet Union eliminated any chance that Thälmann would be released, the Bulgarian Communist Dimitrov described a meeting with Stalin and Molotov. At the end of the gathering, the Soviet leader commented on the letters he had received from Thälmann over the past two years. "He [Thälmann] is not true to Marxist principles, and his letters exhibit the influence of fascist ideology." Although it remains unclear exactly which of Thälmann's epistles Stalin considered objectionable, the Soviet leader went on to say that "he wrote about plutocracy, meaning England [should be] smashed—incredible."[32] With the 22 June 1941 German attack, Great Britain became an ally of the Soviet Union. The fact that at the time that Thälmann wrote his letters the Soviet party chief, too, considered Britain an enemy was irrelevant. The German Communist had for once failed to anticipate the twists and turns of the party line, which earned him the disdain of the Soviet leader, the man whom he addressed as "Dear Comrade!"[33]

In spite of the fact that Thälmann was out of Stalin's favor, an accusation of having opposed Thälmann at any time, especially during the 1928 Wittorf Scandal, could have serious consequences during the purges. In July 1939, for example, Adolf Ende was purged because he had belonged to a faction opposing Thälmann in 1928. One of Ende's accusers, Herbert Wehner, a close confidant of Thälmann, got into difficulty as well, accused of having handed over the party leader's papers and personal effects to the Gestapo. In November 1937, Erich Birkenhauer came under scrutiny, charged with undermining the Free Thälmann crusade, in which he was a leading functionary.[34] On the night of 27–28 April 1938, Heinz Neumann, formerly Thälmann's political rival, and his spouse, Margarete, were arrested and disappeared into the People's Commissariat for Internal Affairs (secret police) prison system, as did Hermann Remmele, another ideological critic, sometime in 1939. None of these people was ever heard from again. Having disagreed with Thälmann—Stalin's loyal ally in the KPD—at any time could become a liability, but then so could practically anything else. All three men were under suspicion for allegedly undermining the position of the German Communist leader—a man whom Stalin both feared and held in contempt. Yet they were only a few among the millions who were shot by the secret police or disappeared into the gulag. Such was the Orwellian world of Stalin's purges.[35]

Even as the German Communist Party and the Comintern privately abandoned Ernst Thälmann in a German prison for the good of the workers' movement, they publicly launched an aggressive propaganda crusade ostensibly to secure his release. On 5 March 1933, two days after the Communist leader's arrest, the ECCI issued a proclamation calling upon all Third International political organs to "resist the most brutal methods of terror" used by the German fascists, even if this meant cooperating with the hated Social Democrats, who remained officially anathema until 1935, when the Comintern ended the so-called Third Period (1928–1935).[36] On 1 April 1933, the ECCI Presidium passed a resolution calling upon all Communists to work diligently for the KPD leader's liberation.[37]

At this point, the Hitler regime had not as yet completely emasculated the German workers movement, and the ECCI proclamation did not go unheeded. In the early spring of 1933, for example, hundreds of illegal flyers, postcards, and newspapers made the rounds among German Communists, and unlawful May Day demonstrations demanded Thälmann's release. The protests were more widespread outside of Germany. In June, for example, the European Antifascist Workers' Congress, with 300 delegates, 120 of them German, elected the KPD leader to its "Honorary Presidium."[38] Even before the KPD leader's imprisonment, Soviet authorities had honored him by establishing a Thälmann Club in Moscow. Created for the benefit of foreign workers in the Soviet Union and with approximately 2,000 members, the club became an important cultural center for non-Russians, especially Germans, living in Moscow. In late 1936, however, the club's chief administrator, Erich Steffen, along with his wife, fell victim to the purges. The association managed to survive another two years under new leadership but was closed in late 1938, one of numerous institutions to fall prey to Stalin's paranoia.[39] But it was not the only Russian organization to bear the German Communist's name. Claiming to show solidarity with the suffering workers of Nazi Germany, the Soviets affixed Thälmann's name to a number of their institutions, including collective and state farms, work brigades, and orphanages. Soviet workers wrote him letters of support, the occupants of an agricultural colony in Ukraine's Melitopol issuing on 8 April 1938 a proclamation demanding the "immediate release of Comrade Thälmann and all other political prisoners from capitalists prisons."[40] Numerous local soviets elected him an "honorary member," as did the Soviet Writers' Congress.[41]

Among the most interesting Soviet manifestations of the Free Thälmann movement was a 1934 *lied* (song) written in both Russian and German, "Ernst Thälmann: [For] Dual Language Chorus with Piano Accompaniment." Hugo Huppert wrote the German text; someone identified only as "Rodionova" penned the Russian lyrics, which were to be sung simultaneously with the German; and Franz Szabó composed the music. The song, which provides an early example of so many of the themes that would come to dominate Free Thälmann propaganda, is worth quoting at some length. Like so much of the verse penned about the Communist leader, this **lied** can only be described as insipid, but it got its message across. It begins:

> Sustain Ernst Thälmann in his prison
> With marching songs of the red world legion.
> They make him younger, make him stronger,
> That old soldier of the revolution.

If the proletariat stands by Thälmann's side, he will become stronger, the song maintains, as will the international workers' movement.

> He stands as he stood, on platforms, as always,
> And millions stand with him.
> Heads have begun to roll at the executioners' hands.
> They hoped to decapitate the German proletariat
> With a single blow.
> They have placed our leader, Ernst Thälmann, in prison.

The Nazis' decision to imprison the KPD leader was an attempt to destroy the German working-class movement. Indeed, Thälmann's fate was closely linked to the destiny of the world's workers. The international workers' movement, millions strong, would stand by its leader, and just as antifascists acting in solidarity had saved Dimitrov, they would likewise rescue the German Communist leader. The piece concludes:

> We are letting the [Nazi] torturers know:
> We are on guard to preserve our leader's head.
> We have rescued Dimitrov from the executioner
> And remain united to preserve Ernst Thälmann's blood.[42]

Thälmann's fate and that of the international struggle against fascism were one and the same. Free Thälmann movement propaganda would repeat these themes countless times over the next several years. These tropes caught on quickly in all of the parties affiliated with the Comintern. The Polish Communist Party, for example, issued a 1934 declaration stating, "We will deliver Ernst Thälmann from the executioner's hand," and the German embassy in Warsaw received a flood of letters and telegrams demanding the German Communist's release.[43]

The Free Thälmann movement was not confined to Europe, however. On the other side of the Atlantic Ocean, in New York City, a red flag bearing the words "Liberate Ernst Thälmann!" was hung from the top of the city's memorial to veterans of the Great War, and, according to Communist sources, the city's German consulate received so many telephone calls expressing concern for Thälmann that regular communications had to be halted for a day.[44] The official organ of the Communist Party in the United States of America (CPUSA), *The Daily Worker*, was intimately involved in the Free Thälmann effort. The newspaper closely followed developments in the KPD chief's case, insisting that his life, like those of thousands of other German Communists, was in constant peril. Fascist thugs tortured him; "Nazis Flog Thaelmann [*sic*], Load Him with Chains in Lightless Cell" accused a headline from 3 March 1934. On the fourteenth of the following month, *The Daily Worker* reported that "Thaelmann [is] beaten when he refuses to answer his Nazi inquisitors in Berlin." The fascists' ultimate goal, however, was even more insidious. The Nazis planned to haul Thälmann and 111 other German Communists before the newly created People's Court, where forged documents would be used to convict him of high treason. All would be executed in the end.[45] Only if America's workers were to launch a massive campaign, similar to the successful one that led to the liberation of Dimitrov, could they hope to save the KPD leader.[46] As a result, the CPUSA launched a major propaganda campaign similar to that carried out by European Communist parties.

During the spring of 1934, the CPUSA organized a series of mass demonstrations across the United States, linking the effort to free Thälmann to the international struggle against fascism. According to *The Daily Worker*, in March alone thousands assembled at Free Thälmann rallies in Chicago, Cleveland, and New York City. American Communists usually organized these demonstrations outside of the local German consulate or another site chosen because of its close association with the Third Reich.[47] Such efforts garnered publicity for the party, contributed to its recruitment efforts, propagated the idea that CPUSA stood for action in the face of fascist tyranny, and created the impression that the party's support was wider than it actually was. As on the other side of the Atlantic, American Communists lionized the imprisoned proletarian leader in political art. On 16 March 1933, for example, a political cartoon appeared on page four of *The Daily Worker* showing a bound Thälmann standing in front of a large tombstone. Carved on the tombstone are the names "Karl Liebknecht" and "Rosa Luxemburg," explicitly linking the imprisoned KPD chief with the two great martyrs of the German Left. Hitler stands beside the prisoner, a sword in his hand, representing the imminent danger to Thälmann's life. In the background stands a factory, representative of the bound captive's proletarian roots.

American Communists exploited every medium at their disposal in the effort to promote the Free Thälmann cause. In 1934, for example, the song "Set Thaelmann Free" became briefly popular in New York City's Greenwich Village. Two women sympathetic to the antifascist cause, Anne Bromberg and Frances May, wrote the words, and Szabó once again composed the music for this little ditty, which included the lyrics:

> Stone Halls and Stairways, sparks from Boots fly,
> Brown-shirted henchmen drag him along;
> Ernst Thaelmann defies them. They wince at his glances,
> Fearing the strength of proletarian hate.[48]

Emphasizing the imprisoned Communist leader's working-class roots was, of course, a central theme of Free Thälmann propaganda. In the American context, this motif was especially prominent in "German Bolshevik," a series of proclamations appearing in the 26 May 1934 edition of *The Daily Worker*. Written by Alan Culmer, this succession of statements about the German Communist leader, composed in verse form, begins by linking him with important figures in the history of American leftist politics, the anarchists executed following Chicago's famous Haymarket bombing in 1886, the year of Thälmann's birth:

> While a Haymarket martyr defied capitalism in a Chicago courtroom ("I speak as the representative of one class to another"), another German leader was born to the workingclass [*sic*] in Hamburg.

Although the German proletarian leader is thousands of miles away, the verse implies, his fate should be important to American workers. After all, the struggle against fascism and capitalist exploitation is international, and Thälmann's struggle is their struggle; his fate is inextricably linked to theirs. The remainder of this bit of doggerel provides an account of Thälmann's lifetime of sacrifice and struggle on behalf of the international workers movement, beginning with his joining the SPD at the age of sixteen, recounting his rise to prominence in the German workers' movement, and concluding with his struggle against fascism:

> In '32 he opposed the Lesser Evil in the elections campaign,
> saw the Junker-Militarist open the door to Hitler,
> beheld the madman unleash a hundred thousand madmen
> to get Thaelmann, to get Thaelmann,
> refused to leave his workers behind. . . .
> They threw him into . . . torture dungeons . . .
> to twist his broad shoulders, to bar his clear seeing,
> to guillotine him.
> Workers, men of culture, SAVE THAELMANN!

The life of the proletarian leader from Hamburg is in danger because of his willingness to sacrifice for his fellow workers. Echoing a theme prominent in Europe's Free Thälmann movement, the KPD chief's comrades in the United States must now come to his aid. In response, the CPUSA launched letter-, telegram-, and postcard-writing campaigns. In 1934, for example, American Communists mass-produced postcards addressed to Hans Luther, the German ambassador to the United States, with the following message printed on the reverse side:

FREE THÄLMANN!
Sir
I DEMAND the release of Ernst Thälmann and all other political
   prisoners
From Fascist dungeons and Concentration Camps!
I DEMAND that the brutal murder of workers who oppose Hitler's
Hangman rule be STOPPED!
I DEMAND a stop to the persecution of the Jewish people.[49]

Communists needed to organize to save Thälmann. Also, like their European counterparts, the American organizers of the effort emphasized the fact that many important non-Communists supported the KPD leader's cause. The prominent Chicago attorney Clarence Darrow, *The Daily Worker* reported, spoke out in support of his release, and even the governor of Maryland, Harry W. Nice, wrote a personal letter to Hitler seeking information concerning "Thälmann's fate."[50]

These actions represent only a handful of the many Free Thälmann actions taking place in Europe and the United States during the months following the KPD chief's arrest. Their spontaneity is questionable, and the KPD, CPUSA, Comintern, and CPSU organized most of these protests either directly or through one of their subsidiary organizations, including local antifascist committees. Further, most of them could have been carried out by a relatively small number of people. A few dozen activists, for example, could keep the phone lines at a German consulate tied up for a day, and a handful of men could raise a banner. The Comintern sought to create the impression of a mass movement to free the leader of the German Communist Party, but the campaign, although impressive and well organized, was probably not as extensive as the Comintern and the KPD maintained. But the real extent of the effort was not the most important concern among Communist propagandists; rather, it was vital that the effort *appear* to be massive. However, there is no doubting the fact that Thälmann was becoming a symbol for the thousands of Communists and other antifascists incarcerated in the Third Reich.

The leaders of the international Communist movement encouraged this result. Willi Münzenberg, who was working in the Comintern's propaganda office in Moscow, received orders to establish a "Thälmann Committee." Münzenberg, who had worked his way up the party hierarchy through his prewar work with the Communist youth movement, had extensive experience in the Comintern's propaganda apparatus.[51] As early as 1921, for example, he oversaw the Foreign Committee for the Organization of Worker Relief for the Hungry in Soviet Russia. Officially an "independent" body under the honorary chairmanship of Clara Zetkin, the committee had the ostensible goal to raise funds for the victims of the 1921 famine in the Volga region of the Soviet Union. It ultimately raised remarkably little money—although most of what it did collect came from the United States. In reality, the organization served two functions. First, it was a Comintern propaganda tool, seeking to mitigate any embarrassment to the Soviet Union that might result because of the success of "bourgeois" relief organizations—especially Herbert Hoover's American Relief Administration—which were much more effective than Moscow's efforts to provide aid to starving Soviet farmers. Second, in organizing the campaign, Münzenberg's Foreign Committee for the Organization of Workers' Relief hoped to absorb radical groups that remained outside of Moscow's orbit.[52] Indeed, even after Hoover's American Relief Administration had mitigated the Volga famine, Münzenberg's committee continued to exist, shortening its name to "International Workers' Relief." Over the next two decades, Münzenberg used Soviet funds to create a vast media empire that included a publishing house as well as a movie studio. His extensive experience as a propagandist would serve him and the ECCI well during the course of the Free Thälmann campaign.

The new Thälmann Committee, created to reorganize the Free Thälmann effort, would, like International Workers' Relief, be international in its membership and theoretically independent of the Comintern—hence the decision to have its headquarters in Paris rather than Moscow. Further, Münzenberg would try to integrate prominent "fellow travelers"—non-Communists who openly opposed fascism and supported at least some Soviet policies—into the effort.[53] This strategy had at least three possible advantages. First, it would create the impression that the campaign to free Thälmann, although surreptitiously controlled by Moscow, was an autonomous international effort, championed by all "progressive" forces, Communist and non-Communist alike. Such an impression would grant the movement legitimacy it would not have if it were openly an ECCI-controlled enterprise. Second, prominent "fellow travelers" could be co-opted for the Communist cause, thereby adding legitimacy not only to the antifascist movement, but also to the broader Marxist–Leninist crusade against capitalism. Finally, a veneer of independence would allow the committee to attract more non-Communist support, assuring that the demonstrations and other activities so vital to the movement would be more extensive than otherwise. But any claims of independence were a facade from the outset; the Comintern controlled not only the campaign's ideological direction, but also its budget. In order to assure continued Communist control of the organization, Münzenberg personally raised whatever funds Moscow did not provide. His experience with famine relief in the 1920s had shown that America could serve as a crucial source of funds for the movement, and he concentrated his efforts there. For example, as his mistress Babette Gross recalled, in 1934 Münzenberg returned from a series of speeches in the United States with a "considerable sum" for his propaganda enterprise.[54] And large amounts of money were needed to carry out a propaganda campaign as extensive as the one to free Ernst Thälmann. The committee's budget would fluctuate slightly, depending on the activities organized. In 1936, for example, monthly expenses ran anywhere between 5,000 and 7,000 French francs (US$306–428, approximately US$4,165–5,825 in 2004 currency), and this amount does not take into account the funds spent by local organizations acting at the behest of the center, not to mention the money spent by the KPD, Comintern, and the Soviet government for the movement.[55]

On 4 January 1934, Münzenberg established the International Committee for the Liberation of Dimitrov, Thaelmann, and All the Imprisoned Antifascists (referred to here as the Thälmann Committee) in Paris.[56] Upon Dimitrov's release in February 1934, however, Thälmann's name assumed pride of place, representing in the Comintern's eyes the thousands of Communists imprisoned in the Third Reich. Meanwhile, Dimitrov contributed to the emerging Thälmann legend upon his 27 February 1934 arrival in Moscow. After thanking his thousands of supporters in the Soviet Union and the rest of the world, whom he credited with securing his release, Dimitrov pointed out that their task was far from complete. "I am convinced that the struggle for the liberation of Thälmann is a question of honor for everyone who wishes to fight against fascism." When asked if he knew the KPD chief personally, he went on to say: "Yes, I saw Ernst Thälmann in March of last year. He is my personal friend. I considered him one of the clearest heads in the international revolutionary movement. Then I met him twice in Moabit prison . . . , his spirit [Mut] is whole and definitely unbroken."[57] Dimitrov's implication was clear: the German Communist leader should be an example for all staunch antifascists. This was just the first of several important contributions that the Bulgarian Communist leader made to the Thälmann Committee's work.

The committee's honorary chairmen were the French writers André Gide, a Nobel Prize laureate, and André Malraux, both "fellow travelers." In 1935, Henri Barbusse, Paul Langevin, and Romain Rolland succeeded Gide and Malraux, who had become disillusioned with Stalinism. It was Barbusse who coined the phrase "Ernst Thälmann must be won like a battle!" which appeared in the committee's letterhead. In light of the intense effort put into the campaign, this simile would prove to be appropriate, relating the seriousness with which the movement pursued its professed goal of freeing Thälmann. His liberation became an important component of the life-or-death struggle between the forces of progress and the forces of fascism. Having famous non-Communist names, such as Gide and Barbusse, at the head of the organization enhanced its legitimacy and undermined any claims that the Thälmann Committee was a front for the Comintern. Further weakening impressions of Communist partisanship, the committee also extended its work to encompass efforts to free non-Communists, such as the German pacifist writer Carl von Ossietzky and the Social Democrat Rudolf Breitscheid, languishing in Nazi prisons and concentration camps.[58] The International Thälmann Committee's French affiliate, the Committee for the Liberation of Thälmann and Imprisoned German Antifascists, located at Paris's 10 rue Notre-Dame-de-Lorette, the same address as the International Committee, listed thirty-two "associated organizations" representing a cross-section of the international Left in the 1930s, including the Friends of the Earth, the Committee for the Aid of the Victims of Hitler-Fascism, the Committee for the Defense of Political Prisoners, the International League Against Antisemitism, the French Communist Party, and the Women's Union Against Suffering and War.[59] From the outset, the Comintern sought to create the impression that the Free Thälmann movement was a worldwide effort comprising all of the forces opposed to the insidious Hitler dictatorship.

Ultimately, however, the Thälmann Committee was indeed only a front for the Third International. Concocted in Moscow and created by an agent of the Communist International, Willi Münzenberg, Communists—such as Wilhelm Pieck and Bela Kun, not to mention Münzenberg himself—performed the lion's share of the committee's work, which consisted of coordinating international efforts to secure Ernst Thälmann's release.[60] Perhaps most important, the committee's secretary, who oversaw much of its daily activities, was Erich Birkenhauer, a Communist. Working under the pseudonym "Belfort," he would later be purged for allegedly undermining the group's work.[61] This reason is ironic given that, at least after 1935, the Comintern and the KPD in exile had no intention seriously to pursue the committee's declared goal. Thälmann had to languish in prison for the good of the movement, an outcome advantageous for Comintern propaganda. The rank-and-file activists who participated in the movement were apparently unaware of this charade, though, and remained sincerely determined to liberate the KPD leader.

The Thälmann Committee coordinated a massive propaganda campaign, one of the largest and most rigorously organized ever undertaken by the Comintern. In order to facilitate this effort, the committee created a massive bureaucracy, including subsidiary organizations in numerous countries, among them France, the United States, Great Britain, Poland, Spain, the Soviet Union, Denmark, and even nations as distant as Japan. Practically every political party associated with the Third International had its own Free Thälmann organization answerable to the International Thälmann Committee in Paris.[62] Through its influence over the committee that was coordinating the Free Thälmann effort, the Comintern could quietly extend its authority over "fellow travelers" and their numerous organizations. In this manner, the Thälmann Committee contributed to the Comintern's long-term goal of fomenting global revolution.

But the organization's most immediate role was to promote a worldwide propaganda effort ostensibly intended to secure the liberation of the German Communist leader held in Moabit prison, and the Thälmann Committee was remarkably effective in pursuing this goal. Coupled with its sister organizations, such as the International Conference of Jurists and the Permanent European Commission for a Total Political Amnesty in Germany (Amnesty Commission) and its worldwide subsidiaries, the Thälmann Committee coordinated a truly impressive global propaganda campaign, carrying its message to several continents. In 1935, for example, the International Conference of Jurists, meeting in Paris, passed a resolution questioning the legitimacy of the indictment against Thälmann and demanding his release.[63] In that same year, other lawyers' associations, such as one meeting in London in June, campaigned against the very real danger that the prisoner would be secretly put on trial. The Interparliamentary Commission for the Defense of the Rights of the People and Their Elected Representatives, meeting in Brussels in November, also demanded Thälmann's immediate emancipation because as a member of the German Reichstag he enjoyed immunity from prosecution. In London, 116 members of Parliament from both houses signed a petition calling for Thälmann's liberation. A British lawyer delivered it personally to the Chancellery in Berlin. In addition, a 100,000-strong (according to the committee's figures) demonstration in Paris demanded the KPD leader's release. Thälmann was a veteran of the 1914–1918 war, and a three-man delegation from an English veterans organization attempted to visit him in Moabit, one of several such groups to try. German officials refused them permission to meet with the prisoner.[64]

Meanwhile, in Czechoslovakia "more than 500,000 Communists, Social Democrats, Christian workers, clerks, civil servants and intellectuals and members of the middle class" signed a petition "against the planned Thälmann trial and demanding his release."[65] At about the same time, the Moscow Thälmann Committee mobilized Soviet workers and farmers to play a part in the campaign. Like its international counterpart, this committee played an administrative role, planning many of the activities carried out by subordinate organizations. Not surprisingly, it seems to have been largely independent of the Paris headquarters.[66] In the Western Hemisphere, *The Daily Worker* published a November 1935 letter, accompanied by a sketch of the German Communist, from Earl Browder, the CPUSA chairman. Writing to Thälmann on behalf of his party's central committee, Browder praised his German comrade to the skies.

> You have now passed nearly three years in prison, barbaric torture chambers of Hitler fascism. We know that no deadly menance [sic] and no torture can break your courageous spirit and resistance against the fascist dictatorship any more than they can crush [the] relentless fight of millions of German workers, farmers, and all other anti-fascists of whom you are the beloved leader. You and your heroic comrades and growing united front against fascism in Germany are the hope of the whole world in [the] struggle against [the] sinister war plans of German Fascism. On behalf of [the] working millions of America we pledge to fight relentlessly for your liberation and [the] liberation of all prisoners of fascism [and] for a liberated Germany.[67]

The Thälmann Committee and its allies, including the CPUSA, rarely missed an opportunity to propagate their message before a mass audience.

The climax of the Free Thälmann crusade centered around his fiftieth birthday on 16 April 1936. The International Committee thoroughly planned the political agitation surrounding this important anniversary. The effort would take place over a span of around six weeks, with the committee overseeing the period from 18 March, which marked the anniversary of the outbreak of revolution in 1848, to 16 April, after which control would be handed over to the Amnesty Campaign overseen by the International Red Relief organization. The crusade would culminate on May Day and employ the efforts of thousands of Communists and fellow travelers in more than a dozen countries—including Germany and concentrating in Berlin and Hamburg, Thälmann's hometown. In the Third Reich, the drive would have to be carried out surreptitiously and would consist of "a flier for illegal distribution," stickers, and clandestine newspapers as well as appeals to Social Democrats and Catholic workers. In addition, pro-Thälmann slogans would be painted on walls and fences.[68] It is worth noting that a handful of men and women could carry out any of these tasks, so all these activities should not be interpreted, as they were by the Comintern, as evidence of the overwhelming strength of the Communist movement in Germany.

The committee's plans for the remainder of the world were much more elaborate. Wilhelm Pieck, for example, was in charge of soliciting "bourgeois personalities," including Heinrich Mann, to write birthday greetings to the Communist leader, which would be published in the many periodicals, such as the *AIZ,* sympathetic to the cause. Pieck's assignment was just the opening salvo of the campaign's so-called literary component. The committee ordered Wilhelm Florin to produce a "brochure" containing a brief biography of the imprisoned Communist leader, and Pieck would write an article, "The Development of the KPD under Thälmann," for the *Kommunist International.* A "collective brochure" of personal impressions of Thälmann and a "Brown Book" concerning the indictment of Thälmann would be published as well.[69]

The production of printed materials was only the beginning of the propaganda effort, the catalyst to involve thousands of activists from all over the globe in the campaign. As always, the mass action would be central to the endeavor. "Arrangement[s]" would be made for "assemblies, resolutions with demands to the German government, and solidarity meetings for the antifascist struggle in Germany." Delegations of Communists and members of allied organizations would visit German embassies across the globe, presenting demands that Thälmann be released. Activists would mail thousands of postcards to German embassies, and the Thälmann Committee would organize "border meetings," where comrades from different countries could meet to show the international unity that Thälmann personified. Finally, "an International Solidarity Day" would be organized "on 16 April under the title 'Thälmann Liberation Day' in order to collect money for the support of the antifascist struggle in Germany." The legislatures of "England, Spain, Greece, Mexico, Holland, Belgium, Denmark, Sweden, Norway, and others" would be asked to place pressure on Hitler's government, calling for Thälmann's immediate release. Finally, the committee planned numerous activities in the Soviet Union, such as mass rallies and radio broadcasts, aimed primarily at the German exile community, the vast majority of whom were already in sympathy with the cause.[70]

The commemoration of Thälmann's fiftieth birthday was a massive undertaking, carefully orchestrated in Paris and Moscow. From the point of view of the Comintern and the Thälmann Committee, the venture was a success, especially in Spain and France, where huge rallies took place in remembrance of the KPD chief. According to Communist estimates, "millions" were involved in the effort. In addition to numerous mass rallies, in which untold thousands participated, German embassies across the globe received millions of postcards and telephone calls demanding Thälmann's freedom.[71] Intellectuals also sought to show their sympathy with the imprisoned Communist leader. Heinrich Mann, marking Thälmann's fiftieth birthday, wrote: "The imprisoned Ernst Thälmann is very strong—much stronger than his persecutors, who would like to let him disappear but won't risk it. Thälmann is a true worker with fortitude and a healthy understanding [of the political situation]. . . . The whole world knows his name." The Danish novelist Martin Andersen Nexö was perhaps even more lavish in his praise, maintaining that Thälmann was "today one of the most popular men in the world."[72] The prisoner also received birthday greetings from Maxim Gorki, Romain Rolland, Arnold Zweig, and the German Communist writers Erich Weinert and Johannes R. Becher. The Comintern and the Thälmann Committee undoubtedly found these endorsements from noteworthy literary figures especially pleasing. As Marxist–Leninists, the leaders of the Thälmann campaign had great—perhaps excessive—respect for cultural luminaries. They believed that art could change the world and create the "new man"—never the "new woman"—who was the ultimate goal of the Soviet experiment. Further, as scholar Boris Groys has pointed out, Leninists considered the building of communism, although a rational exercise, to be analogous to an artistic enterprise. In both instances, one takes raw materials—be they thoughts, paint, stone, or human beings—and molds them into something new, something better, something that would not exist without the contribution of the artist/revolutionary.[73] This notion helps to explain the prominence of cultural figures in the creation of the Thälmann myth, not only in the 1930s and 1940s, but also in the years following the Second World War.

But the masses were just as important, if not more so. Although intellectuals could lead people to the movement, the masses were an essential component of the socialist project. It was they who would build communism under the tutelage of the revolutionary intelligent-sia. Hence, their contribution, in the form of mass rallies and coordinated telephoning and letter-writing campaigns, was vital to the success of the Free Thälmann movement. The masses also made an important contribution to the literary element of the campaign. On his fiftieth birthday, Ernst Thälmann received not only a large bouquet of red roses surreptitiously placed in the entryway to Moabit prison, but also several sacks of postcards and letters from throughout the world relating birthday greetings. The Communist movement sold many of these postcards—100,000 of them in the United States alone.[74] The numbers participating in this effort may appear impressive at first, but one has to take into consideration the untold millions who lived in the countries participating in the crusade. One hundred thousand people can be viewed as a relatively modest number when compared to the total US population of more than 125 million.

Yet the campaign did apparently ruffle some Nazi feathers. Hitler, for example, decided not to try Thälmann publically because of the publicity that would ensue. On 22 April 1936, the German embassy in Paris sent a report to the Foreign Office concerning French observance of Thälmann's fiftieth birthday. Penned by a man identified only as Kühn, the summary pointed out that "[t]he Thälmann case is still mentioned often in the Communist press, less often in the socialist [press]." Further, the Communists rarely missed an opportunity to publicize the KPD leader's plight, and "a resolution demanding the liberation of Thälmann has become an invariable component of every large Communist assembly." The campaign had recently become even more active, with the celebration of the German Communist's fiftieth birthday. Kühn reported, for example, that the Communist newspaper *Humanité* had devoted an entire page to Thälmann on 16 April. Further, "[t]he union newspaper *People* had published an article concerning Thälmann's union activities," and another paper had printed birthday greetings from "Heinrich Mann, Romain Rolland, Léon Blum, and others." The Thälmann Committee also organized a mass protest, as had the Union of German Youth in Paris, held on 18 April. The program for this assembly included music, speeches, and a chorus, Die Jugend und Thälmann (Youth and Thälmann).[75] It is worth noting once again the importance of prominent of non-Communists in the campaign and the emphasis placed on mass demonstrations. Both were apparently effective enough to garner the movement a great deal of publicity, not to mention the Nazi authorities' attention.

Although activities during the spring of 1936 represented the zenith of the Free Thälmann campaign, the effort continued until 1939. A relative handful of examples must suffice. To commemorate the Communist leader's fifty-first birthday on 16 April 1937, the Thälmann Committee published a collection of documents on the "Thälmann case," with the texts translated into French and English. The fact that only six hundred copies of the publication were produced, however, brings into question this effort's effectiveness. Also to celebrate his fifty-first birthday, 189 "English personalities (Members of Parliament, professors, scholars), signed a [birthday] greeting to Thälmann." "Well-known writers and politicians . . . wrote articles about Thälmann," and 50,000 citizens of Czechoslovakia, not to mentions tens of thousands from other countries, sent birthday greetings to the prisoner.[76] From the end of January through March 1938, the Paris Thälmann Committee sponsored an exhibition entitled Five Years of the Hitler Regime. Although not dealing specifically with the Free Thälmann crusade, the committee's sponsorship of the display indicates how integral the campaign was to the overall anti-Nazi propaganda effort. Located in three small rooms on the second floor of Rue de Lancry 10, the exhibition was scheduled to run until 18 March, the anniversary of the start of the 1848 revolutions in Germany. The Paris Trade Union Association and the League for the Defense of Human and Citizens' Rights were among the co-sponsors of the display, which consisted of "photographs, caricatures, and statistics" organized along thematic lines. The first room, of primary interest here, held objects depicting the Nazi seizure of power and the "Hitler Terror," including some information on the Reichstag fire, antifascists imprisoned in Germany, and the concentration camps. The second and third chambers dealt with the economy of the Third Reich and Nazi cultural policy, respectively. In addition, antifascist "experts" would give lectures on daily life in the Third Reich. The exhibit caused something of a minor diplomatic incident, with the German embassy insisting that much of the information presented was "falsified." The German government mounted an official protest, its embassy warning that the display was causing "unrest in German–French relations." As a result, French police closed down the display around one month early. In the meantime, at least according to Communist sources, approximately 15,000 people passed through the exhibit.[77] These Free Thälmann activities were only a few of the innumerable activities carried out in the years immediately before the outbreak of war.

As the start of the conflict grew closer, the momentum of the Free

Thälmann drive waned. The 1939 German annexation of Czechoslovakia sealed off an important route between the Third Reich and Moscow, and carrying out propaganda activities became more difficult. With the signing of the German–Soviet Nonaggression Treaty on 23 August 1939, Soviet and Comintern sponsorship of antifascist activities ceased, and the KPD obediently adapted itself to Stalin's diplomatic revolution. The Free Thälmann campaign came, for all intents and purposes, to a complete halt, although Communist authorities continued to remain in contact with the prisoner. The successful German invasion of France the following year made it impossible to carry out any Free Thälmann activities in that country. It would be misleading, however, to suggest that the incarcerated KPD leader was completely forgotten. In his diary entry for 29 March 1941, for example, Georgi Dimitrov lamented the fact that the Comintern and its subordinate organizations could not participate in any activities celebrating Thälmann's fifty-fifth birthday. "It would be painful if a vigorous campaign took place in foreign countries but we could not undertake one here," where it is "politically hardly possible" because of the "nonhostile policies" being pursued toward Germany. "One must discuss these things in the Central Committee, but the best thing would be if this campaign tapered off," Dimitrov concluded, which is precisely what happened.[78] Even following the German attack on the Soviet Union in June 1941, when there was obviously no longer any concern about offending the Nazi regime, neither the Soviet government, nor the KPD in exile, nor the Comintern considered Thälmann's fate important. Safeguarding the cradle of Marxism–Leninism became the primary duty of all those associated with the Third International and the central theme of Communist propaganda. The dissolution of the Comintern in 1943, the organization bearing primary responsibility for the Free Thälmann campaign, further contributed to the relative neglect of the imprisoned KPD leader. Indeed, even German Communists paid Thälmann very little attention during this period, and the only thing that brought his plight back into the spotlight was his August 1944 murder in Buchenwald Concentration Camp.

But before looking at international communism's response to Thälmann's death, we should take a closer look at some of the Free Thälmann propaganda produced during the years 1934 to 1938, the high point of the campaign. Ever mindful that the Comintern's (not necessarily the individual campaign's) primary purpose for the movement was not to secure Thälmann's freedom, but rather to produce antifascist propaganda, a detailed investigation not only contributes to a better understanding of what the campaign tried to accomplish but also permits a closer examination of the themes incorporated into the crusade's propaganda. In turn, this analysis affords an opportunity better to understand the international Communist movement of the 1930s and how it viewed itself, its role in the struggle against fascism, and the nature of its enemies. Such an endeavor also aids in comprehending the genesis of the antifascism myth and the early development of the closely related Ernst Thälmann legend.

The Soviet Union, the Comintern, and the KPD used every propaganda medium at their disposal: journalism, film, radio, mass rallies, petitions, literature, music, and art. The same can be said for the Thälmann Committee, which oversaw an elaborate propaganda apparatus. Probably the most widely used medium in the Free Thälmann campaign, however, was the political flyer, which had long been a staple of Communist propaganda. The flyer had several advantages. First of all, flyers (*Flugblätter*) were relatively easy and cheap to produce. All that the propagandist needed were paper and ink. If someone were fastidious enough, such flyers could be copied by hand, technically making a printing press unnecessary. But hand copying was not a very efficient method of producing propaganda, and the vast majority of these flyers were printed on small presses secreted away by the KPD's domestic resistance movement or printed in one of the states bordering Germany and smuggled into the Third Reich—which leads to the second advantage of these unobtrusive, usually single-sheet handouts. They could be transported and distributed relatively easily, to be read by several people, it was hoped. The words *read and pass on* appeared in the upper-left-hand corner of many of these sheets. At least within German borders, the KPD's "technical apparatus," consisting of a handful of men, carried out the entire enterprise. Finally, given the Hitler regime's monopoly on the media and its crackdown on left-wing resistance, the flyer was often the only format available to propagandists.[79]

The KPD produced hundreds, if not thousands, of these flyers, dozens of them relating to the Free Thälmann effort, but a few can serve as representative examples. One of the themes linking many of the flyers was the contention that Thälmann's life was in imminent danger. A 10 February 1934 flyer, for example, demanded an organized effort to rescue the imprisoned KPD leader. "Ernst THAELMANN and hundreds of proletarian prisoners [are] in danger!" cries the opening line of one flyer produced by the Berlin section of the outlawed KPD. "SAVE

THE LEADER OF THE GERMAN PROLETARIAT!" it continues. Protests must be organized and "defense committees" created because
"Ernst THAELMANN is in the greatest danger." Evidence of this danger, the flyer continued, can be seen in the fate of his comrades "*Jonny
SCHEER* [sic], *Eugen SCHOENHARR, Erich STEINFURTH and Rudolf
SCHWARZ,*" all of whom were "shot while attempting to escape." The
only possible response to the Nazis' systematic effort to intimidate the
revolutionary workers is to "ORGANIZE MASS DEFENSE IMMEDI-
ATELY!" on Thälmann's behalf. Similar actions had saved Dimitrov,
and the "truest son of the working class" must also be rescued. This
Flugblatt then goes on to present a brief biography of the Communist
leader, who "grew up in a proletarian family in the workers' section
of Hamburg" and went to work at the age of seventeen. He was an
average man who through hard work rose to become the KPD's "most
loved and unchallenged [*unbestrittene*] leader." He was one of them,
and only the German proletariat could save him in his hour of need.
His cause was not lost for "*millions of the masses already stand behind
Ernst THAELMANN today!*"[80] His supporters must stand behind Thälmann, says another flyer, in order to assure that he not be murdered by
Gestapo thugs.[81]

There was a great deal of overlap between the flyer campaign and
political journalism. Many of the *Flugblätter,* both those produced inside Germany and the ones written and printed in foreign countries,
were primitive multipage newspapers. They often contained pieces
written by Pieck, Ulbricht, and other exiled German Communists, not
to mention Dimitrov. These extended flyers were political journalism
on the grassroots level, and many of them advanced the Free Thälmann
crusade. The April 1934 title page of one such underground paper, the
Neuköllner Sturmfahne, incorporated the headline "Thälmann's Life in
Danger!" Like the *Flugblatt* analyzed earlier, this crudely printed illegal
publication called for a "protest and solidarity action" to free the KPD
chief.[82] A similar but even more crudely printed, extended flyer concerned with the "indictment against Thälmann," seeking to establish
that the former dockworker's life was in impending danger, quoted
some verse that had appeared in the organ of the German Workers'
Front, a Nazi organization. Entitled "Off with Thaelmann's Head," the
brief bit of doggerel went:

Herr Teddy is by nature
A man of impressive stature

And add to this
In every way he was the slimmest.
Certainly if he is handsome and thin
He is also *a head too tall!*[83]

Some of these multipage flyers, usually printed outside of Germany, had the appearance of actual newspapers, with individual articles, bylines, photographs, and more elaborate typesetting. *Weltruf für Thälmann* (World Outcry for Thälmann), a publication of the International Thälmann Committee, bridged the gap between political flyer and newspaper. Printed on standard-size stationery rather than newsprint, its modest proportions made it easy to transport and, should the need arise, hide. In brief articles, some of them signed, *Weltruf für Thälmann* augmented the effort to free Thälmann and other imprisoned antifascists.[84]

Political journalism (*Publizistik*) was another integral component of the Free Thälmann movement. Although the majority of this writing appeared in newspapers, periodicals, and books published outside of Germany, the Communist resistance did distribute some of it within the borders of the Third Reich. This form of political propaganda sometimes appeared in camouflaged editions with covers bearing the title of another book or pamphlet, often a Nazi one. To disguise their contents further, these editions sometimes even contained several pages from another publication. The Bible was a particularly popular "front" for these underground pamphlets. Further adding to their stealth, they were usually printed in very small editions, making them easier to conceal if necessary.[85] One of these miniature brochures, two inches by three inches in size, appeared in 1935. Obviously excerpted from a larger publication, the pamphlet had a plain white cover. A superscript at the top of the first page of this pamphlet entitled *The Struggle for Thälmann's Liberation—a Battle Against Fascism and War* claims that it was published in Berlin on 30 November 1935. This assertion is possible in light of the fact that the KPD possessed underground printing presses in Germany, but it is not necessarily true. It is also conceivable that the pamphlet was printed outside the Third Reich and smuggled across the border. The first page of the pamphlet, authored by Wilhelm Pieck, consists of a political caricature drawn by a Russian artist, identified as V. Deni. It shows a line drawing of Ernst Thälmann in the upper-left-hand corner of the page. On the bottom right is a sharp-toothed drooling beast adorned in judicial attire, his right hand a monstrous claw grasping for the KPD leader. The message was clear: the evil Nazi judicial system sought to annihilate Thälmann just as it strove to destroy the German working class. There was nothing new or unusual in this effort to demonize the enemy—a technique as old as civilization.[86]

Pieck's essay, which runs to ten and a half closely printed pages, opens with a survey of Thälmann's legal situation. He had been imprisoned "two years and nine months" earlier, and Nazi authorities had that entire time to build a case against him. Clearly they could not— Thälmann was innocent of all charges. Yet he remained in prison. Even after he finally received a copy of the indictment against him, his case did not come to trial. Finally, through the American press, the international workers' movement heard that he would be tried in November, yet there had been no public announcement. The regime sought to carry out the proceedings in secret, hoping to railroad Thälmann on trumped-up charges, holding him "morally and legally responsible for the acts of terror committed by Communists against National Socialists" in the final years of the republic. "The fascist executioners want to eliminate the best mind of the German proletariat," Pieck wrote. "The life of Ernst Thälmann is in the greatest danger!"[87]

But the German workers could free him through a "powerful campaign," just as they had Georgi Dimitrov, the man who had embarrassed the Third Reich so completely in his Leipzig trial. The effort to free the Bulgarian had succeeded because a "powerful united front of proletarians and workers [*Arbeiter und Werktätigen*] from the entire world [struggled] for Dimitrov's liberation." The Nazis, however, had also learned from their experiences during the trial of the Bulgarian Communist, and the "campaign for the freedom of Thälmann must be even more powerful" if it were to succeed. Further, Thälmann was in even more danger that Dimitrov had been. The German Communist leader was to appear before a "so-called people's court [*Volksgericht*]. . . . But it does not behave as a people's court, but rather as a court of the Nazi Party." The judges would be "two SA men or SS bigshots," and "the most infamous of the blood judgments of these 'people's courts' have been delivered against German workers." Such a court would render Thälmann "dead silent," convicting him with "falsified documents [and] bought witnesses." The Dimitrov trial had shown the duplicity of National Socialist legal authorities, and those proceedings had not taken place before a *Volksgericht* and were bound to be even more unfair.[88]

Yet "[m]illions of workers in Germany and the whole world" stood behind Thälmann because he was the personification of the proletariat, Pieck continues. He was one of them. "Ernst Thälmann is a worker who has sacrificed his entire life to the struggle for his class." He was in the trenches of the Great War and in the "front line" of the "revolutionary struggle." For more than ten years, this staunch opponent of the bourgeoisie had led the KPD, which "under his leadership had become a mass party with 300,000 members and 6 million supporters." Providing several quotations from Thälmann's speeches to prop up his argument, Pieck maintains that the imprisoned Communist leader had become the most steadfast opponent of fascism, that archenemy of the working classes. He represented all that was good in the workers' movement. Pieck concludes his article by quoting the movement's rallying cry: "Ernst Thälmann must be won like a battle. . . . *Freedom for Thälmann!*"[89]

Pieck's political essay is of particular interest because of the role he played in the development of the GDR's Thälmann myth. The piece incorporates several themes that many years later would become important components of the East German version of the legend. First and most obvious, Pieck repeatedly emphasizes the mass support that supposedly stood behind Thälmann and the effort to liberate him, a very common theme that has already been analyzed but bears repeating. Further, he links the struggle to free Thälmann with the successful effort to liberate Dimitrov. The novel and hence most interesting part of Pieck's essay is his analysis of Nazi Germany's "people's courts." In writing about their proceedings, the future GDR president maintains that the "most infamous" sentences handed down by these courts were given to workers. Pieck's implication was obvious: the KPD and its allies were the primary targets of the National Socialist state. Above everything else, the Nazis sought to destroy the working class's political will, which represented the greatest danger to the fascist program of exploitation. This argument anticipates one of the central tenets of the postwar antifascism myth—for the Nazis, it was the Communists, not the Jews, who were the primary enemy. Making this argument legitimized the Communist movement. If the primary enemy of National Socialism, the ultimate manifestation of political evil, is Marxism–Leninism, by this logic the international Communist movement must embody the ultimate good. Similar assertions would be repeated throughout the postwar years, and the Ernst Thälmann myth would become one of its most important manifestations. Pieck's essay anticipated one of the central themes of GDR propaganda.

The future East German president was not the only prominent

figure to produce a tract contributing to Thälmann's defense. Georgi Dimitrov, shortly after his February 1934 release from Moabit and at the height of his fame, wrote a pamphlet entitled *Auf zur Rettung Thälmanns* (On to Save Thälmann). Written in Moscow, the booklet appeared in at least three languages—Russian, German, and English, the German-language version published in Paris by Weltverlag.[90] The size of an average book, five and a half by eight and a half inches, the German version of the pamphlet came with a photograph of Thälmann and Dimitrov's name on the cover and thus could not be easily hidden. The work was published for those in exile from the Third Reich and other German readers rather than for surreptitious distribution in Germany. The most interesting portion of this brochure can be found on pages four and five, where the author introduces his Manichean view of the struggle to set Thälmann free.

The Nazi press, Dimitrov points out, made it clear that the leaders of the Third Reich did not understand why there was such a clamor concerning the fate of a single man. They simply did not understand, as all of Thälmann's supporters knew, that "[h]ere more than the fate of a single leader of workers is at stake. What is at stake is the conflict between two worlds," the forces of fascism and the forces of progress. His explication is worth quoting at length:

> Yes, two worlds stand against each other:
> The world of the struggle for freedom and the world of the oppression of the masses;
> the world of true culture and the world of barbarism;
> the world of communism and the world of fascism.
> Here Ernst Thälmann, the heroic fighter for the liberation of millions of workers,
> of the proletariat, farmers, middle classes and intellectuals.
> There Adolf Hitler the deceiver and oppressor of working-class Germans.
> Here Ernst Thälmann, the untiring struggler for peace between peoples.
> There is Adolf Hitler, the embodiment of war, the alpha and omega of National Socialism.
> Adolf Hitler, supported by his masters, Krupp, Thyssen, and [company], buttressed by lies. Cunning, deceiving demagogue of unlimited terror, ruling in Germany as dictator.
> Ernst Thälmann, the revolutionary proletarian, the champion and

> leader of the workers, supported by the trust and love of workers in Germany and the entire world, sitting, condemned to death, in a German prison.
>
> Millions in the entire world are presented with the decision: for Ernst Thälmann or for Adolf Hitler;
>
> for the chief of the fascist torturers or for the leader of the peace movement;
>
> for the representative of the return to barbarism or for the representative of cultural progress.[91]

Dimitrov describes the struggle to free Thälmann in apocalyptic terms, as a duel to the death between the forces of good and evil, light and darkness. As a result, everyone must choose a side in the controversy. To try to remain aloof amounted to supporting Hitler by default. Hitler, the ultimate force for evil, the instrument of the exploiting classes, at the pinnacle of the German state, is contrasted with the humble KPD leader rotting away in a fascist dungeon because of his peaceful proletarian convictions. Dimitrov clearly implies that the campaign to free Thälmann is about much more than the fate of a single man; the outcome of the Free Thälmann crusade will determine the future not only of Germany, but of the entire world. Thälmann's plight is everyone's concern.

The Free Thälmann campaign also incorporated more traditional forms of journalism. On the proletarian leader's fiftieth birthday, for example, an open letter from the KPD's Central Committee to Ernst Thälmann appeared in *Pravda*. Printed under the rubric "We Swear to Rescue You from the Executioner," the letter begins by extending a "warm Bolshevik greeting" to the prisoner not only from the Central Committee, but also from the "millions of proletarians and workers of Germany," "the millions of the international proletariat, [and] all within the peace movement." The letter, obviously written as a propaganda piece, seeks once again to depict Thälmann as representative of the entire workers' movement. It refers to him as a "true son of the German working class" engaged in an "untiring struggle against war and reaction, against exploitation and surrendering the concerns of the working class." He was a "loyal fighter for our worldwide party, a student of Lenin and Stalin." In short, Thälmann represented the forces of progress, all that was noble in the international workers' movement. On his fiftieth birthday, the KPD Central Committee advises him: "We swear that we will use all the resources at our disposal to free the German land of the shame of fascism." Further, they, along with "many millions of workers from the entire world," promise to "rescue you from the cell of your oppressor, of the deadly enemy of working people. . . . Every hour of your imprisonment . . . is a burning memory for us."[92] Written by Wilhelm Pieck, the letter appears especially cynical, however, when one remembers that by 1936 the KPD and its Comintern allies had abandoned any intention of securing Thälmann's release.

Although *Pravda* as well as German-language newspapers in the Soviet Union were produced primarily for the party faithful, other publications had a broader audience in mind. For years, the KPD had published glossy illustrated newspapers and magazines designed to appeal to the rank and file as well as to win converts from the masses. Following the Nazi seizure of power, many of these titles moved their offices outside of Germany to avoid being forcibly closed. The most famous of the glossy Communist magazines was Willi Münzenberg's *AIZ*, which published numerous articles and photographs pertaining to the Free Thälmann effort. Many of its photographs, for instance, exhibited examples of pro-Thälmann propaganda, supposedly from Germany. Among these pictures were several showing fences or smokestacks with the words "Out with Ernst Thälmann!" or "Save Ernst Thälmann!" painted on them in letters several feet high. Supposedly taken in Germany, such photographs contributed to the myth that worker unrest was rampant in the Third Reich and revolution was imminent.[93] Another popular motif placed emphasis on the scope of the Free Thälmann movement, with photographs showing thousands of protesters from all over the world carrying signs in several different languages. Other photographs displayed boxes of letters and postcards supposedly bound for Moabit prison.[94] Thälmann's visage regularly graced *AIZ*'s pages, photos or drawings of him appearing on several covers.[95]

The most interesting examples of Free Thälmann propaganda appearing in the pages of the *AIZ* were John Heartfield's photomontages. "John Heartfield" was the pseudonym of Helmut Held, an artist born in 1891 in Berlin who grew up in poverty. His experiences as a boy—his parents abandoned him and his three siblings when he was just eight years old—led him into the Communist movement, and he became a staunch adherent of the KPD. Originally trained as a printer, he became one of the editors of *Der Knüppel* (The Cudgel), a Communist magazine, and provided illustrations for children's books. In 1924, Münzenberg established the *AIZ*, which came to have a circulation of 265,000 by 1926. Heartfield began to generate art for Münzenberg's weekly in

John Heartfield's 1936 photogravure of Ernst Thälmann in prison. Courtesy of the Artists Rights Society (ARS), New York/VG Bild-Kunst, Bonn. © 2012.

addition to his work for *Der Knüppel* and *Rote Fahne*, the KPD's official organ. Although he generated other visual images, he became most famous for his photomontages attacking both the Weimar Republic and the growing National Socialist movement. Hitler's seizure of power forced him into exile, first to France, where he had a major exhibition in 1935, then to Britain, where he waited out the war. Throughout his years in exile, Heartfield continued to produce works assailing the Third Reich. Following the war, he moved to the GDR, where he continued to work until his death in 1968.[96] Of primary interest here, however, are his photomontages created for the Free Thälmann campaign.

As Victoria Bonnell has pointed out, "[P]hotomontage was in some ways the quintessential application of socialist realism in the visual sphere."[97] The medium allowed the artist to rearrange the real—the photographs—in such as way as to relate a political message, to participate in the building of socialism. Images from the past, present, and future could be combined to produce an ideal. Heartfield, in many of his photomontages, linked images in order to represent a dystopia, such as the Third Reich, thereby promoting the creation of an ideal socialist society. Among Heartfield's most famous works, for example, is one titled *The Meaning of the Hitler Salute*, which appeared on the cover of *AIZ* in October 1932. It shows the Nazi Party chief in profile, giving the party salute. Behind Hitler stands a much larger, slightly obese figure representing the "fat cats" of capitalism. The capitalist is shown placing money in Hitler's raised hand. The caption reads: "The meaning of the Hitler salute. The little man asks for large gifts; his motto: 'I've got millions backing me.'" The work is a classic case of a "picture being worth a thousand words."[98]

Heartfield created several works incorporating Ernst Thälmann's countenance, but one photomontage clearly stands out, appearing on the back cover of the 22 April 1936 edition of *AIZ*. Quite possibly the most effective visual image to emerge from the Free Thälmann crusade, it shows the Communist prisoner shackled to his bed, which is on the right side of his prison cell. Sitting next to him is a weeping angel, head in hands. A ball and chain is affixed to her right ankle. Although there is a window in the room, it is heavily shaded, apparently to stop the curious from peeking in and to hide the prisoner from the world. The two figures sit in semidarkness, and a metal pitcher and chamber pot in the corner add a note of realism. The contrast between Thälmann's countenance and that of the angel is striking. He sits quietly, a determined look on his face, perhaps gazing off into the socialist future. Both of his hands are balled into fists, reminiscent of the Communist salute. The message is clear: Thälmann is unbowed. He is determined. He is concerned more with the fortunes of others, of the proletariat, than with his personal fate. The angel, in contrast, weeps uncontrollably. She embodies peace, which suffers because of Thälmann's imprisonment. The angel is more concerned with the KPD leader's plight than he is himself, and the heavenly host cries out for his freedom. The caption at the bottom of the page makes all this abundantly clear: "When Hitler speaks of peace, think about this: peace sits with Ernst Thälmann in jail. Freedom for Thälmann—Peace for the World!"[99]

The 1514 Albrecht Dürer print *Melancolia I* clearly influenced Heartfield when he made this photomontage. Dürer's work shows two angels sitting together on the right side of the print, both obviously depressed. Although the photomontage is far less elaborate, Heartfield leaving out many of the details found in the older work—after all, Thälmann was in prison—both works relate the same message: there is a great deal of suffering in the world, and at least some people are concerned about it. Incorporating some of Dürer's motifs allowed Heartfield to assimilate religious imagery into his montage. Like the 1514 print, Heartfield's work integrates religious symbols, but these images are used to relate a secular message.[100] Especially after Thälmann's death in August 1944, religious motifs became a central component of the Thälmann myth, and this 22 April 1936 photomontage provides an early example of this tendency. The past and present, as difficult as they might seem to be, are necessary steps to the glorious socialist future. In spite of its outward dreariness, the montage's message is one of hope. Further, the incorporation of Renaissance motifs into his creation permitted Heartfield to pursue one of the primary tropes of socialist-realist art and subsequently of the Thälmann legend: the linking of the past, present, and future along an ideological continuum. The incorporation of some of Dürer's ideas allowed Heartfield to utilize concepts from German history; socialist-realist artists and writers liked to see themselves as building on the glorious traditions of their "progressive" predecessors. But these historically based themes were not an end in themselves, but rather tools used to depict the present—in this case Thälmann's imprisonment. Further, the viewer's response to the present situation— whether he or she fought for Thälmann's release or not—would affect the future, although the prisoner's obvious resolve makes the future victory of socialism inevitable. Once again, the Free Thälmann movement was, Heartfield's artwork implies, about something much larger than the fate of a single man. The future of humanity itself was at stake.

Closely related themes can also be seen in a poem written by "a Social Democratic worker" and published in the 13 June 1935 edition of *AIZ*, accompanied by a drawing of a tiny imprisoned Thälmann threatened by a huge Nazi executioner's axe. The illustration, drawn by Jacob Burk, originally appeared in the *New Masses*, a periodical out of New York. The poem, authored by Paul Schuhmann, maintains that the struggle to liberate the imprisoned KPD leader is a fight to free all workers held prisoner in the Third Reich, which becomes clear in its concluding stanza and refrain.

> Unity will bring down the walls,
> Destroy the crossbeam, and every jail will fall!
> Go fast,
> Victory is our reward
> And close ranks
>
> In action:
> Thälmann![101]

The KPD leader was the "crossbeam"; if he could be liberated, the entire fascist structure would come tumbling down. Thälmann's fate was inextricably linked with the destiny of the entire working class.

Schuhmann's poem was not the only or even the first verse written about the imprisoned Communist leader. Johannes R. Becher, future GDR culture minister, wrote a poem to mark Thälmann's first May Day in Moabit prison. Entitled "Comrade Thälmann—Our Leader," the poem is reminiscent of the doggerel produced by the Soviet Union's Stalin cult. Not surprisingly, it has many of the characteristics of an intercessory prayer.

> Comrade Thälmann, you [du] are our leader.
> That means that you always stand before us
> And we never let you leave our eyes
> And, where we go, you go with us.
> . . . .
> You vote with [us] at every decision.
> You sit with us when we study Lenin.
> You have taught us that one must learn,
> In order to smell out the class enemy everywhere.
>
> With teeth pressed together,
> We march today on 1 May,
> Secure in your hand,
> The Party, the Party, the German Party![102]

Becher's exposure to the Stalin and Lenin cults in the Soviet Union clearly affected him deeply.[103] As in the images of the Soviet leaders produced during the 1930s, Becher ascribes the qualities of a deity to Thälmann: he is omniscient, omnipresent, and eternal. In this case, it is Thälmann rather than Lenin or Stalin who "is always with us." Once again, the KPD adopted the motifs of Soviet propaganda, in this case the religious imagery of the Lenin and Stalin cults, and there is nothing original in the message of Becher's poem. He merely adapted the themes of numerous odes to Lenin and Stalin to his immediate needs. Although this adaptation of old Soviet Bolshevik themes helped Becher to relate his message, it also added credence to the claims made by many of communism's opponents, including the Nazis, that the KPD represented a foreign ideology. Yet Becher's poem is also strikingly reminiscent of National Socialist political prose and verse, in which the leader (führer) was credited with supernatural powers.[104] Both fascism and communism sought to create secular religions in which the leader was ascribed superhuman abilities, thereby legitimizing the movement and the nascent society that the party created. Both sought to replace traditional religion with a secular one, and religious motifs became increasingly important in their propaganda. The religious tropes found in Communist and Nazi propaganda were eschatological, providing ultimate meaning and assuring the inevitability of the movement's victory, and the nascent Thälmann myth was no exception.

Becher develops the chiliastic component of the Thälmann legend even more thoroughly in another poem, "Dream of a Soviet Germany," in which he writes of the ineluctable Communist victory over fascism:

> Comrade Thälmann poised,
> Uplifted by our cries,
> We carried him on our shoulders
> Into the Reich Chancellery.[105]

Thälmann, the true leader of the German people, would one day secure his rightful place at the helm of a Soviet Germany. The dock worker was the antithesis of Hitler.

Much Thälmann verse arose in the form of song lyrics. In 1934, the German poet Erich Weinert wrote the words for "Raise Your Fist for Comrade Thälmann," also known as the "Thälmann Song." With music composed by Paul Arma, the song takes as its point of departure the Communist salute, in which one raises the right hand in the form of a fist. As in much of the early Free Thälmann propaganda, this song closely links the fate of the German Communist with that of Comintern leader Dimitrov.

> We have liberated Dimitrov
> Because we set the world aflame
> Therefore the damned yell in
> The Executioner's ear:
> The world had awoken, the mutiny rages!
> For Comrade Thälmann
> Raise your fist![106]

Like many other forms of Free Thälmann propaganda, Weinert's song emphasizes the importance of cooperation among antifascists. Only if "the damned" put enough pressure on Thälmann's captors could there be any hope of securing his release. Millions had stood behind Dimitrov and won his freedom, and if the masses worked with equal fervor, they would also succeed in their efforts to free Thälmann.

German Communist writers preferred to immortalize the KPD leader in verse, but the Thälmann myth did occasionally make an appearance in prose fiction. Communist writers exiled in the Soviet Union sought to portray the Germany that their ideology told them existed. In their eyes, the Third Reich was on the verge of collapse because of worker unrest, and it was unthinkable that the fascist regime had the support of the vast majority of the German people, including the workers. Communist writers depicted a country rife with opposition to the regime, and Free Thälmann propaganda, they insisted, was an important component of the antifascist resistance throughout Germany. In a story by Albert Hotopp, one of the Communist characters carves the slogan "Free Thälmann" into the soles of his shoes and covers the soles with paint so as to leave his message wherever he walks.[107] Thälmann also plays an important, if passing, role in Berta Lask's novel *Januar 1933 in Berlin*. In the course of the story, Thälmann gives a speech in which he foresees a bright future for the German workers. "We are witnessing a shift in the balance of class power in favor of proletarian revolution."[108] Action on the part of the workers was imminent, the German writers believed, and Free Thälmann propaganda helped to prepare the path to revolution. Fiction, however, was not as important as verse and journalism to the creation of the Thälmann myth, probably because the latter types of propaganda were much shorter and relied on catch phrases and other easily understood images that did not lend themselves as readily to fiction.

Another medium that related images in an easily understood manner was film. Although film had its advantages in that practically everyone understood it, it was far more expensive to create than other media. In spite of the costs involved, at least one film was made during the course of the campaign, *Free Thaelmann!*—a silent movie released by the British Thälmann Committee in 1935.[109] The film, which lasts around twenty minutes, begins with an elemental question, "Who is Thaelmann?" and goes on to provide a brief account of the life of "this man whose fate has become a symbol all over the world—a symbol of the struggle for human liberty and justice." The KPD leader is then shown giving a speech to the masses. He is a man of the people, it indicates: "Ernst Thaelmann is a worker and leader of workers. He was born in the slums of Hamburg, and as a boy became a seaman and longshoreman. From childhood he struggled to build the trade unions.

He fought on the barricades that ended the war and drove out the Hohenzollerns. Thaelmann became leader of the German Communist Party. He is a common man, a worker, he is 'one of you.'"

Several scenes follow showing the Communist leader speaking before mass audiences. He appears before "Berlin workers mass[ed] at [a] funeral of victims slain by the police on May Day" and speaking to the crowds at the 1930 Sports Union Festival. Another scene shows workers giving the raised fist salute as the KPD leader addresses a mass audience on May Day of 1931. The "workers pledge [to] struggle against Fascism." Other shots record the 1932 presidential elections and Hindenburg's decision to appoint Hitler chancellor. "With the aid of Thyssen, Krupp, Hugenburg and all the forces of finance capital the Nazis come to power," the intertitle explains. The narrative then goes on to recount the Nazi persecution of workers, the Reichstag fire, and the trial of Dimitrov and his alleged co-conspirators for having started the conflagration. The film quotes the Bulgarian Communist, who insists, *"The Nazis burned the Reichstag!"* "A time will come," Dimitrov maintains, "when these accounts will have to be settled, *with interest!*" He continues, "The wheel of history moves slowly on toward the ultimate, inevitable, irrepressible goal of Communism." The film also presents the arrival of Dimitrov and his comrades in Moscow, a joyous look on all of their faces.

Yet all is not well with the world. The Nazi oppression continues, and the film transitions to footage recounting "the burning of books" in Berlin. The fascists are barbarians fit only for destruction, but "in spite of terror, in spite of violence, in spite of rigorous censorship—TRUTH WILL OUT!" A letter from a man whose son was murdered by the Nazis is shown, as are victims of Nazi torture, "[b]ut fascist tortures do not break the spirit of real fighters," Thälmann among them, who was arrested one month after the Nazi seizure of power. The movie then goes on to show examples of anti-Nazi propaganda, an intertitle contending that more than "a hundred daily and weekly antifascist publications are grasped by millions of anxious hands," all of whom stand behind the proletarian leader languishing in Moabit Prison. Numerous examples—newspapers, flyers, the *AIZ*—of Free Thälmann propaganda are also shown. England's Lord Marley and other prominent figures who stand behind the effort to liberate the Communist are shown. A photograph of Lincoln Stephens in New York City, giving the antifascist salute, appears on the screen. "Two years in jail—WITHOUT TRIAL . . . TWO YEARS," the film concludes.

This brief film exhibits why the medium can be such an effective tool for relating political propaganda. In a few minutes, it relates most of the major themes adopted by the Free Thälmann movement: Thälmann is a common man, a decent man, a staunch opponent of Hitler and German fascism, a person willing to sacrifice his own well-being for the benefit of others. Not only do the masses stand behind him, the film maintains, but so do prominent figures in the antifascist movement. He is in danger, but, like Dimitrov, he can be saved from the fascist menace, but only if the masses continue to stand behind him. If the workers support his cause, Thälmann's freedom and the defeat of German fascism are inevitable. As always, the effort to secure Thälmann's liberation is infinitely more important than the fate of a single man, and the future of the entire world is at stake. The film is very effective at relating its message, a masterpiece of propaganda that anyone at the time could comprehend. One did not have to have a detailed knowledge of the situation in Germany to understand its message. The British Thälmann Committee thus made a vital contribution to the Free Thälmann effort, one that would have resonance wherever the film was screened. As the film *Free Thaelmann!* shows, the effort to secure the release of the imprisoned Communist was an international one, extending well beyond the borders of Germany and the USSR.

Nowhere, however, was the international composition of the Free Thälmann campaign more clearly evident than in Spain. In September 1935, for example, a "committee" of "intellectuals and adherents of different parties" organized a protest against Germany's treatment of Thälmann, declaring the fourteenth of the month Ernst Thälmann Day. The group organized a mass meeting "in one of the biggest halls in Madrid." Although the hall held around 5,000 people, 15,000 tickets were sold. Speakers at the rally included representatives of several antifascist parties, including the Radicals, the Republicans, and the Socialists, so non-Communists played an important role in the rally. "The liberation of Thälmann and all imprisoned antifascists in Germany was demanded in a unanimous resolution." On 14 September, Free Thälmann forces also held a meeting in Valencia, in addition to organizing demonstrations in five other cities. Finally, organizers claimed to have collected five million signatures on a petition demanding Thälmann's immediate release![110] As was the case in other Free Thälmann efforts, organizers placed special emphasis not only on the magnitude of support for Thälmann, but also on the movement's nonpartisan and international character.

Spain was at this time a center of political intrigue, and the republican government's hold on power there was tenuous. It is not surprising that the Free Thälmann movement flourished in the months preceding the Spanish Civil War. Supporters of the republic, Communist and non-Communist alike, saw the effort to free Thälmann as part of a larger campaign to defend the Western European tradition of civil and legal rights, prerogatives increasingly in danger in Spain. Hence, it was only natural that the emerging Thälmann myth had its place in the Spanish Civil War, especially among the non-Spaniards, organized into the International Brigade, who came to defend the republic.[111] One hundred men, the "Thälmann centuria," under the political tutelage of erstwhile Communist Reichstag deputy Hans Beimler—who had the distinction of strangling his SS guard before his escape from a German prison—were among the first foreigners to see combat in the conflict. Franz Raab served as the centuria's field commander. In spite of a well-earned reputation for disorganization, the unit grew to battalion strength—about four hundred men.[112] Many of the Germans in the International Brigade, especially the Communists, enlisted in the Ernst Thälmann Battalion, although not all of its members came from the same country as the imprisoned KPD chief. The battalion, consisting of three companies, included Englishmen, Poles, and Hungarians as well as troops from Yugoslavia. Although Thälmann was the battalion's honorary commander, the German writer Arnold Vieth von Golssenau, fighting under the pseudonym "Ludwig Renn," led its troops in the field. Von Golssenau, after serving as an officer in the German army during the Great War, had joined the KPD in the 1920s. After being temporarily imprisoned by the Nazis, he was in Switzerland when the Spanish Civil War broke out. In November 1936, when von Golssenau left the battalion for another post, Richard Staimer replaced him. The group, showing the influence of the Soviet military model on the republican army, also had a political commissar, Beimler, assigned to assure the ideological orthodoxy of its soldiers.[113] Following Beimler's death, he was succeeded by Fritz Vehlov, who fought under the name "Louis Schuster." The unit suffered heavy casualties in a January 1937 battle along the Madrid–Corunna road, its numbers reduced once again to about one hundred.[114] These soldiers had no doubt concerning the reason they were giving their lives. Like the KPD leader whose name the battalion bore, its members supposedly sought to smite the fascist menace in the name of progress and peace among all peoples. They were, as the KPD Central Committee reminded them, to "[g]o forward in the spirit of Ernst Thälmann!"[115]

The soldiers were encouraged to be proud of the battalion's name, which could be seen in some of its political activities. In his account of the International Brigade, Willi Bredel describes the mood of the Thälmann Battalion's soldiers as they celebrated the imprisoned Communist leader's fifty-first birthday.

> The Battalion of the 11th Brigade that bore Thälmann's name invited all its comrades and all inhabitants of the village [outside of Madrid] to a celebration of the 51st birthday of its battalion chief. Young and old, big and small accepted the invitation. Large delegations came from brother battalions in the brigade: from the "Edger André" Battalion and from the French "Paris Commune" Battalion.
>
> The children of the village took part in the birthday feast held in the Battalion's clubhouse, drinking coffee with milk and eating biscuits. The Thälmann Battalion lined up as if preparing to march; spoken choruses, songs, [and] speeches followed one another. A delegation of Communists from Madrid presented the battalion with a new flag, which the battalion's political commissar . . . accepted, with the promise to continue to be worthy of the name of Thälmann.
>
> Whereupon the battalion paraded before the division commander and the brigade staff. Their faces were hard and resolute, their pace was determined. Their guns lay proudly upon their shoulders: Ernst Thälmann's proud, unbeatable, optimistic cadres marched.[116]

The soldiers, Bredel maintained, were the embodiment of Thälmann's spirit, of his determination to fight the fascist hordes and secure a peaceful, prosperous future for the Spanish people. Like Thälmann, the men in the battalion were kind to children, "resolute," and "optimistic," and the masses, ever mindful of the dangers of fascism, supported their cause. As a result, the situation in the present may be tough, but the future will be brighter because of the battalion's efforts. These assertions were similar to those made by others struggling on behalf of the Free Thälmann crusade. A common motif reappeared: the world stood behind the imprisoned Communist leader.[117]

In addition to Weinert's "Thälmann Song," undoubtedly performed at celebrations such as the one Bredel describes, the battalion also had its own tune, "The Thälmann Column." It concludes with the following lyrics:

> Bang the drum! Lay low the bayonets!
> March forward! Victory is our reward!
> With the red flag! Break the chain!
> The Thälmann Battalion goes on to battle!
> Home is far,
> But we are ready,
> We fight and win for you: freedom![118]

Once again Thälmann was linked to such tropes as inevitable victory, international solidarity—the singers point out that they are far from home—and the struggle for freedom, all sentiments that the Free Thälmann movement associated with the imprisoned Communist and that the Thälmann Battalion claimed to adopt as its own. Many of these same themes can be seen in all the Free Thälmann propaganda of the 1930s, be it in the form of prose, poetry, music, or art. Thälmann meant freedom and peace, in contrast to Hitler, who embodied slavery and imperialistic war. Thälmann and the KPD were the antithesis of Hitler and the NSDAP. Their relationship was dialectical—good versus evil.

Yet questions remain: How effective was the Free Thälmann propaganda? Did it achieve any of its goals? As is almost always the case with organized efforts to sway the political opinions of the masses, their effectiveness is extremely difficult to determine. The most obvious conclusion to reach is that the effort failed—after all, Thälmann died a prisoner. But it is important to remember that freeing Thälmann was not the Communist machine's primary goal, and as a prisoner he was a valuable propaganda weapon. With this in mind, perhaps the best way to approach this question is to look at it from the point of view of those behind the propaganda effort. The International Thälmann Committee did make an attempt to assess its results, as can be seen in a June 1937 report.[119]

Written by the organization's secretary, "Belfort," the report begins with an appraisal of "positive tendencies" in the campaign. First of all, the committee's secretary points out, the campaign had been remarkably successful in extending the effort globally. Free Thälmann movements existed not only in many European countries, but also in the United States, Argentina, South Africa, Canada, and New Zealand. The movement clearly had achieved its goal of using the campaign to promote international solidarity in the face of the fascist menace. The local committees, "Belfort" continues, had the added advantage of organizing Communists and fellow travelers behind a movement controlled by Moscow. In short, the campaign had indeed succeeded in extending the influence of the international Communist movement, its primary, although unspoken, goal. In addition, the Free Thälmann crusade had made millions aware of the atrocities committed by the Hitler fascists, most important among them crimes against workers. Further, the propaganda effort had succeeded in making Thälmann representative of the "thousands" of proletarians held prisoner in the Third Reich. Finally, the campaign had helped secure a united front with Social Democrats and other antifascist forces under conditions beneficial to international communism.[120]

"Belfort" then lays out what he and others believe were the greatest weaknesses of the campaign: it was not tightly organized enough, and on the local level the movement had too much independence. Communist control must be extended even further if the campaign were ultimately to promote a global proletarian revolution. As "Belfort" points out, although the socialist youth and trade union movements had indeed participated actively in the Free Thälmann effort, they still had too much autonomy, remaining indifferent to the antifascist position coming out of Moscow. The campaign, "Belfort" insists, had failed to appeal to specific groups within the masses: "trade union members, farmers, small business owners, war veterans, and youth." How specific appeals were to be made while maintaining the movement's universal appeal is not explained. Further, the campaign had not raised awareness sufficiently "against the secret trials, against the chains of death sentences and executions, and against the persecution of Jews." Regarding the last of these issues, the campaign—viewing the Third Reich's assault on the proletariat as paramount—had said practically nothing. In short, although the committee may have been moving in the right direction, much more propaganda work needed to be done.[121]

The report concludes with a series of "suggestions" demanding tighter Comintern control of the movement. Local groups should lose what remained of their autonomy. Although the sentiment remains unstated, the implication is clear: if this tighter control could be accomplished, the life of a single Communist leader was of little significance. Thälmann's ultimate importance was as a symbol that could be used for the benefit of the international Communist movement, and the report says absolutely nothing regarding the prospects of Thälmann's release. The committee based its idea of success on other criteria.[122]

Throughout the 1930s, while Ernst Thälmann sat in a Nazi prison, the international Communist movement led a highly visible campaign ostensibly to secure his release. In contrast to the campaign's avowed goal, however, the Comintern sought not to liberate the KPD leader, but to use him as an important antifascist symbol in the cause of international communism. Opposition to Europe's fascist regimes was often the only sentiment that united the Communists and Social Democrats within the anti-Nazi movement. The Comintern, the Soviet Communist Party, and the KPD sought, therefore, to use antifascism to create a common cause with socialists, radicals, fellow travelers, and even liberals. To promote the cause of Ernst Thälmann was to steer antifascism in a direction favorable to Moscow and its allies, to legitimize the Marxist–Leninist worldview. The Communist Ernst Thälmann, who had committed no crime other than opposing Hitler, served as a key symbol in the effort to accomplish this goal.

With the signing of the German–Soviet Nonaggression Pact in August 1939, an event that shocked the rest of the world, Moscow and its allies promptly abandoned the Free Thälmann movement, providing further evidence that the KPD chief's fate was secondary to his utility as a propaganda weapon. After the German–Soviet rapprochement, the antifascist campaign abruptly ended, as did Thälmann's usefulness as a symbol. Even after the 1941 German attack on the Soviet Union, Thälmann's fate was of little importance to the leaders of international communism, and his plight largely forgotten. The Comintern's propaganda apparatus concentrated its efforts on saving Stalin's Russia from the German invasion, and the Soviet Union became the primary symbol of antifascism. The Thälmann legend of the 1930s was now a thing of the past.

The situation changed dramatically in 1944, however, in at least two ways. First, it became clear that the Third Reich would be defeated and that the Soviet Union would occupy a significant portion of German territory. Those exiled KPD leaders who had survived the purges started thinking about the future fate of Germany and their position in postwar politics. Further, under direct orders from Hitler, Ernst Thälmann was murdered, and he became a martyr to the antifascist cause. This confluence of events assured that Thälmann's image would play an important role in KPD propaganda once again. The Ernst Thälmann myth had entered a critical new phase.

3

"We Are Building upon the Foundations Created by Ernst Thälmann"

By midsummer of 1944, Ernst Thälmann had outlived his usefulness to the Nazi regime. At this point, it was clear to any objective observer that Germany was losing the war and that a negotiated peace with the Allies was impossible; the imprisoned KPD leader could no longer serve as a pawn in German–Soviet relations. Further, as the end of the war drew near, Adolf Hitler became increasingly nihilistic, ever more determined that defeat would mean the destruction not only of his "Thousand-Year Reich," but also of Germany itself. In keeping with this sentiment, the führer wanted to leave no possible successor to replace him. No one should be in a position to rebuild Germany in the wake of the most destructive war in European history, least of all a Communist leader who had long been one of his most vocal critics and a loyal ally of the hated Soviet Union.[1] In Hitler's mind, the imprisoned KPD chief simply had no role to play in Germany's future—indeed, Germany had shown itself unworthy of any future at all.

Thälmann's fate was among the topics discussed at a 14 August 1944 meeting held in Hitler's headquarters in east Prussia, the Wolfsschanze, between the German leader and Reichsführer Heinrich Himmler of the Schutzstaffel (SS). Among the items, the twelfth and final one recorded in the SS chief's brief minutes is Thälmann's name followed by the words "is to be executed." The KPD chief would be secretly transferred under cover of darkness from his prison cell in Bautzen to Buchenwald Concentration Camp, where he would be liquidated. On 17 August, the noncommissioned officer in charge of Buchenwald's crematorium, Oberscharführer Warnsted, received a telephone call instructing him to "heat up" one of the ovens—apparently they had been shut down in response to Allied air activity in the region—in preparation for an emergency cremation. Around midnight, eight SS men entered the crematorium, among them Stabscharführer Wolfgang Otto and Oberscharführer Werner Berger.[2] According to Polish prisoner Marian Zgoda, an eyewitness standing outside of the crematorium, a "large passenger car" pulled up shortly after midnight. Thälmann got out of the automobile, accompanied by two guards dressed in "civilian" clothes, one on either side. Immediately after the three men entered the courtyard of the crematorium, Zgoda heard three shots. Thälmann apparently said nothing before his death, nor did he cry out in surprise. All Zgoda reported hearing was a thud as the Communist leader's body fell to the ground. Shortly thereafter he heard a fourth gunshot, this one evidently from inside the crematorium building. Otto and Berger had shot Thälmann. His body was cremated immediately, camp authorities hoping that their crime would go unnoticed among the inmates. All that was left in the oven the next morning was a pile of ashes and a "pocket watch," "tempered" as the result of having been heated in the oven. Efforts to keep Thälmann's death a secret failed, however, and word of the events of the early hours of 18 August spread quickly throughout the camp.[3]

Apparently concerned about international and domestic reaction to the outright murder of one of its most celebrated political prisoners, the Hitler regime sought to keep secret the circumstances surrounding the Communist leader's death. The 16 September 1944 issue of the official Nazi Party newspaper, *Völkischer Beobachter,* announced not only Thälmann's demise, but also that of the prominent Social Democrat Rudolf Breitscheid, likewise the victim of Nazi thugs. This official account, however, refused to accept responsibility for the deaths, insisting that the two had died as the result of a 28 August Allied air raid.[4] From the outset, almost no one believed the official version of events, and word soon spread concerning the Communist leader's true fate. The result was an outpouring of propaganda produced by the Third Reich's enemies on the political left. The KPD leader's death provided German communism with its most significant antifascist martyr. The most immediate result of the events of 17–18 August 1944 was that the KPD chief—who had long served as the archetype of the determined antifascist fighter—came to represent all those Communists who had given their lives in the fight against Hitler and National Socialism. Thälmann's death at the hands of Nazi assassins made him the stuff of legend.

Never missing an opportunity to spout antifascist or pro-Soviet propaganda, prominent German Communists responded quickly to the news concerning the murder of their titular party chief. On 17 September, those party leaders who had fled to Moscow and survived the purges published a statement in the CPSU's official organ, *Pravda,* outlining their interpretation of Thälmann's death. Signed by fifteen prominent figures in the KPD—including such future GDR luminaries as Anton Ackermann, Johannes Becher, Erich Weinert, Walther Lindau, Wilhelm Pieck, and Walter Ulbricht—the brief article appeared under the title "In Memory of Ernst Thälmann." It begins by relating the true circumstances surrounding the former party chief's death. Evincing the truly remarkable amount of intelligence that the KPD was able to accumulate from its sources in the Third Reich, the article reported that, "[o]n Hitler's command, Ernst Thälmann was murdered in the Buchenwald Concentration Camp near Weimar." Pointing out that Thälmann died as the result of the Nazi führer's direct order reemphasized one of the most prominent themes of the Free Thälmann campaign of the 1930s: the German Communist leader was the antithesis of Hitler and the most important German opponent of National Socialism. Even the führer himself recognized this fact—hence, his decision to have Thälmann murdered. After all, as the article points out, "Thälmann's hatred of fascism was boundless." As the "leader of Germany's revolutionary workers," he represented millions of other progressives across the globe who had fought so long and so hard against fascism, and it was "precisely for this reason" that he was murdered. Such an interpretation of Thälmann's death did much to establish his credentials as a martyr.[5]

The rest of the article continues in the same vein, building on themes initially developed in some cases as long ago as Thälmann's first presidential bid in 1925. The deceased was a longstanding opponent of fascism, of "rapacious [*räuberischen*] German imperialism," who had "called the workers of Germany to unity, to carry out resistance against fascism"—in short, to fight Hitler. But the KPD chief was not a solitary man; he was the leader of a mass movement. "As tens of thousands of Communists and other antifascists were thrown into prison, Thälmann continued his now illegal struggle further." Even while in a fascist prison, he refused to relent, and although the Nazis considered putting him on trial "more than once," they ultimately balked at the idea, recognizing that "Thälmann would [seek to] unmask them from the dock and would exhort [the German people] to the struggle against fascism." Thousands of Germans would have heeded this call.[6]

But Thälmann's death would lead to the same result. "In all of Germany there awakens today hatred against the fascist beasts and those responsible for the war [*Kriegsbrandstifter*]. Thälmann embodies this hatred. He was the antifascist banner of struggle." Following a brief quotation from the fallen KPD chief concerning the inevitability of a Soviet victory, the *Pravda* piece goes on to emphasize the role of Thälmann as the leader of another Germany, the antifascist nation that stood at the side of the Soviet Union. "Millions of people knew Thälmann exactly so: he believed in the victory of the Soviet Union and the leadership of comrade Stalin, he believed that the brown pestilence would be eliminated." Thälmann, a political prophet, foresaw what was approaching; Hitler and his henchmen would pay for their crimes. And one could be assured that "the fascist gangsters will not be able to make the coarse assassination of the leader of the German Communist Party, Thälmann, just go away!" They will be made to pay. German antifascists will demand the just punishment of the "enemy of all of humanity as well as the German people—Hitler fascism."[7]

Although much of the *Pravda* article simply rehashes standard anti-Hitler motifs used in KPD propaganda since the late 1920s, upon closer examination the piece reveals something striking in its tone. Like German opponents of Hitler across the political spectrum, the KPD leadership recognized that it would face difficult questions—questions that remained largely theoretical during the course of the war—in the wake of Germany's defeat: How much did the German people support the policies of the Nazi regime? How much responsibility did the Germans bear for the crimes of the Third Reich? Could the German people ever be trusted again? The KPD leaders dealt with these vexing issues by appealing to Germany's antifascist—and in their eyes Communist—heritage. The fallen party chief represented thousands, perhaps millions, of Germans who had stood up against Hitler and his minions, who had put their lives on the line in the struggle against fascism. It was these antifascist fighters who represented the real Germany, the humanistic Germany, the "good Germany"—not the relatively few "fat cats" and businessmen who stood behind the Hitler regime's predatory policies. In short, the authors of "In Memory of Ernst Thälmann" sought to exaggerate the amount of opposition in the Third Reich, to normalize it, to make resistance against the National Socialist regime the most striking characteristic of Germany during the Hitler years. Here one sees another important step in the creation of the antifascism myth, a legend built on the very real sacrifices of a relative handful of

German Communists who had fought long and hard against Hitler fascism. All good Germans could walk in their footsteps, could participate in the building of a new Germany, could ultimately—in a type of vicarious atonement—avoid responsibility for the Third Reich's crimes. After all, the KPD's Stalinist ideology taught that final responsibility for Germany's crimes lay with the capitalists who had brought Hitler to power in a last-ditch effort to avoid a truly democratic revolution, a revolution that the German people would now have the opportunity to launch. This was the message that the KPD leadership was trying to relate in the *Pravda* article.

Individual leaders of the KPD also wrote obituaries stressing similar themes. Party chief Walter Ulbricht, for example, published a brief account of Thälmann's life and death in *Internationale Literatur,* a German-language periodical published in Moscow. Dated 19 September, the piece begins by informing readers that "[t]he fascist beasts have assassinated our Ernst Thälmann." As in the *Pravda* obituary, Ulbricht emphasizes the fact that the martyred KPD chief had been killed as the result of Hitler's direct order. He had been imprisoned and murdered because the hated führer recognized that "his name was the symbol of a fearless [*unerschrockenen*] struggle against fascistic German imperialism and militarism, for peace, freedom and human rights [*Volksrechte*]." Thälmann represented the millions of Germans, not to mention workers worldwide, who fought so valiantly against the fascist menace. With his death, "[t]he German working people loses its loudest champion and leader." The fact that Thälmann died in Buchenwald, a "site where many tens of thousands of Soviet prisoners of war, Jews and German antifacists were tortured [to death] or killed with gas and their bodies thrown into the death ovens [*Todesöfen*]," was appropriate. After all, he had been among the most important leaders in the struggle against fascism, and his death could serve as a reminder, a symbol, of all those others who died in relative obscurity.[8]

The remainder of Ulbricht's obituary is a highly propagandistic account of the fallen KPD leader's life, emphasizing once again motifs that go at least as far back as the Free Thälmann campaign. The Hamburg native had struggled his entire life against the forces of capitalist exploitation, joining first the SPD and then the KPD. Thälmann was a relentless organizer "who sought, above everything else, to promote the unity of the KPD, social democracy and the trade unions against fascism and the danger of war." He had "many times . . . personally" sought out "Social Democratic workers and functionaries and spoke with them about the path to common action." His efforts were sincere, for he foresaw that under the fascists Germany would become, as Thälmann himself had put it, "a land of gallows and funeral pyres." Perhaps anticipating the 1946 union of the KPD and SPD in the SBZ, Ulbricht insists that Thälmann believed—and events would bear him out—that only a united working class could defeat fascism. The implication is clear: the KPD was not responsible for the failure of the proletariat to unite in the face of the threat posed by Hitler fascism. After all, Thälmann had actively pursued unity, only to be rejected by the Social Democratic leadership. The SPD was responsible for the short-term defeat of Germany's workers. This failure to unite in these circumstances did not cause Ulbricht to despair of possible cooperation between the two parties in the future, however. His obituary of Thälmann, for example, mentions the SPD leader Rudolf Breitscheid, who also died in Buchenwald at about the same time as Thälmann. Although Breitscheid is not subject to the same accolades as the fallen KPD chief, he is at least given credit for a martyr's death. With these two men as examples, the German proletariat could abandon the shortsighted policies of division in favor of a more productive united course.[9] Ulbricht ignores the fact that this solidarity, like the unity that Ernst Thälmann had envisioned on the eve of the Nazi seizure of power, would come only on the Communists' terms. Like other KPD leaders, Ulbricht sincerely believed that such an outcome was possible in the wake of the devastation wrought by the Second World War. They hoped that the Social Democrats had learned their lesson after twelve years of fascist dictatorship. In contrast, the KPD, which had fought the Nazis so long and hard, seeking unity within the working-class movement and sacrificing the lives of tens of thousands of Communists, had nothing to learn. Led by the martyred Ernst Thälmann, the KPD was the only German political force correctly to anticipate the consequences of a Nazi seizure of power, and it was the only movement accurately to diagnose what was needed to avoid this catastrophe. Finally, it was the only faction correctly to anticipate the Soviet Union's decisive role in the military defeat of National Socialism and the resulting liberation of the German people from the fascist plague.

Although many of these themes had long been important components of the Thälmann legend, some originating as far back as the mid-1920s, the obituaries that appeared in *Pravda* and *Internationale Literatur* did add a new dimension to the myth—the importance of the KPD chief's death. Much of the contents of these two relatively brief accounts of Thälmann's life can be found elsewhere, but they provide the first significant examples of comments by the fallen KPD chief's comrades upon his demise. As such, they are the initial examples of what became a central theme of the postwar Ernst Thälmann myth— the importance of his sacrificial death. Although, as John Heartfield's April 1936 photomontage shows (see chapter 2), the early version of the Thälmann legend already contained strikingly religious motifs, as a result of the events of 17 and 18 August 1944 the KPD chief attained the status of martyr. As German Communist and Comintern propaganda had insisted since March 1933, not only had Thälmann suffered intensely because of his opposition to Hitler fascism, but he ultimately gave his life in the struggle against the greatest evil in human history. Indeed, one can see in these obituaries from 1944 the roots of the elevation of Thälmann into a secular Christ, an image that would become so important during the GDR's final years (see chapter 8). In other words, the centrality of Thälmann's death had come to eclipse the importance of his life's accomplishments. Over the course of the next forty-five years—with some noteworthy exceptions, such as the 1986 centennial of his birth (see chapter 8)—Thälmann's death would be celebrated more forcefully than his life. During most years, the anniversary of his death would be commemorated at locations such as Buchenwald Concentration Camp (see chapter 5) more extravagantly than his birthday. Of course, by the summer and fall of 1944, the KPD leaders were far from the only Germans seeking to make sense of the death of a close comrade or family member. By the end of the Second World War, millions of Germans found themselves trying to find an explanation for the death and destruction that surrounded them. At least in the SBZ, the German Communists were able to utilize the antifascism legend—with Thälmann representing thousands of fallen comrades—to find meaning in the terrible destruction wrought by the recent European war.

The motifs of the KPD leadership's effort to present Ernst Thälmann as a Communist martyr were in many ways nothing new. As early as 1919, with the deaths of Karl Liebknecht and Rosa Luxemburg at the hands of a right-wing militia, German Communists had gone to extensive lengths to mourn their dead. Indeed, the martyrology surrounding these two important figures in the history of German communism became the model for rituals commemorating fallen comrades during the Weimar Republic. These rites included such practices as mass processions, marches, speeches, the draping of the deceased's coffin in red cloth, the taking of oaths, and the laying of wreaths—all designed to emphasize the link between the fallen person's sacrifice and his or her surviving comrades. In the name of a martyred party member—often killed in street battles with Nazi Brown Shirts—these ceremonies called on those present to continue the revolutionary struggle in which the deceased comrade had given his or her life in order to ensure that he or she had not died in vain. These ceremonies celebrating the sacrifices of the fallen had the added advantage of promoting unity at a time when there was often a great deal of dissension within party ranks.[10] Indeed, after becoming KPD chief in 1925, Thälmann had played an integral role in propagating German communism's version of the myth of heroic death. He had often spoken, for example, at the graves of fallen comrades, including the monument for Communist martyrs in Berlin's Friedrichsfelde Cemetery—the location of the tombs of Liebknecht and Luxemburg, not to mention those of other deceased heroes in the KPD pantheon.[11] In short, the party already had a long tradition of commemorating its fallen upon which it could draw in its efforts to build a quasi-religious cult around the man who would become postwar German communism's most important martyr, Ernst Thälmann.

On 30 April 1945—a little more than a week before the end of hostilities—representatives of the German Communist Party returned to Berlin after twelve years in exile. With Walter Ulbricht as their leader, they came back to a country that was militarily, politically, economically, psychologically, and morally devastated by the most destructive war in European history, a conflict launched by Germany against its neighbors, during which the Germans and their allies had committed crimes unparalleled in the continent's long history. Germany suffered tremendously as a result of the conflagration that it had unleashed almost six years earlier, and no other German city had endured more hardship than the country's capital. During the last three weeks of the war, almost 305,000 German soldiers lost their lives, became prisoners of war, or went missing, the lion's share in the titanic Battle of Berlin.[12] This figure does not take into account the number of civilian dead. A census conducted in August 1945 determined that Berlin's population stood at slightly more than 2.8 million, down from a little more than 4.3 million in the spring of 1939.[13] To add insult to injury, Soviet troops raped thousands of Berlin's women, a practice that continued even after German capitulation on 9 May.[14] Finally, for all intents and purposes, the former German capital was leveled. Housing was in short supply, with hundreds of thousands left homeless. Once among the most heavily industrialized cities in Europe, Berlin was now a city whose factories lay in ruins and whose once impressive transportation system stood completely immobilized. To make matters worse, the Soviets carted off—as a form of reparations—a significant portion of the city's few remaining resources.[15] Even the most hopeful observer could only conclude that it would take years for the defeated country and its capital city to recover from the destruction.

Yet Ulbricht and his comrades were optimistic.[16] They believed that after the most destructive war in history, the German people would welcome them with open arms. After all, the KPD was the political group that had fought the National Socialists most consistently during the final years of the Weimar Republic, warning that a fascist government would inevitably lead to an imperialistic war against the Soviet Union, which could only end in Germany's ruin. The Communist leadership could legitimately claim to have been at the vanguard of the antifascist opposition. Thousands of comrades, among them Ernst Thälmann, had given their lives in the struggle against the Third Reich. Party leaders believed that this sacrifice served to legitimize their political goals, and they hoped to launch a "progressive bourgeois" revolution that would ultimately lead to a peaceful democratic transition to socialism in *all* of Germany, not just in the SBZ.[17]

German communism's antifascist heritage would become the most important component of Communists' claims to legitimacy, and the KPD and its successor, the SED, justified many of their policies by appealing to this legacy. As a result, the KPD/SED's tradition of opposition to National Socialism played a central role in justifying not only the party's domestic policies, but also the role that East Germany would play in the cold war with the West. The antifascism myth—including one of its most important components, the Thälmann legend—would become the foundation of the legitimizing narrative, first of the KPD and then of the SED. Although the party leadership would seek to tailor the legend to whatever circumstances that it confronted, its options on this score were ultimately limited. The party would continue for more than four decades to base its legitimacy largely on a particular version of historical events. This approach had its advantages, but it also had its drawbacks. The KPD/SED leadership could legitimately claim to have been at the vanguard of opposition to Adolf Hitler, but as the events incorporated into the legend became ever more distant over time, the narrative would lose its effectiveness because ever fewer East Germans had firsthand experience of the events of the 1930s and 1940s. Although the party would make a concerted effort to pass on the legacy of antifascism to future generations (see chapter 6), the myth could never be as effective among young people who had not experienced the Hitler regime's repression or the devastation wrought by the Second World War. The rebirth of fascism would eventually become less of a concern both for the Germans themselves and for their neighbors. Over time, more and more East Germans might very well judge the party and the state's legitimacy based on the concrete accomplishments of "real, existing socialism," a criterion by which they would come to find life under the GDR's socialist system less than ideal. Another potential shortcoming of the antifascism myth was the emphasis that it placed on the role of the Soviet Union, first in the SBZ and then in the GDR. Although the KPD/SED might very well depict the Soviet occupation as an unequivocally good thing—indeed, a "liberation"—events would often belie this interpretation. In the spring and summer of 1945, the Red Army had raped thousands of German women, a reality that many in the SBZ and GDR undoubtedly found difficult to forgive and forget. Add to this the thousands of opponents—real and imagined—that the KPD and its Soviet masters shipped off to the very same concentration camps that the Nazis had built, and the events of June 1953, when the Soviets crushed a popular uprising in East Berlin, and it became increasingly difficult to depict the Soviet presence as entirely benevolent.[18] In short, although the KPD/SED found the antifascism myth useful in the short term, in the longer run that myth would naturally become less effective. Yet the KPD/SED had no choice but to cling to it for more than four decades. To abandon it would bring into question the legitimacy not only of the ruling party and the Soviet presence, but even of the socialist experiment in Germany. As a result, KPD/SED propaganda continued to cultivate the antifascism narrative—much of it centering around the figure of Ernst Thälmann—even after a series of setbacks during the 1940s and 1950s.[19]

Among the earliest postwar attempts to cultivate the Thälmann myth on a large scale—and set in motion what would become the SBZ and GDR's state religion—occurred on 2 September 1945. On this day, the Berlin Communist Party held a memorial service (*Feierstunde*) for Ernst Thälmann. It was among the first of many events in the postwar KPD's antifascism cult that would be scheduled for Sunday mornings. The party leadership undoubtedly planned the ceremony for this time at least in part as a substitute for church attendance. The more secular service could have just as easily been held during the afternoon, when more East Berliners would have been able to attend. A stage was set up in the "area of the Karl Liebknecht House," formerly the location of the KPD's headquarters prior to Hitler's seizure of power and the building's destruction during the war: "A large picture of Ernst Thälmann, our 'Teddy,' greeted [the audience] from the decorated stage. And here at this place, which witnessed powerful assemblies and struggles, here arose, seemingly brought to life, his picture, which holds a special place in the hearts of Berliners, since we, on 28 January 1933 marched by Ernst Thälmann, for the last time, in a parade of hundreds of thousands."[20]

The Berlin party boss, Ottomar Geschke, opened the ceremonies with a brief statement reminding the audience why it had assembled. "Greater Berlin honors its Ernst Thälmann. [It does] so simply and unpretentiously, as he lived [and also] naturally as he struggled, [and] in such a manner seek we also to fulfill his legacy." The emphasis that Geschke placed on the martyred KPD chief's modest lifestyle can be traced all the way back to the mid-1920s, when Thälmann first emerged as a prominent figure in the party. This is only one among numerous instances in which postwar party leaders revived motifs that originated during the Weimar years, clear evidence of the continuity between the prewar and postwar versions of the legend. Thälmann's sacrificial death—beginning with the obituaries published in September 1944—had become a central motif of the legend; indeed, it was rapidly becoming the most important component of the myth. As Geschke pointed out, "[H]e crowned his life through his death."[21]

Among the themes that the featured speaker, Wilhelm Pieck, incorporated into his presentation was the importance of Thälmann's "friendship with the Soviet Union." The murdered KPD chief had correctly understood the importance of the Bolshevik model to any understanding of the situation that prewar Germany faced and, as a result, had sought to emulate the Soviet leadership's policies. The current situation called for a similar loyalty to the traditions of Marxism–Leninism. "We can only hope," Pieck said, "that we, through our work and our behavior, regain the friendship of the Soviet Union."[22] In this statement, Pieck revived one of the major themes from the Weimar years. During the early years of the Third Reich, Communist propagandists had emphasized the political diversity of the Free Thälmann campaign, with its wide array of "progressives," from Communists to left-leaning Democrats, all calling for the imprisoned KPD chief's release. In the postwar era, however, Pieck and other leading German Communists sought to revive the image of Ernst Thälmann that emphasized his admiration for the Soviet Union. The vaguely "progressive" representation of his image had given way to one that emphasized the specifically Communist component of his worldview. This shift should come as no surprise in light of the situation in which Pieck found himself—living under Soviet occupation for the foreseeable future. Add to this the fact that the KPD leadership envisioned a future in which Germany would adopt the Bolshevik political model, and the abandonment of an important component of the 1933–1939 version of the legend should come as no surprise. Indeed, one can see the genesis of this change in strategy in some of the propaganda produced by the KPD and Comintern after the German invasion of the Soviet Union, although, as we have seen, the Thälmann myth played almost no role in KPD propaganda during the years 1941–1944, when special emphasis was placed on the importance of rescuing the Soviet Union from Nazi imperialism.

Like propagandists from the years 1933 to 1939, Pieck also emphasized the suffering that Thälmann endured at the hands of the Nazis, although he, like Geschke, had the opportunity to incorporate Thälmann's sacrificial death into his effort. Thälmann had remained true to his beliefs, even in the face of deprivation and torture at the hands of his captors. He "never lost his belief in the strength of the German working class." This steadfastness should serve as an example for the German people, defeated in a great war and facing difficult years ahead: "This belief [in the German proletariat] of Ernst Thälmann will help us once again to lead the German people on a path, in which [it] will once again win the attention and the respect of other peoples. Whatever consequences and problems stand before us . . . Ernst Thälmann, through his death, shows us the way out [of them]." Hence, Pieck continued, if the German people wanted to "construct a new antifascist democratic Germany," Thälmann's "ideas" must remain on their minds "every free minute." Pieck conceded that a great deal of hard work lay before the German people, but the KPD chief, murdered by Nazi thugs in Buchenwald Concentration Camp, could serve as a role model. "In this work Ernst Thälmann will . . . live on in us as the great leader and son of our German people." In short, Pieck maintained that there was only one path to the rebuilding of Germany and the rehabilitation of its people: to pursue the ideas, the legacy, of Ernst Thälmann. All other paths led to failure.[23] These same themes could be seen in speeches and rallies throughout Soviet-occupied Germany, from demonstrations in Berlin's Neukölln District to ceremonies in Buchenwald Concentration Camp, where Thälmann had bravely met a martyr's death (see chapter 5).[24]

Another propaganda theme that was becoming increasingly popu-

lar at this time was "unity"—in this instance, the unity of the two proletarian political parties, the KPD and the SPD. Wilhelm Pieck alluded
to this issue in his 2 September speech, thereby linking the Thälmann
myth to the effort to create a united proletarian political movement: "It
is therefore important, in his [Thälmann's] memory, every free minute
to seek the creation of the democratic, united front of the workers, in
order to root out all of the powers that led the German people to catastrophe, and [to work] for the construction of a new antifascist, democratic Germany. In this effort, Ernst Thälmann will live on forever in
us as the great leader and son of our German people."[25] The insistence
that the proletariat's failure to unite had contributed to the rise of the
fascism had become an important trope in KPD propaganda, and as
early as 1935 prominent German Communists had begun to discuss
the creation of a unified proletarian political party after the defeat of
Hitler's Germany.[26] In the eyes of the Communist leadership, one of the
most important lessons to be learned from the events of 1930 to 1933
was that divisions among progressives were an important precondition
for the success of the forces of reaction. Hence, it should come as no
surprise that the union of the KPD and SPD would be a top priority for
the postwar Communist leadership. Further, in the wake of the cataclysm of 1933, many members of the SPD—especially on the party's left
wing—supported closer cooperation between, if not outright union of,
the two parties. The Soviets also apparently favored unification, believing that it would make controlling their occupation zone easier. As a
result, with the backing of Soviet forces, the KPD, with the cooperation
of certain elements within the SPD camp, launched a campaign promoting the unity of the two proletarian parties.[27]

This is not the forum to revisit the historiographic controversy concerning the creation of the SED. Although questions concerning how
much force the KPD and its Soviet masters used to cajole the SPD into
agreeing to union are important, they are not the central concern here.
A scholarly consensus seems to be emerging that the creation of the
SED was the product both of coercion on the part of the Soviets allied with the German Communist leadership and of a genuine concern
among rank-and-file Social Democrats about the possibility of a revival
of National Socialism.[28]

What is important here is the role that the Thälmann myth played
in the creation of the Socialist Unity Party. From the point of view of the
KPD leadership, Thälmann's image was in many ways ideally suited
for the unity campaign. After all, he had fought valiantly for proletarian

cooperation, recognizing its importance in the struggle against fascism. Hence, his legend could play a vital role in the effort to join the KPD and the SPD. The martyred Communist leader had warned that the failure of the proletariat to unite politically could only contribute to the fascists' success. The KPD leadership, not to mention many Social Democrats, believed that Thälmann had been right on this issue. The implication was clear: if Germany wanted to avoid another cataclysm like that which had befallen the country in 1933, proletarian unity must be attained. There could, however, also be disadvantages to utilizing Thälmann's image to promote the creation of the SED. Although no one could doubt that the KPD chief had sought accommodation with the SPD in the years preceding the Nazi seizure of power, there was equally no question but that he had insisted on cooperation on his own terms. If Thälmann had had his way, the SPD would have simply adopted the KPD program almost in its entirety, including provisions that would have categorized sympathizers with the SPD's right-wing as "social fascists." To add insult to injury, Thälmann had been largely responsible for the Bolshevization and later the Stalinization of the German Communist Party. As party chairman during the years 1925 to 1933, Thälmann had forged the KPD into little more than an instrument of Soviet foreign policy. Trying to avoid the impression that the proposed new party would also be a tool of authorities in Moscow, the postwar KPD initially sought unity in the western occupation zones as well, hoping that as a result the German people would not view the prospective unity party as a "Russian party." To associate the unity campaign too closely with Thälmann's legacy risked legitimizing the argument that the proposed organization would be an instrument of the SBZ's Soviet masters. Further, such an association also increased the possibility of alienating more moderate Social Democrats, who legitimately feared the Bolshevization—indeed, the Stalinization—of their party.[29] As a result, Communist leaders had to walk a fine line that, on the one hand, incorporated Thälmann's legacy and the myth of antifascism into the unification campaign, while, on the other, avoided estranging moderates who might very well fear the creation of a new party no different from Thälmann's KPD. The KPD leadership and the Soviets ultimately decided to take a series of relatively cautious piecemeal steps, first creating unified proletarian political organizations on the local level before concluding the effort with the creation of the single Socialist Unity Party for the entire SBZ.[30] Even so, the process proceeded quickly, over the course of a few months, and the Thälmann myth would in the end play an important, although limited, role in this process.

The importance of the legend to the unity campaign can be seen in an article in commemoration of Ernst Thälmann's sixtieth birthday published on 16 April 1946 in *Tägliche Rundschau*, a newspaper printed by Soviet occupation authorities. The paper's front-page story, written by S. Sowotjew, opens with a 29 November 1931 quotation from Ernst Thälmann, in which the KPD chief called upon "the Social Democratic workers to fight shoulder to shoulder with us." The piece incorporates the usual themes of the Thälmann myth: the martyred KPD chief's struggle against German fascism, his role in making the KPD a "mass party," and the fact that he was "always an important and uncompromising friend of the Soviet Union." Yet Sowotjew placed special emphasis on the erstwhile German Communist leader's role in earlier efforts to promote united action between the two proletarian parties.[31]

The same edition of *Tägliche Rundschau* also published an interview with Thälmann's widow, Rosa, who would come to play such an important role in the propagation of the official narrative surrounding her deceased husband (see further discussion of Rosa later in this chapter as well as in chapters 4, 5, and 6). In the published version of the interview, Rosa recounts her visits to her imprisoned spouse, held by the Nazis for more than eleven years without a trial. Thälmann's widow remembers how staunchly Ernst believed in the Soviet Union and the inevitability of its victory over German imperialism. In February 1944, upon hearing of a string of Red Army victories, her husband supposedly rejoiced that "[n]ow fascism will soon be defeated!" His concerns also extended to the KPD's welfare, thousands of its members having gone deep underground in order to oppose the imperialist enemy. According to Rosa, Ernst often asked her, "How goes it with father?"—in which "father . . . meant the Communist Party." The motifs found in this interview were often repeated in the propagation of the Thälmann legend. There is nothing new here. Perhaps Soviet authorities hoped that readers would find an exchange with the fallen KPD chief's widow more emotionally effective than the usual highly polemical journalism that appeared in the days close to Thälmann's birthday and the anniversary of his death. If so, the editors failed. Rosa says nothing about her husband's personal life, the psychological trauma that he certainly felt, or the effects that his imprisonment undoubtedly had on their marriage. Even when his wife spoke of him, the Thälmann who emerged during the course of the conversation was a one-dimensional figure, someone interested solely in politics. Indeed, Rosa's account of her husband establishes that even if advocates of applying the totalitarian model—in which everything in Stalinist Germany was politicized—were wrong, it is safe to say that only the political mattered to the Communist leaders.[32]

Although Rosa Thälmann was silent specifically about the importance of workers' unity in the interview published on 16 April, the same cannot be said regarding her participation in a rally celebrating what would have been her husband's sixtieth birthday. Held in Berlin's Palast Theater, the assembly was filled to capacity—at least according to the journalist who covered the event for *Tägliche Rundschau*. Although Social Democrats sympathetic to unity attended the rally as well, the speakers who made lengthy presentations at the ceremony stood firmly within the Communist camp. The two people who addressed the rally—at least at any length—spoke from the "stage decorated with spring flowers." A bust of the fallen KPD chief, likewise bedecked with flowers, stood on the platform. The first person to speak was Wilhelm Pieck, "the friend, comrade and successor [*Nachfolger*] of Thälmann." Paraphrasing the speaker, the newspaper recounts that Pieck began his presentation by talking about the life and accomplishments of his erstwhile comrade. Pieck remembered how "Thälmann also . . . dedicated all his power to a union of the working people of the city and [the] agricultural sector"—an allusion to the ongoing unity campaign. Thälmann, Pieck reminded his audience, had similarly been concerned with promoting the "equality of working women."[33]

Although Pieck only alluded to Thälmann's efforts to promote proletarian unity, Rosa Thälmann, who spoke next, was much more straightforward. She remembered how Ernst and his comrades met at the Thälmanns' apartment in Hamburg, often asking themselves, "How do we create the unity of the working class against the approaching fascist danger? . . . Repeatedly he [Ernst] said: 'We must find the way . . . to unite Social Democrats and Communists in a common struggle against the common enemy.'" Rosa concluded her presentation by reminding those present that the proletariat once again stood at a crossroads, at which it must choose unity and success rather than division and defeat as it had during the final days of the Weimar Republic. "I am happy . . . that, with the creation of the Socialist Unity Party, now, finally, my husband's life's goal will have been realized," she commented. Rosa, standing in for her martyred husband, had vicariously given Ernst's imprimatur to the unity effort, which was entering its final stage. In a far briefer presentation, Erich W. Galfka spoke on behalf of the SPD. "Thälmann," Galfka informed those present, "is for us a constant, brilliant, example of the way . . . to the unity of the working class and to the unity of Germany."[34] In making this brief statement, the Social Democratic functionary seconded the earlier speakers' statements concerning Thälmann's role in promoting working-class unity. Further, he reiterated one of the central themes of the campaign for unity—the insistence that only a single, strong, proletarian party could preempt the reemergence of fascism and assure that Germany would once again be a united country and a trusted member of the family of nations. That is, the creation of the SED became, in the eyes of its supporters, a vital step in the process of rehabilitating the country. Galfka's brief participation in the ceremony also furthered claims that the union of the SPD and KPD was a voluntary one, beneficial not only for the KPD, but for all "progressives" determined to avoid a repetition of the recent catastrophe.

In spite of the fact that Thälmann's legacy assumed an important role in the campaign leading up to the creation of the SED, it played no role at the ceremony officially launching the new political party. The Unity Party Assembly took place in the Deutsche Staatsoper—one of the few large buildings still standing in the German capital after the war—on Berlin's Unter den Linden on 21 April 1946, a Sunday. The stage was decorated with busts of Marx, Lenin, and August Bebel. Conspicuous by its absence—at least in hindsight—was any image representing Ernst Thälmann. Otto Grotewohl, who spoke first, and Max Fechner represented the SPD in the ceremony. Wilhelm Pieck and Walter Ulbricht spoke on behalf of the KPD. At the conclusion of the festivities, Ulbricht announced that "[b]eginning today there are no longer Social Democrats and Communists, with today's assembly there are only socialists." Yet the SED was not simply the union of the KPD and SPD. Ulbricht insisted that "[t]oday is not merely the fusion of Social Democrats and Communists, today is a rebirth of the German workers' movement." Although all of the speakers had a great deal to say about the importance of unity, none of them so much as mentioned Ernst Thälmann in his speech.[35] This omission might not be surprising for the Social Democratic speakers, but, given the importance of the Thälmann legacy to the KPD's unity campaign, it is remarkable that neither Ulbricht nor Pieck so much as mentioned the fallen party leader.

One can only speculate, but it appears that the decision not to incorporate Thälmann's legacy into this important occasion was made on grounds of political expediency. For many Social Democrats, especially moderates, Thälmann might represent the intransigence of the pre-1933 KPD, the party that had completely refused to compromise with more moderate Marxists, even on minor issues. Thälmann's idea of co-operation had been predicated upon the SPD leadership's relenting in the face of Communist demands. Indeed, one might even argue that as much as the KPD chief championed unity between the two proletarian parties, he was largely responsible for their failure to cooperate in the face of the growing Nazi threat. Further, Thälmann had long been an unmitigated champion of the Soviet Union, looking upon it as a model for Germany's future development. To invoke his image at the very foundation of the SED might very well fuel the fear among many Social Democrats that the new party amounted to both the Stalinization and Russification of the SPD. In hindsight, it is safe to say that there was a great deal of resistance among the SPD rank and file to the union. Indeed, many Social Democrats in the SBZ either left the party or simply fled to one of the western zones of occupation rather than acquiesce in what they saw as the destruction of moderate German socialism.[36] As a result, the KPD leadership was willing to go to extensive lengths to placate these fears. Ulbricht, Pieck, and other Communists wanted to present the new party as a relatively moderate, broadly antifascist political organization rather than as a specifically Communist one. This effort helps to explain why the new party, at least at first, did not develop a detailed platform. Indeed, the SED leadership would shortly begin serious overtures to the "bourgeois" parties, eventually cajoling them into a grudging consensus about the creation of a socialist Germany.

Many non-Communists' fears concerning the dangers of unity with the KPD proved to be well founded. The SED would eventually indeed be Stalinized with the adoption of the principle of "democratic centralism" in January 1949. At the same time, the SED leadership also created a Soviet-style politburo to serve as the party's highest governing organ.[37] Hence, it should come as no surprise that German Communists, soon after the 21 April union of the workers' political parties, would return to the Thälmann legacy as an important component of their legitimizing narrative. Indeed, the mythology surrounding the fallen KPD chief would assume an important role in the SED's propaganda offensive during the period between April 1946 and January 1949 as German Communists prepared the way for the Stalinization of the Socialist Unity Party, not to mention the creation of the German Democratic Republic in October 1949.

The foundation of the GDR was not the only important development to take place during the year 1949. The eighteenth of August witnessed the fifth anniversary of the murder of Thälmann in Buchenwald Concentration Camp, a day of remembrance celebrated not only at the site of the KPD chief's death (see chapter 5), but also throughout the SBZ. Wilhelm Pieck set the tone for the commemoration activities with a 15 August radio interview. The reporter opened the discussion by establishing the close links between Pieck and the fallen KPD chief: "Mr. Pieck, you worked together with Ernst Thälmann for many years, indeed decades. . . . You, Mr. Pieck, from personal experience can certainly create a picture of the man Ernst Thälmann." Pieck responded by pointing out the modest roots of the proletarian leader: "Ernst Thälmann came from the people and was a typical son of the German people." The future president of the GDR then went on to outline the major events of Thälmann's life, focusing, as always, on the Hamburg native's political activities. Pieck pointed out that the arrest and imprisonment of both of Ernst's parents "because of support for the illegal Social Democratic Party" was an important turning point in the future KPD chief's political development. Ignoring the facts, Pieck sought to portray his hero as having experienced an exemplary proletarian childhood. Echoing the account contained in Willi Bredel's 1948 biography (see chapter 7),[38] Pieck also assigned Thälmann's class consciousness to his experiences working in Germany's largest port city. Because of his understanding of German imperialism, Thälmann became an important figure in the opposition to the Great War, although Pieck could only trace the future KPD chief's antiwar activities to November 1918. The SPD's support for the war, coupled with its allegiance to the "treasonous republic," led him to the "left-wing" USPD and eventually into the Communist Party. At the same time, the Hamburg native consistently supported "the union of all Social Democrats, standing on the foundations of revolutionary Marxism." Because of his revolutionary zeal, Thälmann rose to the position of chairman of the Communist Party, where, the interviewer pointed out, Pieck had the opportunity to "work closely together with Ernst Thälmann." Pieck responded, emphasizing that he had indeed experienced these things firsthand, by recounting the KPD chief's determination to fight the fascists by "repeatedly calling upon the proletariat for a united struggle against this danger." Further, Thälmann emphasized the "great importance" of the Soviet Union as a model for the German working class. As a result, the Communist leader "was imprisoned right at the beginning of the fascist dictatorship." Next, the interviewer turned to Thälmann's death and legacy. Pieck responded by reiterating the importance of Thälmann's legacy to the situation in Germany. "If Ernst Thälmann were alive, he would stand at the forefront of the struggle for the unity of Germany, for a just peace, and for the withdrawal of the occupation troops." Indeed, Pieck concluded, Thälmann was a "peace-loving" man who believed in "friendship among peoples," which would have led him to support a "just peace treaty" and the withdrawal of all foreign forces from German soil.[39]

Pieck's radio interview established the major themes of the 1949 commemoration of the fifth anniversary of Thälmann's death. The martyred KPD chief stood for an end to capitalist imperialism and exploitation, was in favor of the unity of the working classes under the umbrella of a single political party, and believed in Germany's independence under a single political system, the one most likely to preempt the reemergence of the fascist threat—socialism. Other prominent figures, writing and speaking on the eve of this important anniversary, echoed Pieck's sentiments, which had become the SED line concerning Ernst Thälmann's legacy.

Among those sharing Pieck's thoughts was Willi Bredel, who published a 16 August 1949 article in *Neues Deutschland*, the SED's official organ. Entitled "Ernst Thälmann—Shining Example for Youth," the piece was aimed at younger readers, those who represented the future of German socialism (see chapter 6). Opening with a quotation from Friedrich Engels about the long history of the German revolutionary movement, Bredel tries to place Thälmann's life and sacrificial death in the context of a long tradition of revolution beginning with the Anabaptist leader Thomas Münzer. It had been almost one hundred years since Engels had introduced his pantheon of those who had fought valiantly to improve the lot of the German people, Bredel points out, and there had been many important revolutionary heroes in the meantime, including August Bebel, founder of the SPD, not to mention Karl Liebknecht and Rosa Luxemburg, who had established the KPD in the wake of the 1918 revolution that had ousted Kaiser William II. Among the most important figures in this revolutionary tradition was Ernst Thälmann: "One of these courageous, impeccable revolutionary heroes of our people, who engaged in his activities during the darkness of German fascism like a bright flame of the illegal antifascist . . . revolutionary tradition, was Ernst Thälmann, the leader of the German Communists, the presidential candidate of proletarian Germany." Having established Thälmann's place in Germany's revolutionary pantheon, Bredel proceeds briefly to recount the major events of his subject's life, beginning with Thälmann's having "grown up in his parents' social democratic home," concentrating on his subject's political activities, including his joining the SPD and his rise to prominence in the KPD during the years after the First World War, and culminating with his stalwart opposition to German fascism. Even as things got worse for himself, Thälmann never lost his faith in the German proletariat and the Soviet Union, willingly spending almost a dozen years in prison on behalf of the German people. Here, he languished for a "tragic, bloody . . . twelve years," while "the Nazis tried, with every means at their disposal, to wear down Ernst Thälmann physically and spiritually." The KPD chief had ultimately given his life, one of many victims of the Wagnerian nihilism characterizing the final days of the Third Reich.[40]

The people of the SBZ, Bredel insisted, had learned valuable lessons as the result of the sacrifices made by Ernst Thälmann and so many others. They now understood the shortcomings of Weimar democracy, which engendered capitalist exploitation, imperialism, and war. "The democracy that we have today is rooted in our working people." This development was possible only because the people of the SBZ had learned the lessons embodied in the life and sacrifices of Ernst Thälmann, an eminent example for all Germans to follow. Bredel concludes by pointing out: "Ernst Thälmann's life and struggle are a modern heroic epic of a revolutionary and patriot, a true friend of the people. To choose this great pioneer of socialism as [an] example for one's own conduct . . . is an honorable undertaking."[41]

Bredel's emphasis on Ernst Thälmann as an example for all Germans was nothing new. Thälmann had long been hailed as a paragon of antifascism. Although the article in *Neues Deutschland* did not invoke nearly as many religious images as had Bredel's biography published the previous year, there were some important—and relatively new— themes in the 1949 newspaper article. The most striking among them is what Bredel had to say about democracy. In the immediate postwar period, Communist propaganda in the Soviet zone had said remarkably little about the Weimar Republic—either positive or negative. Perhaps this was because of the KPD's ongoing effort to win the support of Social Democrats—especially in the SBZ. The SPD had been the largest German political party to support the political status quo during the Weimar years. Although in the period preceding the Nazi seizure of power the KPD and its allies in the Comintern repeatedly depicted the

SPD and the bourgeois Weimar constitution as manifestations of "social fascism," after 1933 German Communists largely abandoned this motif, at least in their propaganda. Indeed, the Free Thälmann campaign sought to appeal to all antifascists, regardless of political affiliation, including Social Democrats. To paint the all but defunct SPD with the "social fascist" brush would have been counterproductive. In August 1949, however, the SPD, having been absorbed into the SED and the latter party being thoroughly Stalinized, there was no longer any need to keep up the pretext. A bourgeois democracy, such as the Weimar Republic, was a contradiction in terms. The only truly democratic system was the "people's democracy," such as that which existed in the Soviet Union and was being built in the SBZ, soon to be the German Democratic Republic. Hence, manifestations of the antifascism myth, such as those presented in Bredel's 16 August 1949 article, could safely criticize the Weimar dispensation, viewing it as little more than the herald of full-blown fascism. In short, in the wake of the Bolshevization of the SED in January 1949, there was no longer any need to appeal to non-Communist "progressive" forces such as social democracy. The gloves were off, and the SED was well on its way to creating a polity modeled on that of Stalin's Russia.

Another striking motif to be found in "Ernst Thälmann—Shining Example for Youth," is the concept of the "heroic epic." In his 1948 biography, Bredel had already incorporated millennia-old tropes inherited from Christianity. A year later he integrated yet another theme culled from the ancient world—the "heroic epic." Bredel's article invokes not the religious images incorporated into his *Ernst Thälmann—ein Beitrag zu einem politischen Lebensbild,* but classical motifs instead, some of which were even older than Christianity. By conjuring up the image of the heroic epic—augmenting the view of Ernst Thälmann as the Leonidas of German communism—Bredel invokes images as old as European culture, figures such as Achilles, Hector, and Odysseus, who represented through their struggles what was best in Western civilization. As a result, Bredel associates his fallen comrade with the great heroes of history, linking Thälmann's achievements with something even broader than the German revolutionary tradition. Memory of the martyred KPD chief deserved to live on like the memory of the protagonists in Homer and Virgil. To place Thälmann in the company of ancient heroes was to emphasize not only the role that he played in history, but also the importance that he would have in the future. His legacy would endure forever. Thälmann was a figure like the heroes of

old, to be lauded in poetry and song, with monuments and rituals—
with every means at the disposal of the new Germany.

And this is exactly what the SED leadership did during the ceremonies surrounding the fifth anniversary of Thälmann's martyrdom.
Almost the entire 18 and 19 August editions of *Neues Deutschland* were
dedicated to memorializing Ernst Thälmann and making him the paragon of all that was good in the German people. The newspaper's front-
page headline on the nineteenth announced, "The Proletariat of the
World Honors Thälmann." The SED, the accompanying article pointed out, had received telegrams praising the fallen KPD chief from the
French, Austrian, and Bulgarian Communist parties, in addition to the
Polish Workers' Party, not to mention one from the Swedish Communist Party pointing out that "Comrade Thälmann was murdered not
only because of his name and stature were a flag [*Fahne*] for the proletariat of Germany, but rather also for the world proletariat."[42] One way
of interpreting this litany of countries praising Thälmann is to view it in
the context of Germany's attempts to rehabilitate itself. One must keep
in mind the fact that the war in Europe had ended a little more than
four years earlier, and the Germans' neighbors legitimately continued
to distrust them. But, as *Neues Deutschland* would have it, postwar Germany's neighbors—Poland, Austria, and even France—believed in the
fundamental goodness of Ernst Thälmann. If the German people were
to embrace his legacy, it might very well accelerate the rehabilitation
process. To espouse the heritage of Ernst Thälmann was to inculcate all
that was good in German history, to reject all that was evil, and to carry
out Germany's return to the brotherhood of nations. Another article appearing on 18 August echoed this sentiment, recounting that Thälmann
was a good internationalist and an opponent of all chauvinistic manifestations of nationalism. The author of the article, Roman Rubinstein,
tells how Thälmann traveled to Paris to commemorate the fifteenth anniversary of the Bolshevik Revolution in Russia. While in the French
capital, he had addressed a massive crowd of 15,000. Thälmann spoke
out in favor of peace and "against imperialist war." The deceased KPD
chief could serve as an example of international cooperation, the goal
of which was to avoid a conflagration such as that which had gripped
Europe for six long years. In short, embracing the Thälmann myth was
a path to the redemption of the German people.[43]

Other major themes of the Thälmann myth were also evident in the
editions of *Neues Deutschland* commemorating the fifth anniversary of
the martyred Communist's death. Walter Bartel, a close adviser to Wal-

ter Ulbricht and former inmate of Buchenwald, published a detailed account titled "The Murder of Ernst Thälmann." Opening with a quotation from Nazi propaganda chief Joseph Goebbels claiming that Thälmann had died in an air raid, Bartel insists that this claim "was a foul, wretched lie." Rather, the Communist Party chief had been murdered by the SS on direct orders from none other than Adolf Hitler. Bartel contends that numerous witnesses could attest to the fact that Nazi officials moved the KPD chief from his prison cell in Bautzen to Buchenwald Concentration Camp at around midnight of 17–18 August. The SS shot him outside of the crematorium, taking his body inside the building for disposal. This was not the end of the matter, however. "The murder of Ernst Thälmann had an epilogue [*Nachspiel*]. A group of German inmates carried out a memorial service in a basement room of the disinfection chamber," where they introduced the tradition of commemorating the life and heroic death of the erstwhile KPD chief (see chapter 5).[44]

This account of Thälmann's death would go on to become a vital component of the myth. If the Communist leader had died as the result of an air raid, as the Nazis had claimed, he became just another of the tens of thousands who had died as casualties of war, victims of allied bombers, people who had simply been in the wrong place at the wrong time. Perishing during an air raid was not the stuff of an heroic death. Rather, the Thälmann myth necessitated that he died as the direct result of his conscious decision to oppose the fascist regime. Indeed, the party leader had been such a vocal and consistent opponent of National Socialism that none other than the Nazi führer himself had decided Thälmann's fate. The martyred KPD chief died as the result of his resistance to German fascism, not because of bad luck. The conditions surrounding Thälmann's death became an important device in the SED's efforts to propagate the legend, in order to present itself as the heir of the antifascist struggle. Indeed, the circumstances under which Thälmann perished remained a point of controversy in the rhetorical struggle between the SED and various right-wing groups in the FRG for around forty years (see chapter 8). As a result, the fact that Thälmann died at the hands of Nazi thugs became arguably the most important motif in the myth.

Simply too much material appeared in the 18 and 19 August 1949 numbers of *Neues Deutschland* for all of it to be analyzed here. It is worth, however, examining one more article—a brief piece written by Walter Ulbricht that appears at the bottom of page four. Entitled "The National Salvation of Our People," the short article can best be understood in the context of the recent Soviet effort to drive the Western powers from Berlin by blockading the western half of the city—not to mention the FRG's declaration of independence the previous May. In August 1930, Ulbricht reminds his readers, Germany faced a crisis, the origins of which Ernst Thälmann was the only leading political figure capable of understanding: "Four million unemployed. The middle class in a state of collapse. Foreign capital from the USA and England sought, with the help of the Young Plan, to expand its influence over heavy industry. The bourgeois parties had fallen apart. The chancellor from the Center [Party] undermined further cooperation among the workers through emergency decrees." In short, Germany faced a crisis, and the imperialist powers sought to take advantage of it. There were only two alternatives: one could side with either the "concerns and bankers" in their effort to continue the exploitation of the German people; or one could join with the forces struggling for "peace, the Communist Party under the leadership of Ernst Thälmann." The latter group stood not for exploitation at the hands of international capital, but rather for the "self-determination of all peoples." Because so many Germans responded to the situation by allying themselves with the forces of reaction, Western capitalism had emerged victorious from the interwar catastrophe and Adolf Hitler, the instrument of reactionary capitalism, had taken power. Thälmann and the KPD, however, had "allied with the Soviet Union, and not with the countries that were responsible for the crisis." Indeed, in spite of the reactionaries' temporary victory that Germany experienced in January 1933, "To his last breath, Ernst Thälmann, the most important proletarian leader of the Weimar period, remained true to the interests of the proletariat and working people." Hence, it was the obligation of all good Germans "on this day of remembrance" to struggle to fulfill the legacy of Ernst Thälmann and the Weimar KPD. One must continue his struggle and embrace the fallen KPD chairman's effort to secure "national independence for Germany."[45]

Ulbricht was clearly alluding to recent events. Once again, as in Thälmann's time, Germany stood at a crossroads. The German people could choose association with the Western capitalist powers, the United States and Great Britain, thereby assuring the continued exploitation of the German people, or, like Thälmann before them, they could forge an alliance with the Soviet Union, the only occupying power sincerely to espouse the idea of a truly independent Germany. Ulbricht was appealing to one of the most important SED propaganda motifs to emerge in the early years of the cold war: only the Soviet Union stood for peace and cooperation among peoples; only Bolshevik Russia had the best interests of the German people at heart. Continuing to draw parallels between circumstances in 1930 and 1949, Ulbricht implied that, like the bourgeois parties of the late Weimar Republic, the leaders of West Germany had made a deal with the devil, an arrangement that had the effect of surrendering Germany's autonomy to the great powers. The similarities between the situation in 1949 and the rise of National Socialism almost two decades earlier were, in Ulbricht's eyes, truly striking.

The argument that the party chief constructed was the SED's answer to the Federal Republic's totalitarian model under which the Soviet Union was associated with National Socialism. That is, in the eyes of many Western leaders, Bolshevism was as great a threat to human liberty as the Nazis had been.[46] Ulbricht opposed this Western paradigm with one of his own, the antifascism paradigm. To his understanding, fascism—including the German variety known as National Socialism— was the product of an alliance between international business concerns and the middle class, who cooperated in the face of the imminent collapse of the capitalist system of exploitation. The implications of the SED chief's argument were clear to any reader: the new Federal Republic of Germany was nothing more than the tool of capitalists and imperialists stationed in London and New York. As recent history made clear, West Germany—representing the front-line forces of Western imperialism—was a danger to European peace. The only way to avoid another imperialistic world war was for the German people to embrace an alliance with the Soviet Union and drive the Western powers from German soil. Ernst Thälmann had foreseen the danger during the final years of the Weimar Republic, and in 1949—as the cold war grew ever more intense—Germans must heed the fallen party leader's warning. Ulbricht, like other SED leaders (see, for example, chapter 5), linked the Thälmann myth—not to mention other manifestations of the antifascism legend—to the ongoing rhetorical and political struggle against Western imperialism, a conflict that could erupt into a continentwide war at a moment's notice. The people of the SBZ, soon to be the German Democratic Republic, must be on guard; they must embrace Ernst Thälmann's legacy.

In addition to the wide range of newspaper stories to appear in the SED's official organ, the party scheduled numerous rallies and other events to mark the fifth anniversary of the martyred KPD chief's demise, including ceremonies held at Buchenwald Concentration Camp (see chapter 5). Although the rallies and rituals were concentrated in the SBZ, there was at least one observance staged in the FRG. In Hamburg, Thälmann's home town, a rally was held featuring the fallen KPD chief's widow, Rosa, and a speech by the chairman of West Germany's Communist Party, Max Reimann. Further, as *Neues Deutschland* pointed out, Thälmann's fame had spread beyond Germany's borders, with a commemoration ceremony held at an international youth rally attended by young people from the nations of the Soviet bloc, including members of the Free German Youth (FDJ).[47]

The climax of the observance of the fifth anniversary of Thälmann's death took place in Berlin's Staatsoper on the evening of 18 August. After a ceremony incorporating the FDJ, Walter Ulbricht was the featured speaker at the event. Ulbricht's long speech—of which only a few key passages can be analyzed here—incorporated most of the major themes of the SED's postwar version of the Thälmann myth. His opening included perhaps the most important motifs to be found in the legend: "Five years ago, in August 1944, our Ernst Thälmann, the most important leader of the German workers' movement during the Weimar Republic, was murdered on the orders of the fascist regime. On the 18th of August, the German people and all the peace-loving forces in the world commemorate this great leader of workers, who, during the Weimar period, led the struggle of the working people in Germany for the rights of the people and against the reemergence of German imperialism."[48] Once again the circumstances surrounding Thälmann's death took precedence over the accomplishments of his life. Although this emphasis should come as no surprise in this context—the fifth anniversary of the KPD chief's death—Ulbricht's opening was indicative of a larger trend that placed paramount importance on Thälmann's death, an event that the SED increasingly viewed as a sacrificial offering on behalf of the German people.

This is not to suggest that the party leadership disregarded the power of the narrative of Thälmann's life to instill the proper response among the German people. Thälmann's legacy, as Ulbricht pointed out in his subsequent remarks, went far beyond the martyred KPD chairman's willingness to give his life in the name of antifascism and global proletarian revolution. Not only was his willingness to suffer martyrdom for the benefit of others a worthy model to be followed, but his life was also worth emulating. This "[f]riend of simple people" lived for a little more than fifty-eight years, consistently seeking the benefit of the masses. Incorporating a theme seen in Willi Bredel's essay published two days earlier, Ulbricht depicted the Communist leader from Hamburg as a figure from classical history, "a people's tribune of a new type." Placing the deceased KPD chief in the broader context of the German workers' movement, Ulbricht pointed out that Thälmann—much as his predecessor Karl Liebknecht had defied the SPD leadership by casting his vote in the Reichstag against funding Germany's imperialist war—"forged [schmiedete] the mass party of the German working class into the leadership of the struggle against imperialism and bondage, [and] for socialism." Whereas Liebknecht was instrumental to the creation of the Spartakusbund and its successor, the German Communist Party, "Ernst Thälmann forged the party into a unified party of the working class," in the tradition of "Marxism–Leninism."[49]

Karl Liebknecht was not the only important figure in socialist history from whom Thälmann had learned a great deal. "Ernst Thälmann," Ulbricht insisted, had "tirelessly studied the works of Marx, Engels, Lenin, and Stalin. He studied the laws of social development and the important contributions of Lenin and Stalin to the strategy of the struggle for liberation of the working class. His study of the crisis in capitalism convinced him, in 1929 and 1930[,] correctly to reject the Social Democratic theory about the stabilization of capitalism and to give a correct interpretation of the development of the crisis."[50] In this instance, Ulbricht contended, Thälmann was building upon traditions originating in the Soviet Union, the proper model for Germany's future development.

Thälmann's admiration for the accomplishments of the Bolshevik movement was another major theme in Ulbricht's speech. The martyred KPD chief was a "great friend of the Soviet Union," the SED chairman continued. Indeed, in the midst of the global economic crisis, Thälmann "contrasted the crisis, unemployment, the ruin . . . of the peasantry . . ." in the capitalist countries with "the giant industrial works . . . and the triumph of socialism in the Soviet Union through the realization of the Five-Year Plan in four years." The martyred Communist leader had recognized the importance of looking to the Soviet Union as an example of proper social, economic, and political development.[51] It is likely that Ulbricht was preparing his listeners for developments in the coming months, during which the SBZ would declare its independence as the German Democratic Republic, a socialist German state modeled on the achievements of the "great Stalin" and the CPSU.

The conclusion of Ulbricht's speech, that "the SED will complete the work of Ernst Thälmann," makes the commitment to the martyred

KPD chief's legacy even more explicit. Indeed, the SED party chief viewed the fulfillment of Thälmann's legacy as a solemn obligation, one of cryptoreligious significance. "We swear," Ulbricht vowed, "in the spirit of Ernst Thälmann, to struggle for democracy and socialism, for a happy future for our people in a single, united Germany."[52] The speaker incorporated the Thälmann myth into one of the most important themes of East German propaganda during the late 1940s and 1950s—the imperative to create a united polity under socialist auspices and thereby assure the end of the Western exploitation of the German people and guarantee the long-term peace of central Europe. Only a unified Germany, following the example of Ernst Thälmann, could play a significant role in maintaining harmony on the continent. In spite of the establishment of the FRG three months earlier, the party leadership continued to hope for the creation of a united "antifascist" Germany closely allied with the "progressive" forces led by the Soviet Union.

The SED used this hope to justify the founding of the German Democratic Republic in October 1949. The GDR, the party leadership insisted, would serve as a bridgehead to achieving the ultimate goal of unity under the banner of socialism. Those Germans living in the imperialist West would have the opportunity to view the benefits inherent in humanistic socialism by watching the accomplishments of the new state created under the auspices of the SED. Then—so the party's argument went—the people of the FRG would abandon their imperialistic, pro-Western government. Indeed, SED propaganda would seek to link FRG chancellor Konrad Adenauer's government with the fascist traditions of Germany, never missing an opportunity to criticize the remilitarization of the West and the role that many leaders with Nazi connections played in the FRG. The FRG represented an illegitimate government permeated with "the Nazi spirit because of [the] Western occupation." The GDR's success would ultimately convince the citizens of West Germany of the error of their ways. In other words, the short-term division of Germany was a necessary precondition to the country's long-term reunification.[53]

Unity would be a major theme of the ceremonies and rituals surrounding the official creation of the GDR on 7 October 1949. "Democracy" was another central motif of the celebrations, not to mention the "great service of the Soviet Union" performed on behalf of the people of the former SBZ. Ironically, given the role that the Thälmann myth—with its emphasis on unity and "friendship" with the Soviets—had played in the months preceding the creation of the GDR, the image of the fallen KPD chief played no discernable role in the propaganda campaign announcing the creation of the SED state. None of the speakers at the official ceremony creating the GDR referred to the martyred Communist leader.[54] As was the case with the creation of the SED more than two years earlier, this omission is difficult, although not impossible, to explain. Further, in his speech opening East Germany's first Volkskammer (People's Chamber) on 11 October, GDR president Wilhelm Pieck did not so much as mention Ernst Thälmann. He did, however, make a concerted effort to appeal to FRG leaders. "I appeal . . . ," Pieck said, "to the men and women in the West German parliament and the West German federal government to make themselves aware of the danger in which they are placing the German people in view of the policy of the Western powers, which endangers the unity of Germany, which hinders the [signing of] a peace treaty, which gambles with the existence of the German people," and which increases the possibility of "a new war."[55] The promotion of national unity was so important to the leaders of the new socialist country that one might conclude that, as in April 1946, they made the conscious decision not to invoke the KPD chief's image. Many East Germans and perhaps the majority of the West German population to whom the SED hoped to appeal might have viewed Thälmann—someone noteworthy for his refusal to compromise—as a divisive figure. Although this might very well have been the case, the importance that SED propaganda placed on the role of the Soviet Union—especially its leader, Joseph Stalin—undermined any claims to independence that socialist Germany might make. Yet it is possible that the SED leadership believed that it had no choice but to invoke the legacy of Stalin and the Soviet Union, especially if, as many scholars contend, the Russian leader was not supportive of the creation of a separate socialist German state in the first place.[56] Whatever the reasons that the SED leadership had for excluding the Thälmann legend from the events surrounding the official creation of the GDR, the image of the martyred KPD chief soon returned to its important place in party propaganda.

Numerous developments in the evolution of the Thälmann legend took place in the early years of the GDR. January 1951, for example, witnessed the rededication of the Memorial of the Socialists in Berlin's Friedrichsfelde Cemetery. The locale had been an important commemoration site for the KPD going back at least as far as the funeral of Rosa Luxemburg and Karl Liebknecht in 1919—although famous socialists, including Wilhelm Liebknecht, had been buried at the location even earlier. In 1926, the KPD erected a shrine at the site—arguably the most important one built by the Communists during the Weimar Republic. Designed by Ludwig Mies van der Rohe, the monument became famous for the text appearing in large letters on its front side—"I was, I am, I will be"—emphasizing that the sacrifices of the forty-five socialists and Communists buried there were not in vain. Indeed, Mies van der Rohe's monument became the most important setting for the KPD's version of the myth of heroic death.[57] Recognizing the importance of the locale for their Marxist opponents, the Nazis had destroyed the Communist monument in 1935. Sixteen years later, on 14 January —since 1924 the date for the annual Lenin–Liebknecht–Luxemburg commemoration—the SED leadership dedicated a new memorial at the location. Indicative of the importance of the site to the GDR's legitimizing narrative, none other than Wilhelm Pieck produced the initial plans for the new monument. In addition to the graves of the KPD founders, other prominent figures in the governing party's history were honored at the location. They were buried—in Thälmann's case symbolically because his remains had been cremated in Buchenwald—under a stela reminding visitors that "The Dead exhort us." The setting became important in East Germany's secular religion, with numerous ceremonies held there through the GDR's final years. The message was clear: socialist East Germany embodied the legacy of the fallen buried in this ground, sanctified by the blood of martyrs. The monument and the graves surrounding it stressed the motif of continuity, of "legacy." In order to emphasize the fact that the SED was the product of the union of the KPD and the SPD, two prominent Social Democratic martyrs—Rudolf Breitscheid and Franz Künstler—were buried along with a pair of prominent Communist victims of National Socialism: Thälmann and Johnny Schehr. In addition, four other prominent figures from Germany's Marxist past—including Luxemburg and Liebknecht—were buried immediately around the monument. These eight graves surrounded the monumental structure, two on each side.[58] Although the Friedrichsfelde Cemetery played an important role in the SED's various propaganda campaigns, it was never among the most important sites for commemoration of Thälmann, serving primarily— as before the war—as a spot upon which the party could remember Liebknecht and Luxemburg's legacy, emphasizing the long tradition of sacrifice that was a vital component of Germany's socialist heritage. This is not to suggest that the Memorial of the Socialists played no role in the Thälmann cult. Relatively minor East German government officials and foreign dignitaries, for example, often laid wreaths on Thälmann's "grave" in order to mark the anniversary of his birth or death, not to mention other important dates in the GDR's secular religion.

Among the most important anniversaries to occur during the GDR's early years was Thälmann's sixty-fifth birthday in April 1951. By this point, the cold war between the Soviet bloc and the Western powers was well under way, and the speeches and newspaper articles marking this important date reflected this fact. SED leaders and East German journalists once again sought to draw attention to what they saw as the parallels between the circumstances that Thälmann had confronted on the eve of the Nazi seizure of power and the conditions that the German people faced in 1951. Writing for *Neues Deutschland* on 15 April, Hans Jendretzky, head of the SED in Greater Berlin, made these alleged similarities explicit:[59] "Back then, like now, the creation of a fighting united front of the workers in the struggle against the wage, salary, rent, robber barons—the direct result of American preparations for war . . . stands as a top priority. The warning of Ernst Thälmann is an appeal to all workers opposing this remilitarization and seeking united action against it."[60] The image of Ernst Thälmann had become a central component of East Germany's cold war propaganda directed against the "imperialist" powers, especially the United States. It is worth noting that, unlike the leaders of the SED, the deceased Hamburg native had actually visited the United States. Yet Thälmann's accounts of his experiences while on the western side of the Atlantic Ocean played no role in the GDR's cold war propaganda—probably because the fallen KPD chief's impressions of the United States were generally positive. Nevertheless, SED leaders molded Thälmann's legacy to fit the circumstances in which they found themselves. As a result, the 1951 commemoration festivities placed special emphasis—even more than did earlier ceremonies—on Thälmann's "friendship" and admiration for the Soviet Union. Ernst Thälmann was now a vicarious cold warrior.

These themes can also be seen in a speech that Walter Ulbricht delivered to commemorate Thälmann's sixty-fifth birthday. The party chief's address was a long one—its text consumes two entire pages, in remarkably small print, of *Neues Deutschland*—and a few high points will have to suffice. Ernst Thälmann was "a fighter against imperialist war, [a] friend of all peace-loving people." This made him "the most loyal friend of the Soviet Union." In its most dire hour, Thälmann stood for the "national salvation of the German people." The Communist leader recognized that only a close alliance with Bolshevik Russia

Walter Ulbricht, Otto Grotewohl, and Wilhelm Pieck in the Ziegenhals, February 1953. Courtesy of the German Federal Archive.

could assure the desired outcome, the "unity of the German people," a cause for which the martyred KPD chief had fought so hard and ultimately given his life. In sharp contrast, Ulbricht insisted, stood the FRG chancellor Konrad Adenauer. Instead of fighting, like Thälmann, for the rights of good Germans, all of whom wanted to rebuild a united nation, "Adenauer is against the unity of the Germans. Adenauer is against the unity of the Germans because he is afraid that West German monopolists, who are supported by the American imperialists, could not count upon the excessive profits that they enjoy today." In short, a peace-loving, anti-imperialist, united nation meant a socialist Germany closely allied with the Soviet Union, a circumstance that Adenauer, the tool of "German monopolists" and "American imperialists," could not abide. The implication was clear—only by rejecting the forces of exploitation currently in control of the West and embracing the glorious legacy of Ernst Thälmann, including a close alliance with the Soviet Union, could the German people ever hope once again to secure their independence from the forces of Western imperialism.[61]

In keeping with the theme of struggling against the reemergence of fascism in order to create a united Germany under the banner of social-ism, *Neues Deutschland* published a poem penned by Erich Weinert, a leading figure in East German socialist realism. Entitled "In His Spirit: To the Memory of Ernst Thälmann on His Sixty-Fifth Birthday," this bit of socialist doggerel, like the speeches and ceremonies accompany-ing the celebration, sought to link Thälmann's legacy to the ongoing struggle to create a peaceful, antifascist, socialist Germany in the face of the country's division. Like other poems written about the fallen KPD chief, Weinert's verse emphasizes the importance of its subject's death, opening with the lines, "The executioners had taken him from us / But have not taken him from our hearts." Thälmann lived on, existing in the hearts of all good Germans and in the accomplishments of German socialism. "He knew that Germany would not cease to exist / If the proletariat stood together." Although Thälmann was physically dead, he lived on in the spirit of those who embraced his legacy.

> He fell in his struggle. But his dream is still alive.
> And out of that dream came reality.
> The party of the toilers, united, enduring,
> It lives on today and builds a new world.

In spite of its accomplishments, the SED, the embodiment of Thäl-mann's inheritance, had work to do. The bearers of his glorious legacy would struggle,

> In your spirit to stride . . .
> To the victory of the party,
> For one Germany, cleansed of parasites,
> For one Germany, peaceful, united and free![62]

Like the politicians participating in the numerous rituals marking Thälmann's sixty-fifth birthday, the poet strove to make memory of the martyred KPD chief a central component in the ongoing struggle to build a united Germany free from exploitation, fascism, and imperial-ism. Thälmann's legacy had endured and must continue to do so—for the sake of all Germans.

Two years later, once again at the height of cold war tensions, the SED celebrated another significant date in the life of the fallen KPD chief—the twentieth anniversary of his secret speech given to the KPD's Central Committee in the Ziegenhals in February 1933. This final address had permitted the Communist chief to present his views concerning the situation that Germany faced following the Nazi seizure of power. Twenty years later, on 7 February 1953, Walter Ulbricht visited the location of Thälmann's political swan song, where he dedicated a memorial and display marking the events of two decades earlier. Ulbricht's address commemorating the occasion was an attempt to link himself, his party, and the situation facing the GDR to the accomplishments of the fallen KPD chief. Not surprisingly, Ulbricht opened with a brief description of the event that had taken place at the location two decades previously: "Twenty years ago today, Ernst Thälmann, the leader of the German working class, the leader of the struggle for national and social liberation of working-class German people, spoke, for the last time, to a gathering of the Central Committee of the German Communist Party." Thälmann had correctly recognized that Germany faced a severe situation. Adolf Hitler had become chancellor, the KPD was under attack by the forces of fascism, and a disastrous imperialist war against the Soviet Union loomed on the horizon.[63]

Because Thälmann was a good Marxist–Leninist and a disciple of Joseph Stalin, the SED chief insisted, he clearly understood the situation created by Hitler's chancellorship, and Ulbricht quoted extensively from his predecessor's speech. Thälmann saw the situation from the perspective of an orthodox Marxist–Leninist. The bourgeoisie, in order to avoid the complete collapse of the capitalist system in the wake of the Great Depression, had brought the fascists to power. The Social Democrats—stubbornly refusing to recognize the reality of the situation—had actively participated in the effort to prevent the proletarian revolution that would have avoided this catastrophe. In an allusion to the situation confronting the German people in 1953, Ulbricht pointed out the most important lesson to be learned from 30 January 1933—that as long as capitalism existed, exploitation, imperialism, and fascism would be the natural state of affairs. "Fascism has its roots in capitalism, in its last stage." Linking his hero's approach to the Soviet Union's historic accomplishments, Ulbricht went on to explain how Thälmann had anticipated interpretations presented in *The History of the Communist Party of the Soviet Union*—an essential text for all good Stalinists—in that the KPD chief recognized the roots of the problem that fascism presented: "[T]he immense unemployment and increasing uncertainty of conditions of the propertyless classes, the dissatisfaction of the workers and peasants, had intensified the long delayed crisis of industry and the agricultural economy." In short, wherever capitalism existed, there was the imminent danger of fascism, and this was the case especially in the FRG. Hence, the people of Germany lived under the constant threat of the collapse of capitalism in the West, the resulting resurgence of fascism, and yet another cataclysmic European war. The implication was clear: all good Germans, like Ernst Thälmann before them, must struggle to create a united socialist Germany. Only then could Germany avoid a repetition of the catastrophe that had befallen it a mere twenty years earlier. Ernst Thälmann and the Weimar KPD had created the legacy upon which this new, cold war struggle against fascism could build and ultimately emerge victorious.[64] In his speech, Ulbricht succeeded—at least in his mind—in relating the lessons of the gallant antifascist struggle of the 1930s to the situation in 1953. If the SED and the East German people learned the proper lessons from the collapse of the prewar bourgeois state, they could accomplish great things. Ernst Thälmann, who had properly diagnosed Germany's problems in earlier, similar circumstances, must serve as a role model for all Germans. This lesson was the most vital component of his legacy.

As much importance as the SED leadership placed on commemorating Thälmann's sixty-fifth birthday and the twentieth anniversary of his speech in the Ziegenhals, the governing party of East Germany put even more effort into marking the tenth anniversary of his death in 1954. This important date witnessed what was hitherto the most extensive outpouring of Thälmann commemoration, with East German citizens observing the date in a wide variety of ways.

The SED leadership marked the decennary of Thälmann's death across the GDR, including the usual rallies and speeches by prominent party figures, many of whom had known the fallen KPD chief personally. Building on a major motif long since established, the front-page headline in *Neues Deutschland* read, "The German People Will Complete the Work of Ernst Thälmann." The accompanying story recounted the major commemoration events of the previous day, including a ceremony in the capital city's Ernst Thälmann Park for FDJ members, with Young Pioneers marching under the FDJ banner and carrying placards featuring Ernst Thälmann's visage (see chapter 6). Local party officials held an observance in Leipzig that was accompanied by the opening of an historical exhibition concerning the fallen KPD chief; and the Polish ambassador was among the "hundreds" who laid wreaths at the Memorial of the Socialists at Berlin's Friedrichsfelde Cemetery. Another article recounted the memorial service held in Buchenwald Concentration Camp—one of the most important sites to the Thälmann legend—

on the morning of 18 August (see chapter 5). The "high point" of the commemoration, however, was reserved for a "memorial assembly" held in East Berlin's Friedrichstadt-Palast Theater on the evening of 18 August. Rosa Thälmann was an honored guest at this ceremony, where "Comrade Hermann Matern," vice president of the GDR, "gave the memorial speech," reminding his listeners that "[w]e are building upon the foundations created by Ernst Thälmann."[65] Seemingly every important locale throughout the GDR witnessed some type of commemoration ritual on 18 August 1954. The SED leadership undoubtedly hoped to foster the impression that Germans throughout the country, from all walks of life, idolized German communism's most important martyr and strove daily to complete the work he had begun in his valiant struggle against German fascism.

Other articles appearing in the SED press sought to reinforce such sentiments. On 15 August, *Neues Deutschland* printed the reminiscences of Rudolf Wunderlich, who in March 1939 had occupied a cell next to Thälmann's in a Hannover jail. Wunderlich managed surreptitiously to spy the KPD chief while the latter was taking his daily walk, all alone in the prison yard. The eyewitness had seen the party leader before 1933 and noticed that, in spite of six years in a fascist prison, Thälmann was "pale but unbroken." Wunderlich wished to speak to his political hero, but "that might not be." Instead, he greeted the KPD chief silently, content with "the joy that he [Thälmann] was still alive." Indeed, even while interned in Sachsenhausen Concentration Camp, Wunderlich took comfort in the fact that "he [Thälmann] was still alive." When in August 1944 he heard that the Nazis had murdered his hero, his "thoughts involuntarily returned to this day in March 1939 in Hannover. But they also went forward, to the goal that the party had set," the defeat of fascism and the construction of a new Germany, one built upon the legacy of Ernst Thälmann. The martyred KPD chairman would "be a shining example" for all Germans.[66] In a similar vein, an 18 August article reminded readers that "Thälmann's work lives and is eternal."[67]

In addition to the usual speeches and mass rallies marking the tenth anniversary of Thälmann's death, the party leadership called upon the Marx-Engels-Lenin-Stalin Institute to create an exhibition, to be located at the organization's headquarters on Charlottenstraße, commemorating the fallen party chief's contributions to the history of the German workers' movement. The display would make use of materials— photographs, "books, newspapers, and documents"—and be located

Willy Colberg's *Ernst Thälmann in the Hamburg Uprising.* Courtesy of the German Historical Institute.

in the institute's two "lunch rooms [*Speiseräume*]." In light of the recent release of Kurt Maetzig's film *Ernst Thälmann—Son of His Class* (discussed in chapter 4), those who constructed the exhibition should view it as a companion to the film. "The exhibition would remain [in place for] eight to ten days and then turned over to the [institute's] archive."[68]

The first section of the exhibition, consisting of two tables and two display cases, dealt with the "World War and the October Revolution," the epoch-changing events that would have a decisive effect on the twentieth century. In addition, this first section would be concerned with "Thälmann's youth," his growing up as a member of Hamburg's working class, not to mention the events of October 1923, in which Thälmann played such a decisive role. The next large portion of the exhibition—four display tables and two cases—was concerned with the history of the international workers' movement from 1925 to 1930. Although this part of the display concentrated on events in Germany—including developments in the KPD's Central Committee and the exploitative nature of the Dawes Plan—it dedicated one entire table to the theme of "Thälmann's relationship to the Soviet Union" and another to the Sacco–Vanzetti case in the United States, ample evidence that the international proletariat had been under assault during those trying times. The third part of the display was concerned with the "world economic crisis" and the response of the bourgeoisie through the intensification of political violence against the workers. Thälmann, a prophet who had foreseen these developments, was the leading figure in the effort to improve living and working conditions for the German proletariat. The final section, consisting of four tables and two cabinets, opened with the "fascist seizure of power, the Reichstag fire," and the "imprisonment of Thälmann." Then the display turned to the "international struggle" to liberate Ernst Thälmann, an entire table displaying documents, brochures, photographs, and posters dedicated to the campaign. A third table in this section displayed artifacts concerning the KPD chief's eleven years in prison and the activities of the Thälmann Battalion in the Spanish Civil War. A fourth table consisted of a display concerning the murder of Ernst Thälmann, followed by two display cases, the second one containing items showing how Thälmann's legacy lived on in the GDR.[69]

The exhibition at the Marx-Engels-Lenin-Stalin Institute was typical of East German displays concerning Thälmann, such as the section concerning the fallen Communist leader at Buchenwald's camp museum (see chapter 5). It sought to place Thälmann's life and accomplishments in a broader historical context, as a central component of the proletariat's international struggle for social and economic justice. There was remarkably little in the exhibition about its subject's private life, which was of little importance to the message that the party wished to present. Even the portion of the display concerning Thälmann's youth concentrated on the development of his political consciousness. The Thälmann depicted in these displays was a one-dimensional figure, someone who lived entirely for things larger than himself—a worthy way of life, but one that the average viewer might very well find barren and uninspiring.

Nevertheless, throughout the first postwar decade, it was clear that a great deal of time, effort, and undoubtedly money went into these ceremonies, speeches, and exhibitions commemorating the life, accomplishments, and sacrificial death of Ernst Thälmann. The KPD and SED party leadership left no stone unturned in its efforts to propagate the mythology surrounding the memory of the fallen Communist leader. Party leaders used all of the media at their disposal in their effort to communicate their message to the people of the SBZ and GDR, never confining themselves entirely to making speeches and holding commemorative rallies.

Evidence of the KPD and SED's willingness to use every means at their disposal to propagate the Thälmann legend could be seen in any number of places. The martyred Communist's visage, for example, first appeared on a postage stamp printed in the SBZ in October 1945, just six months after the end of the war.[70] During the more than forty years of the GDR's existence, Thälmann stamps appeared practically every year, images of the Hamburg native printed on East German postage stamps right up to the collapse of the SED regime, with several striking examples released in 1986 to mark the fallen KPD chief's one hundredth birthday (see chapter 8). Images of Thälmann also appeared on

Halle's Ernst Thälmann Platz. Author's photograph.

coins, climaxing in one minted to mark the centennial of his birth. Posters and placards bearing such exhortations as "Fight like Thälmann!" appeared in public spaces throughout the SBZ and the GDR. Perhaps the most extreme example of this phenomenon—one is tempted to call it "Communist kitsch"—was the chocolates shaped like the statue of Ernst Thälmann on the Platz der 56.000 and dedicated in 1956, which consumers could purchase in stores located in Weimar. Further, East German bards wrote poetry and songs lionizing the fallen KPD chief.

Thälmann was also a popular subject in the highly politicized visual arts of the GDR—numerous etchings, statues, and oil paintings. Among the most striking of the oils depicting an episode from Thälmann's life was one painted by Willy Colberg, entitled *Ernst Thälmann in the Hamburg Uprising* (1953). Dominated by earth tones designed to reflect the subject's humble origins—like much of the Soviet art that undoubtedly influenced it—the painting shows the proletarian leader with a group of workers, planning to man the barricades. While Thälmann stands to the right, the worker whom he is addressing is at the center of the work. As always in Thälmann's life, the welfare of the proletariat comes first. There are several other workers standing around, listening to Thälmann plead his case in favor of the German October. In spite of the fact that Thälmann is not at the physical center of the piece, Colberg manages to draw special attention to the future KPD chief. Thälmann has taken off his signature hat, and the sun reflects off of his bald pate, thereby attracting the viewer's gaze. As historian Martin Schönfeld has pointed out, the work shows Thälmann to be "primus inter pares," the "first among equals." He does not merely give orders to his comrades but rather uses the powers of persuasion to lead the men along the proper path. Another oil, this one painted by Walter Eberling and first displayed in 1957—like Colberg's in East Berlin's Museum of German History—reflects similar themes. Eberling's *Ernst Thälmann Discusses the Agricultural Program with the Peasants* shows a scene from 1931, the height of the antifascist struggle. Once again, although he is off to one side in the picture, Thälmann is the central figure in the painting. He is shown addressing a group of peasants, seeking sternly but thoughtfully to convince the assembled farmers of the correctness of the KPD's platform on agriculture. The audience is deeply attentive to the KPD chief; indeed, one or two of those present appear to be spellbound by what he has to say. Colberg accentuated Ernst Thälmann's figure by showing the sun shining off the top of his head, but Eberling goes a step further, encircling the KPD chief's face in light, a motif reminiscent of the aureole so common in Christian art. Both artists portrayed Thälmann as a man of the people, eager to communicate his ideas to the common folk. He was also a man of action, a son of the common people, willing to do what was necessary for his righteous cause. Finally, both oils show Thälmann as an intelligent, thoughtful, compelling speaker, a true leader of the workers.[71] The fallen KPD chief from Hamburg would continue to be an important subject in East German art until the very end of the SED regime (see chapter 8).

Further evidence of the party leadership's willingness to use everything at its disposal to propagate the proper image of Ernst Thälmann can be seen in the naming of numerous awards, factories—a refrigerator plant is only one example—and schools after the martyred KPD chief. Computers built in the GDR bore Thälmann's name, and one would be hard-pressed to find an East German city or town without at least one Ernst Thälmann Straße, not to mention the multiplicity of urban squares dubbed "Ernst Thälmann Platz." The soccer stadium in Potsdam bore Thälmann's name, as did one of that city's major market squares. This tally does not even take into account the innumerable local Thälmann monuments constructed throughout the GDR, not only in larger cities such as Dresden, Weimar (see chapter 5), and Karl Marx Stadt, but seemingly in every village and hamlet, such as Meerane and, of course, Bautzen. There was a plethora of such construction around 1986, Thälmann's one hundredth birthday. Among the most interesting of these local monuments—and arguably the ugliest statue ever made—was the one dedicated in Halle in 1972. Consisting of three massive raised concrete fists, each giving the antifascist salute, the Halle monument is a truly monstrous example of all the shortcomings of socialist realism.[72] To call these memorials "local" is a bit misleading, however, because the party leadership in Berlin was intimately involved in the plans for their construction, the center always concerned that the Thälmann legend be communicated in the proper ways (see chapter 5). There were simply too many of these monuments, distributed throughout the GDR, for more than a small sample to be analyzed here, and the examples found in the following chapters will have to suffice. Given the tremendous resources that the SED leadership poured into remembering the KPD's most important martyr, it is remarkable how long one of the major goals of the East German party's efforts at Thälmann commemoration failed to come to fruition. Indeed, it would not be until 1986, almost forty years into the regime's existence, that Erich Honecker would finally dedicate a

Ruthild Hahne's half-size model for the proposed Ernst Thälmann National Monument. Courtesy of the German Federal Archive.

national Ernst Thälmann monument in East Berlin's Prenzlauer Berg (see chapter 8).

This is not to suggest, however, that the idea of constructing a central national shrine for Thälmann commemoration did not emerge until the final years of the GDR. Although other scholars have analyzed the SED's attempts to construct a national monument to the fallen Communist leader,[73] a brief account of the effort is necessary here for the sake of completeness. The plan to construct a national monument in East Berlin, the GDR capital, can be traced to the regime's infancy. On 3 December 1949, not even two months after the establishment of the new state, the SED central committee called upon German artists to submit their ideas for an Ernst Thälmann national monument. A committee of ten men, chaired by Otto Grotewohl and including party chief Walter Ulbricht, would choose the best proposal. Other members of the jury included art professors, sculptors, and Thälmann biographer Willy Bredel. The winning idea would receive a 20,000-mark prize, with smaller awards for second and third place.[74] The location of the proposed monument was indicative of the importance that the regime placed on this undertaking. It would stand in front of Adolf Hitler's former chancellery at a location previously named after the kaiser and later after the discredited German führer—the erstwhile Adolf Hitler Platz—renamed "Ernst Thälmann Platz" on the fifth anniversary of the martyred leader's death, 18 August 1949. Located on the corner of Wilhelmstraße and Möhrenstraße, the site represented the ultimate victory of German socialism over imperialism and fascism. Further, party leaders planned to construct a major east–west thoroughfare through the square, assuring that the maximum numbers of passers-by would view the statue.[75] In the future, Ernst Thälmann Platz would be surrounded by government buildings, symbolically linking the new regime with the fallen KPD chief's legacy. "A selection" of the artists' ideas would be on "public display" from 30 April to 21 May 1950, allowing citizens of the GDR to view what the jury considered to be the best of the proposals. The committee would announce its decision on 31 May, with groundbreaking to occur on 18 August 1950—an overly optimistic timeline, to put it mildly.[76]

The jury received 183 proposals altogether.[77] Sculptor Ruthild Hahne (1910–2001) won the commission. A member of a famous left-wing resistance group, the Red Orchestra, during the Third Reich, Hahne not only was an accomplished artist but also possessed impeccable ideological credentials, undoubtedly among the jury's considerations when it awarded her the commission.[78] Hahne's proposal, entitled *Die Freiheitskämpfer* (The Freedom Fighters), depicted Thälmann, his right fist raised in the antifascist salute, leading a group of determined workers and peasants on to a better future, a better Germany. Immediately behind Thälmann waved two flags, representative of the revolutionary élan of the German proletariat, the banners fluttering over the workers' heads. Hahne would lead an "artists collective" that would eventually turn her idea into a massive bronze statue—the completed monument would have been around four times life size—to stand at the center of Ernst Thälmann Platz, serving as a call to arms for all good socialists.[79]

In spite of the importance of the enterprise, circumstances conspired to delay the monument's construction. Indeed, over the course of thirteen years, Hahne and her team never got further than the casting of a half-size plaster model of the proposed bronze monument. There were a variety of reasons that Hahne's proposal never came to fruition. There was, for example, a severe shortage of building supplies in the GDR, a fact that delayed the rebuilding of Ernst Thälmann Platz, an undertaking that needed to be completed before the monument could be placed at the center of the square. Indeed, those overseeing the reconstruction of the site could not decide on the proper way to proceed. To add insult to injury, there was apparently dissension within the artists' collective over the question of whether the monument should emphasize vaguely defined "German" or "international" themes.[80] To make matters worse, not only did Hahne at one point suffer a broken leg, further delaying the project, but the building of the Berlin Wall beginning in 1961 had the effect of placing all other construction projects on the back burner. In spite of the lack of results, the effort proved remarkably expensive. By the end of 1956, the collective had cost the state 835,000 marks, and from the "beginning of the work through 31 December 1961"—more than a decade into the undertaking—the project had cost the GDR more than 1.7 million marks, and Hahne had only begun the process of casting a half-size model of the proposed bronze statue.[81] In 1965, almost fifteen years after Hahne had begun work in her studio, the SED, citing cost overruns and lack of significant progress, for all intents and purposes abandoned the project. Ruthild Hahne's *The Freedom Fighters* would never be completed, although a representation of her idea would appear on an East German coin marking Ernst Thälmann's one-hundredth birthday.[82] Indeed, it would be more than two decades before Erich Honecker would finally dedicate the Ernst Thälmann National Monument, constructed on an entirely different site and based on a concept hatched by Soviet artist Lew Kerbel (see chapter 8).

From the time that the leaders of the KPD—and later the SED—returned to German soil in the spring of 1945, they sought to inspire others to participate in their struggle against fascism, imperialism, and exploitation. The image of Ernst Thälmann, martyred in Buchenwald Concentration Camp in the fight against National Socialism, played an important role in this effort. At numerous rallies, in speeches, and in quasi-religious rituals, party leaders sought to link the legacy of the fallen Communist leader first to the KPD's goals and then to the SED's. In their effort, they used every medium at their disposal, including a colossal effort to construct a national monument in the German capital to their erstwhile leader. Although after fifteen long years the SED Politburo felt compelled to abandon this scheme—undoubtedly a bitter pill to swallow—party leaders could take comfort in the fact that they had discovered another medium in which they could commemorate the accomplishments of Ernst Thälmann on a grand scale. This new medium had the advantage of being portable, which meant that, unlike Ruthild Hahne's aborted bronze monument, East Germans did not have to come to the country's capital to absorb the lessons of Thälmann's legacy. This new medium was celluloid. In short, the party leadership chose to make an epic motion picture—indeed, two films—concerning the martyred KPD chief's life and legacy. These films would become the most striking and arguably most successful manifestation of the Thälmann myth produced in the four-decade-long history of the German Democratic Republic.

4

"A Great National Deed"

Thälmann's life was the topic of several East German feature films and television movies, the most important being director Kurt Maetzig's two epics *Ernst Thälmann—Sohn seiner Klasse* (Ernst Thälmann—Son of His Class, 1954) and *Ernst Thälmann—Führer seiner Klasse* (Ernst Thälmann—Leader of His Class, 1955). Both films played a vital role in establishing the parameters of the Thälmann myth and securing its place in the GDR's legitimizing narrative.[1]

East German cultural authorities inherited the traditions and institutions of Germany's famous pre–Second World War studio Universium-Film Aktiengesellschaft (Ufa). Established in 1917 to produce propaganda films during the Great War, Ufa became during the 1920s one of the world's most influential movie-making concerns. Widely respected for its artistic achievements, Ufa produced many landmark silent films that remain classics even today, including Fritz Lang's *Metropolis* (1927) and Robert Wiene's *The Cabinet of Dr. Caligari* (1920). The studio also made several important sound pictures, most famously Lang's *M* (1931) starring Peter Lorre, before the Nazi seizure of power. In National Socialist Germany, film was Joseph Goebbels's favorite medium. His propaganda ministry oversaw the production of numerous movies, such as *Jüd Süß* (Jew Süss, 1940) and *Ich klage an* (I Accuse, 1941), designed to justify Hitler's policies on the "Jewish Question" and euthanasia, respectively. Soviet cinema, however, was the most important influence on film making in the GDR. Russia's Bolsheviks made extensive use of film as a propaganda tool, even building portable cinemas that could be loaded on trains and transported to the most remote regions of Russia. In 1922, Lenin reminded A. V. Lunacharskii, chairman of the People's Commissariat of Enlightenment, "that for us the most important of all arts is the cinema." Hence, productions such as Sergei Eisenstein's *The Battleship Potemkin* (1925), which sought to legitimize the Bolshevik seizure of power, received top priority and generous budgets. The message of this and other Soviet films could be understood even by the most uneducated peasant, making film the most powerful propaganda tool at the regime's disposal. The Bolsheviks went to extensive lengths to produce and distribute motion pictures that justified their policies. As a product of a Marxist–Leninist German state, the GDR's film industry was naturally the heir of the earlier Weimar, National Socialist, and Soviet traditions.[2]

The Soviets began the reconstruction of the film industry in their sector of Eastern Germany with the establishment of Deutsche Film Aktiengesellschaft (DEFA) in 1946. Colonel Sergei Tulpanow, chief of propaganda for the Soviet Military Administration, granted DEFA its license in an elaborate ceremony on 17 May. He ordained the new organization to be part of the "struggle for the democratic reconstruction of Germany and the elimination of the remnants of Nazism and militarism from the consciousness of every German." DEFA, which took over the old Ufa studio in Babelsberg in 1947, would play a vital role in "[e]ducation . . . , especially of youth, in the ideas of true democracy and humanity." In other words, the Soviets gave DEFA a mandate to justify occupation policies as well as those of the German Communists. DEFA's staff consisted mostly of long-time Communists—such as production chief Alfred Lindemann, producer Adolf Fischer, and director Kurt Maetzig—with experience in the prewar German film industry. From the outset, it was clear that DEFA would play an important role in the political education of the German people, and under the guidance of Lindemann and his successors—Walter Janke (1948–1949), Sepp Schwab (1949–1952), and Hans Rodenberg (1952–1956)—film became an important component of the propaganda apparatus in the Soviet zone and later East Germany. During DEFA's early years, the studio, manifesting Ufa's traditions, produced a number of interesting films possessing a great deal of artistic merit. Among them were *Die Mörder sind unter uns* (The Murderers Are among Us) and *Ehe im Schatten* (Marriage in the Shadows), both released in 1946, as well as *Die Affäre Blum* (The Blum Affair) from 1948, each of which candidly confronted Germany's National Socialist past. During the early 1950s, however, the SED leadership began openly to criticize the "formalism" of many of DEFA's films, calling for the rejection of art for its own sake and the introduction of the principles of socialist realism, including the proletarian "positive hero" who could serve as an example for the masses. In light of this emerging agenda, it was logical that Ernst Thälmann should become the subject of two of the GDR's most elaborate feature films.[3]

Willi Bredel's biography *Ernst Thälmann: Ein Beitrag zu einem politischen Lebensbild* (discussed more fully in chapter 7), influenced the tenor of these films. Published in 1948, this brief book is highly hagiographic in tone, complete with portents accompanying Thälmann's birth. The proletarian leader, the product of the Hamburg workers' movement, grows to become the personification of the German working class. He is both a product and a molder of his milieu—the archetypal worker. This same style would characterize the two features *Ernst Thälmann—Sohn seiner Klasse* and *Ernst Thälmann—Führer seiner Klasse*.[4]

In a 1996 interview, director Kurt Maetzig recalled his experiences while making the films, providing an interesting example of the difficulties inherent in the creation of a Marxist–Leninist biographical film.

> I didn't know him [Thälmann] personally, and I felt it would be a difficult task, but I also thought it was an honor to make a film about a workers' politician who, unlike all of the other politicians, had alerted everyone to the danger of fascism. . . . He was a victim, a martyr killed by the Nazis, and so I thought it would be an honor to make a film about him. But after I had accepted I discovered very soon that they didn't want to make the sort of film I had in mind, a film of a worker who despite great difficulties finds his personal path in political life. The leaders of the GDR wanted something totally different. They had young people in mind who during the fascist period had not heard anything about Thälmann, except the worst possible things— that he was a criminal and so on. And so they wanted to build a kind of monument for these young people. Accordingly they put this sympathetic and simple man Thälmann on a pedestal and corrected the scenario all the time. They eliminated anything that was personal and not affirmative in the most obvious sense of the word; they wanted a film of an idealized person.[5]

Although it is easy to conclude that Maetzig's recollections were influenced by hindsight—he also confessed to being embarrassed by the films' propagandistic tone—the documentary evidence supports his account. Further, the director was not the only one of the features' creators to encounter a political elite determined to make films very different from what the filmmakers originally had in mind. The result was a spirited discussion among filmmakers and party officials concerning the films' direction. Hence, a careful examination of the creation of

Sohn seiner Klasse and *Führer seiner Klasse* provides interesting insight into the creative process, especially at a time when, as Maetzig put it, "[a] Stalinist cultural policy was applied to us."[6] In addition, because the importance of depicting Thälmann as a complex, three-dimensional person was often the central issue at stake, such an investigation not only provides an opportunity to analyze SED political mythology in more detail but also affords an invaluable avenue to understand better the politics of biography in the GDR.

As a first step in making the two features, in July 1949 the Politburo ordered DEFA to create a "Thälmann Collective" to oversee the early stages of production. Bredel was among those in attendance at the first meeting on Saturday, 8 October 1949. Others present included Michael Tschesno-Hell, who would coauthor the two scripts with Bredel; Rosa Thälmann, Ernst's widow, who would provide insight into her husband's personality; and various party functionaries and DEFA administrators. At this point, the goal was to make a single film, and, in accordance with the Politburo's order, the group set about planning to make a feature depicting the life of the slain Communist leader. It would be an "historically accurate . . . political and humanistic feature film" that would link the KPD's struggle against fascism with the "great peace movement" under way in the new Germany. Although all present recognized that the project had far-reaching political implications, the collective saw the film as primarily biographical in focus. Hence, a concerted effort would be made to accumulate as much information about Thälmann as possible. Many of the fallen KPD leader's comrades would be interviewed, with Bredel making a trip to Hamburg, which would also provide an opportunity for the screenwriter to visit some of the locations he would depict, further contributing to the historical accuracy of the screenplay, which Bredel would begin to write. The collective also decided to view Soviet films, including *Lenin in October* (1937) and *Lenin 1918* (1939), that could serve as models for the Thälmann project.[7] The Soviet film having the most influence upon the Thälmann project, however, was Milchail Chiaureli's *The Oath*, a 1946 feature emphasizing Joseph Stalin's role as Lenin's ideological heir.[8] Like Maetzig's Thälmann films would be, *The Oath* is highly episodic, depicting Stalin's role at important points in Soviet history, often falsifying events in order to create the proper political effect. As Peter Kenez has pointed out, Chiaureli's ultimate goal was the "deification" of the Soviet leader.[9] Although an ideological course that sanctified the martyred KPD leader was not the Thälmann Collective's goal, the party leadership, however, would insist on it.

The collective's second gathering on 15 October was concerned primarily with practical matters such as directors and actors, but the third meeting on 27 October turned to one of the most difficult problems to be confronted—the film's historical scope. All agreed that Thälmann's life was too eventful to be recorded in its entirety in a single motion picture. A "pure biographical" structure would have to be abandoned on practical grounds. This was not to suggest that the screenwriters foreswore efforts to portray their subject's humanity. Rather, the film's narrative, the collective members determined, should revolve around the KPD chief's interaction with small groups of people, circumstances in which the "radiance of Thälmann's personality" would win others to the cause of proletarian revolution.[10]

There were also important developments at the collective's fourth and final meeting. Tschesno-Hell agreed to coauthor the script, and the group further discussed the film's historical breadth, giving the screenwriters advice on plot line and developing the overall direction of the project. One suggestion would have had the film begin with the "crisis of 1930–1931" but concentrate on the November 1932 Berlin Transport Workers' strike, an event demonstrating the unity of the working class behind Thälmann's leadership. Otto Winzer, speaking on behalf of the Politburo, suggested the alternative that the film incorporate events from Thälmann's "youth and early years." He undoubtedly wanted to assure that the film appealed not only to the "old fighters" of the Weimar period, but also to GDR youth, who were so important to the new regime's future.[11]

With these somewhat ambiguous parameters in mind, Bredel and Tschesno-Hell set about writing a screenplay for a film to be entitled *Ein Sohn des Volkes* (A Son of the People). The authors originally planned to take Winzer's advice and begin with events from Thälmann's youth. The first "treatment" for the film, written in late 1949, begins in Jan Thälmann's "workers' tavern" in 1890 Hamburg, the four-year-old Ernst standing at his father's side. Numerous harbor workers reading socialist literature are present; it is an "illegal meeting of Social Democrats." The police burst into the room, and the workers stuff their outlawed newspapers and pamphlets down the young boy's pants. Ernst flees to his mother, who removes the papers from his trousers. "She praises her son and says, laughing, [that] now the cops have found nothing." Ernst has received his first lesson in proletarian politics. Thälmann's parents play a pivotal role in this early scenario, providing their son with an ideal proletarian upbringing. They love him dearly and seek to instill in him the proper class consciousness. Later, when the teenage Ernst, now employed as a seaman, returns to Hamburg after a stay of several months in the United States, "Mother Thälmann hugs and kisses her son and is beside herself with joy." Although this early treatment is hardly an accurate depiction of the future KPD chief's childhood, it does show Thälmann engaged not only in political activity such as a harbor strike, but also in the events of everyday life. He interacts with his parents, goes to work—in the harbor, at his father's delivery business, and at an industrial laundry—and even falls in love with his future wife, Rosa Koch.[12] At this point, Bredel and Tschesno-Hell sought to depict the proletarian leader as a three-dimensional character, a real person rather than merely a symbol. The proposed film clearly had political overtones, but its focus remained primarily biographical. But this scenario presented practical problems from the outset. If the authors began with their subject's childhood, as they planned, there would be too much material for a single feature. Tschesno-Hell would later recall that he and Bredel found themselves with enough material for three films, and so to open with Thälmann's youth was simply impractical.[13] In response to this problem, DEFA decided to make two films, *Sohn seines Volkes* and *Führer seines Volkes* (Leader of His People), the first beginning in the final months of the First World War and concluding in 1930. The second film would encompass the period from March 1932 to October 1949, concluding with the founding of the GDR. The sources do not record the reasons behind the abandoning of the original titles in favor of *Son of His Class* and *Leader of His Class,* but it is safe to say that political considerations probably inspired the change. The SED leadership— no one else would have made such an important decision—apparently chose to alter the films' ideological focus, decreasing the importance of relating Thälmann's humanity in favor of another type of film, one whose primary goal was no longer to represent the proletarian leader's life, but rather to re-create the entire history of the twentieth-century German workers' movement. As subsequent scenarios and versions of the screenplay show, telling the Communist leader's story became secondary to relating a SED-approved version of recent German history.

Under these circumstances, it is not surprising that Tschesno-Hell and Bredel faced other obstacles as well. Another problem was constant interference from members of the SED Politburo and other political figures concerning the screenplay's ideological direction. The

Politburo regularly discussed the progress of the project, and several of its members edited drafts of the screenplay for political and ideological content. In August 1951, for example, Ulbricht wrote a letter regarding the first draft of the screenplay to the members of the Politburo as well as the screenwriters. The SED chief insisted that Joseph Stalin did not play a large enough role in the proposed script. Thälmann must meet with the Soviet leader in Stalin's Moscow office, he insisted, and have a private talk with him. Further, Ulbricht recommended the addition of a scene "where Thälmann analyzes the general crisis in capitalism."[14] In the party leader's eyes, the film's ultimate purpose was to promote the GDR's legitimacy. Ulbricht's demands were also in line with changes in the SED's cultural policy. During the 1950s, many in the party leadership were increasingly critical of East German filmmakers, accusing them of "formalism," or creating art for art's sake. The party leadership demanded more socialist-realist films showing the inevitable victory of socialism and rendering "positive heroes" who could serve as role models for the masses.[15] The party sought to politicize film, introducing what Maetzig would call "a Stalinist cultural policy." Under these circumstances, it was not surprising that Ulbricht and other party leaders sought to create an icon whose every thought, word, and deed promoted proletarian revolution. The politics of biography had evolved, and Bredel and Tschesno-Hell's ideas would have to be revised in keeping with the new ideological climate.

Hermann Axen was among the DEFA officials most eager to implement the new SED directives concerning film policy. Commenting on a 1951 scenario for *Sohn Seiner Klasse*, Axen, a member of the DEFA Commission, reflected the party's dominant position: "The comrades on the commission are of the opinion that the scenario does not fulfill the primary goal of depicting comrade Thälmann as leader of the working class in the struggle for peace and democracy and as leader of the party that has instituted justice and is today rebuilding Germany."[16]

At a July 1952 DEFA Commission meeting, Axen maintained that the screenplay's "main shortcoming" lay "with the authors in the old primitive depiction of Thälmann," which failed to exhibit his "most important characteristics," including "proletarian class consciousness, grand revolutionary instinct, rapid [political] growth, [and] quick understanding of the teachings of Lenin and Stalin." In other words, Axen wanted to create a cinematic history of the twentieth-century German workers' movement, with a "positive hero" at its nexus.[17]

Axen was not alone in believing that more emphasis had to be placed on the historical context of the Communist leader's actions. Hermann Lauter, another member of the DEFA Commission, maintained that certain events were of such importance to the history of the German proletariat that they must be shown in the films, even if Thälmann did not participate in them. Lauter insisted, for example, that Russia's October Revolution and the founding of the KPD be depicted. After all, "the great historical importance of Thälmann is based on the fact that he properly comprehended [these] developments." Another commission member agreed, holding that the script's primary weakness lay in the fact that there was "no connection with the October Revolution and its influence on 1918 Germany."[18]

By this point, Bredel and Tschesno-Hell were willing to accommodate the party's demands. At a 13 March 1953 meeting of the State Committee for Film Issues, the successor organization to the DEFA Commission, Lauter gave his imprimatur to the revised script of *Sohn seiner Klasse.* "I have the impression," he affirmed, "that the comrade authors and Comrade Dr. Maetzig have carried out all essential recommendations, especially those of comrade Ulbricht." Lauter's conclusion did not make the screenplay immune to criticism, however, and at least one committee member believed that the authors had gone too far in their effort to accommodate the party leadership's demands. Sepp Schwab was highly critical of the script's opening scenes, those taking place during the First World War. In the screenplay, Thälmann, the leader of a small band of soldiers on the Western Front, receives word that German sailors in Kiel had revolted against the imperial government. Overjoyed at the news, the future KPD leader launches a successful rebellion against the officers of his own unit. Schwab pointed out that this scene was "historically inaccurate" because "in 1918 revolutionary soldiers' groups could only be found on the home front." And this scene was not the only falsification of the historical record in the work. Another scene showed future GDR president Wilhelm Pieck in Berlin, fighting alongside Rosa Luxemburg and Karl Liebknecht during the failed revolution of 9 November 1918. As Schwab pointed out, neither Luxemburg nor Pieck "were in Berlin at that time." Indeed, Schwab concluded, the first nineteen scenes of the screenplay were so full of historical fictions that they should be completely scrapped, and the action should open with the twentieth scene, which shows daily life in the Hamburg dockyards.[19]

Schwab's criticisms did not go unchallenged, however, and Hans Rodenberg, although conceding that the opening scenes were the script's "weakness," insisted that they must remain in order to provide the historical background needed to help the audience understand subsequent events. Tschesno-Hell, who along with Bredel attended the meeting as a "guest," defended the screenplay's version of developments on the Western Front even more doggedly. After all, he pointed out, one of the film's main goals was to show Thälmann "as soldier, then as a worker, then as leader. . . . War and peace are therefore important." The committee agreed that the scenes portraying the First World War should remain, but it chose to scrap the one showing Pieck, Liebknecht, and Luxemburg together on 9 November.[20]

In spite of these problems, the script of the first film, *Ernst Thälmann—Sohn seiner Klasse,* was finished by the end of 1952. It finally received official approval at a 20 December Politburo meeting and was published in book form—in anticipation of the premier of the film—about a year later. By now Wilhelm Pieck, president of the GDR, had decided that the film, which would be shot in 1953, would be among DEFA's first color productions. The appropriate equipment and technicians would have to be imported from Moscow, but the project's political importance justified this expense.[21]

The films would be the most expensive produced by DEFA up until that time, the second more costly than the first. *Führer seiner Klasse,* for example, cost more than 6 million marks to produce at a time when the average DEFA production cost slightly more than 2 million. Sets had to be constructed, and costumes for hundreds of actors had to be created from scratch. Granting the cast and crew of the films special training and privileges only added to the skyrocketing costs. For example, members of the production staff traveled to the Soviet Union twice, apparently for some type of technical instruction.[22] Karla Runkehl, the actress who portrayed Änne Harms, the most important female character in the films, received the services of a nanny, apparently at the expense of the Berlin city government, to care for her three-month-old child during the filming of *Führer seiner Klasse.*[23] In addition, the authors of the scripts received the princely sum of more than 57,000 marks for the first film, and the record amount of 96,500 marks for the second—at a time when the average screenwriter received around 37,500 marks for his or her work.[24] The films continued to cost the regime money even after their production was completed—the festivities surrounding the premier of the second film, for example, costing 94,560 marks.[25] Because filming in Hamburg was out of the question, and the appearance of historical accuracy was vital, a great deal of the studio's resources went to the construction of sets. For the first two months of the filming of *Sohn seiner Klasse,* for example, workmen constructed seven major sets, duplicates of sites in Hamburg and the surrounding region, including a city park, a street bordering a canal, and a small country train station.[26] DEFA officials also projected that for the first quarter of 1953 the makers of the first Thälmann film would require several hundred costumes for workers and soldiers, not to mention 70 police uniforms, and 50 sailors uniforms—and securing these resources was evidently a daunting task. The costume department produced only the requested 250 soldier and worker uniforms and the 70 police uniforms, making none of the sailors uniforms available on schedule.[27] At about this time, around 60 percent of the resources of DEFA's men's costume department as well as 30 percent of those of the women's costume department went into the production of clothing for the film. The Thälmann project had first priority for all of the studio's resources at a time when DEFA, like practically every other institution in the GDR, was short of funds.[28] Money was clearly no object when it came to such an ideologically important project.

A great deal of time and money also went into the effort to find a director and cast. Adolf Fischer would produce the film, but it was critical that a director be found who could make a picture meeting both the political and the aesthetic standards established by the party leadership.[29] In May 1952, this challenging assignment fell to Kurt Maetzig, who had already directed a number of highly regarded films for DEFA, including *Ehe im Schatten* (1947) and *Die Buntkarierten* (1949).[30] Finding an actor to portray Thälmann had been a major concern since the project had gotten under way in 1951, and in 1952 DEFA carried out a wide-ranging search for the man who would bring the martyred Communist leader to life. It was looking for an actor of "proletarian origins" from northern Germany, preferably Hamburg or Berlin.[31] DEFA's casting commission eventually bestowed the honor on Günther Simon, who had recently made his debut in *Das verurteilte Dorf* (The Condemned Town, 1952), a film about the effects of a US military base on a small West German town. Simon, unlike most of those who worked on the film, was not a longtime Communist but instead had served as a soldier during the war. There was also the problem of his age; born in 1925, Simon was younger than thirty, and many in the DEFA organization doubted if he could present a credible portrayal of a somewhat older Thälmann. Finally, Simon's bourgeois past also became an obstacle to his securing the role, and ideological considerations had to be overcome. Charlotte

Küter, an East German actress and director, even went so far as to write to Walter Ulbricht raising her concerns about Simon's ideological pedigree. Not only was Simon widely known for his bourgeois sympathies, Küter observed, but he had also been a member of the Hitler Youth—hardly the proper credentials for an actor portraying the greatest hero produced by the German proletariat.[32] The party leadership apparently took such criticism seriously, but in the end Simon's charisma ruled the day, and the casting commission awarded him the role. Simon repaid the casting commission's decision by pouring his heart and soul into the role. In order to prepare himself for the part, for example, he watched film clips of Thälmann speeches as well as "Soviet films about the lives of their great workers' leaders." The actor also read extensively the works of Thälmann, Lenin, and Stalin in order to understand the situation the German proletariat faced during Thälmann's lifetime.[33]

Now that DEFA had found the film's producer, its director, and, most important, its star, shooting could begin. Like those who had already been working on the film, the cast and crew who fashioned *Ernst Thälmann—Sohn seiner Klasse* concentrated on the project's political facets. Maetzig constantly urged his actors to think of themselves as a *Kollektiv* creating a socialist work of art. The spirit of Thälmann and his comrades, their cooperation in the face of a daunting task, supposedly influenced the actors and crew, and the creation of the film itself became a political act. That so many men and women could work together so effectively was only further proof that the GDR, the only country in which this film could be made, was—in Maetzig's mind—a manifestation of Thälmann's legacy.[34]

The first effort, *Sohn seiner Klasse,* premiered on 9 March 1954 in Berlin's Friedrichstadt-Palast. The 127-minute-long motion picture depicts the important events in Thälmann's life during the years 1918–1923, and although none of the major incidents represented in the film was entirely fabricated, the filmmakers clearly did take a great deal of dramatic license, embellishing incidents to make an ideological point.[35] The opening credits, which emphasize the number of National Prize winners who worked on the film, are presented with a red flag fluttering in the background, and this symbolic color of proletarian revolution visually dominates Maetzig's work. Seeking to substantiate its subject's revolutionary credentials from the opening scene, the film begins in the closing days of the Great War, when Thälmann leads a revolt of his comrades in the spirit of the Bolshevik Revolution, establishing from the outset the link between his activities and those of the great Russian leaders. The film ends with the famous Hamburg Uprising, in which Thälmann leads the city's workers in a revolt against the fascist leaders of the Weimar Republic.[36]

From start to finish, the film is laced with images designed to appeal to the allied concepts of *Vermächtnis* (legacy) and *Erbe* (inheritance). No opportunity is missed to relate the party's views on these topics, right down to the pictures on the walls. Photographs of Lenin, Liebknecht, and Luxemburg grace the walls of working-class homes and party offices, and those of Otto von Bismarck, that archenemy of socialism, decorate the rooms of the leaders of the Weimar Republic. Characters in the film read the works of Lenin, with Thälmann at one point diligently studying *State and Revolution*. Meanwhile, the troops who defend the detested Weimar Republic invariably have swastikas, the symbol of the fascist menace, on their helmets. The message is clear: the workers trace their heritage to the transcendent leaders of international socialism: Marx, Engels, Lenin, and Stalin. Theirs is the legacy of the epoch-changing October Revolution and its German progeny, whereas the heritage of the Weimar Republic, the state to which the hated Federal Republic traces its lineage, is that of reaction manifested as the oppression of the proletariat. Further, Americans are conspicuously present at several meetings of the republic's leaders. Once again, the point is clear: the leaders of the Weimar Republic, who had paved the way for Hitler's seizure of power, were the toadies of American capitalism, as were Konrad Adenauer and the leaders of Weimar's successor state. Thus, the film also reflects the SED interpretation of the origins of the cold war, which was well under way by the mid-1950s.

Although *Sohn seiner Klasse* is permeated with images rendering the concepts of *Vermächtnis* and *Erbe*, three points in the narrative stand out: the founding of the German Communist Party; Thälmann's trip to Moscow, where he meets Lenin and Stalin; and the re-creation of the Hamburger Uprising. The first, portraying the founding of the KPD, is quite brief, and Thälmann is not even present, but it had important implications for East German "historical propaganda." It takes place in the meeting hall of the KPD's founding assembly. Pictures of Marx, Engels, and Lenin adorn the walls, and those present are singing the "Internationale," while Wilhelm Pieck, the chairman of the meeting and one of the future leaders of the GDR, is standing at the head table, over which hangs a banner exclaiming "Es lebe der Gründungsparteitag der KPD" (Long live the founding assembly of the KPD). Next to him is Rosa Luxemburg. Karl Liebknecht is at the podium leading the song, after which he, Luxemburg, and Pieck descend into the crowd, where they are surrounded by supportive workers. After receiving congratulations on the founding of the new revolutionary party, Liebknecht warns the workers that although the day is a joyous one, they should not be overly optimistic: "Yes, comrades. But we stand at the beginning of the beginning. There is a world of enemies we must fight and a world of lost humanity to be won. They will be free people, happy people, peace-loving people!"[37]

Like their Soviet and National Socialist predecessors, the makers of East German propaganda films were rarely subtle, and the message of this scene is clear. The SED's ideological lineage and hence its legitimacy are firmly established. The pictures of Lenin, Marx, and Engels authenticate the link between the KPD, as personified in Liebknecht and Luxemburg, and the resplendent socialist past, as embodied in the October Revolution. The presence of Pieck, the future president of East Germany, completes the connection between past and present. Further, the viewer should surmise that the GDR faced the same perils as the KPD did in the early years of the Weimar Republic. Surrounded by hostile forces, the early Communists kept the faith and persevered. The message was eternal and applied as much to the situation in 1954 as to that in 1918.

Another important scene incorporating the motifs of *Erbe* and *Vermächtnis*—the re-creation of Thälmann's trip to Moscow in 1923, where he meets Lenin and Stalin—occurs about halfway through the film. Clara Zetkin, Walter Ulbricht, and Pieck accompany Thälmann on his visit to the Kremlin. Lenin, who is unintentionally portrayed comically by Peter Schorn, addresses his visitors' concerns about conditions in Germany, pointing out that the Versailles Treaty had made many "millions, among them the most civilized, into slaves." As Stalin enters the room, Lenin continues, extolling the KPD as the sole German political organization that had always opposed the "shameful treaty." The only possible solution to such problems is the creation of "Communist mass parties" in every nation, which must struggle to fashion "the dictatorship of the proletariat." Lenin then takes Thälmann by the arm and, drawing him aside as the others look on, asks him how he had "won so many tens of thousands of workers in such a short time." The German's response—"I have tried to learn from you, Comrade Lenin"—is typical of the film's political direction, once again firmly establishing the motifs of *Erbe* and *Vermächtnis*. As those assembled continue to discuss the political situation in Germany, the bell in the Spasskii Tower begins to toll the tune of the "Internationale." Thälmann and Lenin gaze out of the window as the bell rings out, "Wake up, damned of the earth," and Thälmann's gaze segues to Berlin, where thousands of workers are marching under red banners exclaiming, "For Work and Bread!" "Down with Cuno, Down with the Government of National Disgrace!" and "Oust Cuno on the Spree and Poincare in the Ruhr!" As always, even in the heart of workers' and peasants' paradise, the German leader's thoughts are with his people. If only the Germans could have the opportunity to accomplish all that the people of the Soviet Union had achieved.[38]

The scene's message is clear. The KPD leadership's journey to Moscow establishes the party's legitimacy by gaining the official approval of the leaders of the workers' movement in Soviet capital. Lenin and Stalin's blessing is given not only to the current party leadership, but also to the future leader of the GDR, Wilhelm Pieck. Indeed, Thälmann provides the link between the Soviet Union and the KPD, passing on this heritage to the SED in the persons of Pieck and Ulbricht. Further, Lenin is clearly more concerned with the welfare of the German people than were either the French occupying the Ruhr or the leaders of the Weimar Republic. Once again, the implication is clear: just as Lenin cared about the German people's well-being in difficult times, so, too, did Stalin and his successors. Indeed, the GDR and the Soviet Union were linked by the same feelings of socialist brotherhood that characterized the situation in 1923; the legacy continued.

The film's final scenes deal with the 1923 Hamburg Uprising and the events surrounding the arrest of one of the movie's main characters, the humble but devoted worker Fiete Jansen, who kills a particularly sinister army officer. Although the revolutionary attempt to overthrow the republic fails, the subsequent general strike designed to save Jansen from the gallows succeeds, and he is sentenced to seven years in prison. The final scene takes place in the dockyard, where "thousands of workers have assembled" to hear Thälmann speak. Thälmann begins by proclaiming: "Class comrades! Brothers and sisters! The solidarity of the workers of Germany has attained a great success!" "But what now?" a worker shouts out, and Thälmann answers him. The struggle is not over, but the workers have learned an important lesson: "The seizure of power by the proletariat does not happen all at once. . . . We can only obtain the victory of the proletariat after a series of many battles. This is now our task. We will have to put all of our strength into the effort if we are to reach this goal." The faces in the audience are resolute because

Thälmann has struck a chord. He continues: "Today we celebrate the anniversary of the Great October Socialist Revolution. Eventually the day will come on which our Germany is free and the red flag of victory will fly from the Brandenburg Gate!"[39]

Like Hamburg's workers, the people of the GDR had experienced much success, but extensive work needed to be done. The road ahead would be a difficult one, but as Thälmann had told Hamburg's dock workers, the ultimate goal makes the struggle worthwhile. If the people of East Germany can keep Thälmann's inspiring legacy in their hearts and minds, they will achieve their goal: the victory of socialism in all of Germany and eventually the world. All they must do is struggle in the same spirit as the workers of Hamburg. If, like Thälmann and his comrades, they refuse to relent, the victory will be theirs.

Although the message of *Sohn Seiner Klasse* is anything but subtle, DEFA refused to leave viewers to their own devices. The leaders of the GDR had simply invested too much money, time, and effort in the project to risk the possibility that moviegoers might miss the film's message, and the officially controlled media made a concerted effort to orchestrate audience response. In order to strengthen its polemical effect, all the resources at the state's disposal praised the film as a superb example of socialist cinematic art. Important figures, including Willi Bredel and Rosa Thälmann, were interviewed on the radio, urging their audiences to see *Sohn seiner Klasse*. Tens of thousands of placards of various sizes and designs promoting the film were printed and posted in train stations, outside government buildings, and in practically every other public place. One hundred thousand place cards—apparently to reserve seats for important audience members—for the theaters showing the film were printed as well.[40]

In a toast delivered at the premier party, Pieck praised the film as a message to "all peace-loving Germans, especially our youth, to struggle for peace, democracy, and socialism in the spirit of Thälmann," whose inheritance lived on in the film.[41] Moreover, a press packet (*Presseheft*), 50,000 of which were printed, issued in conjunction with the release of the film apprised journalists of the officially approved interpretation. DEFA distributed the packets to the film critics, party organizations, film clubs, and the Cultural Houses (*Kulturhäuser*) of the FDJ and Thälmann Pioneer organizations. The largest number, 11,000, went to schools "of all categories" throughout the GDR.[42] In addition, half a million programs, sixteen pages each, were printed for nonjournalists in the film's audience.[43] The *Presseheft* opens with a statement written by Pieck, pointing out that "[t]he contemplation of Ernst Thälmann is . . . for every decent German holy, his life and struggle a model for everyone." He was the prophet of a new faith: Marxism–Leninism. Pieck concludes, "This film will not only be for German workers, but also for peace-loving people of all countries, who honor and love Ernst Thälmann" and fight to fulfill his legacy.[44]

In light of this ringing endorsement by the GDR president, who had also been a close associate of the movie's subject, it is not surprising that the East German press praised the film to the skies. In an article appearing in the *Tägliche Rundschau* on 28 March 1954, Minister of Culture Johannes Becher presented his views on the film. All who had made the picture had accomplished "a great national deed in the interests of the preservation of peace and the reunification of Germany." *Sohn seiner Klasse* was, in Becher's words, "a masterful depiction of one of the most glorious chapters in the history of the German workers' movement."[45] Other reviewers heaped accolades upon the film as well. *Freie Welt*, lauding its aesthetic quality, reported that "the Thälmann film reaches the exacting [*anspruchsvolle*] level of the best Soviet revolutionary color films," and the *Berliner Zeitung* insisted that "no visitor will remain unmoved by the burning topicality of the film." The film's relevance to the current political climate was also the central theme of a review appearing in the 16 March 1954 edition of the *Tägliche Rundschau*, where Ludwig Turek pointed out the pertinence of the film in a climate similar to the one faced by Thälmann, one where "the same sinister forces" were at work, forces that would like "to destroy our people in a third bloody conflict." In addition to being universal in their praise of *Sohn seiner Klasse*, all of the reviewers agreed that they eagerly anticipated the upcoming release of the sequel, *Ernst Thälmann—Führer seiner Klasse.*[46]

Bredel and Tschesno-Hell began work on the second screenplay in the late summer of 1953. By now, they knew what the party leadership and DEFA officials expected, and the original treatment, completed on 8 September, remained largely unchanged as the authors developed it into a screenplay. The sole significant change involved reducing the film's scope by scrapping several scenes showing events in October 1929.[47]

The second film debuted on 7 October 1955 in the Berlin Volksbühne.[48] It dramatically opens in 1930, with Fiete Jansen's return from prison, next shifts to Thälmann's struggle against the specter of fascism in the closing years of the Weimar Republic, and concludes anachronis-

Günther Simon as an imprisoned Ernst Thälmann in Kurt Maetzig's film *Ernst Thälmann—Führer seiner Klasse* (Ernst Thälmann—Leader of His Class, 1955). Courtesy of the DEFA-Stiftung.

tically with the Red Army's defeat of the Wehrmacht and Thälmann's murder in 1944. As in the case of *Sohn seiner Klasse,* the leaders of the regime took an active interest in the film's political message, and *Führer seiner Klasse* is permeated from start to finish with images designed to link the socialist present with the antifascist past, with the closely connected concepts of *Vermächtnis* and *Erbe* present throughout. In keeping with this motif, the racism—especially the anti-Semitism—of National Socialism is downplayed, and the destruction of Marxism–Leninism at the behest of Germany's capitalists becomes Hitler's primary goal. For example, the Nazis consistently refer not to Jews, but to "Bolshevik subhumans" as their primary enemy. After all, and this was hardly a novel contention, if Nazism was, as any thinking person would agree, the ultimate force for political evil, its foremost aim must have been the annihilation of the movement representing the highest good: international communism. In keeping with this view, throughout the film the Nazis are consistently portrayed as being in league with the masters of big business. This relationship can be seen most effectively in a scene that depicts Thälmann delivering a speech in the Reichstag, where he is shouted down as much by the representatives of the pro-Weimar parties as by the Nazis. Hitler and the captains of industry are linked in other ways as well, and, according to the film, the Nazi leader became chancellor only because the tycoons dominating the Weimar Republic dreaded the prospect of a Communist takeover.[49]

An analysis of three scenes illustrates how the major themes of East German "historical propaganda" worked their way into the film and became the most important components of its message. One of the most interesting scenes appearing early in the film takes place in an Essen cemetery. Dozens of workers, victims of a mining accident, are being buried. The other miners stand by despondently in the rain as the bosses, dry under their umbrellas, hold a rather spiritless religious service in which they fruitlessly attempt to link the sacrifices of the fallen to the republic's supposed accomplishments. Thälmann, "who has arrived too late," works his way through the crowd, which out of respect makes way for the proletarian leader. The Essen KPD chief informs Thälmann that he has spoken on behalf of the KPD Central Committee, and Thälmann is pleased. But the workers are downcast; their comrades have died as the result of capitalist exploitation, and they face a difficult future with the threat of unemployment hanging over their heads. Those who keep their jobs will have to take a 12 percent cut in pay. By now, Thälmann has made it to the front of the assembly, and word spreads, "Thälmann is here." The workers and their wives gather around their leader, and the respect they have for him is palpable. As the workers tell Thälmann about their hardships, some in the crowd begin to chant "Strike! Strike!" while others wonder what they will do without their meager incomes. What will happen to their families? In response, Thälmann speaks of a Mansfeld mine where the workers have been striking for seven weeks. There, a wife of one of the workers told Thälmann: "I swore at the altar to be faithful to my husband, and I have stood by my word, also in the strike." Thälmann exhorts his audience, "Don't underestimate our strength! Don't underestimate our solidarity! One finger can be broken, but five fingers make a fist." An ultimately successful strike is launched.[50]

The themes developed in this scene were obvious to East German moviegoers. First, capitalists, in spite of their protestations to the contrary, do not care for their workers. When dozens die, conditions do not change, but rather the exploiters and their minions in the church simply perform some meaningless rituals devised to placate the workers, and things go on as before. But all it takes to change the world are leaders such as Ernst Thälmann, sprung from the proletariat and guided by the revolutionary principles of Marxism–Leninism. If workers unite under the guidance of a truly revolutionary party, they can bring the exploitative capitalist system to its knees. After all, they are many, and the capitalists are few. As Thälmann eloquently points out, a proletariat imbued with the revolutionary spirit cannot be defeated.

Of course, Thälmann did not come to power, but Adolf Hitler did. *Führer seiner Klasse* assigns the Nazi seizure of power not to the will of the German people but to a deal between the capitalists and the leaders of the Republic. As a result, Thälmann, along with thousands of other Communists, is arrested. Although he spends the next eleven years in prison, he remains undaunted. His bravery in the face of Nazi torture makes him a martyr and a hero, a symbol of the ruthless persecution of the working class that is characteristic of the Nazi years. Members of the working-class resistance unveil a fence painted with the words "Freedom for Thälmann," a sentiment shared by class-conscious workers the world over. Thälmann, clinging to his vision of a future socialist Germany, remains defiant, refusing all deals offered by the Nazi regime. When Germany invades the Soviet Union, the prisoner from Hamburg is pleased, for he knows that Hitler's days are numbered because "Stalin will break Hitler's neck." Because of his strength in the face of overwhelming odds, Thälmann becomes a symbol for the Red Army and the German Communist partisans fighting against the fascists. The Thälmann banner, a red flag with his likeness in the upper-left-hand corner, is flown by the Soviet tanks that turn back the Nazi onslaught. In one scene, in all likelihood fabricated, before a major battle Soviet tank troops kneel in the snow as one of them kisses the banner, and they go on to victory in the name of the German proletarian leader. The Soviets go on to take Berlin, and the final scene depicting the war shows the Reichstag burning.[51]

The scenes portraying the Second World War were vitally important to the development of the concepts of *Vermächtnis* and *Erbe*. An anachronistic rendering of events at the end of the war provides a clear example of how historical accuracy took a back seat to ideological considerations. In the film's narrative, the Nazis are defeated before Thälmann's death is depicted. This is done so that his martyrdom can be more effectively linked with the founding of the GDR. Although there are numerous historical inaccuracies in the film, all designed to increase its political effect, only one of the major events recorded is entirely fictitious.[52] At one point during his imprisonment, Thälmann is approached by Hermann Goering, who offers him his freedom in exchange for the KPD chief's cooperation in bringing the German proletariat to heel. While this scene, if anything, turns actual events on their head, it was important for the regime to establish that Thälmann surrendered his life willingly, further giving credence to the cause for which he died. In addition, the order of events is extensively readjusted for political purposes, and if one judges solely from the contents of *Führer seiner Klasse,* the Soviets were apparently the only people to stand up to Hitler and were alone responsible for the defeat of the Nazis. The Western Front is, once again for political reasons, ignored. Only the Soviets fought the Nazis, not to conquer Germany, but to liberate the German people from their wicked overlords. Indeed, their respect for the German working class—personified in the ever defiant Ernst Thälmann—is what drove the Soviets on to victory in the face of overwhelming odds. The Russians remained the only people truly interested in the welfare of the German proletariat, and the SED, united with the benevolent forces of the Soviet Union, inherited this legacy. Further, German Communists, who consistently recognized the danger posed by fascism, had fought side by side with the Red Army, playing a vital role in the liberation of the German people, which entitled them to govern the GDR. Meanwhile, those who had fought against Soviet liberation, who had actively supported Hitler's

expansionist foreign policy, governed the discredited Federal Republic, and their rule was illegitimate.

The film's final scene re-creates its subject's execution, an important event in the unfolding of the Thälmann myth. Thälmann and an
SS guard are moving through the corridor, and an officer turns to the
proletarian leader and asks, "You know, no doubt, what's coming?"
Thälmann answers, boldly as always, "Yes, a better Germany! A Germany without all of you!" As he proceeds down the corridor, some
of Thälmann's most moving words are repeated in voice over: "The
most precious thing that a human possesses is life. It is given to him
only once. And he should use it in such a way that he can say: I have
dedicated all my strength to the most honorable cause in the world,
the struggle for the liberation of humanity." As he proceeds down the
corridor, the Nazi guards in the background disappear, replaced by the
"victorious fluttering red flag." The "Thälmannlied" begins to play in
the background, and the chorus goes:

> Thälmann und Thälmann vor allen
> Deutschlands unsterblicher Sohn
> Thälmann ist niemals gefallen
> Stimme und Faust der Nation.

> Thälmann and Thälmann before everything
> Germany's eternal son
> Thälmann has never fallen
> Voice and fist of the nation.[53]

In this East German version of what historian Jay W. Baird has
called the "myth of resurrection and return," Thälmann's death is a
sacrificial one, for he dies in order to secure the victory of socialism and
the defeat of fascism, the coming of a "Germany without all of you."
Giving his life, "the most precious thing that a human possesses," he
has made the ultimate sacrifice for the cause, and any cause worth dying for is one worth fighting for. Death under such circumstances is not
annihilation, but the fulfillment of an historic mission, and the legacy
of martyrs such as Thälmann lives on not only in film, but also in the
incarnation of the GDR and its governing Socialist Unity Party.[54]

Once again, in spite of the blatant messages incorporated into *Führer seiner Klasse*, DEFA and the SED left nothing to chance when it came
to the proper interpretation of the film, and DEFA issued a *Presseheft*

designed to inform reviewers of the movie's significance. Reviews of the film uniformly praised it as a significant contribution to the development of socialism in the GDR.[55] In addition, the regime went to extensive lengths to assure that the message of both films reached as wide an audience as possible, staging elaborate—and expensive— premiers in each of East Germany's major cities, where members of the cast and crew were the guests of honor.[56] People who had helped make the films or knew the fallen KPD leader personally, such as his wife, Rosa, made speeches at the premiers. Rosa was especially interested in promoting the films to the GDR's youth, pointing out that "in this film [*Führer seiner Klasse*] we experience the history and struggle of the German working class as well as the life of Ernst Thälmann," who was an "example for youth."[57] Detailed attendance records were kept, indicating not only the number of viewers, but also the number of screenings of the pictures as well as the percentage of seats occupied at each performance.[58] The regime established quotas concerning the number of viewers of each film that it wanted, every region in the GDR being assigned a minimum total audience for the first year after each picture's release. The SED leadership, for example, hoped that 8 million viewers would see *Sohn seiner Klasse* by March 1955. DEFA failed to meet its quota, however, with only 6.7 million attending the first film within a year of its premiere, causing the studio to stress its goals even more strongly for the second film. Even so, this figure was an impressive accomplishment; not taking into account repeat viewers, it represented close to half of the GDR's population. In order to emphasize the importance of Maetzig's films, everyone who saw them, at least during their original runs, had to pay an admission price. On party orders, no one was to attend them for free.[59] In addition to those who paid to see the two movies in theaters during the 1950s, millions more viewed them in schools as well as at FDJ and party meetings over the next thirty-five years. Maetzig's epics became the two most widely seen DEFA movies.[60] They were dubbed into Russian and Czech and shown at numerous film festivals, with *Führer seiner Klasse* winning a major prize in Czechoslovakia. Further evidence, at least according to the regime, of the films' global influence could be seen at "international discussions" of the pictures, such as the one held by Berlin's Club for Filmmakers at the end of March 1954. An account of the meeting written by the Hungarian journalist Miklos Gimes emphasized the participation of filmmakers from Poland, Czechoslovakia, Holland, France, Romania, Hungary, West Germany, and West Berlin. The Germany depicted in

Sohn seiner Klasse was, Gimes concluded, "the inheritance [*Erbe*] of Germany's cultural treasures, the inheritance of all progressive aspirations of German history."[61]

The SED also sponsored meetings at which workers and intellectuals were asked if they understood the films' message, and they apparently did. One young woman reported, "I have seen the film [*Sohn seiner Klasse*] twice—and I want to be just like Änne," Fiete Jansen's love interest and a brave worker's wife who places her life—and virtue—in jeopardy in order to deliver a message to Leipzig. A student in Halle insisted that "[t]he special thing about the Thälmann film is that it shows us German men, heroic fighters from the German working class, who remained unbroken in the face of setbacks and can serve as our models." Another worker also recognized the implicit link between past and present, stating, "Today we fight in our workplace, I, for example, at my lathe."[62] Although it is clear that viewers grasped the meaning of Maetzig's epics, the sincerity of such observations is open to question. Whether the audiences believed the interpretation of historical events presented in the film is simply impossible to determine. It was, however, important to the party leadership that moviegoers voice their approval, and they did.

This is not to suggest that no one dared criticize several components of *Sohn seiner Klasse* and *Führer seiner Klasse,* and as the discussions surrounding the screenplay of the first film show, even the Stalinization of the film industry did not bring about the complete end of debate. Indeed, there was some surprisingly open disagreement concerning the two films among the GDR's cultural elite. Interestingly, much of this debate surrounded one of the central issues that confronted the makers of the two films—how to resolve the tension between the individual's role in events and the forces of history. In other words, how much should the films focus on Thälmann's life and how much on the history of the German working classes? As a 1955 meeting of the Club for Filmmakers—an organization created to encourage discussion of issues concerning film among the country's leading cinematic figures—shows, these questions remained contentious.

Führer seiner Klasse was the subject of a Club for Filmmakers' gathering held in East Berlin's Academy of Sciences on 17 November, but the participants repeatedly referred to the first feature as well, generally agreeing that it was inferior to the second. Those taking part in the meeting included critics and filmmakers from the GDR and other, mostly Eastern European, nations. Among those attending were

Maetzig and Tschesno-Hell (Bredel was ill), who spoke on behalf of the films' creators. Although all present praised the epics for their contribution to the construction of socialism, some participants criticized important components of the films' narratives. Several, for example, questioned the historical accuracy of specific scenes, the way Thälmann's personality was portrayed, and the narrative structure of the last third of *Führer seiner Klasse,* all of which led to a lively discussion concerning the politics of biography in the GDR and the role of "truth" in socialist cinema.[63]

Among the scenes criticized for their lack of historical accuracy were those in *Sohn seiner Klasse* re-creating the 1923 Hamburg revolt. The film assigns the failure of the uprising to the machinations of Thälmann's rivals in the party, who supposedly refused to send the insurgents in Hamburg the weapons that they needed. In reality, as more than one participant pointed out, the German army had used force to stop the planned shipment of weapons to Hamburg, and the failure of the revolt was not the product of sectarianism within the KPD. In addition, a Western critic, Klaus Norbert Schäffer from Hamburg, took the second film to task for ignoring the fact that "the Social Democrats [had] fought together with the Communists, and not only the Communists, but also the Christians and who knows how many other people." Further, Schäffer pointed out, scenes in the film showing daily life in "Buchenwald and other concentration camps" failed to portray the solidarity that developed between Communist and non-Communist prisoners. Also, *Führer seiner Klasse* neglected to show that Thälmann was incarcerated in three different prisons, all of the jail scenes being shot on the same set. Finally, Schäffer and several other participants were quite critical of the last third of the sequel, which turned completely away from Thälmann's experiences in order to concentrate on the Soviet invasion of Nazi Germany. These final scenes, they insisted, were incongruous with the rest of the project because they ignored the film's subject, the KPD's antifascist resistance.

Tschesno-Hell responded by maintaining that these inaccuracies were inconsequential when compared with the "great truths" elucidated in the films. "What you say is not entirely correct," he argued, "there are great truths and minor truths. In art, it is absolutely legitimate to permit the great truths to have precedence. And the great artistic truth is always in agreement with reality." In other words, the "great truth" of the antifascist myth was more important than "minor" inaccuracies introduced in order to make that myth come alive. Faithfulness to historical events had been abandoned in order to foster much more important political truths: that Ernst Thälmann "under the most difficult circumstances" had led the KPD, the only German political movement to challenge Hitler fascism in a significant way; that Thälmann was an "example to millions"; and that the Communist movement was the only political force that "the Nazis feared." Finally, the detailed depiction of the Soviet invasion, the screenwriter asserted, assured *Führer seiner Klasse*'s historical accuracy. The undeniable fact was that, in spite of Thälmann's and the KPD's efforts, the German people had not liberated themselves from fascism, and the GDR was free only because of the Red Army's glorious accomplishments. Tschesno-Hell concluded that the film had to relate this fact in the name of a "greater truth."

Another criticism raised at the meeting held that the films portrayed Thälmann as a "cardboard hero" devoid of any personality. Several of those present responded to this charge. A Bulgarian journalist, for example, pointed out that "Thälmann's personal life is the life of the German working classes." Another participant, Peter Edel, echoed his contention, stating that "Thälmann really had no personal life; it was the life of the German working class." In other words, he lived his life imbued with revolution, his every thought and action for the benefit of the proletariat. All of those refuting the contention that the films portrayed their central character as soulless and void of emotion pointed to the same brief scene, the one showing the imprisoned Thälmann crying in response to the execution of one of his closest comrades.

It is interesting that all three responses cited the same short scene in their argument. Ironically, the fact that three people could provide only a single counterexample ultimately supports the contention that the films portray Thälmann as a "cardboard hero." In order to make him representative of the entire working class, an example for everyone, the screenwriters, director, and actor had to abandon any effort to depict his distinct characteristics. The Thälmann of Maetzig's films is not a human being, but a symbol of "one of the most glorious chapters in the history of the German workers' movement." As Tschesno-Hell put it, "The Thälmann film is therefore a historical-biographical film. The historical events are depicted not in order to illustrate the development of Thälmann, but rather the opposite: Thälmann's development is representative of . . . historical events."[64]

The KPD leader had become, in the hands of East German filmmakers, an icon linking the glorious past with the socialist present and the promise of a better tomorrow. The final scene of *Führer seiner Klasse* re-creates Thälmann's fate at the hands of Nazi thugs, but it does not show his death. Rather, Thälmann marches on, red flag in the background, into the glorious socialist future. Speaking at the November 1955 meeting of the Club for Filmmakers, Tschesno-Hell explained why the film does not conclude with the KPD leader's death: "He was certainly murdered! How should one show that[?] Would it be best to end the film with the massacre, with the murder? That just would not work. . . . We did not want to show it that way. We wanted the great truth, the great truth that lies in the first part [*Sohn seiner Klasse*] and with Thälmann in the second part. Thälmann's function and struggle [today]. And in the German Democratic Republic there are thousands of Thälmanns. Who function and struggle. That is historical unity and that is artistic unity." He was not dead, but rather Thälmann's legacy lived on in the accomplishments of the German Democratic Republic.

The Thälmann portrayed in Maetzig's two features is a far cry from the original intention of filmmakers who, as the director put it, sought to create "a film of a worker who despite great difficulties finds his personal path in political life." Early treatments and scenarios for *Sohn seiner Klasse* sought to depict Thälmann in precisely this fashion, as a three-dimensional individual, not only with strengths to be exploited, but also with weaknesses to be overcome. In short, Maetzig, Bredel, and Tschesno-Hell sought to create a film biography in which a mortal human being overcomes overwhelming odds to emerge as the leader of the German working class. DEFA and party officials wanted a very different sort of film, however. As a result, none of the anecdotes collected from those who knew Thälmann worked their way into the films. Further, Rosa, the martyred Communist leader's widow, the person who knew him best, ultimately had little influence on the composition of the films. Following the fourth and final meeting of the Thälmann Collective at the end of 1949, she disappears from the documentary record concerning the films, participating in none of the committee meetings at which scenarios and scripts were discussed. Rosa reemerged only after the features were completed, serving as an active participant in efforts to encourage the East German people to view the films.[65] Hence, it is not surprising that Thälmann's uniqueness, his childhood experiences, his personal development, and his innermost thoughts are absent from the films. Party and DEFA officials had rejected everything that was "not affirmative in the most obvious sense of the word," that did not portray an "idealized person," as Maetzig puts in the quotation at the beginning of the chapter. Many DEFA and SED officials were willing to go to extensive lengths to create their ideal proletarian leader, even to falsifying events in the name of a "greater truth." The Thälmann of *Sohn seiner Klasse* and *Führer seiner Klasse* is a far cry from Bredel and Tschesno-Hell's original vision, which began with a four-year-old boy with socialist literature hidden in his trousers. It is impossible to imagine the Thälmann of Maetzig's epics getting hugged by his mother or falling in love; rather, his personal existence revolved around "the life of the German working class."

Perhaps the best way to understand the films is as secular hagiography, which becomes abundantly clear when one looks at the general characteristics of Christian sainthood. Historian Richard Kieckhefer has demarcated at least seven characteristics of sainthood: the saint lives an ascetic lifestyle; he or she is contemplative; this contemplation always leads to action; the saint's authority is based on that of a superior "founder and prophet" (e.g., Christ); he or she experiences visions; miracles are associated with sainthood; finally, sainthood is often associated with martyrdom.[66] In *Sohn seiner Klasse* and *Führer seiner Klasse*, Thälmann exhibits every one of these characteristics to some degree.

Although the Communist leader did not take a vow of celibacy, the films do portray him as leading something of an ascetic life. He and his family live humbly in a simple working-class apartment, first in Hamburg and then in Berlin. As a good Communist, Thälmann eschews possessions; rather, he is interested in the ideals of Marxism–Leninism, his religion. He is shown on several occasions thoughtfully reading the works of Marx, Engels, and Lenin, much as a saint might be presented as reading the Bible or another holy book. Further, like a saint, Thälmann's reading leads to action, first in a Hamburg dock strike, and finally in his struggle against Hitler fascism. He takes these actions, not on his own authority, but rather on that of a "founder and prophet." In this case, the role of prophet is filled by three men—Marx, Lenin, and Stalin. Although the East German state's materialist outlook precluded associating the supernatural with Thälmann, he does experience visions and is linked with miracles of a sort. His visions are of a future socialist Germany, "a better Germany! A Germany without all of you!" Once again, as in the saint's case, these visions do not originate with Thälmann, but with the founders and prophets, Marx, Lenin, and Stalin, thus bestowing upon Thälmann's visions a powerful origin in a higher authority. Many of the same things can be said regarding the "miracle" associated with the Communist leader: the glorious Red Army's victory over fascism in the face of overwhelming odds. Although he is not directly responsible for the Soviet Union's victory, he does foresee it—"Stalin will break Hitler's neck"—and tells others. Finally, Thälmann voluntarily suffers a martyr's death at the hands of his class enemies, those who actively oppose the truth.

These hagiographic motifs are incorporated into the films for at least three reasons. First, they are an unavoidable component of Western heroic mythology—all hero cults exhibit at least some of them, and many scholars have pointed out the parallels between Christian hagiography and socialist realism. Although these themes had taken on an undeniably Christian tone by the fall of the Roman Empire, many of them predate Christianity. Second, these images, such important components of Western culture, were familiar to the audience.[67] One did not have to be Marxist–Leninist to understand the films' message. The lessons are universal. Further, these motifs served to make Thälmann's cause holy, beyond reproach. He is continually described with such words as *holy* and *glorious,* transcendent characteristics he bestowed upon his cause. Marxism–Leninism became as much a religion as a political and economic philosophy. Its adherents, the party leadership insisted, should cling to it, even in the face of the FRG's short-term success.

The support of the people—including non-Communists—was important to the SED. The leadership hoped to inculcate its people with socialist values, an effort made all the more important by the recent experience of fascism. *Ernst Thälmann—Sohn seiner Klasse* and *Ernst Thälmann—Führer seiner Klasse* sought to promote this goal. They promised the people of the GDR a better future in the transcendent legacy *(Vermächtnis)* of an antifascist saint, Ernst Thälmann. The present or "real, existing socialism" might present its problems, but the future was much brighter. Just as in Christianity the saints promised a better hereafter in the next life, the SED guaranteed a glorious socialist future in the tradition of Thälmann—one need only persevere and have faith.

Although combining the antifascism myth with the themes of Christian hagiography had numerous advantages, it also caused problems. As Susan Buck-Morss has pointed out, both industrial capitalism and Marxism–Leninism promised a future characterized by material abundance.[68] Hence, over time the philosophical distinctions between the two systems lost their resonance and, as a result, their ideological fervor. The incorporation of these familiar religious themes, a long-standing tradition in international communism, into an avowedly antireligious East German political culture might well have contributed to the reduction in ideological ardor that the people of the GDR exhibited during the last decades of SED rule.[69] Marxism–Leninism became just another ideology, just another failed political religion whose prophets did not deliver on their promises. Kurt Maetzig's two Thälmann epics may have forestalled but ultimately could not arrest the failure of the GDR's secular religion.

Yet these films—especially in light of the regime's failure to create a national Thälmann monument in the East German capital—were nevertheless the most important manifestations of the Thälmann legend created during the 1950s. In some ways, they were superior to the massive bronze colossus planned for the former Kaiser Wilhelm Platz. Films are highly portable, which assured that millions of East Germans could view them throughout the entire country, and they can relate a message and maintain the attention of an audience far longer than any lifeless monument. The apparent success of *Sohn seiner Klasse* and *Führer seiner Klasse*, however, as plans for the former Buchenwald Concentration Camp demonstrated, did not dissuade the party leadership from memorializing the fallen Communist leader in stone.

5

"Out of Your Sacrificial Death Grows Our Socialist Deed"

If the GDR's state-controlled antifascist religion had a central shrine, it was Buchenwald Concentration Camp. The camp, located on the heights of the Ettersberg overlooking Weimar, a city known as the "Athens of Germany," has a complex history, and the site was historically important long before the construction of the camp. The beech groves covering the 1,578-foot-high hilltop were famous for their association with the German-speaking world's most celebrated cultural figure, Johann Wolfgang Goethe. Not only had some of his plays been performed on this site, but the Ettersberg was also the location of Goethe's Oak, under which the eminent writer sat, thought, and composed poetry. It was also among the places where the great man conducted his famous liaison with Charlotte von Stein.[1] SS chief Heinrich Himmler chose this locale so closely associated with "Germanness" to construct one of the Third Reich's most infamous concentration camps.

The history of the camp at Buchenwald was particularly well suited to play a role in the cultivation of the antifascism myth. The SS established the Ettersberg Concentration Camp—which nine days later became known as Buchenwald—on 19 July 1937. Originally holding only 149 male prisoners—52 of them "politicals," many young Communists—transferred from Sachsenhausen, the new camp would serve as part of a regional system of internment sites distributed throughout the Reich. As a post–Second World War report produced by the US Army's Psychological Warfare Division pointed out, "The selection of the site was symbolic in a higher sense: Weimar is the German national cultural monument, formerly the city of the German classicists [Goethe, Friedrich Schiller, and others], who through their works gave German emotional and intellectual life its highest expression. Buchenwald . . . is a monument to the new German sensibilities. Thus a new set of connections was created: the sentimentally preserved museum culture of Weimar versus the uninhibited brutal desire for power of Buchenwald."[2] In order further to emphasize the symbolic link between the Third Reich and German neoclassicism, Goethe's famous oak was within the perimeter of the camp's electrified fence. Not far from the square where the prisoners assembled twice a day in order to be counted, this famous symbol served as a constant reminder of the superiority of German *Kultur*.

In spite of its modest beginnings, Buchenwald became a central component of the Third Reich's system of terror. Although only 2,912 prisoners were admitted to the camp during 1937, 48 of whom died, by the end of the war more than 239,000 people had been held there at one time or another, approximately 56,000 of whom perished at the site.[3] With the start of the Second World War, the composition of the camp population became increasingly diverse, as thousands of the regime's opponents, including prisoners of war (POWs), began to arrive from all over occupied Europe. The attributes of those imprisoned and murdered at the location made it particularly well-suited for incorporation into the antifascism myth. Like the other major camps on German soil, the SS constructed Buchenwald for the "reeducation" of the regime's political opponents. Although the Nazis never introduced any type of reeducation or political indoctrination to Buchenwald, a significant portion of the prisoners, who numbered around 17,000 in 1943 (when significant numbers of French prisoners, many of them Communists, arrived), were detained for political reasons. As opponents of National Socialism, they lived under horrific conditions, characterized by what the US Army described as "crowded quarters, cold, hunger, slave labor, and constant fear." The SS worked inmates to death in the camp's most important "employer," a nearby stone quarry, where thousands met their fate as a result of "blows from stones, caning, 'accidents,' deliberate pushes over the precipice, shooting, and every other type of torment." Many more died of starvation, disease, and overwork, the result of performing other types of backbreaking labor under the direction of the guards, and others were simply shot, often for the most minor infractions. Finally, some of the inmates died as the result of "medical" experiments during which Nazi physicians injected them with deadly bacteria and viruses or of being "inoculated" against disease by means of concoctions that were often more dangerous than the ailments that they were supposed to prevent.[4] Although thousands of Jews passed through the camp, most of them were held only temporarily, until they could be transferred to another location for the "special treatment" that the regime reserved especially for them. The Jewish inmates were segregated from the rest of the prisoners in a separate compound and, as a result, played no significant role in the camp's very active antifascist resistance movement, nor would they have an important place in the SED's postwar cult of remembrance centered around the camp.[5]

Setting aside the common criminals and POWs held at Buchenwald, the largest group of camp inmates consisted of Communists and Social Democrats. It was these leftist groups, longtime opponents of National Socialism, who organized the most effective resistance movement. Members of the KPD had a particular advantage when it came to creating and maintaining an opposition group because they had long been closely and secretly organized. The emphasis that the party placed on unquestioning obedience also worked to the advantage of the Communist resistance. The KPD simply transferred practices developed in the outside world, such as co-opting sympathetic non-Communists to its cause, and adapted them to camp conditions. In July 1943, for example, the KPD created the International Illegal Camp Committee, which was designed to bring non-Communists under the control of the party apparatus. As a result of the committee's tenacity, the party dominated antifascist activity in Buchenwald. Preserving the lives of Communists and fellow travelers as well as the political integrity of the resistance became the two most important functions of Buchenwald's KPD-led opposition group. Enforcing group discipline often proved to be a brutal enterprise as the "rats" who informed to the guards and those who had contact with these traitors—even unwittingly—suffered persecution, at times escalating to murder, at the hands of the resistance. Connections with the KPD underground outside of the camp helped facilitate resistance activity. Other political groups, unwilling to join the Communist-dominated Illegal Camp Committee, were not as well organized and as a result less effective.[6]

Although overt opposition to camp authorities was impossible until the final days of the war, the politically active inmates found numerous ways to resist their captors. The most obvious way to oppose the SS guards was to stay alive in the face of the horrific conditions that the prisoners encountered. But there were other, more overt forms of resistance, and over time the secret underground gained increased control over daily life. The inmates outnumbered the few dozen guards by a wide margin, and the resistance reached an accommodation with the guards, coming to control many of the camp's most important institutions, such as the laundry, kitchen, and even the camp police force created from among the inmates. Using the corruption endemic to the concentration camp system to its advantage, the resistance often bribed guards in order to secure food, clothing, or special privileges, such as a relatively easy job in the kitchen or laundry instead of a highly lethal assignment working in the quarry. Yet another form of resistance resided in the occasional antifascist ceremony, celebration or commemoration. Consisting of the reading of an antifascist text—the poems of Heinrich Heine or Georg Büchner's *Danton's Death*, for example—the marking of an important date on the Soviet political calendar, or the commemoration of a prominent victim of the Nazis—such as the famous September 1944 ceremony memorializing the recently murdered Ernst Thälmann—these rites promoted political solidarity under the banner of the international antifascist movement. Commemorative rituals also allowed participants to remember fallen comrades and served as a reminder of what was at stake in the struggle against Hitler fascism. Finally, these ceremonies were acts of resistance, if for no other reason than the fact that they were forbidden.[7]

The final and most significant act of antifascist resistance occurring in Buchenwald took place in the closing days of the Second World War. As it became clear that Germany was going to suffer a catastrophic defeat, Buchenwald's inmates became increasingly concerned about the possible liquidation of the camp through a Luftwaffe attack or a mass execution through shooting or gassing. The politically organized inmates were determined not to die without a fight, and two groups emerged, each devising a strategy for the final days of the war. In this instance, it was not only the Communists who organized to resist the seemingly inevitable destruction of the camp at the hands of the SS, but also many of the non-Communists under the leadership of Captain Christopher Burney, a British POW. As a result, both of these factions began to spirit away firearms and other weapons, preparing to resist annihilation. Taking advantage of the chaos created by the 24 August 1944 Allied bombing of the site, for example, the resistance surreptitiously stole weapons from Buchenwald's SS armory, hiding them in preparation for the day of reckoning.[8]

In the spring of 1945, as the US Army approached Saxony, the situation changed dramatically. Buchenwald's population increased as the war's end drew near because prisoners from the countries of liberated Europe were transferred to the camp on the Ettersberg. As a result, many of the guards, not to mention the local population outside of the

camp, became increasingly afraid of what would happen once the prisoners themselves were liberated. The guards simply could not control
so many people without their acquiescence, and civilians nearby, believing—as they had been told for years—that the camp's inmates were
the dregs of German society, feared reprisals at the hands of a criminal
element or simply revenge by those whom the state had persecuted. In
short, fear gripped everyone in Buchenwald and the surrounding area,
and an uneasy truce characterized camp life. But this was the proverbi-
al calm before the storm. Circumstances changed dramatically during
the first week of April, as some of Buchenwald's satellite camps were
liquidated. For example, prisoners from Ohrdruf, a subcamp of Buchenwald around thirty miles outside of Weimar, were forced to go on a
death march to the main camp. Of the approximately 12,000 internees
in Ohrdruf, more than 1,500 perished during the evacuation to the Ettersberg, many dying of exposure, starvation, and dehydration, not to
mention those who were victims of SS bullets.[9]

The first act of overt resistance occurred on 4 April, when the Jewish prisoners were summoned for roll call and, realizing that to heed
this summons could have deadly consequences, none of them obeyed
the order. During the night of 4–5 April, Buchenwald's 6,000 Jews attempted to melt into the camp's population, changing their uniforms
with the help of the resistance and taking on new identities. This did
not stop the SS, however, from seeking out the Jewish prisoners on the
next day, assembling all of the inmates and simply choosing those who,
in their estimation, looked Jewish. Fifteen hundred prisoners were assembled through this method, the Jews from Ohrdruf being added to
their number. Altogether, around 3,000 Jews would be compelled to
participate in a death march leaving the camp on 6 April.[10]

The Jews were not the only group forcibly evacuated from the
camp, and during the days between 5 and 11 April several transports
and death marches left the camp, taking the prisoners to unknown des-
tinations. On 11 April, there remained, according to the accounts of former internees, 21,000 prisoners in Buchenwald—most of them either
ill or having jobs vital to the function of the camp—including forty-six
political prisoners hiding among the general population because camp
authorities had singled them out for execution. The SS soon abandoned
its search for the condemned men, however, as the sound of artillery
got louder and American tanks approached. Around 10:30 in the morning, the deputy commandant of the camp announced that Buchenwald
would surrender. Yet rumors continued to spread that dive bombers

from the nearby Nohra Airbase were coming to annihilate the inmates, and the prisoners remained prepared violently to resist any effort to liquidate them. Just before noon, the guards stationed inside the perimeter fled, leaving only their comrades in the lookout towers to oversee the camp's population. The latter abandoned their posts around three hours later. As the US Army's report on Buchenwald records, "Then the comrades of the camp police, who had taken cover with their arms, immediately cut through the barbed wire, occupied the towers themselves, took the gate and the camp entrance, and raised the white flag over the first tower. Thus the first American tanks that rolled in from the northwest found a liberated Buchenwald."[11] Thus was born the myth of Buchenwald Concentration Camp's "self-liberation," a tradition that would become a central component of the GDR's official antifascism narrative.[12]

Returning to German soil during the final days of the war, the KPD leadership and later the SED party bosses incorporated a simplified and highly partisan—although a not altogether inaccurate—version of the history of Buchenwald into their legitimizing myth. In the postwar years, Buchenwald became one of the most important symbols internationally of the crimes of the Third Reich, and a successful effort to link the worldwide Communist movement with the victims of the camp would do much to legitimize the KPD/SED monopoly on power within, first, the SBZ and later the GDR. Hence, the KPD/SED leadership actively sought to manipulate memory at the site to the advantage of the international Communist movement. As a result, a somewhat idiosyncratic version of Buchenwald's past became an integral part of the official historical narrative of the SBZ and East Germany.[13]

The Nazis had constructed Buchenwald as a camp for the internment of political prisoners, and it remained one of the most important sites for the confinement of opponents of National Socialism until the end of the war. As a result, the largest category of those 239,000 people interned at Buchenwald between 1937 and 1945 were political prisoners, and a significant number of them were Communists. The same can be said regarding the 56,000 who died at the site. Buchenwald's inmates were a diverse lot, however, coming from every group opposing the NSDAP, including Communists, Social Democrats, Democrats, liberals, traditional conservatives, clergymen, Jehovah's Witnesses, and numerous other categories. In addition, there were those who were there for reasons other than openly opposing the regime, such as being a homosexual, a common criminal, an "asocial," or, of course, a Jew.

Further, the inmates came from a large number of nations, originating not just from Germany, but from every country occupied by the Third Reich, and some were POWs. Altogether, Buchenwald's prisoners came from thirty-two different countries. Although official commemoration at the location emphasized the fact that the prisoners came from diverse national backgrounds—after all, the international composition of the opposition to Hitler fascism had long been a central component of Comintern and KPD antifascist propaganda—the official KPD/SED account misleadingly homogenized the camp population under the rubric *antifascist*, increasingly synonymous with *Communist* in KPD/SED propaganda. The Jews who died in the camp, for example, became political opponents of the regime in the state-sponsored version of this narrative rather than the victims of Nazi racial policy. In other words, the official account incorporated non-Communists into the Communist version of the Buchenwald legend. Visitors to the camp during the years 1945–1989 were to draw, it was hoped, the false inference that all those who were imprisoned or died at Buchenwald were Communists or at least fellow travelers on the left of the political spectrum. The commemoration at the site ultimately sought to link all significant opposition to National Socialism with the international Communist movement. In it, non-Communist victims were either totally ignored or marginalized. For decades after the war, exhibitions relating events in the camp during the Third Reich displayed only the red triangles worn by political prisoners. It was not until 1985 that the yellow badges sewn onto the uniforms of Jewish inmates made their first appearance in a state-sponsored exhibit.[14]

In a similar vein, German Communists sought to instrumentalize the memory of the anti-Nazi opposition within the camp, emphasizing the role that the KPD played in organizing the prisoners against their oppressors. SED propaganda sought to present the resistance at Buchenwald in specifically Communist terms and mentioned non-Communist resistance only in passing, if at all. Hence, much as GDR discourse on Buchenwald's victims homogenized them as antifascists, the resistance movement in the camp became synonymous with the KPD's glorious struggle against Hitler. In keeping with the KPD/SED party line going back at least as far as Hitler's seizure of power, the official Buchenwald narrative presented the Communist Party as the only political movement consistently to oppose National Socialism. Antifascist propaganda in the SBZ and the GDR conveniently ignored the interlude of the years 1939 to 1941, during which both the KPD and the Comintern discontinued most of their anti-Hitler propaganda in the wake of the August 1939 German–Soviet Nonaggression Pact.

In the official KPD/SED narrative, not only had the Communists been at the forefront of the resistance against the Third Reich, but in the case of Buchenwald the opposition had ultimately emerged victorious. The myth of Buchenwald's "self-liberation" assumed a vital place in the GDR's antifascism narrative. The Communist resistance stood up against the Nazis, refusing to "go like sheep to the slaughter," and had liberated the camp on its own before the American army had arrived. Hence, the official account of Buchenwald's history could present the Communists as both victims *and* victors—a compelling trope—who had withstood fascist persecution because of their undying faith in their cause. This same resolute belief in the ultimate victory of socialism enabled them, when given the opportunity, to cast off the fascist yoke and liberate themselves. Only the Communists in Buchenwald could make this claim, and they could do so only because of their belief in the inevitable victory of Marxism–Leninism. The notion of the Communists as both victims of and victors over National Socialist oppression was a powerful propaganda motif, becoming a central component of the postwar antifascism myth and hence the German Democratic Republic's legitimation narrative.[15]

The Buchenwald site, conveniently for the KPD/SED, could also play a key role in the cultivation of the Ernst Thälmann myth, a central component of the party's antifascism narrative. On 24 August 1944, a Russian inmate identified only as Krutik composed what was apparently the first poem commemorating Thälmann's death. Entitled "Höre Welt!" (Listen, World!), Krutik's verse anticipated many of the motifs of the postwar Thälmann legend. The poem opens with an obvious allusion to Marx: "Listen proletarians of the world / Hear the news of Thälmann!" It then goes on to memorialize the fallen KPD leader as an example for everyone:

In August 1944
In Buchenwald's crematorium
A bright light burning for freedom
Was extinguished
By the bloody assassin's hand.
We lost the leader of the proletariat,
whose name rings out like the sound of the downtrodden.
. . .

> Ernst, you have not left us.
> We swear to follow your battle cry.
> The executioner has only killed your body,
> Your idea remains with us.

Krutik's bit of doggerel concludes with a solemn promise "To live after Your example."[16] Here, in their infancy, were many of the motifs that would become integral to the propagation of the Thälmann myth after 1945: sacrificial death, eternal life within the hearts of the Communist faithful, and the necessity to take up the challenge created by the legacy of the fallen. Thälmann's death in Buchenwald helped to assure that the site would become one of the most important to German communism's antifascism myth.

Not only was the first bit of poetry to commemorate the fallen leader written in Buchenwald less than a week after his death, but one of the earliest and most important ceremonies commemorating Thälmann's sacrifice took place there only a month following his murder. In spite of the fact that officials insisted that Thälmann had died as the result of the August 1944 air raid on the camp, the inmates knew that the former KPD chief was never imprisoned in Buchenwald, and the true circumstances surrounding his death became common knowledge remarkably quickly.[17] As a result, the Communist prisoners organized a commemoration ceremony. Although not the only observance organized following the death of a prominent leftist figure—there was also a commemoration service organized in October 1944 following the death of the trade union official Albert Kayser, for example—the September ceremony would go on to become, during the postwar years, the camp's most important commemorative ritual. After some discussion concerning security—secretly assembling large numbers of inmates outside of the gaze of camp guards always presented a problem—inmates from each of the resistance groups working in the disinfection chamber as well as the nearby building where prisoners' property was stored held a service commemorating the fallen KPD leader on Sunday, 18 September 1944.[18] As an officially sanctioned account of the ritual recorded, "[E]ighty to ninety reliable comrades from nearly all of the Nazi occupied European countries assembled in the basement rooms of the disinfectant section" for the ceremony.[19] One of the participants, Robert Siewert, later recalled that the disinfection chamber was elaborately decorated, with red and black fabric adorning the room. "In the foreground of the room," Siewert remembered,

The site of Ernst
Thälmann's execution in
Buchenwald Concentration
Camp, December 1985.
Courtesy of the German
Federal Archive.

"was affixed a large portrait of Thälmann, bordered by red and black fabric," and "pylons were set up to the right and left of it."[20] A Russian inmate, Roman Jefimenko, had used coal to draw the likeness of the fallen Communist leader on a piece of cardboard. To add solemnity to the occasion, a lamp illuminated Thälmann's likeness. Soviet POWs in full uniform served as an honor guard for the image of the fallen KPD leader.[21] As the ceremony opened, one of the prisoners, the writer and amateur violinist Bruno Apitz, played "the Russian funeral march," entitled "Undying Sacrifice," while some of the participants hummed along. Although another inmate spoke first, Siewert gave the eulogy, relating the major political events in Thälmann's life and emphasizing his role in the struggle against fascism. He then turned to the situation in which those present found themselves, in the midst of the calm before the storm, preparing for the inevitable armed resistance against their captors, comparing it to Lenin's situation on the eve of the October Revolution. The martyred KPD chief's unrelenting struggle would serve as a valuable example during the trying times ahead. After singing a proletarian song, the "Warschawjanka," in the several languages of those assembled, the participants closed the observance with a moment of silence, their balled fists raised in the air, giving the antifascist salute in tribute to their fallen comrade.[22]

In the end, concerns about the security risks involved in staging such an elaborate ritual proved legitimate. It turned out that one of those attending the ceremony, an Austrian recently admitted to the camp and identified only as Strand, was an informant. The information that he gave to the guards led, beginning on 30 October, to the arrest of more than a dozen participants in the Thälmann observance, including the *Kapo* (prisoner functionary) who oversaw the disinfection chamber, Willi Bleicher, and Siewert, who had delivered the eulogy, as well as some other opposition leaders. As a result, several of these inmates were tortured, and some were sentenced to death, which only had the effect of further sanctifying the ceremony in the eyes of the postwar German Communist leadership.[23] Once again, Communists had suffered for their beliefs and activities at the hands of the Nazis, a fact that justified and consecrated the policies of the postwar party leadership. This emphasis on the Communists as the Nazis' prey as well as on the KPD's willingness to stand up to its oppressors became important motifs in postwar antifascist propaganda. The Communists were again both victimized and victorious.

This theme became a central component first of KPD and then of SED commemorations at the camp. Former prisoners created the first monument in the camp themselves, constructing a wooden obelisk just a few days after the liberation, one of several temporary memorials set up in the camp and the surrounding area.[24] The KPD leadership, returning from exile in the Soviet Union even before Germany's surrender, staged commemoration ceremonies at the site as soon as it was possible to do so. But this ultimately took some time. In August 1945, the Americans handed the camp over to the Soviets—it was in the USSR's occupation zone—and Buchenwald became "Special Camp Number Two," holding thousands of former Nazis as well as real and potential opponents of Soviet occupation policies.[25] Even so, small commemorative services took place. On 10 and 11 April 1946, for example, more than "600 former prisoners" attended a ceremony observing the first anniversary of the camp's "self-liberation." Among those attending was Rosa Thälmann, the "partner in life and struggle of the unforgettable leader of the German working class[,] Ernst Thälmann," as East German historian Heinz Koch put it.[26] The Soviet-run camp, however, made it impossible to use the site for the major commemorative activities that would come to characterize later years, and extensive SED-sponsored remembrance did not begin until 1948.

Among the most important party-sponsored rituals to be held at the site in 1948 was an assembly of around 3,000 members of the Association for the Victims of Nazi Persecution (VVN), arguably the most important organization for the propagation of the antifascism myth during the Soviet occupation and the GDR's early years. Held between 9 and 11 April, the anniversary of the camp's "self-liberation," the meeting focused on the theme "Fighters Against Fascism, Fighters for Peace." Such slogans were a common motif of the SED's antifascist propaganda, which sought to link antifascism with the worldwide peace movement, thereby implying that the party's political opponents were not only sympathetic to fascism, but also supportive of the forces of German militarism. In a speech given to the assembly, VVN official Stefan Heymann thanked the Soviet army for its role in the defeat of fascism and welcomed all those who had been the victims of National Socialism, including the Jews who were present. Heymann, like other speakers at the gathering, sought to equate the victims of Nazi racial and political persecution. Walter Bartel, speaking on behalf of the International Buchenwald Committee, similarly tried to link Nazi persecution of the Jews to the Left's political struggle against Hitler and the legacy of antifascism to the contemporary "fight for peace." SED-controlled memory at the site was highly politicized from the outset, and speakers such as Heymann and Bartel consciously sought to associate the legacy of antifascism with current political conditions.[27] As in other political religions, the living in this case had to look to their deceased predecessors for examples of proper conduct.

The party leadership had higher aspirations for Buchenwald than using it as the site to hold rallies for aging antifascists. As early as April 1949, party chief Walter Ulbricht wrote to Bartel about the prospect of a commemorative tower at the site. Although officials introduced plans to clear some of the rubble from the location in July 1949, it was not until 1951 that the scheme bore significant fruit, when the leadership allocated the money for the project.[28] Even then, progress occurred at a glacial pace, and authorities had to wait until 1954 for the plan really to get off the ground. As was often the case in the GDR, the main obstacle to construction was a shortage of funds. Throughout the 1950s the regime faced a severe housing shortage, and the construction of apartment buildings remained a high priority, often at the expense of such schemes as the one developed for the Buchenwald site. Further, much of the labor at the site would be done by "volunteers," who often lacked the skills needed to perform exacting construction work.[29]

In 1954, the party leadership created a committee, chaired by GDR minister-president Otto Grotewohl, to oversee plans to construct a major monument complex at Buchenwald. Grotewohl's role was largely honorary, and the driving forces behind the committee's activities were Johannes R. Becher, the minister of culture, and his lieutenant, Alexander Abusch. Among the more than forty members of the committee were former VVN chief Bartel, the novelist Anna Seghers, and Rosa Thälmann, who played a vital role in cultivating the Thälmann myth during the 1950s. Although other former concentration camps would play an important role in propagating the antifascism myth in the GDR, the budgets assigned to constructing memorials at the major camps on East German soil showed the centrality of Buchenwald to this effort. On 22 November 1955, Grotewohl's Buchenwald Committee learned that its budget was 10 million marks over the next two years, more than the combined totals of the budgets for Sachsenhausen (7 million) and Ravensbrück (2 million), the other two major memorial sites located in former concentration camps.[30] In keeping with one of the major themes of the antifascism myth, the Buchenwald Committee would use these funds to create a series of stone edifices linking the heroic antifascist past with the emerging socialist present and the glorious future of the people of the GDR. As historian Jeffrey Herf describes the situation, "The memorials were [to be] Hegelian monuments set in stone, intended to encourage optimism about the future based on memory of past heroism, rather than reflections of an unredeemable tragedy."[31] Needless to say, commemoration of the sacrifice that Ernst Thälmann made in the courtyard outside of Buchenwald's crematorium would play an important role in perpetuating this version of events.

Plans to memorialize Thälmann at Buchenwald originated even before the creation of Grotewohl's Buchenwald Committee. In October 1950, the Central Committee's Secretariat introduced a scheme to create a "memorial site" (*Erinnerungsstätte*) outside of the crematorium on the spot where the KPD chief was shot a little more than six years earlier. Nine months later party chief Walter Ulbricht signed an order to create both a memorial and a museum at Buchenwald in honor of Thälmann. Bartel and Central Committee member Franz Dahlem were given the assignment of putting together a proposal, complete with sketches of the projected memorial, to be completed in 1953. As a result, the ninth anniversary of Thälmann's murder witnessed a dedication ceremony, overseen by GDR propaganda chief Paul Wandel, held in the crematorium's courtyard, the epicenter of the memorialization of Thälmann in the camp.[32] As Klaus Trostorff, director of the Buchenwald National Memorial during the mid-1970s, put it, "[A] focal point of the crematorium, as well as a site for contemplation, is the memorial in the courtyard of the crematorium at the location where Ernst Thälmann was murdered by the fascists. An unpretentious plaque bears witness to this horrible deed. Hardly a visitor passes by this location without thinking of the great leader of the working class and placing flowers. Thousands of students have sworn at this location to live in the spirit of Ernst Thälmann and to work for progress [and] for socialism."[33]

Even more noteworthy developments in the propagation of the Thälmann myth at Buchenwald marked the tenth anniversary of the martyred KPD chief's death. The party leadership chose 18 August 1954 as an appropriate date to open Buchenwald's Museum of the Resistance Movement. Rosa Thälmann and the fallen KPD leader's daughter, Irma, were among the important figures participating in a dedication ceremony that included the laying of a wreath to commemorate the sacrifice of Thälmann and all the others who died at the camp. Representatives of the Central Committee, Karl Schirdewan and Fred Oelßner; the Soviet ambassador, G. M. Puschkin; as well as delegates from the "Brother Parties" of Czechoslovakia, China, Poland, Hungary, Bulgaria, and Australia took part in the ceremonies. Speaking on behalf of the Central Committee, Schirdewan invoked the name of the martyred KPD chief: "Thälmann . . . is our struggle for peace in Germany. In Ernst Thälmann we similarly honor all victims of the fascists, the Communists, Social Democrats, and Christians." Note that he did mention non-Communist groups, the SED still hoping that the antifascism myth might win outsiders to the party's cause, the long-term goal being to reunite Germany under socialist auspices. Schirdewan concluded his speech with a promise to the fallen leader and a call for proletarian unity: "We swear to you, Comrade Thälmann, to use all of our strength in order to realize the unity of the working class in all of Germany."[34] This was neither the first nor the last time that East Germans had been called to swear an oath to continue the work started by Thälmann or some other figure from the antifascist movement of the 1930s. Such a solemn pledge created a covenant between participants and the martyred leader, obligating those present to embody the KPD's legacy and build a socialist Germany. Schirdewan's use of the word all (ganz) reflected the fact that the SED had not yet officially given up on the prospect of the unification of Germany on its terms. Throughout the early years of the SED's propagation of the Thälmann myth, the party leadership sought to depict the martyred Communist leader as a model for all Germans, not just for those living in the GDR. All Germans, East and West, should work together in Thälmann's spirit to create a new, antifascist, progressive, socialist Germany. They should strive to create a country in which, because everyone remembered Thälmann's and other antifascists' sacrifices, the mistakes of the recent past could not be repeated; in other words, a Germany very different from that being established in the west, where capitalism, class exploitation, and militarism—the conditions that had led to the advent of Hitler fascism—were being re-created.

Although Schirdewan's speech was designed to rally those present to the socialist cause as embodied in Ernst Thälmann, it was not the most emotionally charged portion of the museum dedication ceremony. As bells rang out the "Warschawjanka"—the proletarian song sung at the conclusion of the September 1944 commemoration ceremony for Thälmann—and "Undying Victims," another melody appropriate to the commemoration of Thälmann's and other martyred Communists' sacrifice, "hundreds of wreath-bearing delegations" marched down a lane composed of the 2,400 Thälmann Pioneers participating in the ceremony and lay their wreaths at the foot of a bust of Thälmann. Located in the courtyard outside of crematorium number two, on the site where the former party chief was murdered, the statue and a plaque commemorating Thälmann's sacrificial death remained one of the sites most closely associated with the propagation of the Thälmann cult. This elaborate wreath-laying ceremony, coupled with Schirdewan's address, allowed those present symbolically to link the newly opened museum with the most important of the KPD's antifascist martyrs.[35]

The Museum of the Resistance Movement originally fell under the auspices of the Museum of German History in Berlin, but then Weimar city authorities gained control over it in December 1954.[36] The new museum's function, like its Berlin sponsor's, was to advance the official GDR version of recent German history. The new exhibits were at least in part a response to the supposed "emergence of fascism [*Faschisierung*] [in] West Germany" and contributed to the effort to "avoid a repeat of the catastrophe" experienced by "our fatherland" because of "militarism and fascism." This comparison between the socialist, humanistic GDR and the fascist West was already an omnipresent theme in East German propaganda by the mid-1950s, the product not just of the SED's legitimation narrative, but also of an increasingly hostile cold war discourse. According to *Neues Deutschland,* the function of the exhibition in the newly dedicated museum was to educate the East German people about the recent past and thereby to avoid a repetition of the calamity of the 1930s and 1940s. The display would do so by tracing the origins of German fascism and the Left's response to the threat it posed. The German Left, to which the SED traced its origins, had long resisted the twin evils of "militarism and imperialism," necessary preconditions for the rise of a fascist state. The exhibits, housed in ten rooms, traced the fight against fascism from the "struggles of the left wing of the SPD during the First World War against these crimes [imperialism and militarism] against the German people." Highlights of the first section of the display included accounts of the "assassination of Karl Liebknecht and Rosa Luxemburg," the two most important martyrs of the interwar KPD. "Similarly the ways that the right-wing leadership of the SPD often surrendered to the forces of German imperialism . . . [were] exhibited. Yet this treason could not break the working class's strength and willingness to struggle." Exhibits analyzing such events as the proletariat's "defeat of the Kapp Putsch" made this strength abundantly clear.[37]

The next series of exhibits dealt with events following the onset of the "world economic crisis" beginning in 1929. As in the earlier portion of the exhibition, the photographs and documents in this section sought consciously to link the government of the Weimar Republic with the Third Reich, the latter being the natural result of the policies of the former. In GDR historical discourse, the KPD had opposed Weimar's liberal democracy because it was just an earlier, if less overt, manifestation of what was to follow. Capitalist exploitation, militarism, and imperialism were the order of the day, and the fascist government that succeeded the republic was just another, more openly criminal manifestation of bourgeois democracy—with its facade of liberal humanism torn away. These displays showed the horrific economic conditions that the Depression created, the millions among the proletariat who lost their jobs and went hungry, as well as the workers' attempts to secure the employment, food, and housing to which they were entitled. The display also sought to expose "the German imperialists'" effort to wage "a new war of conquest," seeking "the salvation of their faltering hegemony through an [ever-]increasing terror against the struggling workers [who sought] wages and bread." The text accompanying the items on exhibit also recorded "the right-wing leadership of the SPD's rejection of all of the KPD's efforts to organize a common struggle" against the forces of fascism and capitalist exploitation. Ernst Thälmann, of course, was at the forefront of these aborted efforts to unite members of the working class against the fascist menace, efforts that had failed because of the SPD right wing's decision to embrace the forces of reaction rather than to heed the KPD leader's call to fight the common class enemy.[38]

Although remembrance of Thälmann was admittedly not the central purpose of the Museum of Resistance, he did make more than one appearance in the displays. For example, the exhibit depicting the antifascist resistance during the years 1933–1939 showed him as an important figure who "hardened [*stählte*]—although in a fascist prison—the resistance of all antifascists through his resolve and courage." Other displays honored those who willingly gave their lives in the KPD's struggle against Nazi imperialism. Among these figures were several of Thälmann's former comrades, including John Schehr. The remainder of the museum's exhibit showed the KPD's antifascist activities in the international arena, including the 1935 KPD conference in Brussels, which called upon all antifascists to unite to destroy German militarism and imperialism. The representatives at this conference also elected Wilhelm Pieck as temporary chairman of the KPD, and Thälmann remained official party chief, even though he could exercise no influence from his prison cell. The party leadership continued to recognize the symbolic importance of the imprisoned party chief. Another display portrayed the Thälmann Battalion's contribution to the progressive cause in the Spanish Civil War, which the museum interpreted as yet another example of the KPD's role in promoting international solidarity in the face of the menace posed by the international fascist movement. Indeed, several of the battalion's Communists gave their lives in Spain's antifascist struggle.[39]

Although the museum sought to stress the role that the "other [antifascist] Germany" played in the effort against Hitler, it simultaneously emphasized the international composition of the antifascist struggle, and Thälmann's image played a small but significant role in the propagation of this theme. An entire wall was dedicated to the commemoration of the fallen KPD chief. Here, museum officials placed a bust of Thälmann, flanked on either side by display cases in which "[n]umerous documents [were on exhibit] from Ernst Thälmann's struggle as well as [from] the global campaign [to secure] his release." His image was, as always, a central component of the GDR's antifascist mythology. The Thälmann display established not only that there was "another Germany" that had been opposed to Hitler fascism, but also that this movement had been part of an international alliance of progressive forces. Yet another section of the exhibition depicted the activities of some of the more famous non-Communist resistance fighters, including "workers, intellectuals, and [military] officers," many of whom gave their lives in the struggle against Hitler. Representing their activities in the broader context of Communist resistance undoubtedly had the intention of co-opting them for the GDR's legitimation myth. In a motif that was typical of memorialization efforts at the Buchenwald camp, all of those progressives who resisted National Socialism had in a sense made a significant contribution to the creation of the GDR, the only true antifascist state on German soil.[40]

The final segment of the exhibition was concerned with the heroic military effort undertaken to defeat fascism. Needless to say, the items on display and the accompanying text lionized the Soviet Union's role in the defeat of National Socialist Germany. One of the important results of the Soviet victory was the liberation of Buchenwald, which became possible only because of the success of the Red Army, not of the US armed forces: "The victories of the Soviet Army also brought liberation to the prisoners of Buchenwald." Those antifascists languishing in the camp were not the only beneficiaries of the Soviet conquest, however. Indeed, the Soviet victory was portrayed as a liberation, an emancipation, all the more noteworthy because, *Neues Deutschland* explained, it continued to benefit a considerable portion of the world's population, including the people of the GDR. The museum "show[ed] how the Soviet Union has already led a third of humanity to victory in this struggle [against fascism] and [remains] a secure refuge for all warriors against fascism."[41]

The lessons instilled by the Museum of the Resistance Movement, according to *Neues Deutschland,* should serve as a cautionary tale in light of the ongoing events in West Germany, where Konrad Adenauer's "policy of militarism and creation of fascism, in alliance with the American imperialists, shows . . . [the] new threat of war." But the exhibition also demonstrated that all hope was not lost, "but [rather that] the oath of the resistance fighters against war and fascism . . . , in spite of all of the policies of the Adenauer state, [was still] living in the proletariat of the western part of our homeland," where "millions sign petitions" in opposition to "atomic and hydrogen bombs, . . . the stationing of atomic cannons, against the confiscation of land [for military purposes] and the creation of deserts in the wake of military maneuvers." These antifascists, living in West Germany, were similarly fulfilling the legacy of those remembered in the Museum of the Resistance Movement. The museum sought to relay a message of hope to all those who wanted to avoid the reemergence of fascism in Germany and who sought to continue the struggle of those remembered in the exhibit.[42]

The 18 August 1954 ceremony was among the most important in the years preceding the opening of the Buchenwald National Monument in 1958. But it was far from the only ceremony to promote the Thälmann legend. Commemoration of the martyred party chief's birthday and, more important, the anniversary of his death was always a central component of the SED's efforts to propagate the antifascism myth at the Buchenwald site. On the eleventh anniversary of Thälmann's death, for example, around 5,000 people assembled to memorialize his life and sacrifice. Local officials usually oversaw the ceremonies marking anniversaries of secondary importance. Heinz Kiefert, first secretary of the SED's Erfurt region, was the featured speaker at the 1955 observances, for example.[43]

The year 1955 was an eventful one at Buchenwald, and the eleventh anniversary of Thälmann's martyrdom was not the only occasion upon which the party leadership invoked the KPD chief's name. The eleventh of April witnessed a massive celebration marking the tenth anniversary of the camp's liberation. The official announcement calling upon the people of Weimar to attend the ceremonies emphasized that the upcoming observance was important to the struggle "against the attempt of West German fascists and militarists to permit the reemergence of the ideology of fascism [and] against the participation [*Einbeziehung*] of West Germany in a new war."[44] After all, the FRG was about to join the North Atlantic Treaty Organization (NATO), which, putting aside the military threat that the alliance posed to the GDR, made it abundantly clear that Germany would be divided for the foreseeable future. Further, NATO placed the very existence of a socialist Germany in jeopardy. But the rhetorical attack on West Germany did not stop there. Party authorities also drew up a series of seventeen resolutions, to which all of those attending were expected to agree. The "central resolution" and overarching theme of the ceremony read, "Our promise on the tenth anniversary of the liberation: forward to the triumph of the nations [*Völker*] over militarism and fascism," but the sixth resolution specifically invoked the legend of Ernst Thälmann. It read: "Struggle like Ernst Thälmann for the concerns [*Sache*] of the German nation and for a unified, democratic Germany."[45] Whereas the central resolution, which emphasized the role that the "nations" would play in the defeat of fascism, was clearly designed to invoke the international nature of the struggle against "militarism and fascism," the sixth sought to link this effort more specifically to the fate of Germany, calling for the creation of a "unified, democratic Germany" as an important precondition for the permanent defeat of fascism. The image of Ernst Thälmann was clearly a central component of the ongoing effort—through appeals linking his legacy to antifascism, antimilitarism, and internationalism—not only to legitimize a socialist East German state, but also to support the GDR

leadership's rhetorical attempt to promote the unification of the divided country under the SED's leadership.

Indeed, the Thälmann cult was to become such an important
component of antifascist remembrance at Buchenwald that the party
leadership originally planned to dedicate the National Buchenwald
Monument on 16 April 1956, the martyred leader's seventieth birthday.[46] Circumstances conspired, however, to delay the site's dedication
for more than two years beyond the initially proposed date. First of all,
party leaders had to decide what they were going to do with the Ettersberg location, choosing among rival proposals for the project. To make
matters worse, the Politburo repeatedly altered the plans for the undertaking, hoping to create a monument that would have a maximum ideological effect. Further contributing to the series of postponements was
the shortage of funds and building materials that plagued the East German economy. After all, the SED was simultaneously attempting to expand production in heavy industry, but with only limited success. The
resulting shortages of resources had a dramatic effect on the regime's
construction plans, even delaying such important projects as Berlin's
proposed Ernst Thälmann National Monument as well as the party's
plans for the Buchenwald site.[47] This effect does not take into account
the renovations that had to be made at the camp before construction
on the Buchenwald Monument could be completed. The remnants of
the camp's barracks, which were apparently in an unredeemable condition, had to be torn down and hauled away. Tons of other debris had
to be moved. In addition, the crematorium, the camp canteen, the main
gate, the SS barracks, the delousing building, and the stables all had to
be renovated in order to prepare them for the housing of the several
museums that would be located in the camp. Needless to say, all of
this cost money and used scarce manpower and resources, undoubtedly delaying the construction of the national monument one kilometer
from the camp. Although all of the clean-up and renovation work was
completed by the end of 1954, it was too late to meet the original target
date for the project's completion.[48]

The SED's construction plans for the national monument outside
the camp perimeter as well as a smaller memorial located in the nearby city of Weimar would use scarce resources and cost a great deal of
money, as would the ongoing construction of the national monuments
at the Sachsenhausen and Ravensbrück camps. As part of its endeavor
to raise funds for these projects, the Board of Trustees for the Construction of National Memorials decided to sell white porcelain medallions

with a profile of Ernst Thälmann on one side. Designed by Leipzig's Eyermann porcelain firm, the medallions were fifteen centimeters in diameter and would cost fifty marks for one with a case, but only thirty marks for one with a glass stand. Beneath the profile of the fallen KPD leader was the inscription "Ernst Thälmann 1886–1944." The words "Die Toten mahnen—nie wieder Faschismus" (The dead admonish—never again fascism) appeared around the edges of this side of the medallion. On the reverse side, the following words were inscribed:

KURATORIUM
FÜR DEN AUFBAU
NATIONALER
GEDENKSTÄTTEN
IN BUCHENWALD
SACHSENHAUSEN
U. RAVENSBRÜCK

The Memorials Board, which coordinated the construction efforts at the three former concentration camps, hoped that the porcelains would not only raise funds for the projects at Buchenwald, Sachsenhausen, and Ravensbrück but also increase awareness of the sacrifices made by those imprisoned there.[49]

How much money this project raised remains uncertain—10,000 of the porcelains would be produced, but half of them would be presented to the Thälmann Pioneers, apparently free of charge. The Memorials Board's motives went beyond pecuniary concerns.[50] The board also reissued a stamp, originally printed to commemorate Thälmann's seventieth birthday. Initially printed as a twenty-pfennig stamp in 6 million copies, the new version, of which 750,000 copies were produced, was printed in a block style, obviously for collectors, and cost forty pfennigs. The stamp shows Thälmann from the shoulders up, the omnipresent dockworker's cap atop his head, a red flag behind him. Workers, dressed in a similar fashion, appear in the background. The block made it clear that the money collected from the sale of the stamps would be used "For the Construction of National Monuments in Buchenwald, Ravensbrück, and Sachsenhausen."[51] Eyermann's porcelains and to a lesser extent the stamps would also play a role in political education. Indeed, education might very well have been the primary motivation for selling them. Once again, an organ of the East German state sought to link the sacrifices made at Buchenwald with the memory of Ernst

Thälmann. Although he had never spent a single day imprisoned in the camp, the fallen KPD chief became symbolic of everyone who had suffered within its walls. Thälmann, a Communist, was emblematic of all those who had fought fascism, especially those 56,000 who had given their lives in the infamous concentration camp. Representing the martyred Communist leader in this way, like so much of the propaganda surrounding Buchenwald, had the effect of equating—at least by implication—the antifascist and Communist causes. The medallions had the added advantage of personifying Buchenwald's fallen in the sacrifice of an archetypal individual. Thälmann was paradigmatic of all those who had paid the ultimate price in the struggle to destroy fascism and create an antifascist, humanist Germany. Because Thälmann's lifeless body had been cremated at Buchenwald, there was no burial site at which he could be commemorated. Buchenwald would have to serve as a substitute, and the medallions might serve as a surrogate for historical relics that could bring the possessor closer to Thälmann. Like the medieval relic, items such as the Eyermann porcelains—not to mention the stamps—served to promote memory of the dead individual by making his presence more tactile and immediate.

The summer of 1958 witnessed a series of events important to the propagation of the Thälmann myth in Weimar and Buchenwald. The first National Thälmann Memorial was dedicated in the city of Weimar in August, and the National Monument at Buchenwald was consecrated the following month. Although local authorities played a part in the planning of the ceremonies surrounding these important events, the documentary evidence makes the national party leadership's heavy-handed role abundantly clear. As always, local party officials found the Politburo constantly looking over their shoulders, and Weimar authorities exercised their limited prerogatives within the confines of ideological constraints imposed by Berlin. Regional authorities, for example, chose as the theme for the two dedication ceremonies "Glory and honor to the heroes of the resistance movement and the victims of fascist terror[;] they exhort: Uphold the greatest good of humanity, peace!" The ceremonies would seek to link the "peace-loving progressive forces in our city" to the sacrifices made by Thälmann and all those who had suffered at the hands of the fascists, especially those who had given their lives. Local organizers chose this theme, which had to be approved by officials in Berlin, in accordance with a recent pronouncement by the Fifth Party Congress concerning the links among antifascism, socialism, and international peace. Following the lead established by the Soviet Union, the GDR was engaged in a major propaganda campaign promoting not only a "cessation of all testing with atom and hydrogen bombs," but also the creation of an "atom weapon free zone in central Europe." The West's rejection of these proposals and FRG chancellor Adenauer's consideration of the prospect of an independent nuclear deterrent served as further proof that only socialism could assure the permanent defeat of militarism and fascism and with that defeat the long-term preclusion of international conflict.[52] In short, the dedications at Buchenwald and the Platz der 56,000 would be placed in the larger context of the ongoing "peace offensive" against the West, a policy determined and carried out by central authorities in Berlin acting under the guidance of their allies in Moscow. Not for the first time, party leaders adapted the antifascism myth to the needs of the moment. In order to maintain each ceremony's ideological coherence, the national leadership severely limited the autonomy of Thuringian authorities, and, as always, the important decisions would be made at the highest level.

Weimar officials chose the fourteenth anniversary of Thälmann's death to dedicate a memorial to the Buchenwald martyrs on the Platz der 56,000, not far from Weimar's train station. Thälmann was murdered on the night of 17–18 August, and the party leadership undoubtedly chose the seventeenth because it was a Sunday, which enabled a larger crowd to attend the ceremonies. The fact that this choice would keep people out of church was probably an added bonus. Although the plan to commemorate Buchenwald's fallen on this site was the brainchild of Weimar's party leadership, the SED's Central Committee had to approve of the proposal, which it did in 1956. In the year and a half preceding Berlin's approval, a fund-raising campaign in Weimar netted 80,000 marks to fund construction; following the Central Committee's approval, local officials raised a further 50,000 marks to erect the monument. In addition, the local party leadership held "gatherings" (Versammlungen) at which it sought to solicit the opinions of the area's population concerning the memorial's location and composition. How much influence such public meetings had upon the decision-making process is, as always, difficult to determine in the context of the GDR. The gatherings sought at least to create the impression that the undertaking was the result of a grassroots campaign. But in the highly centralized GDR, the party sought to control grassroots movements, and the final proposal was in all likelihood really the brainchild of local party officials, who in turn operated under tight restraints imposed by Berlin. The SED's Central Committee in the national capital played an important role in the decision-making process. Both officials in Berlin and the artist charged with designing the memorial had to approve of the plan. The Central Committee picked Walter Arnold, a sculptor, professor of art, and candidate member of the Central Committee, to perform this task. The assigning of Arnold to oversee the planning of the monument was indicative of the importance that the SED leadership placed on the propagation of the Thälmann myth. Party leaders in the East German capital wanted to assure that they maintained ultimate control over memorialization of prominent KPD martyrs, which included the victims of Buchenwald, chief among them Ernst Thälmann, and Arnold's influence over the planning process was decisive. Although the intention to construct the memorial might have originated on the local party level, it very quickly came under the purview of national authority. Such developments were hardly unique; indeed, they were typical of the way that the GDR was governed.[53]

Perhaps an even more striking example of the subordinate relationship of regional authority to national authority can be seen in the area of fund-raising for the Weimar and Buchenwald projects. The notion of raising money by selling porcelain medallions featuring Thälmann's visage apparently did not originate with the Memorials Board, but rather with local authorities in Weimar. In October 1956, the National Front Workers' Committee for the Thälmann Memorial in Weimar informed the Memorials Board that local officials had come up with the idea of raising funds by selling porcelains six months before the board made the suggestion. In spite of the fact that regional officials had laid the groundwork, they had to yield to Berlin. Indeed, the national Memorials Board went so far as to choose the same artist and porcelain firm that the National Front had selected earlier. It seems that central authorities stole the idea from the planners of the Ernst Thälmann Memorial constructed on the Platz der 56,000, yet another example of how tight Berlin's reins on local party officials were—at least when it came to propagating the Ernst Thälmann myth.[54] Given the fact that Weimar authorities had the national party leadership looking over their shoulders and had to have all of their substantive decisions approved by the Central Committee, it should come as no surprise that the 17 August dedication ceremonies followed the official line concerning the commemoration of Thälmann and other antifascist martyrs.

Preparations for the ceremony, many of which did indeed fall under the purview of local authorities, began well in advance. Invitations had to be issued, the regional FDJ and Kulturbund organizations needed to be organized for the event, streets needed to be cleared for a parade, and East German flags and portraits of Thälmann had to be displayed throughout the city, especially along the streets leading to the Platz der 56,000. In addition, the local party press had to publish pieces designed both to increase attendance at the upcoming ceremony and to put the crowd in the proper frame of mind for the dedication. On 16 August, for example, *Das Volk,* the official SED organ of the Erfurt region, which included Weimar, published an article written by Fritz Kroh, a former political prisoner in Sachsenhausen. Entitled "Struggle Onward in His Spirit," the piece begins with an account of Thälmann's martyr-dom. Kroh then reminds his readers of their obligation to contribute to Thälmann's "great legacy" by joining in the next day's celebration. He concludes by specifically linking memory of Thälmann with the con-struction of socialism in the GDR: "If we struggle onward in his spirit, then we can be certain that this goal, for all of Germany, will . . . no longer be distant." Perhaps even more interesting is a poem written by Louis Fürnberg and published in the same number of *Das Volk.* Entitled "Requiem for Ernst Thälmann," Fürnberg's verse is especially striking for at least two reasons. Thälmann is never mentioned in the poem, nor, for that matter, is Buchenwald. Instead, Fürnberg repeatedly refers somewhat broadly to "die Toten," all of those who died. Thälmann and the others who lost their lives in Buchenwald become representative once again of all of those who perished in the struggle against fascism. Perhaps even more noteworthy is the Christian imagery that pervades the poem. Not only are the victims depicted as having, like Christ, "broken bones" and "disfigured faces," not to mention the falling of rain upon the deceased, but there is a powerful motif incorporating resurrection. "We . . . have seen the wounds of the dead / and want to assure / that they rise up again." Of course, this resurrection was not a literal rising from the dead, but rather the revitalization of the goals es-poused by the martyrs—a resurgence of their ideas in the people of the GDR. These same powerful tropes can be seen in the dedication service that took place the next day.[55]

The 17 August ceremony began at 9:30 AM, Beethoven's "Eroica" symphony—considered especially appropriate for the occasion—playing on the loudspeakers. East German flags, posters of Thälmann, and banners with slogans such as "We promise to struggle in the spirit of Ernst Thälmann!" decorated the Platz der 56,000. Representatives from the Central Committee and the Soviet embassy were present at the dedication. Although Rosa Thälmann attended, she was unable to

participate actively because she was somehow physically "impeded"—
she was well into her sixties and apparently at this point suffering from
poor health. She was, however, among those officially greeted by "Comrade Gephardt," chairman of the local party council, who opened the
ceremony. Rudi Jahn, acting chairman of the Buchenwald Committee,
gave the keynote address. He began by specifically linking the proceedings with the tradition of German humanism, a heritage closely associated with the city of Weimar. "Here in the heart of Germany, in the city
of German humanism, we seek to dedicate a memorial to the leader of
the German working class, Ernst Thälmann," he began. Jahn continued
in this vein, emphasizing the recent pronouncements of the SED's Fifth
Party Congress, which sought to eliminate the threat of nuclear annihilation in central Europe. The Party Congress's pronouncements were a
natural outgrowth of the traditions of German humanism, the legacy of
the German proletariat, and the longstanding example established by
the Soviet Union. In short, the present ceremony represented the will of
"all [of the] peace-loving forces in the world." To honor Ernst Thälmann
and the 56,000 others who had given their lives at Buchenwald was to
make a valuable contribution to the ongoing struggle to vanquish fascism and militarism and assure a secure future for generations to come.
Only the triumph of socialism could guarantee perpetual peace, making it incumbent upon all those present to continue Thälmann's efforts
to bring Marxism–Leninism to all of Germany. Jahn's speech concluded
with a pledge typical of such ceremonies in the GDR. "We swear, in the
spirit of Ernst Thälmann, to struggle for democracy and socialism, for a
happy future for our people in a single Germany!"[56]

Jahn's speech was characteristic of such occasions in the GDR. It
sought to link eternal principles—German humanism, the struggle
against fascism, antimilitarism, sacrifice for the common good—with
the needs of the moment. In this case, he associated these longstanding
socialist values with the Fifth Party Congress's recent decision concerning nuclear weapons and the role that they should or should not play
in central Europe. Although Jahn or one of his subordinates probably
wrote the speech—there is no archival evidence that it was composed
by or had to meet the approval of the central party leadership—he was
aware of what he should say. Jahn knew how to link a local event to
Berlin's concerns and to develop themes on a local stage that were part
of a national agenda.

Yet, as we have seen, to refer to the 17 August ceremony as "local"
is misleading, the protestations by the planners of the observance not-

withstanding. Not only did the Central Committee in Berlin oversee the entire process, but the statue on the Platz der 56,000 was the first national monument constructed to commemorate Thälmann's legacy. Although the bronze dedicated in Weimar was not *the* national memorial being planned for Berlin, it was *a* national monument, celebrating the patrimony of all of the people of the GDR. Hence, central authorities in Berlin maintained a compelling, even decisive, interest in Arnold's memorial. Thälmann's legacy was simply too important to the national SED leadership for it to permit local party leaders to place their own interpretation upon the mythology surrounding the fallen Communist leader.

Walter Arnold, an appointee of the Central Committee, led the "collective" that laid out the monument dedicated on 17 August. In addition to Arnold, two professors from the College of Architecture and Building—Otto Engelberger and Siegfried Tschirschky—designed the monument, which consisted, first of all, of a wall, two meters tall and twenty meters long. A quotation from Max Zimmering, a prominent German socialist-realist writer, was carved into the wall. Reminding all visitors of the responsibility that they had to those who sacrificed their lives at nearby Buchenwald, the quotation consciously linked the concentration camp's fallen with the GDR: "Out of your sacrificial death grows our socialist deed." The use of the plural form of *your (eurem)* made it abundantly clear that all those who had died at Buchenwald supposedly contributed to the socialist project as embodied in the GDR. Just in front of the wall stood a 2.85-meter-tall statue, erected on a stone base, of Ernst Thälmann, balled right fist giving the antifascist salute. On the base of the statue was a simple inscription, "Ernst Thälmann, born on 16 April 1886, murdered on 18 August 1944 in Buchenwald Concentration Camp." *Neues Deutschland* pointed out that the Platz der 56,000 was surrounded by "modern blocks of apartments," clearly an effort to link the antifascist past with the progress engendered by the GDR.[57] At the conclusion of the dedication ceremony, the representatives of the local and national party organs as well as members of the Soviet delegation laid wreaths at the foot of the Thälmann statue as "Undying Victims" played in the background.[58]

The 17 August ceremonies did not conclude with this gesture, however. At eleven o'clock, there was an assembly in Weimar's stadium, where Alois Bräutigam, an important figure in regional party circles who had joined the SED Central Committee earlier that same year, was the featured speaker. His audience consisted of thousands of members of party organizations. Journalistic accounts of the speech emphasized the number of FDJ members present, pointing out not only the support that the youth gave the regime, but also that the GDR's young people were receiving a proper education in the principles of antifascism. Bräutigam's speech was in keeping with the tenor established earlier in the day. The theme of the rally was "Forward in the Spirit of Ernst Thälmann," and Bräutigam's address emphasized the importance of remembering the antifascist resistance fighters' contribution through their sacrifices to the construction of socialism in the GDR and the defeat of fascism and militarism across the globe. In the course of his speech, Bräutigam read a telegram sent by the Thälmann Pioneers from the city of Halle. "We swear that we will do all in our power to defeat our enemies who seek to disrupt the construction of socialism!" the telegram concluded. The speaker went on to emphasize the importance of the party's numerous auxiliary groups *(Kampfgruppen)*, including the Committee of Antifascist Resistance Fighters (the successor to the VVN) and the FDJ, to the construction of socialism. This contribution was, the speaker insisted, in keeping with the tradition of Thälmann and other antifascist martyrs.[59]

While Bräutigam was giving his speech, the "guests of honor"—local and national party bigwigs as well as the Soviet representatives—had assembled on a platform located on Weimar's Goetheplatz in preparation for a parade. Beginning in the stadium and consisting of "tens of thousands" of members of party auxiliary groups, many holding aloft posters bearing Thälmann's visage as well as banners sporting important party slogans, the parade passed by the platform before reaching its end.[60] With the conclusion of the parade, the ceremonies dedicating the Platz der 56,000 had concluded. It had been an eventful day.

The rituals surrounding the dedication of the Buchenwald National Monument on 14 September of the same year were even more elaborate than those of the previous month. This day's events served as the culmination of a series of holidays celebrating the triumph of socialism over German fascism, beginning with the dedication of Weimar's Thälmann Monument on 17 August. The first of September had been a national Day of Peace, a theme closely linked in the late 1950s with the antifascism myth, and 7 September had served as the Memorial Day for the Victims of Fascism. The fourteenth of September 1958 would witness the GDR's most impressive ceremony extolling the achievements of the antifascist resistance during the Third Reich.[61] It was no coincidence that each of these days was a Sunday, the traditional day of rest in

Germany, which allowed more East Germans to attend the dedication at Buchenwald than would have been the case during the week. The traditional Christian Sabbath was being replaced by a secular equivalent. Those attending the ceremonies would find it impossible to attend church services, the party leadership undoubtedly seeing the missing of church as an added advantage in the officially atheistic GDR. It turns out, however, that 14 September is also the traditional Feast of the Holy Cross, a holy day that commemorates the most important symbol of Christ's sacrificial death. Buchenwald's fallen, among them Thälmann, would serve as secular messiahs in the GDR's state religion, men who had freely sacrificed their lives to save others. Of course, the Buchenwald martyrs did not die to save humanity from sin, but rather to save it from imperialism, capitalist exploitation, and militarism. Whereas Christianity taught that Jesus died to give humankind eternal peace, SED propaganda maintained that the Buchenwald martyrs had given their lives in order to assure the German people earthly peace. Once again, the Christian imagery incorporated into the antifascism and Thälmann legends was striking.

The dedication of the Buchenwald National Monument and Memorial was hitherto the largest ceremonial gathering held in the GDR. Party authorities anticipated a crowd of 50,000, slightly more than half of whom would come from Weimar and the surrounding area. Although the lion's share of the other participants would come from the GDR, officials anticipated 2,000 from the FRG and West Berlin as well as 3,000 foreign guests. Antifascist resistance fighters from all over Europe, including Western countries such as France and Belgium, were among the twenty-one delegations represented at the ceremony. In addition, between 7,000 and 10,000 members of the FDJ camped out on the site during the night of 13–14 September. Although the ceremony did not attract the numbers that planners anticipated—only around 30,000 people showed up—the dedication at Buchenwald was, by SED standards, an impressive accomplishment.[62]

The ceremony's success was at least in part due to the fact that GDR officials made a concerted effort to encourage East Germans to attend. Newspapers, both local and national, promoted the upcoming event in the weeks preceding 14 September. Other media, as always at the state's disposal, called upon all Germans, both in Saxony and throughout the country, to participate in the effort to commemorate the fallen martyrs of Buchenwald. The committee in charge of planning the dedication ceremony issued a flyer entitled "Appeal of the

Committee for the Dedication of the Monument and Memorial [at] Buchenwald." The flyer begins by recounting the theme of the forthcoming ceremony: "Praise and honor the heirs of the resistance movement and the victims of fascist terror! They remind us: peoples of all countries—defend humanity's highest good—peace!" The appeal then goes on to emphasize the importance of the event. After all, antifascists from all over the globe would be attending: "Heeding this call, people from all over Europe, people of all worldviews and religious confessions will assemble on 14 September 1958 to dedicate the Buchenwald Monument and Memorial upon Weimar's Ettersberg." The flyer then turns to the ultimate purpose of the commemoration of Buchenwald's fallen, to "Honor the Dead out of Obligation to the Living!" The peace of Europe was in peril. In an obvious reference to the Federal Republic of Germany, the appeal insisted that "German militarism has once again become the greatest danger to peace in Europe." West Germany, controlled not by the "Bonn Parliament" but rather by "the fascist murderers of millions of patriots from almost every European country," had acquired "weapons of mass destruction" *(Massenvernichtungsmittel)*. Military bases were once again being constructed on German soil, and "old Nazi generals" controlled these vast resources. FRG chancellor Konrad Adenauer was even considering the prospect of West Germany's acquiring its own, independent nuclear deterrent—a prospect that truly frightened the East German leadership. In contrast, the GDR was going to hold a ceremony to honor those who had given their lives in the struggle against imperialism and militarism. Commemorating these martyrs would help to assure the ultimate defeat of the fascist cancer emerging in the FRG. "Peace for the dead! Peace for humanity!" demand the forces of antifascism. "The living must act!" The cold war must end. "All nuclear powers"—especially the United States—must negotiate in good faith with the Soviet Union in order to eliminate the danger. "On 14 September 1958," the appeal states, "we seek" to dedicate a "worthy monument and memorial" on what had once been a site of "fascist inhumanity." The memorial on the site of the camp and the nearby monument would help the people of Germany, indeed of all Europe, to remember the results of earlier policies, similar to those now being pursued in the West. Only if the sacrifices made at Buchenwald are remembered can humanity end the danger to peace. By recalling this sacrifice, all people will be united in the effort to end the threat. Participation in the dedication will allow peace-loving people to fight

for the immediate cessation of all atom and hydrogen bomb
   testing,
for the creation of an atomic weapon free zone in central Europe,
for the prohibition of the proliferation and storage of nuclear
   weapons,
for the easing of international tension and for a commitment to
   disarmament,
for world peace so that human happiness will flourish and
   humanism will triumph.[63]

GDR officials sought from the outset to relate commemoration of Buchenwald's fallen with their nation's current international goals. The
antifascism myth, as manifested at Buchenwald, had become an important component of East Germany's cold war propaganda. Having
unofficially given up on the idea of a unified socialist Germany, the
SED leadership amplified its rhetorical assault on the FRG. Party leaders had adapted their antifascism narrative, including the Thälmann
legend, to the current international situation, one characterized by a

The stela showing the illegal Thälmann commemoration, Buchenwald National Monument. Author's photograph.

cold war not only between the superpowers, but also between the two Germanys. Like the dedication at the Platz der 56,000 a month earlier, the ceremonies consecrating Buchenwald on 14 September 1958 consciously sought to create a link between remembrance of those who had given their lives in the struggle against Hitler fascism and the contemporary effort against the new fascism being created in the FRG. The planners of the 14 September event sought to build on this foundation. This carefully orchestrated observance sought to link the GDR's Buchenwald myth to the ongoing cold war, especially as manifested in the intensifying rivalry between East and West Germany.

The dedication ceremony was to begin at 11:00 AM, and those attending were told to arrive a half-hour earlier. The ritual opened with the raising of the flags of all of the participating countries, followed by two minutes of silence. Then the bells in the newly constructed bell tower tolled for the first time, after which Minister-President Otto Grotewohl approached the podium to deliver the keynote address. Following his speech, local party officials received the opportunity to say a few words. Next Wolfgang Langhoff, a member of the Central Committee's Cultural Commission, led those assembled in the Buchenwald Oath (Buchenwald Gelöbnis), in which they solemnly swore to "remain true to the ideals of the antifascist struggle for peace," which meant securing a Europe free of atomic weapons. Only then could the peoples of the world assure that there "would be peace on earth!" As the crowd took the oath, 10,000 doves were released, symbolic of the pledge to "carry this promise to the entire world." The ceremony concluded with the singing of the East German national anthem, "Resurrected from Ruins."[64]

Grotewohl's address took up the lion's share of the dedication ceremony. His speech related the usual platitudes about the glorious legacy of the antifascist resistance as represented at Buchenwald and the importance of remembering the sacrifice made by those who had been confined in the camp, linking that sacrifice to the ongoing struggle to create a central Europe free of nuclear weapons, a prominent theme in official discourse at this time. Grotewohl also emphasized the importance of the GDR's maintaining its close friendship with the Soviet Union, the nation responsible for the defeat of Hitler fascism. Placing what had happened at Buchenwald into a larger context, he also invoked the memory of the 57 million people who had died in the previous world war, making special mention of the 18 million imprisoned in the Nazi concentration camp system, among them 11 million who died at the hands of fascist criminals. This moment was an opportunity to memorialize all of these victims, and the minister-president's speech emphasized the vast numbers of those who had perished, underscoring the enormity of fascism's crimes, so he alluded to Thälmann only once, near the opening of his speech, when his rhetoric turned to those who had died at the nearby camp. Fifty-six thousand had given their lives freely for the greater good, knowing that when they passed through the camp gates with the inscription "To Each His Own" above the entrance, they would never leave the confines of the Ettersberg. "Upright and courageously they took their last steps, such as the Communist Thälmann, the Social Democrat Breitscheid, Pastor [Paul] Schneider, the untold numbers of Soviet prisoners of war, the tortured slave laborers from every nation and the nameless thousands."[65] Although Thälmann was one among thousands, Grotewohl gave him pride of place in his litany of Buchenwald's victims. The fallen KPD chief could serve as a shining example for all of those who wanted to continue the struggle against fascism and participate in the endeavor to build, on the ruins of the Third Reich, a new Germany characterized by humanism and socialism, a nation standing firmly on the foundations of the sacrifices made at Buchenwald. As a result, "[t]he monument is not lifeless stone. It should bear witness to future generations of the eternal glory of the courageous struggle against tyranny, for peace, freedom and humane values."[66]

The permanence of the monument not only represented the ultimate victory of the fallen—the victims had become victors—but was also emblematic of the enduring nature of German socialism as embodied in the GDR. The site chosen for the monument had during the Nazi years become the location of mass graves for tens of thousands of the victims of Buchenwald, not to mention those who had died during the violent liberation of the camp as well as others who, in spite of being liberated, ultimately succumbed to death because of what they had endured.[67] The new monument, in the eyes of the East German leadership, would serve as a fitting symbol for the new, socialist Germany. Both the monument on the side of the Ettersberg and the GDR were built upon the sacrifices made by the antifascist martyrs. Both were solid and permanent, aptly representing not only a glorious past, but an even better future.

Hence, it should come as no surprise that the Thälmann legend, which played such a pivotal role in the GDR's legitimizing myth, would serve as a central motif of the narrative presented at the Buchenwald

Location of the ceremony marking Thälmann's one hundredth birthday, Buchenwald Concentration Camp. Author's photograph.

Monument. Visitors would approach the monument complex from Blutstraße (Street of Blood), the famous bell tower off in the distance, a stunning view of Weimar behind it. From here, one proceeded down the twenty-meter-wide Stelenweg, walking past seven stelae, each engraved with a relief depicting some important aspect of life in Buchenwald.[68] Designed, like the monument's famous bell tower and striking bronze *Revolt of the Prisoners,* by an artists' collective headed by Fritz Kremer, the stelae cost 35,000 marks. On the reverse side of the stelae was inscribed a poem, "Memorial Words" (Mahnworte). Composed by Minister of Culture Johannes Becher in the spring of 1957—Bertold Brecht's untimely death made it impossible for the GDR's greatest poet to pen the appropriate lines—the poem lionized Buchenwald's fallen.[69] Beginning with the words "A death camp was built here" and incorporating such quasi-religious motifs as "The stones cry out—oh the stones also cry out," the poem contains seven stanzas, each one on the reverse side of each stela.[70]

Of primary interest here, however, are the sixth and seventh stelae, those depicting the 18 September 1944 memorial service for Thälmann and the camp's "self-liberation" in April 1945. Both designed by René Graetz—who also created the statue *Liberation* in Sachsenhausen—these stelae are approximately five meters wide by three meters tall. Each relief is bordered by a frame and consists of numerous blocks, each of the blocks cast in such a way as to create the relief on the front side. The sixth stela shows a highly stylized depiction of the "illegal Thälmann commemoration," with an image of Roman Jefimenko's portrait of the fallen Communist leader appearing at the top of the relief, just left of center. The representation of the portrait used on 18 September is cut more shallowly into the cement, indicative that it was a two-dimensional portrait in contrast to the other figures shown on the stela, which are clearly intended to be three dimensional. The relief even incorporates representations of the red and black cloth that originally framed Jefimenko's coal drawing. To the left of the portrait are eight men, representing those who had participated in the 1944 ceremony. To the right of the portrait of Thälmann is a camp inmate who is giving the antifascist salute with his left hand. Behind his hand is an eternal flame, representative of the need to continue to remember the fallen KPD chief's sacrifice. This figure, like all of those in the stelae, is gaunt, clearly the victim of months or years of starvation rations. In this case, his shirt is open, exposing a torso through which the viewer can clearly see his ribs, an image reminiscent of many depictions of Christ on the cross. Yet the camp inmate, unlike Christ (who did not resist efforts to kill him), remains strong, muscular, and upright. His features, like all of those depicted in the stelae, are angular; he is the archetypal worker seen so often in the socialist-realist visual arts. He has suffered but remains undaunted. The right third of this relief shows six men secreting away weapons behind a brick wall. No border separates these figures from those attending the Thälmann commemoration. The two events are clearly linked. The commemoration of Thälmann's sacrifice leads directly to the decision to hide weapons and resist the fascists violently.[71]

The seventh stela, depicting the "self-liberation" of Buchenwald, continues the narrative. The prisoners have now taken their weapons out of hiding; one, slightly left of center, is raising his rifle above his head in a gesture reminiscent of the antifascist salute. The former inmates are armed and taking their erstwhile persecutors prisoner. Camp guards are being seized throughout the left two-thirds of the relief. Some have their hands over their heads, others have them tied behind their backs. Several of the guards are shown on their knees, even their dogs have seemingly turned upon them. The right third of this final stela shows an archetypal worker, now liberated, standing under a tree, Goethe's famous oak. As with the inmate on the sixth stela—it is possibly the same man—his shirt is open, and his ribs are protruding from his chest. But he remains unbowed, having carried out the promise he had made the previous September: to put Thälmann's legacy into action and seize control of the camp from his fascist oppressors. Goethe's oak links this figure to the traditions of German humanism, made manifest not only in Thälmann's decision to give his life freely, but also in the accomplishments of German socialism as embodied in the GDR. All of these accomplishments grew out of the legacy of Thälmann's sacrifice, made just a few hundred yards from where the relief stood.

If the scenes depicted in these two reliefs do not make the link among Thälmann, the antifascist resistance, the workers' liberation of Buchenwald, and the GDR clear enough, the poetry on the back of the two final stelae removes any doubt. Inscribed on the reverse of the sixth stela, entitled "The Illegal Thälmann Commemoration," are Becher's words:

> Greet Ernst Thälmann, Germany's distinguished son!
> In a bright light he stood before us.
> And all around was a celebratory sound,
> It was, as all peoples raised their voices—*The International*,
> ringing out its chorus:
> "And this world must be ours, ours!"
> And Thälmann hoisted the flag high aloft.[72]

Carved into the reverse side of the seventh and final stela, which is entitled "The Liberation," are the concluding words of the poem:

> What Thälmann saw happened one day.
> They dug up their hidden weapons,
> The consecrated dead rose from the grave.
> See their arms stretched out into the future:
> See a monument in numerous forms,
> That testifies to us, never forget—The dead remind us:
> "Think of Buchenwald!"[73]

Thälmann has the distinction of being the only person whose name is used in the entire seven stanzas of the poem. Like his position in the narrative depicted on the stelae, the Communist martyr plays a central role in the development of the major motif of Becher's verse: he links the past, present, and future. It is he who stood before German Communists like a "bright light," he who hoisted the flag of socialist resistance. His sacrifice served as the model for those who chose to resist Nazi tyranny at Buchenwald. He never lost hope but rather foresaw the "consecrated dead" rising up in order to assure the ultimate liberation not only of Buchenwald, but of all of Germany. Thälmann served as the paragon for the many people who not only fought the fascist menace, but also for those who never lost hope, maintaining their belief in the victory of socialism even in the face of overwhelming odds. He would likewise serve as an inspiration to visitors to the monument, reminding them not to despair, but rather to maintain their faith in the certain victory of socialist humanism. Thälmann, like so many others, perished at Buchenwald, but as long as his cause lives on, he is not dead, but rather manifest in the GDR's ideas.

After passing along the Stelenweg, the visitor proceeded past three immense mass graves, each encircled by a wall, in which the ashes of approximately 10,000 of Buchenwald's victims lay. Then one turned to the left, walking down the Straße zur Freiheit (Street of Freedom) and past numerous massive rectangular monuments, each commemorating the fallen of Buchenwald from a particular country. The victims who died in the camp, like the socialist movement that they represented, were international, from every country in occupied Europe. After treading down the Street of Freedom, the visitor turned left again, heading back up the side of the mountain in the direction of the Feierplatz (Place of Celebration), where he or she encountered Cremer's bronze showing eleven of Buchenwald's inmates. Clearly on the verge of starvation, these figures commemorated the suffering that the victims of fascism endured on the Buchenwald site. Behind the bronze statue stood the bell tower, standing upright, a symbol of the ultimate victory not only of the camp's inmates, but also of the antifascist cause.[74]

Of course, the newly dedicated monument was not the only place on the Ettersberg that played a role in propagating the Thälmann legend. The nearby concentration camp also held two sites that became important to remembrance of the fallen Communist leader. The first was the basement of the camp's erstwhile disinfection building, the site of the illegal September 1944 commemoration ceremony. From the outset, this location played an important role in promoting the Thälmann myth and was a popular site for commemoration services, *Jugendweihe* (youth consecration) ceremonies (see chapter 6), and a display—built at a proposed cost of 92,000 marks—commemorating the martyred KPD chief.[75] An English-language pamphlet describing the camp, after reminding visitors that "German anti-fascists were the first victims of nazi [sic] barbarism," depicts the exhibition during the mid-1970s: "There is today a Thälmann Memorial in the cellar of the disinfection department. Pictures and documents testify to the life and struggle of Ernst Thälmann, the chairman of the Communist Party of Germany, and to his legacy." After explaining that the fascists refused to put Thälmann on trial because they did not want the proceedings to "turn into an accusation of the regime," the printed guide points out that "[o]n 18 August 1944 he was murdered at the crematorium of Buchenwald concentration camp." Finally, the pamphlet reminds English-speaking visitors why the disinfection chamber was so important to remembering the fallen KPD chief:

> Anti-fascists organized an illegal commemoration ceremony in honour of Ernst Thälmann in the cellar of the disinfection department. A prisoner spoke about the life of Ernst Thälmann and on the pledge to continue his work.
> The SS was informed about this gathering and arrested several participants.
> Their heroism protected the illegal resistance organization.[76]

The guide included a photograph of the camp's Thälmann Memorial, complete with a portrait of the fallen party chief, an eternal flame, and a wreath. Next to the portrait were the words "Eternal Sacrifices You Perished Here."

During the mid-1980s, the site was renovated in order to prepare for the celebration of Thälmann's one hundredth birthday.[77] The updated display, "a memorial worthy of Ernst Thälmann,"[78] reflected the party leadership's concerns during the final years of the GDR. The first thing that a visitor encountered upon entering the basement of the disinfection chamber was a wall-size photograph of Thälmann standing among a group of workers. In the upper right of the photograph, in large letters, was a quotation from Thälmann: "Communism will survive; it will be the social system [Gesellschaftsordnung] of tomorrow." Even during the final years of East Germany's existence, at a time when we now know that Soviet-style socialism was in its death throes, the SED leadership clung to the notion that communism would ultimately triumph. Indeed, it is possible that the choice of this quotation at the entrance to the Thälmann display was a defiant reply to the ongoing reform program recently launched in the Soviet Union, the goals of which the GDR leadership—who saw glasnost and perestroika as a betrayal of socialism—did not approve.

The display itself consisted of a series of plywood panels presented in groups of three and hence reminiscent of triptychs. The opening series of panels concentrated on the highlights of Thälmann's life, the first panel displaying a quotation from Thälmann: "I am proud that I have struggled my entire life." The middle panel presented the bare essentials of the fallen Communist leader's life:

> Born on 16 April 1886 in Hamburg.
> Harbor worker.
> Member of the Central Committee of the KPD and Reichstag representative.
> Elected chairman of the KPD in 1925.
> Member of the Executive Committee of the Communist International. Arrested by the fascists on 5 March 1933 and[,] after resolutely [enduring] more than eleven difficult years in imprisonment, [was] during the night of 18 August 1944 murdered in Buchenwald Concentration Camp.

This first triptych concluded with a 1936 quotation from Martin Anderson Nexö, a Communist activist of the 1930s and 1940s: "Ernst Thälmann embodies, as few others do, not only the coming Germany, but also the coming world[.] In the contemporary struggle between culture and barbarism, between man and animal, spirit and beast—which is being fought at its bloodiest in Germany—Ernst Thälmann has become the most powerful symbol of the forces of humanity."

The second trio of panels dealt with the KPD chief's murder. The first of this group consisted of a copy, taken from SS chief Heinrich Himmler's desk calendar, of Hitler's direct order to kill Thälmann. "Thälmann is to be executed," read item number twelve on Himmler's list. The next panel contained a long quotation from Marian Zgoda's eyewitness account, recorded in 1948, of Thälmann's murder. Not only did the text provide a detailed firsthand description of the fallen proletarian leader, but it also mentioned Wolfgang Otto, whose guilt would become an important theme in a subsequent triptych, as one of the SS men participating in the shooting. The third panel in this grouping consisted of a sketch of the murder scene drawn by Zgoda. It was reminiscent of nothing so much as the Stations of the Cross, complete with numbers drawn throughout the diagram and a key below it indicating where the car carrying Thälmann entered the courtyard, the place where the car stopped, the location where the assassins stood as they shot their helpless victim, the exact place where the KPD chief died, as well as the location of the crematorium in which his murderers incinerated his lifeless body.

The third set of panels provided an account of the commemoration ceremony at Buchenwald, which had become a vital component of the Thälmann legend as propagated at Buchenwald.

> On the evening of 18 September 1944 over fifty prisoners—Germans, Austrians, and Czech nationals, in addition to Soviet prisoners of war—assembled of their own accord in this room in order to commemorate the life of the great German workers' leader and internationalist.
>
> They swore not to end their struggle against fascism until its complete destruction.
>
> Because an informer had betrayed the commemoration several prisoners were interrogated and tortured by the Gestapo.

The inmates participating in the ceremony had risked their lives officially to remember their leader, several sacrificing a great deal.

Yet the resistance in Buchenwald remained undaunted. The final panel of this group contained a quotation from Walter Bartel, former chairman of the International Illegal Camp Committee, providing evidence that the resistance had lived up to its solemn promise made on 18 September 1944: "In the spirit of Thälmann we prepared ourselves for the final battle. On 11 April 1945 the inmates of Buchenwald liberated themselves under their own power with their weapons in their hands." Even after his death, Thälmann continued to inspire the opponents of fascism on to ever greater accomplishments.

The next triptych, displayed under the rubric "The murder that has not been legally punished," was concerned with a subject central to the Thälmann myth during the mid-1980s (see chapter 8). As the first panel pointed out, one of the men directly involved in the KPD chief's murder, Wolfgang Otto, "lives in the FRG." Yet "in spite of numerous incriminating accusations against him—the first appeared in 1947 on page one of the 'Frankfurter Rundschau'—a trial against Otto has been put off for four decades." Western leaders had no interest in pursuing justice for the fallen proletarian leader. The central panel in this triptych sought to establish that the FRG government ignored the case in spite of a popular outcry, providing as evidence numerous newspaper articles bearing such titles as: "Should the Thälmann Murder Remain Unpunished?" "Murder of Ernst Thälmann Should Finally Go before a Court," and "Unprecedented Delay of Justice." The final panel exhibited photographs of Rosa and Irma Thälmann, the two survivors who had waited in vain for justice.

The final series of panels displayed a long quotation designed to sum up the lessons of the exhibition. Attributed to Erich Honecker, it began: "Ernst Thälmann was among us in the Weimar Republic as we led the struggle against the approach of fascism." He was, the text continued, also "among us" as "we led the struggle against the Nazis" during the Third Reich. He was "present" when the KPD returned from exile following the victory of the Red Army. "Ernst Thälmann was among us when we established the Republic [in] 1949." Finally, "Ernst Thälmann is among us today because we have sworn, in his spirit, to protect and strengthen our republic and forever to carry the banner of socialist revolution forward." The martyr might have perished, but he was "among us," the German people, whenever "we" took a step forward in the construction of socialism. He was omnipresent, his spirit alive as long as the struggle against fascism, militarism, and capitalist exploitation continued. It was the sacred duty of the German people to remember him and live up to his glorious legacy.

After viewing this series of displays, visitors entered the delousing chamber, where the 18 September 1944 ceremony had taken place. Camp officials had changed this location slightly from the 1970s, introducing a larger portrait of Thälmann, no longer bordered by a red piece of cloth, but rather completely surrounded by a red border. Urns for commemorative flames were on either side of the portrait, and the wreath remained in place. For the Thälmann centennial, however, an altarlike edifice had been added, bearing the dates "1886–1986." The display had been updated for the commemoration of this important anniversary, remaining unchanged during the GDR's final years. The exhibit sought to re-create the solemnity of the original 1944 commemoration, but only proved to be a classic example of the kitsch that was so typical of the GDR's political culture. Even so, the 1989 guide to Buchenwald insisted that "[a] visit to the Thälmann memorial is a moving experience. There are pictures of this great working-class leader telling of his life and struggle for the cause of his class. Prisoners of different nations held a secret ceremony of memory in this cellar on September 18, 1944, when it became known that the Chairman of the German Communist Party had been murdered in Buchenwald."[79]

Perhaps even more important to the propagation of the Thälmann legend were Buchenwald's crematorium and the adjacent courtyard, where the KPD leader was shot and his body destroyed. A draft of a pamphlet written in 1959 that served as a guide to the camp records that "[t]oday there is a plaque in commemoration of Ernst Thälmann, the chairman of the KPD, mounted next to the door entering the crematorium."[80] The plaque reads:

ETERNAL REST
TO THE GREAT SON OF
THE GERMAN PEOPLE, TO THE LEADER
OF THE GERMAN
WORKING CLASS
ERNST THÄLMANN
WHO[,] ON THE 18TH OF AUGUST 1944[,]
WAS MURDERED BY FASCISTS
ON THIS SPOT

To the left of the plaque was a bust of Thälmann with the dates of his birth and death as well as the "remark [that he was] murdered in Buchenwald." Flowers, ribbons, and wreaths were placed on the ground between the plaque and the bust. An eternal flame, not quite two meters tall, was eventually placed at the site. It would later be replaced by an even more elaborate eternal flame, slightly taller, with its base encircled with barbed wire.[81] From 1966, the location of the flame played an important role in the GDR's sports festivals, both summer and winter. The Thälmann flame served the role of its Olympic counterpart, with a torch lighting in the crematorium courtyard. From there, this "Flame of Antifascist Heroism" would be relayed to Berlin, where it would be used to light the ceremonial fire associated with the games. Thus, the undying flame linked so closely with the martyred KPD chief would be distributed throughout the GDR, symbolically joining the entire nation with this holiest site in the Thälmann myth. The flame played a similar role in local sporting events, such as the Buchenwald Monument Run.[82]

After viewing the bust, plaque, and eternal flame in the courtyard, a visitor could then enter the reconstructed crematorium. This building housed six ovens, organized into two groups of three. Each of the ovens could burn as many as three bodies simultaneously.[83] Before the first oven on the left, where Thälmann's remains had been incinerated, there was a wreath and some flowers commemorating his sacrifice. The oven itself contained a watch, all that was reportedly left of the martyred Communist leader following his liquidation by the Nazis. Since nothing remained of Thälmann's corpse except for the ashes mixed among thousands of the other victims of Buchenwald, the crematorium site, including both the courtyard and the oven, was as close as the SED leadership had to a tomb for its fallen leader. This location became an ersatz grave, among the holiest sites in the Thälmann myth, where mourners could go to memorialize his sacrifice. It was not only the spot where his fascist enemies had disposed of his lifeless body, but the very place where he had given his life freely in the struggle against the forces of fascism and for the creation of a socialist Germany.[84] No place was more closely associated with Thälmann's sacrificial death. To the very end of the GDR, party organizations, school groups, and international delegations performed ceremonies at the location, paying homage to the most important martyr in socialist Germany's legitimation myth. For the sake of brevity, a handful of examples will have to suffice.

Although the 1950s—when the antifascism myth was most integral to the legitimizing narrative of the GDR—witnessed the peak of Thälmann commemoration in Buchenwald, the SED regime continued to celebrate its hero's life and, more important, his sacrificial death right up until 1989. No anniversary of Thälmann's birth or death went unobserved, with important dates—most notably his one-hundredth birthday (see chapter 8)—witnessing major commemoration ceremonies. However, most of the remembrance rituals were relatively low-key affairs performed annually on 16 April, Thälmann's birthday, or on 18 August, the anniversary of his death.

The twenty-fifth anniversary of Thälmann's murder fortuitously fell in the same year, 1969, as the twentieth anniversary of the founding of the GDR. The regime made a conscious effort to link the two events, and commemoration of the fallen KPD chief became a "high point in our [the party leadership's] efforts in preparation for the twentieth anniversary of the GDR."[85] Officials scheduled a "large rally and a commemorative wreath laying at the monuments" to Thälmann and the Social Democratic martyr Rudolf Breitscheid. The theme of the ceremony was given as follows: "To fulfill the legacy of Ernst Thälmann and Rudolf Breitscheid means: overall strengthening of the GDR—universal struggle against Neo-Nazism and the imperialistic war-mongering policies of West Germany, for peace and European security." The 1969 commemoration contrasted the GDR's accomplishments with its western neighbor's shortcomings. Several hundred people—both adults and children—from the FRG and West Berlin would participate in the ceremonies, which included a "symposium" based on the theme "In which German state has the legacy of the antifascist fighters been fulfilled?" Maintaining a major motif of SED propaganda since the late 1940s, the 1969 celebration sought consciously not only to link the GDR with the traditions of German antifascism, but also to emphasize the continuity between the heritage of National Socialism and the capitalist Federal Republic.[86]

The year 1974 witnessed lower-key commemoration ceremonies. On 16 April, "leading personalities of the party and mass organizations of the Erfurt region and the city of Weimar" participated in a less extravagant ritual marking Thälmann's birthday. Although soldiers from the Soviet army took part in the celebration, no East German politician of national importance was present.[87] Party leaders marked a more important anniversary in August of that year with a much larger ceremony solemnizing the thirtieth anniversary of Thälmann's death. Werner Krolikowski, a member of the Politburo and the SED's secretary of economics, one among numerous prominent GDR politicians present, was the featured speaker. In keeping with the tradition of linking the Thälmann myth with the political needs of the moment, Krolikowski demanded an "end to the mass terror in Chile" and "[f]reedom for Louis Corvalan and all Chilean patriots" in the name of Thälmann and all the other victims of German fascism. In addition, Walter Wimmer, a scholar employed by the Institute for Marxism–Leninism in Berlin and a leading East German authority on Thälmann's life, hosted a colloquium on the theme "work, learn, and live in Thälmann's spirit." Among those attending were 130 members of the FDJ, the future of the party, who were urged to continue the struggle against the FRG's fascist traditions and to be worthy representatives "of the lives and struggles of the heroes of the antifascist resistance."[88]

The year 1984 saw even more elaborate ceremonies at Buchenwald, among the last major examples of Thälmann commemoration in the history of the GDR. Elaborate rituals marked the fortieth anniversary of the KPD chief's death. Hundreds, especially members of the FDJ, participated in the usual—if more extensive than previously—regimen of parades and laying of wreaths. Among the featured speakers at the ceremonies was Walter Bartel—who had previously given major addresses at Buchenwald. He talked about one of the major themes of Thälmann commemoration that appeared during the final decade of the GDR: "A murder that is not beyond punishment." Bartel recounted his experiences during the Third Reich—how the local population pelted him and his fellow inmates with stones upon their arrival at the train station in nearby Weimar. Passing through the camp gates, over which hung the words "To each his own," he and his comrades entered a new world, one where he became "prisoner number 3225." Working twelve-hour days at backbreaking labor, Bartel faced the constant threat of violent death at the hands of the SS. The creation of the Illegal Camp Committee in July 1943, however, provided the hope for the future that he might otherwise not have had. The committee's program promised "solidarity, [and] aid for everyone, regardless of nation, party, or religion." It was this group of inmates, the staunchest opponents of German fascism, who, upon hearing of Thälmann's death, risked their very lives in order to assure that his martyrdom would not go unnoticed. Whereas the antifascists sought to remember Thälmann's sacrifice, the West sought to forget it. In 1947, for example, the SED leadership appealed to authorities in the American Zone of Occupation to punish the perpetrators of this horrific crime, at least one of whom, Wolfgang Otto, resided in their jurisdiction. Although an American military court sentenced Otto to twenty years, he, like so many other former Nazis living in the West, served only a small portion of his sentence, leaving prison after five short years to "teach at a Catholic boys' school in Geldern." Bartel reported that this murderer of the eternal leader of the German proletariat now lived in retirement, never having paid the price for his most horrific crime. Not only was Otto responsible for Thälmann's death, but as an SS man in Buchenwald, the blood of "8,450 Soviet soldiers and officers" was on his hands. Yet Otto remained unpunished in spite of Rosa and Irma Thälmann's repeated requests to right this wrong.[89]

The West may have forgotten Thälmann's legacy, said Bartel, but neither the inmates of Buchenwald nor the people of the GDR had done so: "Comrades of the disinfection chamber carried out a memorial service for Ernst Thälmann on 18 September. Revolutionary songs were sung. . . . Robert Siewert gave a speech and called upon everyone to continue to fight in the spirit of Thälmann until we had reached the final victory." Bartel concluded by thanking those present who continued to remember the sacrifices made by Thälmann and other antifascists, who had demanded justice for the victims of German fascism, who had refused simply to sweep the past under the rug. It was they who were responsible for the GDR's accomplishments. They represent-ed the future of German socialism.[90]

Bartel's speech is remarkable for its continuity with themes first developed at Buchenwald in the immediate postwar years. Bartel, like the speakers of the 1940s, emphasized the centrality of the antifascist movement to the traditions upon which the GDR had been built. His speech incorporated the same motifs that had become so important al-most four decades earlier, especially the 18 September commemoration ceremony and the "self-liberation" of Buchenwald in the spirit of Ernst Thälmann. Indeed, the GDR's legitimizing narrative had changed re-markably little over the course of two generations and undoubtedly lost much of its resonance in that time. In the face of the shortcomings of "real, existing socialism," appeals to an ever more distant tradition came increasingly to ring hallow. As the heritage of antifascism moved ever further into the past, the SED proved incapable of creating an al-ternative source of legitimacy. Yet to justify its monopoly on power the party continued to appeal to an ever more distant past, one increas-ingly unfamiliar to the GDR's population.

As can be seen in the 1984 video documentary *Oh, Buchenwald*, even when the SED made use of new technologies to legitimize its so-cialist alternative to the West, GDR leaders continued to make appeals to traditions developed during the 1930s and 1940s. A mere twenty-five minutes long, the film is remarkably well made, with footage from the period interspersed with artists' renderings of life and death in the camp. The narration is, by GDR standards, remarkably even handed. Although there is a reference to the Nazis pursuing the policies of the "economic cartels, concerns, and bankers," *Oh, Buchenwald* does con-cede that the opposition to the Nazis was not confined to the Com-munists but also incorporated the "Social Democrats, trade unionists, Christians," and even "bourgeois opposition" groups. The documen-tary, however, does insist that the Communists were at the forefront of the opposition, with Thälmann making a prominent, if brief, appear-ance as the leader of the antifascist movement during the final years of the Weimar Republic and early days of the Third Reich. The Na-zis succeeded in arresting the leaders of the opposition, the KPD chief among them, and the film turns to a series of stills showing an impris-oned Ernst Thälmann. After a comment stating that "Thälmann will later be murdered in Buchenwald," he disappears from the narration.

The remainder of the film is a standard—if well done—GDR account of the history of Buchenwald Concentration Camp, concluding with the "self-liberation" and footage of the 1958 dedication of the national monument, the participants taking the Buchenwald Oath. As always, the message is clear: the GDR has inherited the antifascist traditions established in Buchenwald during the darkest days of German history. Although *Oh, Buchenwald* made only a minor contribution to the Thälmann legend, the film did a good job of summing up the major themes of the antifascism myth as propagated during the GDR's final years. Harkening back to the ceremonies of the 1950s, one of the final images in the documentary shows the explosion of an atomic bomb. To be an antifascist was, as had been the case from the 1950s, to oppose the proliferation of nuclear weapons.[91]

From the final days of the Second World War, when word spread that Ernst Thälmann had been murdered in Buchenwald Concentration Camp, German Communists closely linked commemoration of the fallen KPD leader's sacrifice with the camp's antifascist traditions. After all, the site contained not only the location where Nazi thugs had murdered Thälmann, but also the oven in which his lifeless body had been cremated and the location of the first major Thälmann commemoration ceremony. As a result, his legacy became an important component of the antifascism legend at the camp and hence the GDR's state religion. Although Buchenwald's version of the Thälmann legend evolved over time—such as when GDR leaders placed a new emphasis on opposition to the spread of atomic weapons—overall it remained remarkably consistent. The leaders of the SBZ and then of the GDR relied so heavily on the Thälmann legend for their legitimacy that any significant change in the narrative risked undermining that legitimacy. As a result, although the antifascism myth might have been useful in justifying the establishment of the SED regime, in the long run it hamstrung East German leaders, who simply could not find new ways to defend their monopoly on power in the face of the shortcomings that became ever more apparent in "real, existing socialism."

6

"We Can Look Forward to a Happy Future"

Having recognized that the future of revolutionary socialism depended on it, Germany's Marxist political parties had long made concerted efforts to organize and mobilize the country's working-class youth. As early as December 1906, the SPD had formed the Union of Free Youth Organizations of Germany as well as the League of Young Workers of Germany, seeking to protect the interests of younger members of the proletariat and instill in them the proper revolutionary spirit.[1] The socialist youth movement would later be united under the banner of the Free Socialist Youth, or FSJ. In the wake of the 1917 division of the SPD, the newly formed KPD inherited this tradition of organizing working-class young people, a tendency that the new political faction's close ties to the CPSU only intensified. In November 1919, on the advice of Willi Münzenberg, the KPD formed the Communist Youth International, the group's name emphasizing its close links to the Comintern. In 1920, the KPD's youth organization assumed the name "Communist Youth of Germany" (KJD) and five years later donned the new title of "Communist Youth League of Germany" (KJVD). Unlike the youth movements of other Weimar parties—which emphasized sports or cultural activities—the KJVD focused its efforts almost entirely on political concerns, which may help explain why it never had more than 50,000 members. The KJVD was extremely militant, playing an active role in disseminating KPD propaganda. As historian Klaus-Michael Mallmann has pointed out, members of the KJVD "sold newspapers, painted slogans, glued posters, collected dues, engaged in agitation, and made up voice choruses" on behalf of the party.[2]

After the Second World War, the KPD/SED leadership could legitimately claim that Ernst Thälmann had been deeply concerned with coordinating the proletarian youth of the Weimar Republic. Throughout

Thälmann Pioneers in Halle.
Courtesy of the German
National Archive.

his years as party chief, Thälmann had encouraged the growth of the KJVD, insisting that the organization was vital to the future of Marxism–Leninism. Thälmann's experiences as a young socialist growing up in Hamburg undoubtedly contributed to the urgency that he gave this issue as party chairman. In March 1927, for example, speaking at the KPD's Eleventh Party Conference, he reminded his comrades "that the majority of the population consists of women and youth, of both the masculine and feminine genders." If the party wished to succeed, it needed to increase its success with both of these constituencies.[3] Under Thälmann's chairmanship, the KPD did indeed seek to appeal to these groups, but with very limited success. Class consciousness always trumped gender in the eyes of the party leadership, and young people found the demands that KJVD membership placed on them distasteful. The party offered German youth little more than a uniform and a sense of belonging in exchange for often arduous work.

Given the rhetorical emphasis that the former party chief placed on attracting Germany's young working-class population, it should come as no surprise that the Thälmann myth became a central component of the KPD/SED's efforts to win over the youth of the SBZ and the GDR.[4] As in its appeals to the general population, the party leadership used every means at its disposal to propagate the Thälmann legend and thereby legitimize the creation of a separate socialist Germany. Among the most important weapons that the SED had at its disposal for the propagation of the Thälmann legend was the Free German Youth, or FDJ, among the party's most important institutions.

Although Walter Ulbricht officially re-created the KPD's youth organization on 31 July 1945, given the role that the Hitler Youth had played in recent German history, the Soviets exhibited serious misgivings about allowing individual political parties to form their own youth movements. This reluctance resulted in the creation of a theoretically nonpartisan organization aimed at children and adolescents. Anticipating the unity of their two parties the following month, on 7 March 1946 prominent figures in the KPD and SPD established the Freie Deutsche Jugend (Free German Youth). The result was a self-described "nonpartisan, united, democratic youth organization"—the realization of the goal of creating a single, united youth movement. Like the political party that had begotten it, the FDJ came into existence under the banner of antifascism. Much as the division of the working-class parties had made possible the triumph of National Socialism, the existence of two proletarian youth organizations had undermined the effort to preempt a Nazi takeover. The creation of the FDJ would address this shortcoming and play a vital role in assuring that fascism would never reemerge on German soil. Indeed, the fact that a single youth organization became a reality six weeks before the KPD and SPD were unified throughout the entire Soviet zone was an indication of the importance that Ulbricht and his comrades gave to appeals to Germany's young people. Although a number of organizations—among them the Christian Democrats, the Liberal Democrats, and the church-affiliated youth groups—officially had representation on the FDJ's Central Council, the SED dominated the FDJ from its inception. The naming of Erich Honecker, a dedicated Communist, as the movement's first chairman quickly belied the organization's supposed independence. In the years after 1946, as the SED came ever more closely to embrace the model established by the CPSU, so did its youth organization, evolving like its Soviet counterpart into a multitiered system. Children between the ages of six and fourteen belonged to the Children's Association of the FDJ. In 1949, this group became known as the "Young Pioneers," and in fourth grade children moved up to the Thälmann Pioneers. The latter group's name had the effect of placing Thälmann in the same pantheon as Lenin in that the Soviet Communist youth organization was called the "Lenin Pioneers." From 1956—when SED officials launched their own very modest de-Stalinization campaign—Thälmann assumed a place second only to Lenin in the hierarchy of socialist deities.[5] At the age of fourteen, members celebrated their *Jugendweihe* (youth consecration), which served as a secular substitute for the rite of confirmation practiced in the Roman Catholic and Lutheran churches. The *Jugend-weihe* ceremony was often held at sites important to the Ernst Thälmann cult, such as the basement of the disinfection chamber at Buchenwald Concentration Camp. Following this ceremony, East German adolescents joined the FDJ, to which they belonged until the age of twenty-five. Over time, the Pioneers and the FDJ became closely linked to the East German educational system, having the effect of making membership mandatory for all intents and purposes. The result was that those handful of East German children, adolescents, and young adults who somehow escaped membership in the SED's youth movement suffered a variety of disadvantages—difficulties getting good jobs or gaining admission to a university, for example.[6]

From their inception, the Young Pioneers and the FDJ played a central role in the indoctrination of youth into good antifascists—that is, socialists. As the SED minister of culture Johannes Becher put it, the FDJ's most important goal was to promote an "antifascist–democratic consciousness" among the SBZ's young people first and then later among the GDR's youth. Party leaders took quite seriously their contention that "Keines zu klein—Kämpfer zu sein" (No one is too young to be a fighter),[7] and the organization indoctrinated East German youths from the age of six as staunch antifascists and militant socialists. Stints in the Thälmann Pioneers and the FDJ became prerequisites for membership in the SED as well as for the privileges that resulted from affiliation with the ruling party. Given the centrality of the Thälmann myth to the SED's legitimizing narrative, it should come as no surprise that the political group's youth movement made a concerted effort to instill its members with the proper admiration and respect for the fallen KPD chief. It is interesting to note that the organization never extended similar practices to martyred Social Democrats such as Rudolf Breitscheid—further evidence that the Pioneers and FDJ evolved in an increasingly Stalinist direction alongside the SED. The cult surrounding the martyred KPD chief became a central component of the effort to mold the young people of the SBZ and GDR into good internationalists, intense admirers of the Soviet Union, and staunch opponents of fascism in all of its forms. The things young people learned in their youth organizations would, the party leadership hoped, encourage them to play an active role in the struggle to build socialism and mold them into unswerving cold warriors determined to participate in the struggle between good and evil, light and dark, and one day to defeat the forces of reaction embodied in the FRG. The result was a massive outpouring of agit-prop aimed at the young people of East Germany, encouraging them to look upon Ernst Thälmann as "an example for us all," someone to be admired and emulated because of his love of Germany, the Soviet Union, and the international workers' movement.

This propaganda effort aimed at young people manifested itself in every way imaginable. The East German youth movement published an untold number of books and pamphlets, both fiction and nonfiction, about the fallen Communist hero. The textbooks that children and adolescents used in school came replete with lessons drawn from Thälmann's life and death. The Pioneers' and FDJ's symbols were redolent with images invoking the sacrifices that "Germany's eternal son" had made on their behalf. The songs that they sang at youth meetings and in school invoked the "legacy" that the governing party had inherited from the martyred Hamburg dockworker. The GDR's children regularly swore "solemn oaths" promising to live up to the example set by Ernst Thälmann, and photographs of the erstwhile KPD chief hung in classrooms throughout the GDR. Members of the SED youth organizations could win medals and other awards bearing the martyred KPD chief's name. Indeed, the highest award that a member of the FDJ could win was the Thälmann Medal. First presented to participants in a massive peace demonstration held in East Berlin on 15 August 1951, the honor was also known as the "Ready for the Defense of the Homeland Award." Each medal, bearing a likeness of the fallen KPD chief, was individually numbered, adding value to the honor by pointing out that the number of recipients was limited.[8] Efforts to propagate the Thälmann legend went well beyond such awards, however. Seemingly everyone who grew up in East Germany, for example, saw Kurt Maetzig's epic films at least once, if not in a theater, then either at school or during a youth meeting. Young people also regularly made field trips to places important to the Thälmann legend, such as Buchenwald Concentration Camp or the site of the KPD chief's February 1933 speech about the dangers confronting the workers of Germany in the wake of the Nazi takeover. In short, the image of Ernst Thälmann was an all but omnipresent part of the daily existence of East Germany's children and adolescents.

Space here is limited, and other scholars—Alan Nothnagle, John Rodden, and René Börrnert come to mind—have dealt quite effectively with the employment of the Thälmann myth in appeals to East Germany's young people.[9] For the sake of completeness, however—not to mention the importance of placing these appeals to youth in the broader context of East German political propaganda—it is vital that this subject be examined yet again. It is impossible to analyze every instance in which the party leadership molded the Thälmann myth in order to appeal to young people, so once again a handful of examples will have to suffice.

As Nothnagle has pointed out, "The antifascist myth was generally represented by the symbolism of the oath and the covenant."[10] Hence, it should come as no surprise that from the earliest days of the Pioneers and the FDJ their members would be called upon to swear solemn oaths promising to live up to Ernst Thälmann's legacy. For example, all comrades in the Thälmann Pioneers took the following vow:

> We Young Pioneers, sons and daughters of the German people, swear on our Pioneer honor before our president Wilhelm Pieck, that we will show that we will become worthy of the name of Ernst Thälmann, who struggled for the happiness of our people and gave his life for it.
> We swear, that we will dedicate all of our strength to the struggle to build a unified, peace-loving, democratic and independent Germany.
> We swear, constantly to stand for the uncompromising victory of socialism.
> We swear to cultivate friendship with the Soviet Union, and to watch over it like Ernst Thälmann and Wilhelm Pieck.
> We promise, to live and learn [in an] exemplary [fashion], in order to become worthy citizens of our German Democratic Republic.
> This, we swear![11]

The Pioneers emphasized the relationship between the fallen KPD chief and the head of the East German state, Wilhelm Pieck. As GDR president, Pieck stood as a concrete example of the link between the fallen KPD chief and the leadership of the new socialist Germany. Indeed, at least in the years preceding Pieck's death in 1960, the symbolism of the Thälmann Pioneers was redolent with images linking the martyred Communist leader and the East German head of state. For example, the group's official flag was a red banner with the visages of Pieck and Thälmann in the upper-left-hand corner. Some of the medals awarded to members in the organization depicted the two men side by side, Thälmann representing the glorious accomplishments of the German workers' movement in the past and Pieck emblematic of the links between the GDR and this rich legacy. Some of the first Pioneer Parks would be named after the East German president, closely associating him with the promises embodied in Thälmann's legacy and engendered in the GDR's accomplishments. The images of Walter Ulbricht and Erich Honecker would later replace Pieck's, and Thälmann Pioneers would swear their oaths in the presence of other leaders, but the image of Ernst Thälmann remained a constant in the group's symbols.

Throughout the regime's history, oath taking continued to play a vital part in efforts to promote the Ernst Thälmann myth among East German youth. These oaths were often taken at locations sacred to the Thälmann legend, such as Buchenwald Concentration Camp, where the KPD chief had perished in August 1944. There were numerous instances when party leaders called upon East German youths—not to mention adults—to swear a solemn oath to fulfill the martyred party chief's legacy on this most sacred of sites. Among the many examples of this practice, one such instance occurred on 12 July 1961. This assembly, the Congress of the Central Leadership of the Pioneer Organization "Ernst Thälmann," was important enough that Max Zimmering—who had earlier written an important children's book about the slain party leader (discussed later in this chapter)—wrote a special oath, somewhat longer than most others, for the occasion. "We Thälmann Pioneers," it opens,

> assembled in Buchenwald,
> to honor the fighters who have fallen
> for our future, and to honor the Hamburg harbor worker,
> the son of his class, Ernst Thälmann,
> who grew up into the leader of his class,
> him, whose name we bear,
> in order to fulfill his legacy,
> we want to remain worthy of it
> always and everywhere!
>   This we swear!
> Because his people, the German people
> lay in his heart,
> he hated fascism and war,
> because he loved the working people,
> who created all of the beauty and all
> of the wealth of this earth,

he struggled for socialism.
We, who bear his name,
will dedicate all of our youthful energy,
[so] that peace [will] be victorious
and socialism will bloom in our land.
   This we swear!

The oath continues in this vein, with those present solemnly swearing to participate in the effort to build the "world for which Ernst Thälmann had fought." This was a world with "neither hunger nor war, exploitation nor racial hatred," a world "of knowledge and joy"—in other words, a socialist world such as that being created in the German Democratic Republic.[12] It is worth noting that both oaths emphasized the obligation incurred by those who had taken on the appellation "Thälmann Pioneers," a name sacred in the eyes of the workers' movement, a title that came with an awesome responsibility—the duty, as one children's book put it, to "live like Ernst Thälmann, learn like Ernst Thälmann, [and] struggle as he did for the happiness [Glück] of our people."[13]

East German children continued to swear such oaths and engage in other quasi-religious rituals right up to the SED regime's final days. Thälmann's one hundredth birthday in 1986, for example, witnessed some of the most elaborate commemoration activities in the entire history of the GDR, and it should come as no surprise that many of them centered on East German youth. Indeed, one of the themes of the centenary celebrations was "Thälmanns Namen tragen wir—seiner würdig, Pioneer" (We bear Thälmann's name—Pioneers be worthy of it).[14] According to a party report written just after the events surrounding the Thälmann centenary, these observances included "[c]eremonies honoring Thälmann, Thälmann Exhibitions, Thälmann Memorial Parades, Cultural Programs . . . at community organizations, . . . [and] Agitation during the XI Party Congress."[15] In addition to the many activities targeting children and adolescents, books were published to mark the occasion, and special lessons were given in East German schools. On 12 May 1986, one of the last events marking the centenary took place when the Pioneers held a massive commemorative ceremony at East Berlin's recently dedicated Ernst Thälmann Park, where a fifty-ton bronze likeness of the martyred KPD chief stood (see chapter 8). Among those in attendance were members of the Politburo, including Kurt Hager, the party's propaganda chief, and Egon Krenz, who would replace Erich Honecker as SED general secretary three and a half years later. Also present was Wilfried Poßner, member of the Central Committee and chairwoman of the Thälmann Pioneers, and the slain party leader's daughter, Irma Thälmann—who had played a vital role in the SED's appeal to youth for more than thirty years. Among the thousands of Thälmann Pioneers present was a "Banner delegation" consisting of a handful of children who led those present in the oath-taking portion of the ceremony. At the start of this "Verbal Recitation," the banner delegation stood to the left of the podium of the massive bronze. As this deputation marched slowly to the front of the statue, the Pioneers recited:

> Ernst Thälmann, born on 16 April 1886 was maliciously
> murdered by fascist executioners in Buchenwald Concentration
> Camp!
> He no longer lives. But the thoughts, for which he
> struggled with all his strength[,] do, the class front [*Klassenfront*]
> that does not totter in a storm, the Party of the Proletariat.

During his life, Thälmann had sought to "waken the pride in his [social] class," the recitation continued, to increase the proletariat's "consciousness and its confidence." Although the martyred KPD chief might not have survived the struggle against fascism, his legacy lived on in the GDR's accomplishments.

> He fell in [his] struggle. But his dream lives on.
> And from this dream has come reality: the
> party of the creative [people], united, constant
> [*beständig*], is alive today and builds a new
> world [*neue Zeit*].[16]

The message had not changed since the early days of the regime. Ernst Thälmann's legacy lived on in the SED, and it was incumbent upon German youth to fulfill his heritage. Almost forty-five years after Ernst Thälmann perished as a result of the antifascist struggle, East German children were taught to look to him as an example. On this score, the motifs of the Thälmann myth had changed very little. Yet it is important to note that the message did evolve in one significant way. During the early days of the SED, the promised accomplishments of socialism were reserved for the future; they were to be accomplished "one day."

In the May 1986 "Recitation," however, the promises of socialism were being fulfilled in the present. During the GDR's final years, Honecker and his associates sought to praise the accomplishments of "real, existing socialism," abandoning the motifs of the Ulbricht regime, which had repeatedly promised the East German people little more than additional sweat and toil as integral to the building of a better future. In the 1980s, as Mikhail Gorbachev sought to save Soviet-style socialism through a series of major reforms, the Honecker regime insisted that Ernst Thälmann's hopes were being fulfilled in East Germany. As the 12 May "Recitation" implies, there was no need for "restructuring" in the GDR (see chapter 8).

Efforts to inculcate East German youth with the Thälmann myth went far beyond ceremonial oath taking and the reciting of pledges. Young people also learned songs commemorating the martyr from Hamburg. Songs had been written about the KPD chief going all the way back to the Free Thälmann campaign of the 1930s. The most famous was written by "Kuba," the pseudonym of writer Kurt Bartel. Set to a tune composed by Eberhard Schmidt, this song's chorus was familiar to every East German child and adolescent.

> Thälmann and Thälmann before everything!
> Germany's eternal son—
> Thälmann has never fallen—
> Voice and fist of the nation!
> Thälmann has never fallen—
> Voice and fist of the nation![17]

Although the "Thälmann Song," which featured so prominently at the conclusion of Kurt Maetzig's *Ernst Thälmann—Leader of His Class,* was undoubtedly the most recognized anthem written about the fallen KPD chief, other popular youth hymns also memorialized the worker from Hamburg. On 10 December 1973, as part of a ceremony marking the twenty-fifth anniversary of the founding of the Young Pioneers, participants sang yet another "Thälmann Song":

> We want always to learn, work and struggle—
> like our Ernst Thälmann!
> We want to become good Patriots—
> like our Ernst Thälmann!
> We want eternal friendship with the

Soviet Union and to defend proletarian
internationalism—
like our Ernst Thälmann!
In the spirit of Ernst Thälmann means
our love, our faith, and our strength to
our German Democratic Republic![18]

Because the party leadership sought to encourage young people to embrace proletarian education, the importance of "learning like Ernst Thälmann" was a common theme in this East German youth propaganda, as was the centrality of books—especially the works of Lenin—to the martyred KPD chief's life.

As in other areas of the SED propaganda, the effort to indoctrinate East Germany's children and adolescents with the Thälmann legend made use of every medium at the party's disposal. Articles with titles such as "Ernst Thälmann—Leader of and Example of Youth, Fighter Against Militarism and Imperialist War" and "Ernst Thälmann—Friend of Youth" appeared in *Neues Deutschland,* the SED's official organ.[19] The FDJ had its own newspaper, *Junge Welt* (Young World), which regularly published articles lionizing the martyred KPD chief. Neither Thälmann's birthday nor the anniversary of his death ever went unnoticed on the pages of the party youth organization's official organ. For example, the article "The Man of the People," written by Willi Bredel, author of what was then the standard biography of Thälmann, marked the fallen Communist leader's seventy-eighth birthday.[20] Another piece, printed in commemoration of the thirteenth anniversary of Thälmann's death, informed young readers "how Thälmann helped us." The fallen KPD chief had, the article suggests, seen the role that youth could play in the struggle against fascism. As a result, he had been instrumental in promoting the success of the Communist youth organization, the KJVD, the forerunner of the FDJ. Throughout the final years of the Weimar Republic, Thälmann regularly spoke to young people, informing them of the "danger of fascism and war," providing valuable lessons for the youth of the GDR—who confronted a similar threat from West Germany.[21] The paper reviewed both of director Kurt Maetzig's Thälmann epics—positively of course—pointing out, for example, that *Ernst Thälmann—Leader of His Class,* was a "worthy assessment of the life of Ernst Thälmann" and hence an important film for the children of the GDR.[22] And the FDJ's publishing house distributed numerous books throughout the forty years of East German history.

Among the earliest of these works was *Ernst Thälmann—Vorbild der Deutschen Jugend* (Ernst Thälmann—Role Model of German Youth), published some time during the 1950s.[23] This brief work—little more than a hard-cover pamphlet—consists of fifty-six pages of small print (paper was always in short supply in the GDR), with illustrations. Although several of the photographs in the book show the fallen KPD chief at various stages of his political life, most of the illustrations consist of pictures taken in the GDR, showing some of the benefits that the party had bestowed upon young people. For example, all of page 37 consists of a photograph showing three young girls—with somewhat sullen looks on their faces—participating in the "opening of the Pioneer Republic 'Ernst Thälmann.'" Another photograph shows the "Gate of the Pioneer Republic 'Ernst Thälmann,'" the entrance to a heavily wooded area where East Germany's young people could spend time communing with nature—an old German tradition, even among socialists—and attending mass rallies. This park, located in the Berlin suburb of Wuhlheide, was the Pioneers' answer to summer camp and could accommodate thousands of visitors at a time, playing an integral role in the effort to indoctrinate children with the GDR's state religion.[24] The book's compilers clearly wanted to provide evidence of the things that the party was doing to promote their readers' welfare.

Yet the book contains no other references to the Pioneer Republic. The text consists of an essay written by Wilhelm Pieck, "Honorary President of the FDJ;" a speech delivered by Walter Ulbricht, SED chairman, to commemorate the fifth anniversary of Thälmann's death; and an epistle, often reprinted by the FDJ, "Answer to a Letter from a Fellow Prisoner in Bautzen," that Thälmann wrote in January 1944. The frontispiece is a photograph of the KPD chief wearing his renowned dockworker's cap, along with a quotation from Walter Pieck dated 3 March 1938. Pieck's words, often repeated during the postwar years, invoked Eucharistic motifs and used the terminology surrounding marriage in the book of Genesis. "Ernst Thälmann is one of the best of the German people. Flesh of its flesh, blood of its blood; Ernst Thälmann is the banner of the toiling masses of Germany, which is the flag of peace, freedom and prosperity." Such religious imagery had been a central component of the Thälmann legend since the 1930s, and the East German president clearly hoped to pass on this hagiographic tradition to the young people of the GDR. Pioneers were to view the fallen KPD chief as a secular saint, an incorruptible model to be followed by all good socialists (see also chapter 4).

Pieck's seven-page introduction incorporates most of the other major motifs to be found in the FDJ's version of the Thälmann myth. Among them is the KPD chief's "love of the people—hatred of war." The proletarian leader—unlike so many others—had long recognized the danger of fascism and the inevitability of a war with the Soviet Union following the Nazi seizure of power. He was "our Teddy" in the eyes of the German proletariat, someone who understood the plight of the workers because he had toiled among them. The "son of his class" had grown into the "leader of his class." Further, Pieck invokes the fallen leader's legacy, insisting that "[w]e want to struggle in his spirit." In keeping with the hagiographic tone introduced at the outset of the book, Pieck concludes by reminding his readers that "Ernst Thälmann lives in us!" if "we" will embrace the martyr's legacy and actively participate in the building of socialism on German soil.[25] These motifs, repeated at seemingly every available opportunity, would remain major themes in appeals to youth through the SED regime's final days. East German publishers continued to reissue much of this material, originally written during the 1950s—and in some cases even earlier—through the 1980s.[26] As was the case with other targets of East German propaganda, when it came to appeals to young people, the fundamental themes of the Thälmann legend were established in the years after the Second World War—indeed, in some instances as early as the mid-1920s.

The FDJ and its subsidiary, the Thälmann Pioneers, were not the only institutions available for the indoctrination of youth. The East German education system also played an important role in the SED's efforts to disseminate the Ernst Thälmann myth. This should come as no surprise given the importance that that education had in the building of socialism. Indeed, a great deal of overlap developed between school and FDJ activities, resulting in a concerted—and highly centralized—effort to promote the Thälmann myth in East German educational institutions. Schools, for example, assigned students to read books about the fallen KPD chief, including Irma Thälmann's memoir *Memories of My Father* and Max Zimmering's novel *Buttje Pieter and His Hero*. Textbooks used in East German schools, especially *Lesebücher* (readers), also lionized the fallen KPD chief. One story to appear in a grammar school reader, for example, was titled "Hang Together!" Taking place in the context of Thälmann's childhood years, it records an instance in which a couple of proletarian boys are fighting. Another boy boldly inquires of them: "Why are you hitting each other? Make up! Be friends!

Working-class boys are friends!" The narrative concludes by revealing the identity of the peacemaker: "The boy . . . was called Ernst Thäl-mann. Later, as head of the Communist Party of Germany, he said to all workers: 'Hang together, so that you can beat your enemies!'"[27] Even as a child apparently, the future KPD chief promoted the unity of the working class.

Reading assignments were not the only medium used to promote the Thälmann legend among East German school children. In 1954, for example, party officials called upon students to create Thälmann Corners in their classrooms. These nooks contained photographs of the martyred KPD chief, brief biographies of Thälmann, and reproductions of documents important to his life and legacy. The 1950s also witnessed the construction of Tradition Rooms in East German schools. These displays encompassed a much larger area than the Thälmann Corners. Providing a forum for "the study of the life and struggle of heroes of the working class," these exhibitions universally incorporated information about the Communist leader from Hamburg. Indeed, in 1974, as part of the effort to mark the twenty-fifth anniversary of the founding of the GDR, FDJ officials instructed students to increase dramatically the amount of material concerned with Ernst Thälmann in these rooms.[28]

Yet another resource at the party's disposal was the fallen KPD chief's widow, Rosa. Although bad health limited her activities during the final years of her life—she died in 1962—Rosa worked tirelessly on behalf of the SED as long as she could. Indeed, she was probably the most visible woman in the SBZ and GDR, regularly making appearances at almost every major rally and other event that the SED sponsored. She was also extremely active in the dissemination of the myth surrounding her husband in places such as the Buchenwald and Sachsenhausen concentration camps, and she played a role in both the creation and promotion of Kurt Maetzig's two epic films concerning her martyred spouse. Rosa regularly made public appearances to mark the anniversary of Ernst's birth or death and played a pivotal role, standing in for her fallen husband, in the propaganda offensive preceding the creation of the SED. When on 17 August 1956 the FRG outlawed the KPD as a threat to West German democracy, Rosa was at the forefront of the SED's propaganda offensive. In a public statement that she made for East German radio, Rosa pointed out the irony of the Adenauer government's actions. "Exactly twelve years earlier, on 18 August 1944, Comrade Ernst Thälmann was murdered. On 17 August 1956 the Adenauer regime issued its judgment concerning the Communist Party."

The current government of West Germany was clearly built upon the heritage of the Third Reich, a tradition of oppressive measures against the political arm of the proletariat—the KPD.[29]

If Ernst Thälmann should serve as a model for the children of the GDR, the party leadership sought to depict his spouse as an exemplar for the young people of East Germany, specifically as an archetype of socialist womanhood. In this role, Rosa was instrumental in the SED's efforts to appeal to both the women and the youth of the country, the two groups who composed the majority of Germany's population—as her husband had pointed out so many years earlier. Not only did Rosa belong to many East German women's groups, but she also became an "honorary" FDJ member.[30]

Rosa Thälmann often spoke to FDJ and Pioneers meetings as well as to groups of schoolchildren, standing in for her husband on the party's behalf. She sometimes even signed photographs of her deceased spouse, which the children could take home as mementoes of her visit.[31] Speaking to a group of children in Ettersberg, Rosa lauded the sacrifice of those who had perished at Buchenwald Concentration Camp, insisting that they had died in order to assure a better future for Germany's children. "They wanted good schools for you [and] good teachers who don't beat the children [die Kinder nicht prügeln], who instead educate [children] for peace. [You] see, dear children, that was the wish of my husband, Ernst Thälmann. The fascists also murdered him here in Buchenwald. I want to explain to you: who was Ernst Thälmann?" Rosa went on to recount the characteristics of her martyred spouse, a man whom those present should emulate. Ernst struggled for peace, which he wanted for all of Germany's children. He was a good friend of the Soviet Union, recognizing that it would assure the permanent brotherhood of all nations. Rosa exhorted the children to develop a similar worldview because it was the only way that future generations of Germans could secure the better life that her spouse had wanted for them. She admitted that the children faced a daunting but not insurmountable task. "We are now at the point [where we must] rebuild our country anew." Unlike their counterparts in the West, East Germany's children would accomplish this task without becoming beholden to anyone. Alluding to the Marshall Plan, Rosa insisted that the people of East Germany would rebuild "with our [own] hands, without money from America, which we would have to repay, which would lead to new problems, new difficulties, and a new war."[32]

Speaking to a group of Thälmann Pioneers on the third anniversary of the founding of the GDR, Rosa reminded her audience of the responsibility the organization assumed by taking on her husband's name. "Dear Pioneers, you now bear the name 'Ernst Thälmann,' commit [yourselves] to this name because Ernst Thälmann was a great man, an effective fighter, and a good father. . . . He always stood by his word. Word and deed were one. He was uncompromising against the enemies of the people. His life belonged to his people. In his . . . youth, he learned that one must fight for socialism. . . . He was always ready to sacrifice and always thought of his friends while performing his work." Leaving nothing to chance, Rosa drove her point home. "Every Pioneer has also assumed a great duty: to live as Ernst Thälmann." Although the speaker conceded that to do so "will not always be so simple for you," this difficulty did not release those present from this solemn obligation. East Germany's children, like their model, Ernst Thälmann, should strive to be good examples for others, to be someone whom their "classmates [and] friends" will admire. Further, it was beholden upon all good Pioneers "to help your parents to become [party] activists." In short, the future of socialism on German soil, the success or failure of the German Democratic Republic, depended on the Thälmann Pioneers' willingness to live up to the commitment engendered by the name that they had assumed.[33]

The relationship between Rosa Thälmann and the young people of the SBZ and GDR was not a one-way street. Parents, teachers, and FDJ leaders encouraged their charges to write to the martyred KPD chief's widow, informing her of how important Ernst's example was for them in their daily lives. Many of these letters mention either the authors' reaction to what he or she had seen while viewing Kurt Maetzig's epic films or the effect that reading Irma Thälmann's book about her father had upon them. The children, likely at the instigation of their adult supervisors, often decorated the letters, drawing FDJ and Pioneer symbols in the margins. The letters usually sought to relate the child's sympathy to Rosa for having lost her husband under such painful circumstances. These letters reflect the major themes of the FDJ's version of the Thälmann myth, providing relatively rare evidence concerning the effectiveness of SED political propaganda.[34]

Among the children to write to Rosa Thälmann was Margitta H. Penned in 1958, the margins of her missive contain several FDJ symbols, including the "TP" of the Pioneers, drawn in crayon in the margins. The letter is fairly typical of what children wrote to Rosa and has the tone of something written as the result of a school assignment. The brief letter is worth quoting in its entirety.

Dear Comrade Rosa Thälmann!

We Pioneers of the Zwickau-Auerbach grammar school, Group I, send you our most heartfelt greeting. Now, at the time of the 72nd birthday of your husband, we think especially of the heroic [*tapfer*] and courageous [*mutig*] leader of the workers. We Young Pioneers also want to follow his compelling example [*kämpferlichen Vorbild*], especially now, where [*sic*] there is death at the hands of West German atomic bombs to be rebuffed. In (his) [*sic*] Ernst Thälmann's honor we decorated the Ernst-Thälmann Grove [*Hain*] on the sixteenth of April, and swore, in his spirit [*in seinem Geiste*], to continue to fight for peace and friendship among peoples.[35]

Similar themes and a stiffer tone can be seen in Ekkehard F.'s letter to Rosa Thälmann, which was also decorated with several FDJ symbols drawn in crayon.

Dear Comrade Rosa Thälmann!

We have read many books about Ernst Thälmann. Your spouse was an honorable leader of the working class. We Pioneers of the Friendship [the smallest organizational unit of the Thälmann Pioneers] "Ernst Thälmann" will bear the name honorably. I . . . would also like one day to become a fearless [*kühner*] leader like Ernst Thälmann and defend my fatherland.[36]

Another student informed Rosa that "[h]is [Ernst's] picture is hung on the wall of our classroom [standard practice in the GDR] because he is an example for us all. He reminds us to be hard-working and to learn diligently."[37]

These letters and many others like them are evidence of at least three things. First, they show the extent to which the SED regime was willing to go to instill the lessons of the Ernst Thälmann myth in East German children. From a very young age, the children of the GDR became familiar not only with who Thälmann was, but also with the legend surrounding his activities. Second, the letters show that—in the schools and in the FDJ—East German officials sought to keep a tight rein on the myth, assuring that children imbibed what the SED considered the proper version of the narrative. The children learned nothing even remotely critical about the fallen KPD chief. The Ernst Thälmann about whom East German children learned was more of a monument than a man.[38] Their model was a one-dimensional figure whose sole significant concern, from a remarkably young age, was the welfare of the German proletariat. Contrary to the GDR propagandists' intentions, this portrayal might have rendered him inaccessible rather than worth emulating. Finally, the letters provide a relatively rare insight into the effectiveness of the Thälmann myth specifically and East German political propaganda more generally. These students had clearly learned how to echo the political slogans that their teachers, youth leaders, and parents had taught them. They were learning, at least abstractly, how to become good socialists, admirers of the Soviet Union, and concerned citizens of the GDR. To the extent that this was the case, the political education of East Germany's young people was effective. However, one does not want to read too much into children's ability to parrot ideological catchphrases. Germans who grew up in the GDR can still mouth the slogans and sing the songs that they learned at school and in the FDJ. Some of them even fought, in the years after the *Wende* (the "Turning" or the end of the Communist state), to preserve the tradition of memorializing Ernst Thälmann as a paragon of the struggle against National Socialism (see chapter 9). The extent, however, to which they as children actually believed the version of events that they were taught is impossible to say. The complexity of this matter can be seen in Hermann Weber's memoir of the time that he spent in the Parteihochschule "Karl Marx," an institution created for the training of the future SED elite. Photographs of the fallen KPD chief also hung on the walls of its classrooms and lecture halls. According to this account, which narrates events from the late 1940s, Weber's response to the legend surrounding the martyred KPD chief can best be described as Janus-faced. "For me, Thälmann was, on the one hand, a symbol of the struggle against Hitler; meanwhile [*inzwischen*] it had become clear to me that he bore a great deal of responsibility for the Stalinization of the KPD."[39] Such a response was not what Rosa and others who sought to promote the official narrative had envisioned. In short, although the effectiveness of the effort to instill the GDR's young people with the Thälmann myth can be debated, the importance of Rosa to the propagation of the legend is beyond dispute.

The GDR's children were not the only group to whom Rosa sought to appeal. In keeping with her husband's observation that young people and adult females composed the majority of any society, she regularly spoke to women's groups not only in the GDR, but throughout the Soviet bloc. The relationship between the SED and the women of East Germany remained complicated throughout the country's forty-two-year history.[40] Party leaders insisted that the only way to deal effectively with the problems confronting German women was to build socialism. Indeed, at least in theory, sexism, like organized religion, would eventually perish in the wake of the defeat of capitalism. Although the GDR, like every other socialist (and nonsocialist) state, continued to be dominated by men, the SED leadership at least paid lip service to the idea of approaching East German women differently from the male population, to appeal to women *as women*. Rosa Thälmann, as postwar Germany's most visible female Communist, played a vital role in the governing party's effort to mold the SED's vision of socialist womanhood.[41]

Rosa appeared on behalf of the SED in every country of the Soviet bloc at one time or another. These appearances included an address that she gave in 1955 in Moscow, the epicenter of the international socialist movement, to a Soviet women's group. Not surprisingly, in this presentation Rosa emphasized the importance of the Soviet model to her husband's political development. "Ernst studied everything that Lenin wrote about the October 1917 Revolution." It had a dramatic effect on his thoughts and actions. In 1923, for example, Ernst repeatedly reminded his comrades during the Hamburg Uprising about the lessons that the Russian experience had to teach the German workers' movement. Further, as a good parent, Thälmann made a conscious effort to raise his daughter to love and admire the Soviet Union as much as he did. Indeed, women across all of Germany looked to the Soviets as an example of the proper way to fight against imperialism and war. "Our women in West Germany will [also] struggle . . . against militarism and for peace and for the fortunes of their children. They will fulfill the legacy of Ernst Thälmann."[42]

Rosa sought to address what she considered the concerns of East German women, such as the possibility of another war, which can be seen in a speech she delivered in September 1956. This talk begins with another recurrent theme seen in many of her public presentations—the modesty of her origins. "I was born in the North of our homeland [*Heimat*], in the area around Wasserkante."[43] Rosa's use of the word *Heimat* is interesting. The notion of *Heimat*—which incorporates a strong sense of belonging to, not to mention loving, the region of one's origins—was problematic to socialist ideology. Much as class consciousness trumped gender concerns, official ideology spurned individual narratives that emphasized the importance of a person's local roots. The proper proletarian outlook should supersede, indeed exclude, a self-understanding based on regional origins. Yet, as was the case with gender considerations, the SED eventually had to abandon the ideal in favor of a more realistic approach to building a socialist society. That is, much as party leaders had not only to accept but also to help construct political narratives incorporating gender considerations, the SED had ultimately to embrace the idea of *Heimat*. In spite of the fact that figures as prominent as Rosa Thälmann came to incorporate this notion into their rhetoric, the effort was never successful, contributing to the ultimate failure of the socialist experiment in the GDR.[44]

Later in the same speech, Rosa tells a story that relates a more socialist understanding of *Heimat*, rejecting the nationalist conception of the idea and embracing a more nuanced, class-conscious, and indeed feminine understanding of *Heimat*. When Ernst was a young man, Rosa recalls, his family owned a shop that sold vegetables. One day the future KPD chief returned home to discover, so the narrative goes, that his mother had hung an imperial flag in front of her tiny store, which was filled with female customers from the neighborhood. When Ernst asked his mother why she had done this, she replied, "Tell me, young man, don't you know that we have won a great victory?" Ernst's reply, which his widow quoted, was immediate and to the point: "'Mother, have you forgotten the untold numbers of husbands and sons of many mothers who have paid for this victory with their lives. But Krupp [the arms manufacturer] and the bankers have benefitted from this war. Thousands of soldiers lie wounded outside, and you celebrate that? Mother, I beg of you, take down the flag. Father thinks as I do, and the women who stand here don't know if their husband [*sic*] might be among those who have perished.' Most of the women nodded in agreement, because most of those who shopped in this store were working-class women."[45]

Much like her effort to adapt the conventional, conservative role of women as wives and mothers, Rosa sought to incorporate, albeit in a more politically acceptable form, the traditional German idea of *Heimat* to the needs of the moment. Although the people whom she describes in the previous tale—probably a manufactured one because it is "too good to be true"—did indeed come from a single location, a proletarian section of Hamburg, their place of origin was of far less importance than their working-class roots. In short, Rosa, like the SED leadership, hoped to build a "homeland" for the German proletariat, not one—as in the bourgeois version of the concept—that would have included the exploiting classes. It was necessary to redefine *Heimat* not only because the traditional understanding of the idea ignored class concerns, but also because a conventional *Heimat* perpetuated the exploitation of one person by another, thereby assuring the continuation of fascism and imperialistic war. Rosa's speech made it abundantly clear that her understanding of *Heimat* precluded such a possibility. Only a properly constituted socialist *Heimat* could assure continued peace and prosperity for *all* Germans.

Rosa was not the only surviving member of Ernst Thälmann's family to play a significant role in perpetuating the legend surrounding the fallen KPD chief. Irma Thälmann (born in 1919) also participated in the effort to propagate the myth being built around her martyred father. At first, Irma played a secondary role, supporting her mother. She regularly appeared at rallies and other functions alongside Rosa, although she rarely spoke. As her mother aged and especially after Rosa's death in 1962, Irma increasingly took center stage. Assuming a role that her mother had held previously, she made public appearances more often, delivering speeches more frequently than in the past. Her words were similar to her mother's, and she stuck closely to the party-approved version of her father's life and contribution to the cause of the German proletariat. For example, in one speech given at a youth rally she pointed out that "Ernst Thälmann's life was an example for all German patriots. He loved the German people and his Fatherland above everything else, so that the capitalists and hyenas of war would not be allowed to lead it [once again] into ruin." As such, he was a valuable model for all of Germany's youth. "The Young Pioneers must study the life and struggle of Ernst Thälmann in order to understand why he lived such a life of struggle and endured twelve years, before his death, behind prison walls."[46] Irma dedicated much of her life to the effort to keep the politically approved image of her father alive. She played an important role in the propagation of the Thälmann legend to the very final days of the SED regime, participating, for example, in the effort to force West German officials to prosecute her father's murderers during the 1980s (see chapter 8).

Perhaps the most interesting contribution, however, that Irma made to the propagation of the Thälmann legend was the book *Memories of My Father,* which she published in 1954.[47] If the correspondence between her mother and the children of the GDR is any indication, tens of thousands of East German students and members of the FDJ read this book. The volume, written for children ten and older, is a firsthand account of Irma's experiences growing up in the home of "Germany's eternal son." Although *Memories of My Father* opens with Irma's earliest recollections of Ernst and concludes with the establishment of the GDR and the creation of the Thälmann Pioneers, the author does sometimes relate stories about her father that she heard secondhand. Measuring a mere 138 pages, the book was ideally suited to its target audience—older children and young adolescents. The book is also liberally illustrated with photographs of Ernst Thälmann, his family, and comrades—thereby putting faces on the major figures in the narrative, an expensive practice but undoubtedly helpful for the targeted readership. In spite of its brevity, a detailed account of the entire text of *Memories of My Father* is impossible here, and only a handful of passages can be analyzed, but these passages are representative of the major themes contained in the text as a whole.

The volume opens with a foreword written by Wilhelm Pieck and dated 21 December 1953. After a paragraph reminding his readers of the awesome responsibility that they bear because they hold the appellation "Thälmann Pioneers," the East German president turns to the book's purpose. *Memories of My Father,* Pieck points out, relates not only Irma Thälmann's account of her father as a political leader, but also "how he enjoyed being with children, how he laughed, cracked jokes, and made himself happy." As a result, it provides "all Young Pioneers and all German children a living and vivid portrait of the Great [*sic*] Ernst Thälmann, who was rooted in the working class and in his German people." In short, his daughter's memoir seeks to depict the martyred KPD chief as a flesh-and-blood human being, someone who was, in many ways, much like them. Pieck reminds his young readers that although Thälmann was an ordinary man, he was also a hero. He led the KPD during the darkest days in the history of the German workers' movement, struggling against "[material] need and injustice," standing at the forefront of the struggle against Hitler fascism. Arrested by the enemies of the German proletariat, "He also remained, during the darkest days of the Hitler regime—for the German workers—the model of unyielding opposition against the criminal Hitler regime." As a result, the fallen party leader became a paragon for all East Germans, indeed for socialists everywhere, and so "[e]very Young Pioneer must . . . strive to serve the German working class as selflessly and bravely . . . [as the] murdered leader of the German Communist Party." Thälmann was a good example, someone to be emulated in so many ways. Young East Germans must, "like Ernst Thälmann, struggle to learn from Lenin," to play a central role in promoting "friendship with the Soviet Union." In short, the GDR's Thälmann Pioneers must embrace the legacy of Ernst Thälmann as embodied in socialist Germany. "The Nazi murderers could indeed kill Ernst Thälmann, but he had won in the end." If Germany's young people embraced this legacy, they would ensure that the benefits of Thälmann's ultimate victory could be handed down to future generations.[48]

Although Irma's text is not as polemical in tone as Pieck's foreword, it is just as didactic. Irma may indeed have sought to present her father as a living human being, someone to be admired and emulated, but her success was limited. That Ernst Thälmann was not only a great political leader but also a loving father and husband and a loyal friend to his comrades is asserted in the book much more frequently than it is demonstrated. He consistently placed the welfare of others above his own well being, Irma insists, providing a model not only of socialist politics in action, but of a truly decent person who viewed people not only through the prism of economic class, but also as real human beings with concrete concerns about surviving in the midst of difficult times. In other words, Irma seeks to portray her father as a combination of ideologue, pragmatist, and secular saint who loved those around him and, as a result, struggled on behalf of all that was good and decent, all the while hating all that was evil in Germany in the years preceding the Second World War. Thälmann was, in his daughter's eyes, the greatest enemy of imperialism and class exploitation, while maintaining his basic humanity. Yet, one might argue, Irma fails in her portrayal, and the Ernst Thälmann who emerges in her text is often the typical one-dimensional figure interested primarily, if not exclusively, in proletarian politics. In truth, Irma's memories make it abundantly clear that her father consistently placed political considerations ahead of his family's welfare—a trait common among political true believers. Irma's narrative presents her life as having been exciting, but also chaotic.

The sometimes frightening consequences of her father's actions were among Irma's earliest memories. In the opening section of the book, she recounts several instances in which his political enemies sought to kill or otherwise injure her male parent. Indeed, as early as

1922, as a failed plot to murder the future KPD chief with explosives showed, "the fascists wanted to kill the workers' leader Ernst Thälmann." Yet his primary concern was for the welfare of the proletariat; Thälmann's own well-being was of secondary importance to him.[49] Indeed, the Thälmann household—even at the expense of a normal family life—remained a center of working-class politics in spite of the constant threats posed by political opponents. During the Hamburg Uprising, for example, the Thälmanns' apartment remained a center of revolutionary activity, workers constantly consulting with Irma's father about the appropriate strategy. It was abundantly clear that Irma was extremely proud of the role that her father and mother played in the political life of the proletariat. Yet a reader cannot help but notice that she records nothing concerning her father's efforts to comfort her in these difficult times.[50] Indeed, Irma makes it clear that she and other children of party members were also expected to make sacrifices on behalf of the revolutionary workers' movement. In the wake of the Hamburg Uprising, she recalls, many working-class parents had to go to prison or went into hiding, "leaving their families behind." As a result, their children suffered. Food was often in short supply, and "ever more children slept in a single bed." These painful sacrifices were, Irma insisted, justified. The workers "had nothing to lose in a fight. If they would have been victors in this struggle, then Germany would have had no fascism and no air war, but rather a new, improved life."[51] The resulting difficulties facing working-class children were merely the unavoidable consequences of the path to progress. In short, working-class children also had a role to play in fomenting revolution, and Irma and her comrades' willingness to suffer for the common good could serve as an example for the children of the GDR. After all, "Keines zu klein—Kämpfer zu sein."

In keeping with this sentiment, German Communists began to view the Communist Party as an extended family. Indeed, Irma "often heard my father and his comrades speak of the party as the 'big family.'" Evidence of this attitude can be seen in the help that Communist women gave to each other when one of them was sick. The party's ideology, putting the common welfare of the proletariat ahead of one's individual advantage, was a natural extension of the family ideal.[52] As a result, political concerns influenced even the most intimate moments of family life.

> When father was at home [he was often absent because of his responsibilities as a party leader], he often sat at his table and worked. I said "good night" to him and went to bed.

> When I got up in the morning to go to school, he remained at work, sitting with his books. Mother then said: "When you have finished dressing, you may go out and invite your father to drink coffee with us."
>
> Father was always so happy on these days. He picked me up, whirled me around the coffee table, and then *he talked about his work.*[53]

In short, the KPD leader's political activities seemingly affected every aspect of the family's existence. Ernst viewed something as private as playing with his daughter, Irma recalled, as an opportunity to share with her the lessons that he had learned as a result of "his work."

The importance of books and education is a central theme in *Memories of My Father.* Of course, in this context, reading and learning meant absorbing the ideas of Nikolai Lenin and the Russian Bolshevik movement. Thälmann regularly exhorted not only his daughter but also his comrades to assimilate the great lessons found in the works of this giant who had labored for the benefit of the international proletariat. Irma remembered her father, during a discussion of one of Lenin's writings, urging a comrade to "'[l]isten good! That was written for us! We in the party must learn much more. Our example is . . . the Communist Party of the Soviet Union. Our mistakes have arisen for the most part only because our comrades have not sufficiently studied and applied Marxism–Leninism.'"[54] This passage not only relates the importance of a proper education in Marxist–Leninist classics—a lesson not lost on Irma Thälmann's readers, it was hoped—but also reflects another central theme of the book: the importance of the Soviet Union as a model for the German working class and, by extension, the proletarian youth of Germany. Of course, the appearance of this theme here should come as no surprise. Thälmann's admiration for the Soviet Union had been a major motif of the myth since the mid-1920s. Irma Thälmann's *Memories of My Father* provides yet another example in which Germany's most important proletarian hero, Ernst Thälmann, gives his imprimatur to the official SED view of the Soviet Union's vital role in the success of the international workers' movement.

As Ernst Thälmann became an increasingly prominent politician, and Irma got older, her memories of her father continued to be highly influenced by political concerns. Indeed, it is safe to assume that after he became party chief in 1925, Ernst spent even less time at home than he had earlier, and Irma records an instance in which "we had not heard from father for weeks." Ernst "traveled more frequently to the Soviet Union," and much of the book describes the remarkable things that he had seen there—enormous factories, efficient collective farms, new construction everywhere, and full employment. In short, Irma's father, while visiting the Soviet Union, got a firsthand glimpse of Germany's future. The party chief eventually began to rent an apartment in Berlin because he was spending so much time there, and politics consumed even more of the family's life. The Thälmanns' 1929 Christmas celebration, for example, turned into a lecture about how "[i]n Hamburg and the whole world, except in the Soviet Union, unemployment and need dominate" daily life.[55] In all likelihood, there were even more comrades coming by the Thälmann home at all hours of the day and night than previously. Yet Irma provides no indication that such a life had a negative effect on her childhood. She always knew that what her father did was important and would one day change the world. The value of her father's actions became even more important as the Nazi seizure of power approached, and Ernst Thälmann and the KPD became the only significant obstacles between Germany and the catastrophe engendered by the Hitler regime. It is concerning this period, the years of struggle against Hitler fascism, that Irma Thälmann goes into the greatest detail. Indeed, Irma's account of the years after 1930 comprises the lion's share of the text.

Irma relates how proud she was when her father stood against Hitler in the 1932 presidential election. A "hateful caricature" of her father in the window of a Social Democratic tavern drove young Irma to tears, she later recalled. Yet, in keeping with the example set by her father, she was defiant, informing those observing the caricature that "[w]hoever votes for my father, he votes against war, he votes for the workers, for peace. That much I know for certain."[56] The message to Irma's readers was clear: stand up for what is right—the workers' interests—no matter what, even in the face of ridicule and embarrassment; it was the Communist version of "Be not ashamed of the Gospel." Only forthrightness in the face of adversity can assure the victory of good over evil, of socialism over imperialism and capitalist exploitation.

Some of the most interesting passages of Irma Thälmann's memoir, however, record the events following her father's arrest. After Ernst was imprisoned, Irma's grandfather, Jan, began to share stories with her about her father's difficult childhood. Ernst had very little in the way of material goods as a child, Jan recalled, and had to go to work at a very young age. This adversity, however, had served Ernst and the workers' movement well in the long run. "Irma," Jan told her, "all of the difficulties that your father experienced in his childhood had the effect of making him into a fighter [*Kämpfer*]. His great love of children also resulted. He, who did not have a happy childhood, whose life was filled with hard work, he bears the strong conviction in himself to create a much nicer and better childhood for working-class children." Ernst, Jan insisted, had learned the importance of educating proletarian youths, "who were just as smart as the children of rich people," to be "technicians, engineers and builders" who could contribute to the future welfare of the German people.[57]

Irma also records her visits to her imprisoned father. Irma first visited Ernst while he was in jail in Moabit, where she and Rosa waited three hours to see the KPD chief. In this "visitors' room," twelve-year-old Irma witnessed the devastation wrought by the new Germany. "We were not there alone," she recalled. "Many wives and mothers waited as we did. Most had the same concerns as we did. They anxiously asked each other: 'If my husband is still alive?'—'Is my daughter still healthy? Will I see get to see my son?'—'Hopefully they'll allow me to give him clean clothes today!'" Like Willi Bredel's biography of Thälmann, *Memories of My Father* goes into detail concerning conditions in Nazi prisons and concentration camps, pointing out the extreme brutality of German fascism. In short, the German people suffered under National Socialism; there were many others in a similar situation to Rosa and Irma, constantly in fear for their loved ones' well-being.[58] In this regard, Irma, like the authors of many other books about Ernst Thälmann and the proletarian resistance to Hitler, sought to depict the German working classes as having been the victims of fascism, not active participants in the crimes committed by the Nazi regime. As the final section of the book shows, these same workers supposedly rose up to create the GDR, to give birth to a socialist Germany, to fulfill Ernst Thälmann's legacy. In doing so, they emerged victorious over the forces of imperialism and capitalist exploitation.

Irma and Rosa had one advantage, however, over all of these others: their father and husband was a prominent politician, and millions of people throughout the world were concerned with his welfare. Irma describes the Free Thälmann campaign of the years from 1933 to 1939 in some detail. Thälmann's birthday, for example, resulted in "great agitation at the post office. Many, many letters and cards from all over Germany and the outside world had arrived in Berlin for Ernst Thälmann." The KPD chief later revealed to his wife that he had not received a single piece of this correspondence.[59] These greetings from all over the globe, however, had the effect of securing her father's life. His captors dared not kill Ernst Thälmann; to do so would garner too much opprobrium from the international community, something that the Nazis wished to avoid. Like other East Germans who wrote about her father, Irma fails to mention the party's abandonment of the struggle to free the KPD chief following the signing of the Ribbentrop–Molotov (Nonaggression) Pact in August of 1939. She does point out, however, that her father was not the only one to suffer at the hands of the "Gestapo-bandits," and she records instances of surprise searches inflicted on other proletarian families, not just her household. Such harassment only escalated. She found herself, for example, driven from school in March 1934. Rosa—and later Irma—could not get a job, making it increasingly difficult for them to support themselves, and they increasingly relied on the goodwill of party comrades for their sustenance.[60]

Circumstances only deteriorated further. Irma visited her father in the Gestapo headquarters on Prinz-Albrecht-Straße, only to see him in the wake of a bad beating, his "face swollen" and his "eyes black." She could not even speak to Ernst because she "was so shocked."[61] Indeed, Ernst Thälmann's experiences in the basement dungeon on Prinz-Albrecht-Straße, not to mention the horrific things that Rosa and Irma witnessed when they went to visit him there, became one of the most important tropes in the legend surrounding the KPD chief. It was important to point out that although Thälmann never spent the night in a German concentration camp, he experienced firsthand all of the brutalities that the Nazi regime had to offer. Yet he remained steadfast in the face of eleven and a half years' imprisonment. Even after the number two man in the Third Reich, Hermann Goering, came to Ernst's cell and promised him freedom in exchange for his cooperation—another important trope in the Thälmann myth—the KPD chief stood by his convictions. It was important to the legend that the martyred party leader sacrifice his life of his own free will. Until the very end of his life, Thälmann continued to believe that "Stalin will break Hitler's neck" and that socialism would ultimately triumph. In spite of the grisly sight that greeted them, even as the deprivation that they suffered escalated, Rosa and Irma continued to visit Ernst Thälmann. Like their husband and father, they were also examples to be emulated. Both Rosa and Irma ended up in a Nazi concentration camp because of their refusal to renounce Ernst's convictions. Yet they were not alone in this ordeal. The international solidarity that resulted in response to the

KPD chief's imprisonment helped his family to persevere, not to give up, to continue to fight for Ernst's release or at least an amelioration of his conditions. The "big family" of the party and its allies had come through. Irma Thälmann provides numerous quotations from those involved in the Free Thälmann movement, providing evidence of how far Ernst's fame had spread and how many people—from all walks of life—were concerned with the KPD chief's well-being.[62]

Irma did have the opportunity to receive letters from her father—and even to write to him on occasion. The author of *Memories of My Father* quotes from some of these letters, which reflect the fact that even as he sat in a Nazi prison, facing possible death at any moment, Ernst Thälmann's primary concern was for the German workers' movement. Writing to Irma on her sixteenth birthday, Ernst reminded his daughter of the awesome responsibility that she bore. "You are the only child of a man, who has placed his entire life at the disposal of the workers' movement. You must live your life in such a way that you, as a girl, as my daughter, show yourself worthy." He went on to assure his daughter that even more difficult days approached, when "[y]ou will get to know the strong and weak sides of your character." The KPD chief urges his daughter to remain steadfast, to stay the course. He writes to her of the difficult days of the "harbor workers' strike before the war," the "Dreyfus trial in France," and other great political events that had shaped his life. She must view her current experiences in a similar vein. Irma should, Ernst wrote, learn the proper lessons from them. Only then could she persevere and live to see socialism triumph.[63] As always, even when writing to his daughter from a Nazi prison, sitting in a cell-block that he could never leave, the KPD chief's primary concerns were not for himself or even for Irma, but for the party's well-being. Ernst Thälmann remained first and foremost a socialist politician.

Irma's response, dated 7 May 1936, is much more personal than her father's missive, which makes no mention of love and closes simply with "Your Father." Irma's letter opens, rather, with "My dear Father." The language that she uses is much more personal. She refers to Ernst repeatedly as "Dear Father," and she writes of the difficulties that she is experiencing and the "anxiety" that separation from him has caused her. She writes "[t]hat there comes once again a new hope to my breast [*Brust*]—to see you and speak with you again." Irma closes her letter on a much more personal note as well: "With the steadfast, loyal love of a child[,] your Irma." The contrast between the two letters is striking.[64] Whereas Ernst's epistle is concerned almost exclusively with political matters, Irma makes no mention of politics. She was a young woman writing to the father whom she expected to die in prison. This passage is perhaps the most compelling in *Memories of My Father,* reflecting the distance between a man obsessed with political concerns and a sixteen-year-old adolescent who is suffering tremendously because of his convictions. Although the passage is clearly designed to show the strength of Thälmann's convictions and thus provide a role model for Irma's readers, the KPD chief comes across as rather cold-hearted, even by the standards of the reserve stereotypically associated with northern German culture. Indeed, it is hard to imagine a young person wanting to emulate the martyred KPD chief on this score or for that matter hoping that his or her parents would behave in the fashion of "Germany's eternal son." In short, in spite of what Irma Thälmann and the SED leadership might have thought, *Memories of My Father* had severe limitations as effective propaganda. Many young East German boys and girls might have absorbed the book's historical lessons—that Thälmann had sacrificed everything, including his family, for the benefit of the coming socialist revolution—but the KPD chief comes across in yet another instance as a one-dimensional character, someone to be admired, but not a person who could be emulated. There is more in the book concerning Ernst's love of the Soviet Union than about the love he felt for his daughter. As a result, however accurate her account might have been, Irma Thälmann's memoir suffers from the same deficiency as much of the rest of the materials created for the legend propagated around her fallen father. The martyred party chief emerges as more of a political icon than a real human being with whom Irma's readers could empathize.

From the perspective of propaganda, however, the final five pages of the text were arguably the most important. Here Irma describes the "liberation" both of the concentration camps in which she and her mother were held and of Germany as a whole. "Liberation through the Soviet army!" She recalls "hugging" the Russian soldiers who arrived in the Neubrandenburg Concentration Camp where she was imprisoned. "We cried for joy." The victory was complete: "The red flag now waved over our camp." Yet her father had not lived to see the Soviet triumph that he had anticipated. Irma remembers having discovered that "[t]he fascists had murdered father." Her account of the circumstances surrounding her father's death is brief and to the point. Ernst had met his end in Buchenwald Concentration Camp. "He was—on 18 August 1944—taken to the crematorium there and foully murdered. Afterward, the executioners burned his corpse. They wanted [to ensure] that nothing of Ernst Thälmann remained."[65]

But the fascist murderers had ultimately failed. The final four pages of *Memories of My Father,* appearing under the section title "Fight and Win in His Spirit," make the contention that Thälmann was not really dead, but that his legacy lived on in the GDR's accomplishments. "And we saw: The great goals, for which Ernst Thälmann lived and struggled, for which he had given his life, were realized." The "[j]unkers and capitalists had been stripped of their power in a part of Germany," the implication being that they continued to cling to influence in the West. The division within the workers' movement that had made the temporary victory of fascism possible ended with the "joining together of the KPD and the SPD into the great Socialist Unity Party of Germany." "Agricultural reform" had brought the workers and farmers closer together than they had ever been. The permanence of these accomplishments had been assured because "on the seventh of October 1949 the German Democratic Republic was created, at the top of which stands a worker: the old companion of Ernst Thälmann in struggle, our president Wilhelm Pieck."[66]

These developments benefitted not only the working class as a whole, but even more especially, Irma Thälmann insists, proletarian children. "In our republic," she contends, "children can be happy; here they experience the love and sincere care of the state." East German children need not rely only upon the GDR's largesse, however, because "Side by side we stand with the Soviet Union, with China, with Poland, Bulgaria, Albania, Romania, Hungary, the Czechoslovakian Republic, with the peace-loving people of the whole world, united in friendship in the struggle for a happy, peaceful life." The forces of history were on the side of the GDR's children, and they should be glad of this fact. "Life in our German Democratic Republic is pleasant. We can look forward to a happy future."[67]

Yet although victory was inevitable, it was not complete because "in West Germany the very same executioners who murdered Ernst Thälmann, the very same war mongers who set the last war in motion, are in power again." The children of the GDR must learn to "hate" these powers aligned against the forces of antifascism. Indeed, "[y]ou children, you Pioneers and students[,] must fan this hate in your hearts into a holy flame." Only then can the fascist menace be permanently eradicated from German soil. As a result, the children of the GDR bear an enormous obligation—to help build socialism in *all* of Germany. In order to do so, they must "[l]ive like Ernst Thälmann, learn like Ernst Thälmann, fight like he did for the happiness of our people, and live up to the oath" that all Young Pioneers took to struggle to fulfill Ernst Thälmann's legacy.[68] Like other manifestations of the Thälmann myth, *Memories of My Father* closes with a call to action, a demand to live up to the legacy created by Ernst Thälmann and the others who had struggled so long and hard so that German children could live in the world that the antifascists hoped to create. It ultimately was the youth of the GDR who bore the responsibility of taking the benefits of socialism to the children of West Germany—indeed, of the entire world. Irma Thälmann's brief memoir helped the SED to share this message with thousands of East German children, further establishing many of the tropes that would become central to the version of the Ernst Thälmann legend propagated among the GDR's young people. The book calls upon East German children and adolescents to play an active role in the construction of socialism, to place the general good far ahead of their own mundane concerns, to be a staunch friend of the Soviet Union. Further, as *Memories of My Father* made abundantly clear, children should anticipate—indeed expect—that their parents will place the SED's concerns ahead of the everyday cares of raising a family, especially in difficult times. The experiences recorded in Irma Thälmann's little memoir might very well lead its readers to conclude that the children's family lives were ultimately a function of socialist politics and that the daily discussion of political concerns from a Marxist–Leninist perspective should be a component of even their closest personal relationships—in this case, with their parents.

Irma Thälmann's *Memories of My Father* was far from the only children's book to promote this agenda during the GDR's early years. Another important "literary" contribution to the effort to promote the Thälmann myth among East German youth was Max Zimmering's *Buttje Pieter und sein Held* (Buttje Pieter and His Hero), published in 1951, three years before Irma Thälmann's memoir. Whereas her book was a work of nonfiction, *Buttje Pieter and His Hero* was a children's novel written in the socialist-realist tradition with the twelve-year-old Pieter Jensen as its hero. The book's author, Max Zimmering (1909–1973), was the son of a Jewish watchmaker who perished during the Holocaust. Zimmering had become involved in left-wing politics even before the Nazis came to power, joining the KPD in 1930. Shortly thereafter, he began to write for various party publications, including *Rote Fahne* and Willi Münzenberg's *Arbeiter Illustrierte Zeitung* (see chapter 2). After the Nazi seizure of power, Zimmering fled to Paris, eventually ending up as a party functionary in Palestine. In 1935, he returned to Europe, settling in Prague for a brief period. Zimmering had to flee the Nazis once again, though, seeking refuge in England and later Australia. After the war, he returned to Dresden, where he had grown up. At this point, Zimmering became involved in SED cultural politics in the city, working both as a party functionary and a writer. A journalist, novelist, and poet, Zimmering wrote the lyrics for Günter Kochan's "Ernst Thälmann—Three Songs," which was first performed in 1949. *Buttje Pieter and His Hero* was, however, his most important publication of the immediate postwar years, distributed widely at the time and reappearing in a new edition during the 1970s.[69] As a young man, Zimmering had attended many KPD rallies and heard Thälmann speak, later recording his impressions of the fallen KPD chief. The Communist journalist, for example, attended a Thälmann presidential rally in 1932, and he recalled the passion that the party chief stirred in the crowd. In response to the candidate's presentation, the thousands assembled began to chant such things as "Long live Ernst Thälmann!" "Red Front, Teddy!" and "Vote KPD!"[70] His experiences made Zimmering eminently qualified to produce a children's book about the slain KPD chief.

The idea of writing a children's novel about the martyred party leader first came to Zimmering, he later recalled, in 1949, when party officials from Czechoslovakia approached him, asking him to "[w]rite a story about the great German leader of workers for Czech children." As a result, he consulted Willi Bredel's recently published biography (see chapter 7), concluding that although Bredel's book was a very valuable resource for adults, it was "hardly the right [book] for young readers." There was more than enough material in Bredel's *Ernst Thälmann: Ein Beitrag zu einem politischen Lebensbild* to produce a book for young people, but Zimmering sought to avoid simply writing a watered-down version of the earlier work. "I had to find a way," Zimmering later wrote, "to tell the story of Thälmann's life and struggle in a form understandable and interesting [*spannenden*] for children." The result of Zimmering's task was the children's book *Buttje Pieter and His Hero.*[71]

The novel, like the memoir later published by Irma Thälmann, is relatively brief, 171 pages, and made for easy reading. It is illustrated with forty-four simple pen-and-ink drawings, providing, as *Memories of My Father* would three years later, visual aids designed to help readers better identify with the characters. Most of the action takes place in Thälmann's native city of Hamburg, and the central character is the adolescent Peter Jensen—whose parents and friends call "Pieter." Zimmering makes it abundantly clear that Pieter—as Ernst Thälmann had been in his youth—was a *Buttje*, or a "simple Hamburg youth." He does what is right and "never leaves his friends in the lurch—in short: he is a good comrade."[72]

The simple plot takes place in August 1944. The German army has long been defeated at Stalingrad, and American and British planes repeatedly bomb Hamburg. One day while rummaging through his father's bookcase—once again books play an important role in a children's story about the fallen KPD chief—Pieter discovers a photograph of someone, a man with "clever, friendly eyes," whom he does not recognize.[73] Pieter is afraid to ask his father, Fiete, who is exempt from military service because he is disabled. His parents had hidden it so carefully, so they clearly did not want anyone else to find it. As a result, Pieter hides the photograph under his shirt, hoping to show it to Hannes, his closest friend. Hannes does not recognize the photograph either, so he takes Pieter to visit a friend of his, an elderly furniture maker named "Grandpa" Holm. It turns out that Holm is an old Communist who personally knew the man in the picture. Holm informs Pieter that the impressive figure in the photograph is none other than Ernst Thälmann, leader of the German proletariat. This revelation piques Pieter's curiosity, and he asks Holm to tell him about the man. As a result, the furniture maker regales the two boys with yarns concerning the adventures of this great leader of workers, "our Teddy," who, like Pieter and Hannes, had once been a boy growing up in Hamburg. Holm recounts stories about Thälmann's long struggle against the fascists, insisting that if the KPD chief had had his way, Germany would be living in peace with its neighbors, and Pieter's older brother would not have perished on the Eastern Front. This observation makes the young Jensen even more curious, and he asks Holm about Thälmann's current whereabouts: Is the KPD chief in a concentration camp like so many other workers? No, "Grandpa" Holm responds, because the fascists feared Thälmann's influence among Germany's workers, they had imprisoned him in Bautzen, outside of Hannover. Pieter decides that he must see Ernst Thälmann, who has become his hero.

Pieter then concocts a plan, part of which he shares with Hannes, who, although informed that his friend is taking a trip, does not know where Pieter is planning to go. Pieter decides to take the train to Hannover, where he hopes to see Thälmann for himself. Mentioning to Holm that he is traveling to Hannover to visit an aunt, the furniture maker reveals that he has a brother, Jürgen, living in that city. Holm provides Pieter with Jürgen's address in case the boy needs some help while visiting a city with which he is unfamiliar. Realizing that his parents will be worried—his trip will be an overnight expedition—Pieter asks Hannes to tell his parents that he has left town, but that he is all right. Hannes, however, is not to tell the Jensens where Pieter has gone. Pieter leaves Hamburg on the train, riding without a ticket—no one is asking questions during these final days of the war. Pieter takes the train to Hannover, where he exits the station without any idea concerning where he should go to find the jail. Fearful of asking people on the street, lest they inquire why he seeks the Bautzen prison, Pieter ends up going to Jürgen Holm's house. When hearing that Pieter is interested in discovering the location of the imprisoned KPD chief, Jürgen informs him that Thälmann is dead. The Nazis have murdered him, hoping to cripple permanently the proletariat's political will. Because Pieter cannot see Thälmann, Jürgen—who also knew the recently deceased KPD chief—shares with Pieter some of his experiences struggling alongside the "Buttje's" hero. Pieter spends the night in Jürgen's apartment, falling asleep with his martyred hero foremost in his thoughts. Jürgen decides to accompany Pieter on his return journey—times are difficult, and it is dangerous for a boy to travel alone.

In the meantime, Hannes, also a "Buttje" who keeps his word, has gone to the home of the Jensens to inform his friend's parents that although Pieter has gone on a trip alone and will be gone over night, they must not worry. Fiete and his wife (her name is not given) are nonetheless disconcerted, demanding that Hannes tell them where their son has gone. Hannes does not know, but he thinks that "Grandpa" Holm might. Fiete knows Holm from years ago, when the Jensens were active in the KPD, before the Nazis had come to power. The Jensens decide to pay a visit to the old furniture maker, who is shocked to discover that in spite of what Pieter had told him, the boy was not visiting relatives in Hannover. Holm does, however, recommend that the parents not be too hard on the boy. The Jensens consider calling the police, but Holm—intimately aware of the dangers of dealing with Nazi authorities—advises caution. He suggests that the Jensens return the next morning, and if Pieter has not yet shown up, he will take the train to Hannover with Fiete to search for the boy. Needless to say, Pieter, who has innocently fallen asleep on Jürgen's couch, does not return, and the Jensens arrive at Holm's shop bright and early the next morning. As the two men are about to leave for the train station, Pieter comes walking through the front door, accompanied by Jürgen. Pieter confesses that he had gone to Hannover to see Ernst Thälmann, only to discover that his hero had died at the hands of Nazi thugs. Fiete is angry with Pieter but does not punish the boy. After all, because he never told his son about the great man in the hidden photograph, he bears partial responsibility for Pieter's behavior. He feared telling his son, Fiete explains, about the family's erstwhile connections to the KPD. After all, as workers, the Jensens had constantly to be on their guard for the Gestapo, and his parents wanted to keep Pieter out of trouble. Holm points out that such thinking is counterproductive. "Hitler has become powerful," the old furniture maker points out, "because too many people have thought only about themselves."[74]

Later, when father and son are at home, Fiete concedes that Holm had a point and that, as Pieter's father, he should have shared the story of Ernst Thälmann with Pieter. Indeed, Fiete concedes, his son taught him a valuable lesson. The Jensens' misfortunes and by implication the problems facing the German people were in large part of their own making. Cowed by the overwhelming force brought to bear by the Nazis, they had done nothing, taking refuge in their quiet family existence rather than being moved to action. "When a guy sits at home with his hands in his lap and hurls insults at the Nazis and the bombs, it does him absolutely no good," the father concedes. Fiete promises Pieter that he will remember this valuable lesson in the future. Indeed, Pieter's refusal to stand idly by while his hero faced the threat of death every day should be admired, Fiete concludes. The twelve-year-old had proven to be an excellent example for his politically indifferent parents. "You are a fine young man," Fiete concludes, "I am convinced that Thälmann would also be pleased with you."[75]

But there is more to *Buttje Pieter and His Hero* than Zimmering's insipid story. The book, like *Memories of My Father*, seeks to create a state-sanctioned image of the fallen Communist leader, to transform Ernst Thälmann into an example to be emulated by all German youth, to mold the martyred KPD chief into an icon of the East German state. The SED leadership hoped that East Germany's young people, having read *Buttje Pieter and His Hero*, would seek to build upon his legacy, to pursue Thälmann's goals, which although envisioned in the past could be realized in the present and the future. The slain Communist leader should serve as a bridge between the past and the future. Only then could fascism, as embodied in the West, be completely and utterly defeated.

In keeping with this effort, Zimmering incorporated a second, parallel story into *Buttje Pieter and His Hero*—it comprises far too much of the book to be categorized as a "subplot." This second narrative relates some of the major events of Ernst Thälmann's life, culminating in his martyr's death on the night of 17–18 August 1944. Zimmering uses two methods to relate Thälmann's biography. The first is the stories that "Grandpa" and Jürgen Holm tell Pieter about Thälmann's accomplishments. The second involves bringing the imprisoned KPD chief directly into the narrative, recounting the events of Thälmann's final days. In addition, as he waits for the inevitable shot in the back of the head, the Communist leader reminisces about some of the major events of his life, especially about his youth in Hamburg, the city in which Pieter Jensen is growing up. Using these narrative methods, Zimmering not only tells the story of Pieter Jensen's effort to set eyes upon his hero but also provides an account of some of the most important moments in Ernst Thälmann's life. Hence, Zimmering's novel is more than just a politically approved work of fiction. It is also among the first East German biographies of Ernst Thälmann written for young people. As such, it made a vital contribution to the effort to propagate among East German youth of the 1950s a particular, politically advantageous version of Thälmann's life.

It is worth noting that all of the events running through the fictional Thälmann's mind are concerned with politics. Although Zimmering's Ernst Thälmann thinks about both his wife and daughter, it is always in a political context, as an aspect of his determination to create a better future for the entire German proletariat. Like Irma Thälmann three years later, Zimmering depicts the KPD chief as a figure concerned exclusively with politics. Thälmann was, readers of *Buttje Pieter and His Hero* were to understand, someone who put the welfare of the international proletariat above everything else, including his own well-being and that of his family. In this he was to serve as an example for the young people of the GDR. At the same time, Zimmering's narrative devices permit him to create the desired version of recent history. The German proletariat, Thälmann at its helm, standing side by side with the Soviet Union, led the struggle against Nazism both before and during the war, just as it stood at the forefront of the opposition to the postwar version of fascism emerging in the FRG. Zimmering's account seeks to create the impression that the proletariat universally opposed the fascists—even if many workers were too timid to act upon their convictions. Ernst Thälmann had led this effort for the entire decade preceding the Nazi seizure of power, and East Germany's young people could learn a great deal from his example. History was once again presented in a monumental fashion (see chapter 7), and some of the major events in Ernst Thälmann's life took on iconic status. Seemingly every book, film, or other narrative dealing with the life of the fallen KPD leader dealt with at least one of these major events from his life. The two most important historical developments in which the KPD chief was involved—at least as reflected in the regime's appeals to children and adolescents—were the Hamburg Uprising of October 1923 and his sacrificial death at the hands of Nazi thugs in August 1944. Max Zimmering's *Buttje Pieter and His Hero*, like Irma Thälmann's memoir, covers both of these developments in some detail.

Pieter hears about the famous Hamburg Uprising while visiting Jürgen Holm in Hannover. It was the event—the German October—that had made the dock worker from Hamburg a major force in German politics. Holm, who was present at the events he describes, depicts the brief period of the uprising as among the most glorious days in the history of the German workers' movement. "For three days and three nights . . . we showed the big shots in Hamburg what a powerful force a few hundred armed workers is, above all when they have a leader so clever, prudent, and decisive as Ernst Thälmann." Indeed, in spite of the overwhelming odds against them because the "superior strength of the enemy was so great, and because the people had not taken up their weapons in other parts of Germany," the workers had shown the fat cats who was boss, and "the rich people could not return for days and weeks to their Hamburg villas. That pleased me," says Jürgen, "a great deal." Evidence of how close the workers had come to seizing power in the city could be found in the fact that "the Communist Party was prohibited after the uprising, and the police force of Hamburg's big shots [*Pfeffersäcke*] was always going after Teddy." Jürgen continues by sharing humorous stories about how the clever "Teddy" eluded his incompetent pursuers.[76]

Like other party propagandists going back to the mid-1920s, Zimmering sought to depict the KPD chief as the Leonidas of German communism. Like the Greek hero who had lived so many years earlier, Thälmann had led his comrades in a battle against overwhelming odds. A struggle in which the forces of good, although massively outnumbered, had to stand up against evil. They stood three days and nights against insurmountable odds because they fought for a sacred cause. Also like Leonidas and his Spartans fighting in the valley at Thermopylae, Thälmann and his men—in spite of their tremendous determination and bravery—were temporarily defeated. The forces stacked against them were simply too great. Others who could have tipped the scales in the workers' favor had refused to stand up for what was right. Yet Thälmann and his comrades had set an example that ultimately influenced others to take action. Like the ancient Greeks who, inspired by the sacrifice of the three hundred at Thermopylae, ultimately defeated the Persian invaders, the "several hundred" workers who had stood up against injustice during the German October had ultimately been vindicated. The defeat of Nazi Germany and the establishment of the German Democratic Republic bore this out. Thälmann and his comrades' persistence should serve as an example for East Germany's young people. The workers would experience serious setbacks, but their ultimate triumph was assured, and East German youth would play a pivotal role in securing this victory.

Another major trope of the officially sanctioned version of the Thälmann myth was the sacrificial death endured by the KPD chief. In *Buttje Pieter and His Hero,* Zimmering seeks to present an account of Thälmann's martyrdom that would appeal to young people. Thälmann had suffered over the course of the entire eleven and a half years during which he was imprisoned, and Zimmering—like so many others—invoked the image of the party chief enduring torture in the bowels of the Gestapo headquarters.[77] The oft-repeated story of how the Nazis lied about the circumstances surrounding the death of Pieter's hero is also related here. Thälmann was brutally murdered on direct orders from Adolf Hitler—that paragon of evil. To the very end of his life, because Thälmann garnered the support and respect of Germany's workers, the leaders of the Third Reich feared him and were determined that the KPD chief would not live to see the Soviet victory and the birth of socialist Germany.

Zimmering's book is a work of fiction, which permitted the author to take even greater liberties than the historical accounts of Thälmann's life. As a result, Zimmering, unlike Willi Bredel (see chapter 7) and Irma Thälmann, provides a detailed account of the party chief's thoughts concerning the prospect of his own death. According to Zimmering's story, Thälmann recognizes that his violent demise is all but inevitable and that he will not live to see the glorious day of the Soviet triumph over German imperialism. He resigns himself to spending the rest of his brief life imprisoned by fascist thugs. Zimmering's account of Thälmann's martyrdom begins with "It is the 17th of August," a date that should be familiar to all his readers. On that day, the SS walk into his cell, demanding that Thälmann prepare himself to take a trip. Although he knows that his captors can murder him at any time,

> [h]e had never feared them, and did not fear them now, although he had known for eleven-and-one-half years, that every day can be his last.
>
> But he knows that the working class will emerge victorious, even if the fascists should kill him. He knows that the great Soviet Union exists. He knows that Stalin—who leads the struggle of the Soviet army of freedom, which moves ever closer to Berlin—lives in the Kremlin. The two Gestapo men who stand before him will not escape punishment.[78]

The Gestapo men lead the KPD chief out of the prison to a waiting automobile, where Thälmann sits, "flanked by his armed escort," not knowing where he is going until one of the guards eventually mentions Buchenwald. The KPD chief does not care—"Buchenwald or another concentration camp," it is a matter of indifference to him. The time in the car allows the party leader one last opportunity to think back over his life's accomplishments. He remembers his days in Hamburg, the early, heady days of the German revolutionary movement. As his mind harkens back, Thälmann looks out of the car window, gazing at the people he sees, Germans for whom he has sacrificed a great deal. During the early evening, the party stops in Saxony to eat. People in the street, knowing who Thälmann is, stare at him. Although no one is brave enough to talk to him, "the daughter of the innkeeper" winks at him.[79]

Once the car begins to move again, Thälmann—as always unconcerned about his personal destiny—repeatedly dozes off to sleep. During his waking moments, Thälmann considers the job ahead. "He is less concerned with his own life than with the tasks that lie before him, because Hitler will soon meet his end." In spite of the fact that he does not expect to survive the war, Thälmann is determined "to work and struggle for a new, better, peace-loving Germany. Above everything else must the unity of the working class and all creative people be accomplished," so that the "capitalists and Junkers" can never regain power. His contemplation of Germany's future leads Thälmann back once again to the noble-minded days of October 1923, when he and his comrades had fought for "work and bread." More than two decades might have passed, but "[o]nce again, the working class faces the decision, to relinquish power or to seize it." To build socialism or to acquiesce in continuing capitalist exploitation. Thälmann knew which choice he hoped—and believed—the proletariat would make.[80]

As the KPD chief rides to his death, reminiscences of October 1923 remain foremost in his mind. Indeed, "Thälmann has almost forgotten both the Gestapo officials next to him, because these Hamburg days have become so real before his eyes, as during the hours among his comrades, leading the struggle." He remembers many of his companions from those days personally. Among them is Wilhelm Pieck—"his old comrade"—who, alongside Karl Liebknecht and Rosa Luxemburg, created the party, and "the clever and energetic" Walter Ulbricht, who had stood by Thälmann's side at some of the most important events in the history of the German workers' movement. Finally, his thoughts turn to Stalin, whose party had served as such an important "example" to Thälmann as KPD chairman. Indeed, because the German working class could draw upon the examples established by these valiant revolutionaries, because it had inherited the legacy of such people, its future is bright and its ultimate victory assured. In short, Thälmann is about to go to his grave as an optimistic man deeply satisfied—not so much with his own accomplishments, but with those of the social class in whose benefit he has labored so long and hard.[81] Zimmering's account of Thälmann's martyrdom ends with the KPD chief entering the courtyard of Buchenwald's crematorium, "then three shots ring out. The German working class has lost its greatest son."[82]

Zimmering's story of these last moments of Thälmann's life seeks to link the past, present, and future as vital to the effort to build socialism. Thälmann remembers the past not only out of nostalgia, but because of the lessons it teaches. They are lessons that the KPD chief applied to the circumstances that he faced in the past. His hours might be numbered, but he knows that he has done the right thing. His own willingness and that of others to sacrifice their lives to make socialism a reality establish that the future will be better. Readers will, Zimmering hoped, learn from Thälmann's example. They should look to the past for models of proper behavior, apply these models to the situation they face as young people living in the GDR, and thereby help build a better future. No better example for young people existed than Ernst Thälmann. Indeed, writers of children's books sought to invoke the martyr from Hamburg until the very last days of the SED regime. In doing so, they summoned the same events from Thälmann's life, hoping to instill similar lessons in their readers.[83] As in other manifestations of the Thälmann legend, appeals to youth remained remarkably consistent throughout the more than forty years during which the SED dominated first the SBZ and then the GDR.

As is the case with other examples of the Thälmann legend, the success of Zimmering's effort is difficult to determine. Although it is clear that most East German children read the book, which was assigned reading for children younger than thirteen even up to the GDR's final years, it is difficult to determine if the lessons of *Buttje Pieter and His Hero* became properly ingrained in its readers.[84] Children in the GDR clearly learned the book's story and came away from their encounter familiar with the state-sponsored version of Thälmann's life and legacy. But in every society children often learn things simply in order to get the desired grades, often not putting the lessons that they learn to use. In spite of this uncertainty, it is safe to conclude that the SED placed a high value on *Buttje Pieter and His Hero.* The party leadership was willing to assign valuable resources over the coming years to the effort to maximize the distribution of Zimmering's novel. The book, for example, was reprinted at least twice—in 1954 and 1969. Indeed, Zimmering's didactic tale would go on to appear in at least one other medium. In April 1958, GDR broadcasting aired a radio version of *Buttje Pieter and His Hero.* The performance—"[a] sound play based on the book by the same name by Max Zimmering in commemoration of the 72nd birthday of Ernst Thälmann"—was transmitted during the school day so that the broadcast would have a captive audience. The SED leadership could thus be assured that the radio version of the story would have a maximum effect and that children would have the opportunity to discuss what they had heard with their teachers and classmates.[85]

Over the course of more than forty years, the Socialist Unity Party used all of the resources at its disposal to inculcate the children of the German Democratic Republic with values consistent with socialism: class consciousness, anti-imperialism, a willingness to sacrifice for the common good, a deep admiration for the Soviet Union, and the spirit of antifascism. A vital component of the effort to instill these qualities in young people was the Ernst Thälmann myth. Hence, from an early age East German children learned about the life and legacy of this worker from Hamburg who, the product of a modest proletarian childhood, grew to become "Germany's eternal son," an heroic figure who developed from a "son of his class" into the "leader of his class." As such, Thälmann could serve as an example for all East German children.

7

"Ernst Thälmann Is Still among Us"

Because the governing SED based its legitimacy on the legacy of antifascism, presented as a dramatic narrative that took the form of myth, the study of contemporary history from a Marxist–Leninist perspective played a vital role in East German political propaganda. Scholars in the GDR developed a highly didactic historiography—*Geschichtspropaganda*, "historical propaganda"—that came to play a critical part in the development of the antifascism myth. East German historians played an active role in creating the legitimacy that their government sought, and their profession made many of them instruments of the ruling SED. They were not mere erudite observers of past events, but active participants in the shaping of the socialist present and the Communist future. Like scholars in other Marxist–Leninist states, GDR historians recorded, explained, and encouraged the ineluctable march of class conflict that had culminated in the creation of the German Democratic Republic and that would one day assure the global victory of communism. The historians' goal was, as Karl Marx said of philosophers, not merely "to explain the world, but to change it." Their calling was a moral and political one, and they rejected the spurious notion of "objectivity" in favor of participation in the struggle to liberate the proletariat, to link the past, present, and future along an ideologically predetermined continuum. In other words, GDR scholars were to write what Friedrich Nietzsche called "monumental history" designed to help build the myths necessary to the dissemination of the socialist worldview, rather than the "critical history" to which Western bourgeois scholars supposedly ascribed. In order to promote this functionalist East German historiography and thereby contribute to its quest for legitimacy, the SED created scholarly academies such as the Institute for Marxism–Leninism (IML, founded in 1957) and the Central Institute for History. Scholars working at these institutions as well as at East German universities generated an enormous quantity of historical propaganda, and the IML became especially important to the dissemination of the antifascism myth. Historians produced their work not for other scholars, as was often the case in the West, but for the masses, who needed to be educated in the fundamental principles of Marxism–Leninism. As a result, journals such as the *Beiträge zur Geschichte der Arbeiterbewegung* (Contributions to the History of the Workers' Movement) published scholarly articles on labor history written from a Marxist–Leninist perspective. State-controlled publishers, most important among them being Dietz Verlag, printed and distributed collections from the writings of important socialist thinkers, scholarly monographs, and party histories designed to contribute to the task of historical propaganda.[1]

Although the GDR's Marxist–Leninist historians insisted that social classes made history and, in theory, deemphasized the necessity of "great men," biographical works played an important role in historical propaganda. Great figures from the socialist past—including Karl Marx, Friedrich Engels, Nikolai Lenin, Rosa Luxemburg, and Karl Liebknecht—could serve as models of the proper way to organize and lead the masses, the true creators of historical change. These figures from the past came to represent the socialist archetype, and scholars participated in the development of cults of personality surrounding them. Such historical personalities came to embody the ideals of socialist humanism, the forces of progress in history. The GDR was, according to the Marxist–Leninist biographers, the embodiment of these figures' political struggle. As such, their legacy served to legitimize socialist Germany.[2]

Lenin and, at least until the mid-1950s, Stalin remained the most important figures around whom historians from the Soviet bloc fostered the growth of personality cults. It should come as no surprise, however, that Thälmann became a central figure in the German socialists' historical propaganda, first in the SBZ and then in the GDR. Over the course of the years from 1948 to 1989, numerous books and journal articles, many written by academic historians, chronicled the life of the fallen KPD chief. An analysis of these works provides another fruitful opportunity to understand the evolution of the Ernst Thälmann myth over the course of four decades. For the sake of brevity, I concentrate on the two most important books written about Thälmann during these years: Willi Bredel's *Ernst Thälmann: Ein Beitrag zu einem politischen Leb-*

ensbild (Ernst Thälmann: A Contribution to a Political View of His Life, 1948) and *Ernst Thälmann: Eine Biographie* (1979), written by an author collective at East Berlin's IML.[3] These two works are noteworthy for a variety of reasons. Bredel's book, the original manuscript of which he completed in 1945, was the first postwar biography and established the overarching motifs of the Thälmann myth upon its publication in 1948. It helped create the tradition of basing the legitimacy of the SED on Thälmann's legacy. The book says much regarding the party leadership's worldview during the period immediately preceding the creation of the GDR. Bredel's book was also the principal source for Kurt Maetzig's two epic films, *Ernst Thälmann—Sohn seiner Klasse* and *Ernst Thälmann—Führer seiner Klasse*, which came to play such an important role in the propagation of the legend. The other Thälmann biography of concern here, *Ernst Thälmann: Eine Biographie,* is also among the most important manifestations of historical propaganda based around the Thälmann myth. The result of a direct order issued in 1973 by the Politburo to the IML, this sizeable work says much regarding the way that the SED leadership viewed the socialist past during the final decade of the GDR's existence.[4] Finally, there is documentary evidence available concerning the actual writing process of both books, which permits an analysis of the mechanics of how German Communists wrote history, both during the era of the antifascist struggle of the 1930s and 1940s as well as during the final years of the cold war. Sources exist that record the influence that the party leadership had on the writing of history in both the SBZ and the GDR. An investigation of both books also provides the opportunity to trace the evolution of the GDR's historical propaganda over the course of four decades.

Willi Bredel (1901–1964), like Ernst Thälmann, was a native of Hamburg. Coming from a working-class family, Bredel took a job as a metalworker when he was a young man. After the First World War, in which he did not serve because of his youth, he became active in leftist politics, supporting first the Spartakusbund (Spartacus Union) and then the KPD. A political associate of Ernst Thälmann, Bredel participated in the Hamburg Uprising of 1923 and as a result served two years in prison. In 1928, the twenty-seven-year-old became editor of Hamburg's Communist newspaper *Die Volkszeitung* (the People's Newspaper). Because of his activities with the paper, Weimar authorities prosecuted Bredel for treason, and he was sentenced to a further two years imprisonment. This second incarceration provided him with an opportunity to pursue his literary ambitions, and in 1930 he published his first novel, a socialist-realist work entitled *Machinefabrik N&K* (Machine Works N&K), followed the next year by *Die Rosenhofstraße* (Rosenhof Street). The Nazis arrested him in 1933, and he was detained in Fuhlsbüttel Concentration Camp. After being released the following year and renouncing his German citizenship, the Hamburg native sneaked across the border to Czechoslovakia and from there on to Moscow—a route that many German Communists traveled. Bredel's experiences in Fuhlsbüttel provided the background to his first significant work, *Die Prüfung* (The Test, 1935), a novel set in a concentration camp, which was translated into seventeen languages.[5]

In Moscow, Bredel served as one of the editors—alongside Bertolt Brecht and Lion Feuchtwanger—of *Das Wort*, the literary journal of the German Communist Party in exile. In 1937, he left the Soviet Union to fight in the Spanish Civil War. Joining the famous International Brigade, Bredel became a commissar with the Thälmann Battalion. After Francisco Franco's victory, Bredel returned to the Soviet Union, eventually joining the Red Army and fighting in the Great Patriotic War against the Nazis. After the war, he returned to Germany, serving as a KPD official in Mecklenburg. Over the next decade, Bredel became an increasingly influential member of the cultural elite. During the immediate postwar period, he became an influential figure in the Kulturbund, an officially nonpartisan organization created to lead German culture in a more "democratic" direction, which meant the creation of a uniquely German version of socialist realism. During the years 1947 to 1954, the Hamburg native served as the chief editor of the periodical *Heute und Morgen* (Today and Tomorrow) and in 1950 was a founding member of East Germany's Academy of Arts. He continued to hold a number of important posts in the GDR's cultural establishment, including three years as chief editor of *Neue Deutsche Literatur* (New German Literature, 1953–1956), arguably his country's most influential literary journal. In 1954, he joined the SED's Central Committee and from 1962 until his death in 1964 served as president of the Academy of Arts. In spite of all of his postwar political activities, Bredel found time to complete work on his magnum opus, a trilogy of novels published under the title *Ein neues Kapitel* (A New Chapter).[6]

Willi Bredel had impeccable credentials for a biographer of Ernst Thälmann. Born and bred in Hamburg, the socialist-realist writer was intimately familiar with the milieu that molded the Communist martyr. Not only had he walked the same streets and had many of the same experiences as his subject, but he had also actively participated in the famous Hamburg Uprising that had made Thälmann the Leonidas of German communism. Bredel had known Thälmann personally and could provide insight from his own experiences with the KPD chief. Further, like Thälmann, Bredel had served time in prison because of his political beliefs. He also had impeccable credentials as an antifascist, having been arrested by German authorities shortly after the Nazis came to power and serving a term in a concentration camp. The writer from Hamburg, as was typical for many German Communists, had fled his homeland for the birthplace of Marxism–Leninism, the Soviet Union, where he had emerged as one of the German-speaking world's most influential socialist-realist writers. The fact that Bredel had served in the Thälmann Battalion during the civil war in Spain and the Red Army during its conflict with Nazi Germany added further legitimacy to the idea that he understood the mindset of the fallen Communist leader, who had also sacrificed a great deal in the name of the socialist cause. In short, Bredel had a great deal in common not only with Ernst Thälmann, but also with the leaders of postwar German communism. He was representative of the generation who would build socialism, first in the SBZ and—one day in the future, it was hoped—in all of Germany.[7]

Willi Bredel's *Ernst Thälmann: Ein Beitrag zu einem politischen Lebensbild* was the product of a long gestation, perhaps as much as a decade. The earliest extant documentary evidence of Bredel's thinking systematically concerning the life of his fellow Hamburg native is a typewritten sixteen-page-long précis entitled "Thälmann's Meaning for the Development and Bolshevisation of the K. P. D." Held in the archive of the former GDR's Academy of Arts, this outline is contained in a file labeled "Moscow, Paris, 1935–1945." As a result, the exact year in which Bredel produced this summary remains uncertain. There is evidence, however, that permits considerable narrowing of this ten-year window. First and most obvious, the document fails to mention Thälmann's sacrificial death. Further, it repeatedly refers to the party leader using the present tense, providing additional evidence that Bredel produced the outline while his subject was still alive. Add to this detail the fact that the novelist submitted his finished manuscript—far more extensive than this relatively brief synopsis—in April 1945, and one can safely conclude that the outline was produced before 1944. An examination of its author's very busy life during the years 1935 to 1945 leads to the conclusion that he created the document several years before 1944, probably during 1935 or 1936, the period during which he worked for

Das Wort and contributed to the Free Thälmann campaign. He spent the years 1934 to 1937 exiled in Moscow, writing extensively and editing a literary journal, and the following two years were extremely busy for the novelist from Hamburg. In 1937, he left Moscow to fight in the Spanish Civil War, and although it is possible that he began work on *Ernst Thälmann* while in Spain, as a commissar in the International Brigade he would have had less time for writing than he had during his years in Moscow. Of course, Bredel left Spain for Paris in the wake of Franco's victory, and it is possible that he began work on his book during the two years before he joined the Red Army in 1941. This date is less likely than the earlier one, however. First of all, the document does not mention the Spanish Civil War or the Thälmann Battalion. Further, with the signing of the Hitler–Stalin Nonaggression Pact and the rapprochement between Nazi Germany and the Soviet Union, the Comintern abandoned its insincere effort to secure the KPD chief's release. Hence, the production of a full-scale biography of Thälmann was of far less importance in 1939 than it had been during the years 1935–1937. Indeed, a biography of a leading Communist still imprisoned by the Nazis might very well have served to remind the international socialist movement of the sudden change in the "partly line" taken in 1939. In short, the publishing of a biography of Ernst Thälmann in the context of the years between 1939 and 1941 might very well have been an embarrassment to the Comintern and the KPD in exile, both of whom had abandoned the German party chief to a dreadful existence in a Nazi jail cell. Indeed, it is likely that Bredel temporarily abandoned his plans to write a life of Thälmann during this two-year period.[8]

Further evidence for an early dating of this document lies in its contents, which reflect the propaganda motifs of the Free Thälmann effort of the years 1933 to 1939. From its inception, Bredel envisioned the biography as a work of propaganda. The outline, for example, emphasizes Thälmann's alleged roots in Hamburg's working class. This background, alongside his "[u]ncompromising struggle for the interests of the workers" and his "fundamental" (*grundsätzlich*) study of the works of Marx, Lenin, and Stalin, assured his popularity among the masses and hence his position as a leader of the antifascist movement. In other words, Bredel depicts his fellow Hamburg native as "[t]he archetype of a revolutionary leader of workers." Throughout the sixteen pages, Bredel develops themes that depict Thälmann as a noble but humble man, whose primary concern was with the well-being of others, specifically the international proletariat. Historical conditions molded him for greatness and assured that he would become the leader of the German proletariat in its most difficult hour. The outline emphasizes milestones in Thälmann's ideological development that became components of his public image and played such an important role in the Comintern's 1933–1939 propaganda offensive: his struggle against the forces of reaction during the 1918–1919 revolution; the Hamburg Uprising of 1923; the determined worker's ascent to the KPD chairmanship; the Bolshevization of the KPD under Stalin's tutelage; his strong support for the international workers' movement; his quest for the unity of the workers in the SPD and the KPD in the face of the emerging fascist menace; and, of course, his 1932 presidential bid, in which he ran against Adolf Hitler. Finally, Bredel sought to portray the KPD chief as "a sincere friend, comrade, helper, and leader of youth."[9] In short, all of the major motifs of the Thälmann myth—save the subject's death and martyrdom—can be found in Bredel's early outline, evincing a great deal of continuity between the prewar and postwar versions of the legend.

Although a degree of uncertainty remains concerning when Bredel began the work on his biography of Ernst Thälmann, the time at which he completed his manuscript can be determined with a great deal more accuracy. In April 1945, Bredel submitted the manuscript to Wilhem Pieck, then chairman of the KPD. This practice—in which leading figures in the party vetted scholarly works for ideological reliability—was something that the KPD and SED leadership inherited from their Soviet mentors. Indeed, it was one of the central characteristics of the culture of "high Stalinism," which had so much influence in the SBZ and early GDR. In the accompanying cover letter, Bredel asks Pieck to write a foreword for the book, which the author characterizes as an analysis of how "Teddy's life and actions is [sic] among the most important parts of the history of our party and the German workers' movement between the two imperialistic World Wars." As had been the case at least since the launching of the Free Thälmann effort, the central party leadership remained closely involved in the creation and dissemination of the legend. Although Bredel was one of the most prominent literary figures among postwar German Communists, and his ideological orthodoxy was thus not in question, it was essential that Pieck examine the manuscript. "Teddy's" image was vitally important to the party leadership, and it had to be closely guarded. Hence, it is likely that other members of the KPD's Central Committee read the manuscript as well.[10]

Bredel points out that his forthcoming book is organized into "three sections": "First part: youth. Third part: imprisonment and death. Second part: the party leader. And this second part is of as great a bulk [*Umfang*] as the other two sections combined." In other words, the manuscript emphasized the years 1925 through 1933, during which Thälmann oversaw the Bolshevization of the KPD and led the proletariat's struggle against the emerging fascist menace. The book is, as the subtitle suggests, a political biography, and it says remarkably little about its subject's private life. In his letter to the party chief, Bredel points out something that Pieck might have seen as a weakness in the manuscript. Recognizing that mentioning the absence of certain material might very well delay the publication of the biography, Bredel concedes that "I must remark specifically . . . [that] I have written nothing [*kein Wort*] about Thälmann's comrades [*Mitkämpfer*], nor concerning You [*sic*], his successor [*Nachfolger*]." Bredel remarks that Thälmann was "such an important subject" that he wanted first to get Pieck's advice on the matter before proceeding. The missing material on Thälmann's contemporaries and his successors, such as Pieck and Ulbricht, would ultimately appear in the finished book. In the meantime, this deficiency at least in part explains why it would be another three years before *Ernst Thälmann: Ein Beitrag zu einem politischen Lebensbild* would appear in print.[11]

In 1948, Bredel's Thälmann biography finally rolled off the presses, becoming one of the canonical works of East German historical propaganda. The book cannot be considered a work of scholarship—it is void of any serious critical analysis and scholarly apparatus. Rather, Bredel's *Ernst Thälmann: Ein Beitrag zu einem politischen Lebensbild* is a piece of propaganda that is clearly aimed at a wide audience. It is written in simple, easy-to-understand prose, and Bredel assiduously avoids the verbose academic style so notorious in German historical writing. The straightforward quality of his prose should come as no surprise, given the fact that Marxist–Leninist ideology insisted that history must be written for the masses in order to play its vital role in fomenting proletarian revolution—that is, in such a manner that workers can understand it. Bredel concentrates on political matters, and he depicts his subject as one dimensional, a man without flaws who lived entirely for Germany's approaching socialist revolution. Divided into eleven chapters, the book, published by East Berlin's Dietz Verlag, is a mere 167 pages long, and a persistent reader can consume it in a single sitting. The chapter titles often incorporate the major themes of the Thälmann legend: "Against Militarism and Reaction," "The Avant-Garde of the Working People," "Toward the Construction of Antifascist Unity,"

"In the Struggle Against Fascism and War." Even a quick reading of the book makes it clear that Bredel had a message to share and that he wanted to ensure that his readers would not have to put too much effort into understanding his point. In this goal, he was undoubtedly successful. In spite of the relative brevity of *Ernst Thälmann,* a careful examination of the entire text would be unmanageable, but a close inspection of a handful of carefully chosen passages serves to characterize succinctly its major themes.[12]

The book, as Bredel had hoped, opens with a foreword written by the future president of the GDR, Wilhelm Pieck, in which Pieck, among other things, emphasizes Ernst Thälmann's credentials as an antifascist. Seeking to justify the forced alliance of the KPD and the SPD carried out two years earlier, Pieck points out that Thälmann "knew . . . that the workers' movement can only resist fascism if it is united and has a united leadership." This was, in the party leader's estimation, just one of many ways in which the SED embodied Ernst Thälmann's legacy, for "what he created in his decades-long trade union and political activities lives on. It lives on in a unified socialist party, it lives in the mass organizations of a unified independent trade union movement, it lives in the intrepid example of the antifascist and anti-imperialist struggle, it lives in the quest for socialism." Pieck's foreword seeks to establish the major themes of Bredel's biography. Ernst Thälmann, the former KPD chairman who willingly gave his life in the struggle against fascism, should be a model for all Germans. He is the archetype of those who sought to avoid the repetition of the disaster of the years 1933–1945. He was a determined advocate for socialism and a staunch opponent of fascism. The erstwhile KPD chief was an unswerving champion of proletarian unity, and his legacy lived on in a united proletarian party, the Socialist Unity Party. Thälmann was, in Pieck's eyes, among the most important influences—alongside Marx, Lenin, and Stalin—on postwar German socialism. Like these other giants of the international proletarian movement, he was a man to be admired and emulated.[13] Thälmann was a secular saint, the major prophet of the postwar German socialist movement, who had given his life so that proletarian humanism might live.

The first chapter of Bredel's biography, "The Home of Ernst Thälmann's Parents," is even more hagiographic in tone. Indeed, a useful way of understanding the Thälmann myth is to view it as a secular version of Christian hagiography. Among the characteristics of Christian sainthood is the assertion that portents accompanied the birth of the anointed one.[14] Bredel's *Ernst Thälmann* opens with a series of seven—symbolic of completeness in Christianity—portentous events that the author seeks to link with his subject's birth in 1886. *"In the year 1886,"* Bredel begins, "fifteen years after the establishment of the Reich . . . Germany experienced a mighty industrial collapse." Workers and the owners of small businesses suffered as a result, while the welfare of "corporations and cartels" was the imperial government's primary concern. *"In the year 1886,"* Bredel continues, "the Bismarckian socialist law had already been in effect for eight years and would be extended for two more years." The working classes were under assault from all sides, and "the leader of the German workers—August Bebel—was thrown into prison many times." "In this time of the emergence of monopoly capitalism and imperialism in Germany, of the time of the sharpening of all social contradictions and of the heroic struggle of the young workers' movement against the reactionary enemies of the people, Ernst Thälmann was born on 16 April 1886." The list of portents supposedly accompanying Thälmann's birth continues with the description of Hamburg as a "republican island in the Prussian–German monarchical federal state." Lest the reader conclude that Thälmann's hometown was a democracy, Bredel points out that "[i]n *the year 1886* there was in Hamburg, with a population of nearly one-half million, only 30,500 registered citizens, of whom, however, only 19,500 possessed the right to vote." These portents as well as the others that Bredel incorporates into the opening of his narrative serve to establish that at the time of Ernst Thälmann's birth the toiling masses of Germany were in dire straits. At this time, the German proletariat's greatest hour of need, the forces of history sent Thälmann into the world. The future Communist leader would one day launch a mission to address all of the problems faced by the German people, to rescue Germany from the clutches of "monopoly capitalism and imperialism." Thälmann's early experiences in combating the conditions confronting the German proletariat would one day serve him well in the struggle against fascism and imperialist war.[15]

Ernst's experiences growing up in the home of Jan Thälmann would also help pave the way for his success as a proletarian leader, Bredel contends, and his youth is the next matter to which the author turns. Bredel's biography served to consolidate the mythology concerning the events of Thälmann's youth—much of it patently false—first introduced during the final years of the Weimar Republic. Thälmann, Bredel asserts, was the product of a prototypical working-class family.

Although moving to Hamburg from the northern German countryside, Jan quickly joined the ranks of the proletariat in Germany's largest port city. His "coworkers" introduced him to the SPD. Jan, like his future son, became an active participant in proletarian politics, "and, in spite of the furious persecution of the reaction[ary state], Johann Thälmann became, in the years of the Anti-socialist Law, a comrade [*Mitkämpfer*] of the Social Democrats." Jan married a "working-class girl [*Arbeiter-mädel*]," with whom he opened a tavern, supposedly a center of underground SPD activity.[16]

Into this idyllic proletarian household, Ernst Thälmann was born on 16 April 1886. When young Ernst was only two years old, his father was thrown in jail. Although Bredel confesses that he does not know why Jan was imprisoned, he maintains that in all likelihood it was because of the political activities taking place in his pub. Not only did Jan go to prison, but the family lost its livelihood, the guesthouse owned by the Thälmanns being seized by the authorities. "Hard days came for Mother Thälmann and her little son." The mother, Maria—whose name Bredel does not even use—had to get a job, working hard to support herself and her two children over the course of the next two years. Jan would eventually be released from jail, but only following the expiration of the Anti-socialist Law and Otto von Bismarck's fall from power. As a result of his jail sentence, however, Jan could not open another tavern. Having no means of support, he turned to his "political friends," who helped him to open a tiny business, located in a "small cellar," that sold "potatoes and vegetables." Over the course of the remainder of his childhood, young Ernst worked for his father, helping Jan deliver produce. "At the age of fourteen, Ernst was [working] in his father's delivery business . . . ; he was on his feet from four o'clock in the morning until late at night, [but] numbered among the best students . . . in his school." Indeed, Ernst was such a good student, Bredel reports, that one of his teachers suggested that the youth might eventually become a teacher himself. Jan, however, class conscious as always, would not hear of it. His son, he insisted, would one day become an "honest worker." Indeed, Thälmann's youth served as something of an apprenticeship for the young boy, and Ernst became aware of the suffering of Hamburg's workers. His years living and working for his father were important ones to the future Communist leader's political awakening, Bredel insists. They nurtured his class consciousness, preparing the youth one day to lead the struggle against exploitation, fascism, and imperialism.[17]

Bredel's account of Thälmann's childhood stretches the truth—to put it charitably. Although Jan Thälmann did indeed move to Hamburg from the countryside, he did not become an archetypical worker. Jan, as Ernst himself confessed, was apolitical. He might very well have joined the SPD, but he was not politically active and was hardly the determined revolutionary whom Bredel depicts. For that matter, Maria Thälmann cannot be considered to be a prototypical proletarian wife and mother. She apparently came from a bourgeois family, providing the money that she and her husband needed to open a guesthouse. Further, although it is true that Jan spent some time in prison when Ernst was young, it was not for political activity. Indeed, *both* Jan and Maria went to jail, not for supporting the revolutionary workers' movement, but rather for the unheroic—and politically embarrassing—crime of receiving and selling stolen goods. In short, much of Bredel's account of Thälmann's childhood, and much of the rest of the book for that matter, consist of a series of omissions of bothersome truths and outright falsehoods.[18]

One can only speculate concerning the motivation behind these misrepresentations and half-truths, especially when one considers that a more accurate rendering of Thälmann's life story fits so well into the paradigm of socialist realism, a concept with which Bredel was intimately familiar. Scholars have recognized for some time the influence that hagiography had upon the development of socialist realism in all of its forms, including fiction, a literary medium in which Bredel frequently worked.[19] This influence helps to explain why it was more important to depict Ernst Thälmann's childhood in an idealized, unsullied fashion than to portray his youth accurately. One must keep in mind that Bredel spent two years working as a writer and editor in the Soviet Union, not to mention the time he served in the Red Army. As a result, not only was he familiar with the traditions of Stalinist culture, but Bolshevik historiography clearly had a dramatic effect on his writing. The falsification of history for political reasons was a Bolshevik tradition that only intensified during the Stalin years. The study of history, even within the academy, meant the production of propaganda.[20] Like Winston Smith in George Orwell's *Nineteen Eighty-Four*, Bredel chose to confine unfortunate facts to a metaphorical dustbin. Indeed, it is best to understand *Ernst Thälmann: Ein Beitrag zu einem politischen Lebensbild* as hagiography, and among the characteristics of this millennia-old medium is that the hallowed one lives an ascetic lifestyle. This theme is consistent throughout Bredel's book, beginning with his account of his subject's childhood—one characterized by hard work and deprivation. To say that Thälmann's parents were petit bourgeois would undermine this very important trope. Hence, in keeping with the paradigm that Bredel adopted, Thälmann must have had a proletarian childhood. To admit otherwise was neither politically nor ideologically beneficial. In short, Bredel's book was propaganda, modeled on long-standing traditions within the Western world generally and within Bolshevik historiography specifically.

The influence of hagiography on Bredel's writing becomes more apparent when one looks at other passages in *Ernst Thälmann*. Among the characteristics of hagiography is that the subject is contemplative and acts as a result of his profound rumination. Bredel's version of Ernst Thälmann meets this criterion as well. In the second chapter, "Political Apprenticeship," Bredel traces the ideological evolution of Ernst Thälmann from working-class youth to proletarian revolutionary. After all, it was possible that Thälmann's youthful experiences might lead him to democratic, or "utopian," socialism. That is, many who have witnessed the shortcomings of industrial capitalism have called for a reform of the existing socioeconomic system. It is one thing to grow up in a model socialist home, but quite another to witness firsthand the systematic inhumanity inherent in capitalism. Indeed, Bredel takes it as given that Ernst, in light of his upbringing, would become a Social Democrat. It took personal experience—coupled with careful reading in the works of Marx, Lenin, and Stalin—to forge the young Hamburg native into an ardent revolutionary, an *Arbeiterführer* (leader of workers). Proletarian leaders are not created in a loving family environment, even if both parents are good socialists, but rather on the front lines of the proletariat's struggle for the basic human rights embodied in the socialist ideal. As a result of deep thinking concerning his personal experiences, the young Thälmann reached the conclusion that the political and economic status quo must be fundamentally changed—indeed, replaced by an entirely new social order.

Among the events that influenced Thälmann's ideological metamorphosis was a strike among Hamburg's dock workers when he was an adolescent. Seeing how the bourgeois state dealt with these men, who were only demanding tolerable living conditions, had a profound effect on the future Communist leader. In spite of his tender years, Thälmann was sympathetic to the labor movement. But the experience forced him to begin to reconsider the local trade union leadership's "reformist track." "The young worker, hungry for knowledge, threw himself into the study of political and trade union problems." Acting upon his growing concern, "[h]e took part in study circles" in order to learn more, which led him to turn against "the reformists within the party," who sought peaceful accommodation with the capitalist system in the name of short-term concessions from the exploiting classes. Thälmann's experiences as a front-line soldier in the Great War, the subject of chapter 3, only further consolidated his growing revolutionary worldview. The result of these experiences was that Ernst Thälmann became a faithful and uncompromising revolutionary.[21] This secular "conversion experience" molded him into the leader of the Hamburg Uprising and forged him into the revolutionary leader of German communism.

Yet another major trope of the sainthood paradigm is temptation. The consecrated individual is often enticed by something unholy— usually involving sex or some type of material gain. Bredel's secular saint once again exhibits the attributes of his Christian forerunners, and he experiences profound temptation on several occasions during the course of the narrative. The first incident occurs during the years of the antifascist struggle, when Thälmann recognizes that he can secure the SPD's cooperation in the struggle against fascism if he is willing to abandon the party's revolutionary program. Needless to say, Thälmann resists. Bredel sees this refusal not as wrongheaded intransigence, but rather as principled consistency. In spite of the short-term gains to be won from embracing "social fascism," Thälmann remains steadfast, always thinking of the long-term goal of creating a truly socialist Germany. His ideological purity stays unsullied.[22] An even more striking example of this motif can be found near the end of the book, where Bredel recounts his subject's experiences in prison. As Bredel points out repeatedly, throughout the "eleven and one-half years" of his imprisonment, the KPD chief is tempted to fall into despair, but he does not. Rather, he is determined to do what is advantageous to the international socialist movement, placing his personal well-being a distant second. Bredel records the most striking example of this temptation, which supposedly took place in 1938. "Shortly after Ernst Thälmann's fifty-second birthday, Prosecutor Opitz came into his cell and said to him derisively that he was all but forgotten in the outside world. He had received no flowers, no letters, not a single card for his birthday." The prisoner knows, of course, that this is not the case. Nazi authorities have simply chosen not to deliver these items to him. Thälmann, "knowing that this blackguard of a Gestapo man had something up he sleeve . . . [is] silent." Finally, Opitz reveals the purpose of the visit. "Now write a booklet [*Broschüre*]," the Nazi official suggests. "You write that you have changed your mind and abandoned your idiotic worldview." Opitz implies that his prisoner might reap benefit from this action. Thälmann's answer is, as always, steadfast and true. "You are truly a complete scoundrel," the imprisoned KPD chief immediately responds. "You will never have that experience, even if I croak." Thälmann not only suffered for his cause, but it is also important, in the hagiographic model, that he suffered voluntarily. On another occasion, attempting to break the prisoner's spirit, a policeman shows Thälmann a German newspaper story pointing out that the prisoner's beloved Soviet Union will soon collapse. Thälmann, once again resisting the impulse to fall into despair, responds, "The Soviet Union will still exist in twenty years. The Third Reich will not last so long." In another instance, as the German army stands at the gates of Moscow, one of Thälmann's guards begins to taunt the prisoner regarding the imminent collapse of the Soviet Union. The prisoner's response is typical of Bredel's portrayal of Thälmann: "Stalin will break Hitler's neck!"[23] Like a medieval saint, the German Communist leader repeatedly resists temptation, refusing either to surrender hope for a better future or to accommodate his captors in order to improve the conditions of his imprisonment.

Yet another common theme in Christian hagiography is the motif of the suffering and dying servant of God. Of course, Thälmann did not endure imprisonment, torture, and death in the name of the deity, but rather on behalf of the promise of international socialism, yet Bredel's depiction of the KPD chief's death fits the model of sainthood. One passage in *Ernst Thälmann* describes the KPD leader stoically exiting his cell, leaving behind eleven years of imprisonment in order to suffer a martyr's death. Bredel quotes extensively from firsthand accounts of events in Buchenwald Concentration Camp during the summer of 1944. Everyone in the camp knew within a few days that the SS had shot Thälmann on the night of 17–18 August. He was but one of many victims of the "bloodbath in Buchenwald." Bredel also records how the Nazis concocted a story claiming that the erstwhile KPD chief had died as the result of an American air raid, clear evidence that they feared taking responsibility for the death of the leader of the German proletariat.[24]

In the final three pages of *Ernst Thälmann: Ein Beitrag zu einem politischen Lebensbild*, the author deals with what is probably the most important theme of his book, "Ernst Thälmann's legacy [*Vermächtnis*]." "Ernst Thälmann is dead," this last section begins. Bredel links his martyrdom with a new era in German history, a "turning point in the unwholesome [*unheilvoll*] thousand-year history of the German people" had arrived. The complete collapse of Germany's traditions of imperialism, Prussian militarism, and capitalist exploitation has come. "This new beginning on the top of graves and ruins is only possible" because of the sacrifices made by Ernst Thälmann and millions of others who resisted the seemingly unstoppable tide of fascism. "During the darkness of [the] Hitler [years] that lay over Germany, Ernst Thälmann, even in the face of torture and imprisonment, remained true to the spirit of peace, freedom, and socialism. Steadfast, like no other German antifascist, he fought against imperialist reaction, militarism, and Nazism. . . . No one was more concerned about the friendship between the German and Russian peoples and occupied with [developing an] understanding with all other nations. No German had more selflessly and truly loved his homeland [*Heimat*]." Such sacrifice could serve as a model for all Germans—indeed, for all of humanity. The fallen KPD chief "was a decent man, a practical fighter and a person of honorable character, a man whose word and deed were unified."[25] His vision, if enacted, would assure the German people a better future, one without racism, class conflict, and imperialist war.

> Ernst Thälmann saw in the German proletariat, the most numerous, strongest, and progressive component of the people, the . . . power through which the German people can once again become healthy. He had confidence in the insurmountable revolutionary strength of the German worker. . . . He endured an eleven-and-one-half-year martyrdom for him [the German worker]. He offered his blood for him, drop by drop. Following an incomparable path to Golgotha, leading through the horrors of the Second World War, the German proletariat and the entire German people have the duty to fulfill Ernst Thälmann's legacy.[26]

It is impossible to imagine language more religious in tone than that used by Bredel in his account of Thälmann's death. The imprisoned KPD chief, throughout his "eleven-and-one-half-year martyrdom," maintained his faith in the "German worker." Martyrdom is a motif that runs throughout Christian hagiography. Saintly figures have frequently surrendered their lives rather than renounce their Christian faith. Indeed—at least in Bredel's eyes—Thälmann's martyrdom was especially noble because the KPD chief's demise did not occur suddenly, with a simple beheading or boiling in oil, but rather over the course of eleven and a half years. Thälmann not only perished for his cause but suffered for more than a decade, giving his "blood . . . drop by drop." Bredel's portrayal of Thälmann's relationship to the German proletariat is also described in deeply religious language. Although the KPD chief's contribution to the salvation of Germany was important, it was the "German proletariat"—not Thälmann—who experienced an "incomparable path through Golgotha." That is, in Bredel's rendering, it is "the German proletariat . . . and the entire German people" who stand in for Christ. It is they who suffer Golgotha, not Thälmann, who only suffers "martyrdom." The best way to understand the bond between the German people and the KPD leader is to view it as a Communist version of the relationship between Christ and John the Baptist. Just as John had faith in a future in which Jesus of Nazareth would come to deliver the Jewish people, Thälmann believed in the redemptive mission of the proletariat—the proletariat would one day rescue Germany from its legacy of fascism and imperialist war, replacing that legacy with a heritage of socialist humanism and eternal peace. Thälmann's role in the salvation of the German people was an important one. He laid the foundations of the legacy upon which the Germans could build—much as John prepared the path for Christ. Also like John, the KPD chief paid a heavy price for his faith, freely surrendering his life rather than abandoning his belief in a better future. Although Thälmann played a vital role in the salvation of the German people, he was but the harbinger of things to come. He had not yet been elevated to the position of a secular Christ—as he would in later years—and instead played the role of the KPD and SED's most important saintlike figure. Even before the inception of the German Democratic Republic—as Willi Bredel's *Ernst Thälmann: Ein Beitrag zu einem politischen Lebensbild* shows—the mythology surrounding Ernst Thälmann had come to play an integral role in the SED's historical propaganda. The book played a pivotal role in establishing many of the themes that came to dominate the Thälmann legend for the next forty years.

Although writers such as Willi Bredel were avid Communists and willing contributors to East German historical propaganda, the same could not be said initially of professional academic historians in the new Communist state. By 1950, the party leadership had become increasingly concerned about what East German philosopher Peter Bollhagen called the "ideological neutrality" of academic historians. The

attitude of historians who wrote about contemporary events was especially troubling. Party leaders became concerned that far too many
scholars concentrated on the "misery concept," emphasizing the events
leading to the Nazi seizure of power and the destruction of Germany
as the result of the Second World War. As Wilhelm Pieck put it at the
SED's Third Party Congress in 1950, "The study of the revolutionary
movements" has been "undervalued by us." He called upon university
lecturers to emphasize the examination of the past from the perspective of "dialectal and historical materialism, political economy, [and
the] history of Germany and the German workers' movement." In 1952,
Kurt Hager, the SED's propaganda chief, urged East German scholars
to immerse themselves in the works of Marx, Engels, and Lenin. Only
once they had done so could they assume their rightful place among the
builders of socialism in the GDR. Academic historians, the SED leadership insisted, should become concerned less with a careful analysis of
the suffering caused by German fascism and more with the "progressive" forces in history and with the role that they played in Germany's
historical development. In short, party leaders called for the creation
of a highly didactic historiography that could play a central role in the
creation of German socialism.[27]

As a consequence, throughout the 1950s the Politburo issued a series of decrees, the goal of which was to force academic historians to
abandon "bourgeois" historiography in favor of an approach consistent with a Marxist–Leninist world view. Perhaps the most important
of these edicts appeared on 5 July 1955. Entitled "The Improvement of
the Research and Teaching in the Historical Discipline [Geschichtswis-
senschaft] in the German Democratic Republic," this document called
for the abandonment of the traditional historical models so prevalent in
the FRG. Party leaders demanded the "complete adoption of Marxism–
Leninism" as the only legitimate historical paradigm to be followed in
the GDR. Only after historians had accomplished this transformation
could they assume their rightful place in building German socialism
alongside the workers and peasants. In short, the academic study of
history would become a component of East Germany's massive propaganda apparatus.[28]

The result was the centralization of historical writing and teaching.
New state-sponsored research organizations were established, such
as the IML—founded in 1957 after several earlier permutations originating in 1949; the Institute for German Military History, opened in
1958; and the Historical Society of the GDR, created in the same year as

an umbrella organization for all East German historians.[29] The GDR's Academy of Sciences also played a role in the oversight of historical scholarship. These organizations published journals promoting the study of the past from a Marxist–Leninist perspective. The journals enabled East German scholars to produce an enormous amount of historical propaganda. An historian had to be a member of one or more of the GDR's officially sanctioned historical organizations in order to have his or her work published.[30]

The party leadership increased its control over the writing of history in a variety of other ways. Among them was the creation of "scientific cadres" of scholars and the encouragement of "author collectives." These practices had at least two functions. First, they fostered ideological homogeneity by reducing the possibility that idiosyncratic scholars would produce philosophically unsound work. In addition, collective scholarship replicated the experience of German proletarians laboring on the shop floor. Such working conditions led to proletarian cooperation, an important precondition for the construction of socialism. In 1964, party leaders went even further, and the Academy of Sciences began to issue annual "research plans" modeled on the centralized planning of the East German economy. By the end of the decade, centralized planning of historical scholarship had come under the auspices of the IML's Council for History. As a result, the SED increased its authority over the historical profession.[31]

German historians accepted their lot for a variety of reasons. First and most obviously, as the SED increased its oversight of teaching and writing, scholars faced a stark choice: either write and teach in the politically approved vein or stop practicing their profession. But this was not the only reason that so many scholars adapted themselves to the new research conditions. Many found appealing the importance that the SED placed upon historical scholarship. In keeping with the traditions established by their Soviet allies, the East German leadership insisted that the writing and teaching of history were integral to the construction of socialism. As Ernst Hoffmann, a leading historian in East Berlin's Academy of Sciences, put it, "Well-being and hardship, victory and defeat, rapid progress or stagnation depend to a large extent on a correct scientific analysis. . . . Historical scholarship thus is a precondition of the continued existence of every Marxist party, one of the laws by which alone it can live. And a Marxist party that would neglect history, that would not engage in the constant scientific exploration of historical developments, would be self-destructive and would undermine one of its existential foundations."[32] In other words, the GDR leadership attached a great deal of importance to the study of history from a Marxist–Leninist perspective. Academic history was a path to an important position in East German society. Historians in the GDR—unlike their opposite numbers in the West—could claim to be accomplishing something concrete, the establishment of a socialist state on German soil. Along with this distinction came recognition by the ruling party, material advantage, and a modicum of political influence.[33]

One of the results of the accommodation that academic historians reached with the ruling party was the production of massive amounts of historical propaganda. Much of this work was concerned with the years between Germany's defeat in the Great War and the Nazi seizure of power, the years during which the glorious KPD stood up against Hitler fascism. As a result of this focus, East German scholarship concerning Ernst Thälmann thrived. Much of this scholarship consisted of such publications as collections of reminiscences of the fallen KPD chief, among them *Deutschlands unsterblicher Sohn* (Germany's Eternal Son), edited at the IML and published in 1961.[34] Such works sought to humanize German communism's most important martyr by compiling accounts written by those who knew Thälmann personally. They failed, however, to do so. The carefully selected firsthand portraits of Thälmann, published in *Deutschlands unsterblicher Sohn* and similar compilations, like Bredel's biography, depicted a paragon of a socialist revolutionary, a man without faults who could ultimately not be emulated—a problem that socialist propagandists inherited from Christian hagiography. Editions containing selections from Thälmann's speeches and writings, many of them multivolume collections, also began to appear, edited by both the IML and the FRG's Communist Workers' League of Germany (KABD).[35] The official IML journal, *Beiträge zur Geschichte der Arbeiterbewegung*, also published edited versions of documents concerning Ernst Thälmann. For example, in 1970 a selection of letters that the KPD chief wrote to Soviet workers in the 1920s—ample evidence of Thälmann's love for the Russian proletariat—appeared in the journal. The journal also provided evidence of the martyred KPD chief's progressive thinking concerning agricultural issues when it published several documents about the KPD's farm policy during the Weimar years.[36] This does not even take into account the massive number of articles published in other important academic journals, such as *Deutscher Militärgeschichte* (German Military History) and *Einheit* (Unity).[37] In addition, the figure of Ernst Thälmann played a significant role in many of the monographs and general works written about the German workers' movement. Among the latter is the massive, fifteen-volume *Geschichte der Deutschen Arbeiterbewegung* (History of the German Workers' Movement), written by a collective of authors at the IML under the chairmanship of none other than Walter Ulbricht—a clear indication of how important the party leadership considered the generation of historical propaganda.[38] In addition to these general works, local histories, such Annemarie Lange's *Berlin in der Weimarer Republik*, made a contribution to the dissemination of Thälmann legend, although such work was just one of many things that they sought to do.[39] As a result, they made no significant contribution to the development of the Thälmann legend, and only full-scale biographies of the former KPD chief could contribute to the official narrative in any significant way.

The modus vivendi that East German academic historians reached with the SED was a Faustian bargain—although they were in no position seriously to negotiate with the regime. The price they paid was a heavy one. In exchange for all that the ruling party gave them, academic historians, whether they were employed in a university or an institute, surrendered any pretext of academic freedom. Scholars found themselves in the grip of a heavy-handed ideological orthodoxy, the Marxist–Leninist model of historical discourse. Although East German scholars made important contributions to German historiography on occasion, for the most part they produced a massive amount of propaganda of very little use to serious intellectual inquiry.[40] The result was a calcification of East German historical writing that would only begin to soften during the regime's final years.[41] Whatever loosening of the ideological reins that historians experienced during the GDR's last decade did not apply to biographers of Ernst Thälmann, however. His image and the mythology surrounding his life and death were simply too important to leave in the hands of any but the most ideologically reliable scholars, and the SED leadership continued zealously to guard the integrity of the Thälmann myth. Indeed, the legend became a bone of contention within the Politburo itself and an issue in the power struggle between Erich Honecker and Walter Ulbricht.

In 1973, for example, the SED Politburo debated the distribution of a biography originally written in Russian and translated into German. Penned by D. S. Dawidowitsch, a scholar at the Soviet Union's Institute for General History, the Russian-language version of *Ernst Thälmann: Aspects of His Life* was published in 1971. In 1973, the book was translated into German so that it could be distributed in the GDR by the

Dietz Verlag. On 23 January 1973, however, the party leadership, on the recommendation of Erich Honecker, by this time the general secretary of the SED Central Committee, and Franz Dahlem, one of Honecker's allies on the Politburo, had decided that the book "should not go on sale." The IML, Honecker pointed out, would publish a Thälmann biography some time in 1975, and there was little point in assuming the expense of printing and distributing two Thälmann biographies in such a short span of time. Meanwhile, Dahlem objected to one of the photographs appearing in the book. Ulbricht, however, demurred, pointing out in a memo to the Politburo that Honecker and Dahlem's grounds for canceling distribution of Dawidowitsch's book were illegitimate:

> The [decision] not to publish this book was based on [the fact that] comrade Dahlem does not appear in a picture contained in the book. This is a pretense raised by comrade Dahlem; after all, the same picture is printed in my book[,] *On the History of the German Workers' Movement.* No one raised an objection against the distribution of this book. The book about Ernst Thälmann, published by the Soviet Academy of Sciences, does not make the claim to be a biography. It is, however, written with expert knowledge and love [of its subject]. The book came out in 1971, and no one raised any objections. But now, [in] 1973, objections are raised out of thin air. The German edition now lies in the Dietz Verlag. Concrete arguments against the release and sale [of the book] have not been raised.[42]

In the erstwhile party chairman's eyes, Honecker and Dahlem's arguments did not hold water. Ulbricht went further, insisting that the issue be raised at the next Politburo meeting, to be held on 6 February. The former party chairman, of course, would be disappointed.

On the one hand, this minor episode displays the petty behavior of two political rivals, one with his fortunes on the rise, the other experiencing a precipitous decline. On the other hand, the disagreement demonstrates the importance that those at the helm of the GDR ascribed to the Thälmann legend. The myth was so critical that the SED leadership—despite undoubtedly facing more immediate concerns, both domestic and foreign—spent time and effort considering the publication of an individual book. Control over the legend was a precondition for political power. As a result, the propagation of the Thälmann myth was highly centralized, be it a question of a book produced by an obscure

Soviet author or the construction of a monument in the city of Weimar. In addition, this incident establishes that although the SED leadership publically presented a remarkably uniform version of the Thälmann narrative, there was occasional disagreement on the matter. Those with power—such as Honecker and Dahlem—controlled the legend. Those whose station had fallen—such as Ulbricht—lost their influence over the myth. In other words, Erich Honecker, now the dominant figure in East German politics, was determined to harness the story of "Germany's eternal son" for his personal political ends. The mythology surrounding Ernst Thälmann mattered; it was of the utmost importance to the SED, even playing a role in at least one intraparty struggle.

The decision not to publish Dawidowitsch's biography was not the only determination concerning the Thälmann myth made at the 23 January 1973 Politburo meeting. At this same gathering, the party leadership drew up plans to publish a new book, to be titled "Ernst Thälmann: Eine politische Biographie," about the Communist hero. An author collective at the IML would write the book, which would be published in December 1975, in time for the celebrations surrounding Thälmann's ninetieth birthday. The party leadership went much further than merely deciding when a biography would be published and by whom it would be written. Seeking to oversee closely the ideological direction of the project, the Politburo provided a six-page "Konzeption" for the proposed book. This document consists of five sections, the first of which—the "Zielstellung"—states briefly the project's overall goals.

> A comprehensive, scholarly, easily understood biography of Ernst Thälmann is to be produced. It should portray the life and influence of Ernst Thälmann, should illuminate all the important results of his personality—of the politician and the man—should stress . . . compellingly his place in the history of the German and international workers' movement. The Thälmann biography should strive—as much as possible—to have a . . . direct ideological and educational effect, [written] not only for historians, but rather appeal to a wide circle of readers. It should be . . . a direct contribution to the propagation of the revolutionary traditions of our party and to the construction of socialist consciousness. . . . The biography should expand and deepen the research into the history of the German workers' movement. . . . Hence, the conceptual design, assertions, and argumentation of the biography are to be vigorously scholarly.[43]

Lest the experts at the IML be uncertain concerning how these goals should be achieved, the Politburo went a step further, letting the authors know in another document what developments in Thälmann's life must be covered as well as the proper interpretation of events. "The biography should make comprehensible Ernst Thälmann as a class-conscious worker and important defender of the interests of the working class and all laborers, as a typical embodiment of the fighter formed by the Communist International on behalf of the party of a new type, his development into a leading German Marxist–Leninist, and his historical role at the forefront of the revolutionary German workers' movement, and as a leading functionary of the Comintern."[44] The Politburo went further still to avoid any misunderstanding, instructing scholars about the individual themes they were to address.

> Ernst Thälmann was a class-conscious worker and grew from a son of his class into its revolutionary leader. He remained, in all phases of his life, strongly rooted in the working class, closely bound to the life and struggle of this class, closely familiar with its living and working conditions. His political work was consistently oriented to the working class, constantly originating from [the proposition] that the working class can only liberate itself. Ernst Thälmann grasped—clearer and more distinctly than many others—the necessity of the Communist Party, its development into a party of a new type, and of the penetration of Leninism into the party.[45]

Thälmann had used the CPSU as his organizational and ideological model for building the party, and as a result he was instrumental in the "Leninization" of the KPD. This approach assured that the KPD would "oppose fascism and after the liberation from its yoke could lead the socialist revolution to victory. . . . Unconditional loyalty to the Communist International and steadfast affirmation of the Soviet Union as the achievement and bulwark of the international workers' movement were characteristic tendencies of his personality."[46]

The Politburo, leaving nothing to chance, went well beyond these relatively broad ideological considerations, providing the IML with a list of twelve "main points [*Schwerpunkte*]" to be dealt with in the forthcoming biography. These points began with "Ernst Thälmann's development into a revolutionary Social Democrat, his opposition against the opportunistic policies of the right-wing leadership of the party and the trade unions, [and] his espousal of a policy on behalf of the proletarian class." As a result, the second main point insisted, he "recognized clearly and (relatively early)" the importance of the "Great Socialist October Revolution" to political and ideological developments in Germany. Indeed, several of the main points emphasized that scholars at the IML should place a great deal of emphasis on Thälmann's admiration for and imitation of the Soviet Union. The Bolshevik experiment in Russia consistently served as his model, which led him—among other things—to oppose "Trotskyism and other anti-Leninist tendencies" within the KPD. In short, the dozen main points that the Politburo provided, although more specific, were in keeping with the project's overall ideological tenor.[47]

The Politburo's concerns went well beyond ideological considerations, however, and included issues relating to the nuts and bolts of the writing and publication process, such as a section on the "apparatus" of the forthcoming book, with "footnotes (in [the] character of scholarly monographs)" as well as an "index of persons . . . a Thälmann bibliography, a time line, [and] an index of geographical names." Going a step further, the party leadership even made decisions concerning the biography's "organization [*Aufbau*]" and exact size, determining that it would consist of "675 manuscript pages." The finished book would be divided into six sections, beginning with an "introduction," followed by four main sections, concerned, first of all, with Thälmann's childhood and youth. The second part of the book would deal with his development into a Marxist–Leninist revolutionary, concluding with Thälmann's elevation to the position of party chairman in 1925. The next subdivision—arguably the most important to the propagation of the antifascism myth—would be about the years 1925 to 1933, during which the proletarian leader fought valiantly against the danger of German fascism. Next, the authors should turn to the years of Thälmann's imprisonment, concentrating on "actions of solidarity for Ernst Thälmann" that sought to secure his release from a Nazi prison. Finally, the narrative would end with a conclusion emphasizing "his place in the German and international workers' movement [and] his political legacy [*Vermächtnis*]."[48]

Such a detailed outline of the proposed book was indicative of the importance that the SED leadership assigned to the project. The myth was too important to the regime's legitimacy to leave its creation solely in the hands of a collective of scholars, even if they were Marxist–Leninist historians working at arguably the most important institution propagating the official view of recent German history. The fact that the scholars who would write the biography had long since been vetted for ideological reliability proved irrelevant to the party leadership. The Politburo's "conception" of the project also shows that scholars had almost no independence in the GDR, especially when it came to components of the state's legitimizing narrative. Although all historians in the GDR were subject to central planning and the decisions of the Council of History, the authors of the forthcoming Thälmann biography experienced intense direct intervention from the highest echelon of the SED leadership. Under such circumstances, there was no place for independent thought and even less for imagination, which had the effect of making this Thälmann biography, when it finally appeared in 1979, extremely dry and uninteresting reading. This outcome, of course, made the book ineffective as a propaganda tool. It is hard to imagine the East German public eagerly devouring the 804-page, dry-as-dust behemoth that appeared as a result of the painstaking process that the Politburo initiated in January 1973. Nor was it possible for scholars outside of the Soviet bloc to take the book seriously. Like the products of East Germany's industrial and agricultural economies, the results of East German historical scholarship were almost always second rate. Günter Hortzschansky, one of East Germany's most prominent academic historians, would lead the collective. Hortzschansky, born in 1926, was educated at Humboldt University in East Berlin during the postwar period. Although he took a job at the House of the Child, a department store selling goods for children, he continued to pursue his academic endeavors, taking a post at the Institute for Social Sciences in 1951. In 1958, the future Thälmann biographer finished his dissertation, "Der nationale Verrat der deutschen Monopolherren während des Ruhrkampfes 1923" (The National Treason of the German Monopoly Lords during the Ruhr Struggle of 1923). Published in 1961, Hortzschansky's dissertation argued that only the overthrow of capitalism could have led to an effective resistance against the French and Belgian occupation of the Ruhr River valley. As a result, only the KPD, Hortzschansky argued, was in a position successfully to lead the struggle against the Franco–Belgian invasion of Germany. The failure of the bourgeois parties to appreciate this fact doomed the insurrection from the outset, he contended. "The National Treason of the German Monopoly Lords" earned Hortzschansky a reputation as one of the GDR's leading historians of the workers' movement during the Weimar Republic. As a result, in 1962 he became deputy leader of the

Section for the History of the German Workers' Movement from its Beginnings until 1945 at the IML, assuming the position of leader in 1969, a post that he would hold for the next twenty years. In appointing Günter Hortzschansky chief of the author collective assigned to produce Thälmann's biographer, the SED Politburo chose a reliable, ideologically orthodox scholar who was intimately familiar with the history of the KPD during the first half of the twentieth century. His work on the biography would earn him the National Prize of the GDR, First Class, the highest award that the SED bestowed on scholars and artists.[49] Hortzschansky would lead the team of ten historians who would write the proposed biography—to be entitled *Ernst Thälmann: Eine Biographie*—which would finally appear in 1979, more than three years after the planned publication.[50]

As historians approaching their subject from a Marxist–Leninist perspective, the team of scholars from the IML was interested almost exclusively in Thälmann's political role, both in the KPD and the international workers' movement. As Hortzschansky put it, "I concerned myself—together with my colleagues—with the personage of Ernst Thälmann, with his public actions, with his role in history." Building upon historiographical traditions going back to Bredel's 1948 biography and the Kurt Maetzig films of the 1950s, Hortzschansky assured that the forthcoming book would be an important addition to East German historical propaganda, making a vital contribution to the didactic role of historical writing in the GDR. Thälmann, he asserted, "in his life and struggle embodied . . . a socially just society, [an] antifascist orientation, a world of peace, of friendship among peoples, a democratic . . . influence." The KPD chief's "sacrificial death [*Opfertod*]" only served to enhance his role as a model for all Germans, especially in the GDR, which embodied his legacy. These oft-repeated motifs would become the major themes of the definitive East German account of Ernst Thälmann's life.[51]

The tome that finally appeared in 1979, *Ernst Thälmann: Eine Biographie*, met or exceeded all of the Politburo's expectations. The book consisted of 804 pages, 780 of which were text. In accordance with the Politburo's orders, the book is divided into six sections, although the divisions within the text are slightly different from those originally planned. After an epigram written by Erich Honecker (discussed later), *Ernst Thälmann: Eine Biographie* opens with a brief foreword, followed by the first section, which is concerned with the years 1886 to 1920, covering events from Thälmann's birth until his joining the Communist

Party. The second part of the book recounts the years 1921 to 1925, giving special attention to the Hamburg Uprising of 1923 and concluding with Thälmann's elevation to the position of party chairman. The next section, dealing with the years 1925 to 1929, focuses on the Leninization—in actuality the Stalinization—of the party under Thälmann's leadership. The fourth part, arguably the most important to the propagation of the antifascism myth, deals with the struggle against Hitler fascism, culminating with the situation that the KPD faced during the weeks preceding the Nazi seizure of power. Finally, part five records events that occurred as a result of Adolf Hitler being named chancellor, beginning with the new regime's "declaration of war on the workers" and moving on to Thälmann's famous 15 February speech assessing the efforts of the antifascist movement in light of recent events; the KPD chief's arrest and imprisonment; the Free Thälmann campaign; the outbreak of the war—emphasizing the Soviet Union's role in defeating the Third Reich; and Thälmann's death in August 1944. The final chapter of the book, "Ernst Thälmann Is among Us," analyzes the martyred KPD chief's legacy, which has lived on in the GDR. All of the events that the Politburo had outlined more than six years earlier are covered in the book, and Thälmann's life and accomplishments are interpreted in keeping with the ideological orthodoxies created by the party leadership.

Ernst Thälmann: Eine Biographie incorporates the SED leadership's other demands as well. The book has all of the trappings of a scholarly work, including footnotes, an "Index of Geographic Names," and an "Index of Persons." Probably in order to avoid further increasing the bulk of the work, it does not have a bibliography. The sources cited in the footnotes come from a wide variety of places, although the writings of Ernst Thälmann and the KPD newspaper Rote Fahne are the most frequently referenced. In addition, the notes cite numerous primary works, such as memoirs and documents from the IML's own archive. Further, the authors reference primary sources available only in the West, including files from the Federal Archive in Koblenz. Although the notes incorporate numerous secondary works published in the Soviet bloc, Western secondary sources concerning the history of the German workers' movement are conspicuous by their absence. Nevertheless, the authors of Ernst Thälmann: Eine Biographie consulted an impressive array of sources while researching their book.

Günter Hortzschansky and his team failed to approach their sources critically, though. They simply take officially sanctioned source materials—such as *Rote Fahne,* the writings of Thälmann and other prominent German Communists, and documents held in East German archives—at their word, which helped to assure that the new biography would be of little use to Western scholars interested in more than just the basic facts surrounding Ernst Thälmann's life. Western scholars, however, were not the primary target audience of the book; rather, the East German reading public was, who now had the opportunity to study yet another work of historical propaganda relating the ideological orthodoxies monopolizing the GDR. The 1979 book, like Bredel's biography written thirty years earlier, was written in a straightforward manner, rendering it easily accessible to the average reader. In 1980, a paperback edition of the work appeared. Sold in bookstores, department stores, and even kiosks in East Berlin, the paperback was readily available to anyone interested in its subject.[52] No effort was made to make a novel contribution to the historiography of the German workers' movement—all of the major arguments made in the book concerning Thälmann's role in German history during the first decades of the twentieth century could be found in numerous other writings published in books and scholarly articles. In short, by Western criteria, the book failed to live up to the standards of a serious work of scholarship, but from another perspective it ably fulfilled its main purpose of providing a detailed published account of Ernst Thälmann's life and the history of the KPD during the Weimar Republic and was easily accessible not only to scholars, but also to GDR's general reading public. In short, although the IML failed to meet its original deadline, the finished book met or exceeded the goals of both its authors and the party leaders who had launched the project several years earlier.

Although the copyright page at the end of the book lists which member of the author collective was responsible for each section of the book, the text is written in a markedly homogenous manner. It is impossible to tell where one author leaves off and another begins—even after a careful reading of the text. Of course, this effect was exactly what the author collective sought. Günter Hortzschansky and his associate Walter Wimmer edited the entire text, undoubtedly in part to assure stylistic and ideological consistency.[53] In this, both the authors and the editors were, from the point of view of Marxist–Leninist scholarly traditions, quite successful. In other words, *Ernst Thälmann: Eine Biographie* serves as a noteworthy example of the type of historical writing produced by scholars in the GDR: it is ideologically and stylistically consistent and void of any serious critical approach to the events the book describes or the sources that the authors use. Add to these qualities the fact that the authors—once again in keeping with the standards of Marxist–Leninist historiography—pay remarkably little attention to their subject's private life, and the result is an ideologically overwrought, uninspiring, and indeed tiresome book to read.

Given the length of *Ernst Thälmann: Eine Biographie,* it is impossible to analyze the entire text here, so a handful of examples has to provide an overview of the major themes incorporated into the biography. For the sake of a comparison, the passages drawn upon here overlap with those cited in the earlier examination of Willi Bredel's 1948 biography. Such an approach permits an investigation of the evolution of the methodology of East German historical propaganda over the course of more than three decades. Although as a work of historical propaganda *Ernst Thälmann: Eine Biographie* had much in common with Bredel's brief book written decades earlier, the differences between the two biographies are often as striking as the similarities.

Yet it is clear from the outset that the IML biography, like Bredel's *Ernst Thälmann: Ein Beitrag zu einem politischen Lebensbild,* is a work of historical propaganda. Much as Bredel's work opens with a foreword written by Wilhelm Pieck, *Ernst Thälmann: Eine Biographie* starts with an epigraph written by SED party chief Erich Honecker:

> Ernst Thälmann was among us,
> as we led the struggle against the
> approach of fascism in the Weimar Republic.
>
> Ernst Thälmann was among us,
> as we, from the deepest illegality,
> under the conditions of Hitler-fascism
> led the fight for the downfall of Nazism. . . .
>
> The ideas of Ernst Thälmann were with us,
> as we, in the year 1946, created,
> from two workers' parties,
> one party, the Socialist Unity Party of Germany.
>
> Ernst Thälmann was among us,
> when we founded our Republic
> in 1949.

Ernst Thälmann is still among us,
because we have sworn
to defend and strengthen our Republic
in his spirit
and carry ever further forwards the
banner of socialist revolution.[54]

As always, the party leadership left nothing to chance when it came to the Ernst Thälmann myth, leaving no doubt concerning the primary goal of the biography to follow. The book was a work of historical propaganda designed from the outset to disseminate a particular interpretation of the fallen KPD chief's life, one promoting the legitimacy of the East German state and its governing Socialist Unity Party. The GDR was the embodiment of Thälmann's legacy.

This is not to suggest that the 1979 biography simply apes on a larger scale the methodology and motifs of Bredel's book. From the outset, it is clear that the IML author collective is more interested in presenting its version of Thälmann's life and contribution to German history in a scholarly fashion. There are no portents to accompany the future KPD chief's birth. Indeed, the scholars from the IML are clearly more interested in factual accuracy. For example, the view that Thälmann was the product of an archetypal proletarian upbringing is absent. Although *Ernst Thälmann: Eine Biographie* is far less interested in its subject's childhood than the 1948 biography, probably because that topic added little to the myth, the version of events created in 1979 is more factually accurate. Whereas Bredel recounts that Thälmann's father Jan went to prison because of his supposed revolutionary activities, the scholars working three decades later concede that *both* parents went to jail for "buying stolen goods or for embezzlement [*Schuldung in Zahlung*]." Indeed, in sharp contrast to Bredel, the IML historians were willing to concede that their subject's childhood can best be described as "petit bourgeois."[55] Yet the later work nevertheless has a considerable number of shortcomings as an account of the Hamburg dock worker's life. As one reviewer points out, the inaccuracies in the book can be found in sins of omission rather than in outright fabrication. For example, no mention is made of the ideological divisions within the KPD leadership in the period preceding the 1923 Hamburg Uprising, leading the reader to conclude that the KPD was ideologically homogenous from its inception. Further, Günter Hortzschansky and his comrades imply that the October 1923 revolution was a well-planned, although unsuccessful, attempt to overthrow the Weimar Republic. The authors ignore the chaos that characterized the planning for the German October, not to mention Thälmann's decision to disobey orders to abandon the coup attempt. In addition, the effects that the power struggle in the Soviet Union following Lenin's death had on developments in the KPD are also ignored, although both Leon Trotsky and Nikolai Bukharin are mentioned, always in a negative context, in the book. Although the 1928 Wittorf Scandal, in which a close ally of Thälmann embezzled money from the party and the KPD chief tried to cover it up, is mentioned, the authors dismiss it as merely an attempt by the party chief's political enemies to undermine his authority. Joseph Stalin's role in rescuing Thälmann from disgrace is also ignored, as are the long-term implications of the Soviet leader's intervention in the KPD's affairs. Finally, although *Ernst Thälmann: Eine Biographie* discusses the Free Thälmann campaign of the 1930s in some detail, no mention is made of the determination that Thälmann was more valuable to the antifascist movement as a prisoner of the Nazis than he would be had his freedom, like Georgi Dimitrov's, been secured.[56]

These numerous omissions should come as no surprise. After all, when the Politburo drew up its plans for a new biography in 1973, nothing in the outline called upon the scholars at the IML to introduce new interpretations of KPD history or to do anything novel at all. The party had long ago established the important facts surrounding the heroic struggle of the KPD and its brave leader Ernst Thälmann. Indeed, the detailed outline that the Politburo provided established the narrow parameters within which Hortzschansky and his nine coauthors could operate, and there was no room for innovation on the part of the scholars at the IML. In short, it was clear from the outset that *Ernst Thälmann: Eine Biographie,* like its predecessors, was to be a work of historical propaganda. The party leadership and the authors did not even exhibit the pretext of breaking new ground or of adding anything to historians' knowledge of this important period in the history of the German workers' movement. This becomes abundantly clear when one reads the final chapter of the book, which takes the reader full circle back to the epigraph with which the biography opens. "Ernst Thälmann Is among Us" briefly describes the meeting at which Adolf Hitler gave Heinrich Himmler the order to murder the Communist leader. The führer had decided that the KPD chairman would "not survive the Hitler regime," and the SS chief noted in his diary that "Thälmann is to be executed." This description of events is followed by a short account of the transfer of Thälmann from a prison in Bautzen to Buchenwald for execution. As a result, "Ernst Thälmann lived no longer," the book points out. "The fascists had viciously killed him." As evidence of the importance of the KPD chief's death, the book points out that "[i]n Moscow, New York and Mexico, in London and Stockholm, everywhere Communists, antifascists, and bourgeois democrats assembled in memorial services" not only to mourn his death, but also to celebrate Thälmann's contribution to the defeat of National Socialism.[57]

Indeed, although the KPD chief was dead, his struggle against fascism lived on. Because, as one German Communist put it, "Thälmann believed in the Soviet Union [and] believed, therefore, that Hitler would be eliminated," his legacy lived on. "The fascists had murdered Ernst Thälmann—but the thing for which he had offered his life [had] won." "The victory of the Soviet Union opened the path to fundamental revolutionary transformation for the German people." The "revolutionary developments in Eastern Germany after 1945 were . . . the triumph of the ideas of Ernst Thälmann." "When the KPD and SPD joined together into the Socialist Unity Party, which developed into a successful Marxist–Leninist party of struggle, the most important legacy of Ernst Thälmann was fulfilled."[58]

These developments made possible the creation of the German Democratic Republic, which was the most important manifestation of the martyred Communist leader's legacy. "The spirit of Ernst Thälmann is in the working class, is living in the workers of the German Democratic Republic." The book concludes with Georgi Dimitrov's famous statement about Ernst Thälmann: "He is blood of blood, flesh of flesh of the German working class and of the entire international proletariat."[59] The religious imagery is unmistakable, and it is hard to imagine a statement less scholarly or more hyperbolic than Dimitrov's. Yet the authors of *Ernst Thälmann: Eine Biographie* chose to conclude their book with this quotation, ample evidence that their primary goal was propagandistic, not scholarly.

This outcome should come as no surprise, however. The international Communist movement had long recognized the importance of the study of history—including the writing of biography—to promoting international revolution. Given the SED's Marxist–Leninist worldview, it was natural that its leadership would co-opt historical writing for its purposes. Although the SED did not invent historical propaganda, it was very interested in incorporating the tide of history into its legitimation narrative and sought to do so even before the creation of the

GDR. As a result, the party leadership promoted the writing of history, including historical biography, from a Marxist–Leninist perspective. Indeed, as shown definitively here, when it came to the most important figure in the SED's antifascist mythology, Ernst Thälmann, party leaders kept tight control over efforts to represent the fallen KPD chief's life in all types of historical writing, especially in biography. The Thälmann myth was so important to the party's and the GDR's legitimacy that the Politburo, the most significant political body in those two entities, supervised the writing of Thälmann biographies in East Germany. From the first postwar biography, authored by the socialist-realist writer Willi Bredel, to the writing of the standard East German biography of Ernst Thälmann produced three decades later, the party leadership was intimately involved in the entire process. The examples of Willi Bredel writing during the 1940s and the author collective working three decades later provide ample evidence of the dangers that historians face when they become compliant instruments of the powers that be. Under such circumstances, they are little more than propagandists, and any claim to be scholars that they may have suffers as a result.

8

"Not All Who Have Died Are Dead"

In hindsight, it is clear that by end of the 1970s the German Democratic Republic was in a state of decline. The heady, idealistic days of the regime's first decade were long gone, and the Berlin Wall remained a blight on the landscape of the East German capital and an embarrassment to the SED. The East German leadership had long recognized that the country faced serious problems. Indeed, the failure of the Ulbricht government's economic policies was integral to the decision to replace him at the SED's helm. The new leadership sought to address the deteriorating situation both by pursuing new avenues in foreign policy and confronting the looming economic crisis. Upon assuming power in 1971, new party chief Erich Honecker promised his Soviet allies that he would pursue a rapprochement with the Federal Republic and assured the East German people that he would improve economic conditions under what came to be called "real, existing socialism."[1]

Honecker's predecessor, Walter Ulbricht, had insisted that the GDR could and must catch up with the West economically by 1980. Only then, when socialism had demonstrated that it could provide a standard of living comparable to the FRG, could the SED hope to unify Germany under a socialist system—a goal that the aging party chief refused to abandon. In order to achieve this end, the Ulbricht government maintained that the GDR had to invest as much as 30 percent of the country's gross domestic product into long-term projects such as the development of advanced technology. Under his New Economic System, Ulbricht envisioned a not-too-distant future in which East Germany would be exporting computers to capitalist countries. The SED chief's plan necessitated a massive investment in economic infrastructure, and average East Germans would have to tighten their belts as a result. Not only would there be a decrease in the production of hard-to-

get consumer goods, but East Germans would be expected to pay higher prices for basic necessities such as housing and transportation.[2] As a
result, the regime became increasingly unpopular among the East German population. To add insult to injury, Ulbricht's stock with his Soviet
allies also began to decline because he maintained that the SED did not
have to toe the Soviet line in the area of economic policy. Indeed, believing that having personally met Lenin gave his views a legitimacy un-
matched even by the Soviet leadership, Ulbricht insisted that the SED's
approach should become *the* model for the socialist world, including
the Soviet Union. Soviet leader Leonid Brezhnev found such hubris
disconcerting, and Ulbricht's perceived arrogance did not win him any
friends in Moscow.[3] For these and other reasons, Ulbricht was forced to
step down in 1971, after twenty-one years in office.

Upon assuming power, Honecker sought to pursue more modest
goals. First of all, the new party chief de facto abandoned the goal of
German unification, openly embracing West German chancellor Willy
Brandt's *Ostpolitik*. On 21 December 1972, the GDR and the FRG signed
the Basic Treaty, and the two Germanys finally exchanged "emissaries"
(but not ambassadors) and joined the United Nations.[4] The following
year Honecker conceded, in a dramatic reversal of East German policy,
that "[t]he GDR is not part of the FRG and the FRG is not part of the
GDR."[5] In 1974, the SED chief even went so far as to have the clauses
calling for a single socialist Germany removed from the GDR's Constitution, a move that the FRG leadership refused to reciprocate.[6]

At least in the short run, Honecker's change in course proved beneficial for the people of the GDR. With Brandt's renunciation of the
Hallstein Doctrine—under which the FRG would not have official diplomatic relations with any country that had exchanged ambassadors
with the GDR—East Germany's international isolation came to an end.
Honecker could legitimately claim to have made socialist Germany
into an actor on the international stage. With the GDR's admission to
the United Nations, the world recognized the SED regime's legitimacy.
West Germany had not only accepted the GDR's right to exist but also,
in effect, recognized the permanence of Germany's division. A two-state
solution to the German question had become an important component
of the European status quo, and the leaders of East Germany could now
concentrate on building a consumer-oriented socialist society.[7]

Honecker hoped that the new international situation would permit
him to pursue economic policies based on a "conservative socialism,"
free of any of the radical plans for reform that had characterized the

final years of Ulbricht's leadership. The new SED chief replaced his predecessor's closest economic advisers and proceeded to seek capital from the international banking system, an option previously closed to the GDR. Bringing the GDR's economic policy more in line with the Soviet Union's, the Honecker regime nationalized the remaining "semi-private" enterprises, holdovers from the Ulbricht years. More modest in his ambitions than his predecessor, Honecker rejected rhetoric calling for the overtaking of capitalism economically in favor of an approach that promised all GDR citizens basic necessities such as decent food and shelter. Although Honecker was unwilling to abandon the ideological components of the SED's legitimizing narrative, the final two decades of the GDR witnessed a linking of more traditional propaganda themes, including antifascism, with an improvement of living standards within the confines of "real, existing socialism." In other words, whereas Ulbricht's version of the antifascism myth had bridged the past and the *future,* Honecker's variant sought to emphasize the importance of antifascism to the *present.* Honecker's *Sozialpolitik* (social policy)—which SED propaganda linked to the accomplishments of the antifascist martyrs, including Ernst Thälmann—led to an increase in pensions, a decrease in rents, and a reduction in working hours. The SED chief also expanded the welfare state, guaranteeing social benefits such as maternity leave and state-sponsored day care. As part of the effort to make the GDR a more livable place, playgrounds and parks were constructed throughout the country. The promises of socialism could be experienced in the present, not exclusively in an apparently ever more distant future. In short, the SED abandoned the long-term goals that had characterized the Ulbricht years in favor of the creation of more tolerable living conditions for the East German people in the present.[8] If in the long-term the East German people persisted in their effort to build socialism, the SED promised them "good housing conditions, child care and shopping facilities, clean streets and pathways, well-maintained gardens, playgrounds and sports facilities, quality restaurants, the care of citizens of advanced age, the shaping of an interesting cultural life, including youth dances, discotheques and harvest festivals, the cultivation of village traditions and the furthering of a sense of *Heimat*[,] . . . civil defense, disposal of rubbish and sewage, ensuring the winter road service and other communal political tasks essential to life."[9] In the short term, Honecker's policies did have some benefits for the citizens of the GDR. International recognition granted access to overseas markets previously closed to socialist Germany, and exports increased. Trade with West Germany also rose dramatically, but imports continued to outpace exports, and the trade deficit with the FRG continued to grow. East Germany's citizens enjoyed the welfare guarantees provided by the SED, and many apparently took the regime's good intentions seriously, appreciating the promise to improve living conditions under "real, existing socialism."[10]

East Germans benefitted from the change in leadership in tangible ways. In 1969, for example, around 66 percent of East German households owned a television set; this portion had increased to 93 percent by the mid-1980s. The country experienced a similar dramatic increase in the number of homes that had washing machines and refrigerators. Perhaps most striking of all, whereas in 1969 only 14 percent of families owned an automobile, the number had risen to 46 percent by the year 1985. These changes occurred in spite of often long waiting periods before East Germans could acquire such items. Although the citizens of the GDR came to enjoy living conditions much higher than anywhere else in the Soviet bloc, the standard of living continued to decline in comparison to the FRG's. In 1970, the average GDR citizen had a standard of living just less than two-thirds as high as his West German counterpart; by 1983, it had plummeted to less than half.[11] Of course, Honecker did not link the SED state's legitimacy as closely with the idea of surpassing the West economically as Ulbricht had. Even so, the new party chief's policies involved a calculated risk. To link the regime's legitimacy to its ability to deliver tangible economic progress left the SED susceptible to severe criticism should the party fail to deliver on its promises. The apparent success of Honecker's policies could be seen in the fact that the problems that the governing Polish Workers' Party experienced throughout the 1970s and 1980s did not spill over into the GDR, which remained remarkably quiescent.

Even these limited achievements imposed a heavy burden on the East German economy. The 1970s witnessed an international credit crunch as interest rates skyrocketed. Dramatically increasing oil prices and a reduction in Soviet exports of raw materials to the GDR only exacerbated the situation. The GDR continued to borrow money at high interest rates, and the country's trade deficit increased substantially. The result was an ever-mounting national debt. In 1970, East Germany had owed capitalist countries the equivalent of around 2.2 billion West German marks; a decade later the total had increased slightly more than tenfold; by the middle of the 1980s, the country's debt stood at 30 billion West German marks; and by the time of the GDR's collapse, the total had risen, in spite of austerity measures, to an astounding 46 billion marks. The regime found it ever more difficult to make the payments on its debt, and as early as 1980 the interest payments on GDR's international obligations were larger than the amount of hard currency acquired through exports. To make matters worse, East German industry could not adapt to changing conditions quickly enough, and exports of technologically advanced goods to the West plummeted. The economic situation continued to deteriorate, even in the face of the influx of the billions of Western marks that entered the country as a result of the FRG's *Ostpolitik*.[12]

The SED sought to deal with the mounting economic crisis in a variety of ways. As Western markets dried up, the GDR began to increase its exports to Third World nations. This market created somewhat lower demands on East German technology, thereby making it easier to sell in the developing world what would have been considered substandard goods in Western capitalist countries. This solution proved illusory, however. Many of East Germany's new trading partners suffered from the same economic problems as the GDR—mounting debt, a shortage of hard currency, and a resulting inability to meet international economic obligations. In far too many instances, these countries simply could not pay for the goods that they imported from the GDR.[13]

The party ultimately could no longer ignore the crisis. In a typically Marxist–Leninist effort to streamline the economy, the East German government combined economic enterprises, acting under the theory that bigger was inevitably more efficient.[14] In spite of this massive overhaul of the East German economy, the trade deficit continued to grow, and foreign debt continued to mount. In addition, the production of consumer goods and the construction of new housing began to decline—all of this in the face of the rising expectations among the people that the SED had encouraged. The party could no longer deliver on its guarantee of improving economic conditions, and, as a result, the Honecker regime found itself facing a deepening crisis of legitimacy.[15] As economic conditions continued to deteriorate, the East German people came increasingly to question the party leadership's wisdom. This skepticism, coupled with the fact that the GDR's citizens needed only to look at the other German state for an example of dramatically superior economic conditions, led many of them to view "real, existing socialism" in an increasingly negative light.[16]

By the mid-1980s, the declining economic situation was not the only problem that the East German leadership faced. Over the course of the latter half of the decade, Honecker would be forced to confront an even more dangerous threat to the SED regime. In this instance, the menacing developments would be as much ideological as material, and they would originate in a most unlikely quarter—the Soviet Union.

In March 1985, following the death of Konstantin Chernenko, Mikhail Gorbachev emerged as the new CPSU general secretary. Gorbachev, like an increasing number of younger, well-educated, Russian Communists, believed that in order for Soviet-style socialism to survive it must be fundamentally reformed. The result was the Soviet leader's closely related policies of glasnost (openness) and perestroika (restructuring). To put it simply, the entire Soviet economic and political system had to be restructured, incorporating elements of both the market economy and an expansion of the Soviet people's political role. In order for this reconstruction of society to be successful, the Gorbachev regime encouraged a new "openness," in which the party called upon Soviet citizens to engage in a public dialogue concerning their country's problems and how best to address them. Only if the Soviet Union's deeply rooted troubles were exposed and confronted in a realistic manner could socialism survive. Not limiting his ambitious reform program to the birthplace of Marxism–Leninism, the new general secretary encouraged his Eastern European allies to pursue their own versions of perestroika and glasnost.[17]

The Honecker regime was initially receptive to the new Soviet leadership, especially when Gorbachev made it clear that the Soviet Union's satellite states would enjoy more national autonomy than had been the case previously. But the differences between the two leaders very quickly became apparent. Whereas Gorbachev, much the younger man, associated traditional socialism with the calcification of the Brezhnev years, Honecker viewed Marxism–Leninism through the prism of the valiant and victorious struggle against fascism in the 1930s and 1940s. Gorbachev thought in terms of technology, modernization, and liberalization. Honecker understood the world along the lines of class conflict, eternal vigilance against imperialistic capitalism, and the unity of the international working class. Gorbachev realized that socialism was broken and needed to be fixed, and so he sought to introduce fundamental change in order to preserve the humanistic traditions of Marxism. In short, although both men claimed the mantle of Lenin's legacy, they looked at the world in two very different and sometimes diametrically opposed ways.[18]

Although the Honecker regime appreciated its increased independence in the sphere of foreign policy, it should come as no surprise that it was unsympathetic to glasnost and perestroika almost from their inception. Whereas Gorbachev's policies emphasized the importance of eliminating the economic legacy of Stalinism as engendered by the highly centralized Soviet economy, the GDR leadership sought to increase the SED's control over East Germany's economic system. Indeed, Honecker and the SED Politburo believed that East German socialism worked and that Marxism–Leninism provided a stable, functioning system for the GDR. There was no need for transparency or restructuring in East Berlin. Honecker's opposition to Gorbachev's policies only increased when dissidents in the GDR, seeking to legitimize their resistance to the SED regime, began to appeal to the changes ongoing in the Soviet Union.[19] To make matters worse, Gorbachev insisted on dredging up some of the most unsavory events from the CPSU's past, and the world witnessed a series of dramatic public disclosures concerning the horrific crimes of the 1930s and 1940s, revelations that made those of the Khrushchev years pale in comparison.[20] For a political movement such as the SED, which based its legitimacy largely on the illustrious accomplishments of socialist heroes from the past, such admissions were anathema. As Honecker informed the Soviet ambassador in 1988, "We are against the practice of the purest slander of the CPSU history and socialist construction in the USSR. We are surprised by the doubtful economic experiments, not to speak of the information sphere [sic]. For years we educated GDR citizens about the example of the CPSU and the heroic struggle of the Soviet people. Now, we learn, however, that it was all a string of failures."[21] The SED, a party that based its legitimacy on the historical legacy of the international Communist movement as well as on the accomplishments of "real, existing socialism," Honecker argued, would lose its ability to govern if perestroika and glasnost were introduced to the GDR. The SED chief viewed Gorbachev's policies as an existential threat to his political movement and the state that it had struggled to create.

As a result, the relationship between the Soviet and East German leaders became increasingly strained. Gorbachev viewed his German counterpart as hopelessly wedded to a failed system, a leader clinging to the past, the proponent of continued economic and political stagnation. In his memoirs, the Soviet general secretary later compared dealing with Honecker to "speaking to a brick wall."[22] Honecker, for his part, saw the Soviet leader as an upstart unfamiliar with the historic legacy of Marxism–Leninism and thus a danger to German socialism.

In April 1986, during the Thälmann centennial celebrations, in response to Gorbachev's urging that the SED more vigorously pursue political and economic reform, the East German leader commented that "[t]he young man [Gorbachev] has been making policy for only a year, and already he wants to bite off more than he can chew!" The result was a deterioration in East German–Soviet relations, especially when it came to such matters as cultural interaction. The SED, for example, banned the German-language editions of two of the most prominent periodicals published in the Soviet Union, *Sputnik* and *New Times*. Further, the words *perestroika* and *glasnost* were stricken from German-language translations of Russian documents. A rather bizarre result of all this was that the US Central Intelligence Agency found itself smuggling *Soviet* publications into the GDR.[23] In light of these circumstances, it should come as no surprise that Honecker's Germany was the only country on earth to applaud the Chinese Communist Party's 1989 decision to use force to crush the students protesting in Tiananmen Square. The East German leadership believed that events in China were the result of the CPSU's pursuing policies dangerous to the survival of socialism: an economic program that had decreased the ruling party's control and a platform that had abandoned the path to socialism while ignoring the historical accomplishments of Marxism–Leninism. It is no wonder that in the midst of the *Wende* (Turning), as hundreds of thousands of East Germans took to the streets of Berlin and Leipzig, Honecker considered pursuing a "Chinese solution" to the protests. In his mind, to do so was simply to defend the progressive course of history, to stand up proudly in defense of the historical legacy of socialism, a movement that, as he saw it, continued to be the best hope for humanity. To do otherwise was to renounce the legacy of the antifascist martyrs, including Ernst Thälmann, who had willingly given their lives for the benefit of humanity.

The economic stagnation that began in the early 1980s, coupled with the ideological tensions brought about by Gorbachev's criticism of the development of socialism in the past, created a crisis for the SED regime. The two pillars upon which the Honecker government had built the SED's legitimacy—the concrete economic accomplishments of "real, existing socialism" and the unsullied legacy of socialism's glorious past—had begun to crumble. Even as the economic situation in East Germany deteriorated, the SED leadership could at least appeal to the antifascist legacy of humanistic socialism, something that Gorbachev's repeated admissions of the CPSU's criminal past made increasingly difficult. The SED's response was a renewed emphasis on the importance of East Germany's tradition of antifascism. Given the economic crisis that the regime faced, it was only natural for the party leadership to join its reemphasis on the antifascist past with the supposed accomplishments of "real, existing socialism." In other words, the antifascism myth would once again be adapted to new circumstances, those characterized by economic and ideological crises. Needless to say, this decision would affect the evolution of the Thälmann myth.

Some of the most striking developments in the history of the Thälmann legend occurred during these final years of socialist Germany. The year 1986 marked the martyred KPD chief's one hundredth birthday. The East German government celebrated this anniversary in a variety of ways: new books were published, historians organized conferences, a four-hour-long television movie premiered, and a special ceremony was performed at Buchenwald Concentration Camp, the site where Thälmann gave his life for the cause of antifascism. The centerpiece of the Thälmann centennial, however, was the April dedication

Stamp with Willi
Sitte's portrait of Ernst
Thälmann, 1986.
Author's collection.

of the Ernst Thälmann National Monument in the GDR capital. It was at this dedication that one can see the most striking effort on the SED's part to link the heritage of Thälmann's martyrdom with the tactile accomplishments of "real, existing socialism."

The celebration of the martyred party leader's one hundredth birthday was not the only important manifestation of the Thälmann myth to develop during the 1980s, however. The decade also marked the Communist hero's ninety-fifth birthday. Although the celebrations in 1981 were relatively subdued when compared to those witnessed five years later, there was at least one expression of the Thälmann myth from this year that is worth closer investigation.

Arguably the most striking image to emerge from the 1981 SED Party Conference (Parteitag) was a painting by perhaps the GDR's most noteworthy socialist-realist artist, Willi Sitte, who had already had a long and distinguished career before creating one of the most visually compelling images of Ernst Thälmann produced in the final years of the GDR. Born in Czechoslovakia in 1921, he immigrated to Germany in order to study art. After serving three years in the Wehrmacht, he deserted, becoming a partisan in Italy, thereby establishing his credentials as an antifascist. Following a brief return to Czechoslovakia after the war, he took up residence in Soviet-occupied Germany, joining the SED in 1947. He became a painter and teacher at Halle's Art Institute, where he would be promoted to professor. Sitte was a leading figure in the GDR's Union of Visual Artists, rising to the post of president. In 1979, he received the National Prize of the GDR, First Class, the highest honor that could be bestowed upon an artist in East Germany. He served as a member of the Volkskammer and Cultural Commission of the SED Politburo. In 1986, he joined the SED Central Committee. As this brief account of his career shows, Sitte was among the most prominent artists in the GDR, at least in official circles. Major museums throughout the GDR and the rest of Eastern Europe exhibited his paintings. His work, heavily influenced by the oils of the baroque period, often depicted his subjects, occasionally nudes, with large, gnarly hands—representative of the toil an unjust system imposed on the working masses. Sitte sometimes portrayed his nudes in a state of despair, the victims of war and the other manifestations of violence visited upon the world by fascism and capitalist exploitation. Other subjects were men and women of action, aggressively engaged in the struggle for the liberation of the international proletariat.[24]

Sitte's 1981 portrait *Ernst Thälmann* clearly falls into the latter category. Dominated by the color red, symbolic of international socialism, the painting shows the martyred KPD chief in typical proletarian garb. Only one of his hands, the left, is visible in the painting. The size of the hand is exaggerated. Representing the assertion that Thälmann was a man of action who was familiar with a hard day's work, the hand is about as large as his head. Over Thälmann's right shoulder is a group of men in uniform, RFB members who had fought so valiantly against the fascist menace. They follow their leader into battle, aggressively asserting their rights as workers. In front of Thälmann, to the right of his enlarged hand, another hand is reaching up from the pits of exploitation, grasping at the hope of a better future. Over Thälmann's left shoulder is the fascist beast, eager to take action against the KPD chief and his comrades. In spite of all of the activity taking place around him, Thälmann's face is serene, unworried, almost fatherly. He gazes off into a better future, one that he would not live to see, but a future of which he is certain—the triumph of socialism. This remarkable painting, which appeared on an East German postage stamp marking the SED's Tenth Party Conference in 1981, is one of the highpoints of the final decade of the state-sponsored Thälmann legend. It incorporates traditional themes of the myth with a more contemporary, frenetic sensibility. Sitte's portrait, like so many components of the Thälmann myth, links the past, present, and future through the prism of antifascism. Viewers of the painting should be as steadfast as the fallen Communist hero, as determined to construct a better future for workers everywhere. Thälmann may have died for his cause, but his sacrifice was not in vain.[25]

The 1980s provided many other chances for the SED leadership to propagate the Ernst Thälmann myth. Among the most important of these opportunities presented itself because of developments that took place within the West German criminal justice system. During the course of the decade, one of the men who had shot Thälmann, Wolfgang Otto, went on trial for the KPD chief's murder more than forty years after allegedly committing the crime. The East German leadership naturally saw this court case as an ideal opportunity to contrast the reactionary justice system of the West with that of the GDR, where the legacy of fascism had long been expunged. That it was so long before Otto came to trial, not to mention the fact that the accused was only charged with the crime as the result of West German leftists' heroic efforts, was evidence, the SED leadership insisted, of the superiority of the East German legal system. It also established that with men such as Otto living freely in the FRG, capitalist Germany not only refused to confront its Nazi past but also remained, forty years after the Second World War, a hotbed of fascist activity.[26]

The controversy concerning Otto's prosecution had begun years earlier. In 1945, an American military tribunal sentenced Otto to twenty years' imprisonment—later reduced to ten—for the crimes he had committed as a guard in Buchenwald Concentration Camp, where he had played a role in the death of at least two hundred non-German prisoners.[27] The tribunal, however, did not hold Otto responsible specifically for the murder of Thälmann, an error of which the German Left would soon take advantage. As early as 1947, Marian Zgoda's account of Otto's part in the execution of Thälmann had appeared in print and on the radio, and the erstwhile camp guard's role in the former KPD chief's death was widely known. Indeed, as early as three years after the murder, the Communist *Hamburger Volkszeitung* (Hamburg People's Newspaper) asked rhetorically, "When will those responsible come before a German court?"[28] To add insult to injury, in 1949 the newly created Bundestag passed the Amnesty Law, which made it clear that the new West German government was far less interested in continuing the process of de-Nazification than the occupation forces had been.[29] East German propaganda interpreted the new law as part of an effort by Western fascists to sweep the Nazi past under the rug, and the refusal of Western authorities to prosecute Thälmann's murderers served as evidence of the continuity between the Third Reich and the Federal Republic. To make matters worse, after only seven years in prison, Otto was released in 1952 and took up a position as a teacher of religion and history at a Roman Catholic *Gymnasium*.[30]

During the years following Otto's release, the West's failure to punish those responsible for the Thälmann murder became an important component of the GDR leadership's claim that the FRG continued to embody the legacy of fascism. Throughout the 1950s and 1960s, the martyred Communist leader's widow, Rosa, and daughter Irma, were instrumental in keeping the case in the public eye, repeatedly insisting that the killers of their husband and father be brought to justice. In 1962, a lawyer from East Berlin, Friedrich Karl Kaul, took the case to the Central Office for the Treatment of National Socialist Mass Crimes in Concentration Camps for the State of Nordrhein-Westphalia, located in Cologne. Kaul began to take depositions, most important among them being one from former camp inmate Marian Zgoda, the only eyewitness to the events of 17–18 August 1944.[31] The efforts to promote a prosecution went nowhere in spite of Kaul's diligent work. Officials in the

Central Office, unwilling to prosecute Otto, countered Kaul's endeavor with a number of arguments: Otto's shooting of Thälmann was "not malicious [*arglos*]," and the camp guard was merely "following orders." Officials in Cologne also held that Otto and the others most directly responsible for Thälmann's death were not "perpetrators [*Täter*]," but rather only "accessories [*Gehilfen*]" and hence no longer subject to prosecution. Finally, in their only convincing argument, the Central Office legal authorities maintained that Otto had already paid for his crime because of the seven years that he had spent in jail. Although the first two contentions were relatively easy to refute, the third was a different story, but Kaul was up to the task. The East German lawyer pointed out that the American tribunal had convicted and sentenced the former SS man for "war crimes" and crimes against "non-Germans," and the murder of the former KPD chief fell into neither of these categories. In spite of Kaul's best efforts, however, Thälmann's alleged murderers did not go to trial, and the case languished. As time went on, everyone involved in the crime died except Wolfgang Otto, and the effort to prosecute the last living participant suffered a serious blow when Kaul passed away. In spite of this setback, Thälmann's daughter Irma refused to give up, and, undoubtedly encouraged by an East German government, that saw propaganda benefit in her efforts, she continued her quest to secure justice for her martyred father.[32]

In February 1982, Irma Thälmann, deciding to employ a lawyer from the FRG, approached Heinrich Hannover about the prospect of pursuing a mandamus action (*Klageerzwingsverfahren*), which would force West German officials to prosecute Thälmann's alleged killer. Although permitted under German law, this method was, as Hannover puts it, "a very seldom [used] and even more seldom successful . . . legal tactic." Hannover, who had often taken up left-wing causes in the West German courts, agreed to help Irma, knowing all along that his chances of success were slim. Because he and his client were accusing Otto of murder, not crimes against humanity or war crimes, the West German lawyer's first task was an appeal to the District Court in Kleve—not the office in Cologne that oversaw the prosecution of war crimes. The judges in Kleve concluded that Zgoda's account was "uncertain [*schwankend*], inconsistent, and hardly conclusive [*kaum nachvollziehbar*]." The Kleve District Court (Landgericht) pointed out that although Zgoda had always identified Otto as one of the murderers, his several accounts of the events of 17–18 August were inconsistent in other ways. Further, Zgoda's deposition was now seventeen years old and had been taken eighteen years after the events it describes, both of which brought its accuracy into question. Hannover, in spite of this serious setback, persisted, appealing the case to the State Supreme Court (Oberlandesgericht) in Düsseldorf. After three years of legal wrangling, he was successful. The higher court reversed the Kleve decision, concluding that Zgoda's account was "as far as the central events [*Kerngeschehen*] of the murder of Thälmann is concerned . . . consistent" and established probable cause for an indictment. The judges in Düsseldorf assigned the case to the state court in Krefeld, where Heinz Joseph Paul was the presiding judge. Because local states attorneys were unenthusiastic about the prospect of pursuing such a difficult case, the burden of prosecuting Otto fell to Hannover. Under German law, because Irma Thälmann was the "secondary accuser" *(Nebenklägerin)*, her representative was entitled to participate in the prosecution. Hannover proved to be a zealous advocate for his client and seems to have played a large role in the prosecution. Hannover's zeal was all the more remarkable given that even if the prosecuting attorneys managed to secure a conviction, there was an excellent chance that Otto would not be imprisoned. Because of his age (he was seventy-four), the court might very well conclude on humanitarian grounds that he was not eligible for imprisonment—although he could lose his pension. Hannover sought to end the "camaraderie of silence" surrounding the crimes that the Nazi regime had committed against German Communists and others, and his efforts in the courtroom would stray well beyond the specific case at hand. In the end, Hannover's primary goal was to reanimate memory of the horrific crimes committed in Buchenwald by forcing Germans to confront once again the terrible actions perpetrated in their name. The West German lawyer would seek to introduce these themes during the course of the trial, and he would eventually get the opportunity to do so.[33]

Under the best of circumstances, such a prosecution was unlikely to succeed, if for no other reason than the passage of time. Hannover, however, was further handicapped by the fact that Zgoda had been dead for eighteen years. In addition, the defense promised to call a witness hitherto unheard from who would back up the Nazi story that Thälmann had died during a US bombing raid. The publicity value of the case, however, ultimately far outweighed the distinct possibility of a failure to secure a conviction. An outright acquittal of Otto might very well have been the better outcome from the East German leadership's point of view. After all, if someone who had clearly participated in the murder of the KPD leader could be acquitted, it would be evidence not only of the West German legal system's moral bankruptcy, but also of the FRG's continuing unwillingness to deal with the legacy of fascism. From the point of view of Hannover, Irma Thälmann, and their supporters in East Berlin, the prosecution of Wolfgang Otto, successful or not, was a no-lose proposition. Hence, in spite of the overwhelming odds stacked against them, Ernst Thälmann's daughter and her legal advocate proceeded with their case.[34]

The trial of Wolfgang Otto began on 5 November 1985. Because Zgoda, "the only eyewitness . . . who had viewed events from a hiding place," was long since dead, the prosecution could produce no one who had firsthand knowledge of Otto's participation in the crime. Although the Zgoda deposition could be submitted as evidence, Otto's attorney would not have the opportunity to cross examine his client's accuser, a fact that would undoubtedly work in favor of the defense. In short, Hannover's case would be a difficult one to prove beyond a reasonable doubt.[35]

Only a brief account of the trial is necessary. What matters is the response of the German media, which gave extensive coverage to the case. Proceedings began in a Krefeld courtroom on 5 November. Irma Thälmann, as "secondary accuser," was in attendance, accompanied by two East German lawyers sent to observe the proceedings. Media from the East and West were present, and newspapers in both countries covered the trial, although news coverage was more extensive in the GDR. The fact that Otto was able to secure Fritz Steinacker for his legal team had the effect of increasing media coverage. Steinacker was among his country's most prominent lawyers, defending numerous Germans accused of war crimes, participating in the famous Auschwitz trial, not to mention serving as legal counsel for Joseph Mengele.[36] The prospect of a clash between two such eminent attorneys—Hannover and Steinacker—undoubtedly had the effect of increasing press coverage of what would already have been a widely reported news story.

The West German Communist Party (DKP) sought to draw further attention to the proceedings. As the *Offenbach Post* reported, "Already, hours before the opening of the trial, some hundred members of the DKP demonstrated with posters, songs, and banners" outside of the courthouse. Anticipating an opportunity for free publicity, Herbert Mies, the DKP chairman, entered the courtroom just before the proceedings began, insisting that "I want to assert my rights"—although there is no evidence that anyone had attempted to prohibit him from

attending the trial. One of Mies's comrades, also present in the courtroom, insisted that he wanted to assure that there was a "place for the
followers of Ernst Thälmann."[37]

Otto's defense was straightforward: "I had nothing to do with the
death or the murder of Ernst Thälmann."[38] Indeed, as far as he knew,
Thälmann had died in September 1944 during the course of an American air raid, and the defense called a witness who testified to that effect.
Knowing that the prosecution would seek to depict the defendant as a
vicious murderer responsible not only for Thälmann's death, but for
the executions of hundreds—if not thousands—of others, the defense
sought to minimize Otto's role, to establish that he was a peripheral
figure in events. Otto's attorney insisted that his client was not someone who made decisions, but rather, a low-ranking individual who had
only followed orders. The defendant's respectable postwar life, serving
for decades as a teacher at a Catholic school, was indicative of his character. Such a man could not shoot anyone in the head, including Ernst
Thälmann.

It is the prosecution's efforts, however, that are of primary interest here. Hannover would seek to depict Otto as a cold-blooded killer
known in the camp as "the Spear," an integral part of the machinery of
mass murder. After all, he was chief of Commando 99, Buchenwald's
infamous execution squad. He received orders concerning whom
would be killed and saw to it that his subordinates would carry them
out. Further, because of his position in the camp, he would most assur-
edly have played a direct role in the murder of Ernst Thälmann. Given
these facts, Zgoda's account of events was the only plausible scenario
surrounding the KPD chief's death. As Hannover argued during the
course of the trial, "The accused filled a role in Buchenwald Concentration Camp that made him into an active participant in the fascist mass
murder [process]." Hannover hoped that his argument would permit
the judges to rule against the accused even if they questioned the reliability of Zgoda's twenty-three-year-old deposition. Even if Otto did
not participate directly in the murder of Thälmann—a concession that
the prosecution was unwilling to make, however—Hannover insisted
that the SS sergeant remained criminally responsible for the murder
because he had passed the illegal order to those who had physically
perpetrated the killing. As Hannover later recalled, "Had the Krefeld
court followed my argumentation, the question of whether the accused
had been present at the Thälmann shooting would not have played a
decisive role." Even if Otto had not pulled the trigger in the murder of

Thälmann, it did not reduce his culpability. After all, the law had held Adolf Eichmann, the most notorious of Germany's "desk-top perpe-trators" *(Tischtäter)*, responsible for the deaths of millions, although he had never physically murdered a single one of his victims. But the pros-ecution nevertheless continued to insist that Zgoda's deposition was accurate and that Otto was among those physically present at the mur-der of Ernst Thälmann. There might very well have been insignificant discrepancies among the several accounts that Zgoda left behind, but every time he recounted the events of 17–18 August 1944 he identified Otto as one of Thälmann's killers. On this point, the prosecution's long-dead eyewitness was undeniably consistent. All of the evidence estab-lished, the prosecution insisted, the accuracy of Zgoda's account and Otto's integral role not only in the crime for which he was on trial, but also in an untold number of other outrages.[39] Given this strategy, it was essential that prosecutors place their allegations in a broad context. As a result, the prosecution's efforts included taking all of the principals in the trial on a trip to Buchenwald Concentration Camp, where the jury could visit the site where Thälmann died. Hannover sought to show the jury what life was like for the inmates and guards in the camp. Such an approach also contributed to the trial's propaganda benefits. As a result of the testimony heard in Krefeld, West Germans would be forced once again to confront the crimes of their fascist past and to face the fact that these crimes had gone unpunished in their country—even after four decades.

In order to achieve his goals, both legal and propagandistic, Han-nover called several witnesses who testified to the horrific conditions under which Buchenwald's prisoners existed. Among those called was a former Russian inmate, Zbiniew Fuchs. Fuchs had worked in Buchen-wald's cremation chamber and testified to the vast numbers of victims brought naked to the camp's furnaces so that their remains could be destroyed. Fuchs recounted an experience he had with a Soviet pris-oner of war, shot in the head like the other victims murdered that day, who had temporarily survived the bullet lodged in his brain. In what can only be described as emotional testimony, the former camp inmate recalled how this POW had called out to him, "Comrade, give me your hand!" Fuchs did as the man requested, comforting the dying soldier as he perished.[40]

Fuchs's primary function as a prosecution witness, however, was to serve as a stand-in for the deceased Zgoda, testifying to the verac-ity of his dead comrade's twenty-three-year-old deposition. Although, unlike Zgoda, Fuchs could not claim to have witnessed Thälmann's being led into the crematorium, his testimony could only be characterized as compelling. He recounted how on the night of 17 August some time between 7:00 and 8:00 PM—"it was still light"—the camp prisoner trustee *(Kapo)* Jupp Müller instructed Fuchs and a comrade to heat up the ovens of the crematorium. Between 10:00 PM and midnight, they "heard noises and German being spoken." They heard the door of the crematorium being opened, more conversation, and then "three shots." Early the next day, 18 August, Fuchs returned to the crematorium, discovering that "the remains of a corpse in the form of ashes" lay in one of the ovens. Other than this, all that survived of the previous night's victim was the "remains of a watch."[41]

Although Fuchs's testimony corresponded with Zgoda's deposition in every way, it was not the only evidence that the former crematorium worker had to offer. Fuchs remembered how on the morning of 18 August, as he and his fellow inmates were cleaning the crematorium and its courtyard, they discovered the "traces of gunshots." Upon being informed of the discovery, Kapo Müller asked Fuchs and his comrades if they knew what had happened. Fuchs testified that "[Müller] told us that the famous Communist leader Thälmann had been [shot]." According to Hannover, Fuchs's testimony made a "deep impression" on those in the courtroom.[42] The testimony of another prosecution witness, the former SS man Helmut Roscher, was perhaps even more damning than that of Fuchs. Roscher's account lent support to Zgoda's deposition. Otto's erstwhile comrade acknowledged that Ernst Thälmann had indeed been shot in the courtyard of Buchenwald's crematorium on the night of 17–18 August 1944 and that the KPD chief had not died during an American air raid.[43]

That the state had not been eager to pursue the case became abundantly clear once again in the closing statement made by the state prosecutor, Dr. Brendle. None of the witnesses to appear in the Krefeld courtroom could claim direct knowledge either of Otto's personal participation in the shooting or the former SS sergeant's passing on the order to execute Thälmann to those who had committed the crime, and Brendle conceded these facts in his closing statement. Given the "unsatisfactory nature of the evidence [*unbefriedigenden Beweissituation*]," the state prosecutor acknowledged that the only possible outcome was a "verdict for the accused."[44]

Needless to say, Heinrich Hannover took a very different position in *his* closing remarks on behalf of the prosecution. In spite of the state prosecutor's admissions, Hannover insisted, he had met the burden of proof. There was no doubt but that Wolfgang Otto was an SS sergeant in Buchenwald, that he was the "Spear" of the camp's murderous SS contingent. There was no doubt but that he had participated in innumerable horrific acts. Further, the evidence that the prosecution presented established that the Zgoda deposition from 1962 was reliable and that Otto had participated directly in the murder of Ernst Thälmann. Common sense could lead to no other conclusion. "The accused Otto fulfilled a role in Buchenwald Concentration Camp that made him into an active participant in fascist mass murder. He was a link in the causal chain, at the end of which stood the horrific murder of untold numbers of human beings whom the fascist regime decided, as policy, to kill." Hannover feared that the judges would look at the seventy-four-year-old former Catholic school teacher and not see the cold-blooded murderer known as the "Spear" of Buchenwald. He pointed out that the "many thousands" of other Germans who had committed crimes in the name of the Third Reich were also "totally normal men." "The accused, like thousands of accused before him, understood his murderous deeds as normality, as the everyday fulfillment of his duties." Taking a page out of Hannah Arendt's book *Eichmann in Jerusalem*, Hannover insisted that Otto was a classic example of the "normality of criminality, the banality of evil." History showed unremarkable people had committed heinous crimes. The former SS guard must be convicted, Hannover concluded, because "the post-Hitler generations must be more aware and more critical of the omnipotence of the state . . . than was the generation of Wolfgang Otto."[45]

On 15 May 1986, just one month after the celebrations surrounding Thälmann's one hundredth birthday, the court announced its decision. The panel found Otto guilty of accessory to murder and sentenced him to four years' imprisonment, which was suspended because of his poor health. In a statement that undoubtedly pleased East German officials, presiding judge Heinz-Josef Paul pointed out that, unlike so many Germans such as Otto who had participated in the crimes committed during the Third Reich, German Communists had "risked their lives" in the struggle against fascism. Although Otto had "gone along [*mitgemacht*]," Thälmann and other Communists had acted heroically. The "N[ational] S[ocialist] crimes" against Communists and others, Paul insisted, "must not be forgotten."[46]

Hannover was overall pleased with the outcome. He had achieved several of his goals: the court had recognized that Otto played a role in

Thälmann's death; he had brought the crimes committed against Germany's Communists into the public eye; he had garnered the publicity that he had sought; and finally, the Krefeld judges had forever put to rest the political Right's claim that Thälmann had died during the course of the US air raid on 14 August 1944. If there were ever any doubt that Adolf Hitler had personally decided to have the KPD chief murdered in Buchenwald Concentration Camp, the German court had discredited it. On all of these points, Hannover, his client Irma Thälmann, and SED officials had been vindicated. However, Hannover was concerned with the verdict, which concluded that Otto was an "accessory" to Thälmann's murder simply because of the position that the former SS sergeant held in the camp's hierarchy. The judges had rejected the prosecution's contention that Otto had actively participated in the crime, that he had been one of those physically present at the shooting of the Communist leader, and that—at a minimum—he had personally passed on Himmler's order, originating with the führer himself, to those who had done the actual shooting. That is, the judges had deemed the Zgoda deposition untrustworthy and had concluded that Otto was merely an "accomplice" (Beihilfer) and not a "perpetrator" (Täter). The judges had not only questioned the reliability of Zgoda's thirty-three-year-old account of the murder, provided by a witness whom the defense could not cross-examine, but also rejected Hannover's argument based on the precedent established by the 1961 Eichmann trial—that those who had served as the administrators of the crimes committed during the Third Reich were as guilty as those who had physically carried out the extermination orders. Hannover correctly anticipated that the Krefeld court's decision would be reversed on appeal.[47]

On 25 March 1987, a higher court in Karlsruhe overturned the decision of the Krefeld judges. The Karlsruhe court pointed out that the fact that Otto was an SS sergeant in Buchenwald and chief of Commando 99 did not prove that he had played a role in Thälmann's death. Mere presence at the location of the crime or membership in the camp's SS contingent was not proof of one's participation; indeed, it was possible that Otto was not even in the camp at the time of the murder. Otto would have to be retried. The appeals court's ruling presented the prosecution with a very high evidentiary burden—prosecutors would have to establish that Otto had actively participated in the crime. The Krefeld court had already rejected the reliability of the most compelling evidence supporting this conclusion. An already difficult case to prosecute had become impossible to win. Indeed, Otto was retried in

Düsseldorf beginning on 10 March 1988, and using the standards of proof established in the Karlsruhe proceedings, the Düsseldorf judges had no choice but to acquit him of the charges, which they announced in a decision rendered on 29 August 1988.[48]

Although ultimately failing to convict Otto, Hannover had succeeded splendidly in achieving what was arguably the most important goal of his client and her supporters—he had garnered publicity for those who sought to revive memory of the past, especially memory of the crimes committed by fascist Germany against Ernst Thälmann and thousands of other Communists. The legal proceedings of the years 1982 to 1988 made an important contribution to the propagation of the antifascism myth during the final decade of the GDR's existence. The East German press, heavily under the governing SED's control, made the most that it could of these legal developments, covering the trials extensively, repeatedly pointing out the shortcomings of the FRG's legal system and capitalist Germany's unwillingness to come to terms with its fascist past.

Given the centrality of the Thälmann myth to the GDR's legitimizing narrative, it should come as no surprise that the FRG's apparent unwillingness to punish his murderer had long been a theme of East German propaganda. This effort had picked up momentum as the result of Kaul's attempt to secure an indictment against Wolfgang Otto during the 1960s.[49] The fact that the case did not come to court at that time had the effect of limiting the scope of the propaganda in the GDR press regarding the topic.[50] There was only so much that East German journalists could say on the subject—West German officials knew who had killed Thälmann and refused to do anything about it. As a result, the subject eventually found its way to the back burner.

During the 1980s, the prospect of a trial had the effect of reviving what would otherwise have been a stale propaganda motif. The East German press and the West German Communist newspaper *Unsere Zeit* (Our Time) paid very close attention to developments in the case from 1982, when Heinrich Hannover launched his effort to secure an indictment, right up to the acquittal of Otto in 1988. *Unsere Zeit*, for example, published a long story just a few days before the first Otto trial began. Entitled "Will the Murder of Ernst Thälmann Be Atoned for?" the article picks up with a motif that had long been central to the propaganda surrounding the Otto case. "The tradition is unbroken," begins the piece. That is, the failure of the FRG's justice system to prosecute Thälmann's murderer was just one of many instances in which legal officials in Germany had refused to pursue those who had committed crimes against Communists, both during the Weimar Republic and during the Third Reich. The paper traced the origins of this tradition all the way back to the first days of the Weimar Republic, when right-wing thugs had murdered Karl Liebknecht and Rosa Luxemburg. Bourgeois justice had failed then, just as it had during the almost four decades since Marian Zgoda first identified Wolfgang Otto as one of the killers of the KPD chief. The DKP newspaper positioned the Otto case in the long tradition of failed justice in reactionary German states, the "tradition" within which the situation must be understood. Indeed, it seemed that Otto had been rewarded for his crimes, working as a *Gymnasium* teacher for decades and now living comfortably on his pension in the Federal Republic. The fact that Otto and thousands of other criminals from the Nazi years remained unpunished was ample evidence of the continuity between the Nazi and West German legal systems. To make matters even worse, Otto had served as a teacher, passing his values on to future generations of German youth.[51]

Unsere Zeit was a relatively obscure newspaper published by West Germany's DKP, with a small circulation. *Neues Deutschland*, the official organ of East Germany's governing Socialist Unity Party, had tens of thousands of subscribers and the resources of the East German state at its disposal. It was among the most important components of the SED's massive propaganda apparatus. It should come as no surprise that this newspaper covered the case extensively. Among the most consistent motifs to run through the paper's reportage of the case is one that emphasized the fact that Otto was in court because of legal action taken by Thälmann's daughter, Irma. Only after Irma had gone through the trouble to secure a mandamus action against the former SS sergeant did Otto appear in the dock. West German authorities had to be *forced* to pursue those who had committed crimes against antifascists. Yet another theme to run through *Neues Deutschland*'s coverage was the overwhelming evidence against Otto. The eyewitness testimony of a staunch antifascist, Marian Zgoda, was apparently unconvincing to West German jurists. After all, FRG officials had known about Zgoda's testimony since the 1960s but had not acted upon it.[52]

The May 1986 decision by the Krefeld court convicting Otto of the crime proved problematic for the editors of *Neues Deutschland* and received remarkably little attention. The newspaper—to a great extent legitimately—refused to give West German legal authorities any credit for Otto's conviction. Indeed, the paper pointed out, the state prosecutor, in spite of all of the evidence assembled against the accused, recommended an acquittal. Only the hard work and determination of Irma Thälmann and her legal advocate, Heinrich Hannover, had assured that Otto would be held responsible for his actions. *Neues Deutschland*'s anonymous reporter pointed out that at least the myths concerning the circumstances surrounding Thälmann's death had been forever put to rest. "Germany's eternal son" had been shot in Buchenwald Concentration Camp as the result of an order issued by Adolf Hitler through his most infamous henchman, Heinrich Himmler. Even the naysayers in the Federal Republic would now have to admit these facts, which had been established in a West German courtroom.[53] The overturning of Otto's conviction breathed new life into the topic for the SED's official organ, although the themes of the paper's reporting remained unchanged.[54]

Perhaps even more important was the West German coverage of the case. All major West German news magazines and newspapers covered the two trials extensively, which provided a rare case in which citizens of the FRG had to recognize the KPD's antifascist traditions.[55] The West German printed media tended to view the proceedings in the context of the Third Reich's crimes against humanity rather than in terms of crimes committed specifically against the KPD and its leadership. FRG reporters also were inclined to emphasize the legal ramifications of the case for the West's system of jurisprudence.

West German periodical accounts of the Otto trial tended to be less polemical than their counterparts in the GDR. Western journalists were generally inclined to emphasize the facts of the case, recognizing that the issues involved were difficult ones and that it would be extremely hard to convict the accused. After all, there was conflicting testimony regarding such issues as the exact circumstances under which the execution took place, how many shots were fired, and if Otto had ever confessed his involvement to his comrades. Indeed, many journalists in the FRG held that the difficulty of convicting Otto was not a bad thing. As the accused, the former SS sergeant had certain rights, and no serious West German journalist suggested that Otto's rights should be trampled upon because of the crime of which he stood accused. After all, the recognition that those in the dock had fundamental rights was one of the things that separated the FRG from the regime for which Otto had allegedly committed his outrages. This is not to suggest that there were not parallels between coverage from the East and West. No mainstream West German journalist questioned the contention that Thälmann had died as the result of a direct order from the führer; none accepted the thesis that the Americans had accidently killed the KPD chief during a bombing raid. There was simply too much evidence in support of the former argument and none to support the latter—other than an article in the discredited *Völkischer Beobachter*. Rather, the unresolved questions concerned Wolfgang Otto's role in the events at issue.[56]

Many Western journalists, like their counterparts from the GDR, were also critical of the slowness with which the case against Otto proceeded. As the unnamed author of an article appearing in *Der Spiegel* put it, "And typical for the development of NS trials in the Federal Republic is . . . the slovenly [*nachlässig*] legal wrangling of the justice system, which drags on the case for years."[57] Lothar Bewerunge, covering the trial for the *Frankfurter Allgemeine Zeitung*, also emphasized the length of time between the original accusations against Otto and the beginning of the trial, opening his article by pointing out that it had been "more than forty years since the murder of the former Communist leader Ernst Thälmann on orders of Hitler and Himmler." Much of Bewerunge's piece deals with the long history of the case, which, in the journalist's words, "has a long prehistory." In its current manifestation, the effort to prosecute Otto traced its origins to 1962, when "Thälmann's widow reopened . . . murder accusations" against the erstwhile SS sergeant.[58] One of the issues upon which East and West German journalists agreed was that justice had been a long time in coming.

West German journalists generally greeted the conviction of Wolfgang Otto positively. Indeed, some journalists saw the conviction as an important step forward in German jurisprudence. In response to the Krefeld court's verdict, the *Deutsches Allgemeines Sonntagsblat* reported that "[t]here are once again judges in this republic"; and Dietrich Strothmann, writing in *Die Zeit*, interpreted the decision as evidence of a "new generation of judges" that was willing to confront its country's often distasteful past. Although in this case, Strothmann went on to say, "the law is late, almost too late" in securing justice for the fallen Communist leader, the Otto case established that there were those willing to take extreme measures to assure that the right thing was done. Strothmann concluded that "there remains only one question: What would have happened if the victim had not been the prominent Communist leader, if over the last twenty years the GDR had not repeatedly [and] loudly demanded a trial for his murderer? Would [these] young German judges have made such an effort for a nameless victim?"[59]

Of course, the May 1986 conviction would be overturned, and Otto would be retried in 1988. Although by this time the accusations against the former concentration camp guard were old news, and there was less interest in the West German media, Strothmann continued to write about the case for *Die Zeit*. Once again he lamented the sloth of the West German legal process, pointing out that "[n]ow Wolfgang Otto is sick and old and not long for this world" and given the circumstances, the Düsseldorf court "would probably have to acquit him." To make matters worse, the second trial would be an even more arduous task than the first. There would be "no witnesses, only transcripts [of the previous trial] that must be read for hours" into the court's records. The accused simply sat there, "barely breathing, hard of hearing. Big eyes behind big glasses . . . Otto the clueless." And all for naught. The outcome of the case was all but predetermined. Justice could not be served under these circumstances.[60] Indeed, Wolfgang Otto died in November 1989, never having paid for his crime.[61] The SED regime would survive him by only a few weeks.

East German propaganda concerning the Otto trials, however, paled in comparison to the celebrations surrounding Ernst Thälmann's one hundredth birthday. The observances of the year 1986 incorporated some of the most dramatic examples of Thälmann commemoration since the 1950s. Indeed, 16 April 1986 was arguably the most important date in the history of the Thälmann cult. In addition to the obvious importance usually associated with the centennial of a cult figure's birth, in hindsight it was clear that the GDR faced a crisis. Within a little more than three years, the regime would be in a state of collapse. The SED's efforts to gain legitimacy through a dramatic improvement in the East German people's standard of living had failed. A celebration of Thälmann's legacy, linking it to the supposed accomplishments of "real, existing socialism," would provide the opportunity to breathe new life into the antifascism myth. The closely related ideas of *Vermächtnis* (legacy) and *Erbe* (inheritance), wedded to the material progress created by German socialism, would serve as the overarching themes of the commemoration. The SED leadership hoped to re-create the glories of the antifascist past, downplaying the problems in "real, existing socialism" and countering the calls for reform emanating from Moscow. As always, the party leadership sought also to convince the East German people that German socialism promised a bright future, characterized by material abundance, if only they would stay the course and embrace Thälmann's legacy.

Given the extent of the activities of April 1986, it should come as no surprise that planning for the celebration began well in advance. As early as February 1973, the SED Politburo began reconsidering the construction of a national Ernst Thälmann monument.[62] The dedication of this monument thirteen years later would serve as the climax of the centennial celebration. The SED also scheduled its Eleventh Party Conference to coincide with the Thälmann centennial. Among the other events associated with the festivities would be the premiere of a four-hour-long television film, special ceremonies at Buchenwald and other sites important to the Thälmann legend, and a meeting of scholars from throughout the eastern bloc. These historians would assemble in Berlin in order to discuss Thälmann's legacy and its implications both for the GDR and the international workers' movement. In addition, East German visual artists would put their talents at the regime's disposal, and several historical works, novels, and short stories about the martyred KPD chief and his legacy would be published.[63]

Among the most interesting works to come out in the centennial year was a short story appearing in the January number of *Neue Deutsche Literatur,* among the most important publications of the Writers' Union of the German Democratic Republic. The story consists of an excerpt from a much longer book, *Das Ermittlungsverfahren: Ein Thälmann Roman* (The Judicial Inquiry: A Thälmann Novel).[64] An analysis of this excerpt—which the leaders of the GDR's literary establishment apparently saw as representative of the entire three-hundred-page work—provides an opportunity to examine the major themes of the novel without producing a long assessment of the entire book. Another reason that this selection is of particular interest and worth recounting in some detail is the fact that it is a noteworthy example of fiction for young adults written about Thälmann. Most of the novels and short stories written about the fallen Communist hero were produced with children in mind. Walter Baumert's "Ermittlungsverfahren Thälmann" (Judicial Inquiry Thälmann),[65] the title under which the excerpt was published, was an exception. The tale is much more graphic in its depiction of the violence that the Nazis inflicted on their victims than the novels and stories usually produced for a younger readership.[66] It also lacks, for want of a better way to put it, a "happy ending." At the conclusion of the story—as is the case with the complete novel—nothing is resolved; socialism has not yet triumphed, and its two main protagonists, Ernst Thälmann and his wife, Rosa, have nothing to look forward to but years of suffering and degradation. The narrative is not void of hope, though—both Ernst and Rosa see clear evidence that German socialism's struggle against Hitler fascism continues in spite of their own suffering. Baumert was a writer for East German television, and his story reads very much like a screenplay. It is not a continuous narrative, but rather a series of related scenes, sometimes separated by days or even weeks. One can very easily envision "Judicial Inquiry Thälmann" being turned into a play or short film.

The narrative, which begins in April 1933, opens with Thälmann imprisoned. "Hard weeks began for Ernst Thälmann." New guards had been assigned to his cell, and he fears that this change could be a harbinger of difficult days ahead; perhaps the treatment he receives from his jailors will get worse as a result. Indeed, this is the case. Fewer letters arrive from Rosa and his father; more of the articles are cut out of his newspapers. Yet the Communist leader remains stoic. His primary concern is not with his own welfare, but with the well-being of the KPD and the international workers' movement. He hears of the systematic "extermination" of the Communists and the "execution orders against all political opponents and peaceful citizens." He is aware of the series of Nazi triumphs on the domestic front and knows that the press depicts him as a "tool" of Germany's enemies. Thälmann fears that the "bourgeois regimes" might be taken in by Hitler's "peace feelers." In short, he is, as always, more concerned about others than about himself.

In spite of the burden he bears, Thälmann maintains his simple humanity. He thanks the guard who brings his meals, although the guard refuses to speak to him. The KPD chief keeps his wits about him by reading the two books allotted to him each week by the prison library. He looks forward to possibly reading a novel by Theodor Fontane, maybe *Effi Breist*. He receives two books—neither penned by Fontane. One is well worn, a selection from the novels of Paul Heyse, and has clearly crossed the tables of many other inmates. The second book is something of an enigma. Clearly a new book, this additional tome is written by Johannes Scherr, whom Thälmann immediately recognizes as John Schehr, one of his closest comrades from the days prior to his imprisonment. He immediately begins to search for a code, discovering a series of water marks in the paper that read "n-e-w-s-f-o-r-e-r-n-s-t." Recognizing that Thälmann's primary concern is most likely the movement's fortunes, the hidden message in the book goes on to assure the imprisoned KPD chief that the struggle against fascism continues, that his "closest associates in the struggle[—]Wilhelm Pieck, John Schehr, Franz Dahlem, [and] Walter Ulbricht"—continue his hard work.

Finally, the secret message discusses his fate: Thälmann will be tried for high treason, accused of playing a role in the February 1933 Reichstag fire. He greets the news with joy. Finally, he will have an opportunity once again to confront the forces of German fascism in a public forum and expose the lies that the Nazis have told about the KPD and the international workers' movement. "Their planned settling of accounts with the Communists will become a general reckoning with the fascists!" "He saw an opportunity before him, a clear new goal, and a possibility, even in the desperate situation of a prisoner, to be able to do something against fascism for the movement." A "show trial" would guarantee him the opportunity to speak publically against the crimes of the Third Reich.

In response to this news, Thälmann pens a letter to his beloved wife, Rosa. He recounts the horrible conditions under which he and "thousands of others" are imprisoned by the Third Reich. In spite of the fact that Easter, the "festival of the awakening of spring," approaches, he can find no joy in it. Yet he extols Rosa to urge his comrades to continue the struggle for "a better life[,] [a struggle] that will not be in vain." Although he stands "accused of the most serious crimes" and will be held responsible "for all of the party's resolutions and actions," she should not despair. The truth will one day win out. In reality, he is communicating with the prosecutor, Walther, who will undoubtedly read the letter. Upon reading the letter, the jurist sets out to visit the accused.

Walther and Thälmann sit alone in the latter's cell and discuss the case. Thälmann stands accused of orchestrating a "nonexistent plan for armed opposition" to the regime. His accuser reminds Thälmann that he is now in a position to help "many people" by pleading guilty to the crimes with which he is charged. Thälmann insists on putting up a fight, pointing out that his legal proceedings will provide the opportunity to point out publically that the Nazis were planning for a war against the Soviet Union. He demands his right to a public trial, to a "lawyer of my own choosing," to the opportunity to call witnesses and confront his accusers. Walther leaves the cell with nothing resolved. Sitting in his office after the interview, Walther decides to allow Rosa—who had repeatedly petitioned for the right to do so—to visit her husband. Walther hopes that "the love of the family will weaken [Thälmann's] resistance." The prosecutor then leaves his office to attend a meeting with the Third Reich's minister of justice, Hans Frank.

Frank is concerned about the situation in Germany. In spite of all of the SA and SS's efforts to crush the German Communist movement, it continues to thrive. Agreeing that a more pliant KPD chief might very well use his influence to quell the unrest among the workers, Frank accepts Walther's plan to make use of Rosa against her husband. Frank's scheme, however, is even more insidious than Walther's. The next scene records Rosa walking through the streets of Berlin. A native of Hamburg like her husband, she has been staying with a working-class family—the Krausens—that is willing to overlook the dangers inherent in the decision to help her out. Rosa remains determined to visit her husband. Like Ernst, Rosa's concerns are not personal so much as political. She eagerly anticipates getting word to Ernst about the KPD and Comintern's continuing efforts against fascism. Rosa also wants to be able to assure the party leadership that her husband is in reasonably good health. Hence, she walks to the office of the judge, Dr. Mittelsbach, who signed the warrant ordering her husband's arrest. She is told that he is not there. Rosa's response is defiant: "Then I'll stay here until he comes!" She sits outside of the office for hours, returning every day for a week—to no avail. Rosa gets the runaround for three weeks before even seeing a legal official, who tells her that her husband is "healthy, and nothing has happened to him since he is under the protection of the justice system."

Frustrated, Rosa does the unthinkable: she decides to call upon the Gestapo, which is really responsible for her husband's illegal imprisonment. She meets with a Gestapo official, who asks her to take a seat; she refuses. She is eventually taken to an elevator—Frank's plan to use Rosa against her husband is to be launched. The SS man on the elevator warns her melodramatically that "[y]ou may never speak of what you are about to see. . . . Although you will not forget it until your dying day." The elevator carries them into the cellar; Rosa is now seven meters under ground. She is frightened, but the experience is not entirely new to her. She has had to stand up to authorities on behalf of her spouse on many previous occasions. She and the SS man walk through a long hallway, "narrow prison cells" on either side. She sees the prisoners, "an old man in carpenter's pants," and a sailor, others staring blankly and silently off into the distance. Rosa notices their bloody wounds. The victims of fascist torture, they had been whipped on their backs. Some had blood on their hands or coming out of their mouths. One of the prisoners cries out "murderers, murderers." Rosa has descended into hell. After walking for some time through the immense basement complex, she is shown an empty cell. Her companion from the SS, pale because of a lack of sunlight, informs her that "[w]e have reserved it, madame. For the Communist leader Ernst Thälmann, madame. For your beloved spouse." Rosa is appalled, but the pale man reassures her: "Calm yourself, calm yourself, madame. It is up to him if he lands here with us or at home, in the arms of his beloved wife. It depends only on him. Don't forget that, Frau Thälmann!"

Rosa does not even remember how she gets out of the SS dungeons. She wanders the streets in a daze. "Eventually the tears came." Not knowing what to do, she gets on a local train and takes it to the outskirts of the city. Exiting the train, she begins to roam the streets of one of Berlin's numerous suburbs, where she sees the decorations that the Nazis have put up for May Day, although no one is celebrating this most sacred of workers' holidays. Rosa turns down a side street where she sees graffiti on the paving stones. It reads, "In spite of terror and murder—the KPD lives." Another Communist resistance fighter has painted "Free Ernst Thälmann!" She is assured that in spite of what she saw at the Gestapo headquarters earlier in the day, the struggle continues. The proletariat will never surrender to the fascist beast. Rosa returns late in the afternoon to the apartment where she is staying with the Krausens. Her friends are shocked by her appearance. Rosa assures them that she is fine. "Don't you want to tell us what has happened?" the husband, Robert, asks. "Not today, later, maybe later," is her laconic response.

What makes Baumert's story more effective than nonfiction accounts is that it personalizes the general. One man represents the suffering of many. One woman, like millions of other working-class wives, sisters, and mothers, stands by her man. Each makes his or her sacrifice, linked by the determination, the staunch belief, that good—socialism—will one day triumph. Both Rosa and Ernst serve as examples for the reader, as paragons of those who place the interests of others before themselves. These are the type of people who build socialism, and these are the kind of men and women whom the GDR needs. Baumert's story—as ridden as it is with clichés—evokes an emotional response. It is about love, the close personal bond between husband and wife in the face of unparalleled suffering, as well as about politics—although the latter, as always, takes precedent. Baumert's fictionalized account of historical events allows the reader to penetrate the inner lives of Ernst and Rosa, to identify with them more effectively than they would in reading drier, nonfiction works. Baumert's characters are, in many ways, much like any other proletarian couple. In short, if nothing else, Baumert has effectively humanized his subject, which cannot be said concerning historians' accounts of Thälmann's life, which so often rendered him a bloodless symbol void of any human emotion, a figure ultimately impossible to emulate.

Although all of the major themes of Baumert's Thälmann novel can be seen in the twenty pages reproduced in *Neue Deutsche Literatur*, it is worthwhile briefly to investigate the final passage from the book, an epilogue that concludes with November 1935, at which point the Nazi leadership abandoned plans to put the Communist leader on trial. The international proletariat had risen up to rescue its favorite son, and, fearing embarrassment if such a rescue proceeded, the Nazi government relented to the mighty force—the workers—that had launched the Free Thälmann movement. Although a major chapter in the imprisoned KPD chief's life was at an end, his difficulties were only beginning. "A new Passion [*Leidensweg*] for Ernst Thälmann began. He also endured this test, upright and honorably, created out of the sources of his inner strength [*sic*], unbroken and never defeated. A German Communist, loyal unto death."[67] Such imagery, likening the fallen leader to Christ, became especially prominent during the SED regime's last five years. Party leaders recognized that East Germany tottered on the brink of collapse. The economy was in shambles, and the Soviet leadership called for fundamental change. The GDR leaders nevertheless hoped that, in spite of these dangers, German socialism could be saved, and so they revived the theme of Thälmann's sacrificial death, especially during the year of his one hundredth birthday. Baumert's novel sought to do so in a way—by bringing to life the inner existence of the fallen KPD chief—that was more difficult to effect in nonfiction works. Here lay the contribution of *Das Ermittlungsverfahren* to the propagation of the Ernst Thälmann legend.

This is not to suggest that the SED gave up on biographical and other nonfiction accounts of the fallen KPD chief's life and sacrifice. The party leadership, as always, insisted on using every medium at its disposal to propagate the Thälmann legend, and several important nonfiction works also appeared to commemorate the Thälmann centennial. Much less emotionally effective than Baumert's story, as Günter Katsch, author of an essay reviewing several of the new Thälmann books for *Beiträge zur Geschichte der Arbeiterbewegung* pointed out, these nonfiction books were meant "[f]irst of all to show leading party functionaries and historians Thälmann's legacy in the present." They also established "that the SED and GDR have fulfilled this legacy." Thälmann struggled for the "unity of the working class" in the face of capitalist exploitation, an idea that came to fruition in the creation of the GDR. All of the works under review, Katsch continued, made a vital contribution to the education of the proletariat regarding its role in history.[68]

Katsch singles out for special praise a work entitled *Ernst Thälmann: Bilder, Dokumente, Texte.* Clearly aimed at a popular audience, this coffee-table book combined numerous photographs, excerpts from contemporary texts written by and about Thälmann, and a brief biography, all assembled by scholars at Berlin's IML. The authors-editors of *Ernst Thälmann* made their agenda clear from the outset—to show "that the life and work of this important son of the people . . . can make a fruitful contribution to the present." The book begins with a brief biographical sketch of its subject, written by historian Günter Hortzschansky, emphasizing the importance of Thälmann's legacy. The book reproduces dozens of documents, each with a sometimes lengthy caption, written by party historians. The final section of the book, "His Legacy Lives in the German Democratic Republic," seeks to link this antifascist heritage with the current GDR leadership. Quotations from Thälmann are printed side by side with some from Erich Honecker, thereby emphasizing the continuity between the two proletarian leaders' ideas. The accompanying photographs show various SED leaders at ceremonies commemorating the fallen Communist leader.[69]

Another 1986 publication, *Ernst Thälmann—unsere Partei erfüllt sein Vermächtnis* (Ernst Thälmann: Our Party Fulfills His Legacy), contains thirty essays written by participants in a scholarly conference held in Berlin on 12 and 13 March. The event, sponsored by the IML, brought together historians and politicians from throughout the socialist and the nonsocialist worlds. Among the speakers were figures from the FRG, the Soviet Union, Poland, Czechoslovakia, Hungary, and Romania. The participants' origins served to emphasize the international character of the Thälmann cult, as did the presentations. Günter Hortzschansky, for example, read a paper entitled "Ernst Thälmann as Pioneer [*Vorkämpfer*] of Proletarian Internationalism," and Polish historian Jan Tomicki made a presentation he called "The Polish Workers' Movement in the Struggle Concerning the Defense of Ernst Thälmann," which examined Polish participation in the Free Thälmann movement of the 1930s. Speakers sought to link this proletarian internationalism closely with Thälmann's legacy. Horst Sindermann, member of the SED Politburo and president of the Volkskammer, served as host of the conference and delivered the opening remarks. He greeted his audience as "Dear cohorts [*Mitstreiter*] of Ernst Thälmann." Sindermann then invoked the antifascism myth and the principle of *Vermächtnis*. Thälmann's "personality," the speaker maintained, "embodies the generation of revolutionaries who set the example for the socialist revolution in our [own] country." The remaining speakers repeatedly made this same point, that the leaders of the GDR stood on the shoulders of giants, of the men and women, beginning with Karl Marx and Friedrich Engels and including Lenin, who had set out to change the world, to end the economic exploitation of one man by another. Such was the glorious legacy upon which the GDR was established and that those attending the conference were there to celebrate.[70]

Such historical propaganda was for the benefit not only of scholars, but also, more important, of the masses as well. The conference received extensive coverage in *Neues Deutschland,* the SED's official organ. On 13 March, for example, the meeting was the subject of a front-page article and all of page four. The newspaper coverage emphasized three themes: *Vermächtnis,* the solidarity of the international proletariat that the conference evinced, and the "scholarly [*wissenschaftlich*] nature of the proceedings.[71] The last of these motifs served to lend the proceedings an aura of legitimacy—they were in keeping with the tenets of Marxist–Leninist "historical science." In short, the speakers were not mere propagandists, as the West might claim, but rather adherents of "scientific socialism" who recognized in Thälmann's deeds the origins of the socialist revolution in Germany.

The scholarly conference of mid-March 1986 was not the first major event held to commemorate the fallen KPD chief's centenary, however. This distinction belonged to the 6 February 1986 premiere of a new television movie. The two-part, four-hour long film, called simply *Ernst Thälmann,* was directed by Ursula Bonhoff and starred Helmut Schellhardt in the title role. Günter Hortzschansky and Walter Wimmer, two biographers of Thälmann who worked at the IML, served as historical advisers for the film. SED party chief Erich Honecker hosted the premiere, which took place at Berlin's Kosmos theater. The guest list included not only members of the Politburo and the chiefs of the "allied parties," but also Irma, the slain leader's daughter; Thälmann's granddaughter, Vera; and representatives of other socialist countries. The public soon had the opportunity to view the film in its entirety on East German television on the following evening, a Friday, at 7:00 PM. The entire program would be repeated on 8 February at 8:00 PM.[72] Although the 1986 film covers many of the same events as Kurt Maetzig's epics from the mid-1950s, the films are different in some noteworthy ways. An analysis comparing the Maetzig and Bonhoff films provides an opportunity to show how the Thälmann myth evolved over the course of thirty years and how memory of the fallen Communist leader was manipulated in order to legitimize the ruling Socialist Unity Party's policies.[73]

The 1986 television film, like the 1950s films *Ernst Thälmann—Sohn seiner Klasse* and *Ernst Thälmann—Führer seiner Klasse*, was an elaborate color production. Clearly designed to compete with West German television for young viewers, the Bonhoff film centers around a choir of young Communists who sing proletarian songs in the working-class sections of Berlin during the years 1929 to 1933.[74] Historical advisers Hortzschansky and Wimmer had done what they could to assure *Ernst Thälmann*'s historical accuracy, which, as Hortzschansky put it, was "not simple with a feature film." Indeed, the 1986 film—unlike the epics of the 1950s—takes no serious liberties with history. *Ernst Thälmann* (1986) opens with the events of 1 May 1929, when several workers died at the hands of the Berlin police, and concludes with the famous secret Central Committee meeting held on 7 February 1933, at which Thälmann declared a state of emergency for the KPD. Hence, the scope of the 1986 film is much narrower than that of the 1950s films, which assured that Bonhoff's effort moved at a much slower pace than Kurt Maetzig's, which at least partially explains why the Bonhoff films never achieved the cult status that Maetzig's movies had.[75]

Schellhardt, who was much older than Günther Simon when the latter portrayed Thälmann thirty years earlier, plays the martyred Communist leader very differently. Schellhardt and Bonhoff create a post-totalitarian image of Thälmann, and the persistent anti-Americanism of the Maetzig films is absent. In 1986, viewers of the biopic saw a "kinder and gentler" Ernst Thälmann, who has lost much of the revolutionary fervor of the 1950s. The 1980s Thälmann is much more sensitive—he gives money to a beggar and helps an evicted family return to its home. He does not preach revolution so much as caution, waiting for the proper time to act. This more serene, thoughtful Thälmann—more like the one depicted in Sitte's 1981 painting than the revolutionary firebrand created by Maetzig and Simon—can be seen throughout the 1986 film.[76]

The television movie opens with peaceful workers celebrating May Day in the streets of Berlin. The police launch an unprovoked attack on the workers, and a little girl is shot. The workers take to the barricades, and the police fire upon them, although the proletarians are unarmed. In the end, 21 are killed, and 160 are wounded. Thälmann, to whom the workers naturally turn for advice, points out that they have learned a valuable lesson. The time is not ripe for revolution, and he counsels against further violence. This attitude stands in sharp contrast to the figure who emerges in *Sohn seiner Klasse* and *Führer seiner Klasse*, a man constantly fomenting revolution. Maetzig's workers are men of action who carefully plan a series of attacks on the capitalist system. The 1986 film portrays the workers as hapless, somewhat confused, un-armed victims of capitalism who must be strongly led so that they will not act hastily and delay the inevitable victory of socialism. The 1950s Thälmann is at the forefront of the revolutionary movement, a man of action; the post-totalitarian Thälmann is a cautious thinker, more of a theoretician than a revolutionary.

The same theme can be seen in another scene in the 1986 biopic. While traveling between Hamburg and Berlin, Thälmann meets a fam-ily of dispossessed peasants. He points out that the workers are not the only victims of the hated capitalist system; so are the peasants and the lower middle class. All must band together to create socialism, for "the industrial proletariat cannot win alone." Cooperation—working together to build a better socialist future—is a major theme through-out the film. After the Nazis kill several workers, Thälmann calls once again for unity: "We workers must stand together against fascism and war." Later in the movie, Thälmann even goes so far as to say that his ultimate goal is to bring all Germans, even the bourgeoisie, into the socialist future.[77]

Like Günter Simon's portrayal, Helmut Schellhardt's rendition re-flected the regime's view of itself and its role in East German society. In the 1950s, the SED was energetic and optimistic. The party still believed that its ultimate victory in *all* of Germany lay in the not-too-distant fu-ture. Hence, Thälmann was depicted as a charismatic revolutionary leading a dynamic proletariat vigorously pursuing the victory of so-cialism. In contrast, by 1986 the SED had been governing the GDR for almost forty years. Honecker's government represented the status quo. The SED saw itself as the guardian of East German socialism, not the vanguard of a global revolution. The party sought to promote unity in the face of a number of serious threats because "real, existing so-cialism" had failed to provide the material abundance that the party had promised. Indeed, by 1986, the dream of socialism was in eclipse. The FRG's economic success made it clear that, for the foreseeable future, the status quo was the best that the SED leadership could hope for. Schellhardt's cautious, pensive portrayal of Thälmann embodied the outlook of the party leadership, which, through the film, sought to share its point of view with the East German people. The SED had in effect abandoned its revolutionary roots in favor of the preservation of the status quo.[78] Thus, the television film introduced some of the most important themes of the 1986 propaganda offensive.

Ceremonies commemorating the Thälmann centennial were held throughout the spring of 1986. This phenomenon became especially apparent during the month of April, when seemingly every East German city and village held a ceremony. On 6 April, the Thälmann Memorial in the Ziegenhals, where the KPD chief had made his famous final speech calling for proletarian unity in the face of the fascist menace, was rededicated after a renovation lasting two months. Members of the FDJ and Thälmann Pioneers, 150 of them altogether, participated in the celebration. New displays created under the auspices of the IML and the Museum for German History were unveiled. *Neues Deutschland* found the renovated memorial especially effective. The SED's official organ summed up the message of the exhibit quite succinctly: "The impressive display covers the struggle for unity of action against fascism and war of the Communist Party under Ernst Thälmann's leadership as well as the realization of this revolutionary legacy in the GDR." Although much of the memorial building had been renovated, the room in which Thälmann gave his speech remained as it was in February 1933, with the exception that photographs of those present at the KPD chief's final public speech hung on the walls. Visitors could stand where the great proletarian leader had called the German workers to action in their most desperate hour and listen to recordings of the martyred KPD chief's speeches and of the address Wilhelm Pieck gave at the dedication of the site in 1953. In the "coming days," *Neues Deutschland* reported, a bronze relief would be placed in the "lobby of the memorial. . . . It shows five fists reminiscent of the greeting given by the Red Front Fighters' League under the leadership of Thälmann." The success of the emotionally moving exhibition, the official SED organ continued, could be seen in the fact that since 1953 "61,000 visitors from 45 countries" had traveled to the site.[79]

The Ziegenhals location was not the only important Thälmann commemoration site to receive a facelift prior to the centennial; so did the sites at Buchenwald Concentration Camp. On 13 April, the basement of the camp's disinfection chamber, where on 18 September 1944 inmates had held an illegal memorial service for the recently fallen KPD leader, witnessed an elaborate ceremony at which a new series of displays was dedicated. The exhibition in the adjoining rooms evolved somewhat as a result of the renovation, but the chamber in which the illegal commemoration took place remained largely unchanged, with the exception of the installation of two windows and a glass door in order to provide natural light for the dark chamber. In addition, the former disinfection room received a fresh coat of paint and a new replica of the charcoal rendering of Thälmann used in the 1944 ceremony. Gerhard Müller, local party chief and candidate member of the SED Politburo, presided at the observance ritual. A total of eight hundred people participated in the rededication ceremony, including members of numerous East German organizations—the FDJ, the Thälmann Pioneers, the Committee of Antifascist Resistance Fighters—as well as Soviet soldiers and workers and representatives of allied governments. Soldiers from the *Volksarmee* took part in a wreath-laying ceremony. Klaus Trostorff, director of the Buchenwald National Memorial and Monument, gave a speech in which he recounted the events that had occurred at the location forty-two years earlier. Like so many others who gave a speech at the site, Trostorff related the international composition of those present in September 1944, evidence of the tremendous amount of respect Thälmann garnered within the worldwide workers' movement. He recounted the moving speeches given at the original commemoration as well as Bruno Apitz's performance on the violin. "The comrades mourned with thanks in their hearts," remembered Trostorff, who had been an inmate of Buchenwald at the time of Thälmann's death. "Not all who have died are dead," he insisted. As long as memory of Thälmann and the other victims of fascism survived, their accomplishments and glorious legacy lived on. The local newspaper, *Das Volk*, insisted that the location was a moving one, vital to the preservation of the GDR's antifascist heritage. "Here visitors," the newspaper opined, "find time to contemplate the achievements of our socialist state, to think about the lessons of the politics of Thälmann, whose ideas and actions live on and whose legacy is fulfilled in the GDR." There was another ceremony, held on the same day, in the crematorium courtyard. Once again Müller presided. As the bells in the nearby tower tolled, East German soldiers laid a wreath at the location where the SS had murdered Thälmann in August 1944. And yet a third wreath laying was carried out at the bell tower.[80] The fact that all of these commemorative functions occurred on a single day is no surprise. By the time of the Thälmann centennial, memorial rituals had been held on the Ettersburg for more than forty years, and the rituals at Buchenwald in 1986 made no significant novel contribution to this longstanding tradition.

As important as Buchenwald was to the propagation of the Thälmann legend, the rituals performed there did not constitute the highpoint of the centenary. This distinction belonged to the dedication of the Ernst Thälmann National Monument in Berlin on 15 April, the eve of the martyred Communist leader's one hundredth birthday. Plans to construct a national monument commemorating the fallen KPD chief had originated in the GDR's first days. An early scheme to build the monument on East Berlin's Thälmannplatz had been abandoned. In 1973, Erich Honecker made the creation of a national site specifically constructed for Thälmann commemoration a top priority once again, although it was not until 1980 that the Central Committee would produce a proposal that would bear significant fruit. The party leadership decided to erect a Thälmann monument in Prenzlauer Berg, one of the largest working-class districts in Berlin. The location chosen was at the time a massive gasworks along Greifswalderstraße. Honecker and other party bigwigs passed the site, which was quite an eyesore, each day on their way to their villas in Wandlitz. The monument would be the focal point of a massive forty-hectare park, a green space to be enjoyed by the people of the East German capital and useful to the party as a setting for mass rallies. The location could hold hundreds of thousands of people. Playgrounds and other recreational facilities would be distributed throughout the park. Symbolically linking the GDR's antifascist traditions with the accomplishments of "real, existing socialism," the park would be bordered by a complex of apartment buildings, six to fifteen stories high. These structures would contain 1,332 flats, which would house around 4,000 people. Further, emphasizing the GDR's scientific and technological accomplishments, a planetarium—to be opened in 1987, Berlin's 750th anniversary—would be constructed on the north side of the park.[81] As *Neues Deutschland* pointed out, the new housing project would be "[y]oung, modern, and full of life," *the* place in socialist Germany for workers to raise their children. A public swimming pool and several playgrounds completed this model environment for urban living.[82] These structures would provide ample evidence of economic growth in the GDR, establishing that living conditions had improved and that the party leadership had kept its promises. The material conditions created by "real, existing socialism" were no longer something to be overcome, but rather to be embraced and enjoyed by

Prenzlauer Berg's Ernst Thälmann National Monument. Note the apartment building in the background. Author's photograph.

the East German people, whose standard of living improved daily. Further, the complex would serve as proof to all of the tourists who visited East Berlin, many of them from capitalist countries, that socialism was working in the GDR. In short, the monument, the park, and the housing facilities would serve as a showcase for the SED's accomplishments, demonstrating in a concrete way the accomplishments of a leadership that embodied the legacy of Germany's greatest socialist hero, Ernst Thälmann. Communicating this assertion became vitally important at a time when the legitimacy of the socialist project was increasingly coming into question across Eastern Europe, even in the Soviet Union, the cradle of Marxism–Leninism.

The Ernst Thälmann Monument, located on one edge of the park along Greifswalderstraße, served to link the material progress in the GDR with the antifascist traditions of German socialism. The complex was Honecker's personal project, so he oversaw the planning of the monument and the surrounding construction. He rejected every suggestion that the East German artistic community made, thus ensuring most GDR artists' undying hatred for the monument. In 1981, the SED chief personally chose Soviet artist Lew Kerbel, most famous for his massive bronze of the father of scientific socialism in Karl-Marx-Stadt (Chemnitz), to design the monument, a decision that guaranteed that it would be a massive construction in the style of 1980s socialist realism and a throwback to the enormous monumental structures of the regime's early years.[83]

The enormous monument was fourteen meters tall and fifteen meters wide, weighing an astonishing fifty tons. The base was made of Ukrainian marble, and the likeness of Thälmann was cast in bronze. Rumor had it that the statue, welded together from two hundred pieces, had an electrified nose in order to assure that ice did not accumulate in Thälmann's nostrils. Its massive size would serve as further proof of the technological and material accomplishments of socialism, linking them with East Germany's antifascist heritage. The statue consisted of a bust depicting Thälmann giving the antifascist salute—a raised right fist—with a Soviet flag waving behind him. As a result, the monument alluded to two of the most important components of the Thälmann myth: his integral role in the struggle against Hitler fascism and his enduring friendship for the Soviet Union, the power that had crushed the horrors of National Socialism in the course of the most destructive war in history. The sheer size of the monument amounted, in the words of historian Thomas Flierl, to a "god-like glorification" of its subject. Kerbel's Thälmann was not a person so much as an idol, the embodiment of all that was great not only in the legacy of antifascism, but also in the contemporary GDR.[84] The monument would serve as the culmination of a four-decade-long effort to link Thälmann's legacy with the creation of the German Democratic Republic and its accomplishments. Only a state that possessed such worthy heroes legitimately represented the rejection of Germany's fascist past and could promise its people not only a future, but also a present characterized by socialist humanism, economic prosperity, and living standards comparable to those in the West.

A Traditionskabinett would also serve as a vital component of the complex at Thälmann Park. Located throughout East Germany, these small museums displayed artifacts—or relics—of the socialist past that visitors could view in order better to comprehend the history of the German workers' movement. As sociologist Eviatar Zerubavel has pointed out, such artifacts are vital to the preservation of historical memory. "Despite the fact that they are not tied to a specific location, the actual material presence of such portable *relics* helps provide some physical continuity, which is why they are indeed used almost exclusively, as their etymology suggests, for storing memories. Like . . . other 'transitional objects' . . . relics basically allow us to live in the present while at the same time literally 'cling' to the past."[85] The artifacts in Prenzlauer Berg's Traditionskabinett would evoke Thälmann's efforts and his legacy as embodied in the GDR. The relics—photographs, leaflets, and a variety of other forms of memorabilia—would provide a material connection between the past and present, physical evidence of the link between antifascism and the GDR. Further, because much of the exhibition concentrated on the struggle against fascism in Prenzlauer Berg, the displays would have the effect of linking events that had occurred in the community with the national struggle against fascism under the leadership of Ernst Thälmann. As Erich Honecker put it, the Traditionskabinett would become an "organic component of the Ernst Thälmann Park." According to the SED chairman, the exhibition's functions were to portray the history of the antifascist movement in Prenzlauer Berg; to give concrete examples of the KPD's antifascist heritage; to encourage friendship with the Soviet Union; to promote good feelings among the East German people, the ruling party, and the *Volksarmee*; and, finally, to foster "socialist patriotism" and "proletarian internationalism." The Thälmann myth would be an important component of the message related at this modest museum. For example, the Kabinett would display not only photographs, paintings, and a bust of the fallen Communist leader, but also relics from his life, including a portion of one of the cells in which he was imprisoned.[86] Thus, the Traditionskabinett would provide tactile, material manifestations of the GDR's antifascist heritage and the Ernst Thälmann legend.

After a wreath laying at the Memorial of the Socialists in Berlin's Friedrichsfelde Cemetery earlier in the day, the party leadership dedicated the Ernst Thälmann Monument and the surrounding forty-hectare complex on 15 April 1986. According to East German accounts, as many as 100,000 people, the largest share from the FDJ, attended the dedication ceremony, which began at 3:40 PM. When the crowds arrived, a large white piece of canvas covered the monument; the approaching ceremony would incorporate an actual unveiling of Kerbel's statue—further evidence of the pride with which Honecker viewed the massive bronze. Notables present included not only members of the SED Politburo, the Central Committee, and other important political figures, but also Kerbel and Thälmann's daughter, Irma. Following music performed by an FDJ band, speeches by various dignitaries, and the singing of the East German national anthem, "Resurrected from the Ruins," Erich Honecker stepped to the microphone to deliver the keynote address and officially dedicate Kerbel's bronze monstrosity.[87]

Honecker's speech began with the usual paeans to the accomplishments of the antifascist movement during the course of the 1930s and Ernst Thälmann's crucial contribution to the effort against Adolf Hitler and the forces of reactionary imperialism. Then the speaker sought to contrast East Berlin, the workers' paradise of the 1980s, with the city as it was at the time of the struggle against fascism.

> Don't remember what was here earlier, not the stench, not the horrible working and living conditions of the people, not the almost daily attacks of the police and SA bandits that cost many workers their lives. Today we proletarians [*sic*] are at last the masters of this city, of this city of peace, the capital of the GDR, Berlin. The people were freed from exploitation and oppression, and the police have become a true police of the people, because we have given police uniforms to the workers, construction workers, metal workers, miners—the great multitude of working people, from the ranks of the best, who today perform their duty with the People's Police [Volkspolizei]. The monument for Thälmann . . . bears witness to the fact that with the construction of workers' and peasants' [political] power, a new capital has been constructed.[88]

Building upon the traditions of German antifascism as embodied in Ernst Thälmann, the people of the GDR had accomplished great things. The location on the Greifswalderstraße, which had for so long been associated with bloody violence against the German proletariat, had become a center of the peace and prosperity built by German socialism. Those present could see the evidence of these accomplishments with their own eyes. Here, on the site of a former gasworks, German socialism had constructed a massive complex for the common people. Here was a locale where Germany's workers would live, shop, be educated, and enjoy a massive green space in the center of an industrialized urban environment. Fittingly, at the center of all of this stood a monument to "Germany's eternal son." These accomplishments were the result of the glorious legacy of antifascism, the firm foundation upon which the people had constructed the German Democratic Republic.

The implications were clear: socialism was working in the GDR. The bygone days of the 1950s, when the SED had called upon the East German people to sacrifice in the name of a better future, were long over. The future had arrived. The East German version of Marxism–Leninism had provided the material and economic prosperity that the SED had long promised. This prosperity had been made possible because of the party's determination to stay the course, to realize the dream of those antifascist fighters who had stood up for basic human decency during Germany's darkest hour. Honecker was addressing not only his own people, but also the leaders of other socialist states, the proponents of glasnost and perestroika in the Soviet Union and throughout Eastern Europe, those who had abandoned the traditions of socialism, who had reached the conclusion that Marxism–Leninism could never deliver on its promises—at least without a significant recasting of the meaning of socialism. The GDR's accomplishments—incarnated in the Ernst Thälmann National Monument, the housing complex, the schools, the park, the playgrounds, the newly constructed commuter train station, and the forthcoming planetarium—proved the naysayers wrong. Socialism could work. It was working. Perseverance had shown the superiority of socialism over capitalism. The future promised a brighter tomorrow that would witness an increase in economic prosperity and material well-being. To abandon socialism now would be a serious mistake.

The day following the dedication in Prenzlauer Berg, Mikhail Gorbachev, the CPSU general secretary and architect of perestroika and glasnost, arrived in the East German capital, where he was to participate in the Eleventh SED Party Conference to begin on 17 April. Among the places where Honecker took the Soviet leader during his first day in Berlin, 16 April, was the newly unveiled Thälmann National Monument. On the one hundredth birthday of German socialism's "eternal son," standing in the shadow of Lew Kerbel's fifty-ton bronze, Gorbachev met with members of the FDJ, who represented the future of Marxism–Leninism. The Soviet leader also toured the nearby housing project, evidence of the accomplishments of "real, existing socialism." The East German leader undoubtedly wanted to show the Soviet general secretary that socialism was working in the GDR. The future was bright for East Germany, and there was no need for openness or restructuring in socialist Berlin. The housing construction along Greifswalderstraße, the beautiful park with playgrounds for East Berlin's children, and the soon-to-be opened planetarium were testament to this fact.[89]

Erich Honecker hammered this theme home the next day in his

opening speech of the Eleventh Party Conference. "The goals of the Tenth Party Congress are fulfilled," the East German leader announced. The GDR's housing shortage had been alleviated. The "people's economy" was in good shape, witnessing a dramatic increase in the production of consumer goods. "With the realization of all of our plans, we can uphold the further deepening of our socialist economic integration," Honecker insisted. In spite of the usual rhetoric about "brotherly cooperation with the USSR" becoming "ever stronger," the message was clear: socialism in the GDR was a success; there would be no turning back, no effort at reform. Perestroika and glasnost would never be introduced to the GDR. There was no need for Gorbachev's heretical policies; socialism worked in the GDR.[90]

The SED leadership had once again adapted the Ernst Thälmann myth to the needs of the moment. By 1986, the martyred Communist leader's one hundredth birthday, East Germany was facing a crisis on at least two fronts. The first was the failure of "real, existing socialism" to provide the standard of living promised by the Honecker regime. In response, the party leadership sought to convince the East German people that in spite of the constant shortage of housing and consumer goods, living standards in the GDR were improving. The construction of the housing development around Ernst Thälmann Park served as proof of this alleged material progress. Of course, providing housing for 4,000 people was statistically insignificant in a city in which many thousands more needed a residence. The approximately 1,300 housing units constructed served as nothing more than a symbol of the party's commitment to improve living conditions. In the context of the changes taking place in the Soviet Union and much of the rest of the socialist world, such symbolic gestures, as important as they might have been during the first four decades of the GDR's existence, were viewed by an unreceptive audience. Although the SED had long had to explain away the East German system's economic shortcomings, with the introduction of Gorbachev's reforms in the Soviet Union and much of the rest of Eastern Europe, the situation had changed dramatically. The legend of Ernst Thälmann and his sacrificial death on behalf of socialism would, Honecker and his comrades hoped, once again serve as a symbol to justify the continued existence of a socialist GDR even in the face of abject economic failure.

Indeed, the Thälmann myth came to play such an important role in the 1980s that, as more than one scholar has pointed out, the SED raised its most prominent martyr from the role of prophet to the position of a socialist deity. Nowhere can this phenomenon be seen better than in a series of charcoal drawings produced by the graphic artist Rolf Kuhrt. Unveiled in 1986 to commemorate its subject's centennial, the series of drawings testifies to the parallels between Thälmann's life and the experiences of Christ. Indeed, the last drawing in the series is entitled *Thälmann's Death and Resurrection*. Kuhrt depicts a suffering, dying Thälmann, his arms spread wide like Christ on the cross. As historian Martin Schönfeld has pointed out, in the artist's and the SED regime leaders' view, "Thälmann died—definitely not for the forgiveness of sins—[but] for the birth of a socialist Germany."[91] During the GDR's final years, confronted by a failed economy and calls for fundamental reform from the Soviet Union, Erich Honecker and other leaders utilized Thälmann's sacrificial, Christ-like death once again to justify the continuing socialist experiment in East Germany and trusted that it would work. They would be sorely disappointed.

9

"Imprisoned, Murdered, Besmirched"

Throughout their history, the Germans have repeatedly found themselves trying to come to terms with their past, and the period following the collapse of the SED state was no exception.[1] After all, over more than forty years the GDR and FRG governments had cultivated widely divergent understandings of what it meant to be German. Each state developed its own master narrative designed not only to justify its own social, economic, and political system, but simultaneously to undermine the legitimacy of the rival German state. In the case of East Germany, as we have seen, the ruling SED fostered an elaborate myth of antifascism, in which the leaders of the GDR were either those who had fought the longest and most valiantly against National Socialism or their heirs. In the eyes of East Germany's leaders, this version of the past not only legitimized a separate, socialist, German state by joining it to the glorious traditions of the international Communist movement and the Soviet Union's defeat of the Third Reich in the Second World War but at the same time linked the FRG with the horrific traditions of fascism, antihumanism, capitalist exploitation, war, and genocide engendered by Hitler's Germany. The FRG also sought to justify its existence through a politically charged interpretation of recent German history. Although, like the GDR, the FRG sought legitimacy through distancing itself from the crimes of the Third Reich, its legitimizing myth was very different from that offered by the East. Yet both legitimizing narratives were based on a common historical experience—the crimes committed during the Third Reich in the name of the German people.

In general, public discourse in the FRG, when it dealt with the issue at all, tended to view the Third Reich and its crimes as manifestations of totalitarianism. That is, Nazi Germany was a one-party state based on mass mobilization of the population, an all-encompassing ideology, complete with centrally controlled media, a command economy, and a secret police.[2] With the advent of the cold war, this understanding of Hitler's Germany became increasingly popular in the West because it explicitly linked Nazism and Stalinism, thereby legitimizing the ongoing struggle against the Soviet Union and its East German ally. As early as 1948, in the midst of the Berlin airlift, the city's mayor, Ernst Reuter, made this association explicit when he informed an American audience that the Germans "[o]nce again" confronted "a dictatorship that wants to oppress our people and is trying to break our moral and political will to resist. . . . This time we must stand up for our freedom."[3] Reuter and others sought clearly to link Germanness with the creation of democratic institutions. If one accepted the contention that Stalinism and National Socialism were "different sides of the same coin," then clearly the FRG was the only legitimate German state and the proper focus of German national identity. Although the totalitarian model lost a great deal of support during the course of the 1970s, it reemerged in the late 1980s.[4]

In other words, both the FRG and the GDR sought legitimacy by seeking to distinguish their social and political systems from those of the Third Reich. Given this ideological dichotomy, encouraged by both governments for more than forty years, it is not surprising that westerners and easterners developed very different views regarding what it meant to be German—differing national identities that remained relatively unimportant as long as Germany was divided. Because of the dramatic events of 1989–1991, however, constructing a unified national identity once again became a major concern. Much like 1918 and 1945, the Germans faced a *Stunde Null* (zero hour) when they had to make some major decisions regarding their future. As is always the case in the German context, perceptions of the past would have a dramatic effect on the present and future understanding of what it meant to be German.

The city of Berlin had long been at the heart of conflict between the rival social and political systems. In 1979, for example, SED chairman Erich Honecker publicly stated that the East German capital should "from today forward" serve as "a symbol for the victorious advance of socialism on German soil."[5] Indeed, both sides of the Berlin Wall became centers for politically charged remembrance of recent German history. East Berlin had its Lenin Monument, Luxemburg Platz, and Karl Liebknecht Straße, immortalizing important figures in the history of German socialism, and West Berlin had its Straße der 17. Juni, recalling the 1953 workers' uprising, as well as the Platz der Luftbrücke, honoring those who had died during the famous 1948 airlift.[6] If after 1989 Germany were to be culturally united, if a single national identity could be forged, Berlin would necessarily be the focus of the endeavor.

Many Germans recognized this reality even before unification, and as a result the SED's version of recent historical events came under attack. In the months following the collapse of the Honecker regime, the historical monuments built by the SED in the East German capital became the subject of controversy. In early May 1990, for example, the East German artist Joachim Scheel published an article in the West Berlin daily *Tagesspiegel* (Daily Mirror) in which he attacked the "monumental propaganda" produced by the defunct regime as "symbols of [the] authoritarian ideology" that had dominated the East German people for too long. This "nonart" *(Unkunst)* should be destroyed, he argued, and the materials used to create real art. Scheel was particularly contemptuous of two of the most massive monuments in the eastern half of the city, those commemorating Soviet leader Nikolai Lenin and the German Communist leader Ernst Thälmann.[7] With his attack on the Ernst Thälmann Monument, Scheel set in motion a five-year controversy that said much about the differences between easterners and westerners concerning the question of national identity.

When Scheel assailed the artistic merit of Kerbel's socialist-realist colossus, he also challenged the legitimacy of the collapsing GDR, not to mention the separate East German national identity cultivated for more than forty years. He also maligned one of the Left's most beloved historical figures. But many Germans who had little sympathy for the Honecker regime believed that the memory of Thälmann deserved to be celebrated because of his impeccable antifascist credentials, and Kerbel's bronze adequately performed this task.

It soon became clear that Scheel's disdain for much of East German public art, including the Thälmann Monument, was not universal. In response to demands simply to destroy East Berlin's monuments and memorials, art history students from the city's universities, both East and West, formed the Initiative for Political Monuments of the GDR. The group, although calling for a careful study of political shrines in *both* parts of the city, concentrated its efforts on an analysis of GDR monuments. In collaboration with the Active Museum of Fascism and Resistance—a group that had played an important role in creating West Berlin's Topography of Terror exhibit during the 1980s—the Initiative opened an exhibit entitled Erhalten, Zerstören, Verändern?—Politische Denkmäler der DDR in Ost-Berlin (Conserve, Destroy, Alter?—Political Monuments of the GDR in East Berlin) in August 1990. The exhibit concentrated on the four most controversial monuments in East Berlin: the nineteen-meter-tall Lenin Monument in Friedrichshain, the Marx–Engels Memorial in the city's center, the monument to the antifascist resistance (Kampfgruppen-Denkmal) in Prenzlauer Berg's Volkspark, and the Thälmann National Monument. As its title suggested, the exhibit presented three possible approaches to GDR monuments. One conceivable alternative was simply to leave the monuments as they were, using them as reminders of the now defunct SED state. A second option was to remove them as instruments of a now discredited totalitarian regime. A third possibility was to maintain these stone and bronze artifacts of the former government, but to provide commentary at the sites, usually in the form of billboards explaining the location's political history. Thus, the monuments could be used for political education, an important consideration in the German context.[8]

The exhibit encouraged open discussion concerning the fate of sites important to the GDR's interpretation of history: What should be done with the East German capital's approximately six hundred historical monuments? Which of them should be preserved and under what circumstances? Should placards be added to make them more valuable for political education? What should be done at the sites of any memorials that were removed? The question most often raised, however, got to the root of the problem: Were the monuments "art or simply monumental scrap metal"? The exhibit led to a lively discussion. Dr. Irina Rusta, an adviser on cultural matters for the Berlin city government, insisted that the monuments "had nothing to do with art" because they were too "burdened by ideology." In contrast, others made the fundamental point that "[p]oliticians may not define what art is."[9] After all, the governing party's monopoly over artistic matters was one of the previous regime's drawbacks. At a 7 August 1990 meeting sponsored by the Initiative for Political Monuments, those who lived near Kerbel's bronze monument had the opportunity to voice their opinions. One woman wanted to see the monument removed, maintaining that "[o]ur Thälmann Monument is simply too massive [großklotzig] and monumental." The majority of those present, however, disagreed with her. One eighty-year-old resident contended that "Thälmann was an important antifascist resistance fighter. We shouldn't simply throw him away just because the SED used him to pull its wagon." Manfred Butzmann, an artist from East Berlin, offered a compromise solution. Hoping to make the site in Prenzlauer Berg more visually appealing by "greening" it, he wanted to plant ivy around the monument.[10] The idea was to hide the socialist-realist colossus from sight by encircling it in foliage but also allow commemoration of Thälmann to continue at the location. It was, however, highly unlikely that the city government would be willing to designate the financial resources needed to complete this project, especially when funds were in short supply.

Even as some Berliners engaged in a lively discussion concerning the fate of the Thälmann Monument, others were putting their convictions into action. On the night of 2 June 1990, two teenagers were arrested after vandalizing the bronze bust. The police apprehended them, but no charges were filed.[11] Although those who had overthrown the SED regime emphasized nonviolence and respect for public property, and no statues of prominent socialist figures were toppled, spray painting graffiti on statues throughout the GDR became common, and the Thälmann Monument was no exception. Perhaps the most interesting graffiti on the monument asked, "Don't you have it in a larger size?" an astute, if sardonic, comment concerning the mammoth fifty-ton bronze.[12] Later in June, hoping to distance the monument from the SED regime, Prenzlauer Berg officials removed a pair of two-meter-high stone tablets engraved with quotations from Thälmann and Honecker.[13] At a 5 September meeting, the district government made the decision not to demolish Kerbel's statue. The monument, local authorities maintained, could play an important role in efforts to educate the population about Germany's past, both the antifascist traditions of the German Left and the GDR's efforts to co-opt this legacy. This education was, authorities maintained, "necessary for the development of a democratic community." A second and more practical reason was that Prenzlauer Berg officials were simply unwilling to take on the expense of removing the monument, which could run to hundreds of thousands of marks. Building upon their earlier decision to remove the two stone stelae, the district approved a Green Party plan to make the site more appealing by "greening" it, planting bushes, trees, and flowers in the vast open space at the site. On 15 September, the Greens carried out their project, only to see their efforts destroyed by persons unknown within a few days. Finally, local authorities also called for an "open competition" of proposals concerning the locale's future.[14]

Regardless of whether any of these plans for the Thälmann site and other monuments came to fruition or not, the discussion promoted by

the Conserve, Destroy, Alter? exhibit played a role in creating a democratic identity. The days between the collapse of the regime and unification were characterized by a heady idealism, during which the East
German people faced the prospect of molding a new society free of the
burdens of "real, existing socialism." Untold numbers of people were
politically active, and an impressive 93 percent of eligible voters cast
ballots in the March 1990 national elections, the only free contest in East
German history.[15] Although some East Germans, especially within the
intelligentsia, maintained a degree of loyalty to the ideals of the defunct
system and hoped to create a "third way" between Soviet-style socialism and Western capitalism, almost everyone supported a dramatic
political liberalization.[16] The people of the GDR were developing a new
national identity based on a civil culture rooted in democratic institutions. Grassroots movements had toppled the previous regime, and local groups such as the Initiative for Political Monuments played a vital
role in the democratization process.[17] The Prenzlauer Berg District government had reached its decisions in an open forum, after careful con-
sultation with its constituents, a classic example of democracy on the
local level. As the debate concerning the Thälmann Monument shows,
East Berliners believed that they could effect change, an important precondition for the development of liberal institutions. They expressed
their opinions openly, and they believed that their views mattered.

The issues debated in the weeks preceding unification had dramatic implications for the East German people. The fundamental question
raised in the early stages of the struggle surrounding the Thälmann
Monument concerned the role of the recent past in East Germany's
future. The "children of the GDR" had to decide what part their East
German identity would play in their future. Should Communist heroes
such as Thälmann be remembered for their struggles against the evils
of fascism or rejected outright because of their role in legitimizing the
defunct system? Although most East Germans wanted to maintain the
generous social programs guaranteed by the SED, they still faced the
question of whether they should preserve their historical identity, nurtured for more than forty years. The ultimate question was whether
those who came of age in the GDR should retain a separate identity
based on their historical experience or simply adopt a broader German
worldview, which in this context meant a Western outlook. But before
the people of the GDR had the opportunity to answer these questions,
unification changed the circumstances under which these decisions
would be made. After the 3 October union of the GDR and the FRG, the

people of the "new states" would not be the only ones making these determinations, and many westerners would also seek to play a role in the process. A new chapter had also begun in the discussions concerning the fate of the GDR's political monuments. Although, with reunification, East Berlin's monuments were defended by the FRG's strict laws regarding historical preservation, the sites were not sacrosanct, and these protections could be lifted. To the chagrin of many easterners, westerners would henceforth play a significant role in the decision-making process.[18]

These new circumstances became abundantly clear in October 1991, when Berlin's senator for municipal development and environmental protection, Volker Hassemer, announced his determination to demolish Friedrichshain's Lenin Monument. Groups such as Initiative for Political Monuments and Active Museum, who favored the preservation of the site for historical purposes, immediately attacked the decision. The nineteen-meter-tall stone statue, designed by the Soviet artist Nikolai Tomsky, had stood in Friedrichshain since 1970, they pointed out, and had become part of a familiar landscape. Hassemer, a member of the conservative Christian Democratic Union (CDU), insisted that Lenin was hardly a figure who should be commemorated in a liberal democracy. In a classic elucidation of the totalitarian model, Hassemer pointed out that the Soviet leader had overthrown Russia's first democratically elected body, established the Soviet secret police, built concentration camps, violently crushed the 1921 Kronstadt rebellion, and betrayed the working classes whom he claimed to represent. "This Lenin," Hassemer contended, "represents not only the idea of socialism, but also the reality of totalitarianism." The monument was a "component of the propaganda for a state that ended through a popular revolution." Throughout Eastern Europe, including Lenin's Russian homeland, statues of the Soviet leader had been razed—so why not in Germany as well?[19] Berlin's mayor, Eberhard Diepgen, agreed, referring to the former Soviet leader as a "despot and murderer."[20]

Many easterners and Western historic preservationists, however, were not convinced, insisting that their concerns grew out of an interest in preserving East German history and had nothing to do with Lenin. As one opponent of the demolition put it, "For me it's not about Lenin, but rather about demonstrating our power and not letting ourselves be pushed around." Foes of the demolition circulated petitions, organized a letter-writing campaign, and staged demonstrations. Some even went so far as to shroud the granite statue with a large banner reading "No

Violence!" In spite of this resistance, the Friedrichshain District Assembly passed a motion supporting the removal of Tomsky's colossus. The relatively narrow margin, forty to thirty-three, indicated the divisiveness of the issue. One legislator, Dieter Hildebrandt, a member of the Party for Democratic Socialism (PDS)—the successor organization to the SED—made his feelings abundantly clear. "Leave us a part of our own history," he demanded, "and don't level everything."[21] Opponents of the removal did not give up, even after the district government's decision. Massive protests marked the beginning of the demolition, which cost half a million marks and lasted twenty-five days.[22] In the meantime, the removal of Prenzlauer Berg's "Fighting Group" Monument engendered little protest. In this case, however, the district government alone had made the decision to remove the bronze statue.[23]

Trying to avoid future controversies like that surrounding the Lenin Monument, the Berlin city government sought to depoliticize the decision-making process concerning the former East Berlin's political shrines and allay fears that the new government sought simply to sweep aside the GDR's history. On 10 March 1992, the city's Senate created the Commission for the Fate of the Political Monuments of the GDR in the Former East Berlin. The special position that Berlin held in the GDR's efforts at legitimation, coupled with its role as the new German capital, made it necessary to deal with the hundreds of "sculptures, statues, busts, memorials, stelae, monuments, [and] commemorative tablets" scattered throughout the eastern half of the city. The commission would consist of a committee of ten experts, six from the former East Berlin. Its members included artists, writers, architects, historians, and a museum director. There were only two politicians on the panel, both of whom were also experts on art, one from each half of the city. Over the following six months, they would make recommendations concerning the disposition of more than two hundred objects. The ten members should not "reduce" their decisions to the purely "aesthetic–artistic aspects" of the works, but also take their "historical" and "scholarly" value into consideration. The Senate ordered the commission to go even further than the law mandated, charging it to take into account the opinions of the local population, which often came to view neighborhood memorials and monuments as part of the urban landscape. The committee should write a report, complete with photographs, in which it suggested whether each item should be "maintained, altered, completed, removed, commented upon, [or] moved to a museum." The ten experts ultimately only had the power to make recommendations, and final decisions would be made by local authorities, such as district parliaments. In addition, the Senate also rejected the CDU's politically controversial proposal to display some of the works in an exhibit of "totalitarian art."[24] Both the composition of the panel and the Senate's instructions made it clear that the commission's inclination favored preservation overall. Prenzlauer Berg's Thälmann Monument was among the most important objects to come under the commission's purview.

Those Berliners with an interest in the ultimate fate of the Thälmann Monument did not wait on the commission's recommendation, however, and the site remained a subject of public interest. On May Day 1992, for example, the neo-Nazi Free German Workers' Party staged a demonstration at the site on Greifswalderstraße. The demonstration succeeded in inciting the monument's supporters, and counterdemonstrators chanting "Nazis raus!" ("Nazis get out!") greeted the skinheads. Violent clashes resulted, and rocks and bottles were thrown. In the end, only one young man, a counterdemonstrator, was arrested and ultimately given a nine-month suspended sentence.[25] On 7 May, the Prenzlauer Berg District Assembly passed a resolution maintaining that "[t]he [Thälmann] Monument should not remain in its current form." Calling upon Berlin's senator for culture to put the process in motion, the Assembly repeated an earlier demand for an open competition in which artists could submit their proposals for changes to the site. Finally, the resolution concluded, "The district office will install a panel at the site containing information about the decision-making process." Local officials hoped for a "hasty resolution" to the entire endeavor.[26] With no end to the controversy in sight and the Monuments Commission's report long overdue, in January 1993 the Prenzlauer Berg Assembly took up the subject of the Thälmann Monument again. Acting upon a resolution introduced by the SPD, it decided to make the area more suitable by planting foliage, the goal being to make Thälmann Park more useful to the neighborhood. The assembly had no idea where it would get the money needed for the improvements, however, and significant changes simply could not be made.[27] Further, whatever alterations were carried out might be affected by the recommendation of the Monuments Commission.

The debate regarding the fate of the Thälmann Monument gained new momentum when the Monuments Commission finally issued its report on 15 February 1993. Concerning the Greifswalderstraße site, the commission's recommendations were brief and to the point. It maintained that Kerbel's work "was monumental Leninist propaganda." The SED had co-opted the memory of the KPD leader, and the monument, which reflected its subject "uncritical[ly]" as a "symbolic figure," had nothing to do with the historical Thälmann and was therefore not an appropriate memorial to his legacy. "By a large majority the commission recommends: The Monument is to be removed." Its ultimate fate should be "[d]emolition and modification of the location," which might involve the creation of a "park with sculptures and the inclusion of artists" whose works could not be "exhibited in the park during the time of the GDR," making the proposed artistic competition redundant. Finally, attempting to placate some of the monument's supporters, the report concluded that "the abandonment of this object must not mean a similar abandonment of remembrance of Thälmann."[28]

There was an immediate response to the commission's proposals regarding the Thälmann Monument. The Christian Democrats and the Free Democrats applauded the recommendation. Hoping to use the socialist-realist behemoth in anti-Communist political education, they had long supported its removal and hoped to see it transported to a monument park similar to those outside Budapest and other Eastern European cities. The Social Democrats, although supporting the Monuments Commission's recommendation, did not back the Christian Democrats' efforts to instrumentalize the fifty-ton bronze politically. Rather, the SPD emphasized the importance of converting Thälmann Park into a green space that would be more useful to the neighborhood.[29] The Initiative for Political Monuments, contending that "the monuments are not only witnesses to the history of the city, but also document worldwide historical developments," continued to oppose the removal of any monument or memorial from the former East Berlin.[30] Allied with the Greens and the PDS, the Initiative sought to maintain the Thälmann Monument, albeit in an altered form. Any changes, they suggested, should have two goals. First, the modifications should make the massive bronze less of an eyesore. Insisting that the Christian Democrats' proposal would remove the bronze from its historical context, the three groups further maintained that any alterations should make the monument more useful to the study of the GDR's history. Taking up the suggestion made by the Prenzlauer Berg District government, all three groups wanted to have a competition, open to all artists and architects, for the best design for the future of the monument. And last, the KPD and the DKP, now only small groups consisting of unreconstructed Stalinists, demanded that the monument remain unaltered.[31]

The situation became even more complicated four days after the Monuments Commission issued its report. On 19 February, Joseph Kurz, who possessed a collection of eight monumental statues from Czechoslovakia and the GDR, offered to remove the monument on Greifswalderstraße for free, providing he could take it to his museum in the city of Gundelfingen in Baden-Wurtemberg. Kurz's exhibit boasted a triple monument commemorating martyred SPD leader Rudolf Breitscheid, Lenin, and Thälmann, which he had removed earlier from the city of Dresden. The private monument park also already had images of Joseph Stalin and Hungarian politician Klement Gottwald, and Kurz eagerly anticipated the delivery of ten statues from Lithuania and Poland. The addition of Kerbel's work would enhance his budding enterprise dramatically. Kurz insisted that his proposal was the best solution for nearly everyone, both those who wanted to remove the monument and the groups who wanted it preserved. The scheme had the added advantage of being efficient. Because he would pay for the removal of the monument, the City of Berlin would save at least half a million marks, and the removal of the fifty-ton bronze would take only a couple of days. Welders would simply cut it into sections with a blowtorch and haul the pieces off to Gundelfingen, where the statue would be reassembled. When asked about his motivations, Kurz insisted that he had "no ideological axe to grind" and that he "simply did not want to see the monuments destroyed." In short, he sought to give the Thälmann Monument "asylum."[32]

The Christian Democrats agreed that Kurz had devised the ideal solution to the controversy. The socialist-realist colossus would be removed—at no cost to the city of Berlin—but not destroyed. Much to their chagrin, however, Kurz's suggestion did not bring an end to the controversy, and numerous objections arose. Some simply objected to the idea of giving away fifty tons of bronze and demanded that Kurz pay for the monument.[33] In addition, the plan did not, as Kurz and the CDU had hoped, placate the groups—such as the Greens, the Initiative for Political Monuments, and the PDS—who wished to see the monument preserved. They maintained that relocating the piece to southwestern Germany would take it completely out of its historical context, rendering it useless in any effort to understand the experience of those who lived in the GDR. The PDS, although conceding that the East German regime had misappropriated the martyred KPD leader's memory and that the "monumental statue does an injustice to Thälmann's reputation," insisted that the monument must be left where it was. Although some wanted to see the Communist martyr erased from

German history, the party demanded "justice for Ernst Thälmann." In spite of what conservatives thought, Thälmann was undeniably an important historical figure. He had ardently opposed the Nazis, and, as a result, they had murdered him. Therefore, the PDS held, the monument "must stay in its place until a better, more artistic and politically correct form of assessment is possible." In the meantime, the party hoped that the site could be made more visually palatable.[34] The objections made by the tiny DKP and KPD went even further. "Ernst Thälmann is a symbol of the resistance against fascism," one of their flyers began, and had died in the fight against Nazism. "Anti-Communists," engaged in "demagoguery," dominated the "discussion concerning the form of the monument" commemorating the KPD leader. These non-Communists sought ultimately to obliterate his memory, so "[t]he Thälmann Monument must remain exactly as it is today, where fascism is being revived." The flyer concluded with an invitation to a demonstration to be held at the monument on 16 April 1993, Thälmann's 107th birthday. Its goal was to "protest . . . against the destruction of our history."[35] The PDS would also participate in the demonstration.[36]

One of the members of the Monuments Commission, Barbara Teuber, publically responded to the pro-preservation organizations. The goals of the commission and the protestors were not all that different, she contended. Her distaste for the mammoth bronze was not politically grounded. She simply found the "unaesthetic, propagandistic monument" unappealing and had no objection to commemorating Thälmann's sacrifice, but she recommended that a new, more tasteful memorial be constructed on the same site. Teuber's suggestion was doomed from the outset, however. District officials did not even have the half-million marks needed to remove the monument, much less to build another one, however modestly designed.[37]

Hoping that the city government would ultimately foot the bill, the Prenzlauer Berg District Assembly voted in mid-May to follow the Monuments Commission's recommendation. Once again, the relatively narrow margin of the vote, twenty-two to sixteen, in favor of demolishing Kerbel's behemoth reflected the contentiousness of the issue. Prenzlauer Berg officials still had no idea who would pay for the demolition, and the monument's supporters took comfort in this fact. In response to the Assembly's vote, Eberhard Elfert of the Active Museum of Fascism and Resistance reiterated his group's position. It would be far better, not to mention less expensive, to keep the monument, "examine [it] critically," and modify it artistically.[38]

Refusing to give up on its plan, the Active Museum, along with the Initiative for Political Monuments and two artists' organizations, sponsored a 4–5 June symposium at the Culture House in Thälmann Park.[39] The symposium would permit artists to share their proposals concerning the aesthetic and political modification of the site. They hoped, Elfert pointed out, that this symposium would lead to an official competition sponsored by the district or city government and the ultimate preservation of this "historical document of the GDR."[40] The gathering witnessed the introduction of some interesting ideas. One proposal would have built a "viewing stand" to permit people "to look deep[ly] into Thälmann's eyes." Ruth Baumeister wanted to put the fifty-ton colossus on a rotating platform, but Fritz Heisterkamp favored the demolition of the monument, seeking to replace it with an "airship" bearing the martyred Communist leader's name. The most popular proposal, however, came from Manfred Butzmann, who in 1990 had suggested planting ivy at the site. By 1993, however, his idea had evolved dramatically.[41] Building upon his vision of "greening" the site, Butzmann now proposed encircling it with trees. Further, the Berlin artist wanted to surround the memorial with water, placing it on what amounted to a small island, leaving it as "a place to reflect and ponder, surrounded by trees and a quiet pool."[42] This configuration would not only hide the socialist-realist colossus from sight by cloaking it in foliage, but also create the impression of an imprisoned Thälmann, thereby emphasizing that the monument would now commemorate his incarceration and murder at the hands of the Nazis rather than his place in GDR political propaganda. Although Butzmann's proposal did have much appeal, it was highly unlikely that either the city or district government would be willing to assign the financial resources needed to bring this or any of the other suggestions to completion, and all of the proposals were stillborn in spite of the publicity they received at an exhibit housed in the Prenzlauer Berg Museum.[43]

The site in Thälmann Park ultimately remained largely unchanged. Kurz's death ended the possibility of the monument being moved to Baden-Wurtemberg, and neither the district nor the city could pay to remove it. Other concerns, such as the economic dislocation caused by German unification, would place the fate of the Thälmann Monument and other East German sites far in the background. In April 1995, the district mayor of Prenzlauer Berg, Manfred Dennert, announced that the fifty-ton bust would remain where it was for the foreseeable future.[44] The only alteration made was to stencil three words onto its

base: "Imprisoned, Murdered, Besmirched." Thälmann had been "imprisoned" and "murdered" by the Nazis and "besmirched" by the SED
dictatorship. This brief comment, it was hoped, would place the massive statue in its proper historical context.[45]

Before unification, the debate concerning Berlin's Ernst Thälmann
Monument could be viewed as an early exercise in democracy at the
grassroots level. Discussion about the monuments of Berlin was carried out in the context of an emerging liberal ethos. The argument
took place almost exclusively among East Germans, and the few westerners involved, such as those who belonged to the Active Museum,
were interested in preservation and were willing to concede that the
monument's fate ultimately lay in the local population's hands. Under
these circumstances, the debate took place in an optimistic environment growing out of the popular overthrow of the SED dictatorship.
As Wolfgang K., a trade union official in the East put it, "It was sort of
a liberating moment. The pressure was gone all of a sudden. When you
have been scared to speak up for such a long time, it just feels incredible to be able to say what you think."[46] The people of the GDR were
determining their own fortunes for the first time in decades and molding a new national identity, one characterized by a democratic political
consciousness.

Following the October 1990 unification, however, the tenor of the
discussion changed dramatically. Henceforward, westerners—some
determined to eliminate every last vestige of the defunct SED state—
would play a central role in determining the fate of the former East
Germany. This encroachment, coupled with the economic dislocation
engendered by the unification process, fostered a great deal of resent-
ment, not to mention cynicism.[47] To add insult to injury, westerners
who had never lived under the SED dictatorship saw fit to explain life
in the GDR to those who had personally experienced "real, existing
socialism." Many easterners, therefore, resented it when the central city
government determined the fate of East Berlin's Lenin Memorial, making them determined to defend the city's Ernst Thälmann Monument,
one of the GDR's most important symbols. Many easterners found
themselves disillusioned in the face of "real, existing democracy." Wolfgang K. characterized this change in attitude: "I think we need to look
out for ourselves. In fact, we should have done that all along. You see,
in the opinion of West Germans pretty much everything we've done,
everything we've had here, was somehow wrong, or at least deficient.
In their eyes we are basically all failures, whether it was our fault or

not. I don't think that's correct, and I certainly don't think it's fair. I am not going to let them steal my whole past, and I don't want to be a second-class citizen for the rest of my life."[48] The brief honeymoon characterizing the weeks leading up to reunion came to an end, and the resulting reemergence of a distinct East German identity should come as no surprise. After all, for more than forty years the governments of both Germanys had cultivated identities emphasizing the distinctions between the two systems. Couple this strong identification with all the problems manifested by reunification, and it should have been expected that East Germans have once again emphasized their distinctiveness, their unique outlook, based on common experiences shared for more than four decades. These intra-German differences have manifested themselves in a widespread nostalgia for the GDR, emphasizing the things easterners perceive as having been the regime's positive accomplishments—hence, the reemergence of an appetite for notoriously inferior East German consumer goods.[49] Overcoming this "wall in the head" will probably take much longer than rebuilding the German economy, and disagreements between "Wessis" and "Ossis" will remain a challenge for the new Germany in the foreseeable future. The dispute concerning Prenzlauer Berg's Thälmann Monument can best be understood within this context. The honoring of Thälmann, who had given his life in the struggle against National Socialism, was in the eyes of many from the East one of these "good" things about the GDR and should continue. Although few would defend Kerbel's metal monstrosity on artistic grounds, many former East Germans, which apparently included most who lived in the shadow of the monument, wanted to maintain it not only as a relic of a flawed but not entirely evil regime, but also as a commemorative site honoring a true German hero. Indeed, even today, well more than two hundred locales—among them streets, schools, memorials, and town squares—in the former GDR continue to bear the name of the martyred Communist leader.

There is, however, cause for hope. The discussion surrounding the fate of the Ernst Thälmann Monument was not carried out entirely along East–West lines. There were a handful of westerners—within the Initiative for Political Monuments, the Active Museum, and the Berlin SPD, for example—who sought to cooperate with the people of the former East Berlin and were sympathetic to the effort to preserve some of the GDR's history. These westerners, unlike the leaders of the CDU and the Free Democratic Party, recognized that it was unreasonable to expect the people of the former GDR to reject the legacy of their past suddenly and completely. The Western preservationists recognized that only cooperation between the "Wessis" and "Ossis" could heal the wounds created by ideological divisions nurtured for more than forty years. Cooperation such as that between easterners and westerners seeking to preserve Berlin's Ernst Thälmann Monument, when applied to other areas of German life, could go a long way to uniting the German people.

The fifty-ton bronze representation of the martyred KPD chief still stands along Berlin's Greifswalderstraße, just a few hundred meters from an S-Bahn station. It has been altered only slightly since Erich Honecker unveiled it to much fanfare in 1986, and the years of unification have done little to assimilate the statue into the political life of the united Germany. Few people visit the site today, which has neither been preserved as an historic relic of the GDR nor effectively altered to make it useful in political education. Indeed, as the chief of the Prenzlauer Berg Museum, Bert Roder, put it, the monument in its current state "has no theme."[50] Perhaps this makes it an appropriate metaphor for an understanding of recent German history. In the end, it is up to the Germans themselves to provide a proper "theme" for twentieth-century German history and thereby to help to create a common identity and a better future for themselves, a process for which all will need a great deal of patience.

Conclusion

The debate concerning the fate of the Ernst Thälmann National Monument was the product of an ideological struggle lasting more than seven decades. In the aftermath of the Great War, a conflict characterized by unprecedented destruction, many Europeans came to view the Soviet model as the last best hope for humanity. These supporters of the Bolshevik experiment earnestly believed that Lenin's Russia embodied the sole possibility of avoiding a similar catastrophe. In Germany, the far Left formed the German Communist Party. During the first years of the KPD's existence, party leaders sought to maintain a degree of independence from Moscow, whereas the enemies of German communism sought to depict the movement as a willing tool of the Soviet Union. Although the amount of influence that the Comintern held over its German subordinate during the first years of the KPD's existence was limited, there can be no question but that from 1925 Ernst Thälmann oversaw the Stalinization of the KPD, and his critics could legitimately accuse him of being the Soviet dictator's lackey. Stalin's decision to intervene on the KPD chief's behalf during the Wittorf Scandal of 1928 made abundantly clear that Thälmann had become vital to the Soviet dictator's German policy. As a result, Thälmann became even more beholden to Stalin, and the KPD emerged as an even more compliant confederate of Moscow.[1]

Here one can see the origins of perhaps the greatest disadvantage facing German communism, not to mention efforts to propagate the Ernst Thälmann myth—they both were ultimately manifestations of a foreign ideology. Although at times German Communists sought to distance themselves from Moscow in order to appeal to a wider constituency, as in the Free Thälmann campaign of the 1930s, any outside observer was aware of who was really pulling the strings. Both the KPD and SED relied on their affiliation with the Soviet Union to legitimize their efforts, and this reliance dramatically affected the Ernst Thälmann myth. In 1925, when the Hamburg dock worker made his first bid for the German presidency, KPD propagandists emphasized that Thälmann sought to introduce Soviet-style socialism to Germany.

The 1932 presidential campaign, if anything, made this goal even clearer. Although the KPD could appeal to workers suffering because of an economic downturn or to leftist intellectuals, it had nothing to offer Germans who were at all nationalistic, dooming the movement to permanent minority status. There were only two ways that the KPD could come to power—either through a violent revolution that would impose Soviet-style socialism on an overwhelmingly unsympathetic population or as the result of a Soviet-led invasion of Germany. The Communists ultimately assumed power in part of Germany as a result of the latter development, of course.

This outcome ensured that from its inception the German socialist state was artificial, a system imposed by a foreign power. As a result, German socialism lacked legitimacy from the outset.[2] Although East German political propaganda sought consistently to depict the GDR's subservient relationship to the Soviet Union in a positive light, socialist Germany's political religion made it abundantly clear who was in charge. One of the central tenets of the Thälmann myth was the emphasis placed on the close relationship between the martyred KPD chief and the birthplace of socialism, to link the modest worker from Hamburg to the legacy of Lenin and Stalin. Perhaps recognizing the shortfalls of this approach, the post–Second World War Socialist Unity Party simultaneously emphasized the image of Ernst Thälmann as "Germany's eternal son," representative of a specifically German path pursued in opposition to National Socialism. The Germanness of the SED's greatest hero could never be embraced completely, and Thälmann's links to the Soviet Union were ultimately more vital to the legitimacy of the GDR than were his roots in Hamburg. Under such constraints, Thälmann could never become the prophet of a uniquely German path to socialism. As long as the SED state existed, it was clearly beholden to a foreign power.

Over the course of more than forty years, the people of the SBZ and later the GDR were fed a steady diet of propaganda emphasizing that good German socialists, inspired by the accomplishments of the Soviet Union, had stood up valiantly against the fascist menace, many of them giving their lives in the struggle. Ernst Thälmann, fallen leader of the KPD, came to represent all of these antifascist heroes, celebrated in an omnipresent state religion, complete with rituals, sacred texts, and an elaborate mythology. This state religion, however, had much in common with theistic religion. Like other, more established belief systems, the GDR's mythology embraced such phenomena as memorial services, oaths, rituals, and the consecration of monuments to important figures in the socialist movement's history. East Germany's Ernst Thälmann myth also developed a notion of orthodoxy, a belief system canonizing the dogmas of an official political faith. As a result, the fundamental dogmas of the Thälmann legend—the Hamburg native's roots in the German proletariat, his admiration for the Soviet Union, his staunch opposition to fascism—remained unchanged. Although the major tenets of the Thälmann legend, like those of theistic religions, could be adapted to conditions as they arose—the establishment of the FRG, the cold war, and material conditions in the GDR, for example—important elements of the official creed simply could not be abandoned. Indeed, in some instances East German propagandists falsified their accounts of Thälmann's life in order to render a narrative consistent with their mythology. Party leaders were hamstrung by a legitimizing narrative that could not be altered in any significant way. As a result, although linking the GDR to the accomplishments of Ernst Thälmann and other antifascists had undeniable advantages, such an effort also had its shortcomings. Over time, in spite of the SED propaganda state's best efforts, a legitimacy narrative derived from historical events lost its resonance. Erich Honecker's decision to emphasize the material accomplishments of "real, existing socialism" in East German propaganda serves as proof that even so staunch an advocate of the official ideology recognized this fact. From the early 1970s, Honecker and his comrades in the party leadership began increasingly to trumpet the accomplishments of socialism in the present. This is not to suggest that under Honecker the SED abandoned the Ernst Thälmann myth. Indeed, Honecker eagerly embraced the legend, adapting it to the situation the ruling party faced. Thälmann became, in the official SED narrative, more than just a harbinger of a glorious socialist future, but also the prophet of the "real, existing socialism" characteristic of the Honecker years. When in the mid-1980s calls urging reform came from the SED's allies in Moscow, German party leaders opposed them, believing that glasnost and perestroika endangered the GDR's antifascism myth and hence the legitimacy of German communism. Honecker and his associates clung to their traditional legitimizing narrative. As a result, the GDR leadership sought to use the image of the fallen Communist leader from Hamburg to link the past, present, and future in a teleological narrative. Thälmann remained a symbol of German socialism's glorious antifascist past and even brighter future, but party leaders also began to link his legacy to the GDR's economic and social conditions. This effort failed, of course. The system that Honecker and his comrades championed had proven moribund, and no effort to re-build traditional mythology—however seriously undertaken—could save the GDR.

Indeed, the pervasiveness of propaganda in East Germany was evidence of a failed system. Political movements that deliver on their promises—who actually improve the lives of their people—have less need constantly to remind citizens that all is going well. Although all states are built on legitimizing narratives, myths that justify the political and economic status quo, not all political movements seek to maintain a monopoly on the flow of information, to create a propaganda state like East Germany's. Only failed systems will launch such an extensive effort to convince their people that the situation is dramatically differ-ent from what it actually is. When the GDR's founders relied on the So-viet Union, the original modern propaganda state, as their paradigm, they not only assured themselves political ascendance in the short term but ironically also set themselves up for failure in the long run.

Here one sees possibly the greatest disadvantage confronting po-litical religions. Unlike theistic faiths, which assure a paradise in the next life, political mythologies must ultimately deliver on their prom-ises on this side of the grave. In the eyes of the East German people, the material abundance promised by socialism appeared to be ever more distant. The existence of the FRG, where economic growth far outpaced that of the GDR, only exacerbated matters. In short, by the 1980s, So-viet-style socialism had little to offer the citizens of East Germany. The people of the GDR found it increasingly difficult to embrace the legacy of Ernst Thälmann and other long-dead antifascists, nor could they look forward to the life of material abundance that the party leadership promised. In short, the East German people lived under a system based on an ideology that had consistently failed to deliver on its promises. To make matters worse, the major institutions of East German society were imposed by a foreign power, the Soviet Union.[3] Given the oppor-tunity to do so, the people of the GDR abandoned this system, which had dominated their lives for more than four decades, with remarkable alacrity.

As a result, one can only conclude that the political propaganda of German communism, which relied so heavily on the antifascism myth and the Thälmann legend, was ultimately a failure. Four decades of indoctrination did not bestow upon the people of the GDR what the party leadership would consider a proper socialist consciousness. In spite of millions of marks spent on a massive propaganda apparatus, socialist values had not been successfully instilled in the East German people. The evidence does establish, however, that the Thälmann myth was on the individual level a very limited success. Children did learn the songs composed about the fallen Communist leader and were able to mouth the platitudes that the party taught them at school or during FDJ activities. East German film audiences apparently did absorb the appropriate lessons from Kurt Maetzig's two Thälmann epics. Indeed, the willingness of so many former East Germans publically to defend Lew Kerbel's massive fifty-ton monstrosity in Prenzlauer Berg in the years following reunification is evidence that at least some citizens of the GDR had grown to respect German communism's most prominent martyr. It is worth noting, however, that when "children of the GDR" sought to preserve the monument in Berlin's Thälmann Pioneer Park, no one justified his or her position by appealing to the former KPD chief's close ties with the Soviet Union. Rather, defenders of the Kerbel statute emphasized Thälmann's role as a German antifascist, someone who should be remembered because he gave his life in the struggle against the greatest evil of the twentieth century. One need not have been subjected to decades of political propaganda to adopt this position.

These conclusions can only be tentative, however. It is extremely difficult to evaluate the effectiveness of political propaganda. Scholars have been debating, for example, the effectiveness of National Socialist propaganda for decades. As we have seen in the case of the Thälmann myth, people can seemingly mouth the major tenets of a political faith one minute and abandon that belief system the next. As can be seen in the case of the GDR, publically voiced popular opinion can change quite dramatically very quickly. Indeed, the idea of public opinion in the context of a propaganda state—in which the ruling party has a monopoly on the media—is problematic at best. As a result, given the current state of research, the only thing that can be said with certainty regarding East German efforts to mold the population into good Marxists–Leninists is that, in light of the fact that the GDR no longer exists, KPD and SED propaganda failed in the long term. Whether Germany's socialist experiment miscarried because of the shortcomings of Communist propaganda remains to be seen. The collapse of the GDR was an extremely complex event, and no one would seriously argue that it was entirely the result of the failure of propaganda. Yet the shortcomings of the antifascism myth clearly did play a role in the failure of East German socialism.

The ultimate failure of the East German propaganda state naturally leads to much broader historical questions. In the modern world, can any political system, even with a monopoly on the media, exist for more than a relative handful of years if it does not deliver on the material promises it makes to its people? The strikingly sudden collapse of Eastern European socialism would suggest that the answer to this question is no. However, Nikolai Lenin's Soviet Union remained an important political and economic model on the world's stage for more than seven decades. Indeed, the leaders of many political systems—the leaders of China and North Korea come to mind—continue at least to pay lip service to the ideas and goals of Marxism–Leninism. Perhaps one day scholars will be able to write histories of the failure of these propaganda states. That is, after all, one of the characteristics of history—it never ends.

Acknowledgments

This book has been a long time in the making, and, as a result, I have incurred a long list of debts, both professional and personal. Regarding the former, I must begin by thanking David Bathrick, who first suggested that the Ernst Thälmann myth would make a good subject for a book. I would be remiss if I did not also thank the members of David's seminar "The Writer and the State in the German Democratic Republic," which encouraged serious discourse on the subject. I am grateful to Bob Shirer, who first pointed out to me the similarities between East German personality cults and the cults of medieval saints. Also important on this score is Don Prudlo, my colleague at Jacksonville State University. Not only did he read the entire manuscript—more than once—but he also encouraged me to make use of the political religions paradigm. The following people at Jacksonville State also contributed to the development of the manuscript in significant ways: Joe Delap, George Lauderbaugh, Paul Beezley, Rebecca Turner, and Earl Wade. I am also grateful to my department chair, Gordon Harvey, who did what he could for me with limited resources. The National Endowment for the Humanities and the German Academic Exchange Service also provided funds that made researching this book possible.

I am indebted as well to the broader scholarly community. Jay W. Baird provided me with top-notch training as a scholar and educated me regarding the role of myth in the building of a society. In addition to Jay, the following scholars have read parts of the manuscript—often unbeknownst to them—and their comments have improved it dramatically: David Murphy, David Meier, John Davidson, Sabine Hake, Silke Arnold-de Simone, and Diethelm Prowe. Needless to say, I could not have written this book without the kind help of librarians and archivists on two continents. In the United States, Jacksonville State's history and interlibrary loan librarians, Linda Cain and Debra Deering-Barrett, were especially helpful. In Germany, Sabine Stein took me on a personal tour of the Thälmann sites at Buchenwald Concentration Camp, and Bernt Roder of the Prenzlauer Berg Museum was similarly helpful. Günter Hortzschansky, arguably the GDR's leading authority on the life of Ernst Thälmann, was kind enough to answer my written questions concerning the Thälmann legend. The number of archivists who aided my efforts is too vast for them to be listed here, and their invaluable aid was often given anonymously. I thank the staffs of the following German archives: the German Federal Archives in Berlin, Potsdam, and Koblenz; the German Federal Film Archive in Berlin; Berlin's Television and Radio Archive; the Archive of the GDR's Academy of Arts; the Thuringia State Archive; the Institute for Contemporary History (Munich); and the Buchenwald Archive. I also made use of the following collections in the United States: the Hoover Institution Archive; the Archive of the United States Holocaust Memorial Museum; and the Library of Congress. Anyone who has performed scholarly research recognizes the valuable contribution such institutions make.

Portions of this book have appeared in different places. "'Germany's Eternal Son': The Genesis of the Ernst Thälmann Myth, 1930–1950" was published in the May 2009 number of *German Studies Review*. Parts of chapter 4 originally saw the light of day as "'Great Truths and Minor Truths': Kurt Maetzig's Ernst Thälmann Films and the Politics of Biography in the German Democratic Republic," in John Davidson and Sabine Hake, eds., *Framing the Fifties: Cinema in a Divided Germany*, 91–105 (Oxford: Berghahn Books, 2007). Finally, chapter 9 originally appeared in a different version as "'Imprisoned, Murdered, Besmirched': The Controversy Surrounding Berlin's Ernst Thälmann Monument and German National Identity, 1990–1995," in Silke Arnold-de Simone, ed., *Memory Traces: 1989 and German Cultural Memory*, 309–334 (Bern: Peter Lang, 2005). I thank all of these publishers for permission to reprint portions of these earlier works.

On a more personal level, I thank "Hardy" Jackson, Carmine Di Biase, and Shakil Khan. I owe these three truly fine men more than I can possibly say—or ever repay. My mother and father always encouraged my intellectual pursuits, and for that I am truly grateful. Finally, I thank my wife, Diana, and daughter, Lauren. Scholars' families are often inconvenienced in unusual ways. My daughter especially has lived with "ET" for as long as she can remember. It is to her that I dedicate this book.

All of the foregoing people are responsible for whatever merits this book possesses. Anyone who knows me already recognizes that its shortcomings are completely my own responsibility. I am, after all, a stubborn man.

Notes

When dealing with archival sources, I have given only as much information as is necessary for readers to find the source to which I refer. When, for example, the pages of an archival file are numbered consecutively—which is usually, but not always, the case with the holdings of the Foundation Archives of Parties and Mass Organizations of the GDR in the German Federal Archives (SAPMO-BA)—I have not cited the document's title, but only the page number(s) of the appropriate file. When the pages of a file are not numbered consecutively, as is usually the case with the archives I used other than the SAPMO-BA, I have provided the title of the document referenced in order to facilitate the tracking down of information.

Introduction

1. Jaroslav Pelikan, *Jesus Through the Centuries: His Place in the History of Culture* (New Haven, CT: Yale University Press, 1985).

2. Peter Brown, *The Cult of the Saints: Its Rise and Function in Latin Christianity* (Chicago: University of Chicago Press, 1982).

3. The literature on martyrdom is immense. See, for example, Caroline Walker Bynum, *The Resurrection of the Body in Western Christianity, 200–1336* (New York: Columbia University Press, 1995), chaps. 1 and 2; Brad S. Gregory, *Salvation at Stake: Christian Martyrdom in Early Modern Europe* (Cambridge, MA: Harvard University Press, 1999); Diana Wood, ed., *Martyrs and Martyrologies* (Oxford: Blackwell, 1993). On Jesus, see Pelikan, *Jesus Through the Centuries.* Concerning early Christian martyrdom, see Brown, *The Cult of the Saints.* On Abraham Lincoln, see Merrill Peterson, *Lincoln in American Memory* (New York: Oxford University Press, 1995). For an overview of the modern West, see Lacey Baldwin Smith, *Fools, Martyrs, Traitors: The Story of Martyrdom in the Western World* (New York: Knopf, 1997).

4. Nina Tumarkin, *Lenin Lives! The Lenin Cult in Soviet Russia* (Cambridge, MA: Harvard University Press, 1997); Nina Tumarkin, *The Living and the Dead: The Rise and Fall of the Cult of World War II in Russia* (New York: Basic Books, 1995).

5. Nachman Ben-Yahuda, *The Masada Myth: Collective Memory and Mythmaking in Israel* (Madison: University of Wisconsin Press, 1996); Tom Segev, *The Seventh Million: Israelis and the Holocaust* (New York: Farrar, Strauss, and Giroux, 1994).

6. George L. Mosse, *Fallen Soldiers: Reshaping the Memory of the World Wars* (New York: Oxford University Press, 1990); Jay W. Baird, *To Die for Germany: Heroes in the Nazi Pantheon* (Bloomington: Indiana University Press, 1990); Allen J. Frantzen, *Bloody Good: Chivalry, Sacrifice, and the Great War* (Chicago: University of Chicago Press, 2004).

7. George L. Mosse, *The Nationalization of the Masses: Political Symbolism and Mass Movements in Germany from the Napoleonic Wars Through the Third Reich* (New York: New American Library, 1975).

8. Concerning the origins of the Liebknecht–Luxemburg myth, see Manfred Scharrer, *"Freiheit ist immer . . .": Die Legende von Rosa und Karl* (Berlin: Transit, 2002), as well as Joachim Hoffmann, *Berlin Friedrichsfelde, ein deutscher Nationalfriedhof: Kulturhistorischer Reiseführer* (Berlin: Das Neue Berlin, 2001), 55–60.

9. For earlier work on the Thälmann myth, see René Börrnert, *Wie Ernst Thälmann treu und kühn! Das Thälmann-Bild der SED im Erziehungsalltag der DDR* (Bad Heilbrunn/Obb, Germany: Julius Klinkhardt, 2004); Allan L. Nothnagle, *Building the East German Myth: Historical Mythology and Youth Propaganda in the German Democratic Republic, 1945–1989* (Ann Arbor: University of Michigan Press, 1999), chap. 3; and the collection of essays in Peter Monteath, ed., *Ernst Thälmann: Mensch und Mythos* (Amsterdam: Rodopli, 2000).

10. Günter Hortzschansky, Walter Wimmer, Lothar Berthold, Heinz Karl, Horst Naumann, Stefan Weber, et al., *Ernst Thälmann: Eine Biographie* (Berlin: Dietz, 1980), 780; I used the two-volume paperback edition from 1986, but it has the same pagination as the original hardcover version of the book.

11. *Ernst Thälmann—unsere Partei erfüllt sein Vermächtnis: Wissenschaftliche Konferenz zum 100. Geburtstag Ernst Thälmanns in Berlin am 12. und 13. März 1986* (Berlin: Dietz, 1986).

12. Randall L. Bytwerk, *Bending Spines: The Propagandas of Nazi Germany and the German Democratic Republic* (East Lansing: Michigan State University Press, 2004), 6.

13. For Eric Voegelin, see *Race and State* (Baton Rouge: Louisiana State University Press, 1997); *The History of the Race Idea: From Ray to Carus* (Baton Rouge: Louisiana State University Press, 1998); "The Political Religions," in Manfred Hennigsen, ed., *Modernity Without Restraint: The Political Religions, The New Science of Politics, and Science, Politics, and Gnosticism*, vol. 5 of *The Collected Works of Eric Voegelin*, 19–74 (Columbia: University of Missouri Press, 2000); *Science, Politics, and Gnosticism* (Chicago: Regnery, 1978); and "Ersatz Religion," in *Science, Politics, and Gnosticism*, 55–102 (Washington, DC: ISI Books, 2005). On Voegelin's life, see Michael P. Federici, *Eric Voegelin: The Restoration of Order* (Washington, DC: ISI Books, 2002).

14. See, for example, the essays collected in Voegelin, *Science, Politics, and Gnosticism*; for an overview, see Michael Burleigh, *Earthly Powers: The Clash of Religion and Politics in Europe, from the French Revolution to the Great War* (New York: Harper, 2006), 249–252.

15. See, for instance, Arthur Jay Klinghoffer, *Red Apocalypse: The Religious Evolution of Soviet Communism* (Lanham, MD: University Press of America, 1996). Klinghoffer even goes so far, for example, as to state that "Stalinism represented the Middle Ages of communist development" (119).

16 . Michael Burleigh, *The Third Reich: A New History* (New York: Hill and Wang, 2000), 10.

1. "Heil Moskau!"

1. Regina Scheer, "'Ich bin kein weltflütiger Zigeuner': Legende und Wirklichkeit einer Jugend—über die frühen Prägungen Ernst Thälmanns," in Peter Monteath, ed., *Ernst Thälmann: Mensch und Mythos* (Amsterdam: Rodopi, 2000), 41.

2. Ernst Thälmann, "Mein Lebenslauf bis zum Eintritt in die KPD" (c. 1935), *Beiträge zur Geschichte der Arbeiterbewegung* 17 (1975), 88. See also the standard GDR biography, Günter Hortzschansky, Walter Wimmer, Lothar Berthold, Heinz Karl, Horst Naumann, Stefan Weber, et al., *Ernst Thälmann: Eine Biographie* (Berlin: Dietz,

1980), 14; I used the two-volume paperback edition from 1986, but it has the same pagination as the original hardcover version of the book.

3. On the provenance of this document, see Horst Naumann's introduction to Thälmann's "Mein Lebenslauf," 86–88.

4. On conditions in Thälmann's Hamburg, see Richard A. Comfort, *Revolutionary Hamburg: Labor Politics in the Early Weimar Years* (Stanford, CA: Stanford University Press, 1966), 17–25.

5. Thälmann, "Mein Lebenslauf," 89–91; translations throughout the volume are mine unless otherwise noted.

6. Scheer, "'Ich bin kein weltflütiger Zigeuner,'" 42.

7. Thälmann, "Mein Lebenslauf," 89.

8. Ibid., 91.

9. Quoted in Scheer, "'Ich bin kein weltflütiger Zigeuner,'" 43–44.

10. Thälmann, "Mein Lebenslauf," 89.

11. Ibid., 89, 91.

12. Ibid., 90–91.

13. Ibid., 91–92.

14. Ibid., 93.

15. Ibid., 93–94.

16. Ibid., 94–95.

17. Ibid., 95.

18. Ibid., 95–96.

19. Ibid., 96.

20. Ibid., 96–97.

21. Ibid., 97–98, emphasis in original poster. Nowhere in "Mein Lebenslauf" does Thälmann explain what these "twelve questions" are.

22. Ibid., 98–99.

23. Ibid., 99–100.

24. Ibid.

25. Ibid., 100.

26. Concerning the German front-line soldier and the political effects that the Great War had on him, see Scott Stephenson, *The Final Battle: Soldiers of the Western Front and the German Revolution of 1918* (Cambridge: Cambridge University Press, 2009).

27. Thälmann, "Mein Lebenslauf," 100–101.

28. Ibid., 101–102.

29. See, for example, Willi Bredel, *Ernst Thälmann: Ein Beitrag zu einem politischen Lebensbild* (Berlin: Dietz, 1948), which is systematically analyzed in chapter 7.

30. Katerina Clark, *The Soviet Novel: History as Ritual,* 3rd ed. (Bloomington: Indiana University Press, 2000), 9.

31. Ibid., 10, 15–16, emphasis in original.

32. Thälmann, "Mein Lebenslauf," 98.

33. Clark, *The Soviet Novel,* 38–39.

34. Thälmann, "Mein Lebenslauf," 98.

35. Clark, *The Soviet Novel,* 55.

36. Ibid., 58.

37. Ibid., 58, 73.

38. Jeffrey Brooks, *Thank You, Comrade Stalin! Soviet Public Culture from Revolution to Cold War* (Princeton, NJ: Princeton University Press, 2000), 111.

39. On the role of love in socialist realism, see Thomas Lahusen, *How Life Writes*

the Book: Real Socialism and Socialist Realism in Stalinist Russia (Ithaca, NY: Cornell University Press, 1997), 134.

40. Clark, *The Soviet Novel*, 49, 54.

41. Ibid., 27–68. Although almost all of the important scholarship on socialist realism agrees that it was an organic development of late Leninist and early Stalinist culture, what is in dispute is the paradigm's supposed pre-Soviet roots. Regarding this controversy and for a compelling argument for the Nietzschean roots of socialist realism, see Bernice Glatzer Rosenthal, *New Myth, New World: From Nietzsche to Stalinism* (University Park: Pennsylvania State University Press, 2002), passim, esp. 1–25.

42. Comfort, *Revolutionary Hamburg*, 111.

43. On Thälmann's ideas concerning an upcoming German revolution, see his article "Vorabend der deutschen Revolution," which first appeared in the 3 October 1923 edition of the Soviet publication *Gudok*. This essay was republished in J. A. L'vunin and I. S. Poljanskif, eds., "Publikationen Ernst Thälmanns in sowjetischen Periodika der zwanziger Jahre," *Beiträge zur Geschichte der Arbeiterbewegung* 15 (1973): 952–955. See also Ben Fowkes, *Communism in Germany under the Weimar Republic* (London: Macmillan, 1984), 75.

44. Comfort, *Revolutionary Hamburg*, 117–119.

45. Ruth Fischer, *Stalin and German Communism: A Study in the Origins of a State Party* (New Brunswick, NJ: Transaction, 1982), 423.

46. Werner T. Angress, *Stillborn Revolution: The Communist Bid for Power in Germany, 1921–1923* (Princeton, NJ: Princeton University Press, 1963), 254.

47. Ibid., 312–313; Heinrich August Winkler, *Von der Revolution zur Stabilisierung: Arbeiter und Arbeiterbewegung in der Weimarer Republik*, vol. 1: *1918–1924* (Berlin: Dietz, 1984), 564–565.

48. Winkler, *Von der Revolution zur Stabilisierung*, 1:624; Angress, *Stillborn Revolution*, 398–399; Comfort, *Revolutionary Hamburg*, 122–123. For a detailed pro-Communist account of the Hamburg uprising, see Larissa Reisner, *Hamburg auf den Barrikaden* (Berlin: Dietz, 1960), 7–82.

49. For a brief but incisive account of the occupation and German reactions, which included not only the KPD revolt but also Hitler's infamous Beer Hall Putsch, see Hans Mommsen, *The Rise and Fall of Weimar Democracy*, trans. Elborg Forster and Larry Eugene Jones (Chapel Hill: University of North Carolina Press, 1996), 129–171. The literature on the German inflation is extensive, but the most important work published on the subject is Gerald D. Feldman's *The Great Disorder: Politics, Economics, and Society in the German Inflation, 1914–1924* (Oxford: Oxford University Press, 1997). In this massive volume, Feldman traces the origins of the inflation to the policies of the German government during the First World War.

50. Angress, *Stillborn Revolution*, 444–446; Karl Heinrich Biehl, *The Thälmann Putsch in Hamburg und Umgebung* (Hamburg: Books on Demand, 2000), 149.

51. Fischer, *Stalin and German Communism*, 339–340; see also Fowkes, *Communism in Germany*, 107.

52. Ibid.; Winkler, *Von der Revolution zur Stabilisierung*, 1:653–654.

53. Biehl, *Thälmann Putsch*, 139–143. Hortzschansky et al., *Ernst Thälmann*, 207.

54. Angress, *Stillborn Revolution*, 451.

55. Biehl, *Thälmann Putsch*, 147–154.

56. Ernst Thälmann, *Ausgewählte Reden und Schriften in zwei Bänden*, 2 vols. (Frankfurt: Marxistische Blätter, 1976), 1:108–111.

57. Fischer, *Stalin and German Communism*, 405.

58. Fowkes, *Communism in Germany*, 123–124; Winkler, *Von der Revolution zur Stabilisierung*, 1:704.

59. Fischer, *Stalin and German Communism*, 419.

60. Erich Eyck, *A History of the Weimar Republic*, vol. 1: *From the Collapse of Empire to Hindenburg's Election* (New York: Atheneum, 1970), 334–335.

61. Hortzschansky et al., *Ernst Thälmann*, 222–224. On the direct links between Soviet, especially Stalin's, concerns and KPD policy, see David Pike, *German Writers in Soviet Exile, 1933–1945* (Chapel Hill: University of North Carolina Press, 1982), 3–21.

62. Hortzschansky et al., *Ernst Thälmann*, 225.

63. *Rote Fahne*, 15, 28, and 29 March 1925.

64. Ibid., 29 March 1925.

65. Ibid., 25 March 1925.

66. Ibid., 24 and 28 March 1925.

67. Regarding the role of the crowd in politics and religion before the twentieth century, see Elias Canetti, *Masse und Macht* (Frankfurt: Fischer Taschenbuch, 1960), 149–194.

68. *Rote Fahne*, 24 March 1925.

69. Ibid., 21 March 1925.

70. Ibid., 29 March 1925.

71. Heinrich August Winkler, *Der Schein der Normalität: Arbeiter und Arbeiterbewegung in Deutschland*, vol. 2: *1924 bis 1930* (Bonn: Dietz, 1988), 235.

72. Eyck, *From the Collapse of Empire to Hindenburg's Election*, 335–336.

73. Winkler, *Der Schein der Normalität*, 2:238–239.

74. *Rote Fahne*, 12 April 1925, quoted in ibid.

75. Winkler, *Der Schein der Normalität*, 2:239–243.

76. Hortzschansky et al., *Ernst Thälmann*, 231.

77. For a detailed account of Stalin's dispute with Trotsky, Zinoviev, and other Bolshevik "leftists," see Robert C. Tucker, *Stalin as Revolutionary, 1879–1929* (New York: Norton, 1973), 292–421. Concerning the collapse of Bukharin's position, see Stephen F. Cohen, *Bukharin and the Bolshevik Revolution: A Political Biography, 1888–1938* (New York: Oxford University Press, 1971), 270–336. On Thälmann's anti-intellectualism, see Fischer, *Stalin and German Communism*, 423.

78. Conan Fischer, *The German Communists and the Rise of Nazism* (New York: St. Martin's, 1991), 81–82; Winkler, *Der Schein der Normalität*, 2: 417–421, 425.

79. Hortzschansky et al., *Ernst Thälmann*, 250.

80. Winker, *Der Schein der Normalität*, 2:421. On the tremendously complex machinations surrounding the Comintern letter, see Hermann Weber, *Die Wandlung des deutschen Kommunismus: Die Stalinisierung der KPD in der Weimarer Republik*, 2 vols. (Frankfurt: Europäische Verlaganstalt, 1969), 1:220–226.

81. Winkler, *Der Schein der Normalität*, 2:433.

82. Klaus Kinnes, "Thälmann und der Stalinismus: Das Ende des eigenständigen deutschen Parteikommunismus 1928/1929," in Monteath, ed., *Ernst Thälmann*, 61–62; Winkler, *Der Schein der Normalität*, 2:661–662.

83. Fowkes, *Communism in Germany*, 149–150. For the correspondence produced by various figures involved in the scandal—including Thälmann, Stalin, Pieck, and Ulbricht—see Hermann Weber and Bernhard H. Bayerlein, eds., *Der Thälmann-Skandal: Geheime Korrespondenzen mit Stalin* (Berlin: Aufbau, 2003), 77–302.

84. Winkler, *Der Schein der Normalität*, 2:445–446, 455–458.

85. On Thälmann's relationship with Stalin, see Hermann Weber, "Thälmann

und Stalin, die KPdSU und die KPD," in Weber and Bayerlein, eds., *Der Thälmann-Skandal*, 11–34.

86. On Münzenberg, see Babette Gross, *Willi Münzenberg: Eine politische Biografie* (Leipzig: Forum, 1991).

87. Fischer, *Stalin and German Communism*, 606–607, italics in original.

88. Ibid., 608.

89. On spectacle in Stalinist Russia, see Karen Petrone, *Life Has Become More Joyous, Comrades: Celebrations in the Time of Stalin* (Bloomington: Indiana University Press, 2000).

90. On the Lenin cult and its role in the Soviet Union under Stalin, see Nina Tumarkin, *Lenin Lives! The Lenin Cult in Soviet Russia* (Cambridge: Harvard University Press, 1983), 207–252.

91. Eric Weitz, *Creating German Communism, 1890–1990: From Popular Protests to Socialist State* (Princeton, NJ: Princeton University Press, 1997), 185.

92. Paul Levi, "Karl Liebknecht and Rosa Luxemburg: Zum Gedächtnis," speech given at the 2 February 1919 commemoration ceremony, Paul Levi Collection, Folder no. 1, Hoover Institution Archives, Stanford, CA.

93. Manfred Scharrer, *"Freiheit ist immer . . .": Die Legende von Rosa und Karl* (Berlin: Transit, 2002), 174.

94. Annelies Laschitza, *Rosa Luxemburg, im Lebensrausch, trotz alledem: Eine Biographie* (Berlin: Aufbau Taschenbuch, 1996), 404–405.

95. Quoted in Weitz, *Creating German Communism*, 183.

96. Quoted in Scharrer, *"Freiheit ist immer,"* 177.

97. For more concerning Thälmann's views on Liebknecht and Luxemburg, see J. A. Lwunin, ed., "Ernst Thälmann über Karl Liebknecht und Rosa Luxemburg," *Beiträge zur Geschichte der Arbeiterbewegung* 19 (1977): 63–66.

98. Quoted in Eve Rosenhaft, *Beating the Fascists? The German Communists and Political Violence* (Cambridge: Cambridge University Press, 1983), 72.

99. Jürgen W. Falter, "Wahlen und Wählerverhalten unter besonderer Berücksichtgung des Afusteiges der NSDAP nach 1928," in Karl Dietrich Bracher, Manfred Funke, and Hans-Adolf Jacobsen, eds., *Die Weimarer Republik, 1918–1933: Politik, Wirtschaft, Gesellschaft*, 484–504 (Düsseldorf: Droste, 1987).

100. Both quotations are taken from Heinrich August Winkler, *Der Weg in die Katastrophe: Arbeiter und Arbeiter Bewegung in der Weimarer Republic*, vol. 3: *1930 bis 1933* (Bonn: Dietz, 1990), 199.

101. Pike, *German Writers in Soviet Exile*, 16–17; Winkler, *Der Weg in die Katastrophe*, 3:600.

102. Rosenhaft, *Beating the Fascists?* 68–69.

103. Winkler, *Der Weg in die Katastrophe*, 3:642, 693.

104. Erich Eyck, *A History of the Weimar Republic*, vol. 2: *From the Locarno Conference to Hitler's Seizure of Power* (New York: Atheneum, 1970), 350–353.

105. Ibid., 355, 360; Andreas Dorpalen, *Hindenburg and the Weimar Republic* (Princeton, NJ: Princeton University Press, 1964), 256–260; Gottfried Reinhhold Treviranus, *Das Ende von Weimar: Heinrich Brüning und seine Zeit* (Düsseldorf: Econ, 1968), 299; Heinrich Brüning, *Memoiren, 1918–1934* (Stuttgart: Deutsche Verlaganstalt, 1970), 533.

106. Russel Lemmons, *Goebbels and Der Angriff* (Lexington: University Press of Kentucky, 1994), 57–58.

107. Hortzschansky et al., *Ernst Thälmann*, 551.

108. Ibid., 562; Eyck, *From the Locarno Conference to Hitler's Seizure of Power*, 351–

352; Karl Dietrich Bracher, *Die Auflösung der Weimarer Republik* (Stuttgart: Droste, 1955), 418–419.

109. See, for example, *AIZ*, 11, no. 15 (1932), 358–359.

110. Ibid., 11, no. 9 (1932), 198–199.

111. See two Thälmann campaign posters from 1932, Poster Collection, Bundesarchiv Koblenz, Federal Republic of Germany.

112. *Der Angriff*, 10 March 1932.

113. Quoted in Hortzschansky et al., *Ernst Thälmann*, 555.

114. Flugblatt no. 92, File 199, Akte XII, Hauptarchiv IV, Geheimes Staatsarchiv preussischer Kulturbesitz, Berlin.

115. *AIZ* 11, no. 9 (1932), 197.

116. Ibid., 11, no. 15 (1932), 358–359.

117. Winkler, *Der Weg in die Katastrophe*, 3:760; Hortzschansky et al., *Ernst Thälmann*, 617–620.

118. Robert C. Tucker, *Stalin in Power: The Revolution from Above, 1928–1941* (New York: Norton, 1990), 228–232.

119. See Fischer, *The German Communists and the Rise of Nazism*, 186. On the transport workers' strike, see Lemmons, *Goebbels and* Der Angriff, 102–106.

120. Quoted in Rosenhaft, *Beating the Fascists?* 81, italics in the original.

121. Thälmann, *Ausgewählte Reden und Schriften*, 2:345–347.

122. Ibid., 2:347–357, italics in the original.

123. Mario Frank, *Walter Ulbricht: Eine deutsche Biografie* (Berlin: Siedler, 2001), 94.

124. Quoted in Michael Schneider, *Unterm Hakenkreuz: Arbeiter und Arbeiterbewegung, 1933 bis 1939* (Bonn: Dietz, 1999), 44–45.

125. Fowkes, *Communism in Germany*, 171; on Thälmann's concealment and arrest, see Reinhard Müller, *Die Akte Wehner: Moskau, 1937 bis 1941* (Berlin: Rowohlt, 1993), 275, 278. The KPD murdered Kattner in 1934.

2. "Ernst Thälmann Must Be Won Like a Battle!"

1. Ralf Georg Reuth, ed., *Joseph Goebbels, Tagebücher, 1924–1945* (Munich: R. Piper, 1992), entry for 7 November 1941, 1698. On the Nazis' efforts to win over their imprisoned political opponents, see Nikolaus Wachsmann, *Hitler's Prisons: Legal Terror in Nazi Germany* (New Haven, CT: Yale University Press, 2004), 119.

2. See Jörn Schütrumpf's introduction to Wolfram Adolphi and Jörn Schütrumpf, eds., *Ernst Thälmann: An Stalin, Briefe aus dem Zuchthaus, 1939 bis 1941* (Berlin: Dietz, 1996), 8–9.

3. Regarding Kippenberger's background, see Hermann Weber, "*Weiße Flecken" in der Geschichte*, 2nd ed. (Frankfurt: isp, 1990), 79.

4. Annette Leo, "Die Berichte der Thälmann-Kuriere," in Peter Monteath, ed., *Ernst Thälmann: Mensch und Mythos* (Amsterdam: Rodopli, 2000), 82–84; Annette Leo, "Kein Platz im Museum für den Helden: Die Geschichte des Thälmann-Kuriers Walter Trautzsch," in Annette Leo and Peter Reif-Spirek, eds., *Helden, Täter und Verräter: Studien zum DDR-Antifaschismus* (Berlin: Metropol, 1999), 133–134.

5. Leo, "Die Berichte," 84–85.

6. Wachsmann, *Hitler's Prisons*, 23.

7. Klaus Scheel, ed., "Dokumente über die Verschärfung der Gefängenschaft für Ernst Thälmann," *Beiträge zur Geschichte der Arbeiterbewegung* 15 (1973), 458.

8. Leo, "Die Berichte," 82.

9. Quoted in unidentified newspaper (possibly the *Daily Telegraph*) clipping from 1935, File 117, p. 1329, Zeitgeschichtliche Sammlung, Bundesarchiv Koblenz, Federal Republic of Germany.

10. Schütrumpf, introduction to Adolphi and Schütrumpf, eds., *Ernst Thälmann*, 9–10.

11. Scheel, "Dokumente," 452–460; Leo, "Die Berichte," 87.

12. Ibid., 87–88; Schütrumpf, introduction to Adolphi and Schütrumpf, eds., *Ernst Thälmann*, 9.

13. For excerpts from the indictment, see "Die Anklageschrift gegen Thael-mann," File 896/4, Willi Bredel Papers, Stiftung Archiv der Akademie der Künste, Berlin.

14. Georgi Dimitrov, *Selected Works in Three Volumes* (n.p.: Balkan State Printing House, n.d.), 3:445–448.

15. Ibid., 1:355, 362–366, 378–379.

16. Ibid., 3:450–451. The campaign to secure Dimitrov's release had been going on since his arrest, but his acquittal gave it more urgency and legitimacy.

17. See Lothar Berthold, ed., "Unbekannte Dokumente Ernst Thälmanns aus dem faschistischen Kerker," *Beiträge zur Geschichte der deutschen Arbeiterbewegung* 6 (1964), 464–467.

18. Reuth, ed., *Joseph Goebbels, Tagebücher*, 905.

19. Quoted in "Lieber drinnen," *Der Spiegel* 31 (27 July 1996), 47.

20. Günter Hortzschansky, Walter Wimmer, Lothar Berthold, Heinz Karl, Horst Naumann, Stefan Weber, et al., *Ernst Thälmann: Eine Biographie* (Berlin: Dietz, 1980), 700–701; I used the two-volume paperback edition from 1986, but it has the same pagination as the original hardcover version of the book.

21. Bernhard H. Bayerlein, "Ernst Thälmann: Vom 'Fall' zur Parabel des Stalinismus?" in Hermann Weber and Bernhard H. Bayerlein, eds., *Der Thälmann-Skandal: Geheime Korrespondenzen mit Stalin* (Berlin: Aufbau, 2003), 60.

22. Ibid. Concerning Trautzsch's account, see Leo, "Die Berichte," 89.

23. Quoted in Leo, "Die Berichte," 86.

24. Quoted in "Lieber drinnen," 47.

25. For an East German version of Schehr's tenure as chairman and his murder at the hands of the Gestapo, see Stefan Weber, "Nach der Verhaftung Ernst Thälmanns leitete John Schehr die illegale KPD," *Beiträge zur Geschichte der Arbeiterbewegung* 24 (1982): 483–498.

26. Regarding Ulbricht's elevation to temporary party leader, see Mario Frank, *Walter Ulbricht: Eine deutsche Biografie* (Berlin: Siedler, 2001), 117. Concerning Thälmann's reelections to the two highest KPD governing bodies, see Michael Schneider, *Unterm Hakenkreuz: Arbieter und Arbeiterbewegung, 1933–1945* (Bonn: Dietz, 1999), 982–999.

27. For Pieck's letter, see Renate Heimann and Hans Vieillard, eds., "Brief Wilhem Piecks an Ernst Thälmann aus dem Jahre 1935," *Beiträge zur Geschichte der Arbeiterbewegung* 18 (1976): 74–78. Concerning the Ulbricht–Pieck alliance, see Frank, *Walter Ulbricht*, 106–111.

28. Quoted in Bayerlein, "Ernst Thälmann," 61, italics in original.

29. Quoted in Leo, "Die Berichte," 87.

30. Schütrumpf's introduction to Adolphi and Schütrumpf, eds., *Ernst Thälmann*, 9–10.

31. For examples of Thälmann's letters to Irma, see Karl Heinz Jahnke, ed., *Ernst Thälmann—Freund und Vorbild der Jugend* (Berlin: Junge Welt, 1974), 33–39. Inter-

estingly, there was tension between father and daughter, the result of Thälmann's having spent so much of his time in Berlin during the years 1925–1933, and Irma did not write to him as often as he and the Comintern would have liked. As a result, Communist functionaries sometimes wrote letters on her behalf. On this topic, see Leo, "Die Berichte," 86. For other examples of Thälmann's letters published in the GDR, see Lothar Berthold and Charlotte Erxleben, eds., *Ernst Thälmann: Briefe aus dem Gefängnis an seine Angehörigen* (Berlin: Dietz, 1965), and Günter Hortzschansky, ed., "Aus den Aufzeichnungen Ernst Thälmanns im faschistischen Kerker," *Beiträge zur Geschichte der Arbeiterbewegung* 28 (1986): 192–198.

32. Georgi Dimitrov, *Tagebücher 1933–1943*, 2 vols., ed. Bernhard H. Bayerlein, translated from Russian and Bulgarian by Wladislaw Hedeler and Birgit Schliewanz (Berlin: Aufbau, 2000), 1:326, 441.

33. For the texts of Thälmann's letters to Stalin, see Adolphi and Schütrumpf, eds., *Ernst Thälmann*, 12–160.

34. Reinhard Müller, *Die Akte Wehner: Moskau, 1937 bis 1941* (Berlin: Rowohlt, 1993), 281, 304–309, 360.

35. Concerning the effects of the purges on the KPD, see Hermann Weber, *"Weiße Flecken" in der Geschichte: Die KPD-Opfer der Stalinischen Säuberungen und ihre Rehabilitierung*, 2nd ed. (Frankfurt: isp, 1990). Weber lists 305 murdered or "missing" German Communists as well as 40 who were imprisoned but survived the purges.

36. For the 5 March quotation from the Comintern, see Hortzschansky et al., *Ernst Thälmann*, 668; on the Comintern and the Third Period, see William J. Chase, *Enemies within the Gates? The Comintern and the Stalinist Repression, 1934–1939*, with Russian documents translated by Vadim A. Staklo (New Haven, CT: Yale University Press, 2001), 16.

37. Hortzschansky et al., *Ernst Thälmann*, 668.

38. Ibid., 668–669.

39. David Pike, *German Writers in Soviet Exile, 1933–1945* (Chapel Hill: University of North Carolina Press, 1982), 322–323.

40. Valentin Ivanenko, "Dokumente der Klassensolidarität: Über die Teilnahme von Werktätigen der Sowjet–Ukrain an der Protestbewegung des internationalen Proletariats zur Befreiung Ernst Thälmanns," trans. C. Remer, *Jahrbuch für Geschichte der sozialistischen Länder Europas* 26, no. 2 (1983): 137–146.

41. Hortzschansky et al., *Ernst Thälmann*, 692–695.

42. NY4003, File 66, SAPMO-BA.

43. Hortzschansky et al., *Ernst Thälmann*, 692–695.

44. Ibid.

45. *The Daily Worker*, 1 and 2 June 1934.

46. Ibid., 4 April 1934.

47. Ibid., 3, 7, and 9 March 1934.

48. Quoted in Sean McMeekin, *The Red Millionaire: A Political Biography of Willi Münzenberg, Moscow's Secret Propaganda Tsar in the West* (New Haven, CT: Yale University Press, 2003), 271. For further information regarding Münzenberg's understanding of propaganda and its role in politics, see Willi Münzenberg, *Propaganda als Waffe* (Paris: Éditions du Carrefour, 1937).

49. This postcard is included with other postcards, letters, and telegrams from 1934 in NY4003, File 57, SAPMO-BA.

50. NY4003, File 56, p. 25 of file, SAPMO-BA.

51. On Münzenberg's early political career, see McMeekin's informative biography, *The Red Millionaire*, 7–99.

52. Ibid., 103–122.

53. Babette Gross, *Willi Münzenberg: Eine politische Biografie* (Leipzig: Forum, 1991), 400.

54. Ibid., 412.

55. NY4003, File 56, p. 81 of file, SAPMO-BA.

56. Gross, *Willi Münzenberg*, 400; Hortzschansky et al., *Ernst Thälmann*, 689.

57. Quoted in Hortzschansky et al., *Ernst Thälmann*, 690.

58. Pike, *German Writers in Soviet Exile*, 96.

59. "Comite pour la Liberation de Thaelmann et des Antifascistes Allemandes emprisonnés," 21 April 1934, in NY4003, File 53, SAPMO-BA.

60. See, for example, the numerous documents from Pieck's office in NY4003, File 56, SAPMO-BA.

61. Ibid., p. 80 of file.

62. On the expansion of the Free Thälmann campaign and the growth of its bureaucracy, see, for example, ibid., File 56, pp. 24–27 of file, SAPMO-BA. On the Japanese Communist Party's "Free Thälmann" crusade, see ibid., File 53, p. 5 of file, SAPMO-BA.

63. Hortzschansky et al., *Ernst Thälmann*, 736.

64. NY4003, File 56, pp. 62–63 of file, SAPMO-BA.

65. Ibid., p. 24 of file.

66. Ibid., pp. 47–49 of file.

67. *The Daily Worker,* 25 November 1935.

68. NY4003, File 56, pp. 36–37 of file, SAPMO-BA.

69. Ibid.

70. Ibid., p. 37 of file.

71. Ibid., p. 60 of file.

72. Both Mann and Nexö are quoted in Hortzschansky et al., *Ernst Thälmann,* 742.

73. Boris Groys, *The Total Art of Stalinism: Avant-Garde, Aesthetic Dictatorship, and Beyond,* trans. Charles Rougle (Princeton, NJ: Princeton University Press, 1992), 3–4.

74. Hortzschansky et al., *Ernst Thälmann,* 742.

75. NY4003, File 53, pp.131–132 of file, SAPMO-BA.

76. Ibid., File 56, pp. 64–66 of file, SAPMO-BA.

77. Gilbert Badia, "'Fünf Jahre Hitlerregime': Eine Austellung des Pariser Thälmann-Kommittees im February/März 1938," *Beiträge zur Geschichte der Arbeiterbewegung* 22 (1980): 552–567.

78. Dimitrov, *Tagebücher,* 1:364.

79. See Margot Pikarski and Günter Uebel, *Einfuhrung zu der antifaschistische Widerstandskampf der KPD im Spiegel des Flugblattes, 1933–1945* (Berlin: Dietz, 1978), 8–35.

80. "Ernst THAELMANN und hunderte proletarische Gefangene in Gefahr!" Zeitgeschichtliche Sammlung, pp. 65–66, italics in original.

81. *Der antifaschistische Widerstandskampf der KPD im Spiegel des Flugblattes* (Berlin: SED, 1978), a boxed set of separate copies of around two hundred flyers reproduced by the SED, Flyer no. 104.

82. *Der antifaschistische Widerstandskampf der KPD im Spiegel des Flugblattes,* Flyer no. 25.

83. Quoted in *"Die Anklageschrift gegen Thaelmann,"* File 896/4, Bredel Papers.

84. NY4003, File 53, pp. 98–101 of file, SAPMO-BA.

85. See several examples in *Der Antifaschistische Widerstandskampf der KPD im Spiegel des Flugblattes,* for instance Flyer no. 25.

86. Wilhelm Pieck, *Der Kampf um die Befreiung Thälmanns—eine Schlacht gegen Faschismus und Krieg*, Box 43, German Subject Collection, Hoover Institution, Stanford, CA.

87. Ibid.

88. Ibid.

89. Ibid., italics in original.

90. On the translations of this pamphlet, see Dimitrov, *Tagebücher*, 1:112–113.

91. Georgi Dimitroff [Dimitrov], *Auf zur Rettung Thälmanns* (Paris: Weltverlag, 1934), 4–5.

92. See the German translation of the letter "WIR SCHWÖREN, DICH DEM HENKER ZU ENTREISSEN!" in NY4036, File 409, SAPMO-BA.

93. *AIZ*, 14 June and 26 July 1934.

94. See, for example, *AIZ*, 1 August 1935.

95. Ibid. and 12 April 1936.

96. For a brief account of Heartfield's life as well as numerous examples of his art, see John Willett, *Heartfield versus Hitler* (Paris: Hazan, 1997).

97. Victoria E. Bonnell, *Iconography of Power: Soviet Political Posters under Lenin and Stalin* (Berkeley: University of California Press, 1997), 40.

98. For this Heartfield work, see Willet, *Heartfield*, 101.

99. *AIZ*, 22 April 1936.

100. For numerous examples of Heartfield's montages—including several incorporating religious motifs—as well as a more detailed account of his career as an artist, see David Evans, *John Heartfield*: Arbeiter-Illustrierte Zeitung, Volks Illustrierte, *1930–1938*, ed. Anna Lundgren (New York: Kent, 1992).

101. *AIZ*, 13 June 1935.

102. Johannes R. Becher, "Genosse Thälmann—unser Führer," quoted in Günter Scholdt, *Autoren über Hitler: Deutschsprachige Schriftsteller 1919–1945 und ihr Bild vom "Führer"* (Bonn: Bouvier, 1993), 47–48.

103. On the Stalin cult, see Barbara Kiteme, "The Cult of Stalin: National Power and the Soviet Party-State," PhD diss., Columbia University, 1989. On the Lenin myth, see Nina Tumarkin, *Lenin Lives! The Lenin Cult in Soviet Russia* (Cambridge, MA: Harvard University Press, 1983).

104. On the image of Hitler in the Third Reich, see Ian Kershaw, *The "Hitler Myth": Image and Reality in the Third Reich* (Oxford: Oxford University Press, 1989), esp. 53 for poems lionizing the *führer*.

105. Johannes R. Becher, "Dream of a Soviet Germany," translated and quoted in Pike, *German Writers in Soviet Exile*, 242.

106. The lyrics and music for Erich Weinert's "Für Kameraden Thälmann Hoch die Faust" can be found in Dimitrov, *Auf zur Rettung Ernst Thälmanns*.

107. Pike, *German Writers in Soviet Exile*, 243.

108. Quoted in ibid., 239.

109. The film is held at the Bundesarchiv-Filmarchiv, Berlin.

110. NY4003, File 53, p. 129 of file, SAPMO-BA.

111. For a highly polemical account of the history of the International Brigade, see Willi Bredel, *Spanienkrieg*, 2 vols., ed. Manfred Hahn (Berlin: Aufbau, 1977).

112. Vincent Brome, *The International Brigades: Spain 1936–1939* (New York: Morrow, 1966), 71–75.

113. Bredel, *Spanienkrieg*, 2:252–253. See also R. Dan Richardson, *Comintern Army: The International Brigades and the Spanish Civil War* (Lexington: University Press of Kentucky, 1982), 27–30, 64–66, 82.

114. Heinz Preiss, *Spaniens Himmel und keine Sterne: Ein deutsches Geschichtsbuch. Erinnerungen an ein Leben und ein Jahrhundert* (Berlin: Edition Ost, 1996), 105; Brome, *The International Brigades,* 144–145.

115. Bredel, *Spanienkrieg,* 1:168.

116. Ibid., 300.

117. Ibid., 299.

118. Quoted in ibid., 179.

119. NY4003, File 56, pp. 83–88 of file, SAPMO-BA.

120. Ibid., pp. 83–84 of file.

121. Ibid., pp. 84–86 of file.

122. Ibid., pp. 86–88 of file.

3. "We Are Building upon the Foundations Created by Ernst Thälmann"

1. On Hitler's nihilism at the end of the war, especially after the failed 20 July coup, see Ian Kershaw, *Hitler, 1936–1945: Nemesis* (New York: Norton, 2000), 753.

2. Emil Carlebach, Paul Grünewald, Hellmuth Röder, Willy Schmidt, and Walter Vielhauer, *Buchenwald: ein Konzentrationslager* (Frankfurt: Röderberg, 1986), 80.

3. Emil Carlebach, *Tote auf Urlaub: Kommunist in Deutschland, Dachau und Buchenwald 1937–1945* (Bonn: Pahl Rugenstein, 1995), 159; see also *Neues Deutschland,* 17 August 1958.

4. Günter Hortzschansky, Walter Wimmer, Lothar Berthold, Heinz Karl, Horst Naumann, Stefan Weber, et al., *Ernst Thälmann: Eine Biographie* (Berlin: Dietz, 1980), 776; I used the two-volume paperback edition from 1986, but it has the same pagination as the original hardcover version of the book.

5. For a German translation of this article, see "Zum Gedächtnis Ernst Thälmanns," in NY4003, File 60, SAPMO-BA; quotations are my translations of the German version.

6. Ibid.

7. Ibid.

8. "Aus 'Internationale Literatur,'" in NY4003, File 60, SAPMO-BA.

9. Ibid.

10. See Sara Ann Sewel's insightful article "Mourning Comrades: Communist Funerary Rituals in Cologne during the Weimar Republic," *German Studies Review* 22, no. 3 (October 2009): 527–548.

11. See, for example, photographs of Thälmann speaking at the gravesides of fallen comrades in Institut für Marxismus–Leninismus beim ZK der SED, ed., *Ernst Thälmann: Bilder, Dokumente, Texte* (Berlin: Dietz, 1986), 95, 178.

12. Concerning this number, see John Erickson, *The Road to Berlin: Continuing the History of Stalin's War with Germany* (Boulder, CO: Westview Press, 1983), 622.

13. Richard Bessel's *Germany 1945, from War to Peace* (New York: Harper, 2009) is the latest of many accounts of the country during the final months of the war and the first months of peace. See page 254 regarding the dramatic decrease in Berlin's population.

14. Concerning the Red Army's campaign of rape against German women, see Norman M. Naimark, *The Russians in Germany: A History of the Soviet Zone of Occupation, 1945–1949* (New Haven, CT: Yale University Press, 1995), 69–140.

15. Wolfgang Ribbe, "Berlin zwischen Ost und West (1945 bis zur Gegenwart),"

in Wolfgang Ribbe, ed., *Geschichte Berlins*, vol. 2, *Von der Märzrevolution bis zur Gegenwart* (Munich: C. H. Beck, 1987), 1027–1035.

16. Michael Kubina, "Der Aufbau des zentralen Parteiapparates der KPD 1945–1946," in Manfred Wilke, ed., *Die Anatomie der Parteizentrale: Die KPD/SED auf dem Weg zur Macht*, 48–58 (Berlin: Akademie, 1998).

17. Dirk Spilker, *The East German Leadership and the Division of Germany: Patriotism and Propaganda, 1945–1953* (Oxford: Oxford University Press, 2006), 10–36.

18. Concerning Germans imprisoned by the Soviets, see Bettina Greiner, *Verdrängter Terror: Geschichte und Wahrnehmung sowjetischer Speziallager in Deutschland* (Hamburg: Hamburger Edition, 2010).

19. Antonia Grunenbert, *Antifaschismus—ein deutscher Mythos* (Hamburg: Rowohlt, 1993), 120–145.

20. *Deutsche Volkszeitung*, 5 September 1945.

21. Ibid.

22. Ibid.

23. Ibid.

24. Concerning the demonstration in Neukölln, see ibid., 9 September 1945.

25. Ibid., 5 September 1945.

26. Mario Frank, *Walter Ulbricht: Eine deutsche Biographie* (Berlin: Siedler, 2001), 202.

27. The literature on the creation of the SED is vast and growing. Among the most concise and informative treatments can be found in Gareth Pritchard, *The Making of the GDR, 1945–1953: From Antifascism to Stalinism* (Manchester, UK: Manchester University Press, 2000), 108–136. Among the most recent accounts is Andreas Malycha and Peter Jochen Winters, *Die SED: Geschichte einer deutschen Partei* (Munich: C. H. Beck, 2009), 16–52.

28. For a discussion of this topic, see Pritchard, *The Making of the GDR*, 123–129. Kurt Hager insists in his memoir that although the Soviets supported the creation of the SED, they believed that it was "an issue for the German Communists and Social Democrats . . . to decide." See Kurt Hager, *Erinnerungen* (Leipzig: Faber and Faber, 1996), 107. However, Mario Frank argues in his biography of Walter Ulbricht that the occupation authorities played a central role in the creation of the SED. Indeed, Frank argues that in creating the SED, German Communists were simply doing Stalin's bidding. See Frank, *Walter Ulbricht*, 205.

29. On this concern, see Malycha and Winters, *Die SED*, 50–51.

30. For examples of unification on the local level—Brandenburg, Turingia, and Mecklenburg—see *Tägliche Rundschau*, 2 and 9 April 1946.

31. Ibid., 16 April 1946.

32. Ibid.

33. Ibid., 17 April 1946.

34. Ibid.

35. Ibid., 23 April 1946; see also Frank, *Walter Ulbricht*, 205.

36. Pritchard, *The Making of the GDR*, 124.

37. Ibid., 164.

38. Bredel, *Ernst Thälmann.*

39. Wilhelm Pieck, radio interview, transcript in NY4036, File 440, pp. 125–128 of file, SAPMO-BA.

40. *Neues Deutschland*, 16 August 1949.

41. Ibid.

42. Ibid., 19 August 1949.

43. Ibid., 18 August 1949.

44. Ibid.

45. Ibid.

46. On the totalitarian model, see Abbot Gleason, *Totalitarianism: The Inner History of the Cold War* (Oxford: Oxford University Press, 1997); for the classic elucidation of this model, see Hannah Arendt, *The Origins of Totalitarianism* (New York: Houghton Mifflin Harcourt, 1950).

47. *Neues Deutschland,* 19 August 1949.

48. Ibid.

49. Ibid.

50. Ibid.

51. Ibid.

52. Ibid.

53. For more on this topic, see chapter 5 as well as *Neues Deutschland,* 6 October 1949.

54. See *Neues Deutschland,* 4, 6, and 7 October 1949.

55. Wilhelm Pieck's 11 October 1949 speech is included in *Reden und Aufsätze: Auswahl aus den Jahren 1908–1950,* 3 vols. (Berlin: Dietz, 1954), 2:301–302.

56. See, for example, Wilfried Loth, *Stalin's Unwanted Child* (New York: Palgrave, 1994).

57. Joachim Hoffmann, *Berlin–Friedrichsfelde, ein deutscher Nationalfriedhof* (Berlin: Das Neue Berlin, 2001), 84–86.

58. See the useful Web site sozialistenfriedhof.de, accessed 21 May 2010, for an overview of the memorial site. See also *Neues Deutschland,* 14 and 15 January 1951, as well as Hoffmann, *Berlin–Friedrichsfelde,* 168–187.

59. Concerning Jendretzky, see "Jendretzky, Hans," in Bernd-Reiner Barth, Christoph Links, Helmut Müller-Enbergs, and Jan Wielgohs, eds., *Wer war wer in der DDR: Ein biographisches Handbuch,* 340–341 (Frankfurt: Fischer, 1995).

60. *Neues Deutschland,* 15 April 1951.

61. Ibid., 16 April 1951.

62. Ibid.

63. Ulbricht's 7 February 1953 address is included in Walter Ulbricht, *Zur Geschichte der deutschen Arbeiterbewegung: Aus Reden und Aufsätzen,* 10 vols. (Berlin: Dietz, 1955), 1:653.

64. Ibid., 1:654–663.

65. *Neues Deutschland,* 19 August 1954.

66. Ibid., 15 August 1954.

67. Ibid., 18 August 1954.

68. DY30 IV2/9.07, Institut für Marxismus–Leninismus, File 129, pp. 129–130 of file, SAPMO-BA.

69. Ibid., p. 133 of file.

70. *Michel: Deutschland-Katalog 1996/97* (Munich: Schwanneberger, 1996), 321.

71. On these paintings, see Martin Schönfeld, "Die Konstruktion eines politischen Idols: Darstellungen Ernst Thälmann in der Kunst der SBZ/DDR und ihre Funktion," in Peter Monteath, ed., *Ernst Thälmann: Mench und Mythos* (Amsterdam: Rodopi, 2000), 153–155.

72. Much of this paragraph is based on my personal experiences traveling in East Berlin, the GDR, and, later, the "new states" of the Federal Republic of Germany. In 1986, for example, I visited Germany and was exposed to the Thälmann myth for the first time during trips to East Berlin. I saw several posters in the East

German capital, such as the one mentioned in the text, and, despite—or perhaps because of—the fact that I was in the country to study Joseph Goebbels, the pervasiveness of propaganda in the GDR, including efforts to inculcate the Thälmann legend, made an indelible impression on me.

73. See, for example, Peter Monteath, "Ein Denkmal für Thälmann," in Monteath, ed., *Ernst Thälmann*, 179–201.

74. DR1, Kulturministerium, File 1799, pp. 121–122 of file, SAPMO-BA.

75. NY4033, File 66, p. 217 of the file, SAPMO-BA.

76. DR1, Kulturministerium, File 1799, pp. 121–122 of file, SAPMO-BA; *Neues Deutschland*, 25 May 1950.

77. *Nationalzeitung*, 25 May 1950.

78. On the Red Orchestra, see Anne Nelson, *The Red Orchestra* (New York: Random House, 2004), and Shareen Blair Brysac, *Resisting Hitler: Mildred Harnack and the Red Orchestra* (New York: Oxford University Press, 2000).

79. *Tägliche Rundschau*, 26 May 1950.

80. Concerning problems with the collective, see DR1, File 7907, pp. 207–208 and 384 of file, as well as File 1799, pp. 80–81 of file, SAPMO-BA.

81. DR1, File 7695, pp. 3–4 of file, and File 1799, p. 38 of file, SAPMO-BA.

82. For more information concerning the delays in the project, see the numerous documents in DR1, Files 1799 and 7695, SAPMO-BA.

4. "A Great National Deed"

1. For a brief analysis of Maetzig's two Thälmann films (complete with stills), see Ralf Schenk, "Mitten im kalten Krieg," in Ralf Schenk, ed., *Das zweite Leben der Filmstadt Babelsberg: DEFA-Spielfilme, 1946–1992* (Berlin: Henschel, 1994), 104–109.

2. On film in Nazi Germany, see David Welch, *Propaganda and the German Cinema, 1933–1945* (Oxford: Oxford University Press, 1983). On Soviet film, see Peter Kenez, *Cinema and Soviet Society, 1917–1953* (Cambridge: Cambridge University Press, 1992). For the quotation from Lenin, see Peter Kenez, *The Birth of the Propaganda State: Soviet Methods of Mass Mobilization, 1917–1929* (Cambridge: Cambridge University Press, 1985), 106. Concerning Ufa, see Klaus Kreimeier, *The Ufa Story: A History of Germany's Greatest Film Company, 1918–1945*, trans. Robert and Rita Kimber (Berkeley: University of California Press, 1996).

3. See Thomas Heimann, *DEFA, Künstler und SED-Kulturpolitik: Zum Verhältnis vom Kulturpolitik und Filmproduktion in der SBZ/DDR 1945 bis 1959* (Potsdam-Babelsberg: VISTAS, 1994), 48–57, 108–109, 131. For the quotation from Tulpanow's speech, see Christiane Mückenberger, "Zeit der Hoffnungen, 1946 bis 1949," in Schenk, ed., *Das zweite Leben der Filmstadt Babelsberg*, 14. Regarding the critique of "formalism"—art founded solely on aesthetic criteria and often too sophisticated for the masses—and the call for socialist-realist films, see Joshua Feinstein, *The Triumph of the Ordinary: Depictions of Daily Life in the East German Film, 1949–1989* (Chapel Hill: University of North Carolina Press, 2002), 30–31. For a brief overview of DEFA's institutional history, see Seán Allan, "DEFA: An Historical Overview," in Seán Allan and John Sandford, eds., *DEFA: East German Cinema, 1946–1992* (New York: Berghahn Books, 1999), 1–21. Concerning the effort to create a "democratic" film industry in the GDR, see R2, Ministerrat, File 1093, p. 1 of file, Bundesarchiv Abteilung, Potsdam.

4. Bredel, *Ernst Thälmann*, passim.

5. Martin Brady, "Discussion with Kurt Maetzig," in Allen and Sanford, eds., *DEFA*, 84.

6. Ibid., 83.

7. See "1. Sitzugn des Thälmann Kollektivs der DEFA," in NY4219, File 9, pp. 1–3, SAPMO-BA. See the same file, pp. 70–72, for examples of reminiscences of Thälmann collected in Hamburg. Concerning the file of the film in East German "historical propaganda," see Detlef Kannapin, *Antifaschismus im Film der DDR: DEFA-Spielfilme 1945–1955/56* (Cologne: PapyRossa, 1997), 63–71.

8. Detlef Kannapin, "Ernst Thälmann und der DDR-Antifaschismus im Film der fünziger Jahre," in Monteath, ed., *Ernst Thälmann*, 128.

9. Kenez, *Cinema and Soviet Society*, 228–232.

10. NY 4219, File 9, pp. 6–8 of file, SAPMO-BA.

11. Ibid., pp. 9–11 of file, SAPMO-BA.

12. See "Ernst Thälmanns Jugend" and "Treatment zu dem Film 'Ein Sohn des Volkes,'" File 1090, Willi Bredel Papers, Stiftung Archiv der Acadamie der Künste, Berlin.

13. Michael Tschesno-Hell, "Einige Gedanken zum Thälmann-Film," *Neues Deutschland*, 5 January 1954.

14. NY 4182, File 1369, p. 97 of file, SAPMO-BA.

15. Feinstein, *The Triumph of the Ordinary*, 30–31.

16. Quoted in Dagmar Schittly, *Zwischen Regie und Regime: Die Filmpolitik der SED im Spiegel der DEFA-Produktionen* (Berlin: Christoph Links, 2002), 65.

17. DR1, File 4352, SAPMO-BA.

18. Ibid.

19. DR1, File 4851, SAPMO-BA.

20. Ibid.

21. Wilhelm Pieck to Walter Ulbricht, 10 December 1952, in ibid., pp. 100–101 of file. On the publication of the film script, see "Ein lebendiges Kapital Geschichte: Zum Film-Szenarium 'Ernst Thälmann—Sohn seiner Klasse,'" *Neues Deutschland*, 22 December 1953. For the published edition of the script, see Willi Bredel and Michael Tschesno-Hell, *Ernst Thälmann—Sohn seiner Klasse* (Berlin: Henschelverlag, 1953).

22. "Die Regierung der DDR, Ministerium für Kultur, Film, Kaufmänische Abteilung, 30.12.1955," and "DEFA STUDIO FÜR SPIELFILME an der Regierung der DDR, Ministerium für Kultur, Kaufmännische Abteilung, 29.10.1955," both in DR1, File 4520, SAPMO-BA.

23. DR1, File 4614a, p. 132 of file, SAPMO-BA.

24. "Realisierte Stoffe," in DR1, File 4150, SAPMO-BA.

25. "Anlage zur Vorlage für das Kollegium des Ministeriums für Kultur betr. Uraufführung und Einsatz des 2. Teiles des Thälmann-Films," DR1, File 4620, SAPMO-BA.

26. "DEFA-Studio für Spielfilme—Produktion—*II Arbeitsplan für März 1953*," DR1, File 4124a, p. 1 of document, SAPMO-BA.

27. "Studio für Spielfilme, Atelierbetrieb, *Erfüllungsbericht*, 11 April 1953," DR1, File 4124a, p. 5 of document, SAPMO-BA.

28. "*Erfüllungsbericht für den Monat Januar 1953*," DR1, File 4124a, p. 2 of document, SAPMO-BA.

29. Sepp Schwab to Walter Ulbricht, 28 November 1952, NY 4182, File 1369, p. 99 of file, SAPMO-BA.

30. "Sondersendung zum Gedenktag der Opfer des Faschismus 'Thälmann ist niemals gefallen,'" Sunday, 11 September 1955, Rep. 07, V.2a, File 14, Kurt Maetzig Papers, Stiftung Archiv der Akademie der Künste, Berlin.

31. Thilo Gabelmann, *Thälmann ist niemals gefallen: Eine Legende Stirbt* (Berlin: Das Neue Berlin, 1996), 275.

32. Charlotte Küter to Walter Ulbricht, n.d., NY4182, File 1369, SAPMO-BA.

33. "Presseheft: *Ernst Thälmann–Sohn seiner Klasse:* Ein farbiger DEFA-Spielfilm," NY 4219, File 10, pp. 17–19 of file, SAPMO-BA.

34. Ibid., p. 20.

35. Susanne Brömsel and Renate Biehl, "Filmographie," in Schenk, ed., *Das zweite Leben der Filmstadt Babelsberg,* 371.

36. Bredel and Tschesno-Hell, *Ernst Thälmann—Sohn seiner Klasse.* I thank Progress Film Verleih for providing access to both Thälmann films.

37. Ibid., 19–20. Stalin was cut out of the film as a result of de-Stalinization.

38. Ibid., 77–80.

39. Ibid., 151–154.

40. "Einsatz-, Agitations- und Werbeplan für den DEFA-Farbfilm 'Ernst Thälmann Sohn seiner Klasse,'" DR1, File 4464, pp. 5–7 of document, SAPMO-BA.

41. "Toast beim Empfang zu Ehren der mitwirkenden Künstler am Thälmann Film," 9 March 1954, NY 4036, File 464, n.p., SAPMO-BA.

42. "*Aktenvermerk,* Besprechung mit Kollegen Schlösser und Oswald, HV Film. Am 19.3.54," DR1, File 4050, p. 1 of document, SAPMO-BA.

43. "Einsatz-, Agitations- und Werbeplan,'" p. 5 of document.

44. "Presseheft: *Ernst Thälmann—Sohn seiner Klasse,*" 3.

45. Johannes Becher, "Eine große nationale Tat," manuscript, NY 4219, File 11, SAPMO-BA.

46. See "Presseheft: *Ernst Thälmann–Führer seiner Klasse,*" in File 1, pp. 45–58, Maetzig Papers, for excerpts from reviews of *Sohn seiner Klasse.* For a Western response to the film, see Erich Wollenberg's "Thälmann: Film und Wirklichkeit," manuscript, File 1100, Bredel Papers. Wollenberg raises some questions regarding the film's historical accuracy, pointing out, for example, that although Thälmann did participate in the Hamburg Aufstand, he was not its overall leader. He convincingly establishes that although none of the events in the film was entirely fabricated, DEFA was willing to manipulate the facts for political advantage.

47. DR1, File 4418, SAPMO-BA.

48. Brömsel and Biehl, "Filmographie," 376.

49. See the manuscript of the *Führer seiner Klasse* screenplay in NY 4182, File 1369, pp. 141–150 of file, SAPMO-BA.

50. Ibid., pp. 9–14.

51. Ibid., pp. 84–120.

52. On the historical inaccuracies in the films, see Erich Wollenberg, "Thälmann—Film und Wirklichkeit," in Monteath, ed., *Ernst Thälmann,* 115–118.

53. Ibid., 121.

54. On the National Socialist "myth of resurrection and return," see Jay W. Baird, *To Die for Germany: Heroes in the Nazi Pantheon* (Bloomington: Indiana University Press, 1992), 73–107.

55. "Presseheft: *Ernst Thälmann–Führer seiner Klasse.*"

56. See "Betr. Festlich Aufführungen mit Schauspielern des DEFA-Farbfilms 'Ernst Thälmann Sohn seiner Klasse,[']" DR1, File 4614a, all three pages of the document, SAPMO-BA.

57. Untitled speech dated 2 September 1955, NY4003, File 82, p. 1 of document, SAPMO-BA.

58. "Erfolgsmeldungen (auszugsweise) unserer Theater anlässlich der Er-

stauffführung des Filmes *Ernst Thälmann—Führer seiner Klasse,*" DR1, File 4655, pp. 1–4 of document, SAPMO-BA.

59. "Sonderwettbewerb mit dem Film 'Ernst Thälmann Führer seiner Klasse,'" DR1, File 4620, p. 1 of document, SAPMO-BA.

60. Michael Tschesno-Hell, "Nur wer kämpft, zählt zu den Lebenden," in NY 4219, File 10, p. 2 of file, SAPMO-BA.

61. Miklos Gimes, "Notizen über Deutschland," a German translation dated 15 June 1954 of an article appearing in a Hungarian periodical, the title of which is illegible in the manuscript, DR1, File 4614, pp. 1 and 21 of the document, SAPMO-BA.

62. Ibid., pp. 4–4a. See also "Diskussion über den Thälmann-Film am 17. November 1955 im Gebäude der Akademie der Wissenschaften, Berlin," in NY 4219, File 10, pp. 26–86 of document, SAPMO-BA, regarding reaction to the films in other socialist countries.

63. A transcript of this 1955 meeting of the Club for Filmmakers is in NY4219, File 10, SAPMO-BA; all quotations come from this source.

64. Tschesno-Hell, "Einige Gedanken zum Thälmann-Film."

65. See the several speeches in NY4003, File 72, SAPMO-BA.

66. Richard Kieckhefer, "Imitators of Christ: Sainthood in the Christian Tradition," in Richard Kieckhefer and George D. Bond, eds., *Sainthood: Its Manifestations in World Religions* (Berkeley: University of California Press, 1988), 11–12, 20; see also the preface, vii. Kieckhefer associates an eighth characteristic with sainthood—relics—and although this characteristic was an important aspect of the Thälmann cult, it is not, for obvious reasons, incorporated into the Maetzig films. See chapter 9 in *Hitler's Rival* concerning Thälman relics. Katerina Clark has also pointed out the hagiographic components in Stalinist culture, especially the socialist-realist novel. See her book *The Soviet Novel: History as Ritual,* 3rd ed. (Bloomington: Indiana University Press, 2000), esp. chap. 2.

67. It needs to be pointed out that this familiarity with such images applies not only to the Roman Catholic parts of Europe, but also to the Protestant parts. Even as staunch a Protestant as Martin Luther—in spite of his rejection of the miracles and relics associated with the saints—recognized that they could serve as examples of a proper Christian lifestyle. See Kieckhefer, "Imitators of Christ," 7.

68. Susan Buck-Morss, *Dreamworld and Catastrophe: The Passing of Mass Utopia and East and West* (Cambridge, MA: MIT Press, 2000), passim.

69. Charles S. Maier, *Dissolution: The Crisis of Communism and the End of East Germany* (Princeton, NJ: Princeton University Press, 1997), 5–6; Sigrid Meuschel, *Legitimation und Parteiherrschaft: Zum Paradox von Stabilität und Revolution in der DDR, 1945–1989* (Frankfurt: Suhrkamp, 1991), 29–122.

5. "Out of Your Sacrificial Death Grows Our Socialist Deed"

1. On the importance of the city of Weimar to German cultural memory, see Georg Bollenbeck, "Weimar," in Etienne François and Hagen Schulze, eds., *Deutsche Erinnerungsorte,* 3 vols., 1:187–206 (Munich: C. H. Beck, 2001); on Buchenwald as a site of memory, see Peter Reichel, *Politik mit der Erinnerung: Gedächtnisorte im Streit um die nationalsozialistische Vergangenheit* (Munich: Carl Hanser, 1995), 129–135.

2. For a concise account of the expansion of the concentration camp system, see Doris L. Bergen, *War and Genocide: A Concise History of the Holocaust* (Lanham,

MD: Rowman and Littlefield, 2003), 90–92. On the establishing of Buchenwald, including this quotation from the US Army's report, see David Hackett, trans., *The Buchenwald Report* (Boulder, CO: Westview Press, 1995), 32–33.

3. The estimates of the number of prisoners held at one time or another in Buchenwald vary, with Wolfgang Sofsky putting the number at more than 306,000. The same can be said concerning the number who died at the location. Sofsky calculates the number of dead at "only" slightly more than 33,000, whereas other estimates run as high as 60,000. None of these mortality estimates, of course, includes prisoners held at one time in Buchenwald but who died in other camps. The totals used in the chapter text here have been adopted because they were the official statistics used in the GDR and would play an important role in the antifascism myth. See Wolfgang Sofsky, *The Order of Terror: The Concentration Camp,* trans. William Templer (Princeton, NJ: Princeton University Press, 1997), 36; James E. Young, *The Texture of Memory: Holocaust Memorials and Meaning* (New Haven, CT: Yale University Press, 1993), 75.

4. See Hackett, trans., *The Buchenwald Report,* 45 and 51 for the quotations; see also "Buchenwald," in Walter Laqueur, ed., *The Holocaust Encyclopedia* (New Haven, CT: Yale University Press, 2001), 97.

5. Young, *The Texture of Memory* , 74.

6. Hackett, trans., *The Buchenwald Report,* 83. On the founding of the Illegal Camp Committee, see the letter dated 13 December 1984 from Professor Dr. J. S. Drabkin in Moscow to Jascha and Irina, Buchenwald Archive, File 04 1–26, Federal Republic of Germany.

7. Hackett, trans., *The Buchenwald Report,* 84–87.

8. Ibid., 98.

9. Ibid., 98–99.

10. Ibid., 100–102.

11. Ibid., 103–104.

12. The issue of Buchenwald's "self-liberation" became a divisive one in the wake of reunification, when many Germans called into question this legend, one of the central components of the GDR's legitimation narrative. On this issue, see Hasko Zimmer, *Der Buchenwald Konflikt: Zum Streit um Geschichte und Erinnerung im Kontext der deutschen Vereinigung* (Münster: agenda, 1999). Zimmer's useful book incorporates numerous facsimiles of documents and newspaper articles regarding the controversy.

13. For brief accounts of the KPD/SED's manipulation of historical memory at Buchenwald, see Young, *The Texture of Memory,* 72–79; Reichel, *Politik mit der Erinnerung,* 129–135.

14. Angelika Timm, *Jewish Claims Against East Germany: Moral Obligations and Pragmatic Policy* (Budapest: Central European University Press, 1997), 42.

15. On the antifascism myth at Buchenwald, see Young, *The Texture of Memory,* 77–79; Reichel, *Politik mit der Erinnerung,* 131–132. See also Manfred Overesch's useful study concerning memory at Buchenwald from the end of the war to the opening of the national memorial in 1958, *Buchenwald und die DDR: Oder die Suche nach Selbstlegitimation* (Göttingen: Vandenhoeck & Ruprecht, 1995), esp. chaps. 4–6. As Overesch points out in chapter 3 of his book, the 1947 American-directed Buchenwald trial threatened the antifascism myth by raising the question of prisoner complicity in enforcing some of the camp's policies. The raising of this issue ultimately had little effect on the development of the antifascism myth at the site, however. For the official view of the KPD's leading the antifascist resistance in Buchenwald,

see Erhard Pachaly, "Die Rolle des illegalen Parteiaktivs der KPD in der internationalen antifaschistischen Widerstandsorganisation im KZ Buchenwald," *Beiträge
zur Geschichte der Arbeiterbewegung* 23 (1981): 851–861. For a brief analysis of the
ways that the GDR commemorated the victims of the Third Reich, see Jeffrey M.
Peck, "East Germany," in David S. Wyman, ed., *The World Reacts to the Holocaust*
(Baltimore: Johns Hopkins University Press, 1996), 447–472.
    16. For the text of the poem, both in German and the original Russian, see Kru-
tik, "Höre Welt!" in Walter Bartel, Internationales Buchenwald-Komitee, and Komi-
tee der Antifaschistischen Widestands Kämpfer de Deutschen Demokratischen
Republik, *Buchenwald: Mahnung und Verpflichtung, Dokumente und Berichte* (Frankfurt: Röderberg, 1960), 476–477. The German version of the portion quoted in the
text reads:

   Hört Proletarier aller Länder!
   Hört die Nachricht von Thälmann!
   . . .
   Im August Neuzehnhundertvierundvierzig
   wurde im Krematorium von Buchenwald
   von der blutigen Hand des Henkers
   ein für die Freiheit brennendes Licht ausgelöscht.
   Wir verloren den Führer der Proletarier,
   dessen Name wie Sturnleuten klang.
   . . .
   Ernst, Du bist nicht von uns gegangen.
   Wir schwören, Deine Losung zu befolgen.
   Der Henker hat nur Deinen getötet,
   uns blieb die Idee.
   . . .
   Und nach Deinem Vermächtnis leben.

    17. Concerning inmates' knowledge about the murder, see Robert Siewert's ac-
count in *Buchenwald: Mahnung und Verpflichtung, Dokumente und Berichte* (Berlin:
VEB deutscher Verlag der Wissenschaften, 1983), 476.
    18. Emil Carlebach, *Tote auf Urlaub: Kommunist in Deutschland, Dachau und Bu-
chenwald 1937–1945* (Bonn: Pahl-Rugenstein Nachfolger, 1995), 161–162; Herbert
Weidlich, "Das Sonderkommando und weitere gefährliche Aktionen der SS," *Buchenwald Heft* 9 (1979), 68.
    19. Günter Hortzschansky, Walter Wimmer, Lothar Berthold, Heinz Karl, Horst
Naumann, Stefan Weber, et al., *Ernst Thälmann: Eine Biographie* (Berlin: Dietz, 1980),
777; I used the two-volume paperback edition from 1986, but it has the same pagination as the original hardcover version of the book.
    20. For Siewert's account of the ceremony, see Bartel et al., *Buchenwald*, 368–369;
the quotations from Siewert's account are taken from this source. See also Erich
Fein and Karl Flanner, *Rot-weiß-rot in Buchenwald: Die österreichishcen politischen
Häftlinge im Konzentrationslager am Ettersberg bei Weimar 1938–1945* (Vienna: Eu-
ropaverlag, 1987), 197–198.
    21. Hortzschansky et al., *Ernst Thälmann*, 2:777; Carlebach, *Tote auf Urlaub*, 162.
    22. Bartel et al., *Buchenwald*, 369; Fein and Flanner, *Rot-weiß-rot in Buchenwald*,
197; Hortzschansky et al., *Ernst Thälmann*, 2:777.
    23. Fein and Flanner, *Rot-weiß-rot in Buchenwald*, 197–198.

24. Young, *The Texture of Memory*, 75.

25. Reichel, *Politik mit der Erinnerung*, 132.

26. Heinz Koch, "National Mahn und Gedenkstätte Buchenwald: Geschichte ihrer Entstehung," *Buchenwald Heft* 31 (n.d.), 9.

27. Jeffrey Herf, *Divided Memory* (Cambridge, MA: Harvard University Press), 96–97. As James Young points out, the SED dissolved the VVN in 1953 because "its aims were now official government policy." See Young, *The Texture of Memory*, 75.

28. Overesch, *Buchenwald und die DDR*, 261, 265.

29. Young, *The Texture of Memory*, 75; concerning the "volunteer" laborers, see Klaus Trostorff, "Die Nationale Mahn-und Gedenkstätte Buchenwald," *Neue Museumskunde: Theorie und Praxis der Museumsarbeit* 18, no. 2 (1975), 85. As is often the case in societies such as the GDR where the state can provide a great deal of incentive to participate in "volunteer" actions, it is difficult to determine how much of the work performed by "volunteers" was actually voluntary.

30. "Protokoll, Berlin, den 22.11.55," DR1, File 7517, p. 1 of file, SAPMO-BA.

31. Herf, *Divided Memory*, 176.

32. Koch, "National Mahn und Gedenkstätte Buchenwald," 25, 32.

33. Quoted in ibid., 91.

34. Quoted in *Neues Deutschland*, 19 August 1954.

35. Koch, "National Mahn und Gedenkstätte Buchenwald," 40–41; *Neues Deutschland*, 19 August 1954.

36. Overesch, *Buchenwald und die DDR*, 309.

37. *Neues Deutschland*, 17 August 1954. Concerning the museum's composition, see also Trostorff, "Die Nationale Mahn-und Gedenkstätte Buchenwald," 87–88.

38. *Neues Deutschland*, 17 August 1954.

39. Ibid.

40. Ibid.; Overesch, *Buchenwald und die DDR*, 308.

41. *Neues Deutschland*, 17 August 1954.

42. Ibid. Ten years later a new museum display was dedicated. It incorporated the same motifs as the 1954 display into a larger exhibition housed in ten rooms. See Trostorff, "Die Nationale Mahn-und Gedenkstätte Buchenwald," 87–88, 91.

43. Koch, "National Mahn und Gedenkstätte Buchenwald," 44.

44. See the reproduction of the announcement in Overesch, *Buchenwald und die DDR*, 310.

45. Quoted in ibid., 311.

46. Koch, "National Mahn und Gedenkstätte Buchenwald," 51.

47. Concerning the reasons behind the repeated postponements in construction of the Buchenwald National Monument, see Overesch, *Buchenwald und die DDR*, 262–263; see pages 262–297 in this same work concerning the debates surrounding construction at the site, a subject beyond the scope of my research. For a brief description of economic conditions in the GDR during the 1950s, see Henry Ashby Turner Jr., *Germany from Partition to Reunification* (New Haven, CT: Yale University Press, 1992), 69–70.

48. Overesch, *Buchenwald und die DDR*, 300.

49. *Leipziger Volkszeitung*, 2 March 1957; *Neues Deutschland*, 6 March 1957.

50. "Protokoll über die Tagung des Kuratoriums für den Aufbau National Gedenkstätten in Buchenwald, Sachsenhausen und Ravensbrück am 1 April 1957," in DR1, File 7521, p. 20 of file, SAPMO-BA.

51. Concerning the stamps, see *Michel: Briefmarken-Katalog Deutschland 1996/97* (Munich: Schwaneberger, 1996), 347.

52. "Plan der Massnahmen des Kreisauschusses der Nationalen Front Weimar-Stadt zur Vorbereitung der Einweihung der Mahn-und Gedenkstätte Buchenwald und des Ernst Thälmann Denkmals am Platz der 56 000," IV/B/2/9.04/325, Karton B490, Bezirkparteiarchiv der SED Erfurt, Thüringisches Hauptstaatsarchiv Weimar, Weimar.

53. "Sitzung des Sekretariats des ZK vom 23.5.1956," in DY30/JIV2/3, File 514, SAPMO-BA; on the centralized nature of GDR governance, see Mary Fulbrook, *Anatomy of a Dictatorship: Inside the GDR, 1949–1989* (Oxford: Oxford University Press), 61–77. Fulbrook states that "[t]he party aimed at total penetration and control of social processes, total persuasion of all the people, total conformity and outward support" (62). At one point, party officials planned to dedicate the memorial in Weimar on 18 August 1957, the twelfth anniversary of Thälmann's death, but as for most construction in the GDR a shortage of construction materials led to delays. On this plan, see the letter from Lepper to Saemerow (no first names shown), 29 October 1956, in volume 1 of the Zeitlicher Umfang Collection, Buchenwald Archive, Buchenwald. Concerning fund-raising after the Central Committee granted its approval, see *Neues Deutschland*, 17 August 1958.

54. Lepper to Saemerow, 29 October 1956.

55. "Plan der Massnahmen des Kreisauschusses der Nationalen Front Weimar-Stadt"; for the quotations from Kroh's article and Fürnberg's poem, see *Das Volk*, 16 August 1958.

56. For an account of the ceremony as well as excerpts from Jahn's speech, see the Weimar newspaper *Das Volk*, 18 August 1958.

57. *Neues Deutschland*, 17 August 1958.

58. *Das Volk*, 18 August 1958.

59. Ibid.

60. Ibid.; *Neues Deutschland*, 18 August 1958.

61. Overesch, *Buchenwald und die DDR*, 325.

62. Ibid., 320–322; *Neues Deutschland*, 13, 14, and 15 September 1958.

63. "AUFRUF DES KOMITEES FÜR DIE EINWEIHUNG DER MAHN-UND-GEDENKSTÄTTE BUCHENWALD," Carton B204, B IV/219.01–16, Thüringisches Hauptstaatsarchiv.

64. "An alle, die an der Einweihung der Mahn- und Gedenkstätte Buchenwald am 14. September 1958 teilnehmen," Carton B490, IV/B/2/9.04/490, 1 Thüringisches Hauptstaatsarchiv. For the text of the "Buchenwald Oath," see *Neues Deutschland*, 15 September 1958.

65. Quoted in *Neues Deutschland*, 15 September 1958.

66. Quoted in Trostorff, "Die Nationale Mahn-und Gedenkstätte Buchenwald," 85.

67. Ibid., 92.

68. Ibid.

69. "Protokoll über die Tagung des Kuratoriums für den Aufbau Nationaler Gedenkstätten in Buchenwald, Sachsenhausen und Ravensbrück am 1 April 1957," in DR1, File 7521, p. 16 of file, SAPMO-BA. See also Jens-Fietje Dwars, *Abgrund des Widerspruchs: Das Leben des Johannes R. Becher* (Berlin: Aufbau, 1999), 771–772.

70. For the text of the poem, see *Das Wort*, 13–14 September 1958.

71. Concerning the reliefs on the sixth stela, see *Buchenwald mahnt: Antifaschistische Kunst in der DDR* (Weimar: Druckhaus Weimar, 1988), 83–84.

72. Although seeking to relate the German original as accurately as possible, I

did take some minor liberties in the translation for the sake of readability. In German, this stanza reads:

Gegrußt Ernst Thälmann, Deutschlands grosser Sohn!
Er stand vor uns in einem hellen Schein.
Und ringsum war ein feierlicher Ton,
Er war als stimmten alle Völker ein—*Die Internationale* klang als Chor:
"Und dieser Welt muß unser, unser, sein!"
Und Thälmann hob die Fahne hoch empor.

73. Once again, I have taken some liberties in my translation in order to promote readability. The German reads:

Was Thälmann sah, sich eines Tags begab.
Sie gruben aus die Waffen, die versteckt,
Die Todgeweihten steigen aus dem Grab.
Seht ihre Arme weithin ausgestreckt:
Ein Mahnmal seht in vielerlei Gestalt,
Das uns beschwört, aus dem Vergessen weckt—Die Toten mahnen: "Denkt an Buchenwald!"

74. Trostorff, "Die Nationale Mahn-und Gedenkstätte Buchenwald," 92.

75. Concerning the use of the disinfection chamber as a site for the Thälmann commemoration, see DR1, File 7524, p. 131, SAPMO-BA. For the cost of construction, see page 1 of this document.

76. *Buchenwald*, pamphlet dated 1974, United States Holocaust Memorial Museum library, Washington, DC. The guide's English-language version is a translation of the original German-language edition.

77. The description of the basement museum is based on a personal tour of the site given to me by Sabine Stein, who oversaw the Buchenwald Monument and Memorial when I visited it in 1996. Ms. Stein graciously permitted me to take photographs and shared some of her reminiscences about the location. She, for example, had her *Jugendweihe*, "youth consecration" or coming-of-age ceremony, at this site.

78. Concerning the "worthiness" of the display, see *Buchenwald: Guide to the National Memorial*, pamphlet dated 1986, United States Holocaust Memorial Museum library. The guide's English-language version is a translation of the original German pamphlet.

79. *Museum Buchenwald*, pamphlet dated 1989, United States Holocaust Memorial Museum library. Once again, I have quoted from the English-language version, which is identical to the original German.

80. DR1, File 7524, p. 131 of file, SAPMO-BA.

81. Ibid. For a photograph of the site, absent the bust—which was eventually removed, apparently to the Thälmann memorial in the basement of the disinfection building—but with a good view of the plaque, the second version of the eternal flame, wreaths, flowers, and ribbons, see Institut für Marxismus–Leninismus beim ZK der SED, ed., *Ernst Thälmann: Bilder, Dokumente, Texte* (Berlin: Dietz, 1986), 381.

82. Concerning these ceremonies, see Rikola-Gunnar Lüttgenau, "Geschichtserinnerung im Wandel: Das Beispiel der nationalen Mahn- und Gedenkstätte Buchenwald," MA thesis, Heinrich-Heine Universität Düsseldorf, 1992, 72–73.

83. Concerning the design of Buchenwald's crematorium, see page 3 of *"IN-SPECTION OF GERMAN CONCENTRATION CAMP FOR POLITICAL PRIS-ONERS LOCATED AT BUCHENWALD ON THE NORTH EDGE OF WEIMAR,"* RG-09.027, Records Relating to Post-liberation Dachau and Buchenwald, United States Holocaust Memorial Museum archive.

84. Concerning the use of memorial sites and statues as substitutes for tombs, see Katherine Verdery, *The Political Lives of Dead Bodies: Reburial and Postsocialist Change* (New York: Columbia University Press, 1999).

85. "Maßnahmen zur Ehrung Ernst Thälmanns anläßlich des 25. Jahrestages seiner Ermordung," DY24, File 12037, p. 1 of the document, SAPMO-BA.

86. DY30/JIV 2/3, File 1527, pp. 106–109 of file, SAPMO-BA.

87. *Nationale Mahn-und Gedenkstätte Buchenwald: Informationen* 3 (1974), 5–6.

88. Ibid. 4 (1974), 3–7.

89. "Rede von Prof. Dr. Walter Bartel auf dem Gedenkappell der FDJ und Pionierorganisation 'Ernst Thälmann' anläßlich des 40. Jahrestages der Ermordung Ernst Thälmanns," DY24, File 1080, SAPMO-BA.

90. Ibid.

91. *Oh, Buchenwald*, documentary directed by Ulrich Teschner, 1984.

6. "We Can Look Forward to a Happy Future"

1. Carl Schorske, *German Social Democracy, 1905–1917: The Development of the Great Schism* (Cambridge, MA: Harvard University Press, 1955), 97–98.

2. Barbara Köster, "'Die Junge Garde des Proletariats': Untersuchungen zum Kommunistischen Jugendverband Deutschlands in der Weimarer Republik," PhD diss., University of Bielefeld, 2005, 36–46; Catherine Epstein, *The Last Revolutionaries: German Communists and Their Century* (Cambridge, MA: Harvard University Press, 2003), 38, the quotation from Mallmann on this page also.

3. See *Ernst Thälmann: Ausgewählte Reden und Schriften in zwei Bänden*, 2 vols. (Frankfurt: Marxistische Blätter, 1976), 1:162.

4. For an overview of the antifascism myth and East German youth, see Alan L. Nothnagle, *Building the East German Myth: Historical Mythology and Youth Propaganda in the German Democratic Republic, 1945–1989* (Ann Arbor: University of Michigan Press, 1999), 93–142.

5. John Rodden, *Textbook Reds: Schoolbooks, Ideology, and Eastern German Identity* (University Park: Pennsylvania State University Press, 2006), 33.

6. Andreas Herbst, Winfried Ranke, and Jürgen Winkler, eds., *So funktionierte die DDR*, 3 vols. (Reinbek bei Hamburg: Rowohlt, 1994), 1:291–294; Nothnagle, *Building the East German Myth*, 117. Concerning the Bolshevization of the SED, see Andreas Malycha and Peter Jochen Winters, *Die SED: Geschichte einer deutschen Partei* (Munich: C. Beck, 2009), 52–102.

7. Quoted in Nothnagle, *Building the East German Myth*, 103, 117.

8. René Börrnert, *Wie Ernst Thälmann treu und kühn! Das Thälmann-Bild der SED im Erziehungsalltag der DDR* (Bad Heilbrunn: Julius Klinkhardt, 2004), 135–136.

9. Nothnagle, *Building the East German Myth*, 93–142; Rodden, *Textbook Reds*; Börrnert, *Wie Ernst Thälmann treu und kühn!*

10. Nothnagle, *Building the East German Myth*, 95.

11. Quoted in Irma Thälmann, *Erinnerungen an meinen Vater* (Berlin: Kinderbuchverlag, 1971), 137–138.

12. DR2, File 5868, p. 15 of file, SAPMO-BA.

13. I. Thälmann, *Erinnerungen*, 137.

14. "Freie Deutsche Jugend, Zentralrat, Beschlußreihe K, 12/28/85." in DY24, Freie deutsche Jugend, File 12073, p. 8 of document, SAPMO-BA.

15. "Freie Deutsche Jugend . . . Schwerin, den 08.05.1986," in DY24, Freie Deutsche Jugend, File 112260, p. 1 of document, SAPMO-BA.

16. "Ablauf des Appells zur Ehrung Ernst Thälmanns am 12. Mai 1986 um 18.30 im 'Ernst-Thälmann-Park,'" in DY24, File 111374, p. 4 of document for the quotation, SAPMO-BA.

17. For the music and text of the entire song, see Walter Bartel, *Ernst Thälmann: Das große Vorbild der deutschen Jugend im Kampf für Frieden, Einheit, Demokratie und Sozialismus* (Berlin: Zentralrat der Freien deutschen Jugend, Abteilung Propaganda, n.d.), 2.

18. "Drehbuch für den Festakt aus Anlaß des 25. Jahrestages der Pionierorganisation 'Ernst Thälmann' am Montag, den 10. Dezember 1973 im Friedrichstadt-Palast," in DY25, Freie Deutsche Jugend, File 2237, p. 5 of document, SAPMO-BA.

19. Both in *Neues Deutschland*, 18 August 1951.

20. *Junge Welt*, 14 and 15 April 1956.

21. Ibid., 17 and 18 August 1957.

22. Ibid., 24 August 1955.

23. The book is undated, but internal evidence indicates that it was published sometime in the early 1950s. See *Ernst Thälmann–Vorbild der deutschen Jugend* (Berlin: Neues Leben, n.d.).

24. See also the photograph in the Bildesarchiv Preußicher Kulturbesitz, "Opening of the Pioneer Republic 'Ernst Thälmann' at Wuhlheide, East Berlin (May 1, 1950)," at http://germanhistorydocs.ghi-dc.org, accessed 9 August 2010.

25. *Ernst Thälmann–Vorbild der deutschen Jugend*, 5–12.

26. See, for example, *Ernst Thälmann—unser Vorbild* (Berlin: Junge Welt, 1986), which consists of a collection of excerpts from secondary sources written during the 1970s and 1980s as well as speeches and writings by Erich Honecker from as early as 1952.

27. Quoted in Rodden, *Textbook Reds*, 35.

28. Börrnert, *Wie Ernst Thälmann treu und kühn!* 112.

29. See "Rosa Thälmann zum Verbot der Kommunistischen Partei Deutschlands," in NY4003, File 82, SAPMO-BA.

30. On Rosa Thälmann's honorary membership in the FDJ, see *Neues Deutschland*, 1 December 1950.

31. Although I have been unable to find documentary evidence concerning this practice, the anecdotal evidence to support it is strong. More than one "child of the GDR" of the immediate postwar generation with whom I spoke—casually, not in the context of an interview—recalled having received such a photograph from Rosa Thälmann, and an archivist in Weimar was also familiar with the practice. In his memoir of growing up in the SBZ and the early years of the GDR, Hermann Weber recounts an instance in which he and his classmates had traveled to the Staatsoper in Berlin to hear Rosa Thälmann give a speech marking the fifth anniversary of her husband's death, only to be informed that she had decided to participate in a ceremony being staged in Hamburg. See Hermann Weber, *Damals als ich Wunderlich hieß: Vom Parteihochschüler zum kritischen Sozialisten* (Berlin: Aufbau, 2002), 343.

32. NY4003, File 81, pp. 7–8 of file, SAPMO-BA.

33. NY4004, File 81, p. 33 of file, SAPMO-BA.

34. See the children's letters to Rosa Thälmann in NY4003, File 83, SAPMO-BA.

35. Ibid., p. 6 of file.

36. Ibid., p. 7 of file.

37. Ibid., p. 9 of file.

38. Weber, *Damals als ich Wunderlich hieß*, 135.

39. Ibid., 343.

40. There is an important and growing historiography concerning the role of women in the GDR. Among the most interesting of these recent publications is Donna Harsch, *Revenge of the Domestic: Women, the Family, and Communism in the German Democratic Republic* (Princeton, NJ: Princeton University Press, 2007).

41. Concerning the ceremonies surrounding Rosa Thälmann's death, see DY30/JIV2/3, File 838, p. 10 of file, SAPMO-BA.

42. NY4003, File 84, pp. 51–57 of file, SAPMO-BA. The name of the women's group to whom Rosa spoke is not given in the document.

43. NY4003, File 82, p. 309 of file, SAPMO-BA. Once again the title of the women's group to whom Rosa was speaking is not given.

44. On this issue, see Jan Palmowski, *Inventing a Socialist Nation: Heimat and the Politics of Everyday Life in the GDR, 1945–1990* (Cambridge: Cambridge University Press, 2009).

45. NY4003, File 82, p. 312 of file, SAPMO-BA.

46. Undated speech in ibid., p. 349 of file.

47. The 1971 reprint is being used here. See Irma Thälmann, *Erinnerungen an meinen Vater* (Berlin: Kinderbuchverlag, 1971). The reverse side of the title page informs the reader that the book was written "[f]ür Leser von 10 Jahren an."

48. Wilhelm Pieck, foreword to I. Thälmann, *Erinnerungen*, 5–8.

49. I. Thälmann, *Erinnerungen*, 10–11.

50. Ibid., 12.

51. Ibid., 15–16.

52. Ibid., 17–18.

53. Ibid.,18–19, italics added.

54. Ibid., 19.

55. Ibid., 22, 30, 37.

56. Ibid., 49.

57. Ibid., 65.

58. Ibid., 65–66.

59. Ibid., 67–68.

60. Ibid., 73.

61. Ibid., 79.

62. Ibid., 90–93.

63. Quoted in ibid., 93–95.

64. Quoted in ibid., 95–96.

65. Ibid., 134–135.

66. Ibid., 135–136.

67. Ibid., 136.

68. Ibid., 137.

69. "Zimmering, Max," in Bernd-Rainer Barth, Christoph Links, Helmut Müller-Enbergs, and Jan Wielgohs, eds., *Wer war Wer in der DDR: Ein biographisches Handbuch*, 825–826 (Frankfurt: Fischer Taschenbuch, 1995).

70. "Wie ich Ernst Thälmann begegnete," File 389, Max Zimmering Papers, Deutsche Akademie der Künste, Berlin.

71. "Warum Buttje Pieter geboren wurde," File 376, Max Zimmering Papers.

72. Max Zimmering, *Buttje Pieter und sein Held* (Berlin: Dietz, 1951), 5–6.

73. Ibid., 11.

74. Ibid., 168.

75. Ibid., 170, 171.

76. Ibid., 138–139.

77. Ibid., 143.

78. Ibid., 144–145.

79. Ibid., 145–148.

80. Ibid., 149–150.

81. Ibid., 150–163.

82. Ibid., 164.

83. For a statistical analysis of the major motifs appearing in children's literature concerning Ernst Thälmann, see Börrnert, *Wie Ernst Thälmann treu und kühn!* 170. For these same motifs found in a book published during the final years of the GDR, see my analysis in chapter 8 as well as Giesela Karau, *Dann werde ich ein Kranich sein: Eine Erzählung um Ernst Thälmann* (Berlin: Kinderbuchverlag, 1980).

84. On children's literature as propaganda in the GDR, see Bernd Dolle-Weinkauff and Steffen Peltsch, "Kinder- und Kinderliteratur der DDR," in Reiner Wild, ed., *Geschichte der deutschen Kinder- und Jugendliteratur* (Stuttgart: J. B. Metzlersche Verlagsbuchhandlung, 1990), 372–401. Concerning the importance of Zimmering's book to the school curriculum in the GDR, see Börrnert, *Wie Ernst Thälmann treu und kühn!* 168–170.

85. "Schulfunk Radio DDR," Berlin, 1 April 1958, File 17, Max Zimmering Papers.

7. "Ernst Thälmann Is Still among Us"

1. On the political role of historians in the GDR, see Andreas Dorpalen, *German History in Marxist Perspective: The East German Approach* (Detroit: Wayne State University Press, 1988), 46–54; Iko-Sascha Kowalczuk, *Legitimation eines neuen Staates: Parteiarbeiter und der historischen Front Geschichtswissenschaft in der SBZ/DDR, 1945 bis 1961* (Berlin: Christoff Links, 1997), passim; and Konrad H. Jarausch, "The Failure of East German Antifascism: Some Ironies of History as Politics," *German Studies Review* 14 (February 1991): 85–102. For an East German perspective on this issue, see Fritz Zimmermann, "Die BzG und ihr Platz in der Geschichtsforschung und Geschichtspropaganda der DDR," *Beiträge zur Geschichte der Arbeiterbewegung* 23 (1979): 510–520, and Walter Schmidt, "Zur Geschichte der DDR Geschichtswissenschaft vom Ende des Zweiten Weltkrieges bis zur Gegenwart," *Beiträge zur Geschichte der Arbeiterbewegung* 27 (1985): 614–633. For a brief description of the IML, see Andreas Herbst, Winfred Ranke, and Jürgen Winkler, *So funktionierte die DDR*, 3 vols. (Reinbek bei Hamburg: Rowohlt, 1994), 1:420–423. On Nietzsche's distinction between "monumental" and "critical" history, see Friedrich Nietzsche, *Vom Nutzen und Nachteil der Historie für das Leben*, in *Werke in vier Bänden*, 4 vols. (Salzburg: Das Bergkbad-Buch, 1985), 3:35–43. In sharp contrast to the SED leadership, Nietzsche firmly maintained that "monumental" history needs to be tempered by the "critical" approach.

2. Dorpalen, *German History in Marxist Perspective*, 43–44. On the Marx cult, see Konrad Löw, *Der Mythos Marx und seine Macher: Wie aus Geschichten Geschichte wird*

(Munich: Langen Müller, 1996). On the Lenin cult in the Soviet Union, see Nina Tumarkin, *Lenin Lives! The Lenin Cult in Soviet Russia* (Cambridge, MA: Harvard University Press, 1983).

3. Willi Bredel, *Ernst Thälmann: Ein Beitrag zu einem politischen Lebensbild* (Berlin: Dietz, 1948), and Günter Hortzschansky, Walter Wimmer, Lothar Berthold, Heinz Karl, Horst Naumann, Stefan Weber, et al., *Ernst Thälmann: Eine Biographie* (Berlin: Dietz Verlag, 1980). For the latter, I used the two-volume paperback edition from 1986, but it has the same pagination as the original hardcover version of the book.

4. "Anlage Nr. 12 zum Protokoll Nr 3/73 vom 23. 1. 1973," in DY30/JIV2/2, File 1431, Politbüro, pp. 86–92, SAPMO-BA.

5. For brief accounts of Bredel's life and literary career, see "Bredel, Willi," in Bern-Rainer Barth, Christoph Links, Helmut Müller-Enbergs, and Jan Wielgohs, eds., *Wer war Wer in der DDR: Ein biographisches Handbuch* (Frankfurt: Fischer, 1995), 98–99; Herbst, Ranke, and Winkler, *So funktionierte die DDR*, 3:46–47; and the Web site "Willi-Bredel-Gesellschaft" at www.bredelgesellschaft.de, accessed 16 February 2010.

6. For these details concerning Bredel's life, see "Bredel, Willi"; Herbst, Ranke, and Winkler, *So funktionierte die DDR*, 3:46–47. On Bredel and the Kulturbund, see David Pike, *The Politics of Culture in Soviet-Occupied Germany, 1945–1949* (Stanford, CA: Stanford University Press, 1992), esp. 215–218. Concerning Bredel and *Neue Deutsche Literatur,* see Wolfgang Emmerich, *Kleine Literatur Geschichte der DDR: Erweiterte Neuausgabe* (Berlin: Kiepenheuer, 1996), 116.

7. Concerning the generation of German Communists to which Bredel belonged, see Catherine Epstein, *The Last Revolutionaries: German Communists and Their Century* (Cambridge, MA: Harvard University Press, 2003).

8. See Willi Bredel, "Thälmanns Bedeutung für die Entwicklung und Bolschewisierung der K.P.D.," File 896/2, Willi Bredel Papers, Stiftung Archiv der Akademie der Künste, Berlin; "Moskau, Paris 1935–1945," Stiftung Archiv der Akademie der Künste.

9. Bredel, "Thälmanns Bedeutung."

10. Willi Bredel to Wilhelm Pieck, 22 April 1945, File 892, Bredel Papers. Concerning the relationship between scholarship and politics in the Soviet Union, see Dmitrii Shepilov's account of working alongside Joseph Stalin in the writing of a textbook on political economy: Dmitrii Shepilov, *The Kremlin's Scholar: A Memoir of Soviet Politics under Stalin and Khrushchev,* ed. Steven Bittner, trans. Anthony Austin (New Haven, CT: Yale University Press, 2007), 21–27. Concerning the relationship between politics and culture during the Stalin years, see Katerina Clark, Evgeny Dobrenko, Andrei Artizov, and Oleg Naumov, *Soviet Culture and Power: A History in Documents, 1917–1953* (New Haven, CT: Yale University Press, 2007), esp. parts 2 and 3.

11. Bredel to Pieck, 22 April 1945. There are a variety of other reasons why it might have taken so long to turn Bredel's manuscript into a printed book, the most obvious being the severe shortage of paper and ink—not to mention other resources needed to print a book—that both the SBZ and GDR experienced throughout their history. It is also possible that party leaders other than Pieck made demands for additions to the manuscript.

12. A later printing of the book, from 1950, is slightly longer because a "memorial speech" delivered by Walter Ulbricht on 18 August 1949—the fifteenth anniversary of Thälmann's death—is included. In addition, some of the section headings were changed, but the text remains unaltered.

13. Wilhelm Pieck, foreword to Bredel, *Ernst Thälmann*, 5–7.

14. On the characteristics of sainthood, see Richard Kieckhefer, "Imitators of Christ: Sainthood in the Christian Tradition," in Richard Kieckhefer and George D. Bonds, eds., *Sainthood: Its Manifestations in World Religions* (Berkeley: University of California Press, 1988), 11–12, 20. Katerina Clark has pointed out the hagiographic components of Stalinist culture in her classic book *The Soviet Novel: History as Ritual*, 3rd ed. (Bloomington: Indiana University Press, 2000), esp. chap. 2.

15. Bredel, *Ernst Thälmann*, 9–13, italics in original.

16. Ibid., 13–16.

17. Ibid., 16–18.

18. For more accurate accounts of Thälmann's formative years, see Regina Scheer, "'Ich bin kein weltflütiger Zigeuner': Legende and Wirklichkeit einer Jugend—über die frühen Prägungen Ernst Thälmanns," in Peter Monteath, ed., *Ernst Thälmann: Mensch und Mythos*, 41–58 (Amsterdam: Rodopi, 2000); and Ernst Thälmann, "Mein Lebenslauf bis zum Eintritt in die KPD" (c. 1935), *Beiträge zur Geschichte der Arbeiterbewegung* 17 (1975): 86–102.

19. See, for example, Victoria E. Bonnell, *Iconography of Power: Soviet Political Posters under Lenin and Stalin* (Berkeley: University of California Press, 1997).

20. See, for example, David King, *The Commissar Vanishes: The Falsification of Photographs and Art in Stalin's Russia* (New York: Henry Holt, 1999).

21. Bredel, *Ernst Thälmann*, 19–26.

22. Ibid., 81–98.

23. Ibid., 150–151, 158.

24. Ibid., 161–165.

25. Ibid., 166, 167.

26. Ibid., 167.

27. Dorpalen, *German History in Marxist Perspective*, 46–54, where the reader can find several quotations from Bollhagen and other scholars concerning the importance of a Marxist approach to historical writing. For the quotation from Wilhelm Pieck, see Kowalczuk, *Legitimation eines neuen Staates*, 163.

28. Concerning the 1955 decree, see Horst Haun, *Der Geschichtsbeschluß der SED 1955: Programmdokument für die "volle Durchsetzung des Marxismus Leninismus" in der DDR-Geschichtswissenschaft* (Dresden: TU Dresden, 1996).

29. Concerning the origins of the IML and its precursors, the Marx-Engels-Lenin Institute (1949–1953) and the Marx-Engels-Lenin-Stalin Institute (1953–1956), see Herbst, Ranke, and Winkler, *So funktionierte die DDR*, 1:420–423. On the German Military History Institute, see ibid., 2:628–630. Concerning the creation of the Historical Society of the GDR, see Walter Schmidt, "Die Gründung der Historikergesellschaft der DDR 1958," *Zeitschrift für Geschichtswissenscshaft* 31, no. 8 (1983): 675–690.

30. Dorpalen, *German History in Marxist Perspective*, 51.

31. Ibid.

32. Quoted in ibid., 53.

33. Ibid., 46–54.

34. Institut für Marxismus–Leninismus beim ZK der SED, ed., *Deutschlands unsterblicher Sohn: Erinnerungen an Ernst Thälmann* (Berlin: Dietz, 1961).

35. See, for example, Institut für Marxismus–Leninismus beim ZK beim SED, ed., *Ernst Thälmann, Geschichte und Politik: Artikel und Reden 1925 bis 1933* (Frankfurt: Marxistische Blätter, 1974); Kommunistischen Arbeiterbund Deutschlands, ed., *Ernst Thälmann: Für ein freies sozialistisches Deutschland, Auswahl der Reden und Schriften 1919–1933*, 3rd ed., 3 vols. (Stuttgart: Neuer Weg, 1977).

36. L. Schorochow, ed., "Ernst Thälmann schrieb an der Werktätigen des Gouvernements Wjatka," *Beiträge zur Geschichte der Arbeiterbewegung* 12 (1970): 949–952; Josef Reinhold, ed., "Thälmann-Dokumente zur Bauernpolitik der KPD," *Beiträge zur Geschichte der Arbeiterbewegung* 24 (1982): 224–233.

37. See, for example, Edgar Doehler and Egbert Fischer, "Ernst Thälmanns Beitrag zur Entwicklung des wehrhaften Kampfes der deutschen Arbeiterbewegung gegen die wachsende faschistische Gefahr (1929–1933)," *Militärgeschichte* 15 (1976): 274–285; Kurt Seibt, "Die Partei Ernst Thälmanns im Kampf gegen Faschismus und Krieg," *Einheit* 30 (1975): 415–424.

38. Walter Ulbricht, Institut für Marxismus-Leninismus beim ZK der SED, *Geschichte der deutschen Arbeiterbewegung*, 15 vols. (Berlin: Dietz, 1968).

39. Annemarie Lange, *Berlin in der Weimarer Republik* (Berlin: Dietz, 1987).

40. One noteworthy exception to this tendency was Ernst Engelberg's massive biography of Otto von Bismarck, the first volume of which, *Bismarck: Urpreuße und Reichsgründer* (Berlin: Akademie, 1985), was published in the FRG by Siedler Verlag and was readily available in stores in West Berlin. Scholars working outside the field of labor history apparently had more intellectual independence than those who wrote about subjects of more immediate concern to the regime. Even so, Engelberg's work clearly falls within the category of Marxist–Leninist historiography.

41. Hermann Weber, "Neue Tendenzen? Differenzierungen der DDR-Geschichtsschreibung über den deutschen Kommunismus," *Deutschland Archiv* 18 (August 1985): 796–799.

42. DY30/JIV2/2, File 1433, pp. 47–48 of file, SAPMO-BA.

43. Ibid., File 1431, pp. 86–87 of file; concerning other plans regarding the celebration of Thälmann's ninetieth birthday, see DY30/JIV2/3, File 2416, pp. 13–15 of file, SAPMO-BA.

44. DY30/JIV2/2, File 1431, p. 88 of file.

45. Ibid.

46. Ibid., p. 89 of file.

47. Ibid., pp. 89–90 of file.

48. Ibid., p. 92 of file.

49. Dorpalen, *German History in Marxist Perspective*, 338–341; Kowalczuk, *Legitimation eines neuen Staates*, 187.

50. Concerning the composition of the author collective, see the reverse side of the title page of Hortzschansky et al., *Ernst Thälmann* (1986 ed.). The exact number of scholars who worked on the book remains obscure. The information on the back side of the title page lists six members of the author collective, along with four associates, *Mitarbeiter*, not to mention "and others." The reasons for the delay in publication are also unclear, but one can surmise that the writers of the book faced a number of problems typical of scholars in the GDR: interference from party leaders; disagreement and confusion among the collective's members; and the constant shortage of paper, ink, and other materials necessary for the publication of the book, for example.

51. Concerning the author collective's goals, see Günter Hortzschansky to Russel Lemmons, 8 November 2002, in author's files. I thank Dr. Hortzschansky for agreeing to answer in writing a series of questions I submitted to him in the summer of 2002.

52. I bought my copy of the paperback during my first trip to Berlin in 1986. Because of the Thälmann centennial that year, the book could be found in every

bookstore in the East German capital. Indeed, it was even available in kiosks in the Friedrichstraße subway station.

53. Hortzschansky et al., *Ernst Thälmann*, 804.

54. Ibid., book epigraph. The epigraph is from a speech that Honecker delivered to the FDJ in 1973; see Erich Honecker, *Reden und Aufsätze*, 12 vols. (Berlin: Dietz, 1975), 2:324.

55. Hortzschansky et al., *Ernst Thälmann*, 15, 20.

56. Brian Peterson, review of *Ernst Thälmann: Eine Biographie*, by Günter Hortzschansky et al., *Journal of Modern History* 53, no. 3 (September 1981): 580–582; for the IML biography's account of the Wittorf Scandal, see Hortzschansky et al., *Ernst Thälmann*, 398–400, 688–702.

57. Hortzschansky et al., *Ernst Thälmann*, 776–777.

58. Ibid., 778.

59. Ibid., 779–780.

8. "Not All Who Have Died Are Dead"

1. Concerning the replacement of Ulbricht with Honecker, see Mary Fulbrook, *Anatomy of a Dictatorship: Inside the GDR 1949–1989* (Oxford: Oxford University Press, 1995), 36.

2. Jeffrey Kopstein, *The Politics of Economic Decline in East Germany, 1945–1989* (Chapel Hill: University of North Carolina Press, 1997), 73. Concerning the role of technology in the GDR, see Raymond G. Stokes, *Constructing Socialism: Technology and Change in East Germany, 1945–1990* (Baltimore: Johns Hopkins University Press, 2000).

3. M. E. Sarotte, *Dealing with the Devil: East Germany, Détente, and Ostpolitik, 1969–1973* (Chapel Hill: University of North Carolina Press, 2001), 29–30. Sarotte assigns Ulbricht's fall from power not only to his political pretensions regarding the Soviet Union, but also to his willingness to cooperate with the FRG without the FRG's first recognizing the GDR's right to exist. Indeed, she argues that Honecker took a harder line than Ulbricht on the issue of inter-German cooperation (32). Sarotte's view is in contrast to Henry Ashby Turner Jr.'s more traditional argument that the Soviet Union decided to support Ulbricht's ouster at least in part because of the SED chief's outright opposition to *Ostpolitik*, a policy to which the USSR became highly receptive in response to its problems with the People's Republic of China. See Henry Ashby Turner Jr., *Germany from Partition to Reunification* (New Haven, CT: Yale University Press, 1992), 150.

4. Werner Link, "Ostpolitik: Détente German-Style and Adapting to America," trans. Richard Sharp, in Detlef Junker, ed., *The United States and Germany in the Era of the Cold War, 1968–1990, a Handbook*, 2 vols. (Cambridge: Cambridge University Press, 2004), 2:38.

5. Quoted in Kopstein, *Politics of Economic Decline*, 74.

6. Charles S. Maier, *Dissolution: The Crisis of Communism and the End of East Germany* (Princeton, NJ: Princeton University Press, 1997), 26; Kopstein, *Politics of Economic Decline*, 74.

7. Kopstein, *Politics of Economic Decline*, 74. Honecker's hopes that the FRG's recognition of the GDR would lead to a decrease in the FRG's influence in his state were largely disappointed. As a result of *Ostpolitik*, thousands of East Germans had the opportunity to visit with family members in the West, and an even larger num-

ber of West German citizens had the chance to visit the East. See Turner, *Germany from Partition to Reunification*, 195.

8. Kopstein, *Politics of Economic Decline*, 74–85. The term *conservative socialism* is Kopstein's.

9. Quoted in Mary Fulbrook, *The People's State: East German Society from Hitler to Honecker* (New Haven, CT: Yale University Press, 2005), 49.

10. On the Honecker regime's efforts to improve living conditions and the East German population's response, see ibid., especially chapter 3.

11. Turner, *Germany from Partition to Reunification*, 204.

12. Ibid., 202–204, 208–209; Kopstein, *Politics of Economic Decline*, 86–87. On the economic benefits of *Ostpolitik* for the GDR, especially in the 1980s, see Fulbrook, *Anatomy of a Dictatorship*, 146–147.

13. Turner, *Germany from Partition to Reunification*, 203–204.

14. Kopstein, *Politics of Economic Decline*, 95–100.

15. Ibid., 190–192.

16. For firsthand accounts of the economic hardships that East Germans faced during the SED regime's final years, see Dirk Philipsen, *We Were the People: Voices from East Germany's Revolutionary Autumn of 1989* (Durham, NC: Duke University Press, 1993), passim.

17. The scholarly literature on Gorbachev, perestroika, and glasnost is vast and growing. For brief accounts of the Gorbachev years, see Robert Service, *A History of Twentieth-Century Russia* (Cambridge, MA: Harvard University Press, 1997), 448–466; Nicholas Riasanovsky, *A History of Russia*, 5th ed. (Oxford: Oxford University Press, 1993), 590–608. For Gorbachev's justification for his policies, see Mikhail Gorbachev, *Perestroika: New Thinking for Our Country and the World*, updated ed. (New York: Harper & Row, 1987); and *Documents and Materials: 19th All-Union Conference of the CPSU*, report by Mikhail GORBACHEV, General Secretary of the CPSU Central Committee, a special supplementary issue of *Soviet Life* (Moscow: Government Printing Office, n.d.), esp. 5–93.

18. A. James McAdams, *Germany Divided: From the Wall to Reunification* (Princeton, NJ: Princeton University Press, 1993), 179.

19. Catherine Epstein, *The Last Revolutionaries: German Communists and Their Century* (Cambridge, MA: Harvard University Press, 2003), 235.

20. For instance, see Gorbachev's admission that the Soviets bore the guilt for the Katyn Massacre, the slaughter of 30,000 Polish soldiers perpetrated by the Soviets in 1940, in Mikhail Gorbachev, *Memoirs* (New York: Doubleday, 1995), 480–481.

21. Quoted in Maier, *Dissolution*, 220.

22. Gorbachev, *Memoirs*, 523.

23. McAdams, *Germany Divided*, 178–185, the quotation from Honecker on 179.

24. For a concise overview of Willi Sitte's life and career, see "Sitte, Willi," in Bernd-Rainer Barth, Christoph Links, Helmut Müller-Enbergs, and Jan Wielgohs, eds., *Wer war Wer in der DDR: Ein biographisches Handbuch* (Frankfurt: Fischer Taschenbuch, 1995), 695–696.

25. Concerning the stamp, see *Michel Briefmarken-Katalog Deutschland 1996/97* (Munich: Schwaneberger, 1996), 458.

26. For an overview of the trial of Wolfgang Otto, see Heinrich Hannover, *Die Republik vor Gericht, 1975–1995* (Berlin: Aufbau Taschenbuch, 2001), 254–278.

27. Falco Werkentin, *Politische Strafjsutiz in der Ära Ulbricht* (Berlin: Christoff Links, 1995), 219.

28. *Hamburger Volkszeitung*, 26 April 1947, for quotations from Zgoda's account

of the murder of Thälmann. The article also identifies Wolfgang Otto as one of the killers.

29. On the Amnesty Law, see Norbert Frei, *Adenauer's Germany and the Nazi Past: The Politics of Amnesty and Integration,* trans. Joel Golb (New York: Columbia University Press, 2002), 5–26.

30. Hannover, *Republik vor Gericht,* 257.

31. Ibid., 255–259; "Kaum nachvollziehbar," *Der Spiegel,* 14 October 1985, 2. For the text of Zgoda's deposition, see "Der Mord an Ernst Thälmann und das Verfahren gegen Wolfgang Otto—Hintergründe eines Justizskandals," in Präsidium der VVN-Bund der Antifaschisten, *AID,* n.d., p. 2, ZSg.1–233, Zeitgeschichtliche Zammlung, File 51, Bundesarchiv Koblenz.

32. Hannover, *Republik vor Gericht,* 259; *Nürnberger Zeitung,* 6 November 1985.

33. Hannover, *Republik vor Gericht,* 259–260; "Kaum nachvollziehbar," 2–3, see especially page 3 for the quotations from the Kleve and Düsseldorf courts' decisions.

34. For a detailed account of the official East German perspective on events leading up to the trial, see Peter Przybylski, *Mordsache Thälmann* (Berlin: Militärverlag der Deutschen Demokratischen Republik, 1986).

35. Ibid.

36. *Frankfurter Abendpost,* Nachtausgabe, 6 November 1985.

37. *Offenbach Post,* 6 November 1985.

38. Quoted in ibid.

39. Hannover, *Republik vor Gericht,* 269–270, quotation from Hannover's memoirs on 270.

40. Ibid., 266.

41. For a long quotation from Fuchs's testimony, see ibid., 264.

42. Ibid., 265.

43. *Neues Deutschland,* 12–13 April 1986.

44. Quoted in ibid., 12–13 April 1986.

45. Hannover provides a series of quotations from his closing statement in *Republik vor Gericht,* 269–271.

46. The quotations from Judge Paul's decision can be found in Dietrich Strothman, "Dornen für den Staatsanwalt: Über vierzig Jahre nach der Tat: doch noch eine Spur von Gerechtigkeit," *Die Zeit,* 23 May 1986, online version at http://www.zeit.de, accessed 14 January 2010.

47. Hannover, *Republik vor Gericht,* 271.

48. Ibid., 272–278.

49. See, for example, an article by Hermann Dünow in *Neues Deutschland,* 16 April 1966.

50. This did not mean, of course, that the East German or even the West German radical press completely abandoned the theme. See, for example, *Unsere Zeit,* 17 August 1979.

51. Ibid., 1 November 1985.

52. See, for example, *Neues Deutschland,* 12–13 and 23 April 1986, 8 July 1988.

53. Ibid., 16 May 1986.

54. See ibid., 8, 15, and 16–17 May 1988.

55. Concerning the benefit that this recognition would have for the GDR, see Josef Streit's afterword ("Nachwort") in Przybylski, *Mordsache Thälmann,* 228.

56. Numerous articles on the trial appeared in West German periodicals and newspapers—for example, *Frankfurter Allgemeine Zeitung,* 31 October 1985; *Süddeutsche Zeitung,* 5 and 6 November 1985; *Frankfurter Rundschau,* 5 November 1985.

57. *Der Spiegel*, 14 October 1985.

58. *Frankfurter Allgemeine Zeitung*, 31 October 1985.

59. *Deutsches Allgemeines Sonntagsblat* quoted in Hannover, *Republik vor Gericht*, 271; Dietrich Strothmann's coverage of the trial can be found in *Die Zeit*, 23 May 1986, online version at http://www.zeit.de.

60. *Die Zeit*, 25 March 1986, online version, accessed 20 January 2010.

61. *Der Spiegel*, 4 December 1989, online version at http://www.spiegel.de, accessed 20 January 2010.

62. For the Politburo records concerning the reemergence of the plan to construct a national monument, see DY30/JIV2/e, File 3291, p. 45 of file, SAPMO-BA.

63. "Maßnahmeplan zur Würdigung des 100. Geburtstag von Ernst Thälmanns," 5 December 1985, DY30/JIV2/2, File 2149, pp. 129–133 of file, SAPMO-BA; concerning planning for the scholarly conference, see *Neues Deutschland*, 13 March 1986.

64. Walter Baumert, *Das Ermittlungsverfahren: Ein Thälmann Roman* (Berlin: Neues Leben, 1985), excerpt on 150–170.

65. Walter Baumert, "Ermittlungsverfahren Thälmann," *Neue Deutsche Literatur: Monatsschrift für Literatur und Kunst* 34 (January 1986): 106–123.

66. Concerning East German literature during the 1980s, see Wolfgang Emmerich, *Kleine Literatur Geschichte der DDR*, exp. new ed. (Berlin: Gustav Kiepenhauer, 1996), 397–434.

67. Baumert, *Das Ermittlungsverfahren*, 304.

68. Günter Katsch, "Kritik und Bibliographie," *Beiträge zur Geschichte der Arbeiterbewegung* 28 (1986), 831–834.

69. For the quotations from the book, see Institut für Marxismus–Leninismus beim ZK der SED, *Ernst Thälmann: Bilder, Dokumente, Texte* (Berlin: Dietz, 1986), 7, 382–395.

70. *Ernst Thälmann—unsere Partei erfüllt sein Vermächtnis: Wissenschaftliche Konferenz zum 100. Geburtstag Ernst Thälmanns in Berlin am 12. und 13. März 1986* (Berlin: Dietz, 1986), quotations from Sindermann's speech on 7.

71. *Neues Deutschland*, 13 March 1986.

72. DY30/JIV2/2, File 2149, pp. 129–132 of file, and DY30/JIV2/3, File 3291, pp. 32–35 of file, SAPMO-BA; "Standard Report über all eingetragene Felder mit Lagernummer," concerning the made-for-television movie *Ernst Thälmann*, Deutsches Rundfunkarchiv, Fernseharchiv, Berlin. See also *Neues Deutschland*, 7 February 1986.

73. As for the Maetzig films, the screenplay of the 1986 production was published in book form. See Otto Bonhoff, Georg Schiemann, and Erich Selbmann, *Ernst Thälmann: Zweiteiliger Fernsehfilm, Szenarium* (Berlin: Henschelverlag, 1987).

74. East German officials had long been concerned about the popularity of Western television among the GDR's young people. See, for example, "Empfang von Schlager-und Unterhaltungssendungen des Rundfunks und Fernsehens der DDR," part of a "Parlamentsstudie" from 1975, in DC4, Amt für Jugendfragen/Zentralinstitut für Jugendforschung, File 615, Bundesarchiv Potsdam.

75. I thank the staff of the Deutsches Rundfunkarchiv, Fernseharchiv, Standort Berlin, for its assistance in viewing this film. The former East Germans to whom I spoke informally about the films remembered that the Bonhoff biopic bored them. For the quotation from Günter Hortzschansky, see Günter Hortzschansky to Russel Lemmons, 8 November 2002, in author's files.

76. My account of the film is based on viewings of *Ernst Thälmann*, directed by Ursula Bonhoff, 1986, in the Deutsches Rundfunkarchiv, Fernseharchiv.

77. A review appearing in *Neues Deutschland* on 8–9 February 1986 emphasizes that German unity was a central theme of the film.

78. The film was also shown in the People's Republic of China; see ibid., 16 April 1986.

79. Ibid., 7 April 1986.

80. Ibid., 14 April 1986; for the quotations from Trostorff's speech, see *Das Volk*, 14 April 1986. See also "Ehrendes Gedenken zum 41. Jahrestag der Selbstbefreiung des KZ Buchenwald und zum 100. Geburtstag Thälmanns," in Nationale Mahn- und Gedenkstätte Buchenwald, ed., *Nationale Mahn-und Gedenkstätte Buchenwald: Information* (1986), 3–5, DR1, File 7181a, p. 205 of file, SAPMO-BA. Concerning the new display, see DR1, File 71816, pp. 315–324 of file, SAPMO-BA.

81. Helmuth Holtz, "Ernst Thälmann Park in Prenzlauer Berg," *Diplomatische Depesche* (November 2004), 60–61; Hartmut Seefeld, "Hunderte auf Hausdächern: Aus der Geschichte des Thälmannparks in Prenzlauer Berg," *Vor/Ort: Stadterneuerung in Prenzlauer Berg, Weißensee und Pankow* 15 (May 2006), 13.

82. *Neues Deutschland*, 16 April 1986.

83. Thomas Flierl, "'Thälmann und Thälmann vor allen': Ein Nationaldenkmal für die Hauptstadt der DDR, Berlin," in Günter Feist, Eckhart Gillen, and Beatrice Vierneisel, eds., *Kunstdokumentation, SBZ/DDR 1945–1990* (Berlin: DuMont Buchverlag, 1996), 382–384; Bruno Flierl, "Politische Wandbilder und Denkmäler im Stadtraum," in Bruno Flierl, ed., *Gebaute DDR: Über Stadtplanner, Architekten und die Macht* (Berlin: Verlag für Bauwesen, 1998), 103–104; Rudy Koshar, *From Monuments to Traces: Artifacts of German Memory, 1870–1990* (Berkeley: University of California Press, 2000), 277–278; Brian Ladd, "East German Political Monuments in the Late German Democratic Republic: Finding a Place for Marx and Engels," *Journal of Contemporary History* 37, no. 1 (2002), 97.

84. Flierl, "'Thälmann und Thälmann vor allen,'" 382–383. The massive size of the Thälmann National Monument stands in sharp contrast to the Marx–Engels monument dedicated earlier in the month. See *Neues Deutschland*, 5–6 April 1986.

85. Eviatar Zerubavel, *Time Maps: Collective Memory and the Social Shape of the Past* (Chicago: University of Chicago Press, 2003), 43.

86. *Dokumentation: Das Traditionskabinett "Antifaschistischen Widerstandskampfs 1933–1945," in Berlin-Prenzlauer Berg*, Prenzlauer Berg Museum Archives, Berlin. For a detailed analysis of the Traditionskabinett, see Annette Leo, "Zerbrochene Bilder: Ein antifaschistisches Traditionskabinett und die Geschichtsauffassung der SED/PDS," in Rainer Eckert and Bernd Faulenbach, eds., *Halbherziger Revisionismus: Zum postkommunistischen Geschichtsbild*, 263–281 (Munich: Olzog, 1996). See also the collection of essays edited by the Kulturamt Prenzlauer Berg und das Aktive Museum Faschismus und Widerstand in Berlin, *Mythos Antifaschismus: Ein Traditionskabinett wird kommentiert* (Berlin: Christoph Links, 1992). For a brief description of the Kabinett, see Koshar, *From Monuments to Traces*, 277–278. Prenzlauer Berg's Traditionskabinett closed in 1993. Bernt Roder, Prenzlauer Berg Museum director, to Russel Lemmons, 2003 (no specific date given), in author's files.

87. *Neues Deutschland*, 16 April 1986.

88. Details of the day come from *Neues Deutschland*, 16 April 1986; for the quotation from Honecker's speech, see Peter Monteath, "Ein Denkmal für Ernst Thälmann," in Peter Monteath, ed., *Ernst Thälmann: Mensch und Mythos* (Amsterdam: Rodopli, 2000), 191.

89. *Neues Deutschland*, 17 April 1986.

90. For the entire text of Honecker's long speech, see ibid., 18 April 1986.

91. Martin Schönfeld, "Die Konstruction eines politischen Idols: Darstellungen

Ernst Thälmanns in der Kunst der SBZ/DDR und ihre Funktion," in Monteath, ed., *Ernst Thälmann*, 167–168.

9. "Imprisoned, Murdered, Besmirched"

1. Concerning the efforts to create a common German identity, see Harold James, *A German Identity, 1770–1990* (New York: Routledge, Kegan and Paul, 1989).

2. The classic exposition of the theory of totalitarianism remains Hannah Arendt's *The Origins of Totalitarianism*, 2nd ed. (New York: Harper, 1973).

3. Quoted in Jeffrey Herf, *Divided Memory: The Nazi Past in the Two Germanys* (Cambridge, MA: Harvard University Press), 265.

4. Concerning efforts to compare Stalinism and National Socialism, see Ljudmila Andreevna Mercalowa, "Stalinismus und Hitlerismus—Versuch einer vergleichenden Analyse," in Eckhard Jesse, ed., *Totalitarismus im 20. Jahrhundert: Eine Bilanz der internationalen Forschung*, 200–212 (Bonn: Bundeszentrale für politische Bildung, 1996).

5. Quoted in *Die Zeit*, 17 August 1990.

6. Brian Ladd, *The Ghosts of Berlin: Confronting German History in the Urban Landscape* (Chicago: University of Chicago Press, 1997), 175–215.

7. *Der Tagesspiegel*, 15 May 1990.

8. Ladd, *Ghosts of Berlin*, 194; *Berliner Morgenpost*, 18 October 1990.

9. All quoted in *Berliner Morgenpost*, 18 October 1990.

10. Ibid., 9 August 1990.

11. *TAZ*, 5 June 1990; author's interview with Bernt Roder, director of the Prenzlauer Berg Museum, 15 August 2002, Berlin.

12. Ladd, *Ghosts of Berlin*, 202.

13. *Berliner Morgenpost*, 9 August 1990; *Die Zeit*, 17 August 1990.

14. "Beschluß der Bezirkverordnetenversammlung vom 5.9.1990," in *Denk-Mal Positionen: Dokumentation zur Ausstellung vom 14. Juli–13 August 1993* (Berlin: Prenzlauer Berg Museum, 1993), 20 (*Denk-Mak Positionen* is a collection of copies of various official documents and newspaper articles that the museum put together as a pamphlet).

15. For the results of the election, see Dirk Philipsen, *We Were the People: Voices from East Germany's Revolutionary Autumn of 1989* (Durham, NC: Duke University Press, 1993), 401.

16. On the optimism of this period, see ibid.; concerning the "third way," see Konrad Jarausch, *The Rush to German Unity* (New York: Oxford University Press, 1994), 75–94.

17. On the collapse of the GDR, see Charles Maier, *Dissolution: The Crisis of Communism and the End of East Germany* (Princeton, NJ: Princeton University Press, 1997).

18. Concerning the depiction of life in the GDR following unification, see Paul Cook, *Representing East Germany since Unification: From Colonization to Nostalgia* (Oxford: Berg, 2005).

19. *Spandauer Volksblatt*, 17 October 1991; on the origins of the Lenin statue, see Brian Ladd, "East Berlin Political Monuments in the Late German Democratic Republic: Finding a Place for Marx and Engels," *Journal of Contemporary History* 37, no. 1 (2002), 94–95.

20. Quoted in Ladd, *Ghosts of Berlin*, 197.

21. Quoted in *Berliner Morgenpost*, 20 September 1991.

22. Ladd, *Ghosts of Berlin*, 197–198 for the quotations; also Helga A. Welsh, Andreas Pickel, and Dorothy Rosenberg, "East and West German Identities: United and Divided?" in Konrad H. Jarausch, ed., *After Unity: Reconfiguring German Identities* (Providence, RI: Berghahn, 1997), 131.

23. "Beschluß der Bezirksverordnetenversammlung Prenzlauer Berg vom 5.12.1991," in *Denk-Mal Positionen*, 28.

24. "Senatsvorlage Nr. 1467/92," Berlin, 19 February 2002, in *Denk-Mal Positionen*, 29–30.

25. *TAZ*, 22 April 1993.

26. "Berzirksverordnetensammlung Berlin–Prenzlauer Berg, Beschlußnummer 451/92," 7 May 1992, in *Denk-Mal Positionen*, 32.

27. "Bezirksverordnetenversammlung Prenzlauer Berg von Berlin, Drucksache Nr. 197/93," 27 January 1993, in *Denk-Mal Positionen*, 38.

28. *Bericht der Kommission zum Umgang mit den politischen Denkmälern der Nachkriegzeit im ehemaligen Ost-Berlin* (Berlin: Stadtregierung Berlin, 1993), 33–34, 85.

29. "Umgang mit den politischen Denkmälern de DDR in Berlin," in *Denk-Mal Positionen*, 5.

30. "Denkschrift der 'Initiative politische Denkmölern' Arbeitsgruppe des Aktiven Museums Faschismus in Berlin," February 1933, in *Denk-Mal Positionen*, 13.

31. "Position 4," in *Denk-Mal Positionen*, 7.

32. *TAZ*, 22 February 1993.

33. Roder interview, 15 August 2002.

34. "Presseerklärung der PDS Prenzlauer Berg zum 107. Geburtstag von Ernst Thälmann," 16 April 1993, in *Denk-Mal Positionen*, 12.

35. "Flugblatt der Parteien KPD und SKP zum 107. Geburtstag von E. Thälmann," 16 April 1993, in *Denk-Mal Positionen*, 14.

36. *Berliner Morgenpost*, 16 April 1993.

37. Ibid., 16 April 1993.

38. Ibid., 14 May 1993.

39. "Einladung zum Ernst-Thälmann-Symposium in der Wabe vcm 4. bis 5. Juni 1993," in *Denk-Mal Positionen*, 40.

40. *TAZ*, 7 June 1993.

41. *Der Tagesspiegel*, 9 June 1993.

42. Quoted in ibid., 19 February 1993.

43. Ibid., 15 July 1993.

44. Ibid., 29 April 1995.

45. Ladd, *Ghosts of Berlin*, 203.

46. Quoted in Philipsen, *We Were the People*, 289.

47. Maier, *Dissolution*, 285–329.

48. Quoted in Philipsen, *We Were the People*, 381.

49. Paul Betts, "The Twilight of the Idols: East German Memory and Material Culture," *Journal of Modern History* 72 (2000): 731–765.

50. Roder interview, 15 August 2002.

Conclusion

1. On Thälmann and Stalin, see Hermann Weber, "Thälmann und Stalin, die KPdSU und die KPD," in Hermann Weber and Bernhard H. Bayerlein, eds., *Der Thälmann-Skandal: Geheime Korrespondenzen mit Stalin*, 11–34 (Berlin: Aufbau, 2003).

2. The scholarly literature on political religions is vast. See the notes to the introduction to this book. For an overview of the subject, see Emilio Gentile, *Politics as Religion*, trans. George Staunton (Princeton, NJ: Princeton University Press, 2006).

3. Regarding East German society and its effects on GDR citizens, see Wolfgang Engler, *Die Ostdeutschen: Kunde von einem Verlorenen Land* (Berlin: Aufbau, 1999).

Index

Page numbers that appear in *italics* refer to illustrations.

CPSIA information can be obtained at www.ICGtesting.com
Printed in the USA
BVOW071054180113

310711BV00002B/4/P